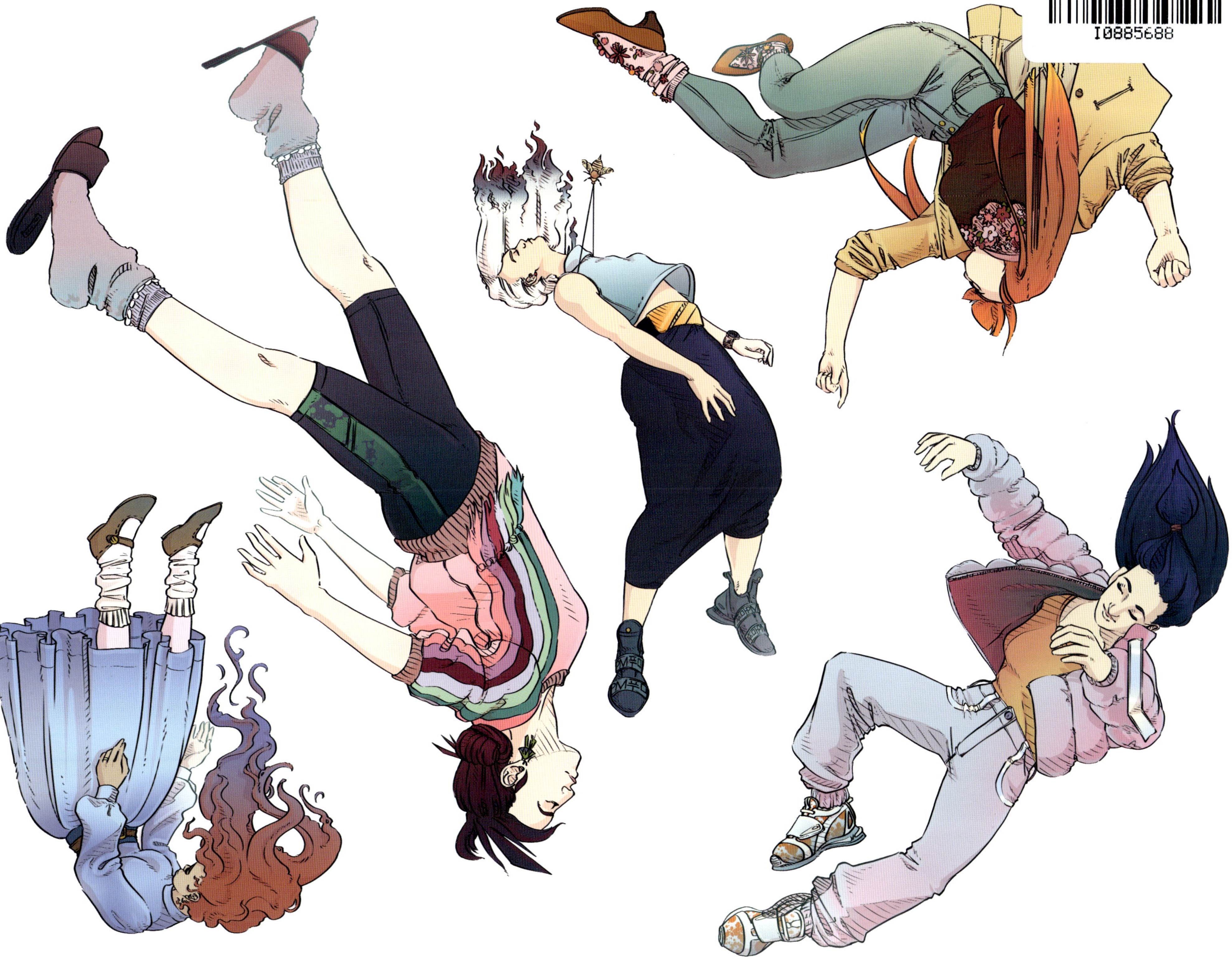

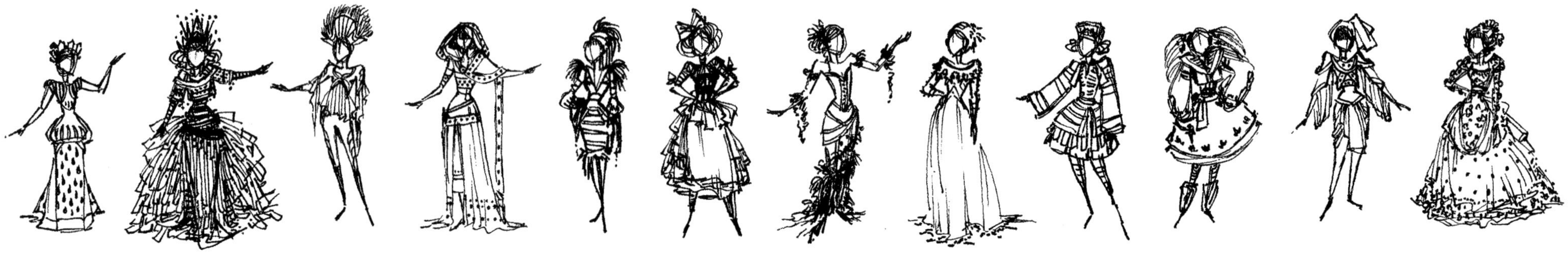

Talking Threads

www.thetalkingthreads.com

Original concept and compilation by Jessie Kate Bui

Editor: Teena Apeles

Proofreader: Sara Richmond

Graphic Design:

The Talking Threads Team

Alyssa Homan

Layout: Christopher De La Rosa

Website: www.designstudiopress.com

E-mail: info@designstudiopress.com

10 9 8 7 6 5 4 3 2 1

Printed in China

LCCN: 2021952358

ISBN: 9781624650482

TALKING THREADS

BUI | CONAWAY | KERCHER | RUSSO | BLACK-GLIKO

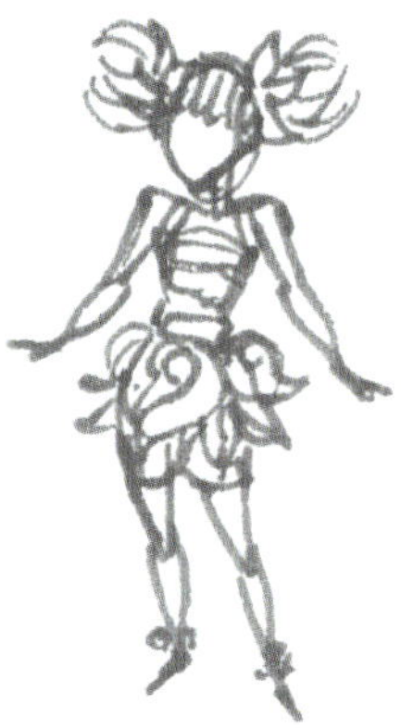
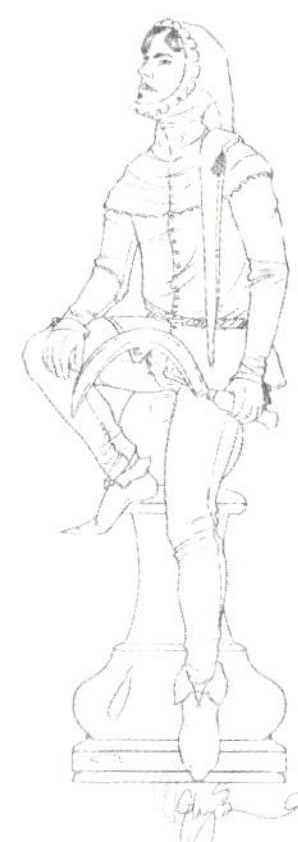
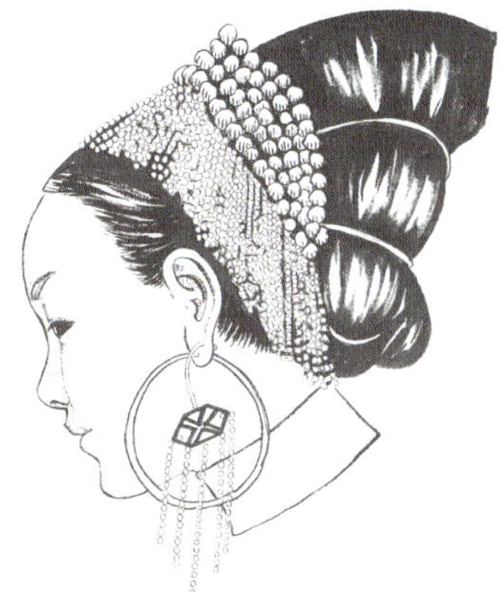
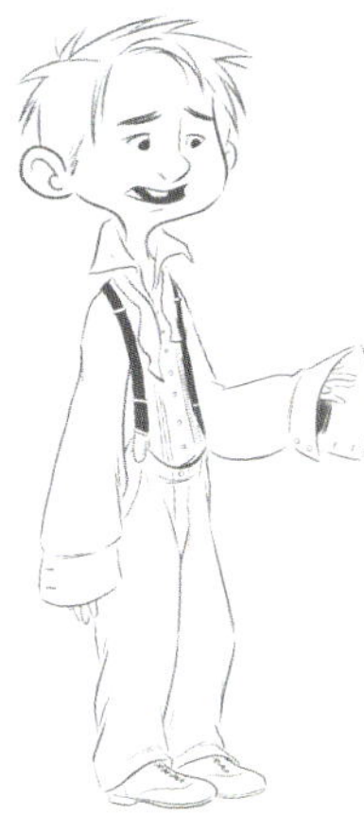
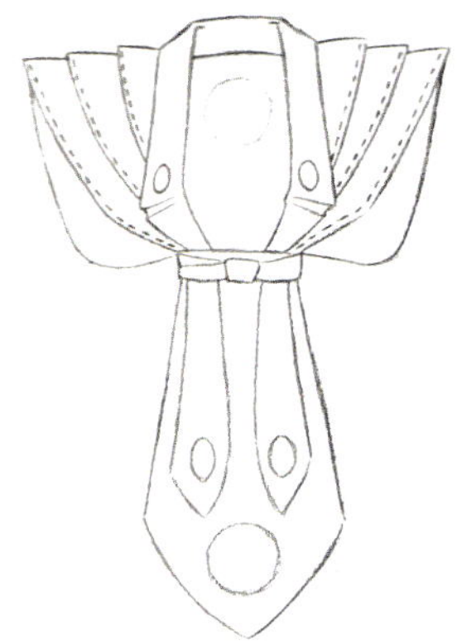

TABLE OF CONTENTS

DEDICATIONS

Jessie Kate Bui

For Chris Oatley, who pushed me to write a book; Matt and Josh, for clarifying the path; Tong, for encouraging me to own it; my art pals, for cheering me on; and to my awesome family, for their support and patience along the way.

Gwyn Conaway

To my husband, my sister, my mother, and Fizzy.

Maria Ferreira Kercher

For my parents, who surrounded me with art since I was small and pushed me to share my artistic voice; Cecília, for always believing in me, I miss you; my husband, Ryan, whom I love and has always been patient and supportive; Chris Oatley, for creating the Oatley Academy community and introducing me to Jessie Kate; and my friends and family, for the constant encouragement and their faith in me.

Blythe Russo

Above all, to my mom and dad, and to all family and friends who have supported me: I love you.

Rebecca "Beki" Black-Gliko

Foremost, to my heart, Raul Ramos, and special thanks also to my family and friends all over the world who make everywhere I go feel like home.

FOREWORD

Whether you're a costume design veteran, emerging talent, or costume enthusiast, *Talking Threads* deserves a place on your desk. It is filled with 21st-century costume design tools that expand on the usual tips and tricks with a much deeper dive. Thanks to the contributions of talented design professionals, *Talking Threads* quantifies the essential nature of the costume designer for live-action productions, animation, digital games, and the theatre. By shining a light on the creative process, *Talking Threads* celebrates the vital role that all costume designers play in helping the director tell the story.

Costumes are so much more than clothes; they embody each character's psychological, social, and emotional condition at a particular moment. We must care about the people in the story and feel invested in the outcome, and costume provides essential information to the audience, answering the question, "Who are they?" Great costumes are the result of astute observation, research, analysis, and imagination. Whatever the genre or period, nothing that appears on stage or screen is casual; every accessory and garment is a deliberate choice made by a designer.

Costume design serves two equal purposes: to support the story by creating memorable characters and to provide balance within the frame using color, texture, and silhouette. *Talking Threads* illustrates that whatever the creative platform, a team of visual artists collaborates to paint and light each moment as meticulously as a canvas. Together they engineer the invented universe of each story as interpreted by the director. Costume designers help make that world—and the characters that people it—come to life.

Deborah Nadoolman Landis, PhD

Distinguished Professor and David C. Copley Chair,

Director, David C. Copley Center for Costume Design

UCLA School of Theater, Film & Television

INTRODUCTION

The Story We Wear

I have always been fascinated by the way clothing could tell a story, but my aversion to sewing machines seemed to put life as a costume designer out of my reach. However, when I saw the Disney film *Tangled* and Claire Keane's gorgeous work in the *Art of Tangled* book in 2010, I was immediately struck. I had never considered using my design skills to create costumes for animation!

So, I set out to learn more about the craft. I experimented with personal projects, asked questions at industry expos, interviewed professionals, received critiques, and taught myself about unique considerations when designing for animation.

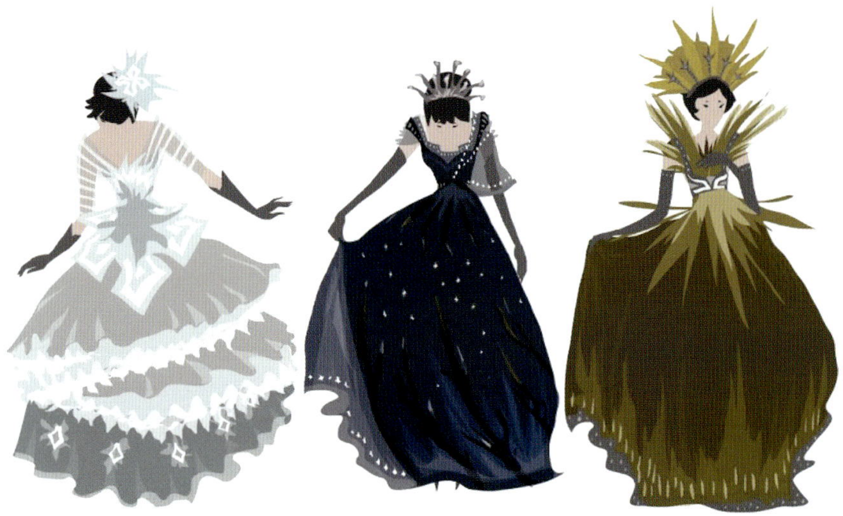

As a result of my research, I collected a variety of techniques and insights that I began to share with others. My mentor at the time, Chris Oatley, suggested I turn them into a costume design book. I was initially overwhelmed at the idea but with some sound advice from family and friends, and a group of talented costume specialist friends to call on—Rebecca Black-Gliko, Gwyn Conaway, Maria Ferreira Kercher, and Blythe Russo—I decided to do it.

I proposed that we share our go-to design tips in a simple "tips and tricks" book for different formats or roles. However, as we took the time to learn each other's approaches to design, we found deeper principles that tied our approaches together. Though the formats the five of us work in vary—from live action and animation to video games and theatre—and each format has specific considerations, the challenges and the ultimate goal of our work is the same: to tell a story.

Whether the job was to create an illustration for a book cover, depict a character in an epic scene as a concept artist, or create and fabricate complex costumes for the protagonists of a fantasy action-adventure video game set in the 1600s, we found that there were five fundamental functions that embedded a design with meaningful context and story:

- **Connects to PLOT AND THEME**
- **Establishes the Structure of SOCIETY**
- **Contextualizes TIME AND PLACE**
- **Indicates PERSONALITY**
- **Reveals a PASSAGE OF TIME**

Each design we created was a unique visual response to the questions that arose as we explored those functions. And so our simple "tips and tricks" evolved into a full-on introductory book for aspiring costume designers and entertainment industry artists.

In each section, we will explore a function and phase of the design process. You'll also find helpful research questions, guides, valuable exercises and examples to inspire your creativity and help you refine your process.

As a disclaimer, this is not a plug-and-play design bible. It's in the gray area between the archetypes, historical rules, and format limitations that you will find your story and create your designs. *Talking Threads* is intended to help you stretch your imagination and consider important questions in order to access the vast potential of costume as a storytelling device—and work more efficiently as a result.

And if you ever feel overwhelmed by the challenge . . . remember that you already have at your disposal the perfect and most accessible source of reference to analyze.

Yourself

Because costume is also the story *we* wear. Even without years of study in fashion and design history, analyzing and understanding how your own clothing choices connect you to your personal story will deepen your comprehension—making it easier, and more enjoyable, to weave your insights and passion into your own imaginary world.

Jessie Kate Bui

Los Angeles, CA

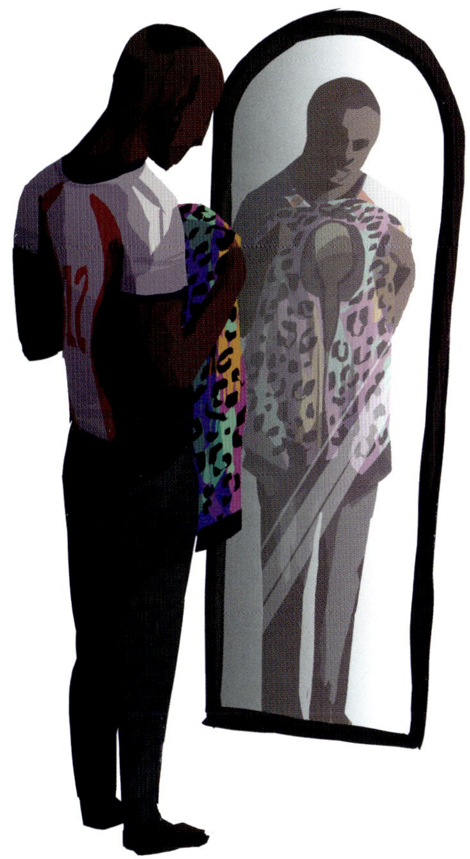

You are first and foremost a storyteller, and the unique connections you make between the story world, character, and costume are what will give your costume life.

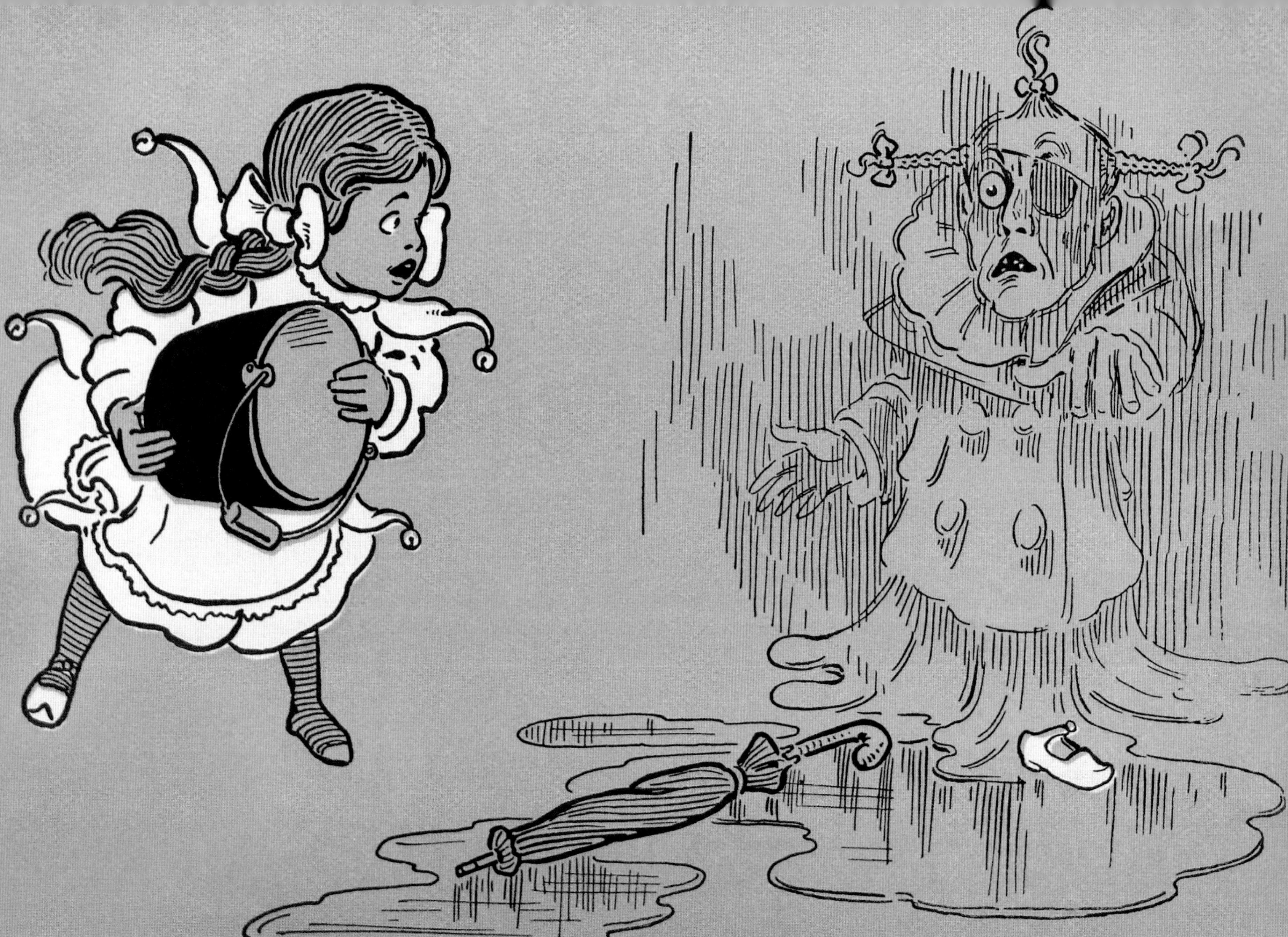

"I firmly believe that with the right footwear one can rule the world."

—Bette Midler

CHAPTER 1 PLOT AND THEME

In fairy tales, a character's costume often gives us a striking and identifying visual that we can follow through his/her journey, such as Cinderella's glass slipper and the Wicked Witch of the East's magical shoes in *The Wizard of Oz*. Not only do these accessories have a plot function—the glass slipper leads the prince back to Cinderella, and the witch's shoes are Dorothy's key to returning home—but they also serve a thematic purpose.

While Dorothy doesn't see the value in the slippers, the Wicked Witch of the West seeks them with intensity. The shoes become a symbol of envy that eventually costs the witch her life. What makes these items and designs special are their narrative context. Take the shoes out of Oz and they're just shoes.

The Elements of a Story

As designers, we must transform the words of the script into visual subtext on the screen or page; you can think of it as visual translation. So it follows that in order to capture nuance in your design, you need to first become more fluent in the language of your story.

Basic Elements of a Story:

Plot: A sequence of events that create conflict and move the character through an arc.

Logline: The plot of the story simplified into one or two sentences. This one may ring a bell: "A troubled boy finds the courage to help a friendly alien stranded on Earth hide from the government and return to its home planet."

Act: A way to divide a story into multiple parts. An example would be a three-act structure consisting of a beginning, middle, and end.

Beat: A major plot point, such as the death of a character or the breakup of a relationship.

Theme: The heart that drives your story or a profound question about humanity or truth that the writer wants to feature. Think "What does it mean to take a life?" and "Cheaters never prosper."

Character Arc: The process of change the character goes through from the beginning of the story to the end of the story, for instance, an ordinary person transforming into a hero.

Character of Change: A character changed by their world. This character will have an internal change by the end of the story or may go through more than one change in the story. Very simply, this can be evil to good or good to evil. In less dramatic examples, characters may change their perspective of the world or reaction to a character or plot point.

Steadfast Character: A character who changes their world. This character will have a predetermined view of the world and themself, remaining steady in their convictions; they are tested to maintain these through the story. Other characters around them may change as a result.

Story Structure

Whether a story uses a simple three-act structure or it follows a more open "hero's journey" style form like Dan Harmon's story circle (you, need, go, search, find, take, return, change), organizing your thoughts and impressions in the same framework will help you identify and translate your characters' inner (thematic) and outer (plot) transformations. This also helps you find opportunities to complement your core message with supporting characters, environments, costumes, and style. Let's examine the narrative of a familiar three-act story.

Logline: A kind but neglected orphan must deal with an evil stepmother and stepsisters as she attempts to escape her life of abuse for just one night.

Theme to Explore: Don't judge a book by its cover; true beauty is on the inside.

SETUP

Stepmother verbally abuses Cinderella when comparing her to her daughters. Tells her she is ugly and worthless.

The lie set up by the stepmother: outer beauty determines happiness.

Cinder Dress

Older, less decorated, saturated style that contrasts with the shapes in her stepsisters' dresses to amplify their differences. "Happier" colors in the stepsisters' dresses that are oversaturated to hide their insecurity.

INCITING INCIDENT

An invitation for the palace ball comes after finishing her chores; Cinderella makes a homemade dress using her mother's old dress to attend the ball.

You can create outer beauty.

Homemade Dress

An update to her mother's old dress; still out of date but moves toward the happier colors.

MIDPOINT

The stepmother goes back on her promise to let Cinderella attend the ball and destroys the dress.

Those who disregard inner beauty will still ignore outer beauty.

Destroyed Dress

Tearing up of mother's dress further disrespects the inner feelings of a character. The stepsisters feel competitive and outer beauty is intolerant of competition with inner beauty.

BUILD ON MIDPOINT

Cinderella's fairy godmother comes to reward inner beauty and help her attend the ball. She meets the prince who notices her amongst the many other beautiful women.

Outer beauty can help others more easily notice inner beauty.

Magic Dress

Transformed dress includes details from mother's dress to respect inner feelings while updating the look to include Cinderella's traits.

CINDERELLA

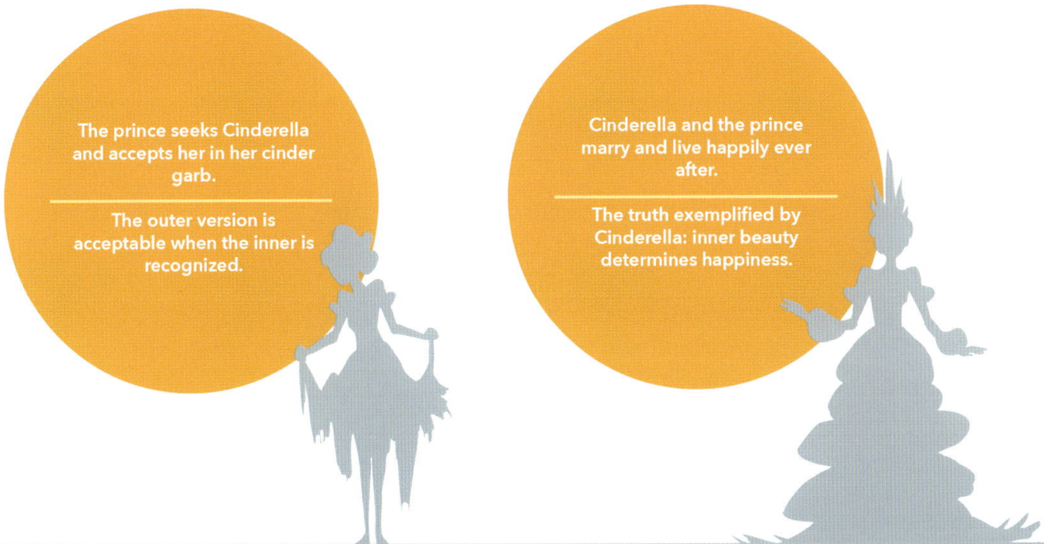

CLIMAX

Cinder Dress

Back to the original dress but add a splash of color, flowers in her belt or hair, to indicate a more hopeful attitude. The happier colors are peeking through.

RESOLUTION

Wedding Gown

Wedding gown is less fussy and simpler than the attendees' attire. Flowers bring in the happier colors, but the dress is a simple pale tone to bring more focus to her face. The stepsisters' and stepmother's costumes are comparatively dull next to the attendees'.

LOGLINE
A kind but neglected orphan must deal with an evil stepmother and stepsisters as she attempts to escape her life of abuse for just one night.

THEME TO EXPLORE
Don't judge a book by its cover; true beauty is on the inside.

Personalizing a Story

Do you see any connections between the character's story and your own personal history?

When making notes about Cinderella's mother's dress, I remembered when my mother let me try on her gunnysack wedding dress for fun.

I also recalled my mother's love of peasant skirts and embroidery when I incorporated her 1970s style; the resulting shapes reminded me of pumpkins, so I added notes of orange, seed shapes, and pumpkin plant flowers to the design.

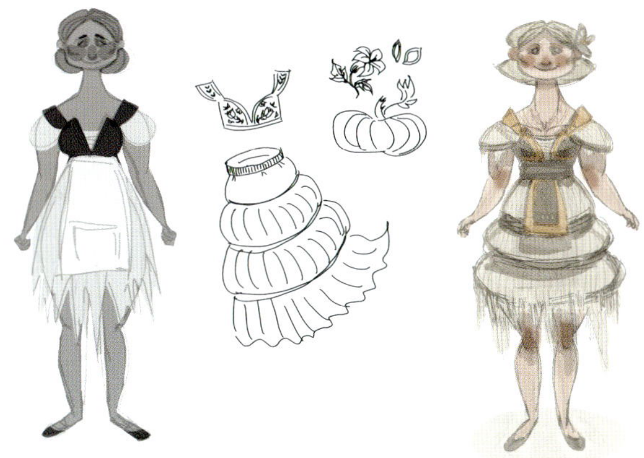

Using the reference of my mother's 1970s dresses allowed me to call on a simple, familiar emotional connection to an aesthetic that others my age may relate to. I can also examine the social context of the 1970s to find the origin of peasant dress styles and possible complementary themes or history that might align with my story.

This personal approach helps me warm up my design thinking and equips me to create aesthetic solutions on the fly; this can be especially handy if the art direction of the project is still being developed.

Exercise: Plotting Your Design

Now try to break down the narrative of a three-act story you're working on.

1. Do an initial read through. Immerse yourself in the story, allowing yourself to experience it as an audience member. This will allow you to comprehend the content organically before switching to an analytical mindset. After you finish reading, note your first raw impressions.

2. Summarize the story's logline, making sure to include the theme and explore the setup to find a lie that is stopping the character from achieving his or her end goal and a universal truth that will be revealed or questioned in the story.

3. Fill in information about the plot and thematic arcs, from the setup to the resolution.

4. Note what items or elements will be required during the course of the story, and include your first impressions. Add any ideas or questions you want to research or explore.

	ACT 1		ACT 2		ACT 3	
BEATS	**SETUP**	**INCITING INCIDENT**	**MIDPOINT**	**BUILD ON MIDPOINT**	**CLIMAX**	**RESOLUTION**
Plot Arc	The everyday world: establishes backstory and relates to the audience	New perspective and results of change	Something happens that triggers a question/need to change	Change of behavior	Insight and new action	New perspective and results of change
Theme Arc	A lie limits the character or world	The lie is transformed or broken down				The truth frees them or they choose a new lie
Costume	Descriptive notes					
Thoughts	Personal connections, or initial ideas					

YOUR TITLE

LOGLINE

THEME TO EXPLORE

Types of Stories

The type of story being told will always greatly affect how you develop your designs. Is it a straightforward good vs. evil tale? Or a story that examines the greater, foggier complexity of humanity?

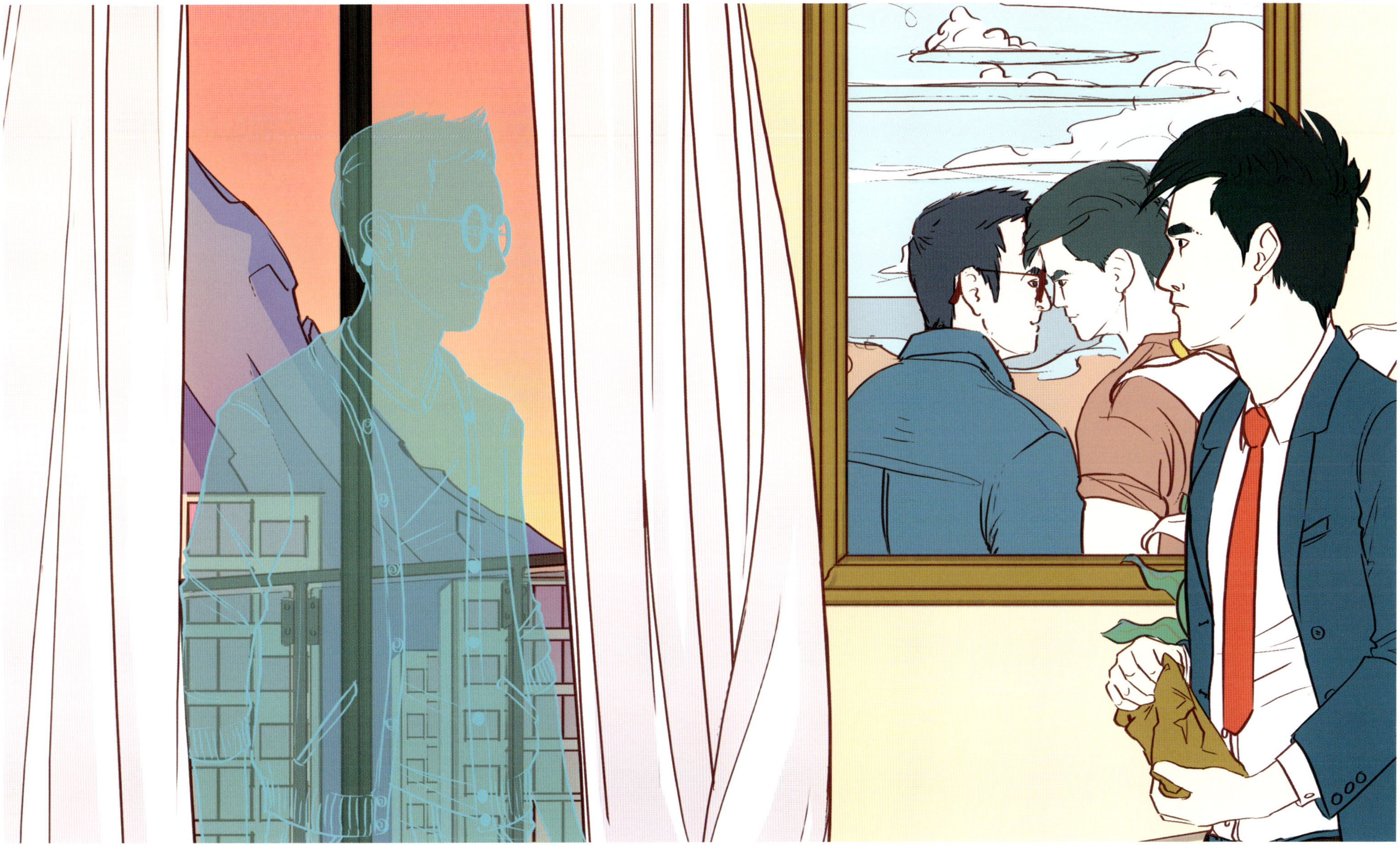

Let's examine the two most popular types of narrative in world-building: the moral compass, which divides conflict by group, and the foggy mirror, which explores the individual. They are extreme opposites of each other. Not every narrative will fit perfectly within either context, but if you were to place a production on a scale, you'll be able to tell which more greatly affects the story and thus your contribution to it.

MORAL COMPASS

Throughout most of human history, storytelling has been used to keep our morality in check, and legends, religious mythologies, and folklore are perfect examples of moral compass tales. These stories are appealing to most people because the protagonist can be anyone. Likewise, the antagonist can be any challenge we face.

In the famous morality play, *Everyman*, the protagonist Everyman goes on a journey with Knowledge to find Confession and heal Good-Deeds. This simple story structure is how we tell hero stories, so that every audience member can put themselves in the hero's shoes.

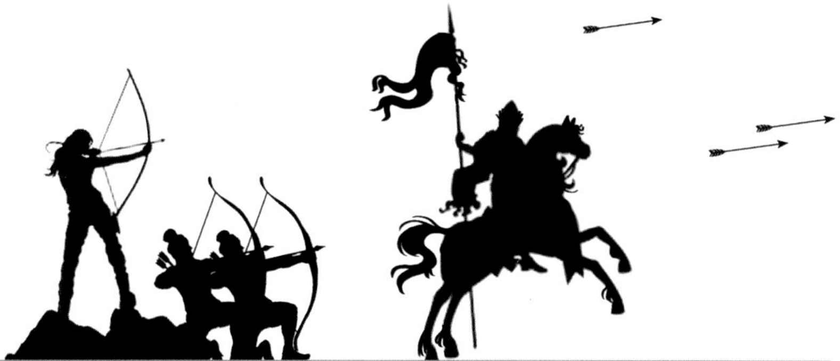

Story Elements

- "Everyman" narratives, religious mythologies, and folklore.
- Morality is black and white.
- Direct metaphors for current events and politics; picks sides in the argument.
- "Us vs. them" mentality.
- Evil is a physical force.
- Patriotism is more important than globalism.
- Context is divided by categories of people rather than individuals.
- Portrays archetypes with moments of great struggle but an overall steadfast character, such as princesses and knights.

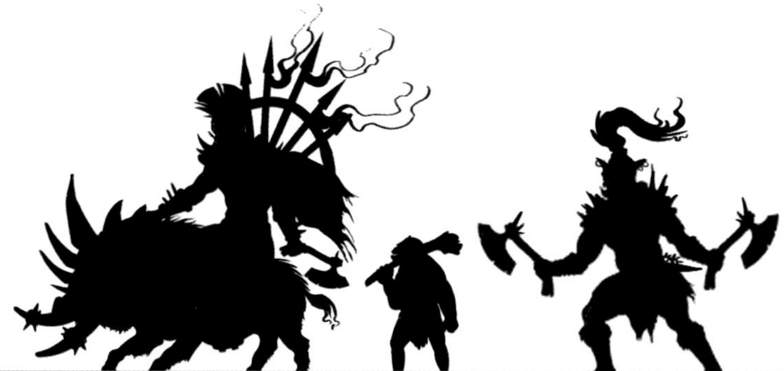

Examples

- **Film:** *Star Wars*, *The Avengers*, *Metropolis*, *Wonder Woman*, *Tarzan*
- **Animation:** *Mulan*, *Snow White*, *Toy Story*, *James and the Giant Peach*, *Coco*
- **Literature:** *The Chronicles of Narnia* series, *The Oz series*, *The Last Unicorn*
- **Games:** *Super Mario Bros.*, *The Legend of Zelda*, *Destiny*, *Final Fantasy XV*
- **Illustration:** *Momotaro*

The Hobbit

J. R. R. Tolkien

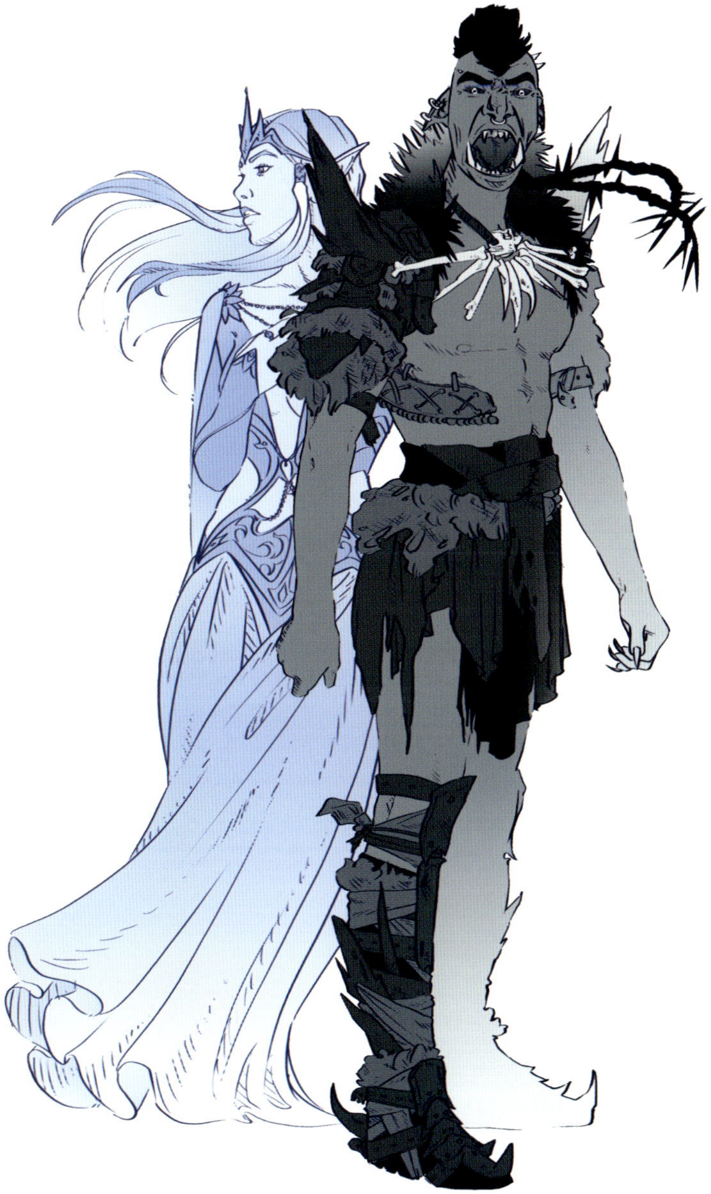

A Closer Look

The high fantasy epic to end all epics, J. R. R. Tolkien's Middle-earth is the quintessential moral compass setting. He used it to criticize the development of weapons of mass destruction. He even referred to their use as "Orc work." The novelist may not have been criticizing the atomic bomb in his masterpiece—the Manhattan Project began after the four major novels were released—but he certainly used *The One Ring to Rule Them All* as a comment on the seductive lure of modern militaristic power, and how quickly it can turn on its wielders.

Despite a huge world of snowy mountains, vast plains, grassy knolls, and towering forests, the people of Middle-earth are defined by race, and in turn, class. Every elf is elegant. Every dwarf is blunt. Every orc is evil. Socioeconomic status is also divided in this way: the elves are the upper crust, the hobbits are suburbanites, and the dwarves are the working class.

This world order is easy to digest. We are able to divide visual language by archetype (elegant elves, gruff dwarves, wise wizards, etc.) rather than based on the individual. Because of this, Tolkien was able to expand upon a vast world that a very wide range of people are dedicated to. Unlike works such as Frank Herbert's *Dune*, for example, readers and viewers don't have to exert much effort to understand the political climate of the world, and can be casual consumers of the story.

THE FOGGY MIRROR

Moral compass narratives feature heroes with a singular tragic flaw, who live in a black-and-white world, where good and evil are clearly defined. Costumes are often very stereotypical, relying on group identity. Foggy mirror stories, on the other hand, place doubt at every turn. Good and evil live in a gray zone, where good intentions might lead to tragedy, and antagonists might be fighting for the greater good. Thus, they call for costume designs that are more flexible as they showcase individuals who may experience personal growth but still maintain their group identity.

Take, for example, Marvel characters Daredevil and Kingpin. Both fight for the good of Hell's Kitchen but in different ways. Our protagonist in this story is clearly Daredevil, but is he our protagonist only because he is our point of view? Imagine the Daredevil comics from Kingpin's point of view. He would be the philanthropist in love, while Daredevil's role might easily shift to that of an evil assassin.

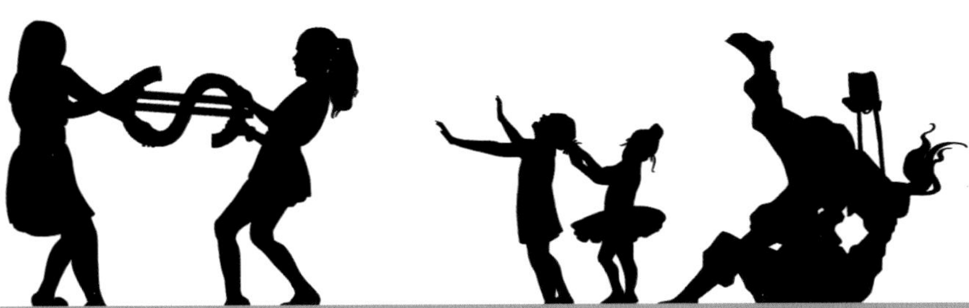

Story Elements

- Hero/antihero stories focusing on personal struggles in an imperfect world.
- Morality is gray and flexible.
- Nonlinear narratives.
- Uses current events directly rather than metaphors.
- Openly examines the repercussions of current events.
- Evil and virtue are explored in the same individual.
- Good and bad people are found on both sides of the conflict.
- Portrays three-dimensional people.
- Even very minor characters struggle with their personal fears and ideals.

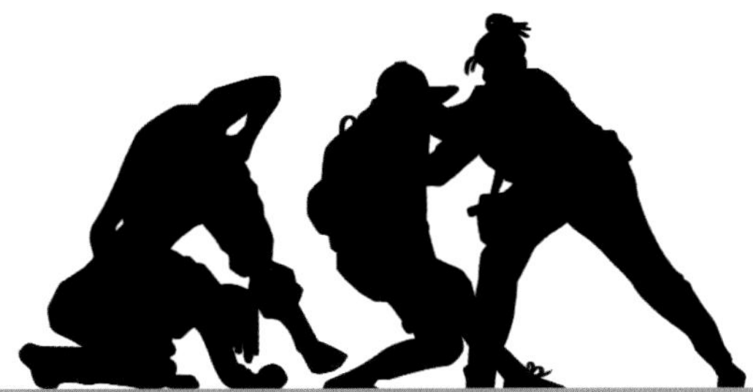

Examples

- **Film:** *Fight Club*, *Seven Psychopaths*, *Maleficent*, *Broadchurch*
- **Animation:** *Shrek*, *Ergo Proxy*, *Akira*, *Steven Universe*
- **Literature:** *American Gods*, *Harry Potter* series, *Dune*, *Ender's Game*, *Wicked*
- **Game:** *Fallout: New Vegas*, *Far Cry 5*, *The Elder Scrolls V: Skyrim*
- **Graphic Novels/Comics:** *Saga*, *Sandman*, *Watchmen*, *Daredevil*

A GAME OF THRONES

George R. R. Martin

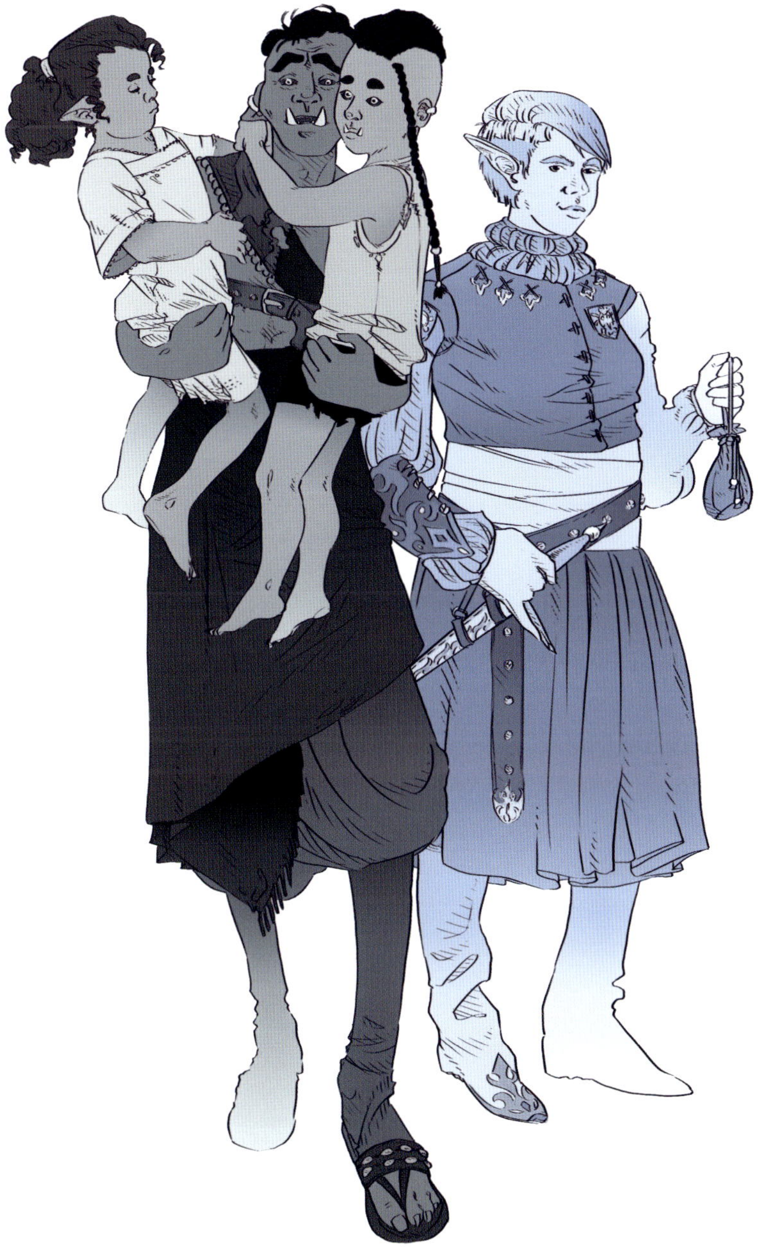

A Closer Look

George R. R. Martin's epic is chaotic. His work is the perfect example of the foggy mirror. Each character is driven by his/her own individual path rather than an overall narrative. Personal goals conflict and contradict. Group identities, such as the Stark family, are quickly fractured, sending beloved characters into the fray of an unpredictable world.

Unlike the characters of Tolkien, there is no way to neatly archetype Martin's work. Every character is an individual and can't be judged by the group they belong to. In fact, Martin often uses these defining traits to challenge the reader's perception of his characters. This requires the audience to be entrenched in the lore of the world to truly understand the motivations of deeply flawed and traumatized characters. His writing reinforces the truth that all humans are capable of both great good and great evil.

How Viewpoint Impacts Design

While the story may be the protagonist's, how you view the story may or may not be representing the character's own view of the world. The director may be trying to give the audience an authentic version of an era or may instead focus on sharing a relatable emotional experience with the audience. We see this choice through the lens of the camera, our eyes in the world. A story may switch between lenses to emphasize moments, but the production is usually dominated by one or the other for the course of the film.

EXPERIENTIAL

The experiential lens captures the way the character feels about his or her world. With this lens, we invite the audience to share an emotional experience with the character. However, because we can't expect our audience to comprehend how people will have felt in the past, or in fantasy or sci-fi situations, we translate it through modern tricks, exaggeration, and intimate shots. This lens is often used for heightened emotional scenes.

In the film *The Great Gatsby* (2013), for example, a raucous party is being thrown. To a modern audience, knee-length flapper dresses and swing music would feel relatively conservative and old-fashioned. The audience wouldn't feel the rebellious atmosphere that those who truly lived in the time would feel. So instead, director Baz Luhrmann chose to use rap and modern interpretations of flapper fashion to translate the emotion to the audience.

VOYEURISTIC

A voyeuristic lens gives the audience a window into the character's world. They are not trying to understand or relate to the characters as much as they want to gossip about them. It is the nosy neighbor of viewpoints. As a result, there is more reservation with visuals and styles overall; leaning on more accurate historical costume, we allow the audience to suspend their disbelief more easily so they can focus on examining the plot in more detail.

Attention is given to the realistic world as shots often pull back to let us see the settings, creating a sense of distance from the characters. Intimate shots are more likely to focus on items rather than people, grounding the audience in the seriousness and weight of the world. This steadier lens is often used in period drama where the complexities of the character's lives are being discussed in quiet detail.

Notice how much the TV series *Downton Abbey* focuses on shots that establish where we are and what the characters are wearing. The meticulous attention to detail helps establish a grounded, realistic world with clear rules. This allows the audience to keep better track of the complex motivations and storylines of the ensemble cast.

Exercise: Levels of Realism

Using your viewpoint as a guide, determine the level of realism you will be aiming to achieve in your project. This will help you understand how to approach your research in later stages.

REALISM

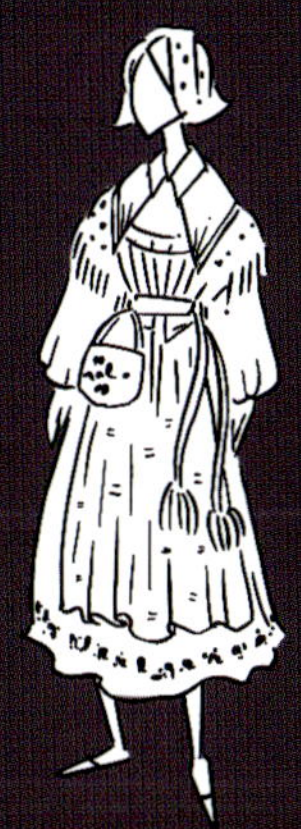

HISTORICAL ACCURACY IS MOST IMPORTANT.

There is a strong association with time and place. The costume can still be playful, showcasing the personal taste of the character and including thematic symbolism so that it can fulfill its basic function: establishing a dialogue between the character, historical time, and the narrative.

Elizabeth (1998)

PARA REALISM

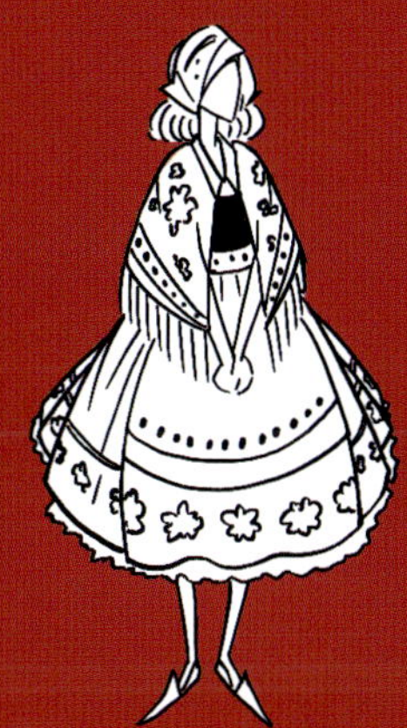

STYLE AND BEAUTY PREVAIL OVER ACCURACY.

Inspired by the fashion of the time, but the vision of what we find beautiful and acceptable will influence the concept of the outfit, and the costume design will end up as more of an interpretation than an exact reproduction of the original.

Sleeping Beauty (1950)

SURREALISM

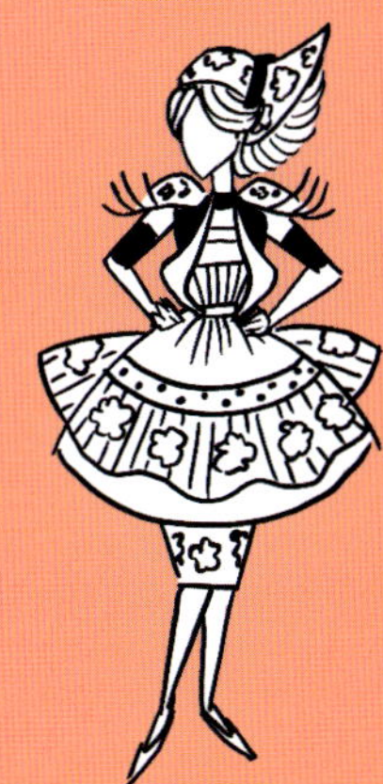

A SYMBOLIC REPRESENTATION IS VALUED OVER ACCURACY.

Historic accuracy loses importance and the costume functions to symbolically translate the character, their state of mind, and/or create dramatic or psychological effects.

Mirror Mirror (2012)

A Take on *Midsummer Night's Dream*

by William Shakespeare

As you begin to search for connections and note your impressions of the story type, lens, and costumes, pick up a drawing tool and think through your hand to begin translating. As adults, we don't always feel confident exploring as boldly and imperfectly as we did as children. Remind yourself that it's okay if you don't know the answers yet. Analyzing, questioning, or exploring takes time. If you rush these important stages, you may easily fall into the trap of spending more time defending your first idea from critique and not enough time humbly questioning if there is another way to look at the idea. Use a personal sketchbook to explore your emotional and aesthetic reactions fully and fluidly without worrying about accuracy or appropriation. Remember, at this stage you are simply analyzing visually.

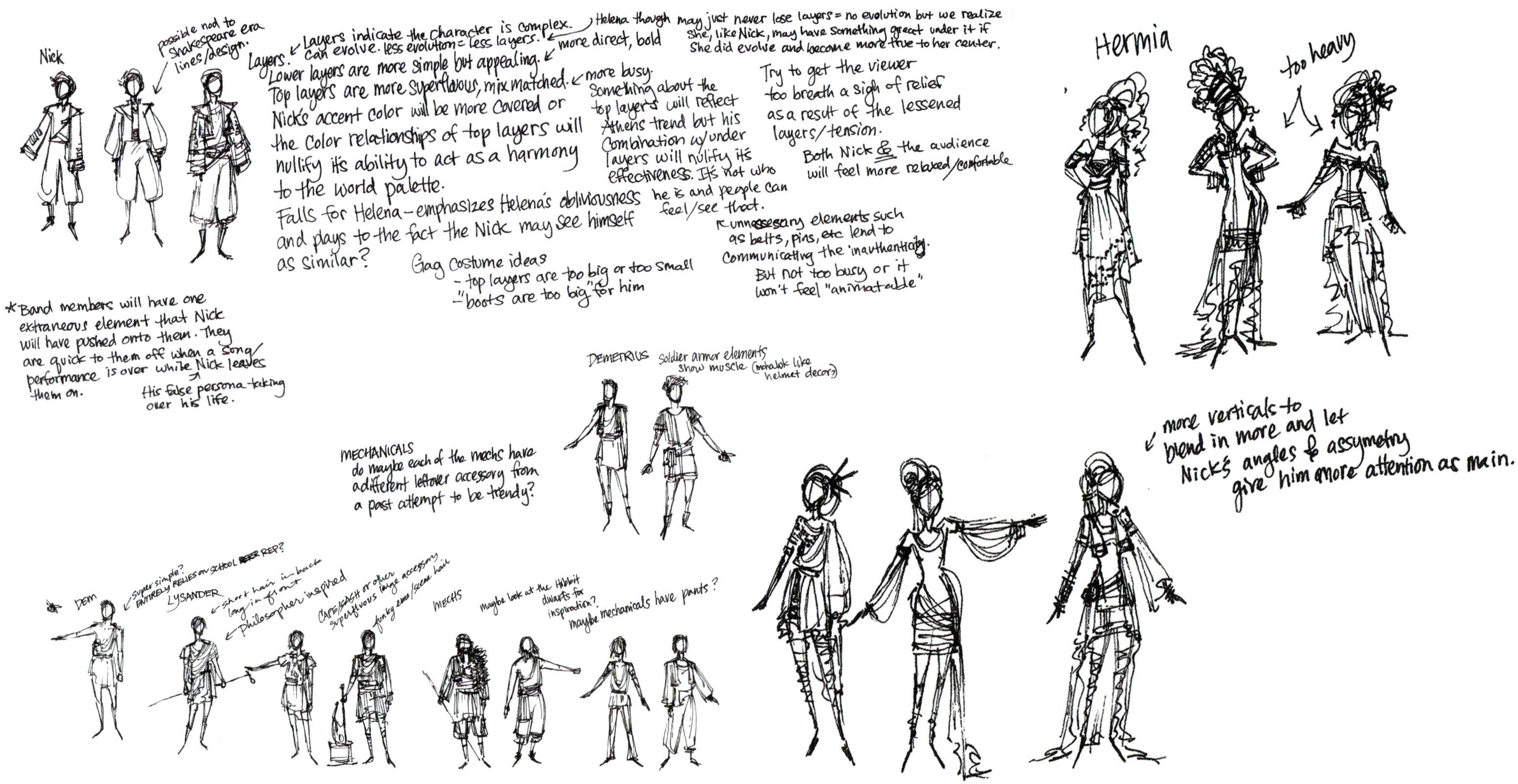

THUMBNAILING

Once you have concepts you like, summarize and clarify the ideas by thumbnailing. Thumbnails will help you push past your first ideas and note any patterns you consistently come back to. As you refine your thumbnails with visual research, clarify the drawings so that a director or collaborator will be able to understand your intent without excessive explanation. And at any point in the process of design, when in doubt, go back to thumbnailing!

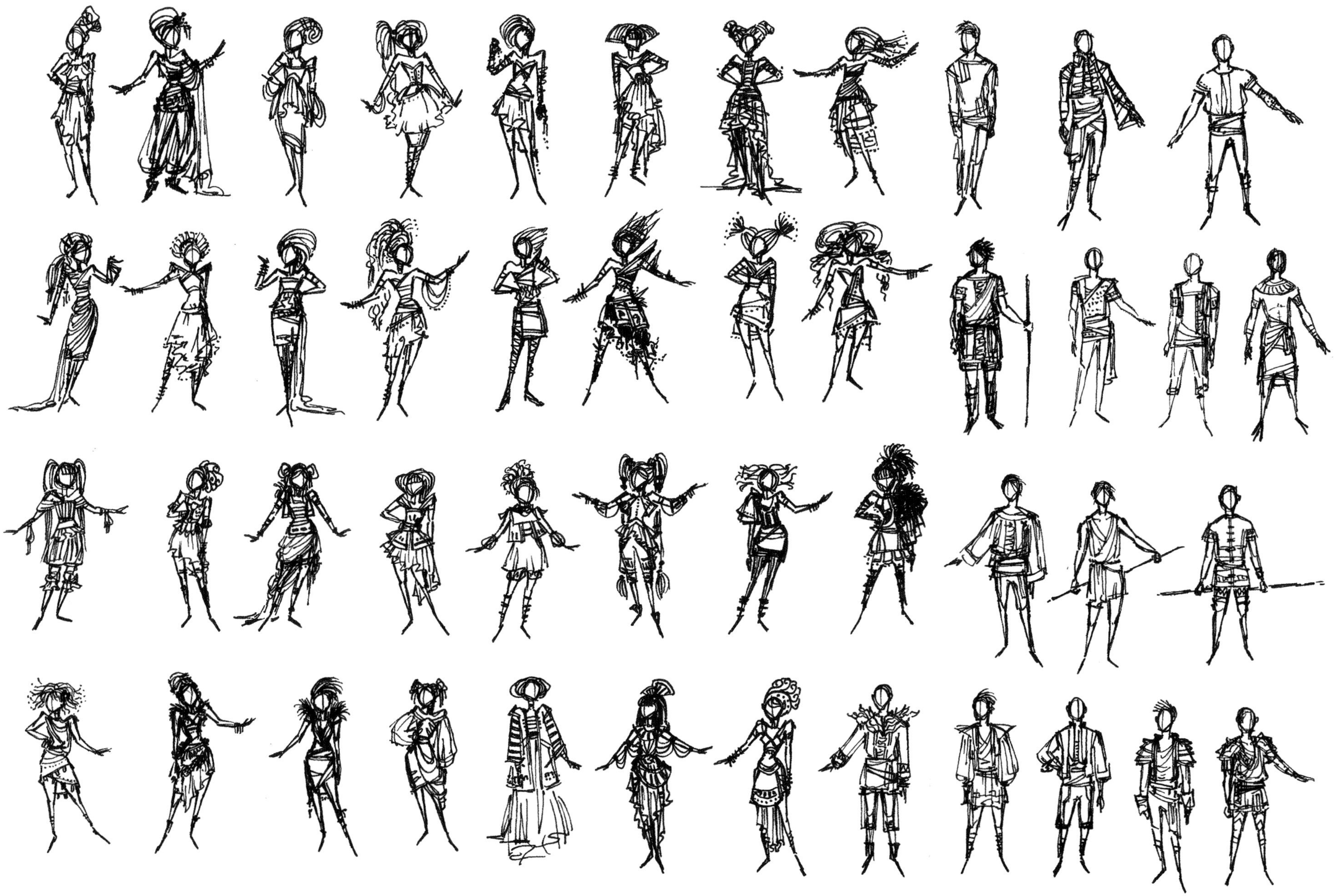

RIFFING

This stage is often called "blue sky" in animation and can be a great opportunity to collaborate as you explore your responses. Riffing with other concept artists, visual development artists, or character designers will allow your team to flow through more ideas quickly and land on the most impactful elements to include. As the production art accumulates, you may even riff off of environment concepts to find more ways to connect the costumes with their settings.

TIP: Find elements you like and mix them to surprise yourself with unexpected options. Don't worry about final style during these initial explorations. At this visual problem-solving stage, you only need to worry about noting your thoughts and questions. Work in whatever style comes naturally.

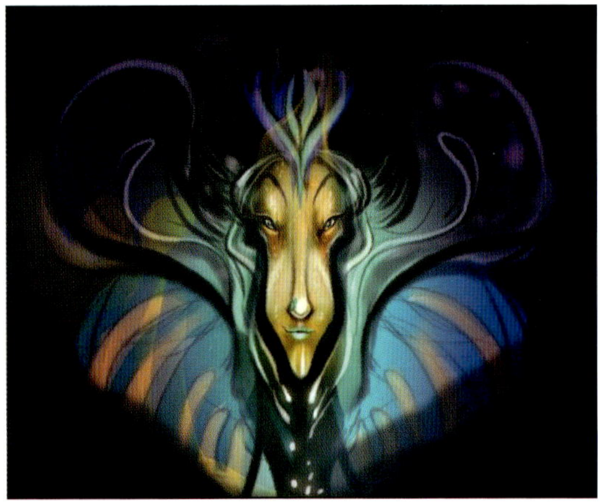
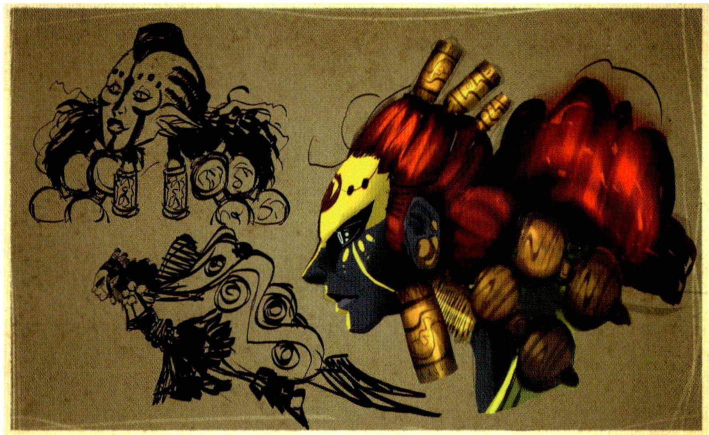
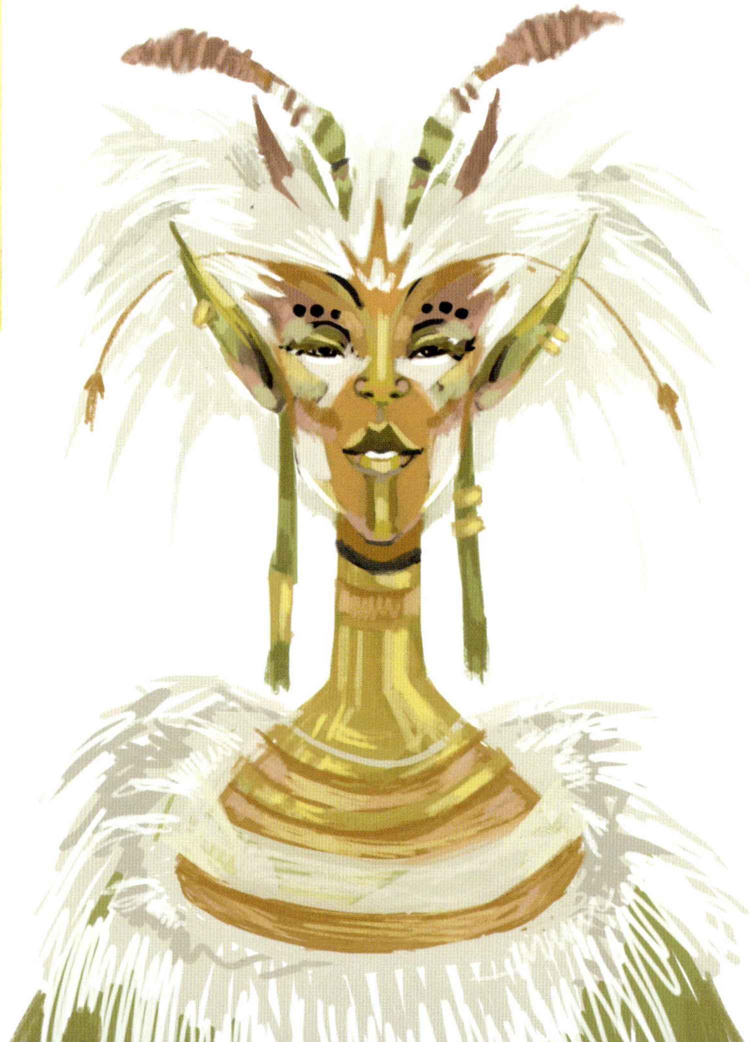
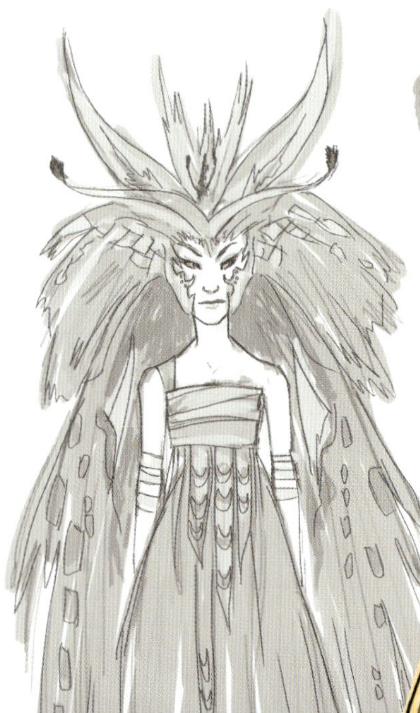
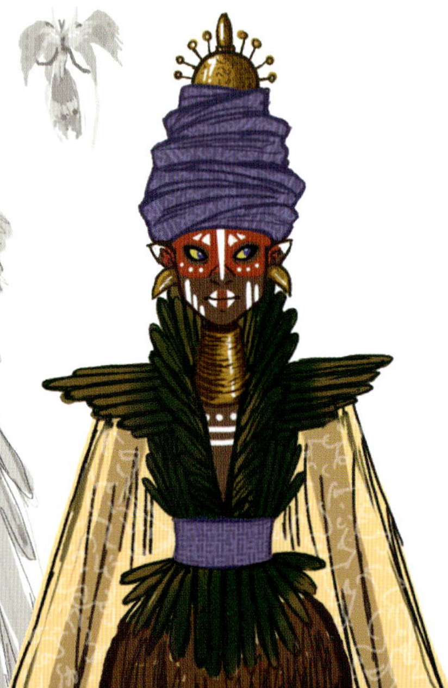
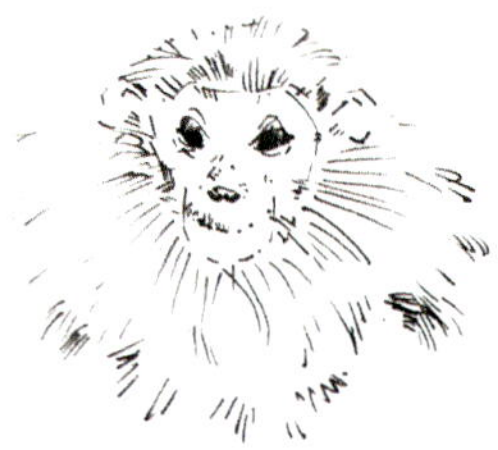
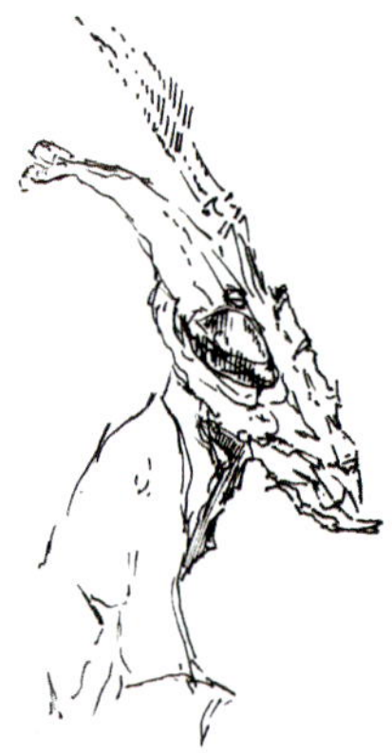

SIMPLIFY

Try using photobashing or digital symmetry tools to surprise yourself and create quick variations. Lowering the opacity of a completed design layer you have already made and creating a new one over it can help you push beyond your first impressions. Make one large opposing choice in your new design and then follow where it leads. Don't worry about posing, lighting, details or "rendering" yet, these are just visual "what-if" questions. You're not selling the idea at this stage; you're just exploring what you want to take further into research. If it's "readable" enough to respond to, it's functional.

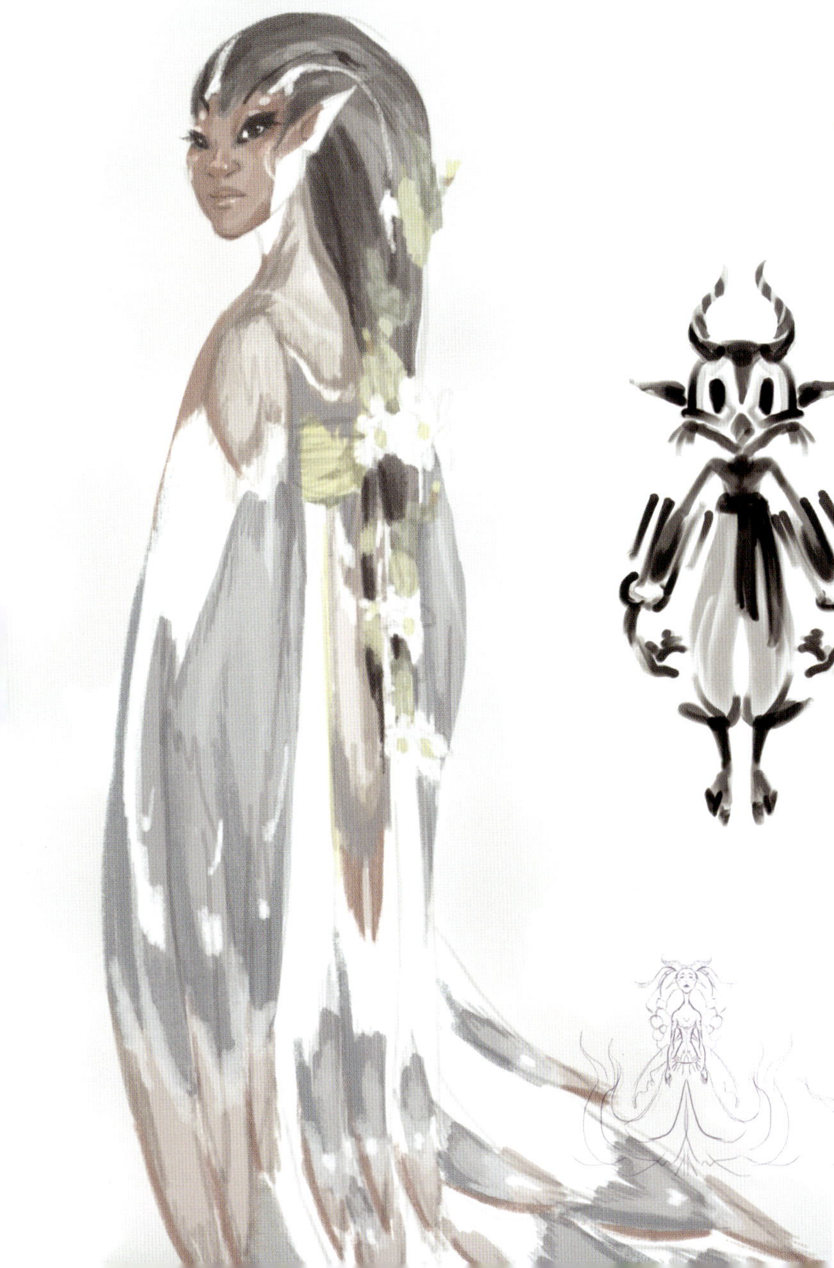

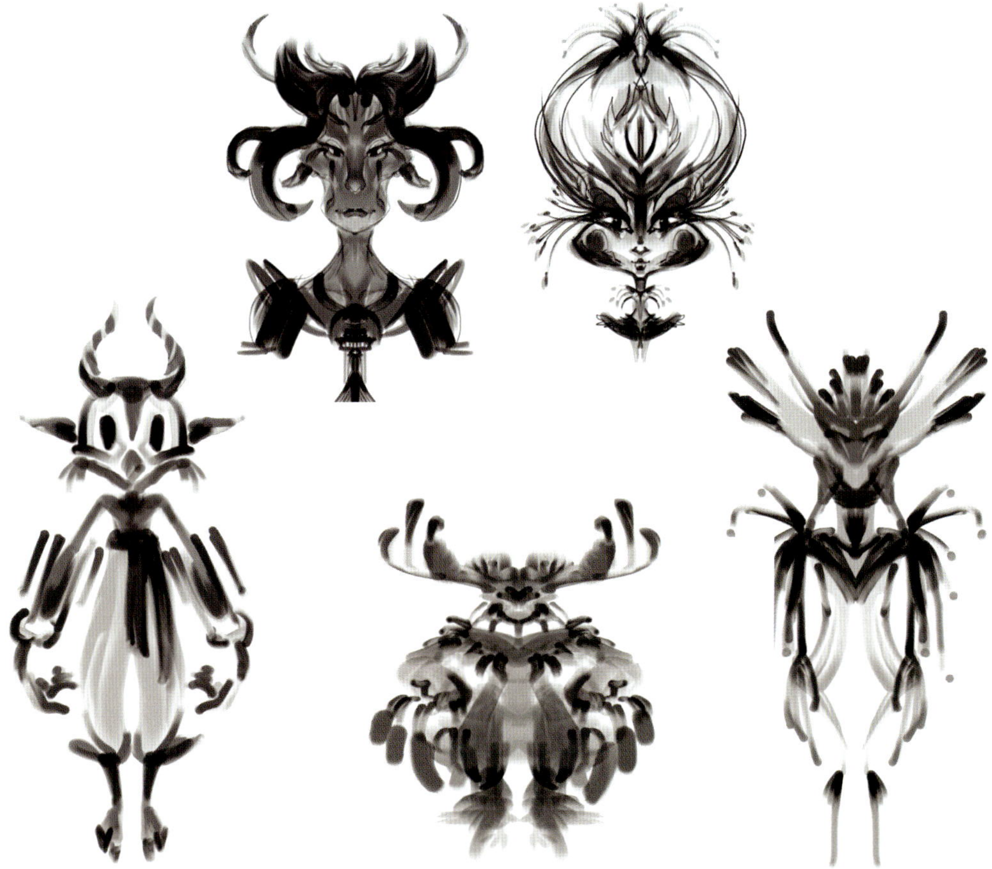

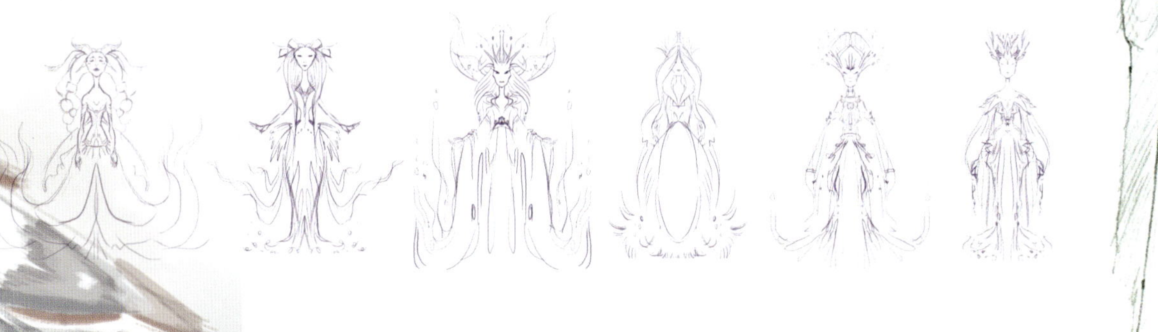

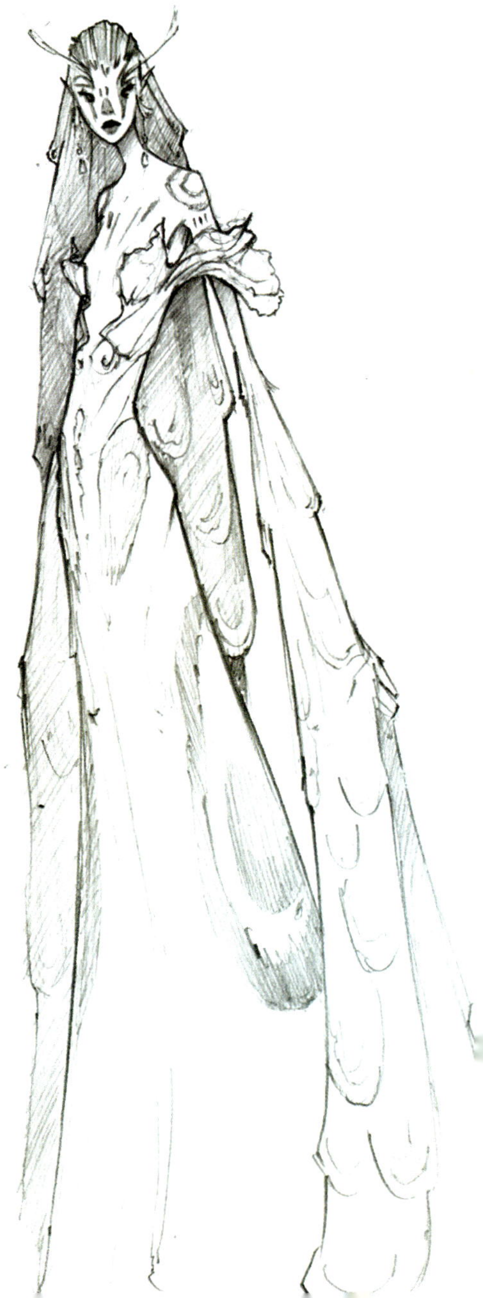

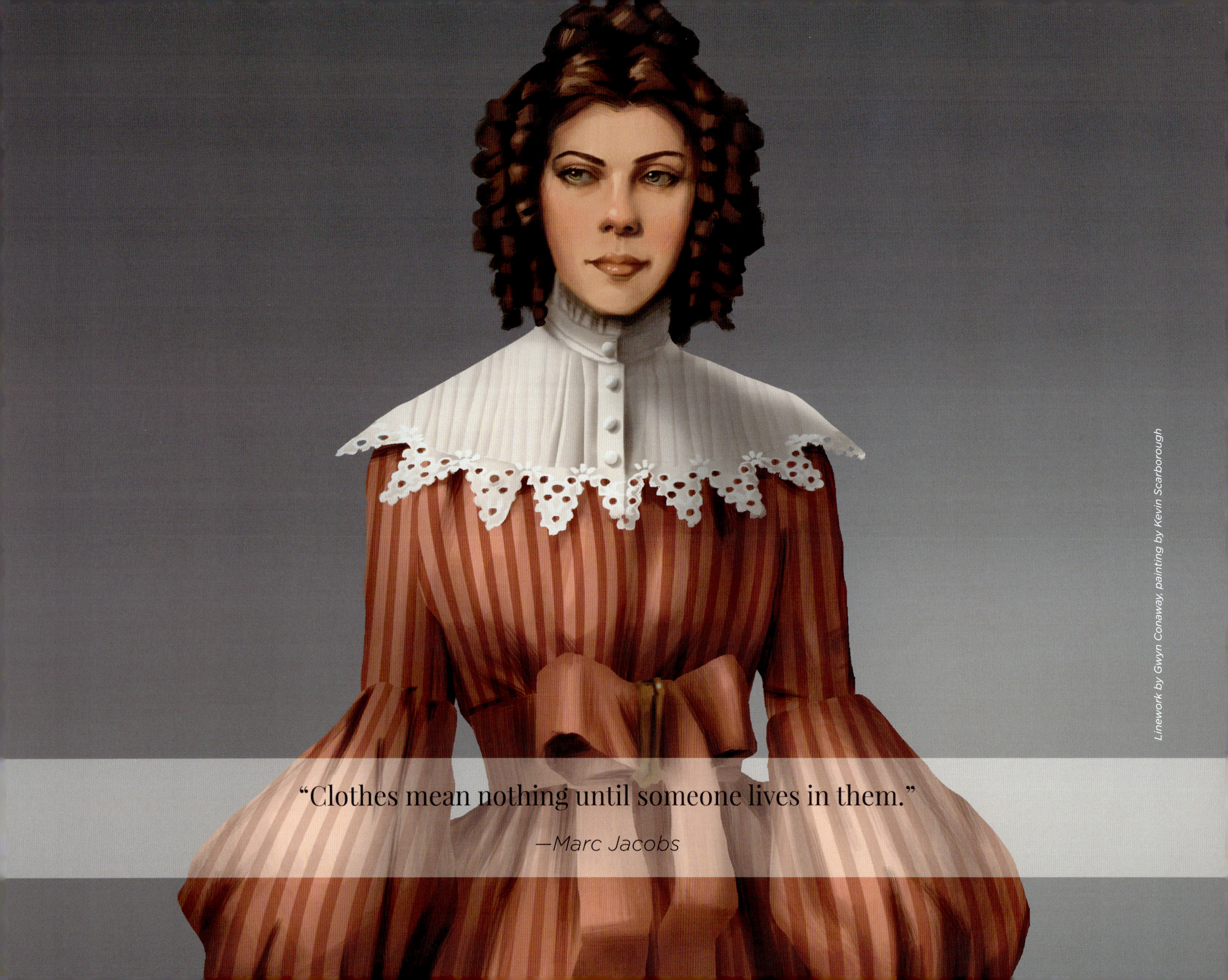

"Clothes mean nothing until someone lives in them."

—Marc Jacobs

Linework by Gwyn Conaway, painting by Kevin Scarborough

CHAPTER 2 SOCIETY

We rely on the human experience to tell meaningful stories. If your protagonist's story is a single thread, context is the entire tapestry. Knowing how to weave together the relationships between power, class, and trade within a story is knowing the larger world. And to know the larger world is to know the character's place within it—the social terrain.

This often isn't easy to recognize, because the terrain isn't physically underfoot. This terrain is defined by the structure of society, expressed through its culture and people. If the social terrain of a character is not carefully considered during your design process, the character may appear to be disconnected, too distant from the world, and in turn, from the audience.

For this section, set your sketchbook aside and tuck away your imagination as we explore different societies to identify what factors (social terrain) influence what people wear and don't wear. This info will help you effectively identify and utilize a character's social terrain during your design process. Knowing both the character and the context well allows you to address one of the biggest questions you should ask as part of exploring any story: Which changes more—"the hero" or the world? This answer will inform your design decisions just as it has the history of fashion.

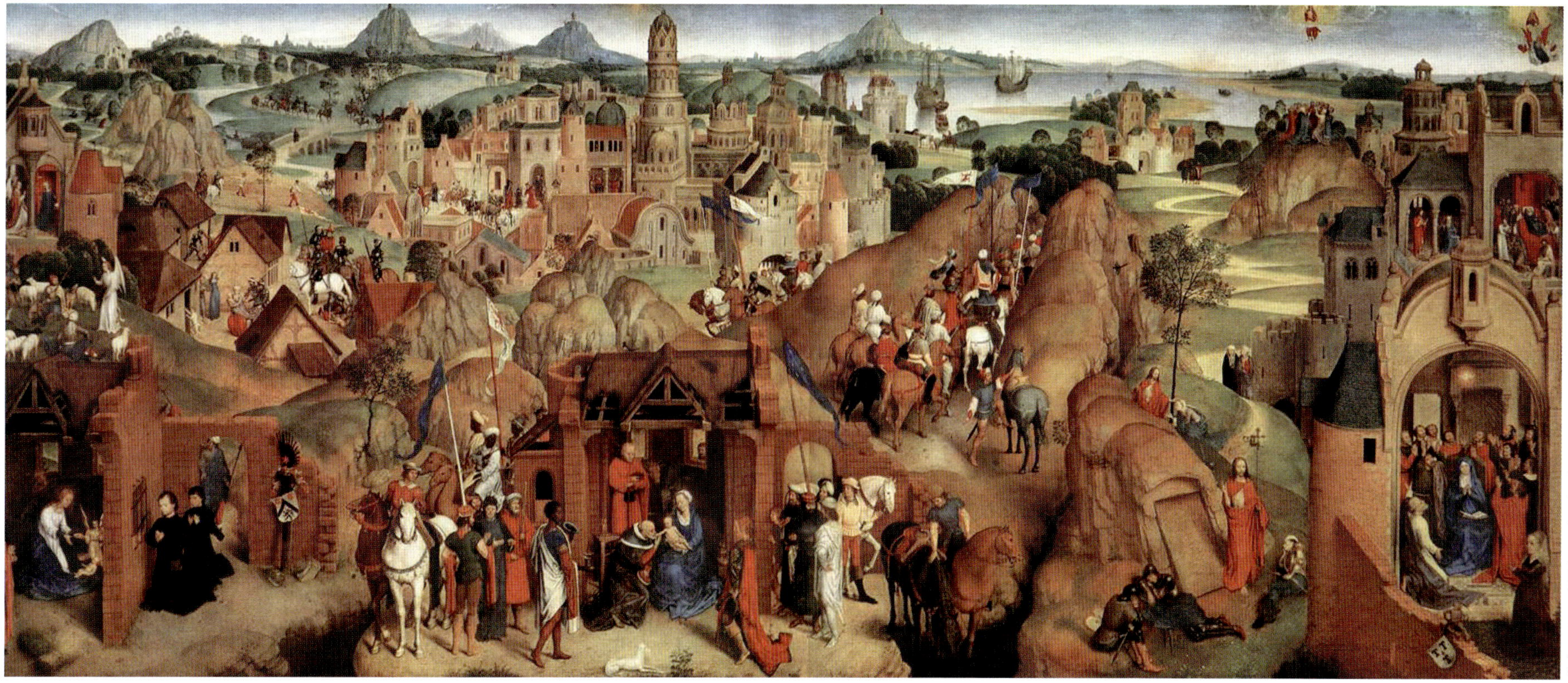

Advent and Triumph of Christ, by Hans Memling, 1480

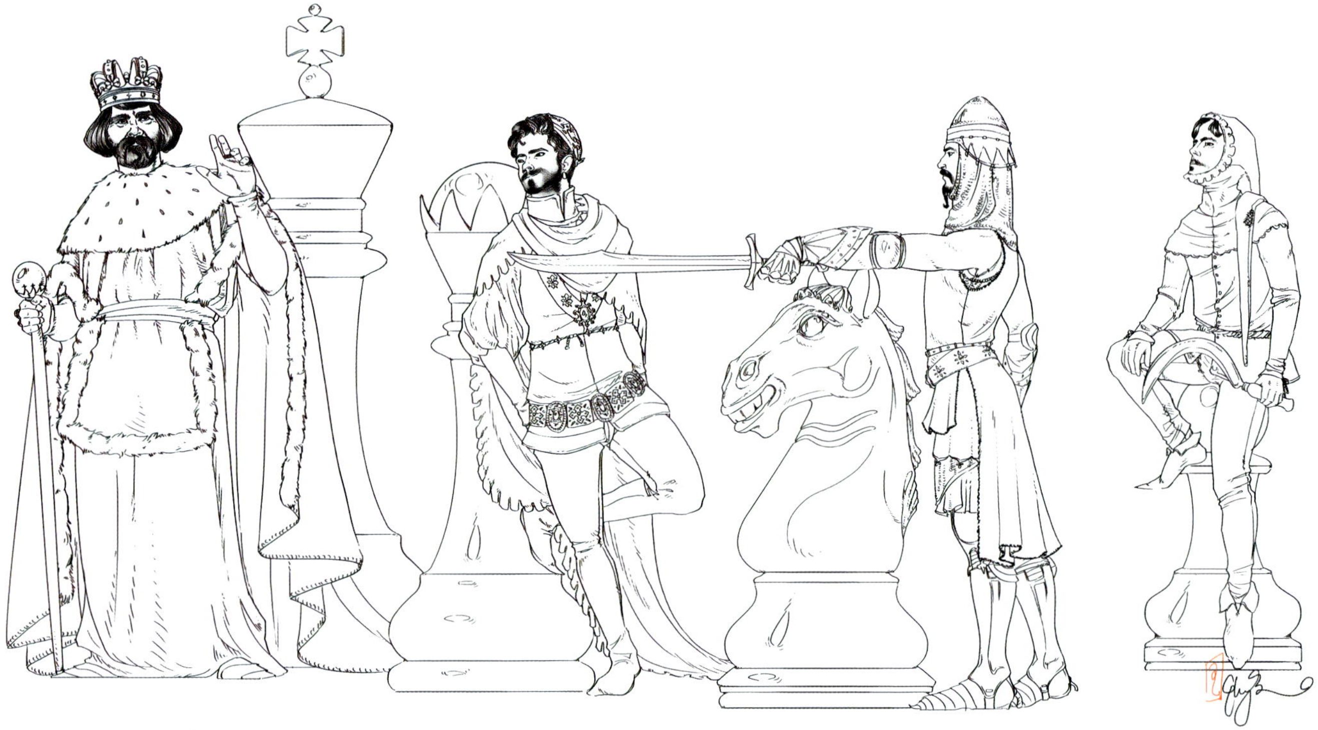

Power Dynamics

An important thing to first acknowledge as you explore the society of your character is that power dynamics exist in all relationships, whether the parties are two individuals or two nations. This carries into fashion as well. Trends don't change just because the next generation wants to separate themselves from those who preceded them. In many cases, change is a conscious decision made by people, let's call them "the Powers," with a specific goal in mind.

The Powers constantly fight for control and can act as an obstacle for the protagonist in a story. As mentioned, one of the biggest questions is, "Which changes the most in the end? The world or the hero?" This is the heart of the story. Understanding these relationships is important for creating costumes that psychologically support the story arc.

Remember, the Powers aren't always a political force. They can be people of trade, philosophy, religion, influence, science, and so on. In a narrative, the Powers can even be individual characters.

Let's meet them, see how their standing in society is expressed through their style, and review some iconic examples from history.

Style Elements

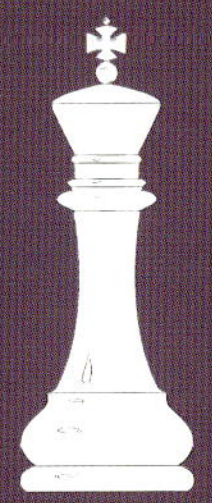

Established Power

Usually a heavier "steeped in tradition" aesthetic.

Rigmarole is important! Complicated status symbols are a must.

Generally, more mature silhouettes with deeper color palettes.

Money is spent on displays of power and social gatherings.

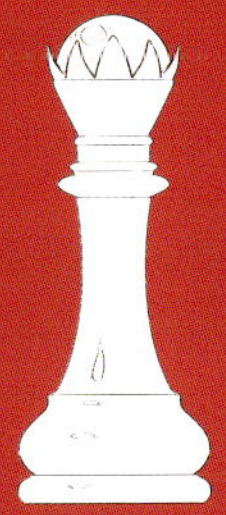

Rising Power

Dreamlike aesthetic with an emphasis on fantasy.

Might mock the status symbols of Established Power in an attempt to shock and offend.

Silhouettes can explode in this dynamic because the rules have been thrown out the window.

Money is spent on personal pleasure and social gatherings.

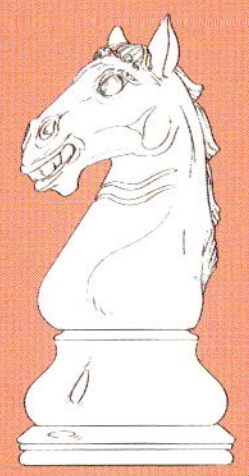

Foreign Power

Aesthetic varies greatly, but will always merge or take over the local aesthetic.

Forces locals to adopt Foreign Power's culture, beliefs, and social structure.

Local clothing is a curiosity for entertainment only, becoming a stereotype over time.

Foreign Power's textiles, sewing techniques, palettes, and other elements may not be suited for the local climate, but will always be considered more refined.

Money is spent on displays of power and assimilation of locals.

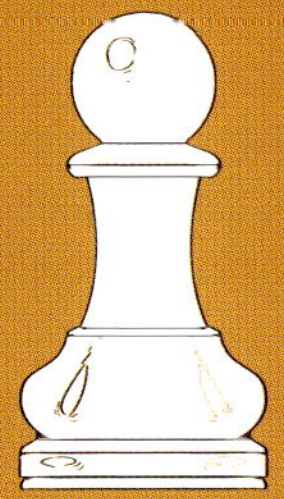

The People

Functional clothing becomes cultural status symbols.

High fashion follows street fashion.

Sometimes wearing symbols of wealth and power can be dangerous.

Money is spent on rebranding and public projects.

Established Power

This is a group of powerful, conservative elite, born into privilege, who have held constant power for generations. They surround themselves with loyalists and are cemented in their ways.

EXAMPLE: QUEEN VICTORIA

Influence: Queen Victoria promoted family ideals and tradition during her reign from 1837 to 1901, therefore small waists, large busts and hips—physical features thought to correlate with fertility—and docility were in style throughout the period.

The Victorian Era had five distinct fashion silhouettes—romantic, crinoline, crinolette, fishtail bustle, and teacart bustle—all of which had elements of Established Power with skirt shapes that were rigid and grandiose and grew in maturity with the queen. When Queen Victoria died in 1901, fashion designers such as Mariano Fortuny and Paul Poiret (Rising Powers) breathed a sigh of relief and dove headfirst into modernism.

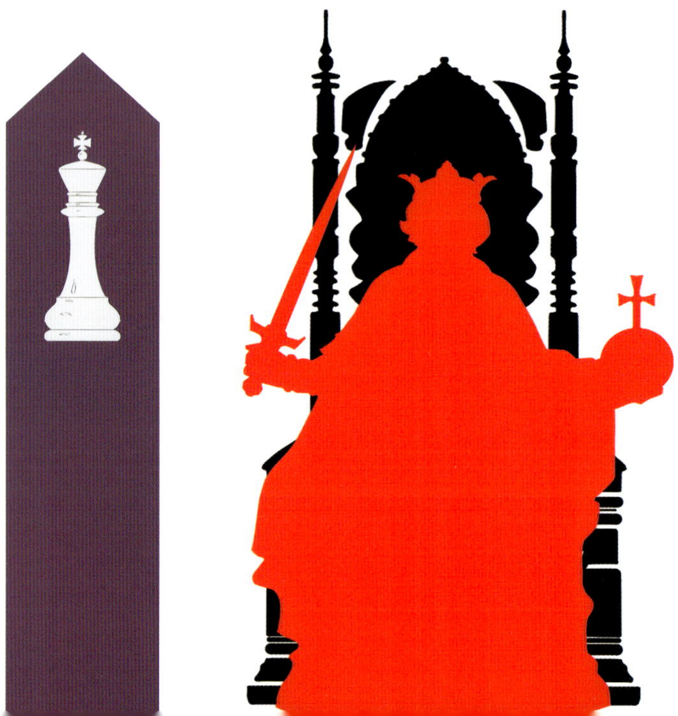

Rising Power

Rising Power may have grown up under the wing of Established Power but they choose to disregard the traditions and duties set up by their predecessors. Instead, they pursue personal pleasure, escapism, or idealism. They often use shock tactics to overthrow the stale philosophies of the past.

EXAMPLE: MARIE ANTOINETTE

Influence: An archduchess of Austria, Marie Antoinette was only 14 when she left her homeland to marry Louis XVI and become queen consort of France in 1774. Labeled an outsider and living under intense public scrutiny, she often looked for relief from royal duty. In the early 1780s, she gently defied the long-held rules of the French courts (Established Power), first by building the Petit Hameau on the grounds of Versailles, a leisurely getaway from life in the palace.

She then introduced a common dressmaker, Rose Bertin (The People), into her inner circle. This alliance sparked a new fashion, insidiously labeled by the public chemise à la reine, or the underwear of the queen. Marie Antoinette shirked the big hoop skirts and corsets, the heavily embroidered and beaded robes, for a light, airy gaulle. This dress, made of multiple layers of fine, delicate cotton or muslin, tied with a simple sash, looked more like undergarments to the established powers of the courts. Once introduced, though, the fashion spread like wildfire, sparking the Rococo age of fantasy and luxury.

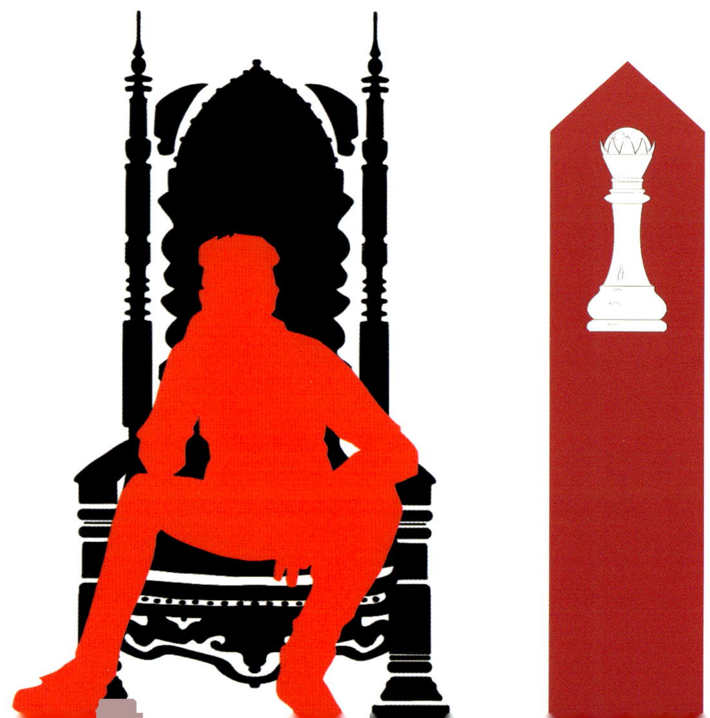

Foreign Power

Hailing from a distant land, culture, language, and/or climate, Foreign Power is usually driven by a combination of philanthropy, evangelism, and imperialism. They are considered invaders who threaten a society's cultural identity and often dehumanize and vilify the native population.

EXAMPLE: PORTUGUESE COLONISTS

Influence: When the Portuguese colonized parts of Africa to Brazil starting in the late 1400s, it enslaved the countries' peoples and forced them to convert to Catholicism. This was an active attempt to pacify slaves by forcing them to adopt the culture of their owners.

The native Brazilian and West African enslaved people were left with a choice: either adopt Catholicism or face persecution. As a result, many dressed their own Yoruban deities, the orixás, as Catholic Saints. A new belief system called Candomblé evolved, and with it, a mixture of West African and Catholic styles.

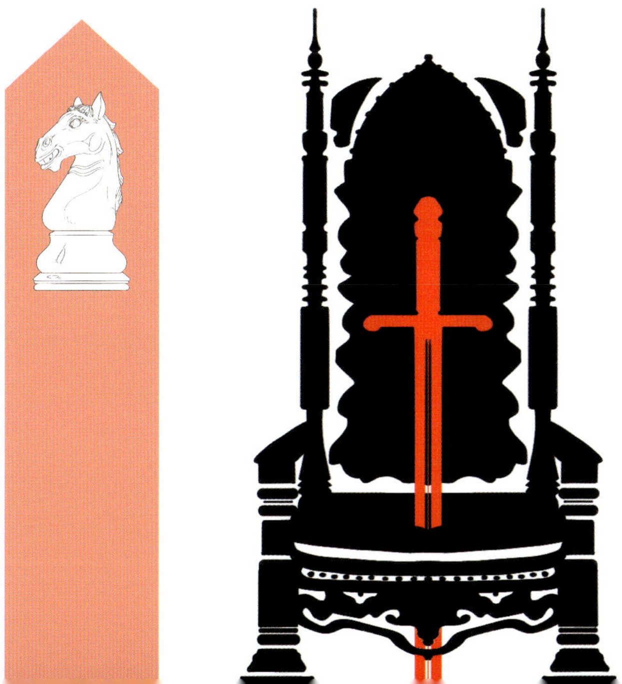

The People

When traditional powers put too much cultural and economic pressure on the masses, the People will rise up and demand change. The disenfranchised and working class mount grassroots movements to challenge the status quo. The People, although perceived as powerless, can topple empires, redefine borders, and change the world. Narratives usually focus on the People because wider audiences relate closely to their modest beginnings.

EXAMPLE: THE BEATLES

Influence: In 1964, the Beatles (Rising Power) performed on *The Ed Sullivan Show* sporting mop-top haircuts and the quintessential slim mod suit and tie. Little did people realize that this new boy band wasn't a passing fad, but a cultural behemoth. By 1966, the band had set aside their mod style and clean-cut hair for sideburns and round tinted glasses. Conservative critics deemed this new style of hair for men as "unsafe" in an attempt to quash the onslaught of rebellious youth. The Beatles, however, weren't done. By 1969, they'd grown out their beards and fully embraced the Summer of Love, writing politically driven anthems.

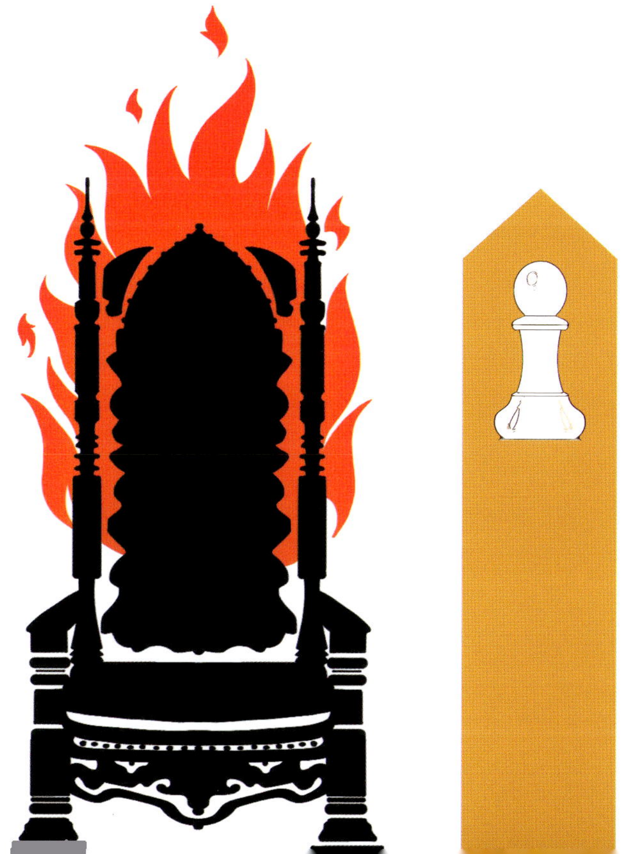

Power Players in Video Games

Can you think of more examples of each of the powers? Or are you able to identify each power in your favorite film or book? Here are some premises from video games:

FAR CRY 3

(Ubisoft, Massive Entertainment, and Red Storm Entertainment)

The islands are in control of the Citra (Rising Power), having stolen it from Rakyat (Established Power) through piracy. Jason (The People) rises up and has the choice to join Citra or kill it.

DRAGON AGE: INQUISITION

(BioWare)

Corypheus (Foreign Power) invades the kingdoms of Thedas (Established Power) and destroys its leaders. Inquisition (Rising Power) throws out the rulebook and elects Herald of Andraste (The People) to lead the charge.

FALLOUT: NEW VEGAS

(Obsidian Entertainment)

The Courier (The People) wakes up the target of Benny and Mr. House (Established Power). The Courier ends up caught in the middle of a feud between Mr. House and New California Republic (Established Powers), Benny (Rising Power), and Caesar (Foreign Power).

BORDERLANDS 3

(Gearbox Software)

The Calypso Twins (Foreign Power) use their social media cult Children of the Vault (The People) to attempt to hijack the vaults of Pandora. The Crimson Raiders (Established Power) call on new Vault Hunters (The People) to help them head off the onslaught.

Asserting Power Through Fashion

Think of fashion in its verb sense, per Merriam-Webster:

1. *To give shape or form to;*
2. *To make or construct, usually with the use of imagination or ingenuity;*
3. *To design or devise for a particular use or purpose.*

If you think of fashion in this way, it becomes an invaluable tool for creating cultures, conflict, characters, and context. As such, an Established Power or Foreign Power may use fashion to placate, control the people, or influence public perception. The clothing of a time and place is the story its people literally wear on their sleeves.

Roping Them In: Christian Dior

During World War II in the United States, many clothing staples were rationed. Fabrics such as wool, cotton, and silk were needed for uniforms and medical bandages. As a result, the US government imposed regulations on the cut of womens wear. Approved garments had to be cut in the most efficient way possible. This meant that the silhouette became boxy and narrow. The war led to the advent of the classic secretarial pencil skirt, for example.

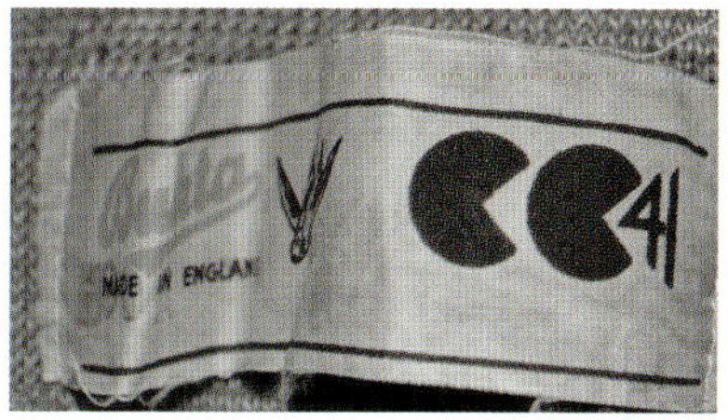

CC41 Utility Label, c. 1944: signified that a garment followed rationing laws.

However, by the time the war was over, women had become accustomed to work and independence. The men returning home found themselves out of their element, surrounded by a highly trained workforce they couldn't compete with. The US government began running domestic ad campaigns to push women back into the home and promote family values. The same could be said for much of Europe.

Around this time, in 1947, Christian Dior launched his first line, Corolle (that roughly translates from French to English as "a flare of flower petals"), now affectionately known as the New Look. Before this, he had worked with other designers, always acknowledged for his potential, but Dior struggled in a war-torn France. He was approached by a man named Marcel Boussac, the richest man in France, who agreed to fund his first collection.

Boussac, the King of Cotton, saw funding Dior's look as good for business, and governments in the West saw it as an opportunity to push their agenda. Dior had designed a line of full skirts and dresses supported by petticoats, paired with highly tailored jackets and overcoats. Many of his designs required an excessive amount of fabric, from 10 to 80 yards. These garments were lush and sweeping, with small waistlines, full busts, and wide hips.

Throughout human history, these proportions have been viewed as a symbol of fertility, and our modern world is no exception. The Established Power of the United States recognized this correlation. The government chose to promote fashions such as the New Look. As a result, it sparked fresh romanticism for femininity and supported the push of women back into the home during the 1950s and 1960s.

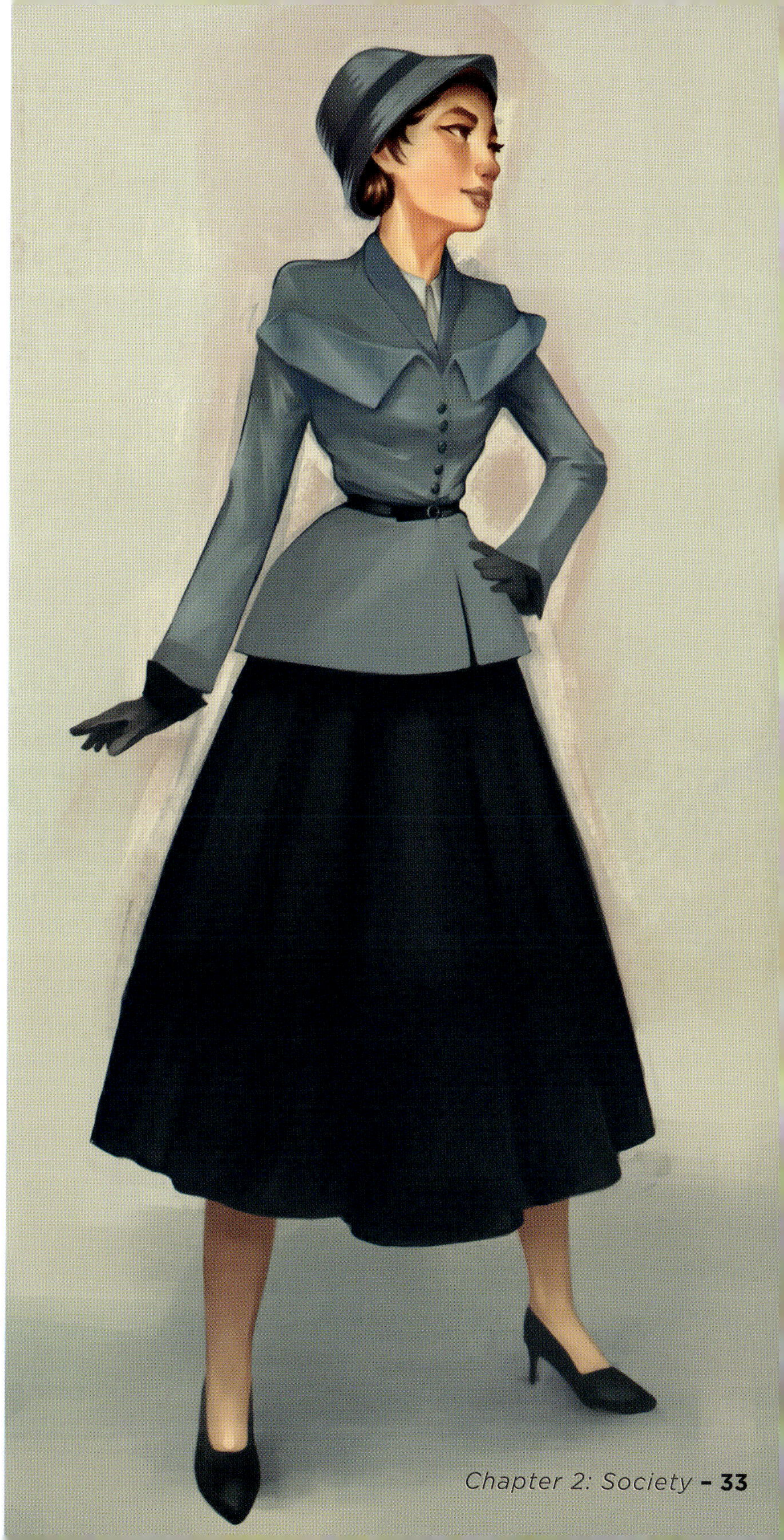

Illustration by Kellan Carranza

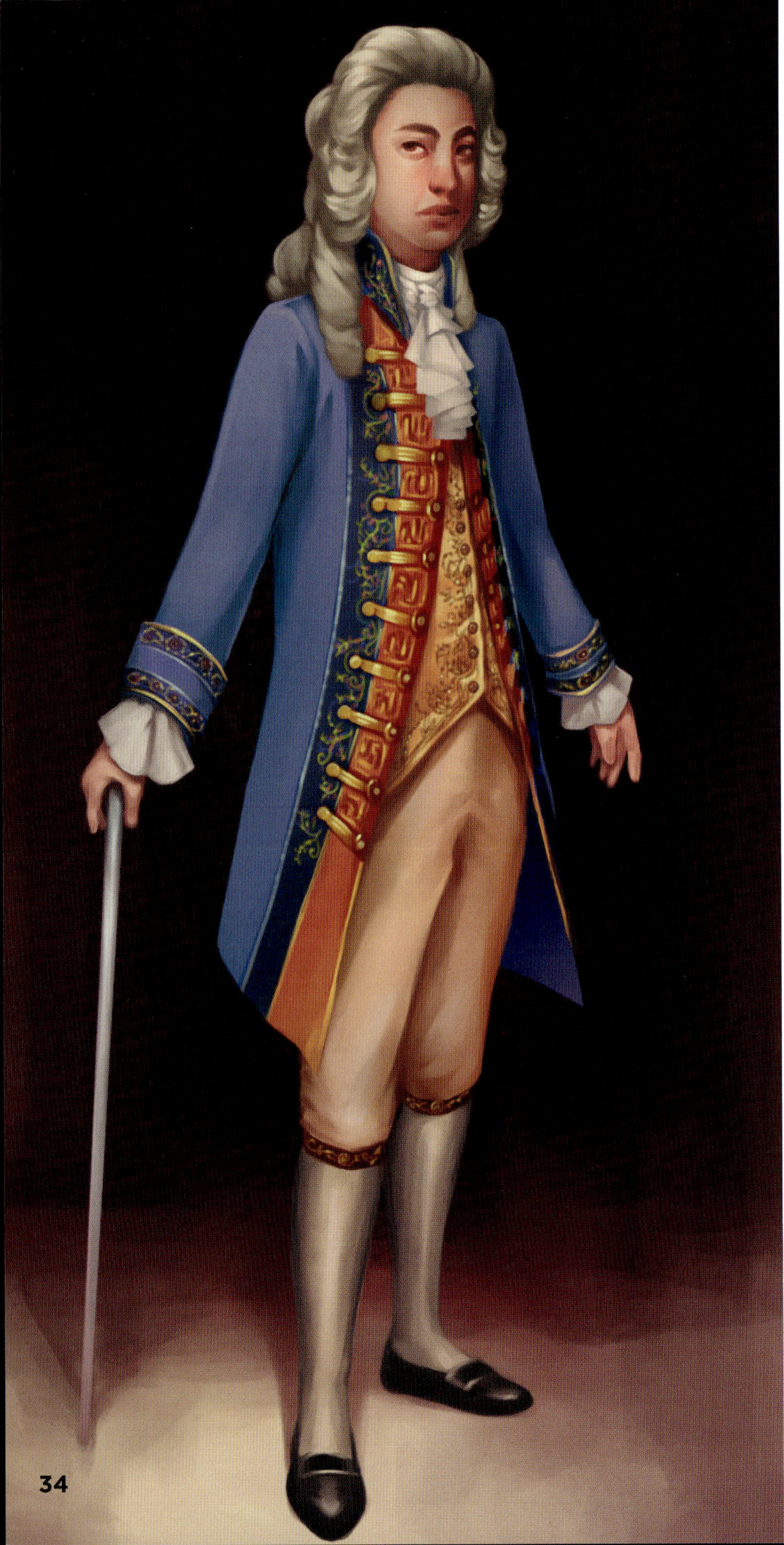

Illustration by Kellan Carranza

Revolutions, Guillotines, and . . . Breeches?

Of course, the rich and powerful don't have a monopoly on fashion. The People can also use fashion as a tool for change and revolution. They can force the hand of those in power by defying social rules or adopting a fashion en masse.

In 1776, American colonists declared that their new nation would be based on an ancient and radical idea: democracy. This incited terror among European monarchies, and with good reason. The People were starting to realize they had the power to lead. While the American Revolution was an actual war, the subsequent uprisings in France and the Caribbean were the stuff of noble nightmares.

As plantation owners in Saint-Domingue (now Haiti) were executed by their African slaves and lost control of the island, the nobility in France were being tried and executed for crimes against the People. During the French Revolution's Reign of Terror (September 5, 1793–July 27, 1794), almost 17,000 were executed by guillotine in the Place de la Revolution in Paris.

As a matter of survival, the nobility dropped their luxurious court ensembles in favor of the People's patriotic fashions. This is when noblemen adopted trousers, called sans culottes ("without breeches"), which were worn by the working class. Breeches, by comparison, were a symbol of a delicate, wealthy lifestyle. By wearing trousers instead, noblemen expressed their acceptance of the People's power.

DID YOU KNOW?

The word sabotage comes from the French word sabot, a type of wooden clog worn over laborers' shoes to protect them from the muck. In the 18th century, French (and English) textile workers would throw their sabots into machines they thought were stealing their jobs!

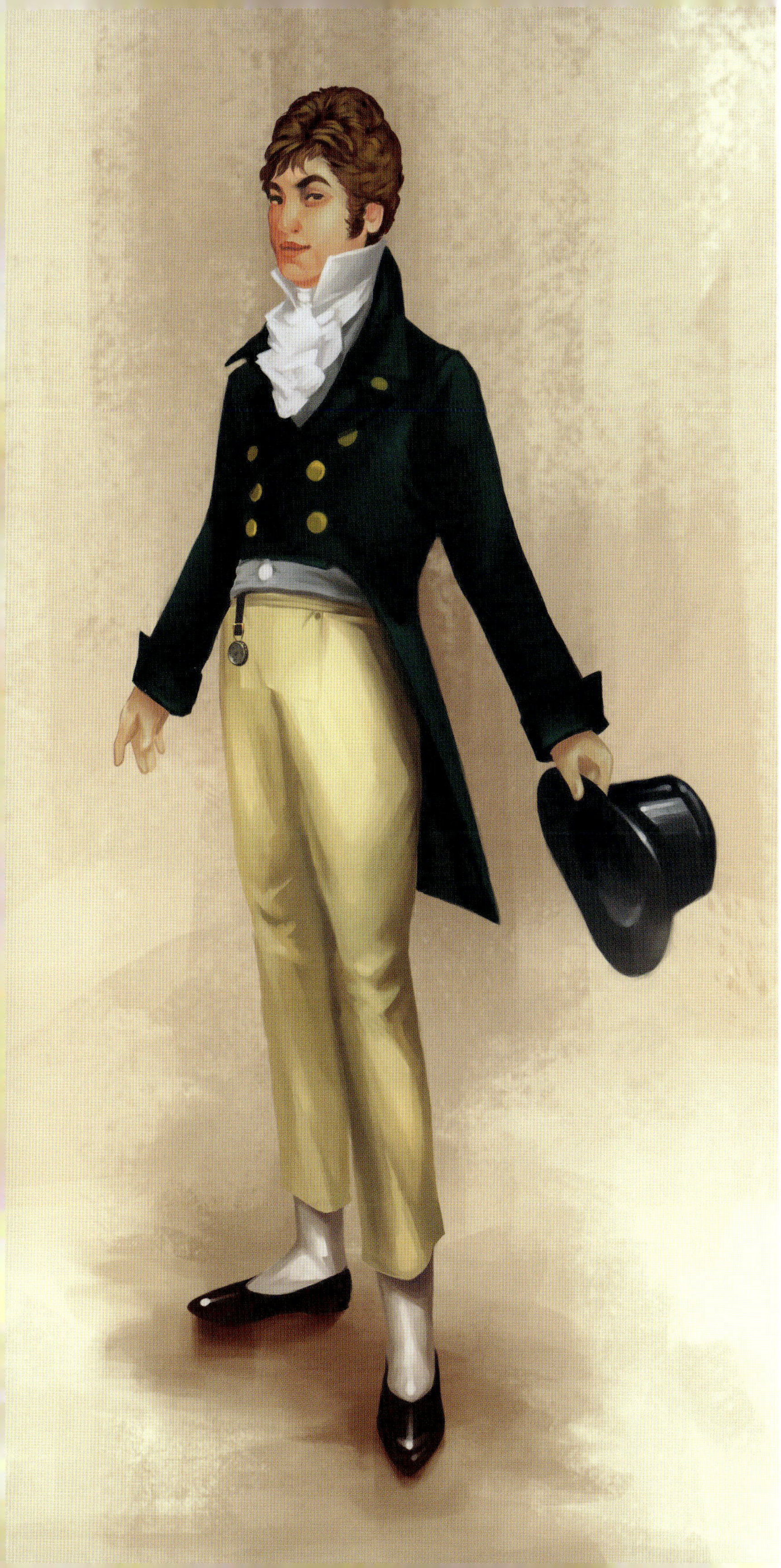

Illustration by Kellan Carranza

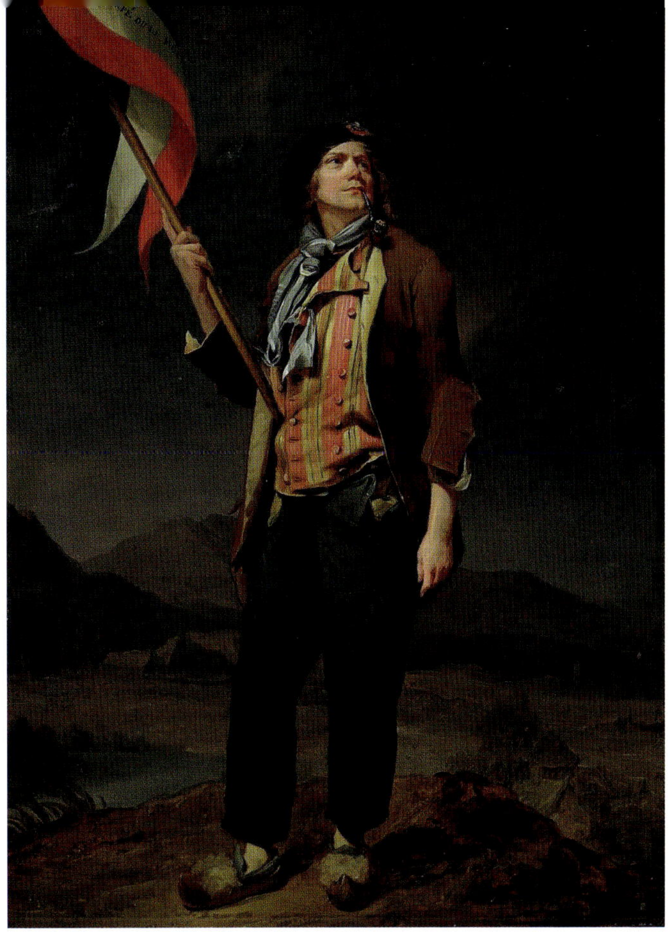

Sans Culotte by Louis-Léopold Boilly, b. 1761-1845

Compare the neoclassical gentleman's clothing on page 34 to the two on this page.

Sans Culotte, above:

- Folded collar and lapel of the waistcoat lead to a large collar and lapel for the gentleman for the first time.
- Long pantaloons rather than breeches.
- Embroidery and metallics are replaced with striped textiles, which are more affordable to the working class.
- The front of the tailcoat is meant to close, unlike the frock coat, reflecting workman's jackets of the time.

Nobleman, on left:

- Silhouette is exaggerated for a long and athletic leg.
- The length of the frock coat leads to the tail of the tailcoat.
- Soft leather slippers or boots.
- The new cravat is tied by hand into intricate bows and cascades around the neck.

Fear and Fascination

The machinations of the Powers have an immediate effect on what we wear. Whether the following fashions come from a place of solidarity, defiance, or unease, their inspirations all originate with the same basic "fight or flight" instinct. Fear is a constant psychological element of costume that is often overlooked. From ancient Mesopotamia to current-day America, many of our clothing and adornment choices stem from normalizing fear and conquest. In our modern time, this is particularly true in the West, where imperialism has been a big part of our cultural history.

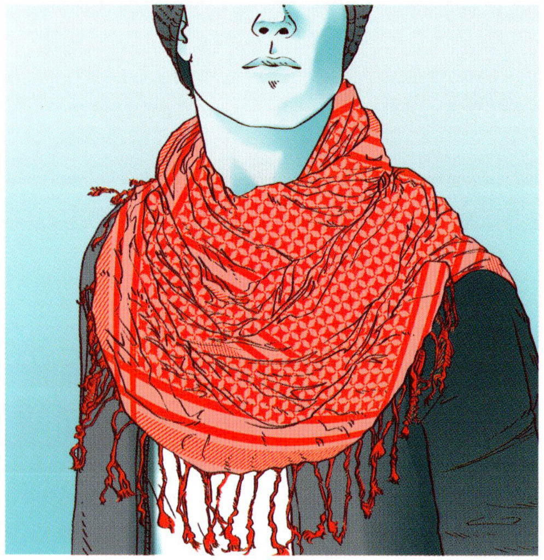

The **shemagh** became popular after September 11, 2001. Although seen in America as a youthful, intellectual fashion trend, its origin is the large tactical scarf worn by Afghan soldiers. The intellectualism associated with these large scarves in the US today is in direct contrast to what we see as a region of chaotic, violent terrorism.

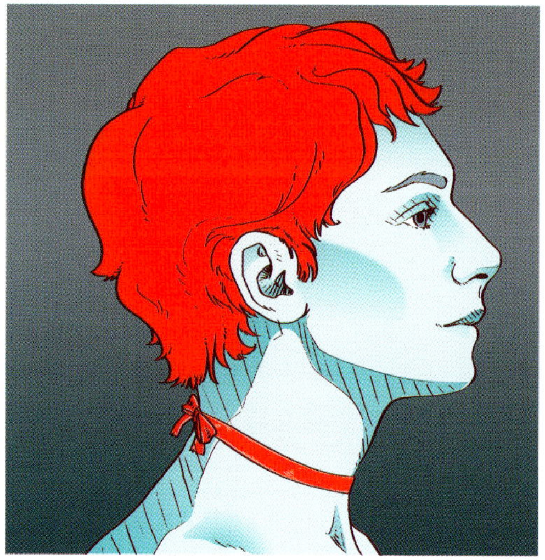

The **coiffure à la Titus** was worn by aristocratic women in the later years of the French Revolution. They wore their hair choppy and short, often with some curls still framing the face. Prisoners awaiting the guillotine were prepared in this way, so the blade would have a clean neck to chop. Morbidly, the hairstyle was sometimes paired with a red ribbon around the neck to symbolize relatives that had lost their heads.

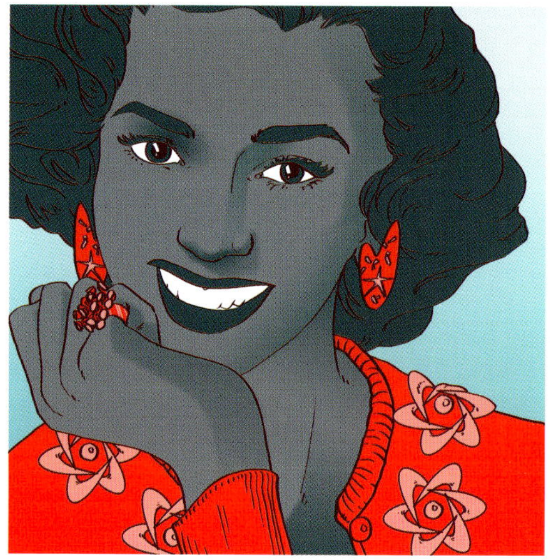

With the Cold War causing mounting international tensions over nuclear war, American families were taught to fear Communism, Russia, and the destruction of the American Dream. This led to **atomic motifs** repeating through the shapes of suburban life, bringing order to an unstable international stage while glorifying nuclear destruction.

Evolving Symbols

Just as these fashion trends have complex origins, the symbols we come across every day (and often wear) can evolve over time to inform, communicate, and convey more complex ideas and beliefs. While symbols can be used in any visual medium, they can be given positive or negative connotations depending on how you use them and the audience.

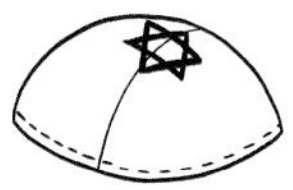

DEVOTED/SUPERSTITIOUS

The piece is worn in the appropriate manner. It is identifiable to others in a way that expresses that they are a devout believer/follower. Examples: yarmulke or a mantilla.

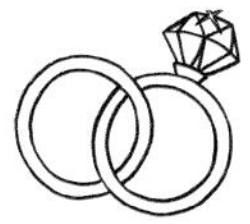

TRADITIONAL/RITUALISTIC

The piece is often worn out of a sense of duty or sacred obligation. The user doesn't necessarily have to believe in the meaning of the symbol but may care about its social value. Examples: a corsage at prom or a wedding ring.

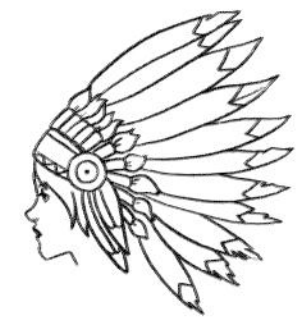

PASSIVE/APATHETIC

The deeper meaning behind the symbol/design is not understood and therefore disregarded. If it's worn, it is because of the shape or a love of the idea of a symbol. This is often where cultural appropriation takes place. Examples: a boho fashion shoot accessorized with a war bonnet.

As you consider different symbols in your designs, examine the history of them, their meanings, how they might shift, especially depending on who is using or wearing them. Two prime examples of this are the pentagram, a once devoted symbol becoming an irreligious symbol, and the swastika, a devoted symbol becoming its opposite.

IRRELIGIOUS

These would be powerful symbols of defiance, an ironic statement after a change of belief, or an aggressive sign of rejection of the value. An inverted cross, Alexander McQueen's bumsters (trousers that revealed bum cleavage), or Lady Gaga's meat dress reject traditional ways these items are worn or constructed.

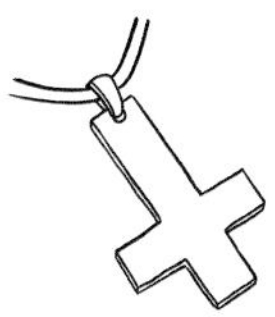

Ranging in use from a religious symbol to one of magical protection, the pentagon's meaning has changed across nations and through time. In the United States, for example, there is perhaps no symbol more sacred and more honored than the Congressional Medal of Honor, which uses the pentagram as its most dominant design feature. However, the pentagram has also come to represent anti-Christian beliefs, in large part thanks to the Satanic Panic of the 1980s in America.

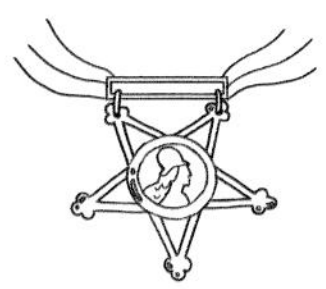

And while most of us in Western nations almost exclusively associate the swastika with the Nazi Party, in religions such as Buddhism, Hinduism, and Jainism, it is a symbol of universal harmony and fortune. At 12,000 years old, the swastika is truly a universal symbol and one of the most ancient, used by the Greeks, Egyptians, Romans, and Celts.

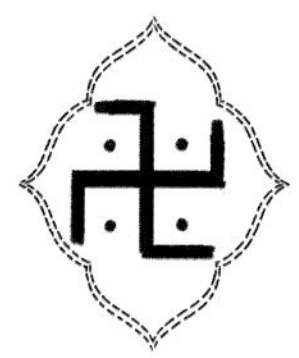

Nobility

Knighthood

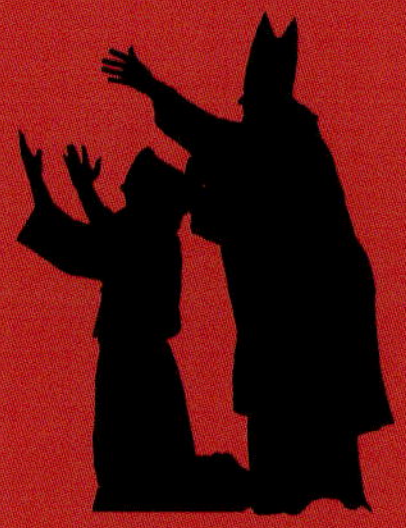

Monkhood

Centuries ago, class was generally defined by a man's occupation and whether or not he held a title. Class was granted through titles that were either inherited or earned through great service, such as to your god or guild. It was possible to be a "pauper prince" and maintain your title as long as you also maintained expectations. In general terms, freemen held no titles but worked within social institutions (church, guild, or military), while bondsmen were tied to the land (serfs or slaves).

Nobility

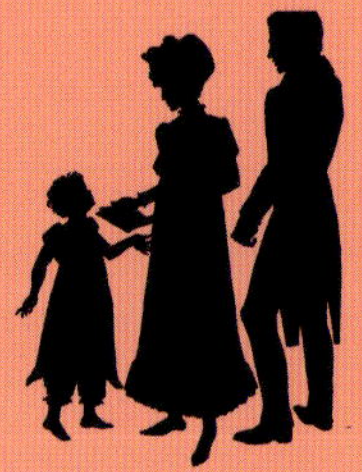

Merchant Class

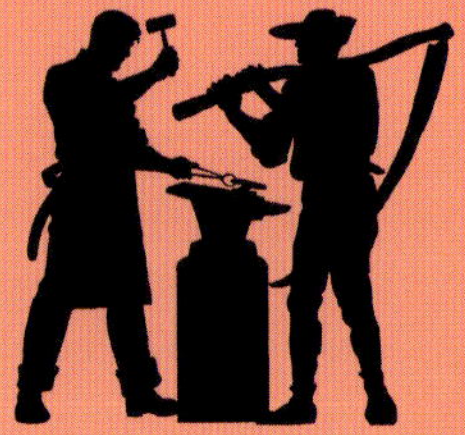

Working Class

As our cities grew, our idea of class actually narrowed in scope to three categories: nobility, merchant class, and working class. Class was associated with pedigree, or blood right, as well as economic status. Social registries and family trees were actively used to prove one's class and virtue. Class became more rigid with the introduction of divine right.

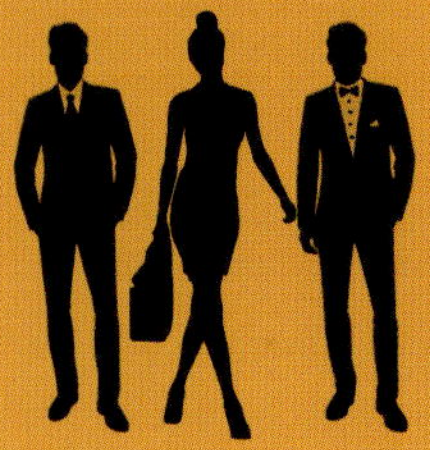

Upper

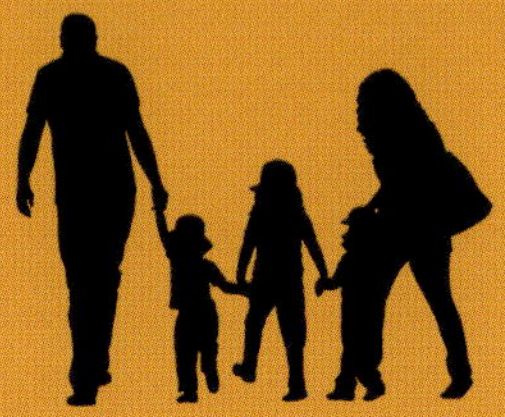

Middle

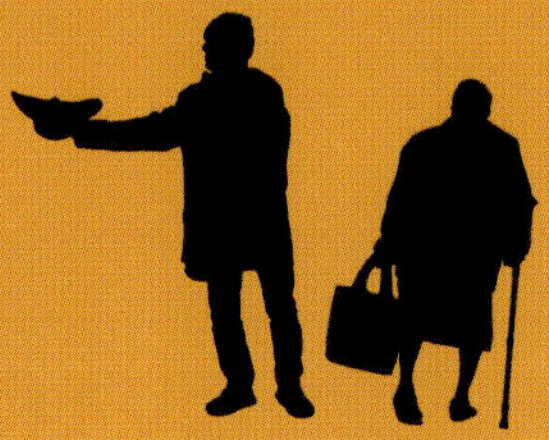

Working

The biggest shift so far in class structure happened in the last 125 years.

We are no longer bound by our pedigree, service, or virtue. Instead, we earn our class exclusively through personal economic wealth. We can also easily lose our status, unlike divine right or titles. This is a modern capitalist social structure.

Middle Ages

Early Modern Age

Modern Age

Class Dynamics

Likewise, over time or distance, the definitions of life, status, influence, gender, power, beauty, and so on, change. As modern storytellers, we rarely recognize this fact. We can't help but tell stories through our own point of view, but that reality is not shared by everyone. Class is part of the social terrain of any world that shapes a person's experience of it. Consider the nobility, the merchant class, and the working class. Who among your main characters is rich or poor? How does each class contribute to society? How do they treat each other?

Here are some of the mechanics of how these different classes interact within society at large in Western Europe over the ages—including fashion's role in expressing (or hiding) one's class—to help inform your design choices for specific characters.

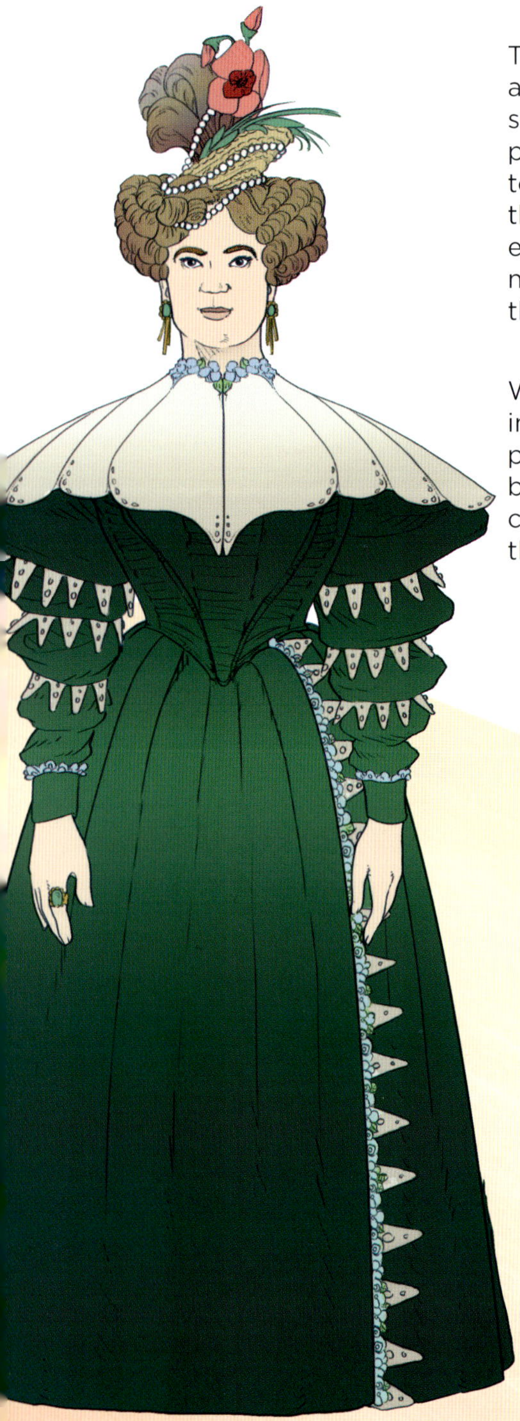

Nobility

The nobility gain their power and influence by birthright and see their status as a very exclusive club. Practices such as intermarriage ensure that no one without the right pedigree can become a member. This is very important to note. The merchant class is often just as wealthy as the nobility, and sometimes even more important to the economy. This threat to the social ladder pushes the nobility to express their elitism through lavish fashion that, thanks to sumptuary laws, are not available to other classes.

Women's fashion, historically, has been extremely important to the nobility. Fine cloth, exotic dyes, and precious materials do not become just a pretty dress, but a symbol of the family's wealth. As a noblewoman's costume can cost more than a house today, it's no wonder that keeping up with trends is a display of power!

Merchant Class

The merchant class rose out of the growing power of guilds in the Middle Ages. This class holds many of the most powerful cards in the deck of life. Why? The merchant class are the merchants, tradesmen, artisans, and entrepreneurs of the early modern age.

Well-educated, comfortable, and ambitious, the merchant class are caught between two worlds: they yearn for the lifestyle and benign power of the courts, but also think the nobility are outdated, wasteful, and greedy. Because they work for their wealth, this class is more conservative and reserved as a whole. Merchant class fashions may resemble the nobility but could swing in the exact opposite direction. Conservatism and religious beliefs may manifest together through somber, pious color palettes and starched white details. Modesty is also highly prized in these circles, especially for young, unmarried women.

The public face of the merchant class may be very different from their private lives, though. Beneath the public veneer, the merchant class may feel more freedom to express themselves and their flaws.

When the merchants and tradesmen earn a threatening amount of influence, the nobility distance themselves through extravagant trends and sumptuary laws. As a result, taxes rise, tempers rise, and people rise.

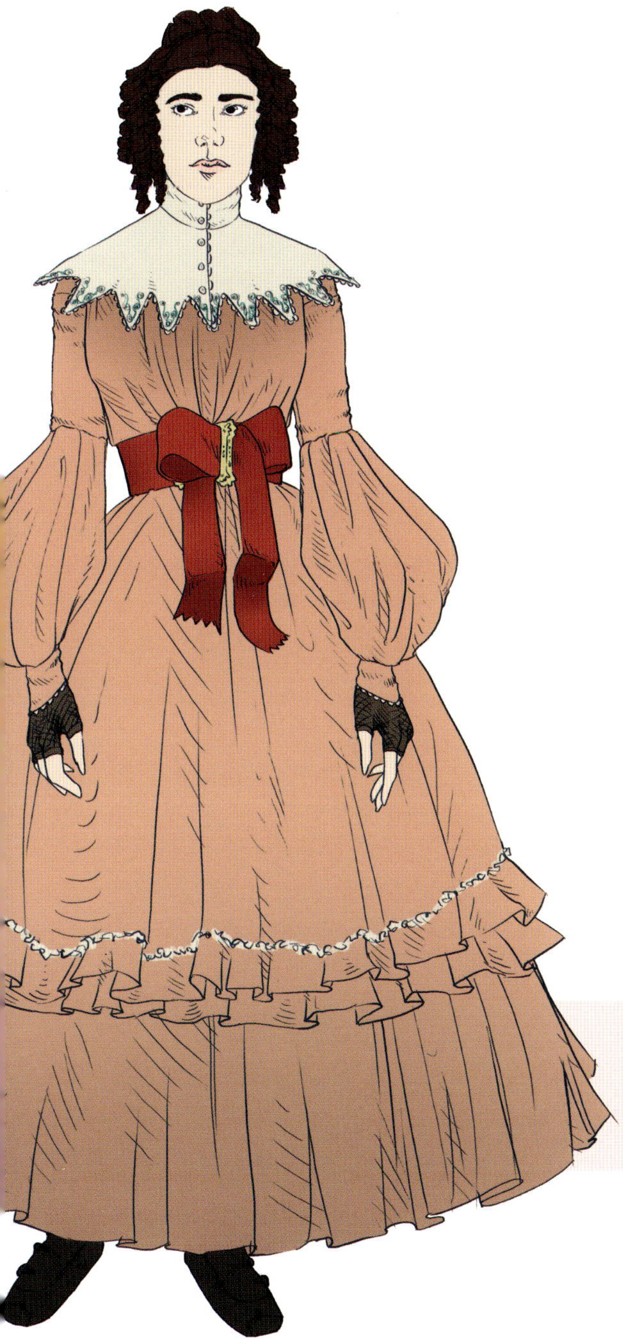

Working Class

The working class is often disenfranchised without access to education, medical care, or savings. Survival is a real concern for the common man, unlike their merchant class employers or noble rulers.

Garments are passed down generation to generation, and good garments are reserved for religious holidays. They rarely bathe, and hot water is difficult to come by. Clothing is usually dyed with clay, or other local pigments. Ribbons are a common accessory, as they are small, relatively inexpensive, and colorful.

To keep up with the fashions of the decade, most women will restyle their ensemble, such as fresh flowers on their hats or a new pair of mitts. Many garments are made at home, and fabrics are recycled for as long as possible.

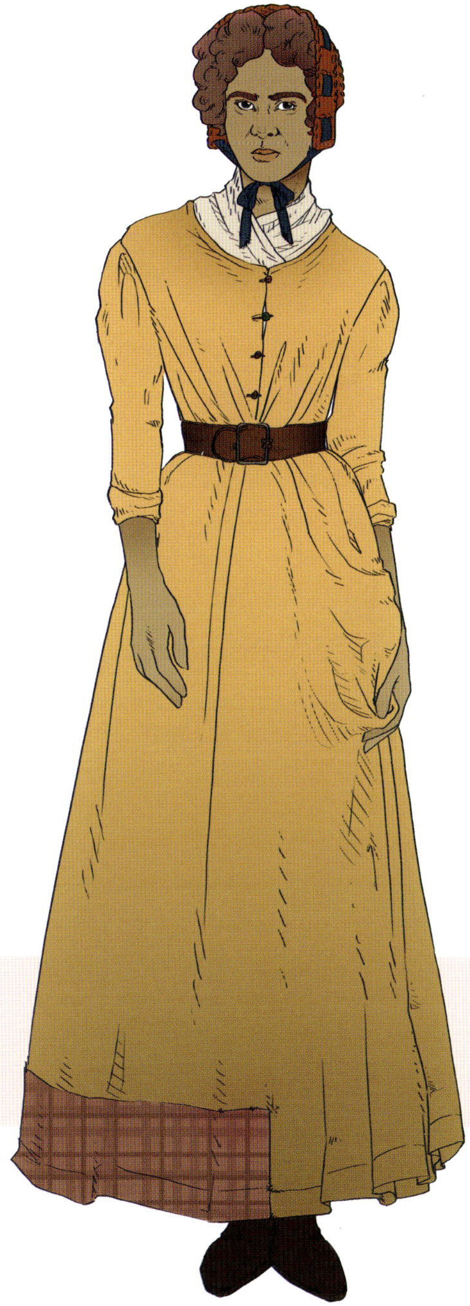

DID YOU KNOW?

Sumptuary laws are used to control what luxuries people have access to. For example, in both ancient Rome and Islam, men weren't allowed to wear silk.

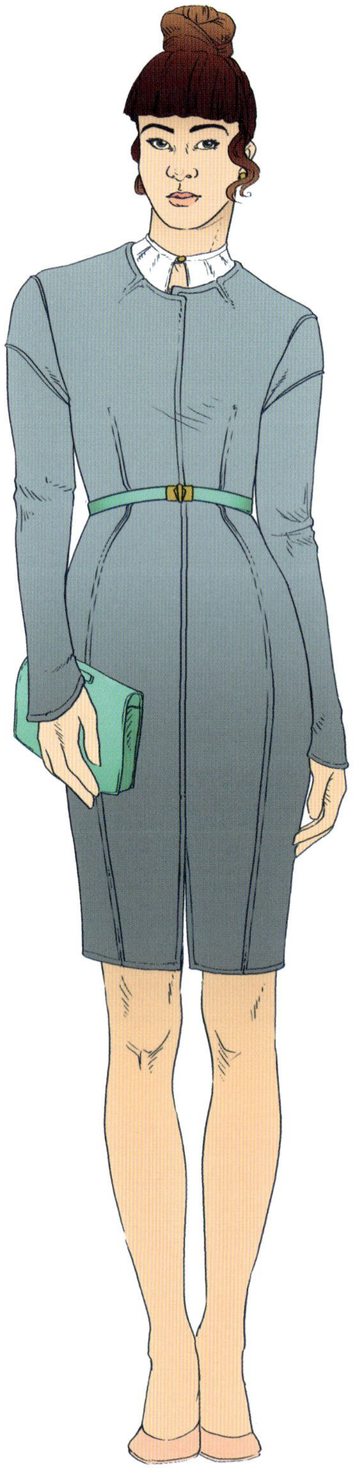

Upper Class

The upper class no longer has a monopoly on fabrics, colors, shapes, or detail. The 19th century marks a major shift in fashion and social psychology. Thanks to standard sizing, industrial looms, and synthetic dyes, fashions are widely available to all classes at different price ranges. As a result, the upper class shifts to fit, technology, and branding as a sign of their wealth.

Vacationing also becomes a large part of life in the Western world. Along with it comes athleticism and escapism. Money is spent on nutrition, exercise, and travel. The ideal female figure loses weight consistently through the 20th century, while the male figure becomes increasingly tanned and muscular. In previous eras, these were the bodies of the working class.

Similarly, purposefully distressed garments, such as jeans, are now more expensive than their durable, evenly dyed counterparts. Intentionally creating durable holes and frayed edges on clothing is time consuming and expensive, not to mention impractical for laborers.

DID YOU KNOW?

Most middle and higher quality casual trends are artificially aged to look fashionably worn in. Inexpensive casual clothing and textiles have flat palettes and textures because they don't go through this additional process.

Middle Class

The middle class, like the merchant class, continues to chase the fashions of the wealthy, but the logistics have changed drastically. Department stores knock off major fashion houses by sacrificing fit for cost. The middle class can follow trendy shapes and colors, but rarely has clothing custom made. They must rely on standard sizing. This means garments are almost always made with some stretch to ensure the widest range of people can buy them.

The middle class errs on the side of caution and invests in timeless fashions (e.g., the little black dress) rather than bold pieces. Because of this, conservative silhouettes saturate the middle class for about five years at a time rather than season by season.

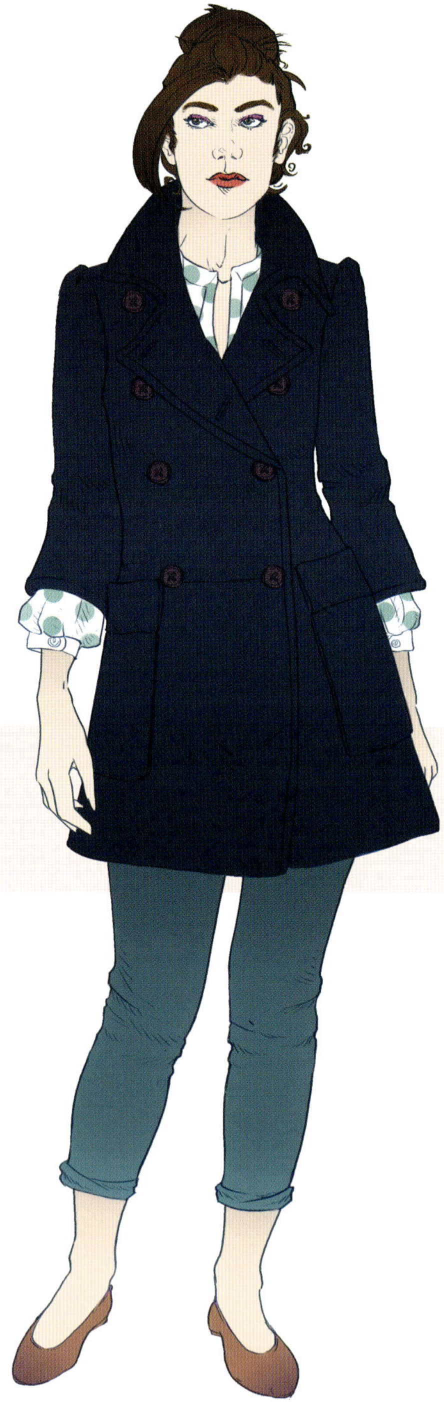

Working Class and Disenfranchised

The working class has always played a balancing act between survival and aesthetic. While members of this group may seek out fashionable garments, they are not always readily available or practical. As a result, street fashion becomes a defiant voice against the overwhelming aesthetic influence of the avant-garde and haute couture fashions of the upper class. In times of social revolt, this anti-fashion ends up becoming the most desirable aesthetic for all classes.

Used clothing is handed down either through family or via thrift stores and donation centers, usually well behind current trends. There is less sense of fit, as most items either pinch or hang loose from age. Therefore, fashionable working-class people often look back to vintage options.

Because they are subject to secondhand clothing, the working class has little control over clashing colors and patterns. They may wear summer colors in the winter and vice versa, causing visual friction with the higher classes.

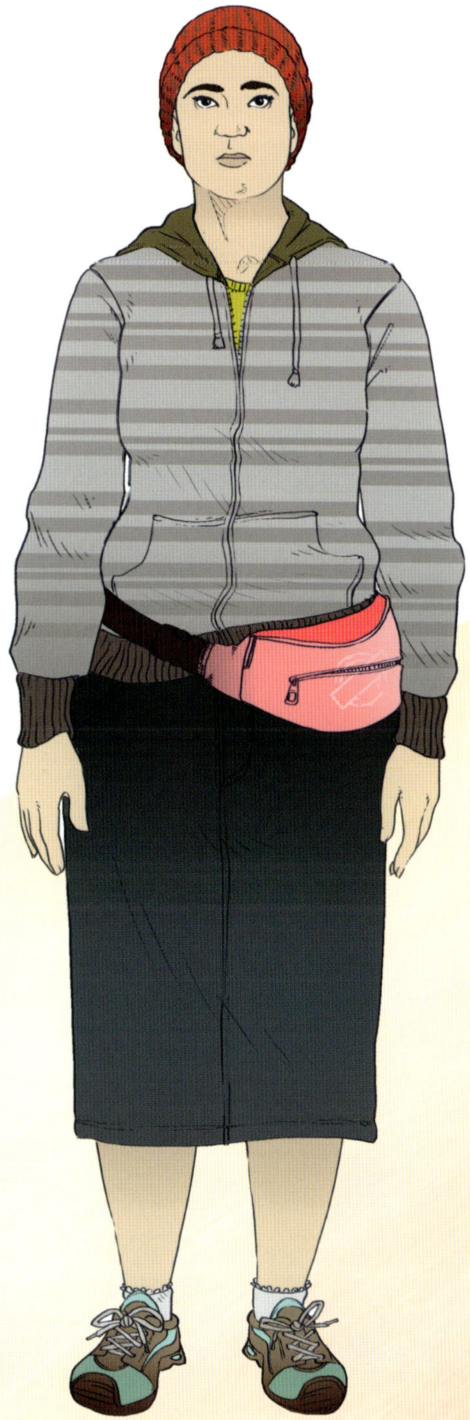

Exercise: Rags to Riches

How does class impact the clothes your character wears? Examine your own wardrobe and choices to see this factor at play.

Imagine what your life would be like if you only owned 10 pieces of clothing. Write or draw them and note the class and values you exhibit with each piece.

Now think of a scenario in which you suddenly needed to shop at very different stores because of a change in your finances and status. Perhaps you lost your job, changed professions altogether, or were starting a family. What would change in your 10-item wardrobe? What would stay the same? Why?

Window shop in two locations that differ in class from your own to design two class variations of your 10-item wardrobe: a thrift store (working class), a mall (middle class), and a high-end boutique or retailer (high class). Compare them, build outfits from each, and write down what you learned.

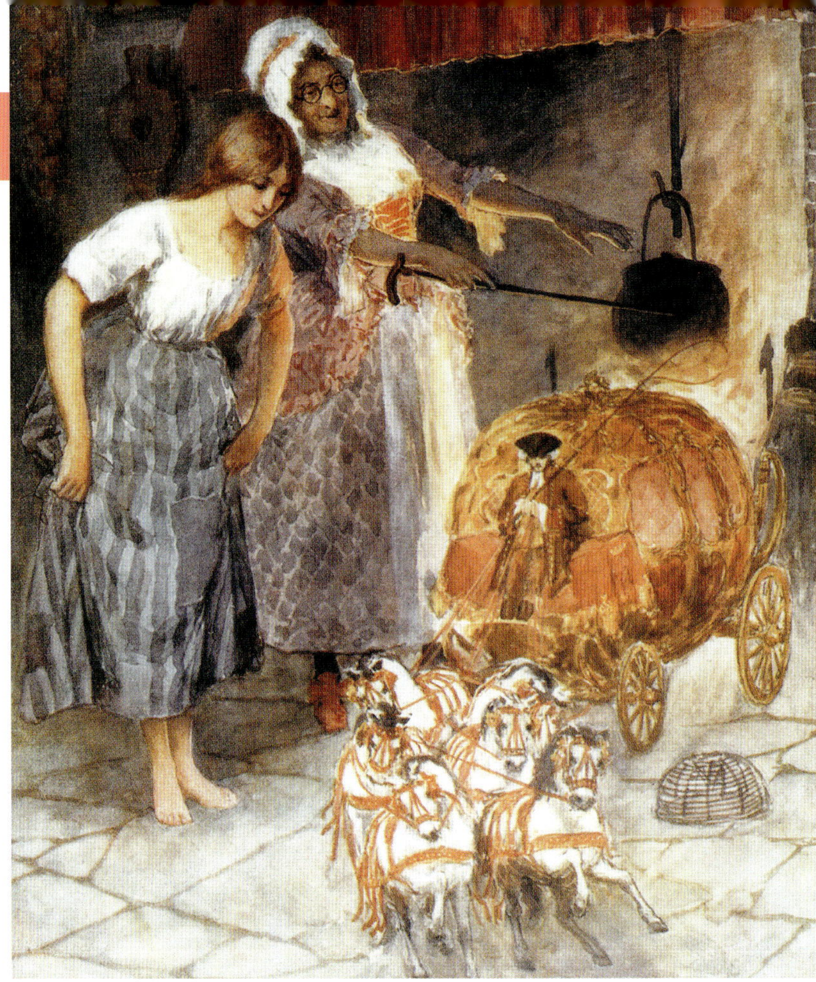

Cinderella and the Fairy Godmother by William Henry Margetson (1861-1940)

A character who suddenly comes into wealth or status may have vastly different taste from a character who was born with it. As you evaluate your choices, ask yourself what drew your attention more? For example, if you were finding a new jacket, did you find yourself more attracted to one that showcased its quality in subtle details and carried its status in the name brand only recognizable to those who also wear it? Or did you find yourself drawn to a flashier display of opulence where the expensive brand name was more identifiable? How would you mix it with other items? Why did you choose those combinations?

How you choose to display a change in wealth or status will depend on your personality and taste, yes, but the social narrative you associate with each class, and the newness of the situation will influence the choice even more. When something is new to you, your lack of experience in that situation initially results in less "refined" taste. Even as you gain more insight into your options and the power of the brands and aesthetics, you still might have less desire to align with the values of traditional upper-class styles—instead desiring to flaunt the way you suddenly rose in rank by creating more experimental, expensive looks and changing your looks often to stay hyper current.

Fitting In: Character and Context

White at a funeral, tattoos on a child—what if your audience isn't familiar with a cultural tradition or symbol you employ? How do you avoid the audience misinterpreting your characters or bringing in prejudices that compromise the impact of your design and story?

We can't possibly guess how everyone in the audience will respond to unfamiliar cultural styles, and the perception of each symbolic element and ethnicity will change according to the country viewing it. However, it's important not to assume that because something is different from your audience's culture that they won't be able to automatically understand. By understanding both the culture of your character and the preconceptions that your chosen audience will have about that culture, you can look for opportunities to bridge their understanding through the visuals. You can do this by sprinkling design clues throughout the narrative to build up to the more unfamiliar moments, or incorporating historical symbolism in your character's costume. These visual clues will help your audience prepare to have their preconceptions challenged. Giving yourself permission to genuinely represent your subject matter adds layers of appreciation for different audiences, and rarely takes something away from the story.

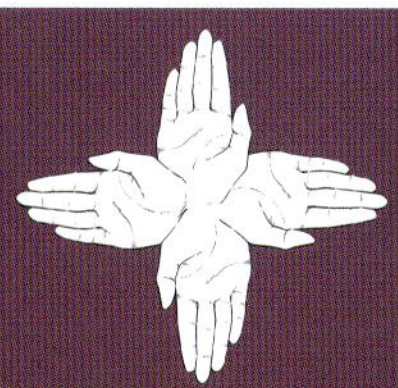

Ethnicity

Expressions of ethnic pride, evidence of ritual, or cultural origin and heritage; an inheritance of knowledge through one's elders rather than larger institutions; the narrative (or point of view) of a cultural group.

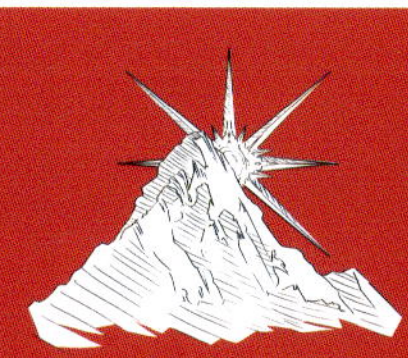

Belief Systems

Connection to, or expressions of, deep religious/spiritual convictions; superstitions that affect daily life; cultural obligations that uphold traditions; convictions that separate cultures into morally exclusive groups which often lead to conflict.

Social Status

Expressions of a political statement, or representing a class or role within society; sometimes divinely ordained, other times earned; in some instances, based upon reverence for a belief system or physical attributes.

TIP: **What if your idea is bad, offensive, and/or wrong?** First, you need to be comfortable with the question. If you don't talk to other people, especially those you might offend, you'll never know the answer to your question. The trick is finding a way to address the question respectfully. And listen before you react. Your intentions and the result do not always align. It is important to acknowledge that just because the result is bad/offensive/wrong, doesn't mean that your initial intention was wrong. Opening up a dialogue with someone you might offend will help you find the best path to your original intentions.

TAILORED EXAMPLE

A Nobleman Rises up against an Oppressive Power

Maria Ferreira Kercher

My character is a person living during the time of the Ottoman Empire. My goal with his costumes was to show his position within society and the impact of Turkish rule. To brainstorm ideas, I asked several questions:

- Who is the character? What is his role in the story?
- Is he a ruler (nobility), member of the merchant class, or working class?
- Is he from the invading culture or invaded nation?
- How did the different cultures represent their status and place in society?
- What is the location like?

By answering them, I was able to set some parameters and my direction:

- A Polish governor (protagonist) whose city is invaded by the Turks (antagonist)—what garments does each culture wear?
- Needs to wear fabrics and garments from the invading culture to maintain peace but is not prohibited from still using some of his original garments.
- Has a defiant personality trying to take back the city: How do I show this?
- Set in Poland during winter: What do both cultures wear in the cold and in the areas they live?
- May need to hide symbols from past life depending on how much tension there is in the invasion; for example, if a scar is in a visible place, character could hide with another costume element.

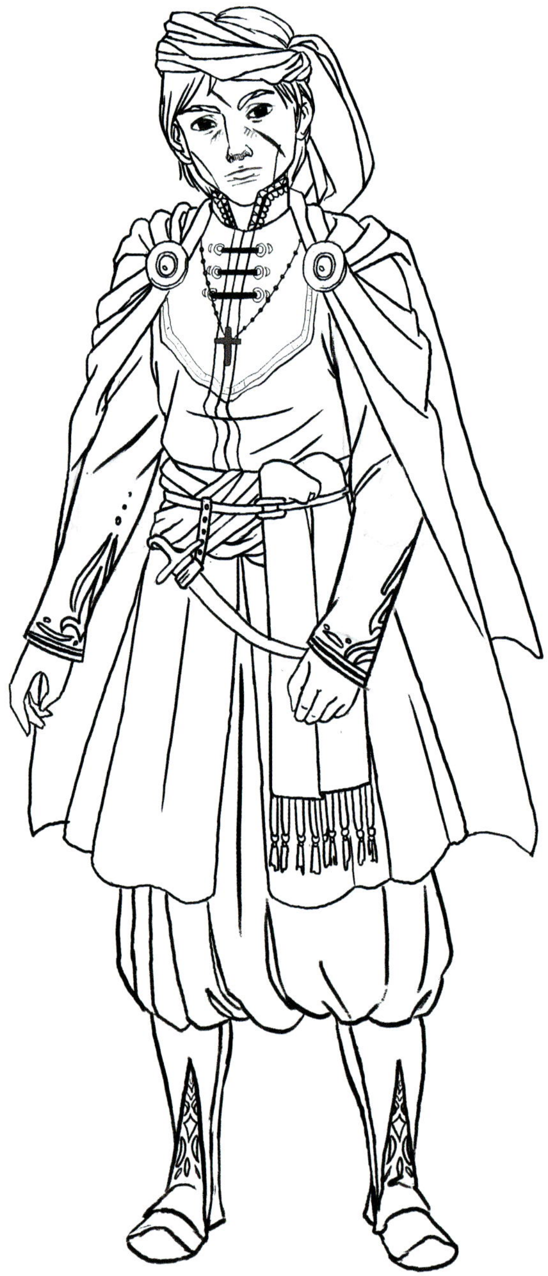

Polish costume

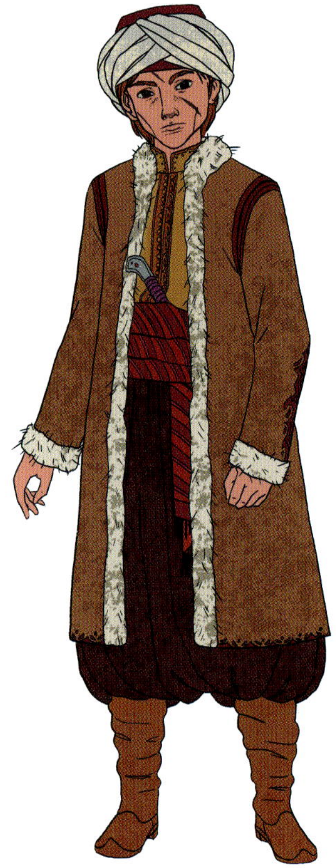

Turkish costume

ETHNICITY

In exploring how Polish/Slavic cultures showed rebellious behavior through clothes, I found that they used ritual scarification, so I chose to put a visible scar on his face.

BELIEF SYSTEMS

I researched adornment that could show his Christian background. Religious jewelry authenticates his position and increases his ability to assert power over the devoted.

SOCIAL STATUS

As governor, he holds the highest leadership position in his city. His costume needs to be expensive and opulent to clearly identify his role and status to his population and foreign visitors. I found in my research that Polish nobles used to wear sashes as a symbol of high social status.

SYMBOLS

The sash not only serves as a decorative element of the outfit but also as a symbol of high social status and wealth, consistent with its use and origin in Eastern European cultures. The sash could be very long, or he could wear multiple sashes to display his wealth. Their patterns or colors might define the group at large or an individual's occupation. Fringe can also communicate important factors such as class, role, religion, and so on.

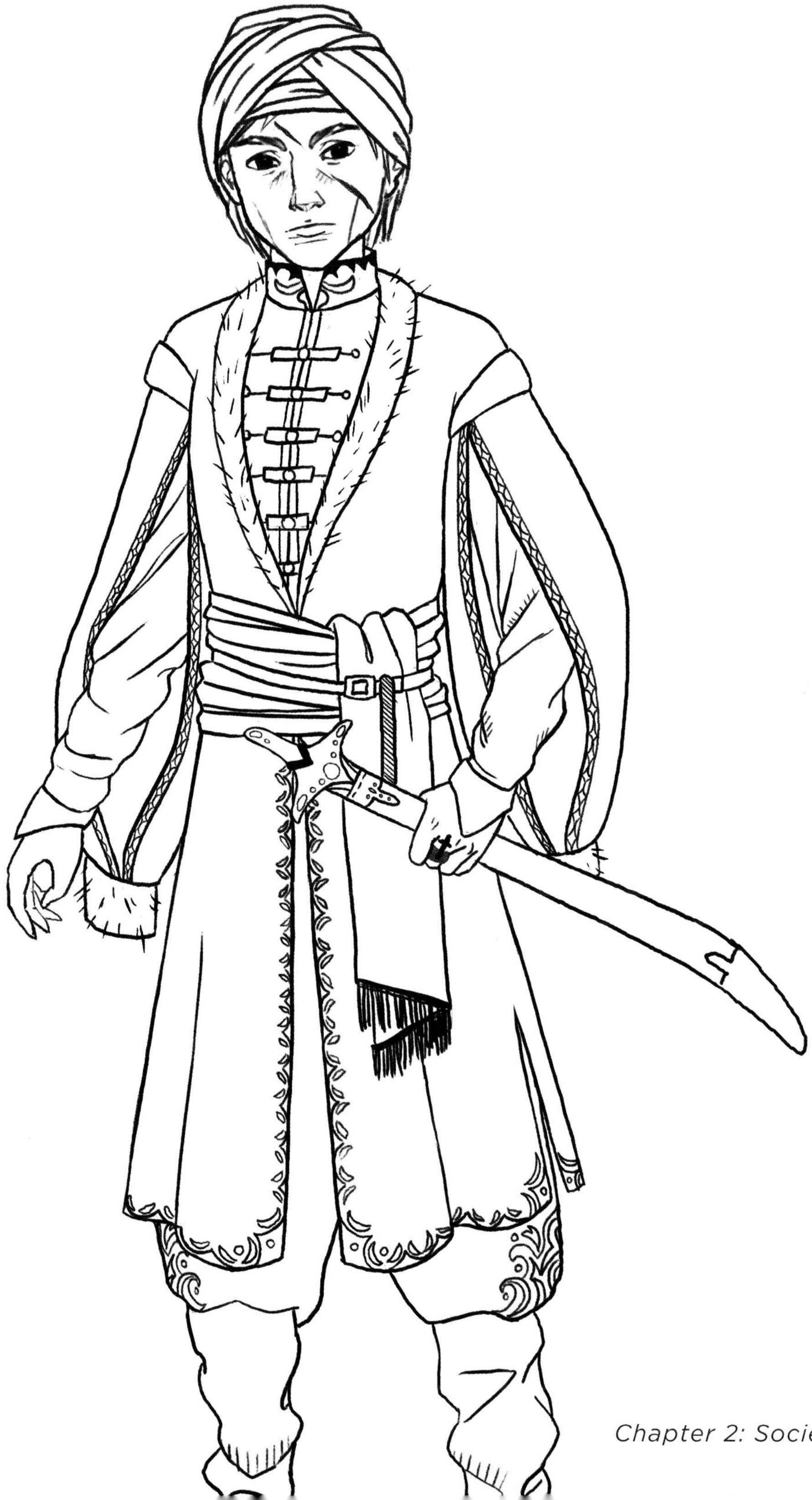

Modern audiences may not know the subtle language of sashes, so it's important to find the modern equivalent. The necktie is used in the same way today in the West as the sash has been used for millennia. While someone might own only one or two suits, they could have several ties. Necktie patterns and palettes are also used in private schools in the United Kingdom and Japan to display school pride.

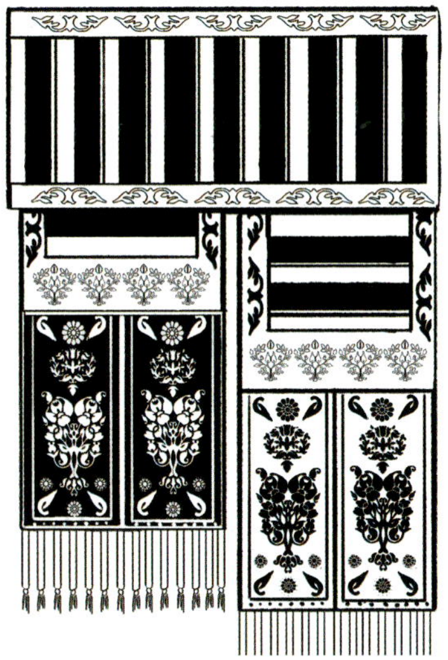

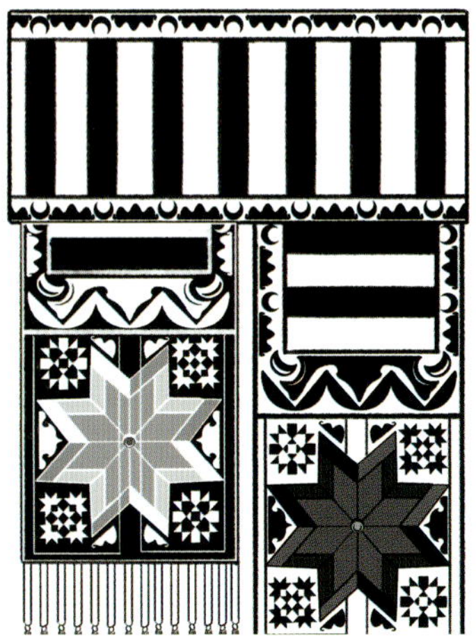

A narrow belt cinching in the sash is used to carry a ceremonial dagger.

The shalwar are voluminous Turkish trousers cuffed at the ankle.

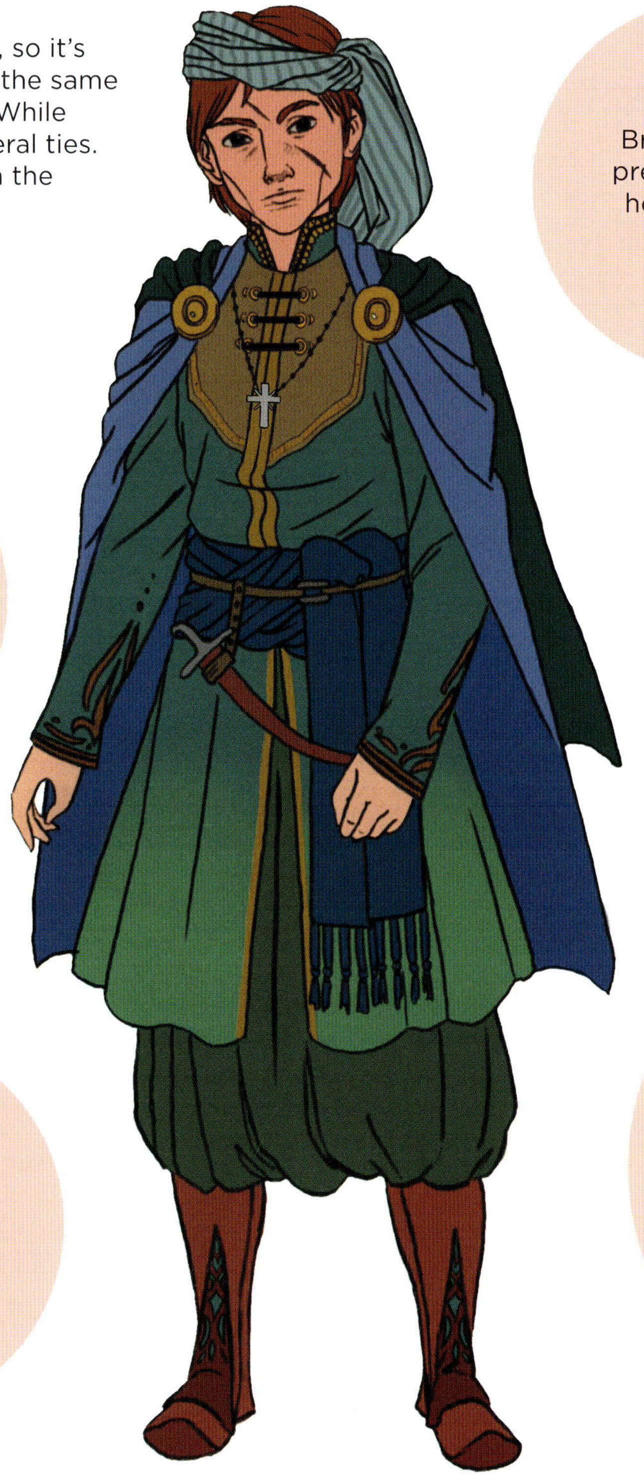

Brooches with precious stones hold the cape closed.

He wears a cape with a long mantle to widen his silhouette. We automatically assign more importance to his status as a result.

Boots are leather, but he otherwise wears only silk and linen. In many eastern countries, wearing animal hides is considered barbaric and brutish. Wools and silks are acceptable, because they don't kill the animal in the process of harvesting.

Wearing symbols of his culture while also being occupied by a foreign power puts him in hot water but is important to his people. The occupying power knows that his people will use these subtle visual cues as symbols of rebellion. As a result, this governor is putting his life on the line by communicating to his people through fashion.

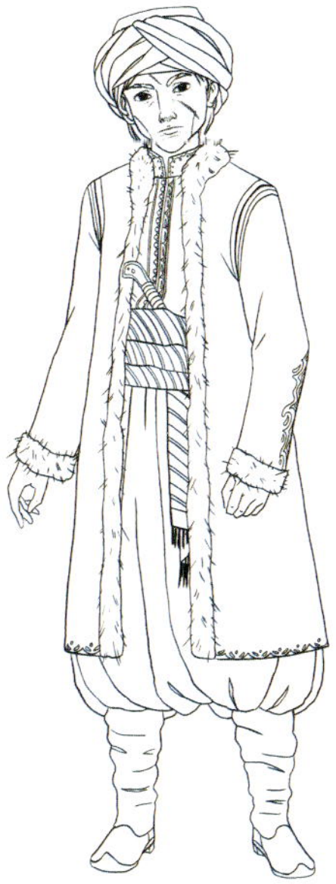

Foreign power

This surcote is called a kontusz. It is made of a fine textile, silk or velvet with precious stones or hand embroidery detailing the surface. The open-slash sleeve is indicative of the Renaissance, showing an imperialistic culture that sees themselves as superior to the "unenlightened."

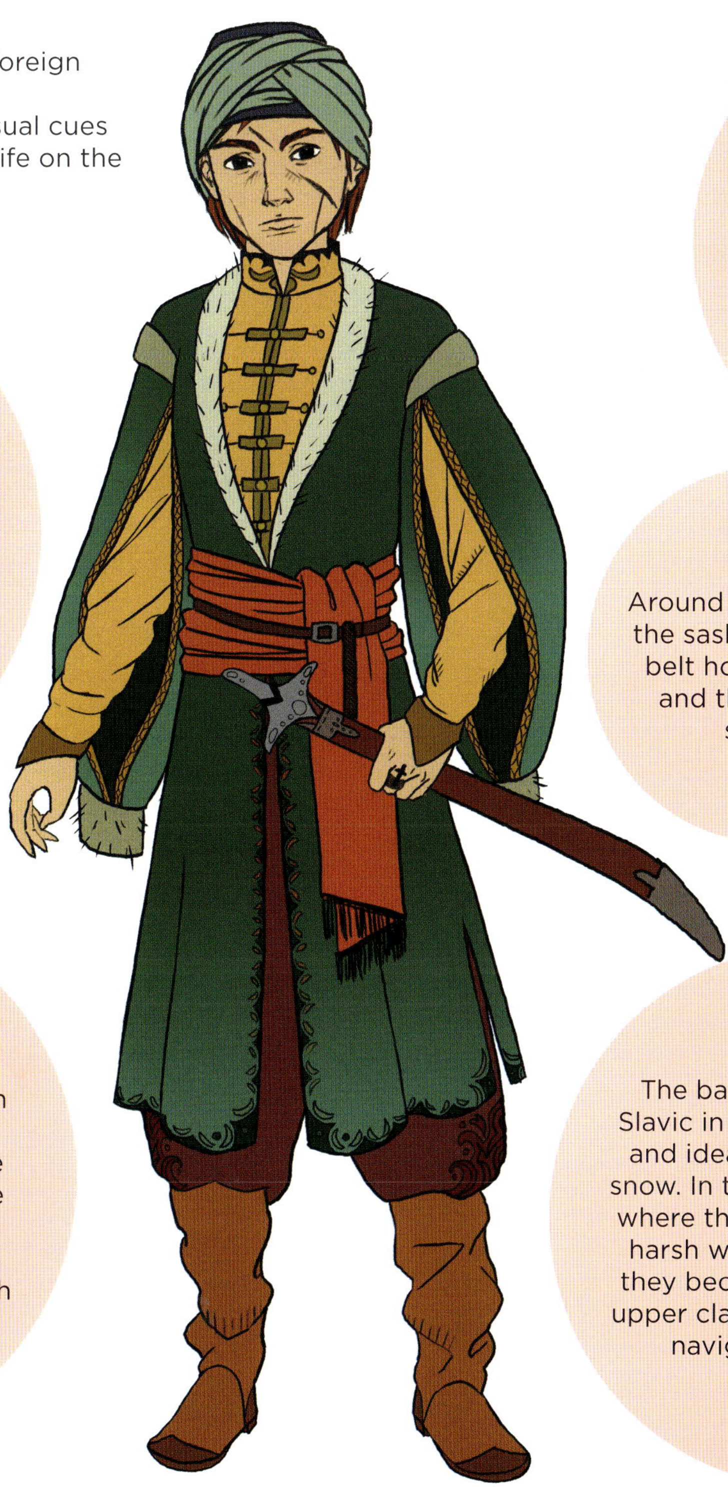

The baggy pants, the long robe, the sash, the Muslim fabric wrapped around the head, the boots, and the shirt being buttoned in the middle reflect the invader's presence as well.

Around the surcote is the sash. The leather belt holds the sash and the karabela sword.

The motifs on the surcote and trousers (spodnie) are motifs that represent his own nation. While he wore some of these motifs subtly on the left side image, they become more prominent after being occupied, because they are now more closely related with his cultural survival.

The baczmagi boots—also Slavic in origin—are flat-soled and ideal for walking on the snow. In this governor's nation, where the terrain is rocky and harsh with no snow in sight, they become a symbol of the upper class, who don't have to navigate steep paths.

Trade Dynamics

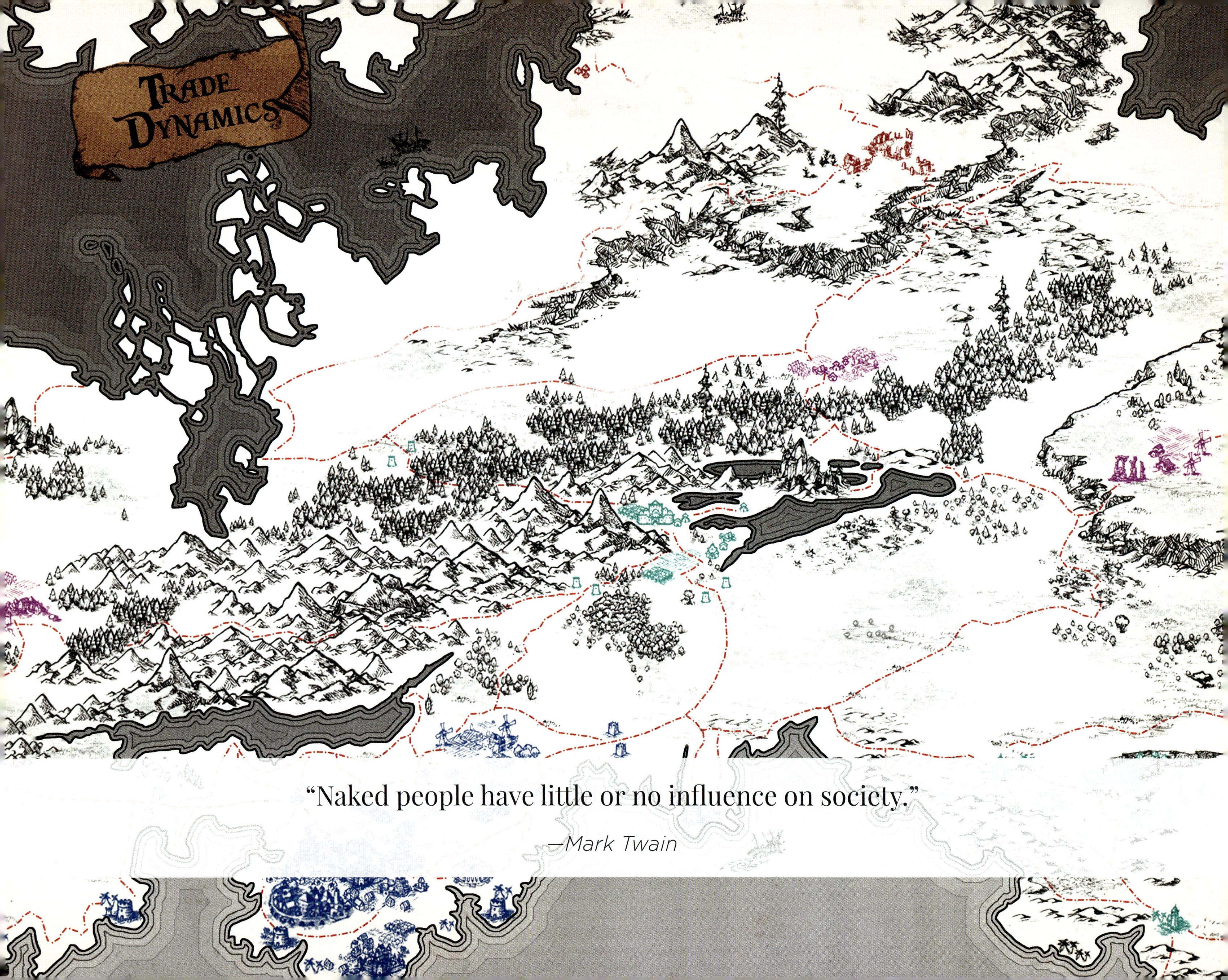

"Naked people have little or no influence on society."

—*Mark Twain*

CHAPTER 3 TIME AND PLACE

From trade dynamics to rules of dress, the time and place your character lives in can inspire valuable boundaries for your designs. Using these tools in your design allows the audience to trust the rules of the world and maintain their focus on the narrative. What sorts of trade dynamics create the scaffolding of your world? Identify what kinds of societies your characters interact with in your project. You'll then be able to shape the costumes with these limited resources in mind. More importantly, you'll be able to tell how a society's priorities in fashion shift as their place within the world evolves.

Trade Dynamics

Trade is the cornerstone of every civilization, whether it be fictitious or real. Although trade inspires conflict, it also encourages cultures to interact in meaningful ways, to learn about each other and distant corners of the world. In large trade hubs and ports, people from many cultures are thrust together. In these places of great diversity, the arts and philosophies flourish. A community's access to trade, stability, and natural resources will shape its outlook on the world. It is a focal point of war, of diversity, and power—and will determine how a society views the roles of fashion and culture. Let's examine four different types of societies and the aesthetics that can result due to their access to trade.

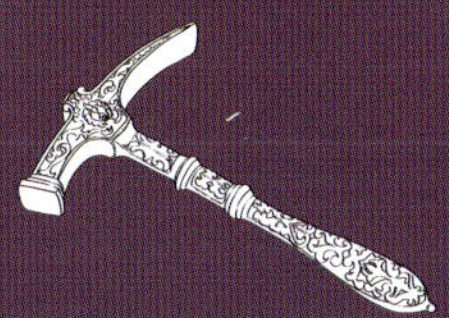

Trade Hubs

All roads lead to Rome! Hubs are the center of culture, politics, and philosophy. Here, new ideas are generated, and heated prejudices boil over. What happens here reverberates out to affect the world, just like waves in the ocean.

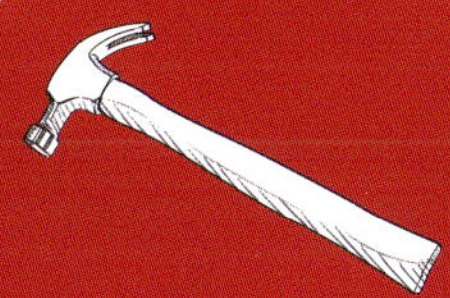

Crossroads

Although there is a sizable population and goods industry, crossroads are a stop along the way to a major trade hub. Life here caters to the merchant class or middle class. Goods might be manufactured here, and life is comfortable. There is less distance between the classes. A few roads lead into these towns, and commerce flows in and out steadily.

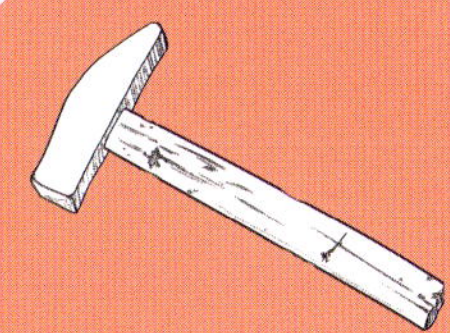

Utilitarian Beacons

Beyond the crossroads are long-standing communities that get few visitors. The people here are almost entirely working class, and the community survives when they work together. They have a one goods economy that maintains most of the population. This means that a single bad haul can lead to hard times. Only one road leads in and out of these villages.

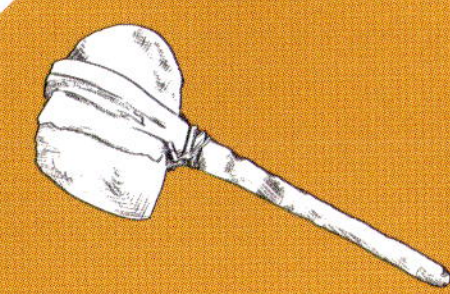

Life Rafts

Groups that either live in harsh conditions or have been devastated over a period of time are more like life rafts in choppy waters than stable communities. Although there are ranks among these groups, there are no real class differences. Communities are small and tight-knit with natural resource trading as their sole source of income, if they have any connection with stable communities at all. Usually the road leading to these settlements is harsh, overrun, or nonexistent.

Trade Hubs

Characteristics:

- Has an economy large enough to sustain master artisans, therefore it has superior quality goods.
- Establishes trends and leads the way for new technologies.
- More focused on decoration and fit with a highly-trained artisan workforce.
- Diverse range of aesthetics originating in or in defiance of many cultural backgrounds.
- More focused on woven textiles than animal by-products because furs, feathers, etc. are not needed for protection against the elements or visual communication across vast distances (e.g., colorful adornment). This leads to animal by-products becoming an exotic, upper-class fascination.
- Location is long-lasting, therefore architecture becomes an important part of ceremony and status.

Examples:

Literary: King's Landing in *A Game of Thrones* and OASIS in *Ready Player One*

Video Game: New Vegas in *Fallout: New Vegas*

Crossroads

Characteristics:

- Quality goods, but often a season behind trends in the major trade hubs.
- Implements tried-and-true technologies.
- More focused on practicality from day to day, but the community puts a premium on formal events and holidays as well.
- More focused on local tradition and conservatism than trade hubs.
- Prefers timeless fashions over shocking trends.

Examples:

Literary/Film: Hobbiton in *The Hobbit* and Career Districts in *The Hunger Games* trilogy

Video Game: Helgen in *The Elder Scrolls V: Skyrim*

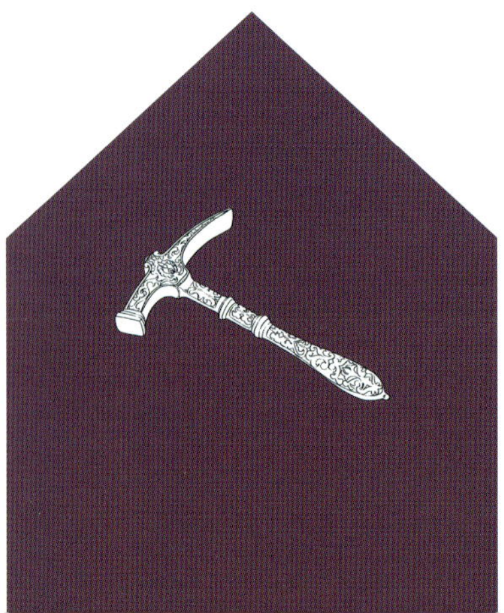

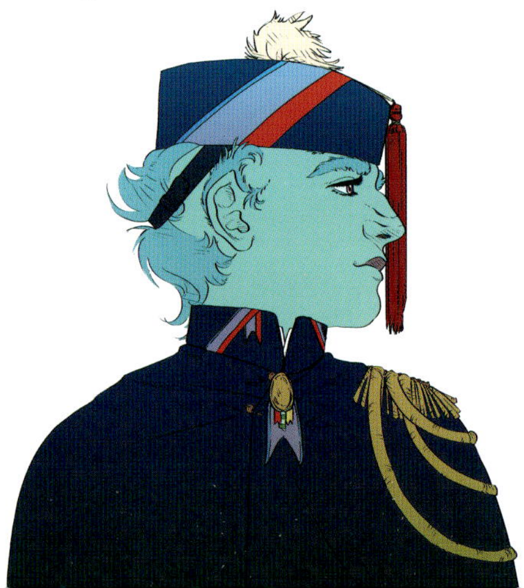

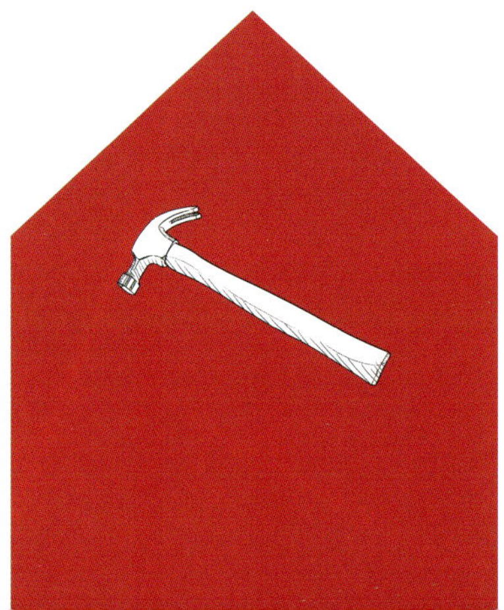

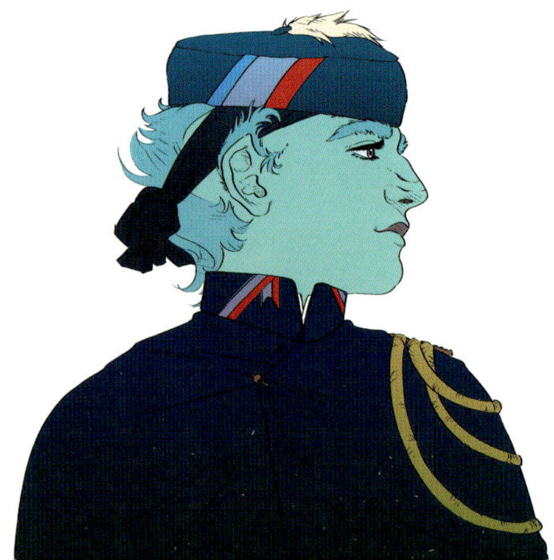

Utilitarian Beacons

Characteristics:

- Often years or even decades behind trends.
- Clothing is passed down the generations.
- Emphasizes durability in both textiles and machinery.
- Prizes animal by-products much more than fashion, though exotic pelts, feathers, or weaving may be their primary industry.
- Tends to favor more traditional gender roles, conservative economic practices, and staunch belief systems blended with local superstitions.
- Rebels often ostracized by the group at large.
- Practical architecture, thus ceremonies rely more heavily on clothing to convey their special nature.

Examples:

Literature/Film/TV: Winterfell in *A Game of Thrones* and Tatooine in *Star Wars*

Video Game: Machine Village in *NieR: Automata*

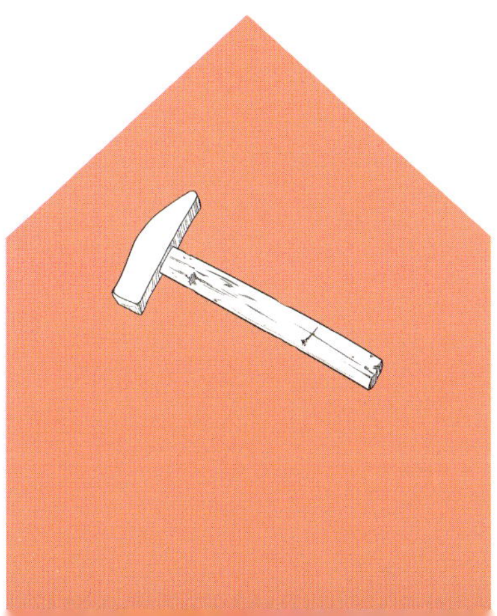

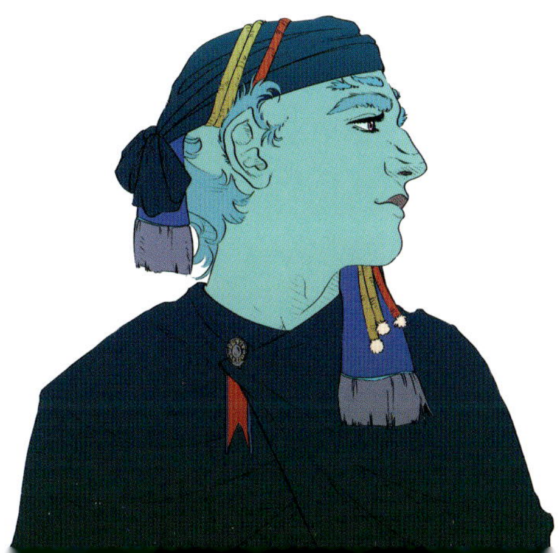

Life Rafts

Characteristics:

- No concept of trend, with garments focused solely on protection either from the elements or from the supernatural.
- Adornment is usually connected to age, gender, and role within the community rather than personal choice.
- Every member of society participates in survival preparation efforts.
- Animal by-products are prized since the community must hunt rather than shop for meat.
- Community strongly believes nature and religion are entwined.
- Ceremonial items tend to be permanent body modification or temporary natural decoration rather than clothing.

Examples:

The wall in *A Game of Thrones*, Arrakis in *Dune*,

Dejima in *Ghost in the Shell*

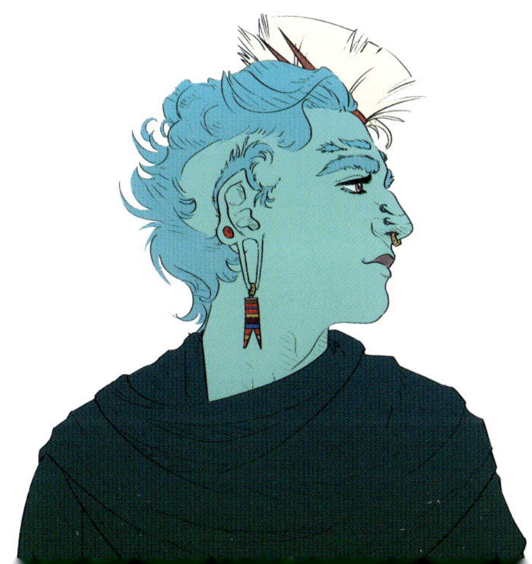

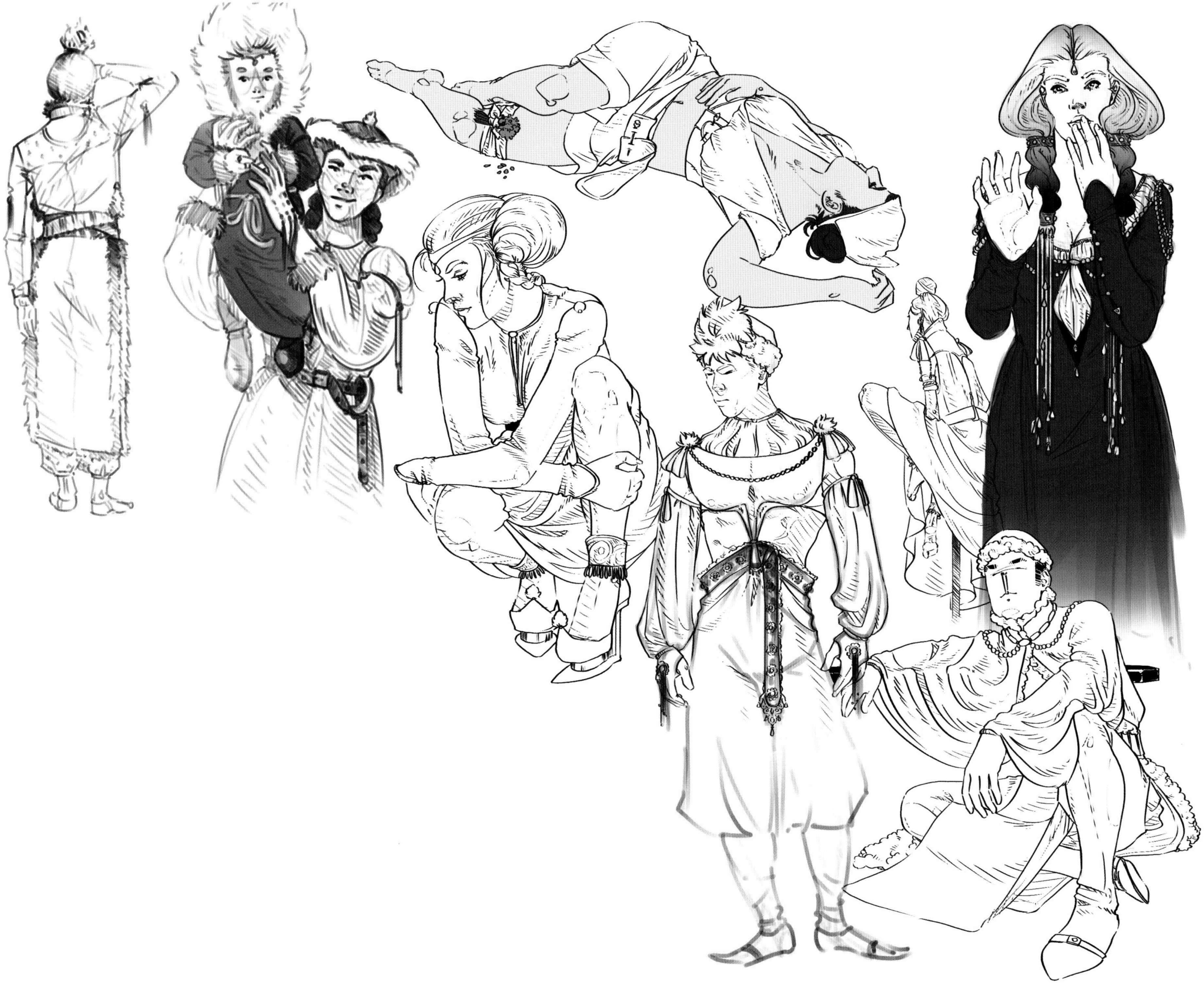

TAILORED EXAMPLE

The Young Orator in the Winterlands

Gwyn Conaway

Prompt: A young orator, the voice of his people, plays a delicate political game in the Winterlands. While his charisma is undeniable, he must convince the people that his plans for the future will be more fruitful than those of their elders. Time is of the essence.

How much does societal terrain change your costumes? Below I've designed the same orator in two different contexts. They are the same class, age, occupation, and personality type, but look at how different they are!

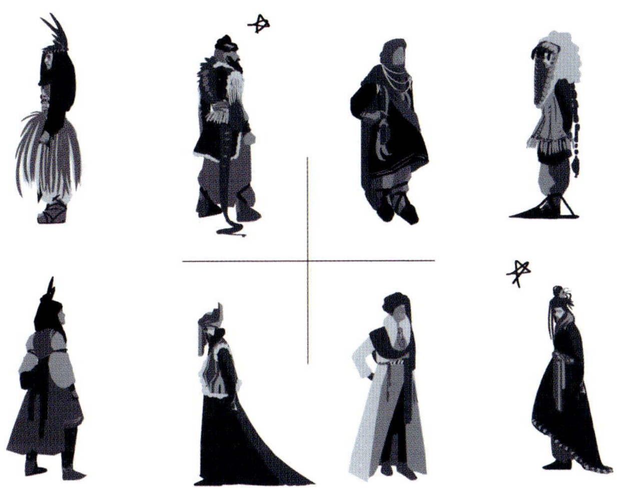

Before I designed these final options, I fleshed out their worlds enough that I could make informed decisions. It didn't take long, and ultimately made the process faster. These thumbnails are divided into two parts. The top two rows are a harsher context while the bottom two rows are milder in every way: climate, power, economic stability, and trade dynamics, which will be discussed in greater depth in the next chapter.

The same prompt, the same location, but drastically different outcomes. Let's compare their societal terrain and see what "invisible" factors influenced these designs.

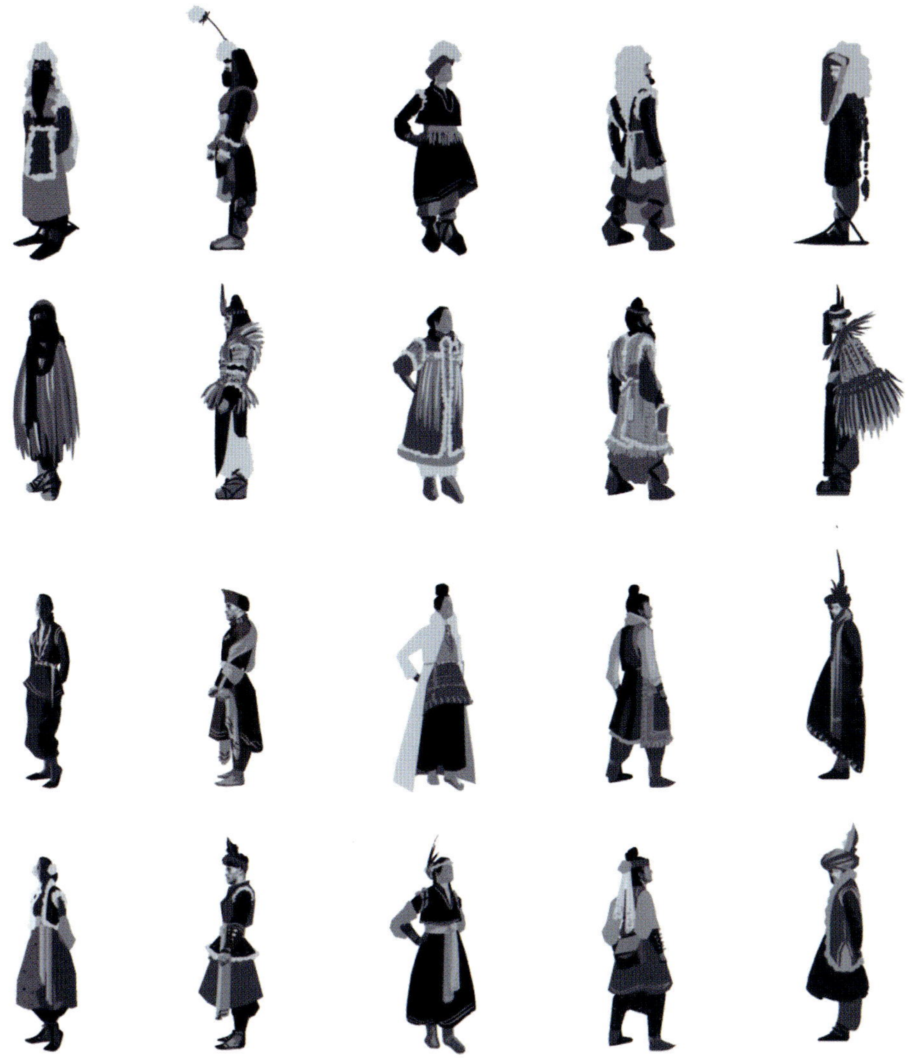

Merchant Wyvern Herder Weaver Apothecary Monk

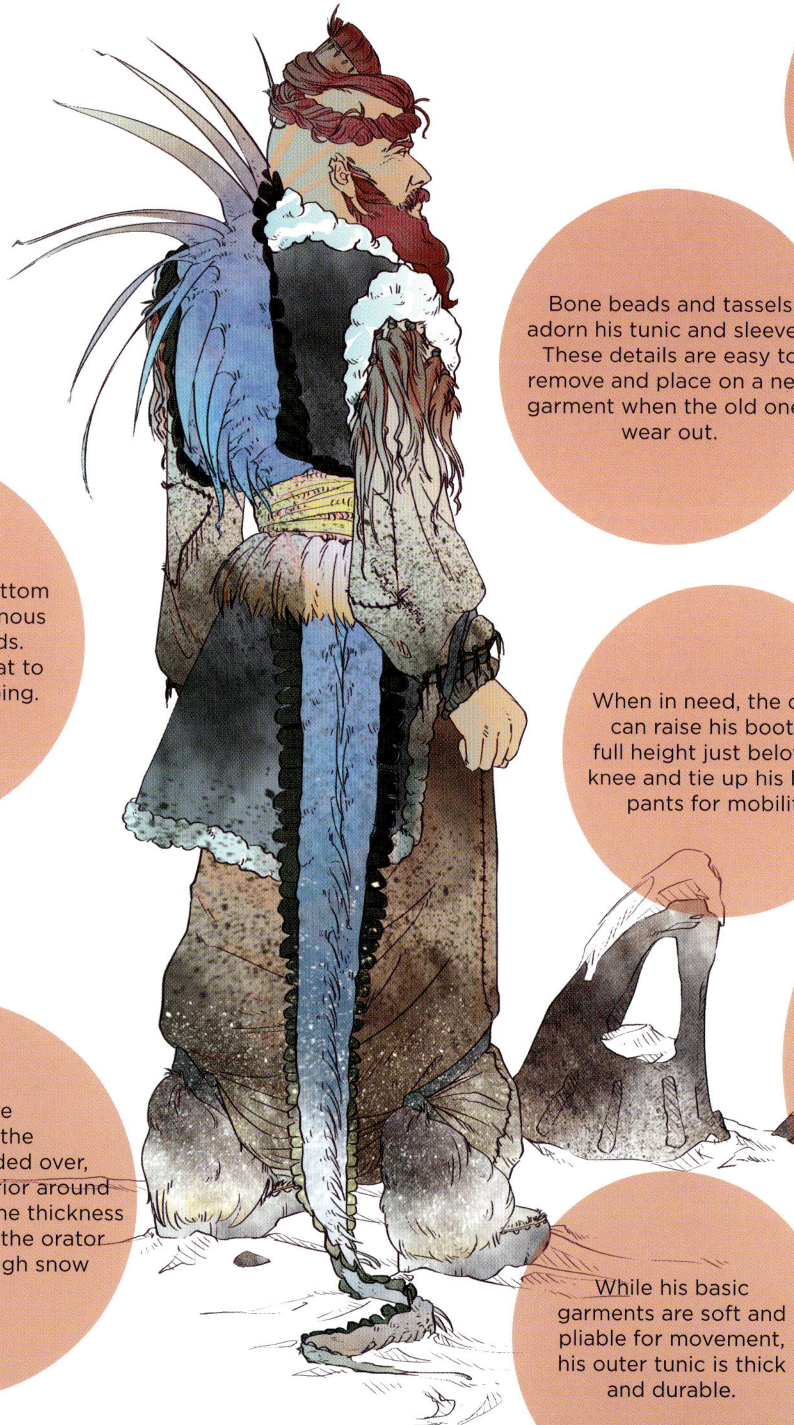

The orator's hairstyle is specific to his status in the group. A single piece of jewelry, a gold clamp, keeps his hair aloft.

Scarification on his right ear shows that he has passed the trials of adulthood.

A wyvern tail adorns his shoulder, a symbol of his spiritual and physical prowess. The only way to earn this status symbol is to slay a wyvern alone.

Bone beads and tassels adorn his tunic and sleeves. These details are easy to remove and place on a new garment when the old ones wear out.

The sash is made on a small hand loom from yak hair, cotton from the valleys, and dye from wild flowers that grow in unusually warm summers. It's of rough quality, but that doesn't matter. Someone honored the orator by making it. It is only as long as it needs to be, wrapping around his waist twice.

His sleeves and drop-bottom harem pants are voluminous and tied off at the ends. This allows his body heat to circulate without escaping.

When in need, the orator can raise his boots to full height just below the knee and tie up his harem pants for mobility.

Although his basic garments look like worn-out cloth, they're actually seal calf or kid leather. Another village, several days away, is where they trade wyvern for this important resource. The route takes nearly a month and is therefore only attempted once per year. As a result, even the orator's basic garments are patched. These may last him for several more seasons though.

The sash around his waist was probably made by a family member or passed down by an elder. The fur fringe is from the mane of a grand wyvern, one of the group's most prized and rare trophies. While other garments he is wearing may be staples of the group at large, this piece is unique, and its rare color communicates his importance, even from afar.

His boots are fur-lined with the top of the boot folded over, exposing the fur interior around the calf. Doubling up the thickness of the boot protects the orator while walking through snow drifts daily.

While his basic garments are soft and pliable for movement, his outer tunic is thick and durable.

TRADE DYNAMICS

Beacons: How do they survive? What do they hunt/eat? How do they clothe themselves? Who are their leaders?

Society: Remote, with a steady stream of pilgrims during the summer months, when the snow isn't so treacherous.

- Main Staple: Wyvern by-products, a sacred animal that, when slain, can feed the group for several weeks and provide money enough for two seasons.

- Group: Tight-knit, fairly democratic, and stern. Steadfastness is their most prized trait. Women make up the majority of elders.

- Education: Focuses on survival skills and trades rather than scholarship. Reading is more metaphorical, learning to read navigational runes, different village colors, and hunting patterns rather than letters.

POWER DYNAMICS

The People: What is the character's place in society? How does he contribute to it?

- Because the society is small, the orator is considered a part of the people. Convincing a small percentage of the group can easily tip the scales in a beacon society.

- Like every other member of this group, the orator comes from modest means, and relies on the respect of others to maintain his influence in society. As a result, he is reserved and thoughtful.

- Because the good of the group comes before everything else, the orator is not politically savvy, and therefore leans toward self-sacrificing.

- It is important for the orator to prove that he contributes to the society through his daily tasks. He will often participate in wyvern hunts, weather fortifications, and other necessary duties, just like his neighbors.

CLASS DYNAMICS

Working Class: Are there clear distinctions?

- Although the orator is highly respected, money does not separate him from the group.

- The concept of class does not truly exist in this society, as everyone must contribute in order to survive. Class is more associated with wisdom and group respect than economy.

OTHER FACTORS

Climate/Geography: What challenges are faced due to their location?

- This beacon is located part way up the Wyvern's Spine, a narrow ridge of mountain peaks.

- The winters are harsh, even for other Winterlings. They must hunker down in the winter months.

Belief Systems: What or whom do they worship? What do they place value on?

- Local superstitions have mixed with the larger Winterland beliefs. Although not everyone is religious, they are all superstitious.

- Wyverns have become a sacred animal. Other animals, such as albatrosses and snow leopards, are also considered deities.

- Luxuries, such as music, needlework, and jewelry, are religious in nature and not for profit.

Stability: What threatens their well-being?

- Although they are stable and have lived in the same location for several generations, this society is one bad year away from wreckage. As such, they plan diligently for the worst.

TRADE DYNAMICS

Trade Hub: How busy is it? What are the popular items?

- City: Bustling, boasting several ports. Though the city is cut off from the world during the winter months, this time of year is considered the most beautiful.

- Society: A vast monoculture, in large part due to the harsh climate. However, its tourism and business reach are quite international. As a result, people live in close proximity, but are distant from their rulers and neighbors.

- Delicacies: Arctic seafood, wyvern leather goods, whaling, carved bone jewelry, luscious fur tailoring, and more.

- Education focuses on letters and has forgotten the importance of survival skills.

POWER DYNAMICS

Rising Power: What is his background, and how has it shaped him?

- The orator questions how his affluent family has ruled in the past.

- It is important for the orator to rebel against his predecessors and carve his own path to success. Although he is defiant, it also ensures that his family will remain in power, as he shifts with the political climate and sides with the views of younger generations.

- Since childhood, his peers have used psychological tactics to challenge one another. This has served to make him a strong political tactician, but also self-centered.

- The orator distances himself from other forms of power, unless strategically beneficial. He does not perform benign tasks and may even find boredom fashionable. Nonchalance is a power game in his world.

CLASS DYNAMICS

Nobility: How connected is he to those rules?

- Economy separates the orator from the people. Although his job is to be the voice of the people, he has little insight to their needs.

- He lacks exposure to the people and has little interest in being close to them. He does, however, want their adoration.

OTHER FACTORS

Climate/Geography: What's the actual terrain?

- This trade hub is located in a glacial bay where warm waters from the south cycle through, leaving the harbor waters open year round despite the frigid temperatures. This allows for trade all year round.

Belief Systems: What is their religion?

- The larger Winterland religion is dominant here, with superstitions passed on through the working class.

- International beliefs influence individual families, depending on their backgrounds and travels.

- The nobility attend religious rituals more faithfully, while the working class is more devout.

Stability: How stable is it?

- This city is centuries old. Thanks to its infrastructure, citizens have more leisure time rather than thinking about survival.

- Nonessential trades such as art, music, and luxury goods have become a profitable way of life here.

He could not be physically active in his orator's headdress, as the towering bun, feathers, and crown would probably fall apart. As a result, he must control impulsive reactions and movements. This helps him look more all knowing and nonchalant in the face of political games.

His beard is clenched in a gold clamp and trimmed neatly. Each braid is also clamped at the ends.

His hairstyle requires a servant to create. Notice that he wears his braids in a relaxed manner. This might separate him from established powers that wear more orderly hair.

The sash also wraps around his neck, insulating him from the cold, though not for long bouts of time. This, combined with his shaved head, conveys that he spends most of his time in a warm space.

Made of delicate, imported silk, his sash is several yards long and wide. It wraps around itself in complex knots, possibly a personal fashion statement or hot trend.

This tailored cotehardie of wyvern leather is a prized commodity among the wealthy. Not only expensive, but time-consuming to construct, each stitch must be hole-punched before being sewn. Wyvern hide, even if softened, is too tough for a sewing needle.

The even finish of the cotehardie is also a symbol of wealth, as it means the prime pieces of leather from multiple wyverns were combined to create it.

Basic garments are made of silk rather than soft leather, including his sapphire blue shalwar pants. He may be wearing as many as three layers underneath his cotehardie.

The tassels along the edge of the cotehardie are raw silk, imported from his family's trade partner across the seas. This is a political statement of solidarity more than a fashion choice.

While most Winterlings must wear thick boots to protect their feet, the orator's wealth is shown in the complex, slim design of his shoes. A seal calf or kid leather bootie is covered by a gold open-lattice poulaine. This shoe is definitely made for the authoritative sound of gold soles on stone floors.

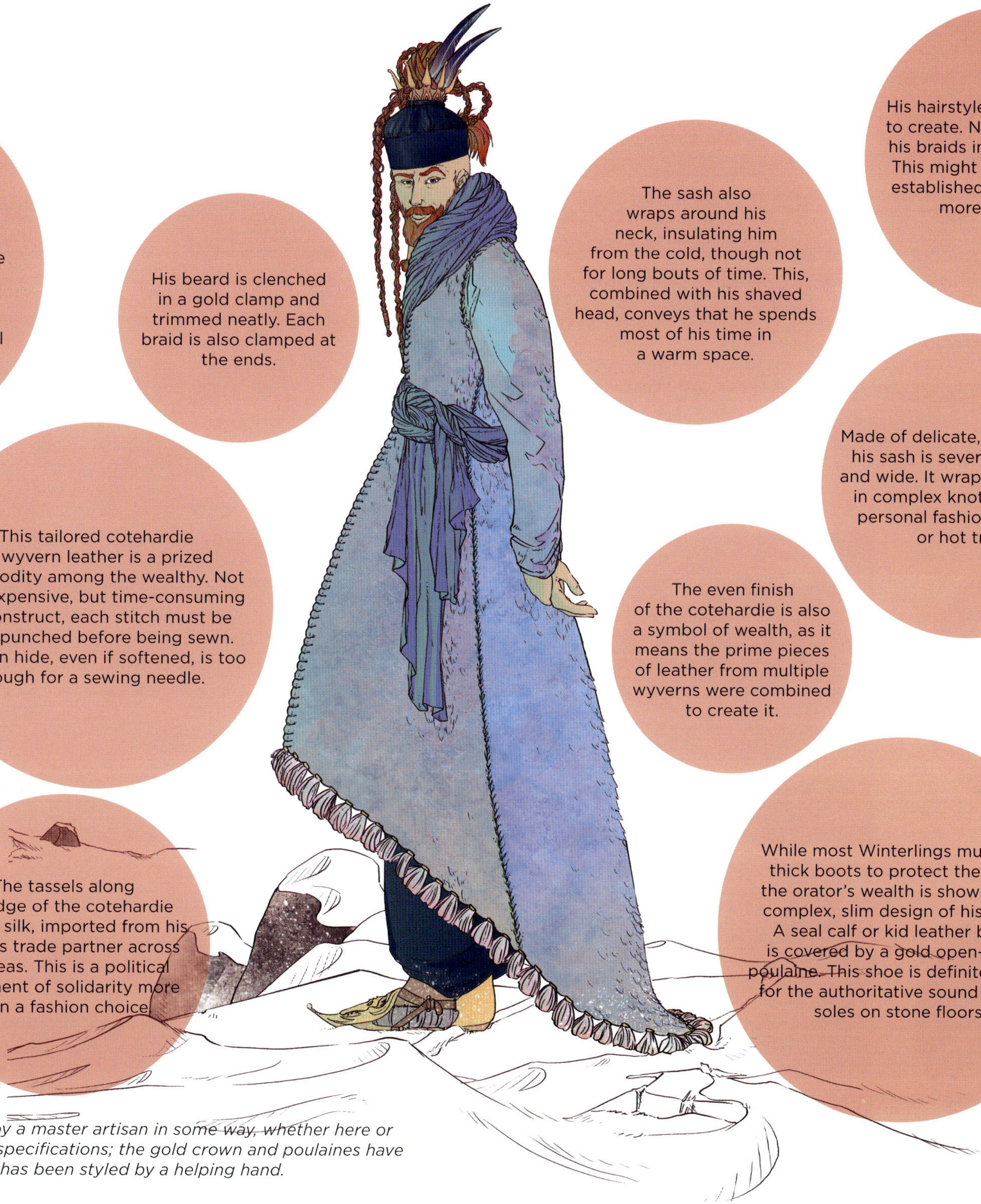

Each garment he wears has been touched by a master artisan in some way, whether here or in another land. Tailors fit every item to his specifications; the gold crown and poulaines have been cast into custom designs, and his hair has been styled by a helping hand.

Camouflage

Camouflage isn't just for hunters and soldiers. Humans subconsciously camouflage themselves in their environments over time. The more comfortable a person is in a place, the more they'll blend in with it.

If a character in your narrative walks into a bar and feels insecure, chances are they don't fit the visual setting. The more time they spend in that bar, the more they will begin to resemble the bar. Similarly, if they've always gone to that bar and start to have a new outlook on life, they will visually separate from it over time.

Let's examine examples of both countryside and urban camouflage across the world. As can be seen below (Vietnam and Greece), farmers from around the world may have their own unique style, but within each culture, coarse, checked, and ribbed fabrics that are durable find their way onto every palette. Their textiles, though ranging in fit, detail, color, and type, reflect farmland patterns and regional crops as well as the demands of working in their natural environment. Though you may see someone similarly dressed in the city, this is a conscious choice on the part of that person to identify their personality as more closely relating to the natural world.

Urban landscapes are no different. Different kinds of cities inspire different kinds of camouflage. If your metropolis is full of towering, reflective glass, then patterns become abstract, distorted repeat patterns. Old brick cities can inspire eclectic layers, net, and distressed fashions with their crumbling facades and stained cement. Ad-lined streets will encourage people to wear neutrals with pops of color that are often text.

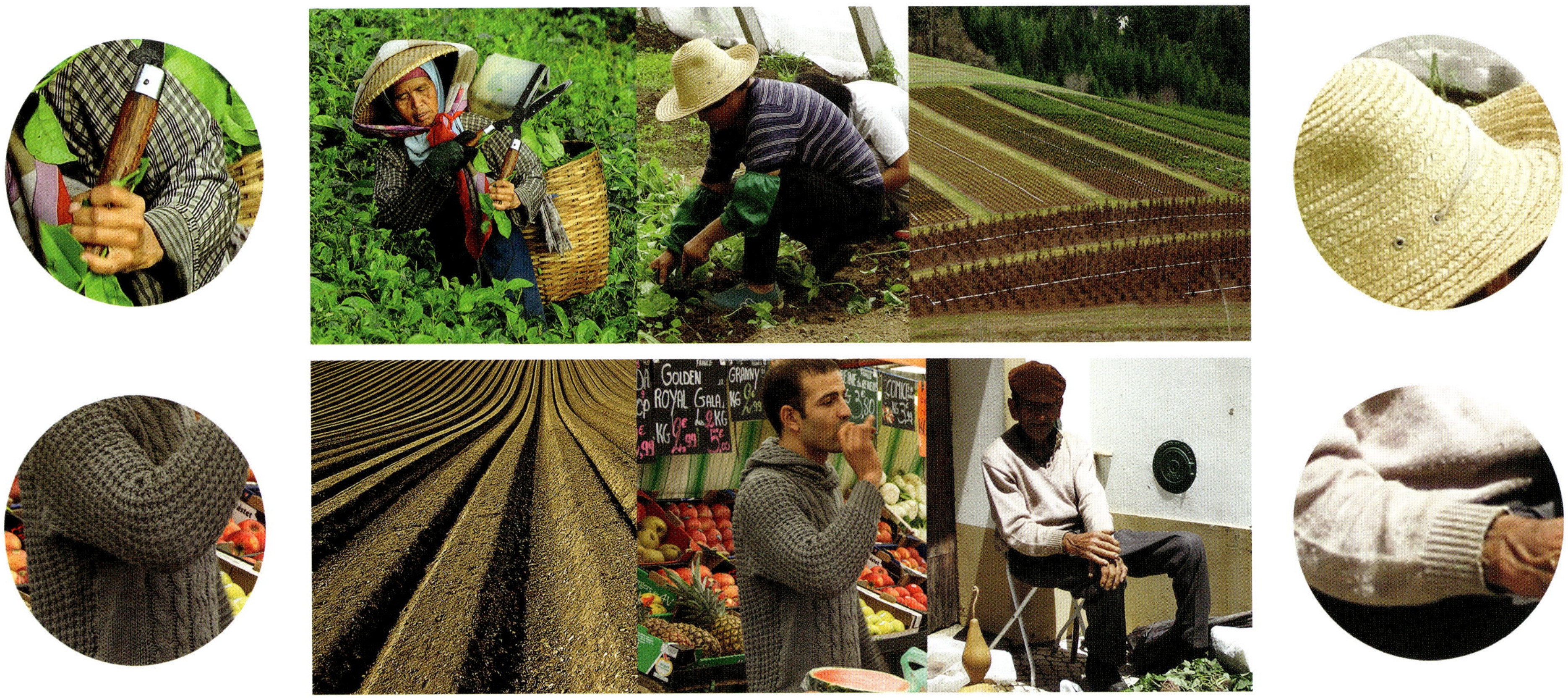

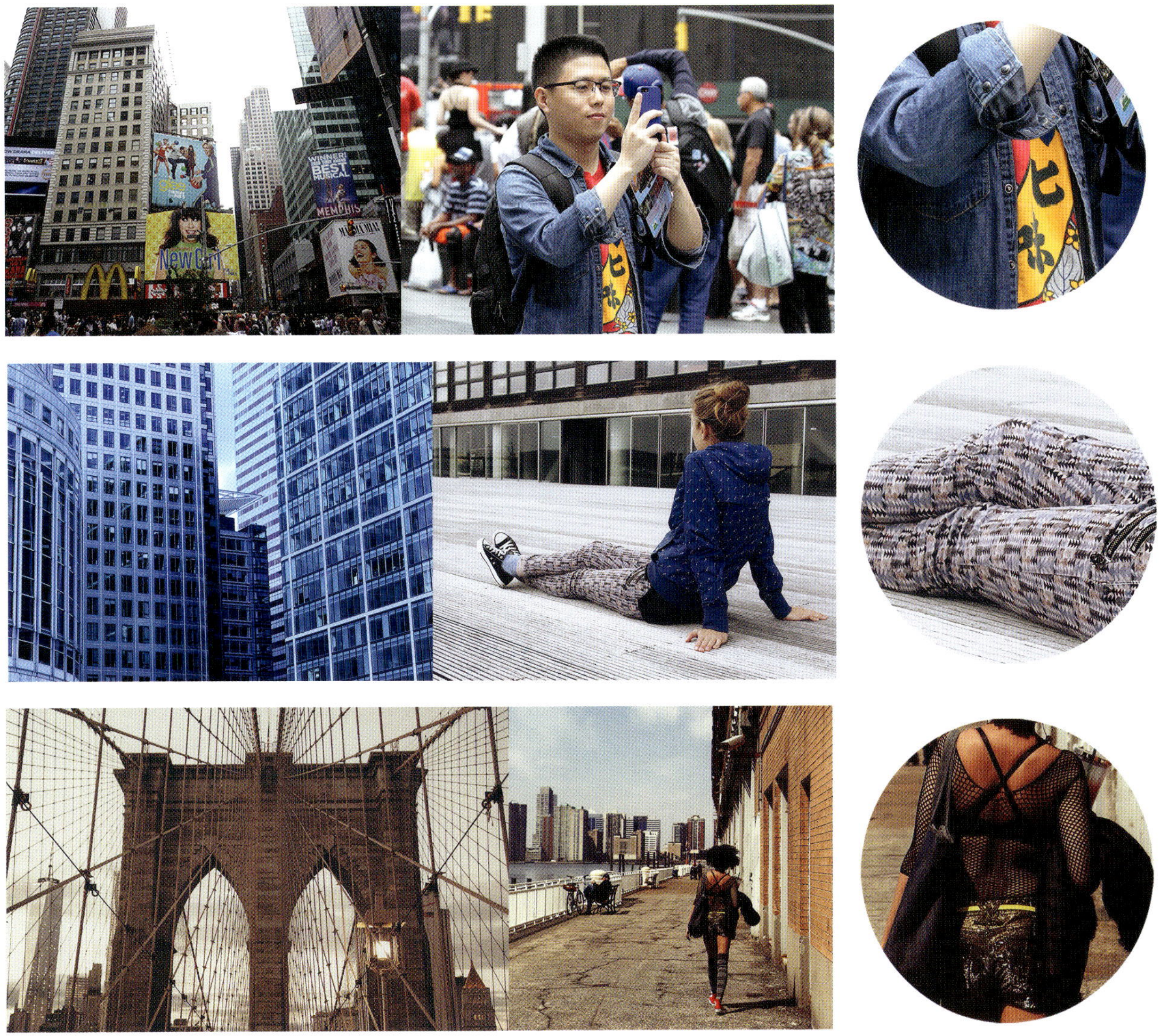

In the film *Back to the Future, Part III*, Doc (Christopher Lloyd) gives Marty (Michael J. Fox), a time traveler, an outfit that is a modern interpretation of fashion from 1885. When Marty goes back in time, the modern materials, sneakers, and color palette stand out like a sore thumb. This not only allows him to stand out amongst the rest of the cast, but it helps the audience recognize that he is out of place. When he changes into a more appropriate outfit for the time, using dyes and materials that were native to 1885, he gains more influence and power over his fate in that world.

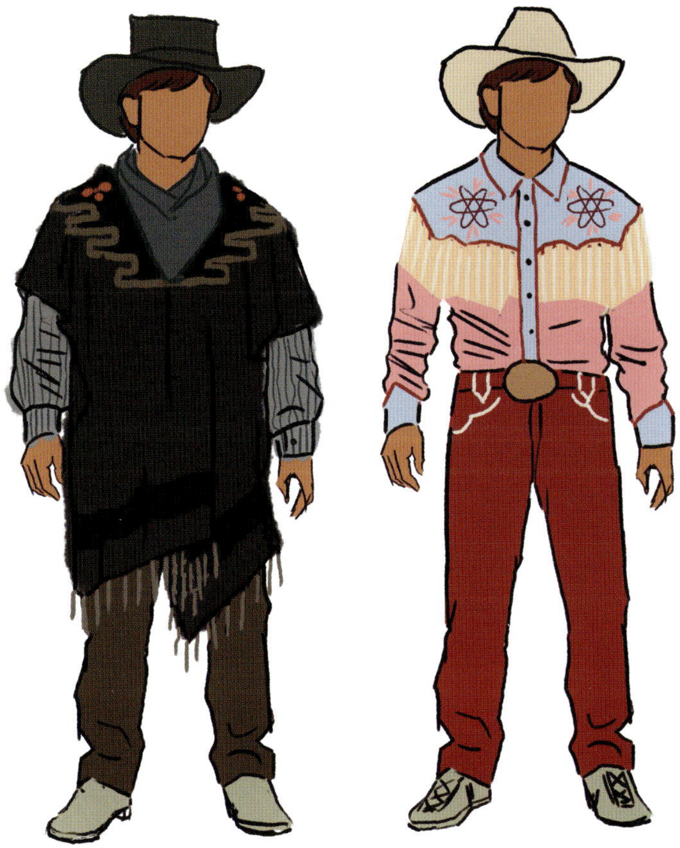

The Value of Live Research

Whether you are creating your story for an adult or a child, nurturing a childlike and humble curiosity about the world is of priceless benefit. Explore a culture or a neighborhood, interview residents, note your sensory impressions, take photos, sketch. The more you understand others and what influences their perception, the more natural it will become to create visual languages that reflect an authentic point of view.

As you dive deeper into a culture, you may find familiar elements that transcend time and place. Personalities may remind you of family or friends back home, or cultural values may echo your own. Familiarity in a foreign country can allow you to better draw from the foreign cultural experiences and combine them with your own context to create something entirely new.

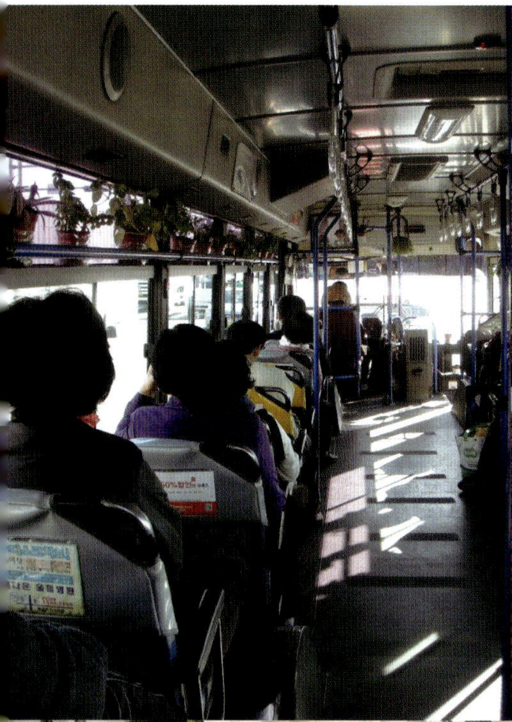

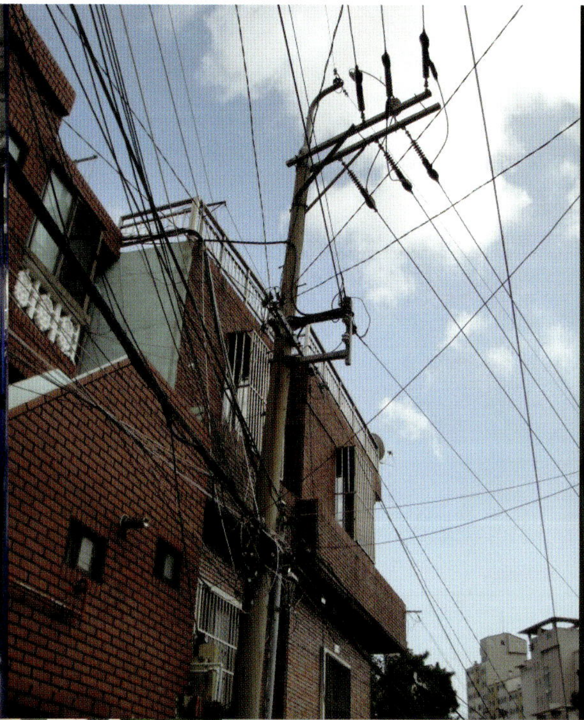

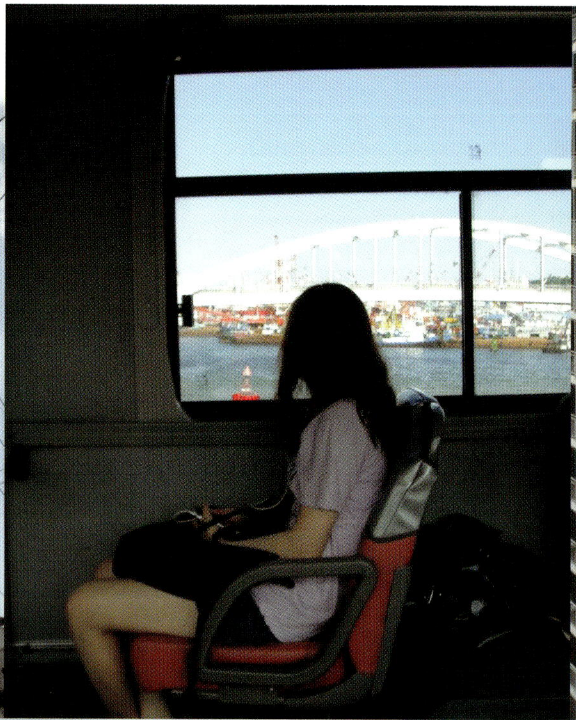

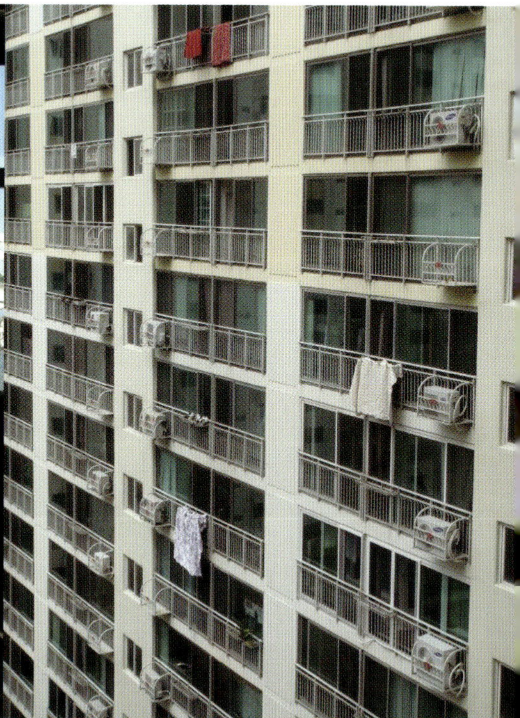

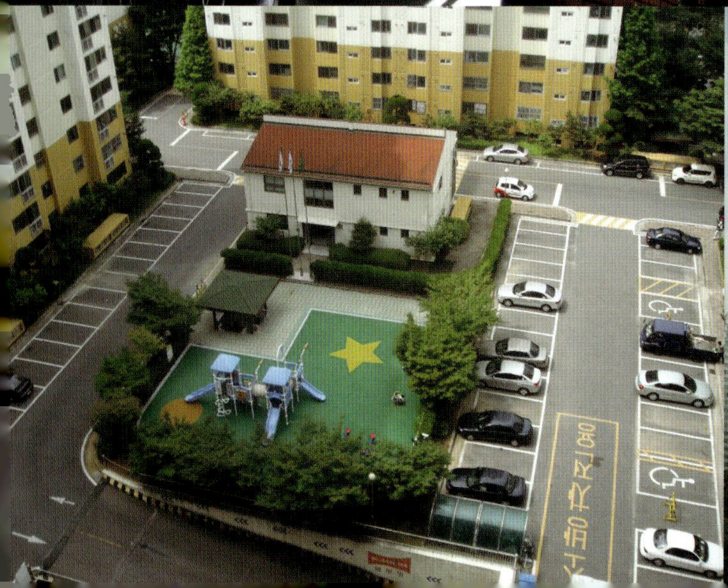

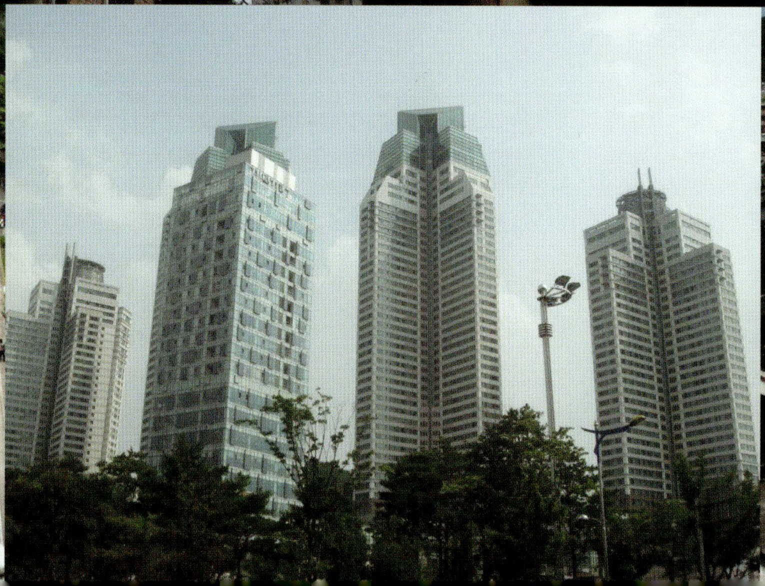

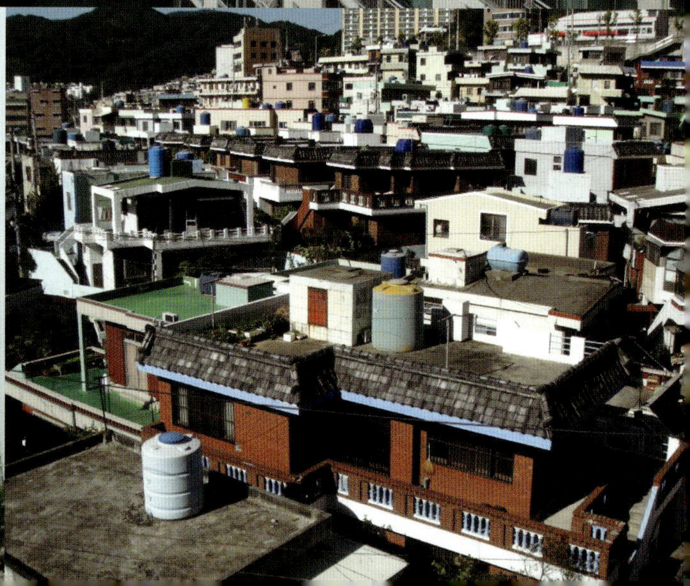

Exercise: Mood Board Explorations

Prompt: Explore a character who travels from one trade archetype to another set in a particular time period.

Gather your resulting photos, thoughts, and sketches into mood boards to note interesting connections, color palettes, compositional cues, and design patterns that have the potential to amplify your story's theme.

When you're limited from traveling, or you are working on an ancient or alien world, you can gather images, read articles, and watch interviews online. However, without supplementing your research with direct sensory feedback, it can become more difficult to narrow in on an authentic and impactful visual language. Try looking for places with similar cultural values or scenery with similar qualities within your own locale—or reach back into your memory to access places or times that relate to the theme or plot in some way.

Beware! Good quality research is hard to find! Locations, dates, and names of garments are often missing or incorrect. Instead of using a search engine or search curator site, go straight to museum archives online and published books.

Take your time and select images that are clear and strongly represent the trade routes you are exploring.

- Note the patterns you see and discard the outliers to clarify them.
- Refine it through more directed exploration and experiments.
- If there is a specific element that you want to bring focus to (something that an outsider wouldn't realize), you can make a note. For instance, say you have a photo of an old house. Do you want to focus on the architecture or the peeling paint? Just jot down a text note on the board or crop the picture.

By calling back to my time living in Korea, I can isolate ideas such as hierarchy, height, order, control, isolation, technology, and desire for support.

My characters will be from a trade hub in space. In this futuristic world, they will struggle to build relationships and feel disconnected from nature, so I focus on architectural patterns, synthetic materials, and reflectivity or translucency.

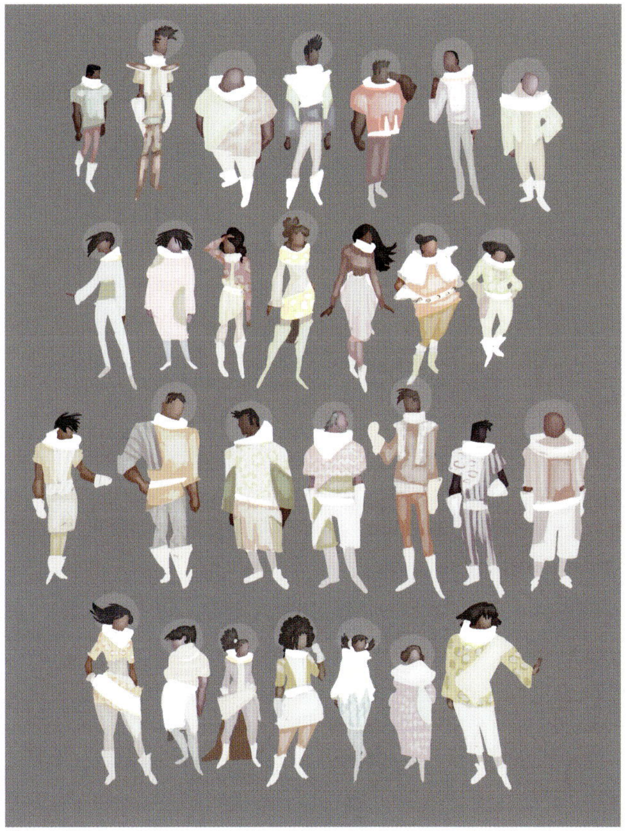

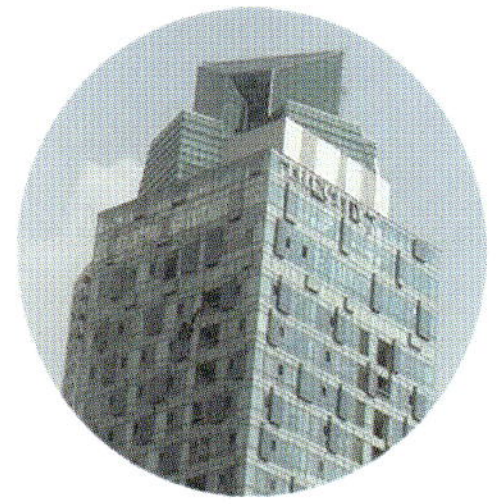

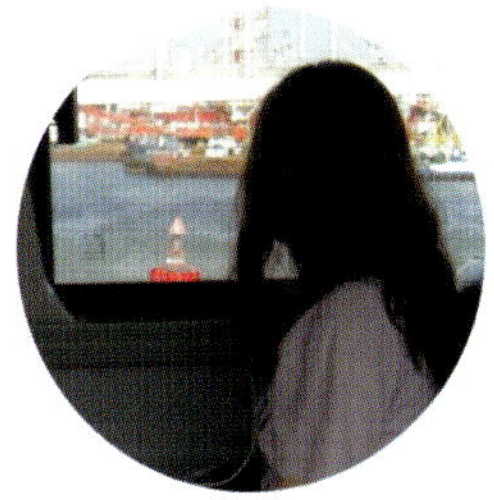

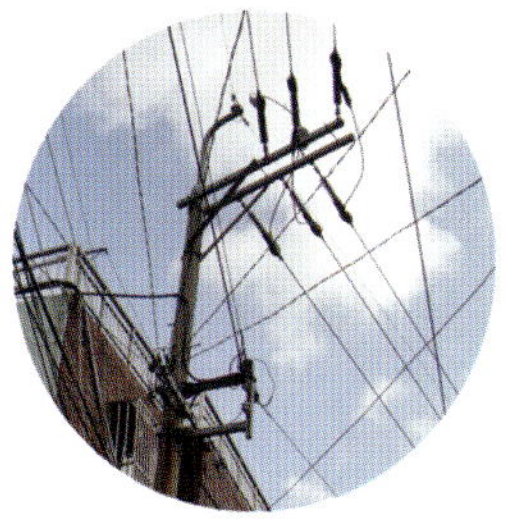

Now let's transport our space travelers to a prehistoric planet where nature is more powerful than mankind and building relationships is necessary to survive.

For example, imagine a life raft on a prehistoric alien planet. What materials would be available and how would you use them? Do they need to be camouflaged? What kinds of shapes make sense in that world?

Materials exploration: by exploring the aesthetics and materials available, you can effectively "shop" in the world as you style costume ideas for your character. This not only speeds up the process of thumbnailing costumes for the main characters but gives you a great context to push and pull within, allowing you to use the full cast of characters to support and complement the costume of the protagonist.

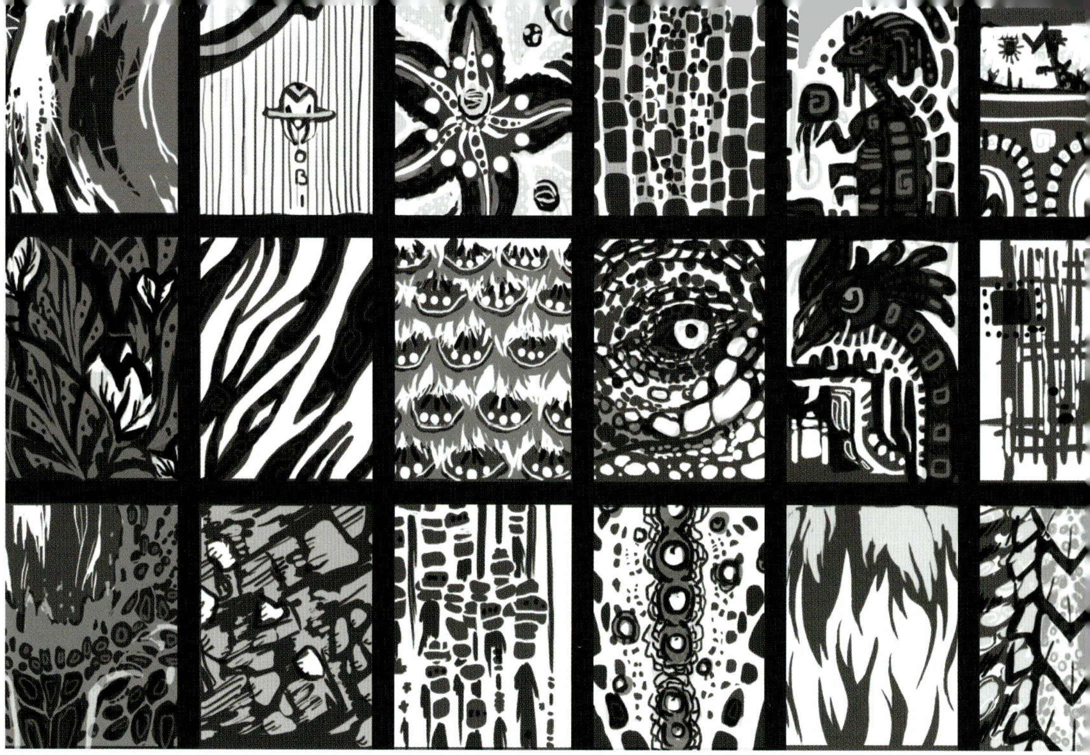

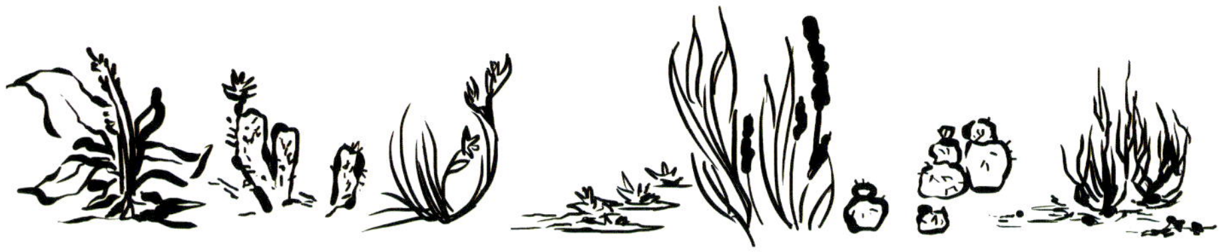

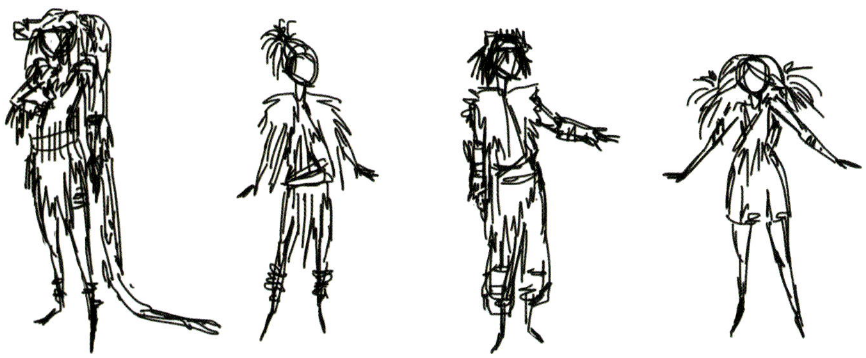

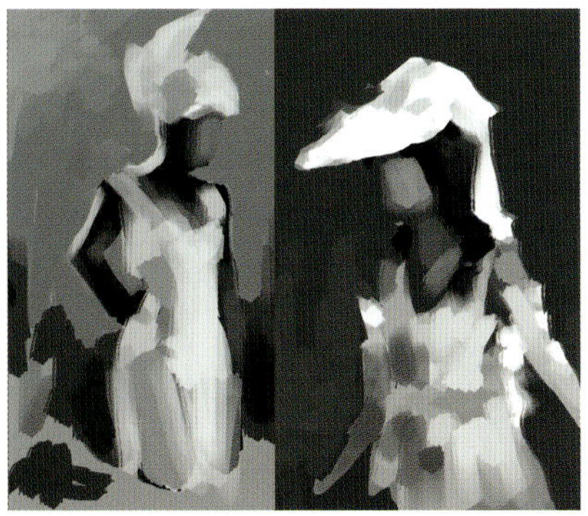

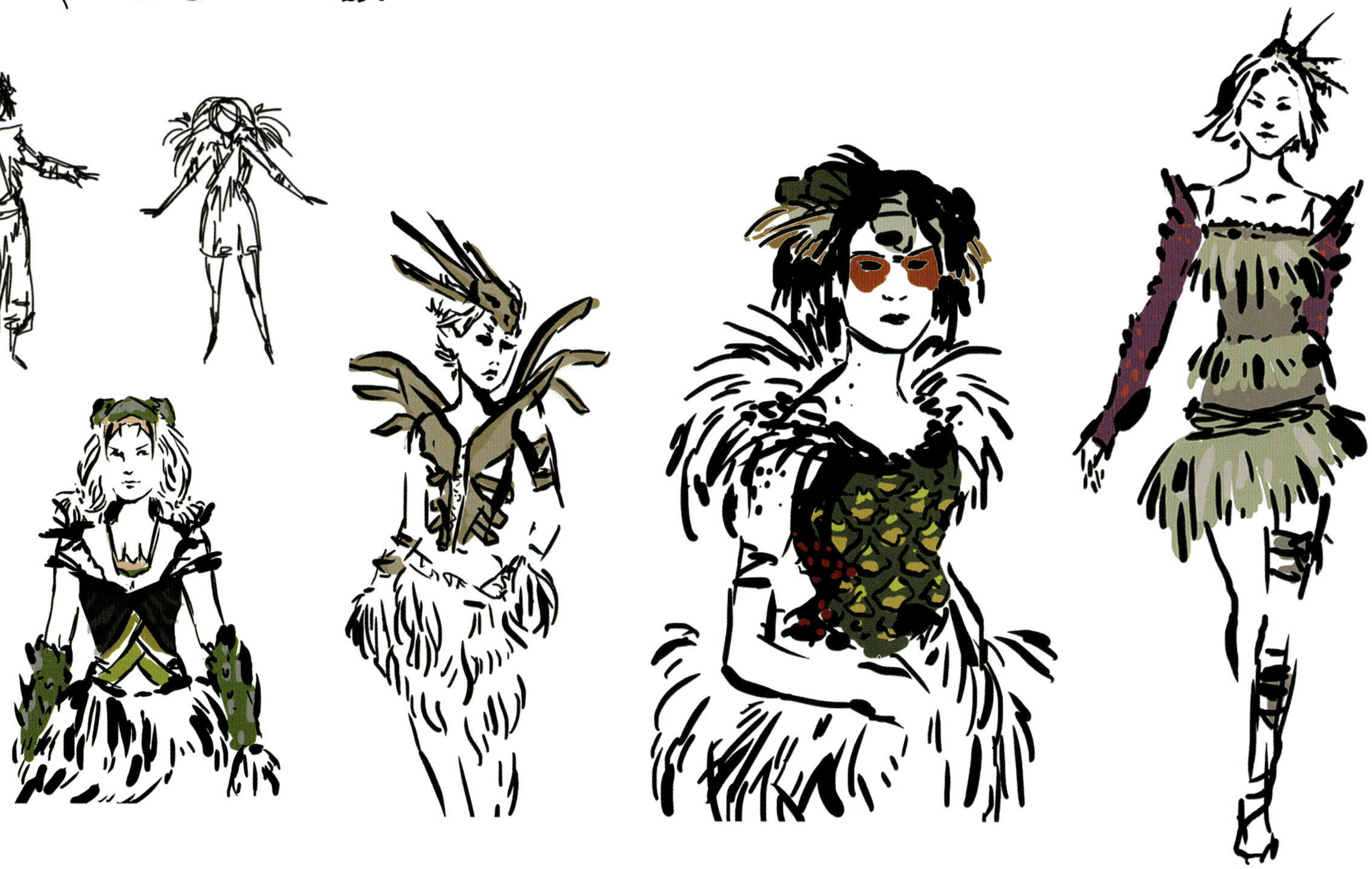

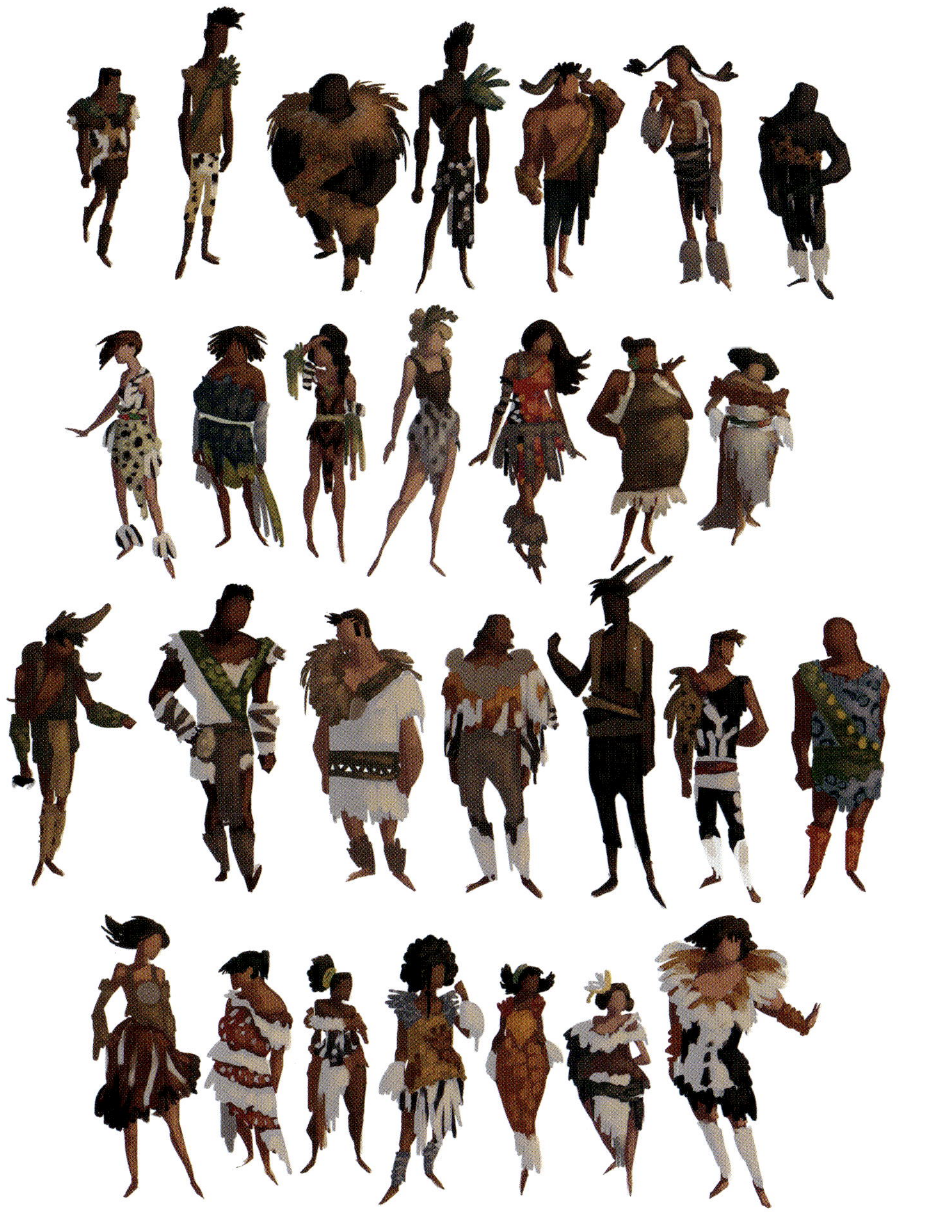

Explore genders, body types, and a variety of roles to get a clearer picture of your world. As you notice patterns you like, refine your thoughts by selecting a small group of characters from your thumbnails.

Use these to create the items you can "shop" from to create your character's altered look. For this example on the right, inspired by *Swiss Family Robinson*, I created a child who embraces the adventurous world.

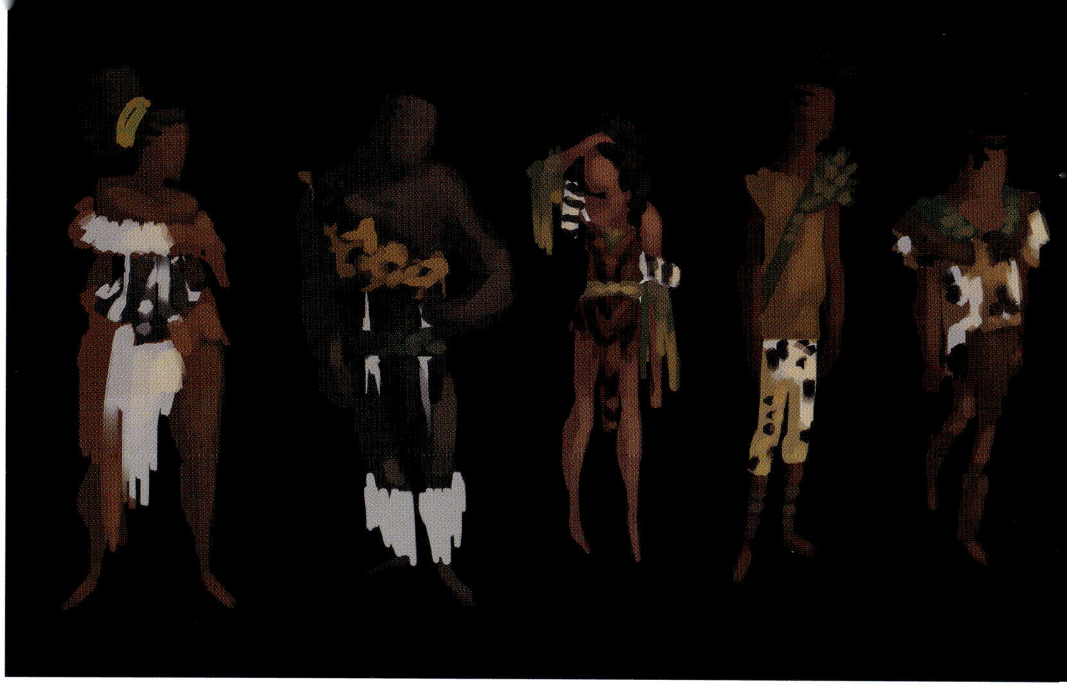

Using the group of characters above as a guide, I pull natural materials from the prehistoric planet to layer over the top of the futuristic costume, adding complexity and flexibility for her costume to evolve as she traverses and explores the alien world. Curious and excited, this young child embraces the life raft aesthetic and layers the animal furs and natural materials over her original trade hub school uniform. She is camouflaged into the new environment while showing flashes of her original costume to remind us that she is not native to it.

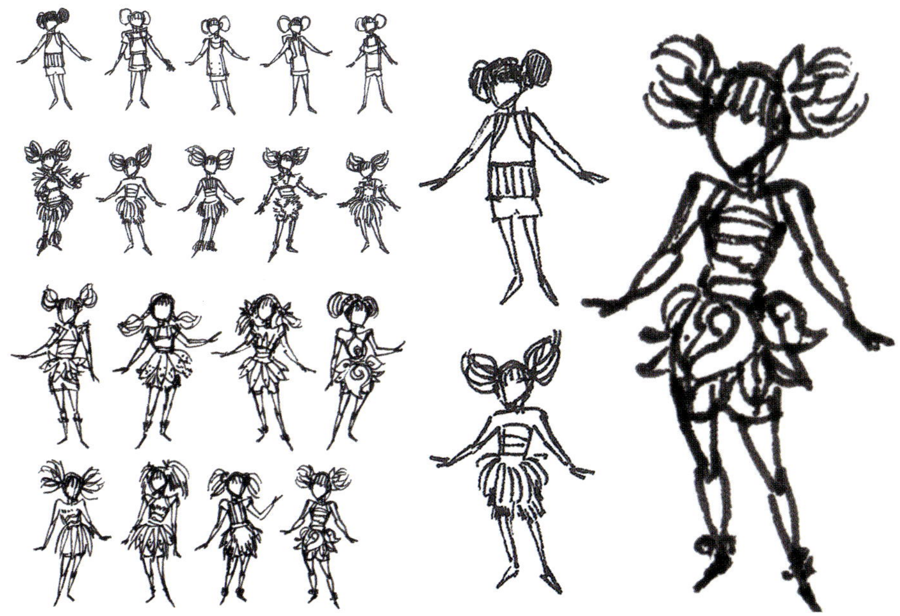

Exercise: Creating a Material Language

Whether your story takes place in the real world, a fantasy world, or a futuristic sci-fi setting, understanding how past and contemporary civilizations used fabrics gives us a strong reference to build our society's story through material choices.

A good rule of thumb is to check the available colors, materials, and manufacturing techniques available in your world—especially for realistic dramas where accuracy creates the foundation for the voyeuristic lens. For example, mauve doesn't exist in nature. The first synthetic dye was (accidentally) invented in 1856 by William Henry Perkin. Some other notable inventions include the cotton gin (1794), spinning jenny/Mule (1764/1779), water frame (1768), jacquard loom (1801), and 3D printers (1980s, but in fashion starting in 2010). For fantasy or sci-fi, find a logical stylization, evolution, or deviation from history that suits the story's lens and thematic intent. Haphazard choices compromise immersion and make consistency across the production design difficult, while logical rules to your material language, however stylized, will help build believability and trust in the story's world.

Here is an overview of basic material and fabric types. Be conscious if the selected material would make sense for your character and his or her world. Choose one of your costume designs and create a page/document/presentation board that clearly communicates the material choice for each element of the costume. This can mean gathering photo reference, including physical swatches or rendering the material.

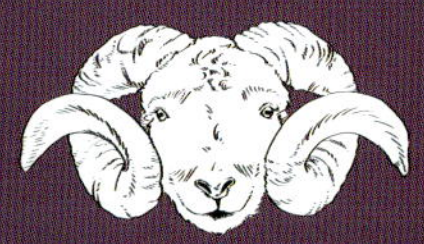

ANIMALS

- leather
- silk
- fur
- wool

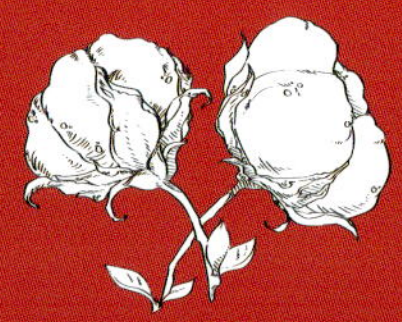

PLANTS

- cotton
- bamboo
- flax
- straw
- grass

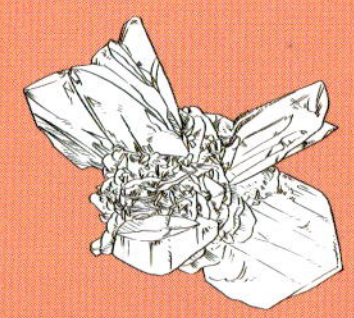

MINERALS

- glass
- metal
- shell
- asbestos

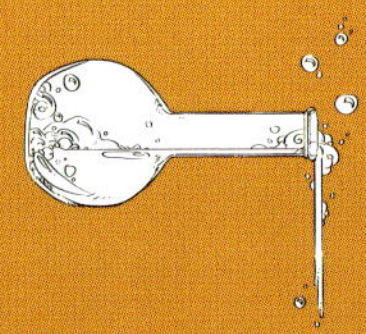

SYNTHETIC

- polyester
- spandex
- nylon
- acrylic

DID YOU KNOW?

Generally speaking, natural fibers such as cotton will char when exposed to fire, whereas synthetic fibers like polyester will melt—and sometimes produce hazardous gases, so, when creating swatch samples, enjoy science with safety in mind!

Fantasy Material Tutorial: The Sugar Sentinel

Logline: In a kingdom flourishing because of their sugarcane, a young, rash warrior apprentice must fight off greedy invaders from stealing their crops. In order to protect their land and the helpless creatures who inhabit the forests, she must come up with a strategy to outwit the persistent intruders.

Ethnicity: Indigenous Brazilian tribe

Religion: Connection to Mother Nature

Social Status: Warrior apprentice

Material Resources: Sugarcane and candy

With an abundance of sugarcane plants, the culture and evolution of Brazilian society developed using sugarcane as its source, and their art and technology are closely linked to cane sugar as a result. To use candy as my material is not too much of a stretch. In this case I decided that instead of the entire world being made of candy, people are fully human but have developed the power to control sugar and substances derived from sugar.

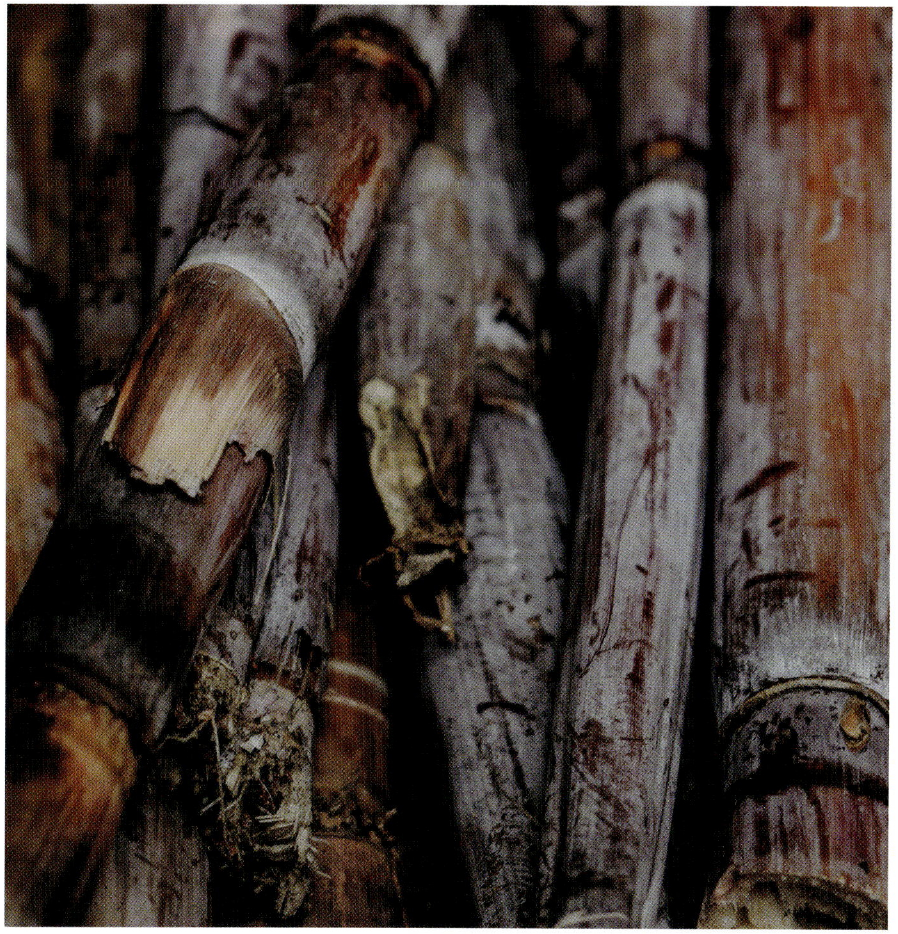

WHERE TO START

I start by researching how warriors of various indigenous tribes dress themselves and why. This way when I create the candy-influenced costume design, I'll have real-life reference to return to if I get stuck. This approach will also help me preserve the identify of the source culture in my concept.

As a warrior apprentice, her outfit requires freedom of movement. Coming from a tribe with limited technology, their garments are handmade; the range of shapes would be basic, and, in this case, I have decided that she would have made most of her own outfit. With that in mind, the different parts of the outfit need to be simple and practical.

TIP:

You may notice the influence of multiple cultures within your chosen culture. Study the costume history of Brazil to see if you can recognize how different cultures intertwine in their clothing and contribute to the evolution of their traditions. These interactions can and did lead to competition, conflict, or a unique blending of identity. Opportunities to base imaginary cultures on these types of dynamics can give you more interesting and complex costumes without sacrificing cultural integrity.

Tattoos and Body Paints

Members of a religion or subculture often tattoo themselves to show integration into a group; the process can even become a ritual (e.g., the Maori's use of Moko in New Zealand). A tattoo can also represent a character's position, rank, or personal devotion. Maui's design in Disney's *Moana* take them to the next level, animating his tattoos to tell his story.

Since tattoos are intended to be permanent modifications to a character's body, they can be used to add extra information about the character's identity, allude to a past event or—in a society where tattoos are uncommon—show us the character's rebellious nature.

Body paints, as impermanent modifications, are more common during special events, for example, Celt warriors in battle or henna at a wedding with a Hindu bride. Since my character is a warrior, and body paint is traditional in Brazil, I gathered reference and explored some possible options.

"Urucu" is the red seed Brazil uses for body paint, and red paint across the eyes is one of the most iconic Brazilian face paint patterns (mostly used by women and children). I referenced the Kayapo tribe who uses body paint to indicate social hierarchy. For this child apprentice, I can use this to indicate her coming of age. The dots or use of geometric shapes turns body paint into a graphic language others can use to communicate within her tribe or camouflage into their environment.

Hair

Throughout history, hair has been an essential part of a person's identity and a representation of status and health. Instead of using the traditional beads in her hair made from glass or stones, her adornments will be made of hard sugar. As a warrior, she needs to have her weapon with her at all times, so I decided to make her scepter part of her costume by allowing her to soften the sugar and put it in her hair when it's not in use. When danger is near, she easily unwraps the scepter from her hair and immediately makes it rock solid.

On the next page, I developed two ideas for her weapon. First, she easily unwraps the candy "ribbon" from her hair and creates a set of nunchucks. Second, her weapon is wrapped around her hair like a hat which she can unwrap, harden, and use as a staff.

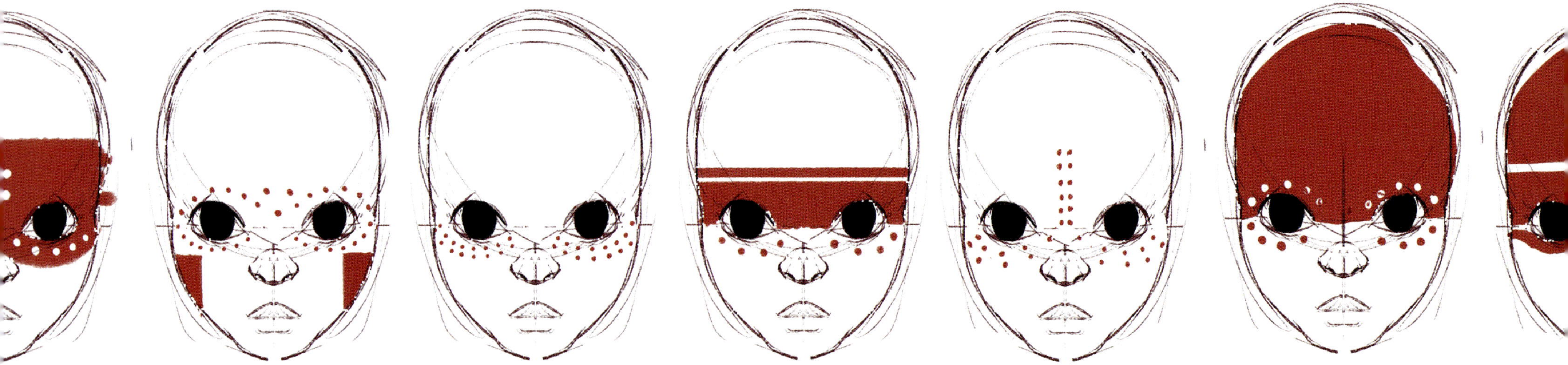

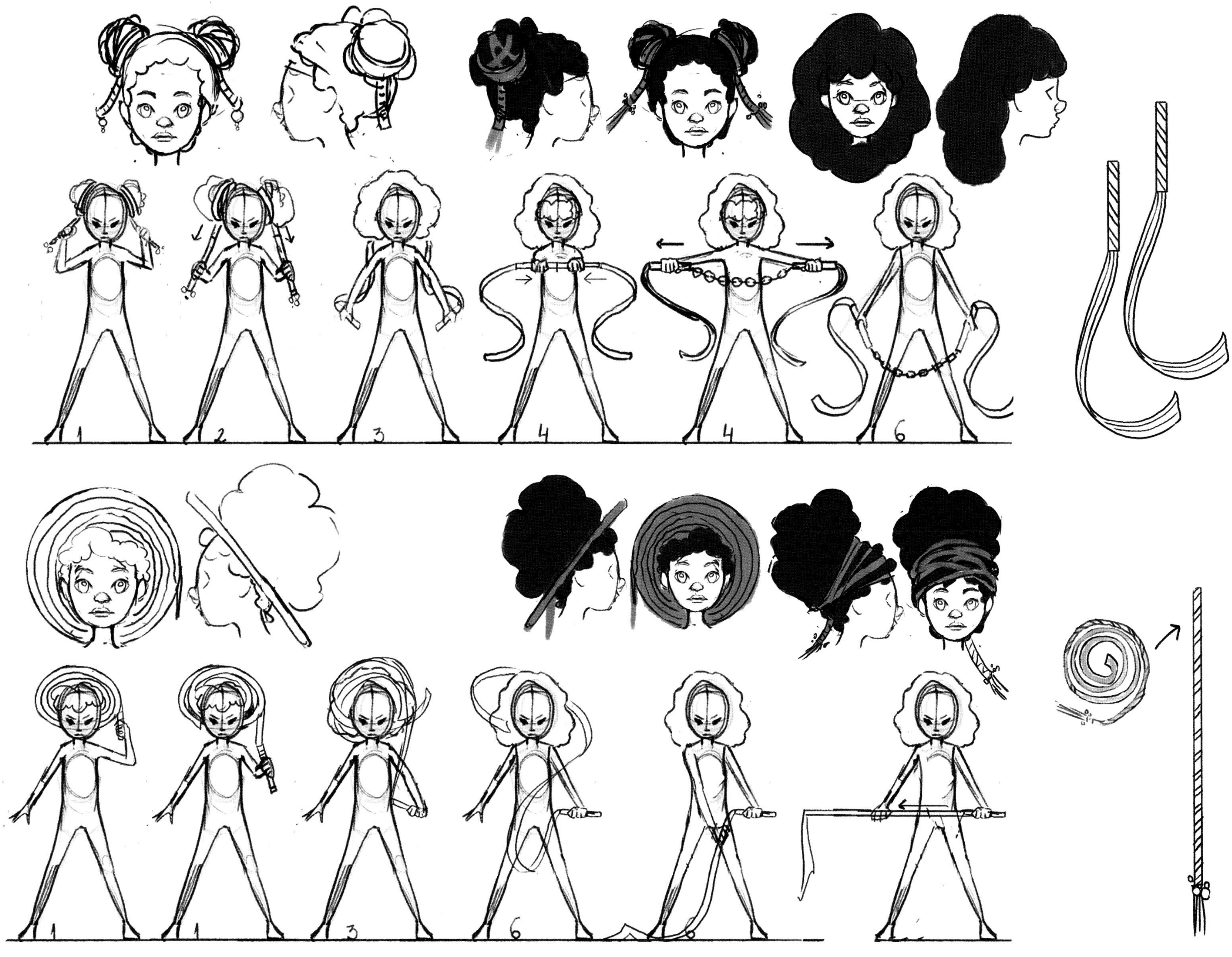

I create a simple pose to incorporate all the elements and present my concept. Her pants open in the center so she can use her knees as much as she needs to without ripping or wearing out her pants. The beaded skirt showcases a unique native flourish while adding opportunities for secondary animation. The addition of the green paint allows her to further blend into the jungle while giving her look another candy allusion (candy cane). Other candy elements: sprinkles in her hair, lollipops for earrings, sweet and sour stripes for the ribbon that holds her hair, sugared almonds for the necklace, colorful button-shaped chocolates for her skirt, and opaque plastic candy wrappers for the pink part of her shoes.

As a warrior, she will dye her outfit colors that she can use as camouflage in her environment, in this case, brightly colored flowers. To fit her strong personality, I chose a combination of dark pink, yellow, and orange. The orange-yellow represents her sensitive and playful side, and the dark pink her determined side.

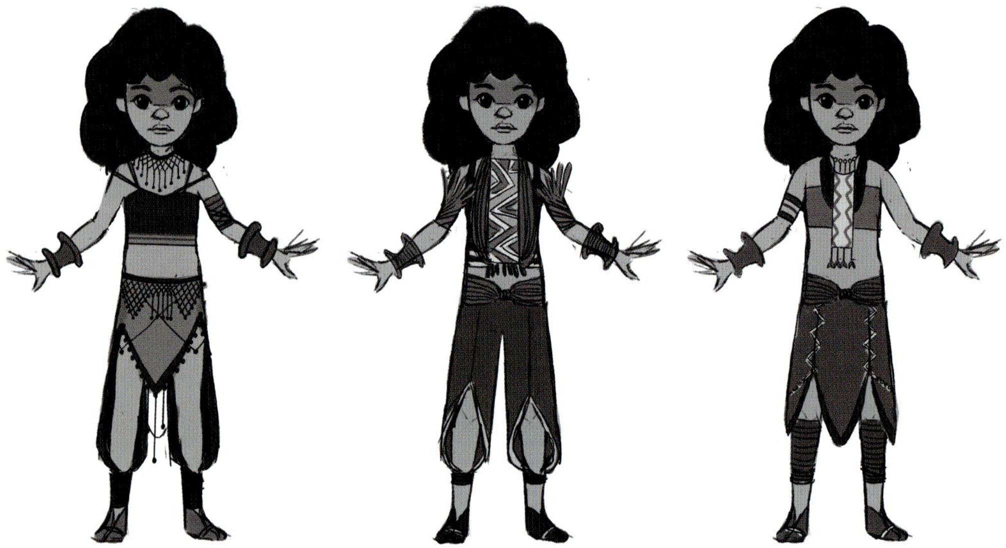

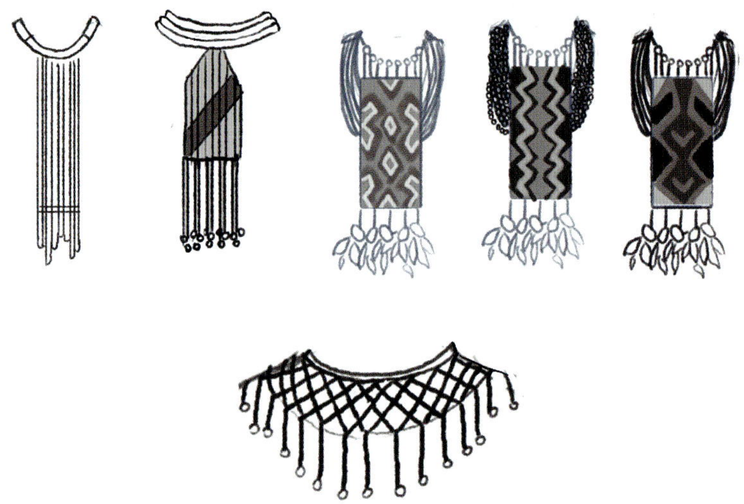

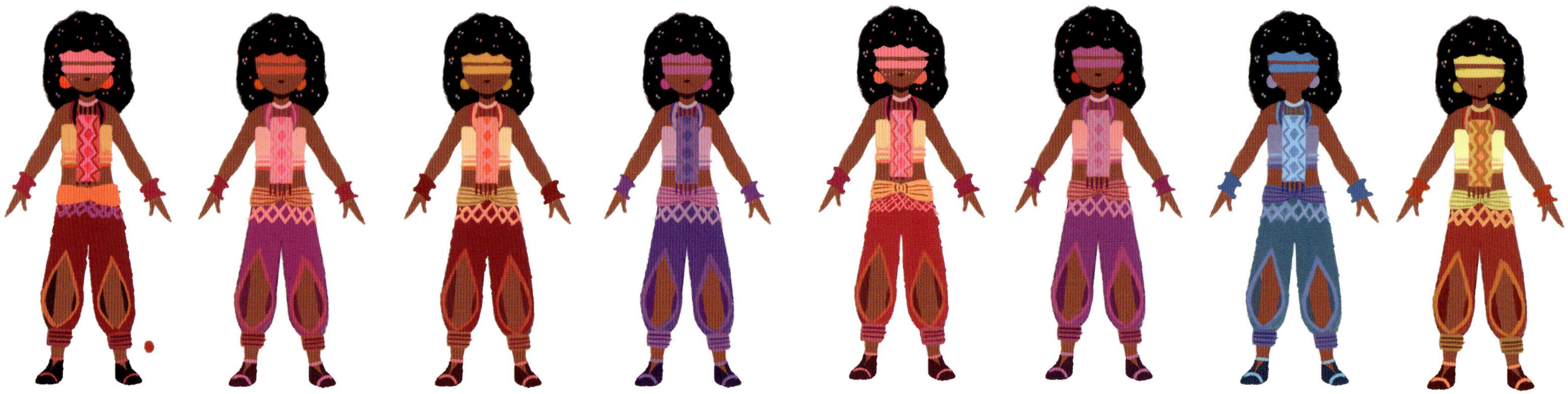

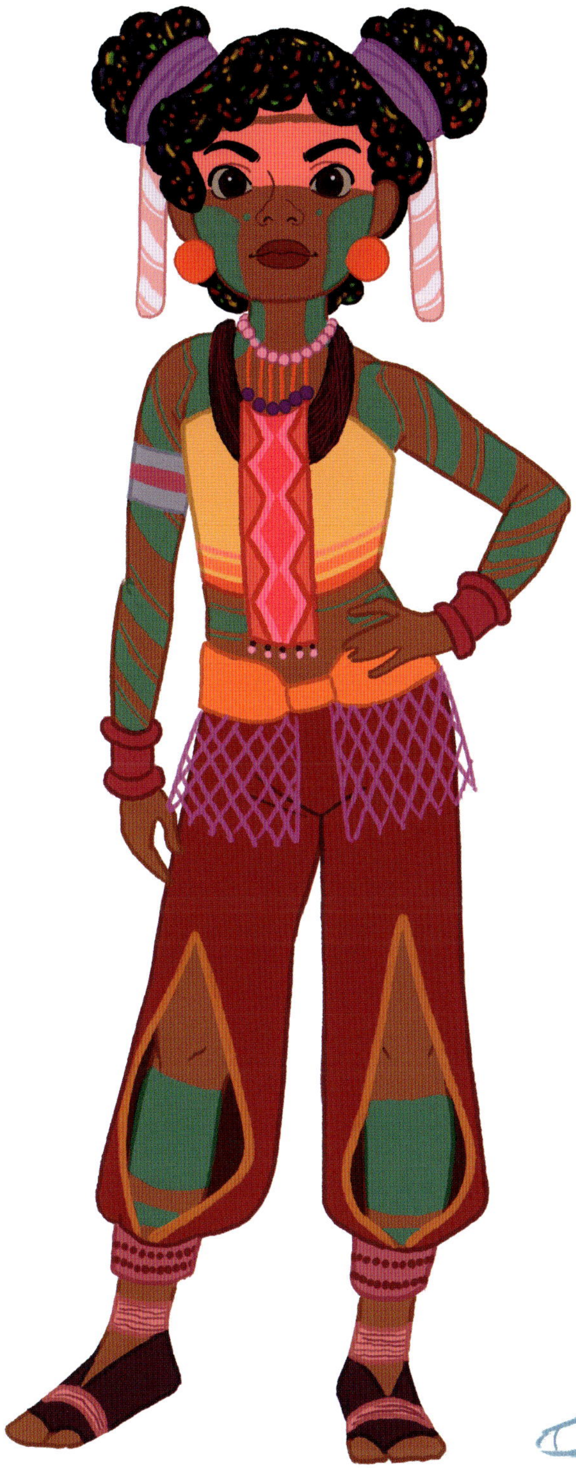

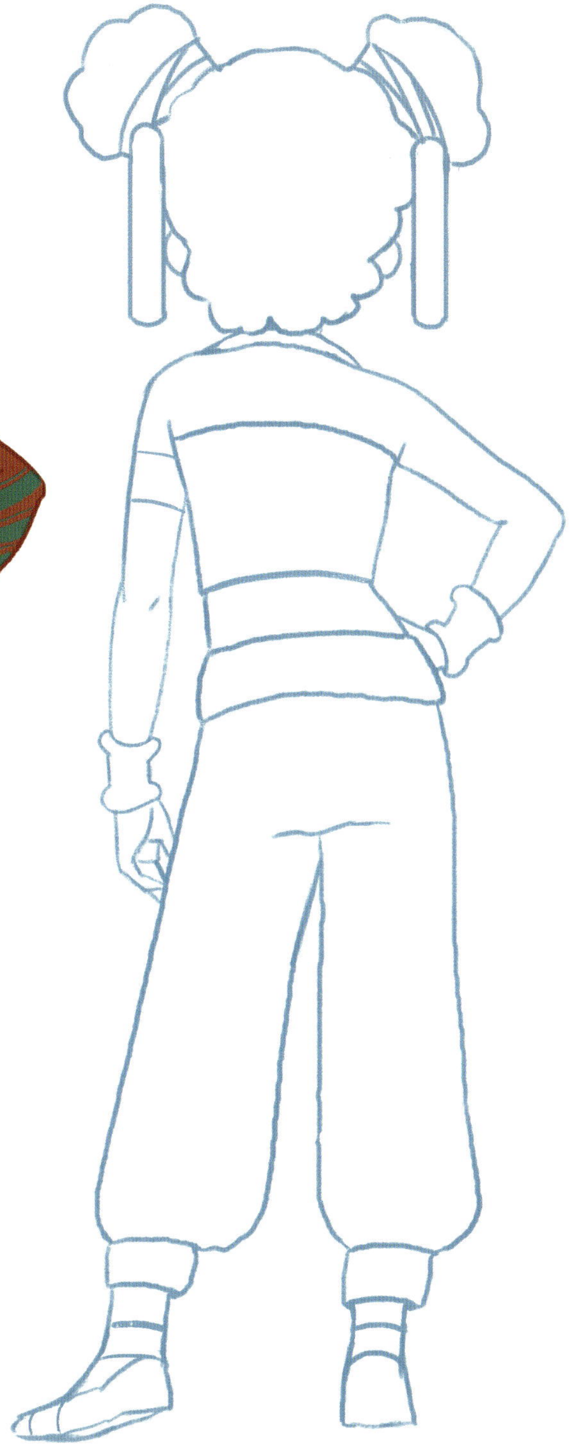

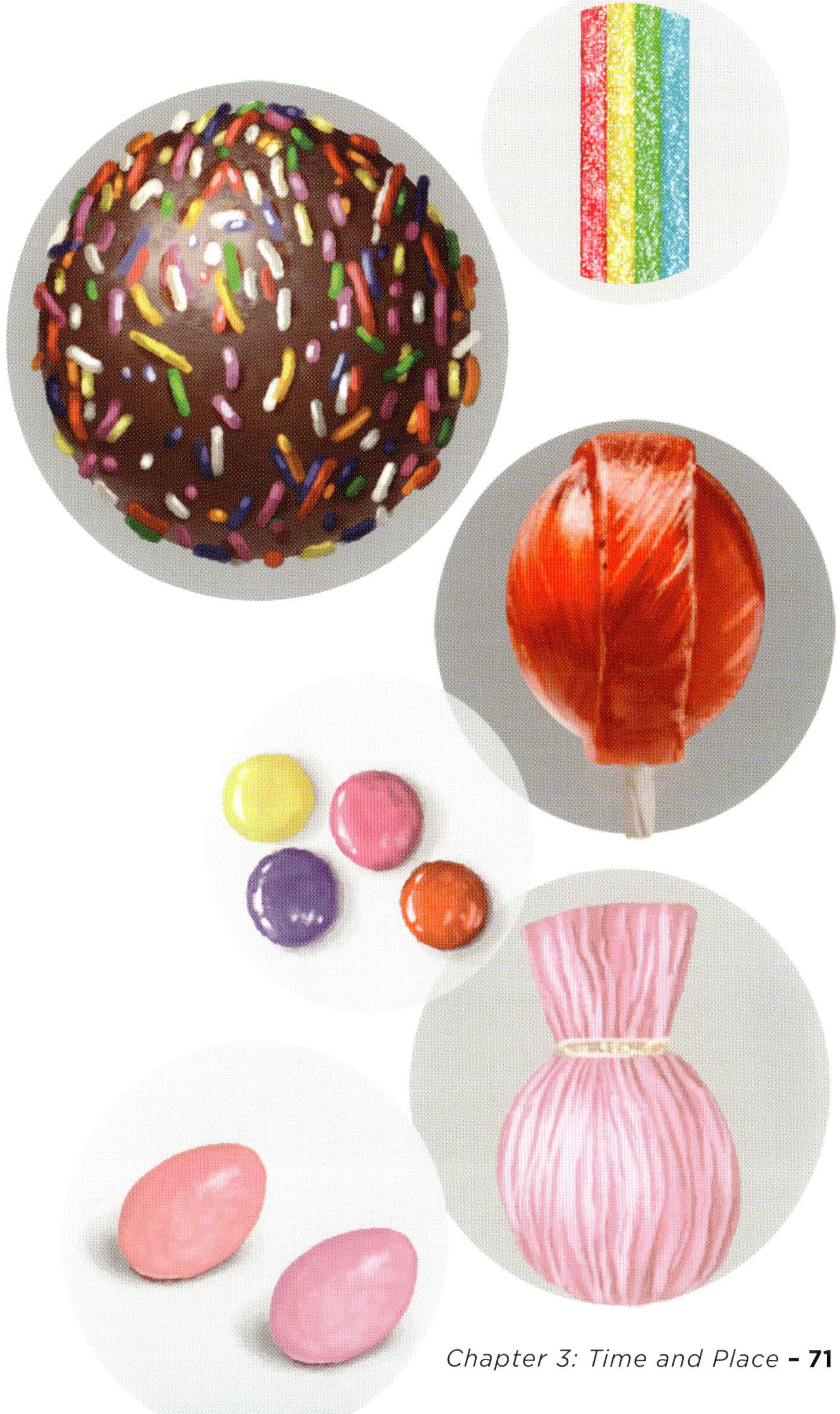

Situational Design

Each society has unspoken rules for different settings and occasions. Establishing solid rules in your imaginary world will help make your visual design more flexible. Your character can then choose to break the rules or maintain them. Often the occasion will dictate the appropriate mode of dress, and people who defy these social laws are considered uneducated, inconsiderate, and/or rude, for example, an adult who wears a T-shirt and jeans to a wedding. While the details of some modes of dress may change, these basics principles ring true the world over.

PUBLIC VS. PRIVATE

In private spaces, socially expected conduct and grooming is not enforced and depends solely on the relationship between individuals. If a stranger or business relation enters a personal space, an individual's comfort level will determine if they adhere to basic public expectations. One scenario would be choosing to answer the door for the pizza delivery guy in your underwear or not.

LOUNGEWEAR

- **Occasion**: Worn in intimate company, such as close family and friends, within the comfort of one's private spaces; over time, these garments become acceptable to wear in public spaces.
- **Examples**: Sweatpants, flip-flops, spaghetti-strap tank tops, teddies, boxers, hot pants, nightgowns, nightshirts, bathrobes, hoodies.

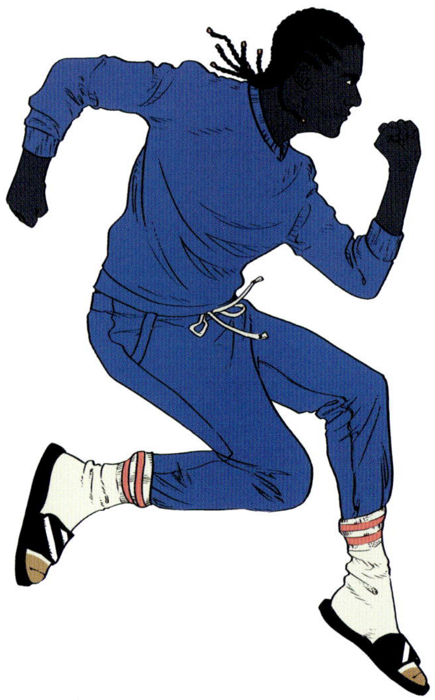

CASUAL OR DAY WEAR

Occasion: Worn within the home to accept guests, take care of daily tasks, or spend leisure time in public spaces

Common Elements:

- Often less durable than athletic wear and blue-collar workwear to promote a quick turnaround in trends and seasonal palettes.
- More daring colors, patterns, and shapes.
- **Examples:** Jeans, jumpers, cargo pants, tennis shoes, T-shirts, blouses, button-down shirts, polo shirts, combat boots, gladiator sandals, capris, palazzo pants, shorts.

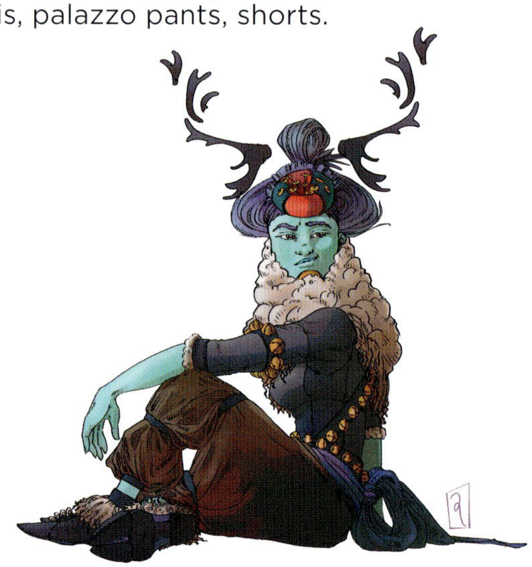

FORMALWEAR

Occasion: worn for events or traditions that have some sense of obligation, such as funerals, weddings, graduations, job interviews, award ceremonies, and high school formals.

Contrary to popular belief, tends to be behind current trends.

Common Elements of Womens Wear:

- Open necklines and exposed collarbones.
- Short sleeves or sleeveless.
- Cinched, defined waist (this is usually a bit of a higher waist than trendy fashion at the time).
- Impractical for physical activity in some way.
- Focus on a stunning display rather than uniformity.
- Examples: Bias-cut gowns, cocktail dresses, little black dresses, pumps, stilettos, and bolero jackets.

Common Elements of Menswear:

- Wide shoulders.
- Narrow hips.
- Muted palette, possibly with a small understated pop of texture.
- Focus on uniformity rather than stunning display.
- Examples: Tuxedos, two- and three-piece suits, Oxford brogues, cummerbunds, neckties, and bow ties.

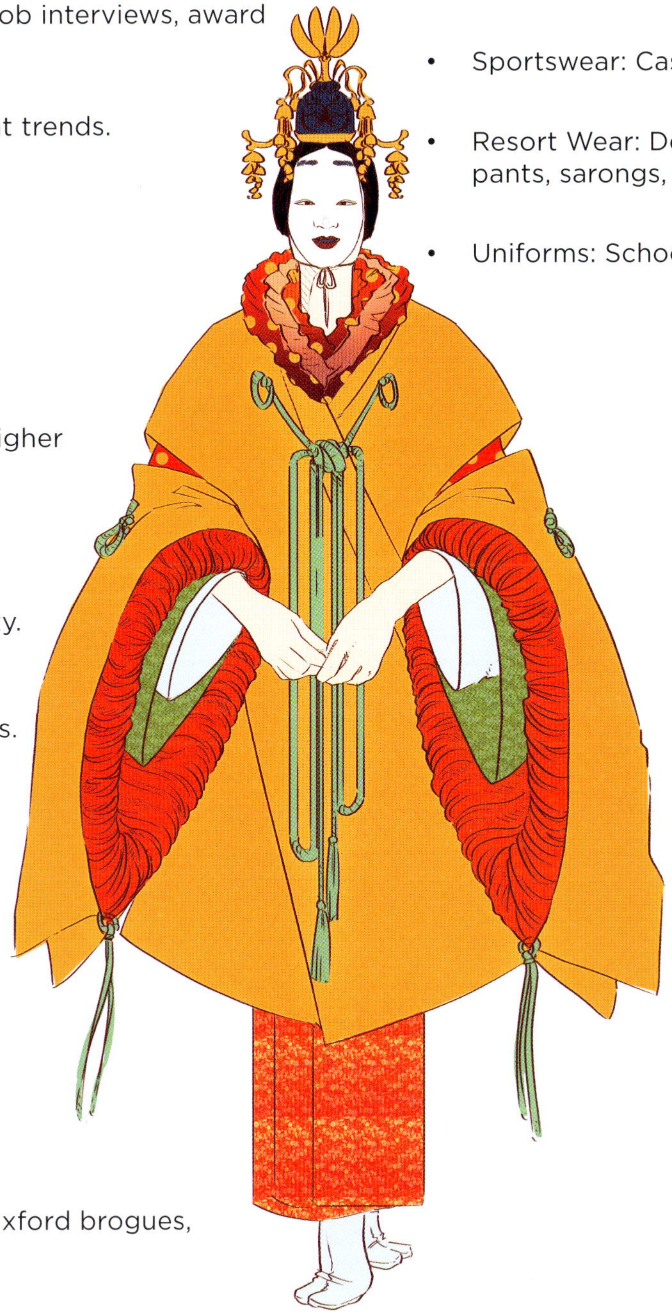

OTHER MODES OF DRESS

- Athletic Wear: Yoga pants, swimsuits, basketball shorts, etc.
- Sportswear: Casual separates with a functional beauty.
- Resort Wear: Designed for seasonal leisure travel; sun hats, palazzo pants, sarongs, kimono robes, sun dresses, linen suit, chinos.
- Uniforms: School, military, police, waitstaff, sports teams, etc.

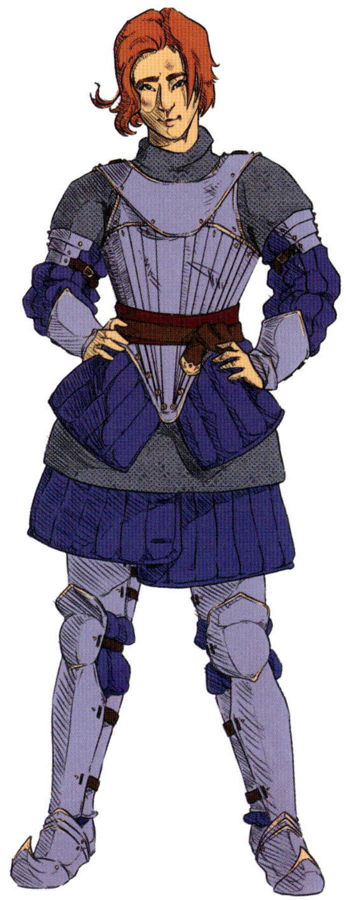

LOUNGEWEAR

At home she can dress more comfortably. This is a pajama set that consists of two layers: a blouse with roomy shalwar underneath, and an open banyan.

All closures for this outfit are in the front, ensuring she can dress herself without the helping hand of a servant.

Shirt made of a breezy and light fabric.

Undergarments are minimal, allowing full range of motion and a natural bust. She wears this for comfort rather than public display.

Puffy pants. Usually made of cotton or linen.

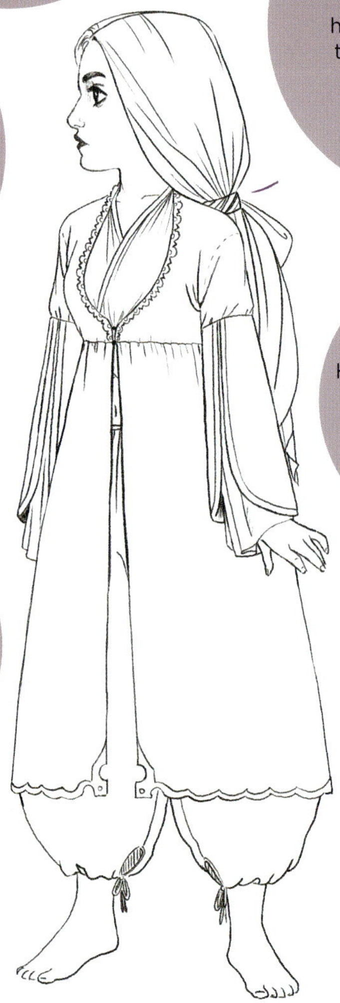

A simple ribbon holds her hair away from her face to allow her to perform leisurely domestic tasks.

Her hair is held loosely with a ribbon and she walks around the house barefoot.

CASUAL OR DAY WEAR

When going outside, she wears more layers for modesty, to exhibit status, and to suit the weather.

White shirt made of light fabric underneath the dress. Because bathing is considered important in the nobility, wearing white is a symbol of good hygiene.

The main undergarment is a simple shift that helps support the bust and protects the more expensive outer garments from body oils and sweat.

The stripes in her outfit represent the family she's from. To show off their level of prosperity, her belts are made of metals such as gold and silver.

Sirwal is a kind of puffy trousers practical for walking a lot in the heat due to air circulation and wicking sweat from the inner legs.

This hat is called Kalpak. The ribbon that holds it covers her ears on both sides.

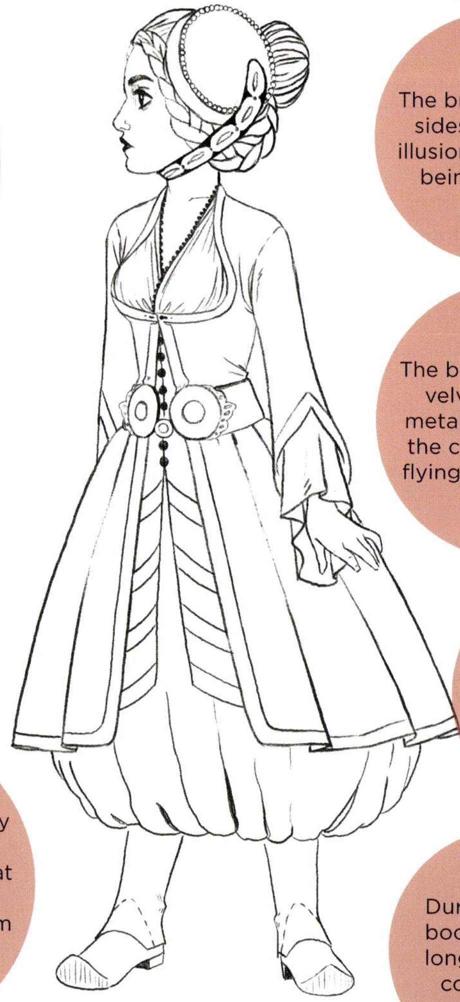

Her hair is in a bun to keep the back of her neck cool, and a small hat helps protect her head from the direct sun.

The braids on both sides create the illusion of the head being covered.

The belt is made with velvet fabric and metals. It helps keep the cote's skirt from flying up in the wind.

Long coat made of silk taffeta.

Durable leather boots made for long walks with cover on the front.

FORMALWEAR

For special events, the most expensive and complex garments are chosen to show status. In some cultures, like Japan, people do this through wearing many layers. This Greek- and Turkish-inspired noblewoman wears three layers and is adorned with pearls and a gold belt.

Pearls adorn the ensemble to showcase a famous, local fashion delicacy. Not only are pearls in style, but also by wearing them, this noblewoman is a walking billboard for local tradesmen, or perhaps even her own family's interests in the trade.

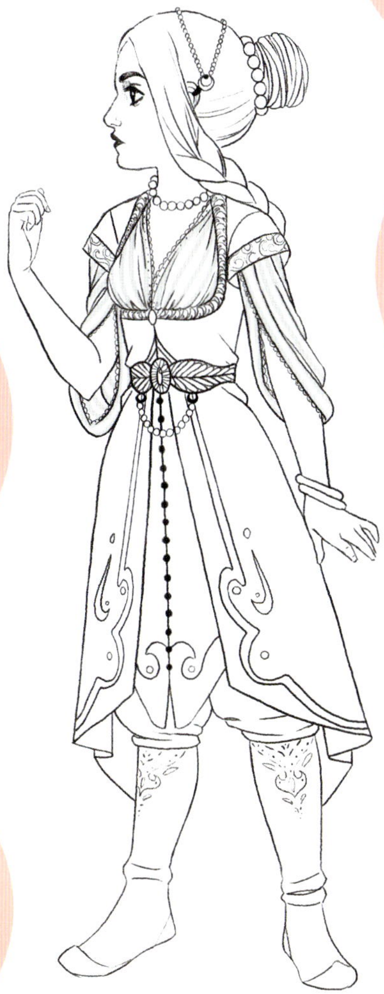

This hairstyle would need the assistance of a handmaiden, reflecting her noble status. She may use hairstyles to influence fashion trends, and thereby gain power in elite political circles.

Vibrant, reflective textiles are used to catch people's attention, such as taffeta, velvet, or silk detailed with metal sequins, bullion thread, small mirror fragments, glass beads, or precious stones.

Hand embroidery is a symbol of the time, dedication, and cost of skilled artisans. The more tedious the details, the more expensive the ensemble.

Leather boots with gold embroidery are worn. Note that they are soft-soled, which means she may even dance through them by the morning.

TAILORED EXAMPLE

A Noblewoman's Wardrobe

Maria Ferreira Kercher

DID YOU KNOW?

Like hand gestures, clothing is a form of communication. Being aware of your audience's vocabulary is important! In South Korea, for example, buying your boyfriend or girlfriend a pair of shoes means you want them to leave. In China, wearing a green hat means your lover is cheating.

OTHER MODES OF DRESS

Utilitarian Design

Tips from designer and illustrator Tom Parrish

For more extreme contexts or climates, you may even be forced to bridge the familiar world of costume with industrial design. With anything that's mechanical—whether it's a vehicle, a weapon, a ship, or armor—you need to consider three factors:

User: Who is wearing it.

Is it an adult human, alien, child, or sentient animal? The user needs don't just entail the "shape" or anatomy of a living creature; the mech also needs to address their state, for example, a cosmonaut in the first trimester of pregnancy or a paralyzed child. These states of being aren't necessarily visible, but the mech needs to accommodate nonetheless.

Purpose: What it's being used for.

Does the user need to carry 1,000 pounds of gear, or do they need to be able to move quickly through a jungle? What is the purpose? Does it need to be armed? Does it need giant claws to pick stuff up? Does it need to have pockets to put moon rock samples in?

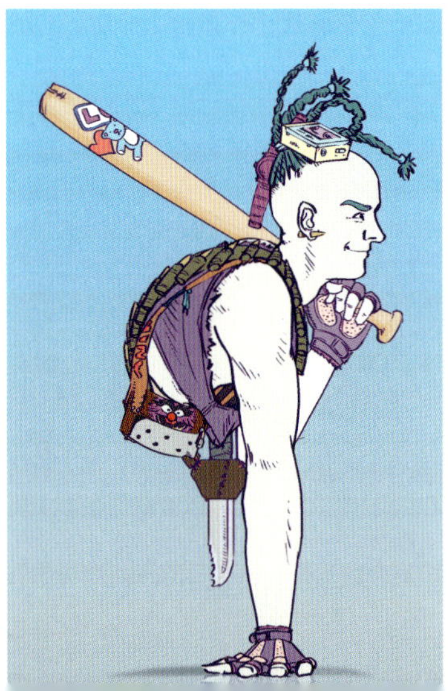

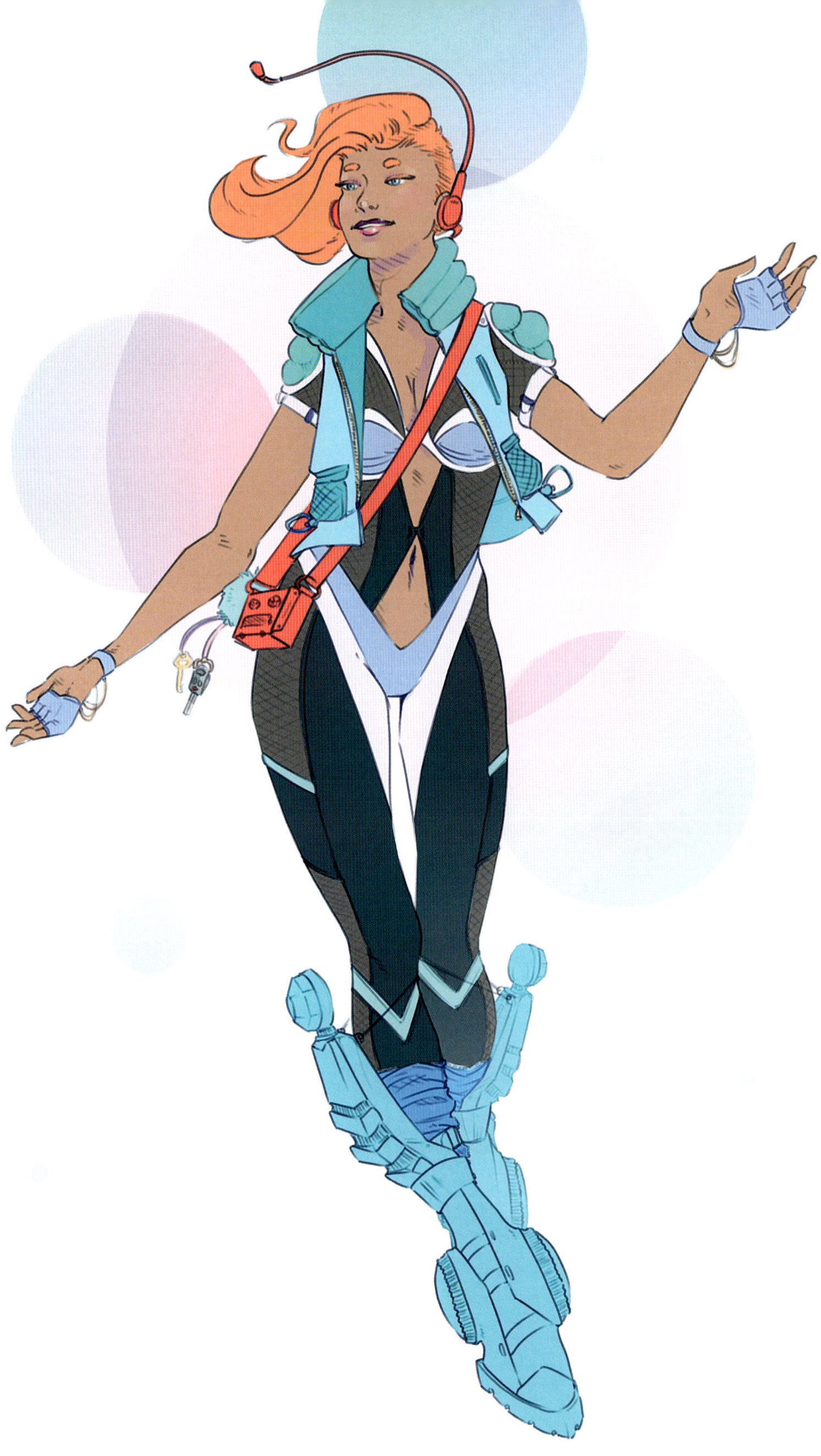

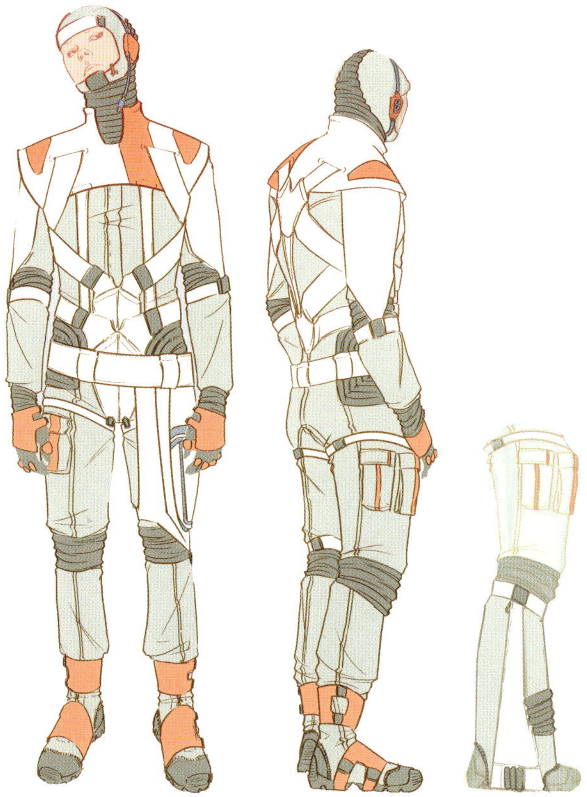

Location: Where is it being used.

Is it for use in the atmosphere, space, in an environment where there's high gravity, or where there are poison gases? Does it shield you from the environment or make you compatible with the environment? For example, an atmospheric diving suit (ADS) vs. a wetsuit and scuba gear.

Once you've determined those constraints, you can start to develop within that. Generally, with industrial design, form is important, but function is king. You need to make sure whatever you're designing is believable, that you can look at it and read what it's supposed to be. We have preconceived ideas of what a helmet or an articulated joint looks like based on what we see around us; you can use these as design cues to inform your audience and assist them in deciphering your design and helping it read quickly.

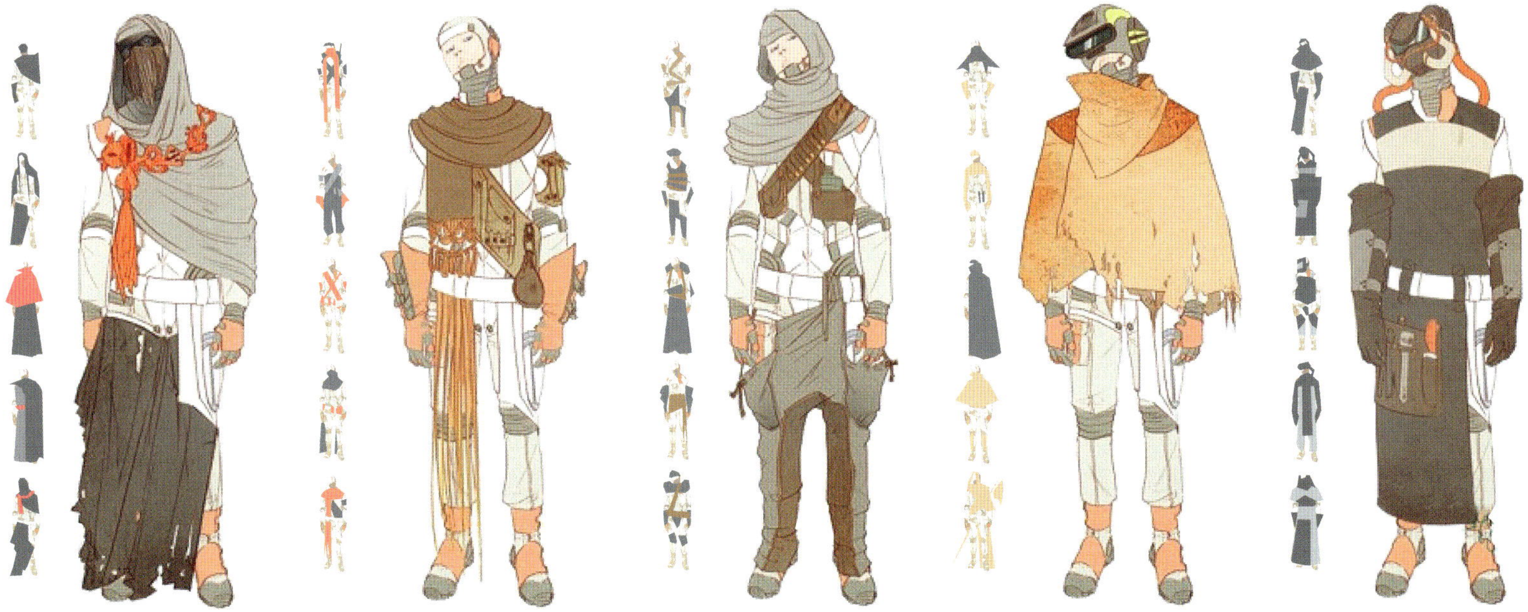

Fremen Stowaway *Medic* *Gunner* *Worm Watcher* *Engineer*

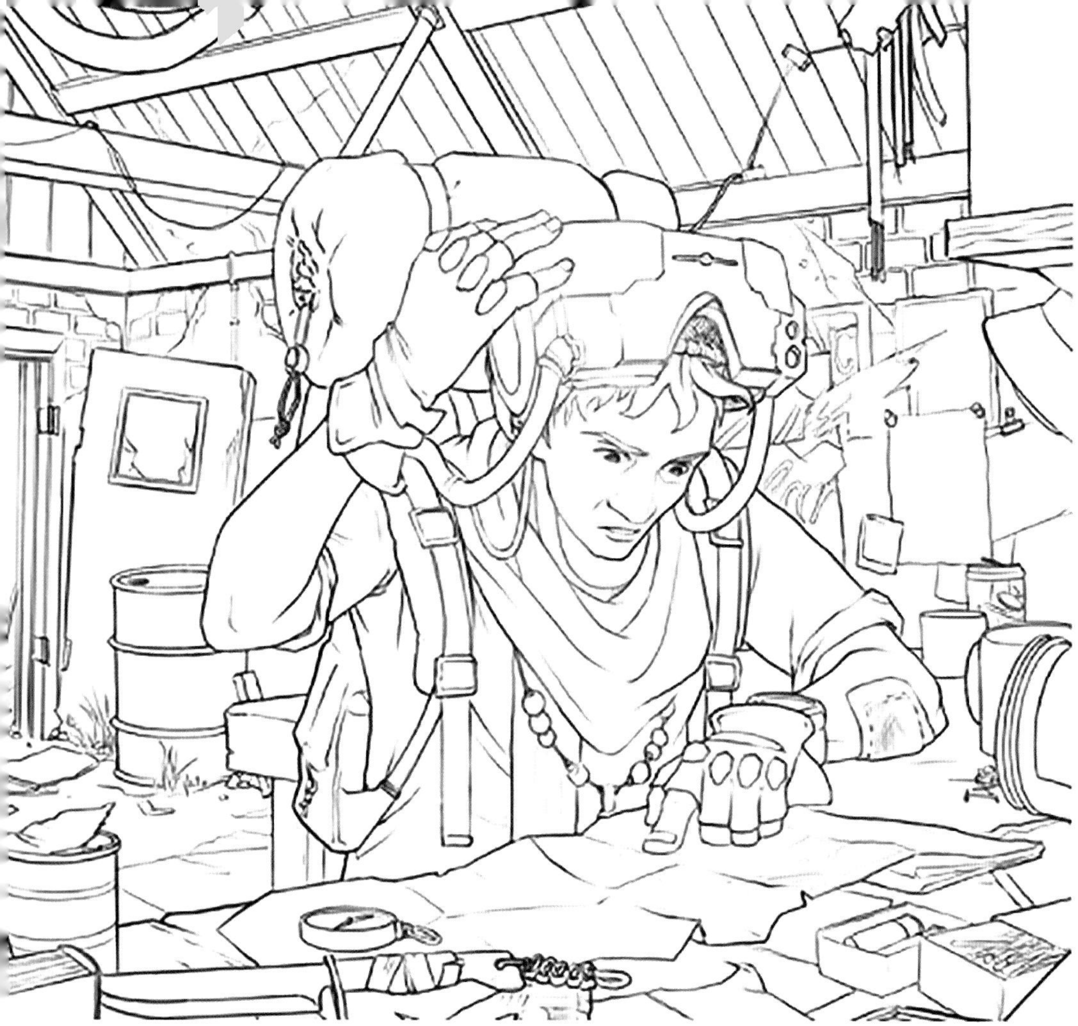

What is the mech made of?

Make sure you've incorporated where each functional part is going to go. And you're not just designing the outer shell, you're putting thought into the inner mechanics. Even if you are making this up completely and the functions are humorous, incorporate each element with equal consideration. Consider these questions:

- Where are the moving parts?
- Does it have an exhaust port?
- Where is the power source?
- What is the power source?

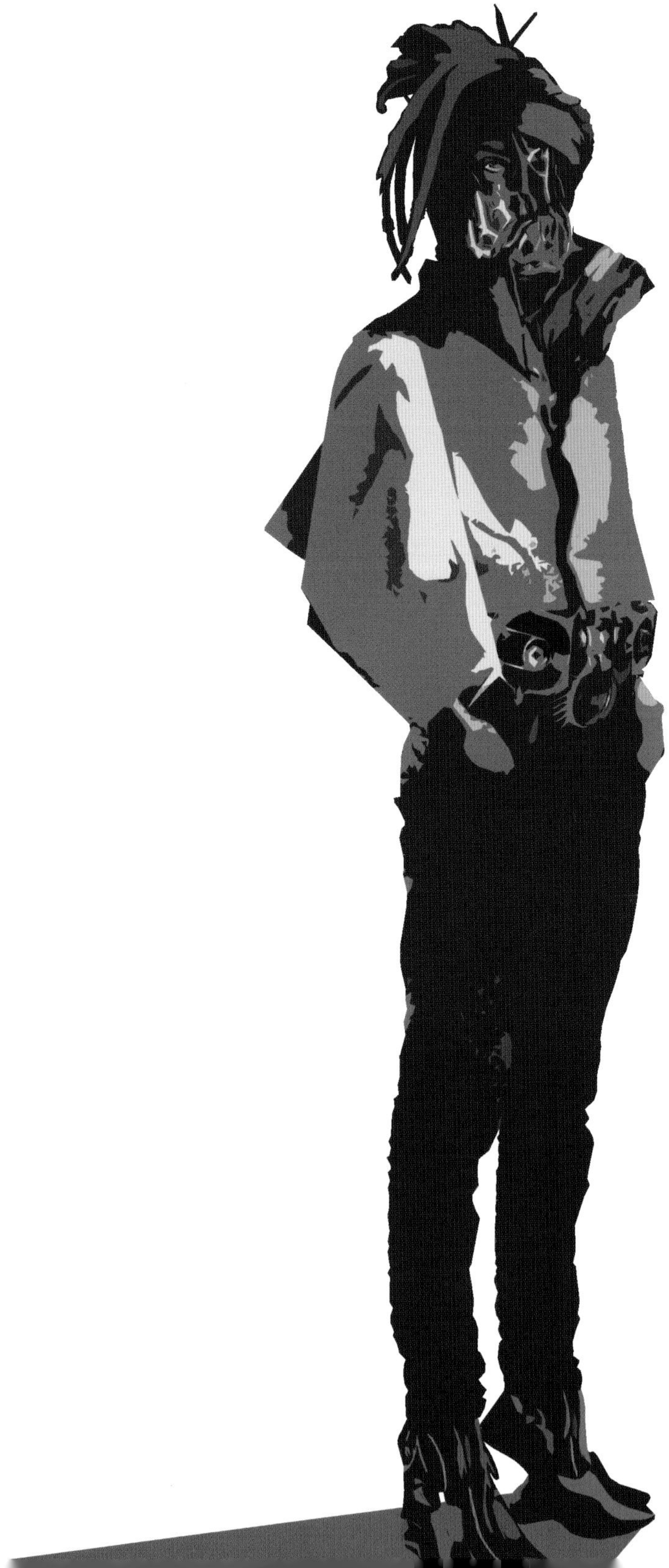

What makes the mech work?

Once I've figured out the function of the mech, what it needs to do, I then think about how it's going to do it. The power source needs to be proportionate to the work that the device is going to have to do, so if you're designing a giant robot, there's a big difference between the amount of energy and the size of the motor that would be required to drive a 50-foot robot compared to a six-foot one.

Visual cues like these will help you denote scale, size, power, and impressiveness. If it has loads of tiny pistons and motors, and it's complex, you're telling your audience that this thing is massive. Whereas if you have single, sleek pistons that are in scale with the rest of the robot, it helps you realize it may just be about five feet.

The resulting aesthetic comes down to the world that you're working in too. For example, if you were doing a steampunk or diesel punk design, look at industrial machinery that's less sleek and sophisticated, and you might notice historical reference featuring the machinery on the outside. Think exposed cogs and pipes, pistons, and valves—form over function and efficiency.

If your design calls for something more sci-fi and sleek, that look would be the result of a refined production process in that world. You'd have cool panels covering the inner workings and everything would be more miniaturized, perfectly designed to fit well together. When you see slick designs with smooth armor panels, grills and vents, your audience can associate that with real world high-end sports cars or gadgets.

I usually make notes, write a half-dozen keywords, and refine my design on paper before I even start drawing. That way, when I start thumbnailing and exploring shapes, I already have an idea of the functions that need to be filled. Then when I start to draw random shapes, I'm looking at them and thinking what those shapes could be. Because I know the functions I need to include, it's easier for "happy accidents" to appear through the chaos.

Consider this related question:

- How do the motors actually work?

On using reference:

It's really easy to switch the brain off and copy reference, but I encourage you to draw inspiration from reference and understand why it looks a particular way (an astronaut suit, for instance). By understanding the why, you'll be able to create something more unique to your prompt and continue to build your mental library of mechanical functions that you can use in the future.

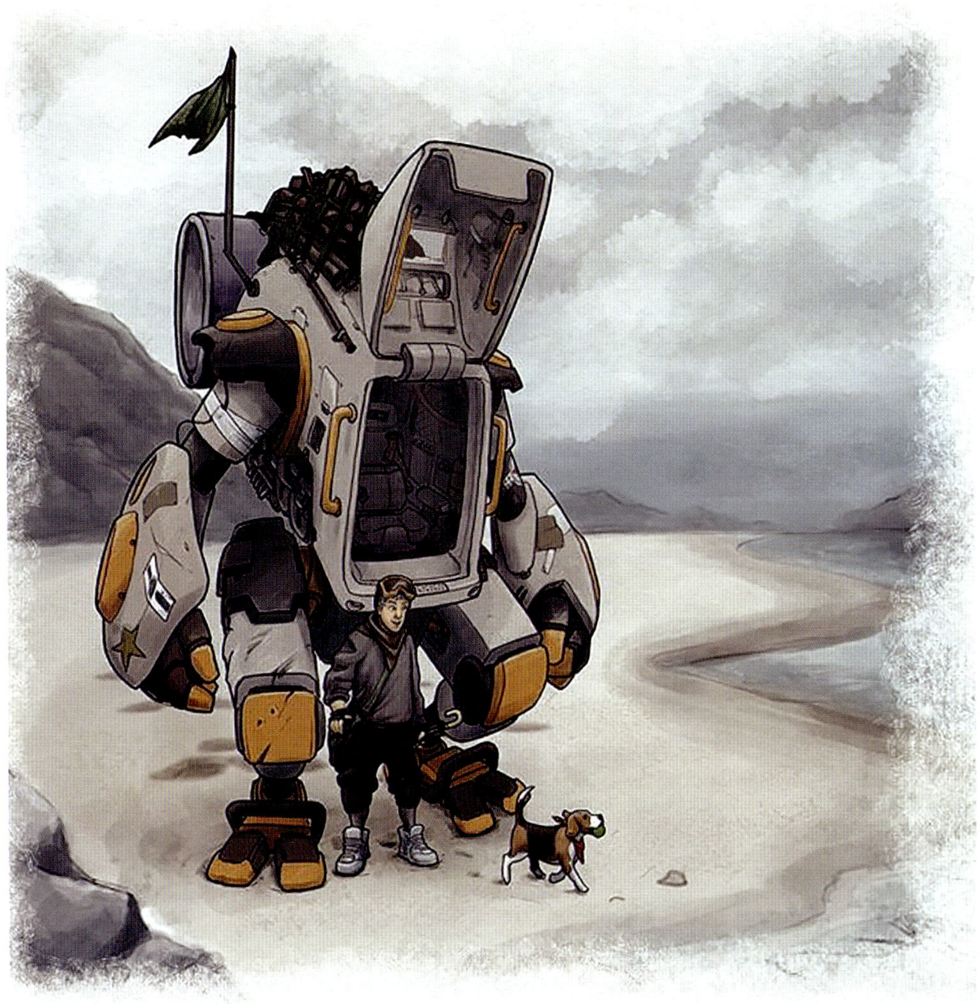

A Story in Three Acts: The Spanish Dancer

Maria Ferreira Kercher

Logline (loosely based on the "12 Dancing Princesses" by the Brothers Grimm):

A princess with a passion for dance faces her impending coronation. Afraid that she will never be able to see the world and will forever be limited to the restrictive dance styles of nobility, she disguises herself and sneaks out of her castle to explore new worlds of dance.

First Act: It's the morning of the annual village festival and the princess has built up her courage to sneak out of the castle, so she can attend. She disguises herself as a commoner and dances with the women of the village.

Second Act: The princess then hears of a ball that is happening in a nearby castle, outside of her family's land. Despite her family's disapproval to attend, she sneaks out again, and dances by herself through the night. When a mysterious man approaches her, she joins him for a dance and receives a flower from him that she adds to her dress.

STEP 1: RESEARCH

To develop my mood board, I researched traditional costumes from each region in Spain. Despite being in the same country, each region had unique influences, and their designs varied as a result. I looked for folk clothing and photographs of cultural events to get high-quality images, as well as sketches of traditional dancing costumes from the 19th century.

Commemorative stamps showcasing the main outfits from each region of Spain and online catalogues from Spanish costume museums were great resources as well.

For the second act, I searched for recognizable motifs, with design elements created especially for dance. "Goyesco"-style dresses, for example, were developed for dance and influenced by the famous painter Goya's work, rather than stemming from traditional designs of a particular region.

STEP 2: SKETCH

I do around 10 variations exploring three major regions. I prefer to sketch in color because it allows me to capture the most basic visual information of the source image in one sketch. Keeping it small forces me to concentrate on the bigger dominant shapes of the design and only roughly indicate the smaller patterns at this point.

TIP:

Existing costume designs by other artists are based on their own narratives and aesthetic interpretations. They can help you identify new techniques, but if you don't want to water down your own interpretations, look directly to history and culture for the highest quality reference.

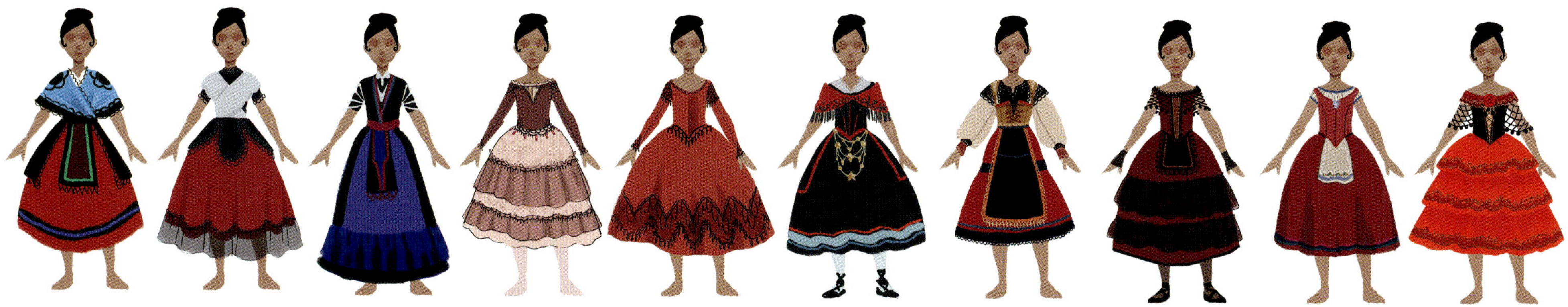

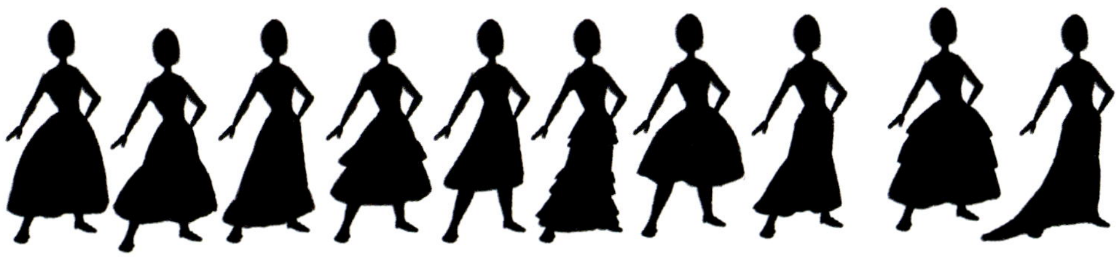

Third Act: On the day of the coronation, the princess is behaving normally throughout the dry ceremony. However, at the ball after the coronation, she surprises everyone by suddenly changing from her gown into her tutu. A dance of triumph, she dances freely in her own personal style now.

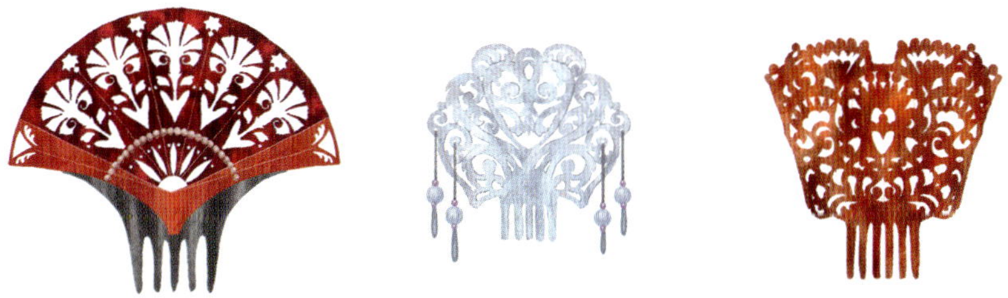

STEP 3: SILHOUETTES

Once I have enough concepts to pull from, I create silhouettes. These help me explore possible variations with my existing shapes before I spend a lot of time on variations of the interior details.

After I decide on skirt silhouettes for the three dresses, I choose my three favorite designs from the color concepts and mix the motifs I found in each region (ruffles, black, apron-like elements, bell shape, flamenco layered skirt, and Goyesco netting) to create iterations of the interior, details, and accessories. Using the tops from my color concepts visually balances the overall silhouettes.

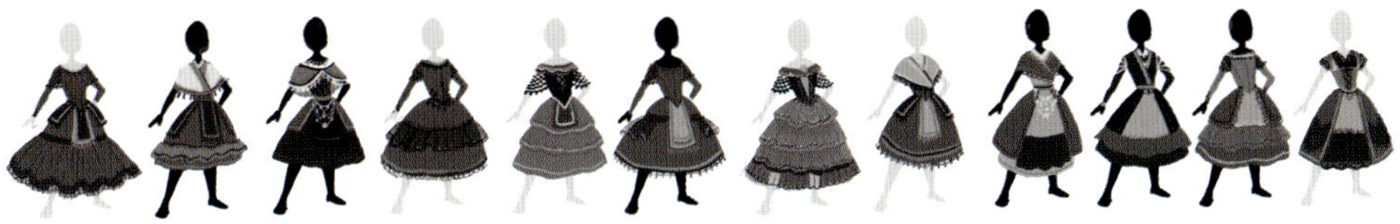

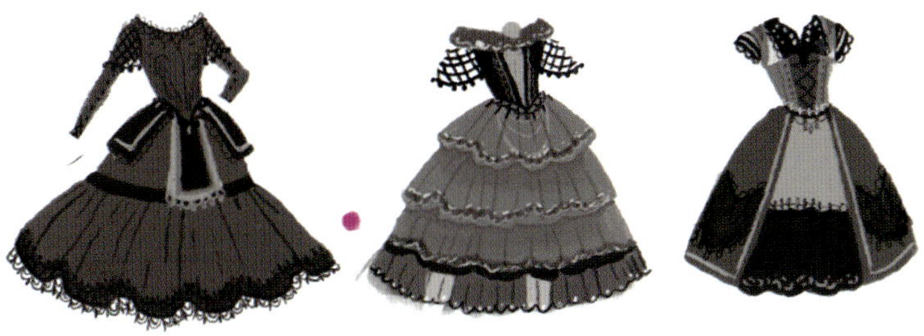

STEP 4: ACCESSORIES

Next, I explore hairstyles and adornments. Based on Spain's history of Moorish invasion, I choose combs with East Asian–inspired, Islamic, and floral motifs, using the national flower of Spain (the carnation) to tie them together. The first design, the fan shape, is made of wood and metal. The second design, with dangling pearls, is made of mother-of-pearl, and the third design is made of wood.

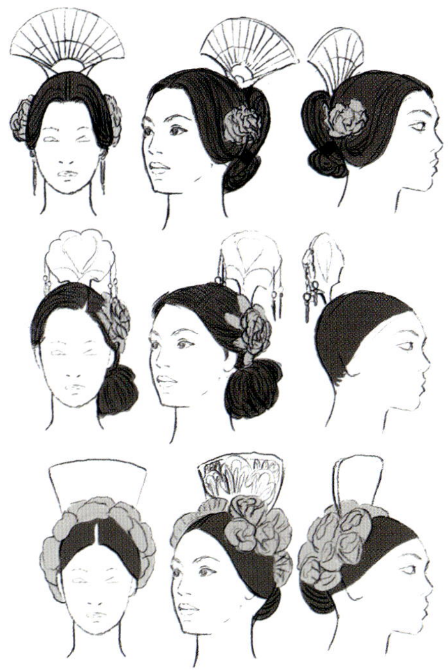

STEP 5: DETAILS

Act One Dress: The Village Festival

I keep the colors flat and the illustration simple, so I can test color options or change details without spending too much time on them. When the details are too small to be seen easily, pulling out elements and enlarging them on the side helps me explore and explain my concept to others.

Colors: For this dress, I thought the salmon color would be perfect. It's a warm, jovial, and energetic color, without being too adult. I kept the black details to show the Moorish influence. I also noticed a deep blue hue in my reference, so I used that to balance out the palette.

Pattern: the flowers are buds to represent that she hasn't "bloomed" into an adult yet.

Detail: The beads on the shoulder and waist are of Goyesco style. I almost added white pearls, but the overall color palette didn't seem right with white details. To bring more energy and color, I added emeralds to contrast with the salmon color and make it pop. The color of the overall design represents her transition into a young adult. It's bright, not too pink/childish, and has touches of more adult colors like black, dark red, dark blue, and green.

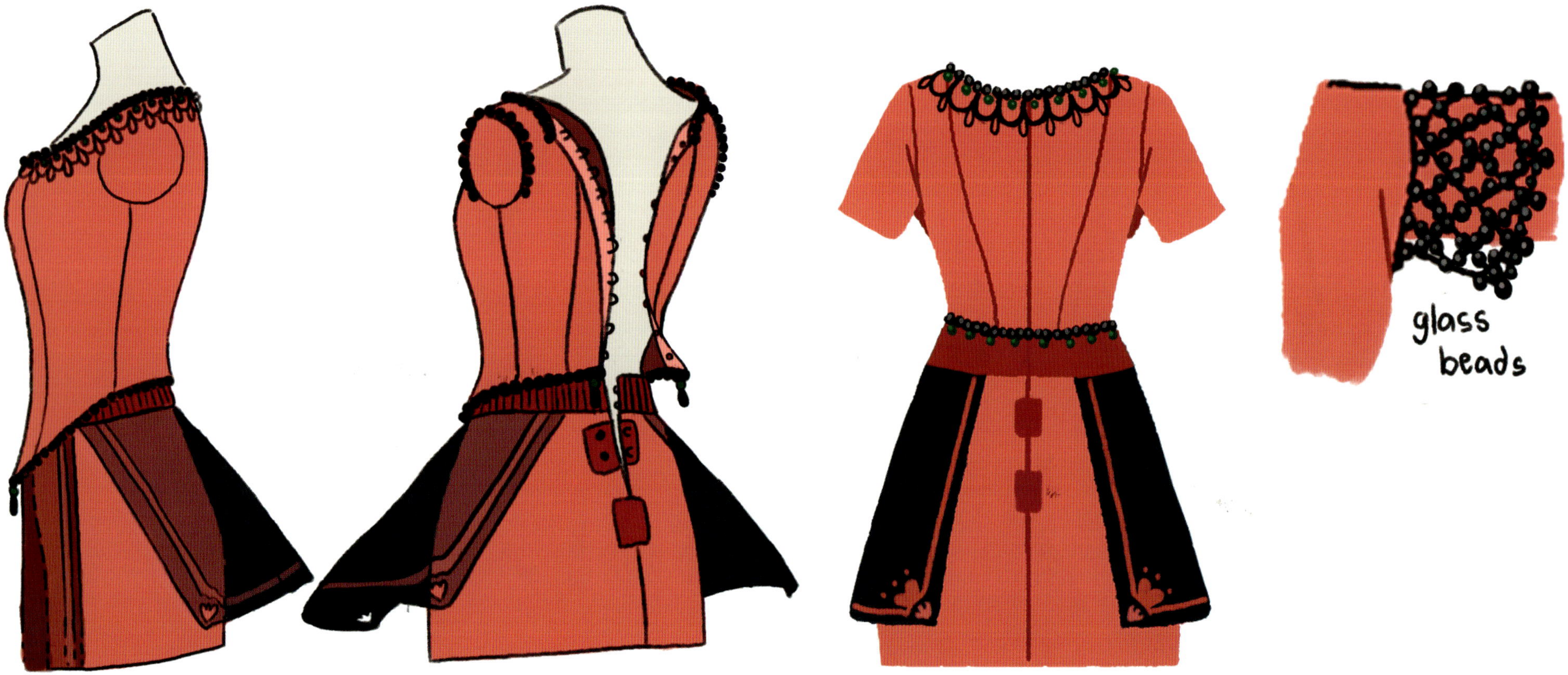

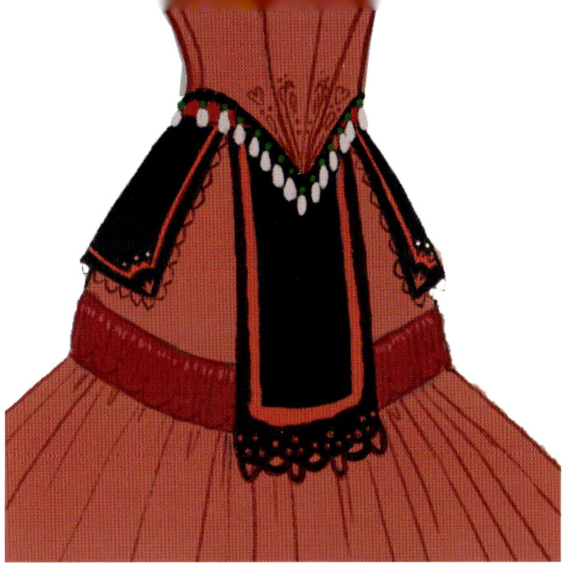

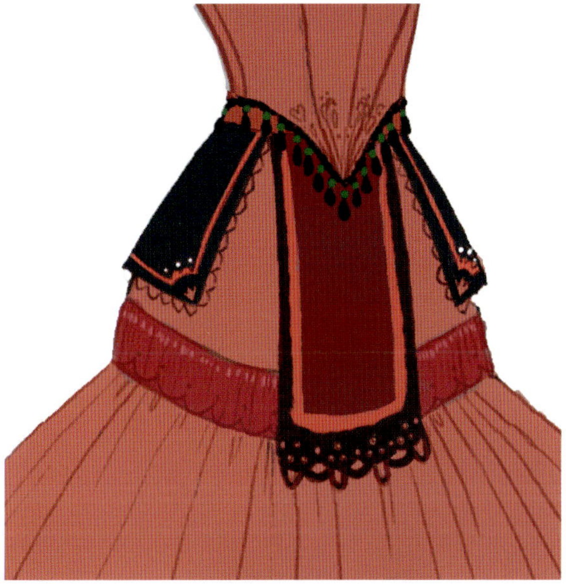

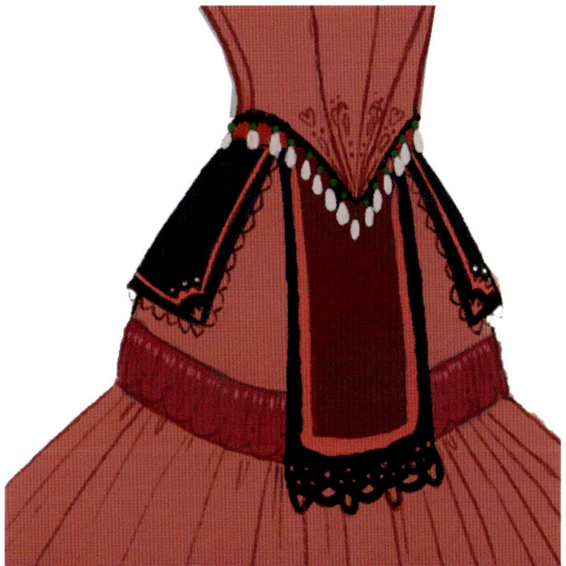

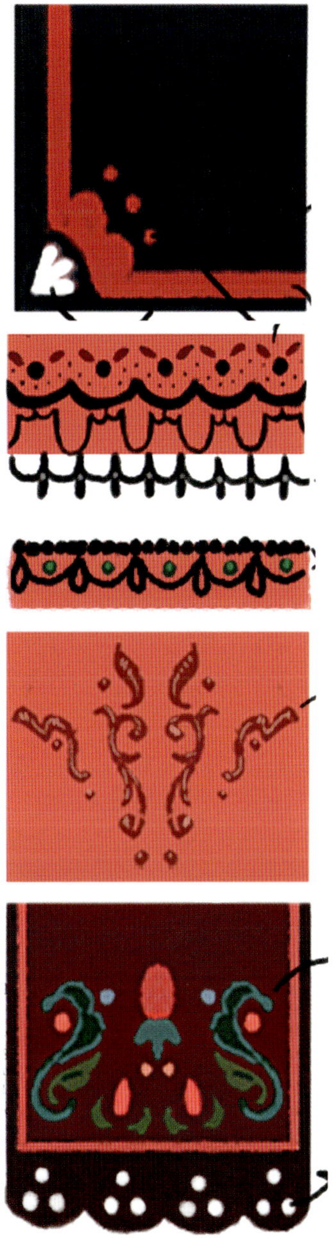

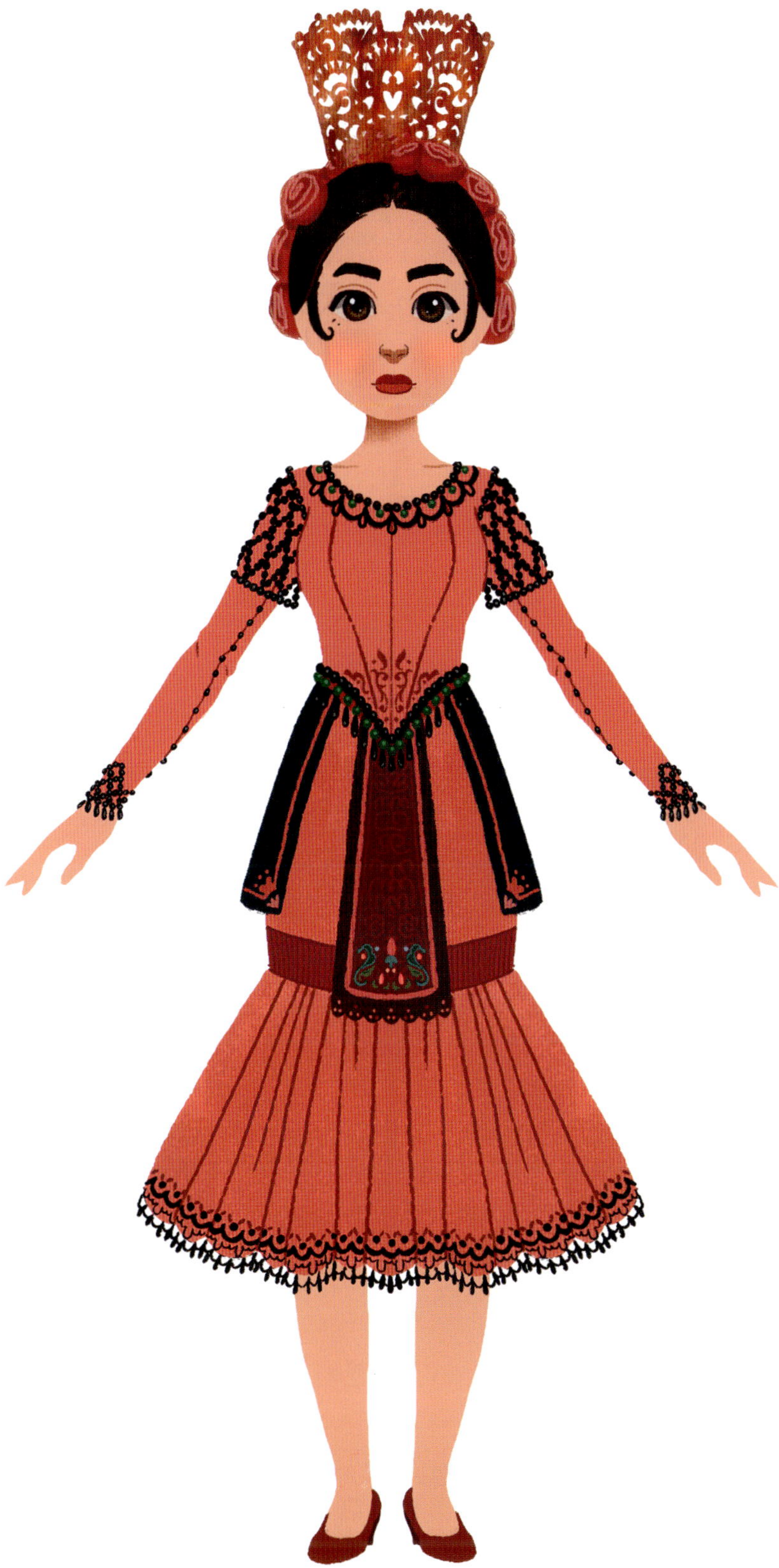

Act Two Dress: The Ball

Colors: To represent her growing independence and express her intention to be the center of the ball, I decided to go with bold and warm colors. The colors are the vibrant orange/red because it was the most youthful option. Her garment will be the most vibrant at the ball.

To pair with the vibrant skirt, I added a deep red top to give it a more sensual look, with the black Goyesco-style net under the shoulder increasing that effect. I used brighter colors like gold and yellow to bring attention to her movements and showcase her wealth.

Details: With lots of black details on her shoulder and top, I decided to use pearls at her waist to help transition the vibrant skirt and the darker top. Since this is a dancing scene, she wears ballet shoes.

Animation Considerations: The main function of this dress is for dancing/performance so elements naturally stray from the common folk designs to serve its functional purpose. Her skirt, having three ruffled layers, and the black Goyesco net coming from under the shoulder create a feeling of youth and sensuality, and were added to create opportunities for secondary animation to her actions, giving her more life as she dances. The skirt with three ruffled layers is also found in the Andalusia region of Spain.

Pattern: The flower pattern on her skirt is carnations.

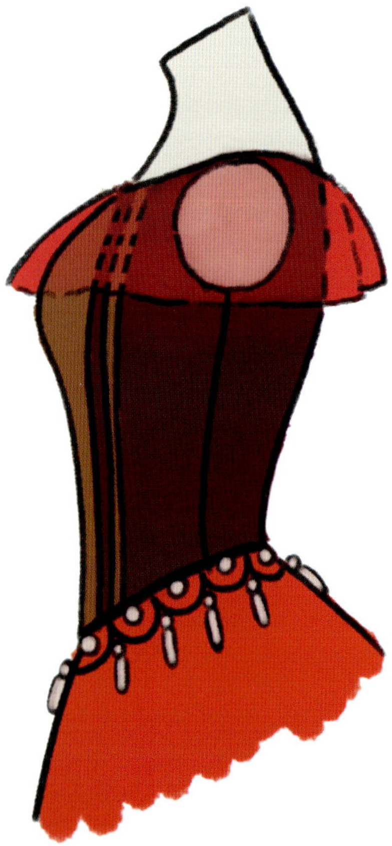

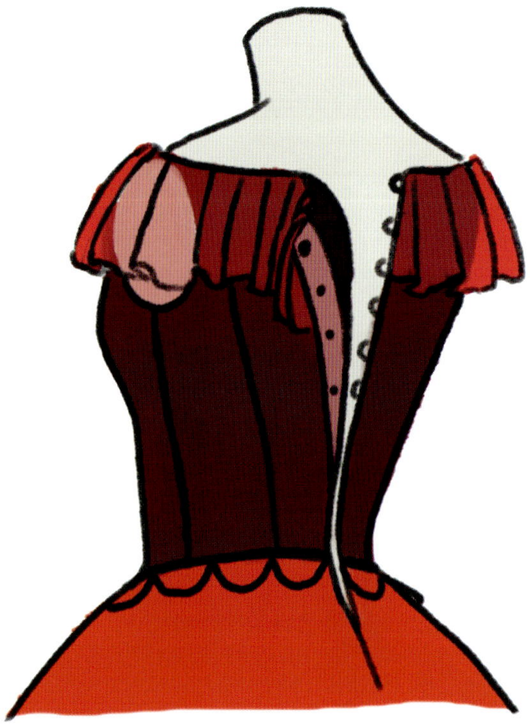

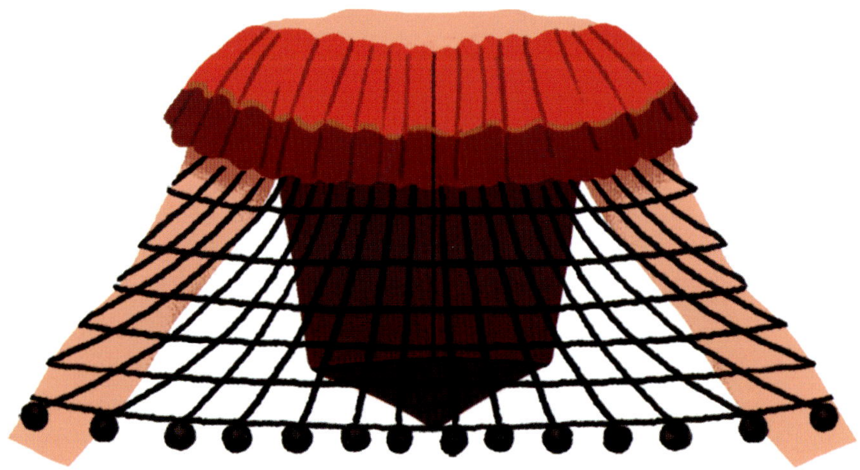

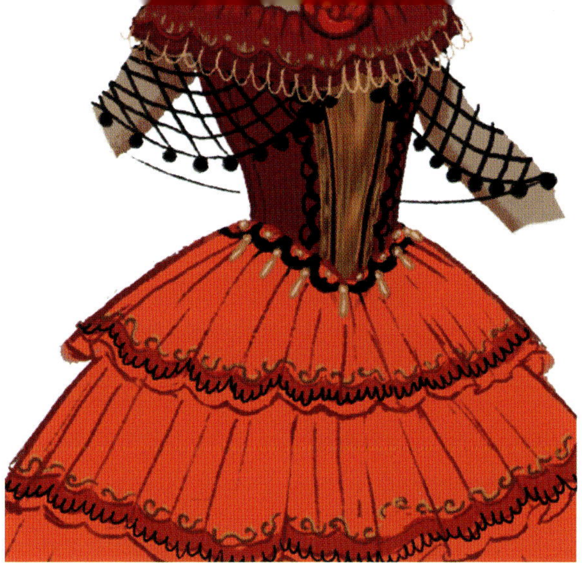

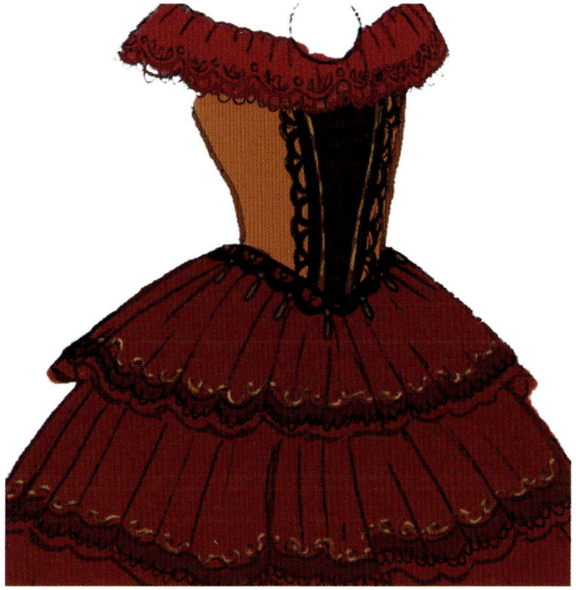

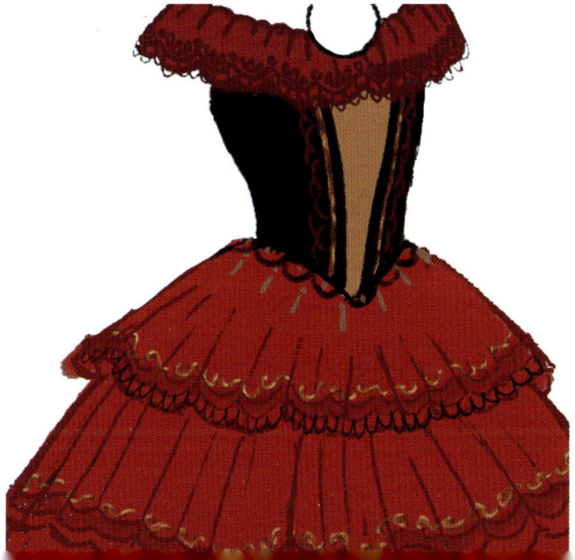

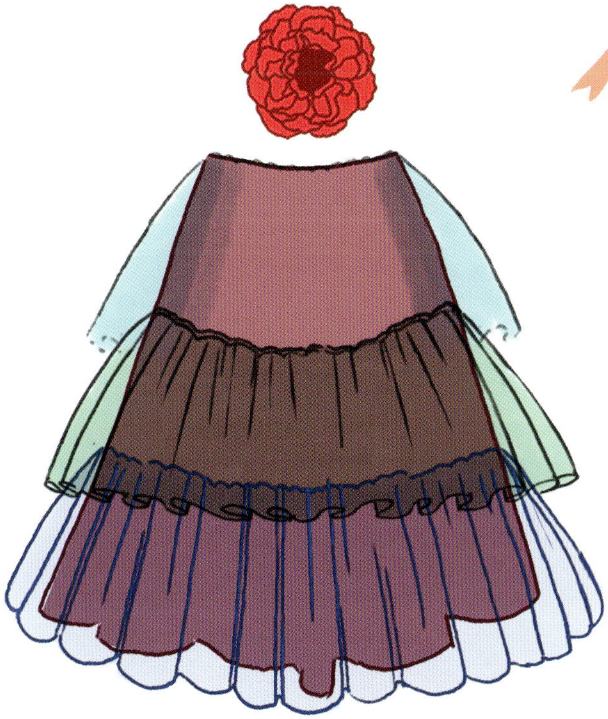

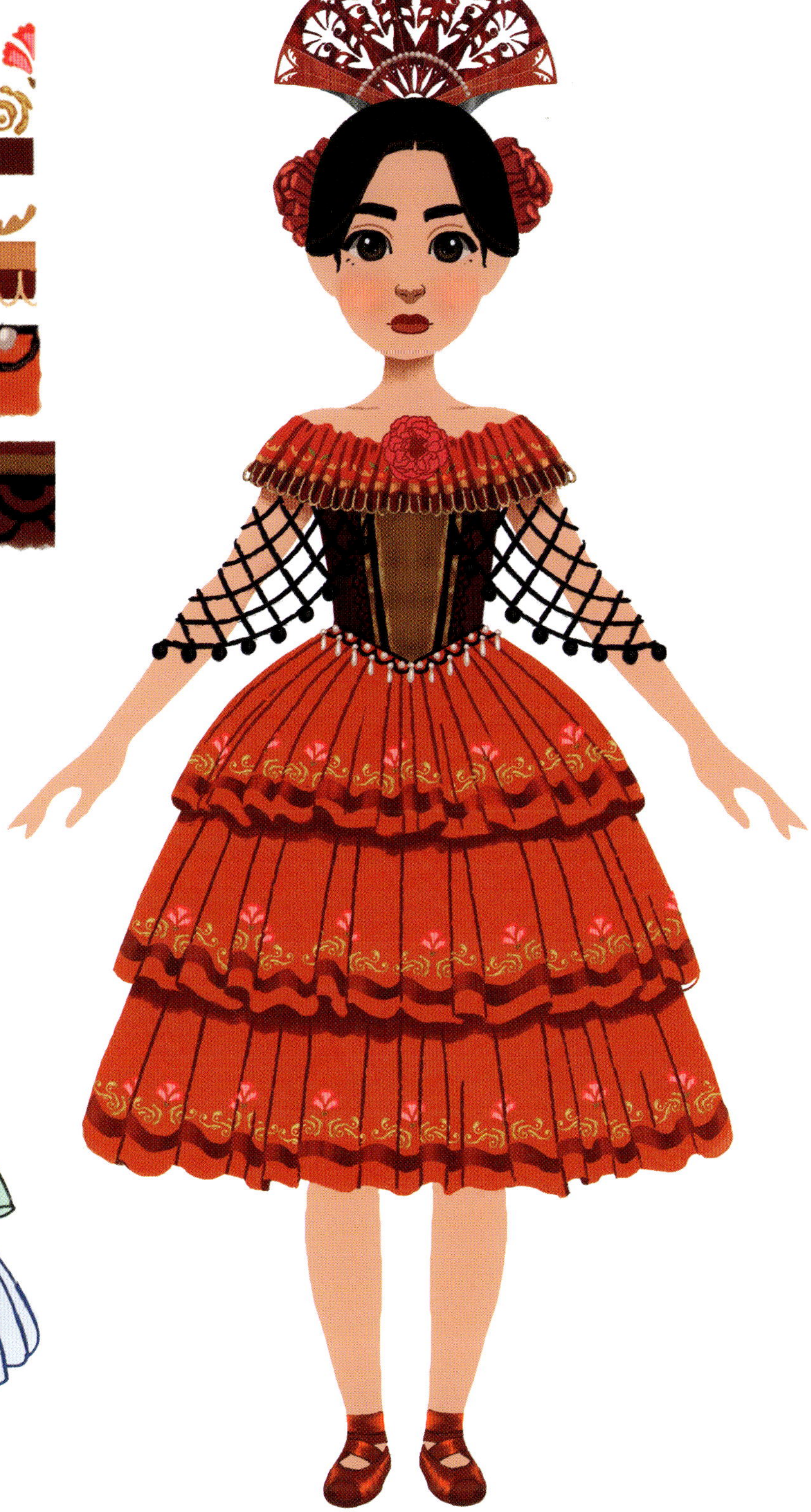

Act Three Dress: The Coronation

Colors: This is the most complex dress so far. As a queen, she needs to represent leadership and stability, so I added the denim blue and cream colors to the skirt and the top. The second layer of the skirt has a dark pink color to link to her youth and fiery personality. The bright details on the skirt represent the vibrant colors from different villages and folk costumes of Spain.

Details: The salmon color details on her top are the same youthful color as her first dress. The black details bring in the adult feel. The beige/golden corset ties the different colors together while bringing in the allusions to wealth. A pattern of gold leaves represent royalty.

The blouse I used here is from Toledo, Spain, and the level of detail felt perfect for the final dress. The beautiful and unique adornment on her waist is from Ibiza and Formentera, islands of Spain, and no queen is a queen without lots of gold jewelry.

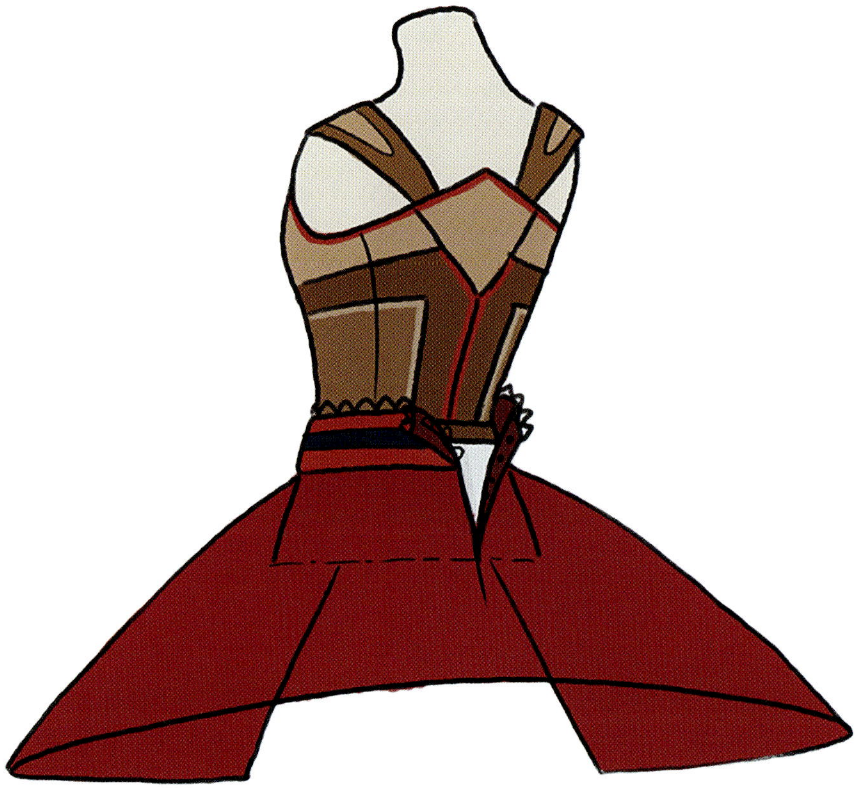

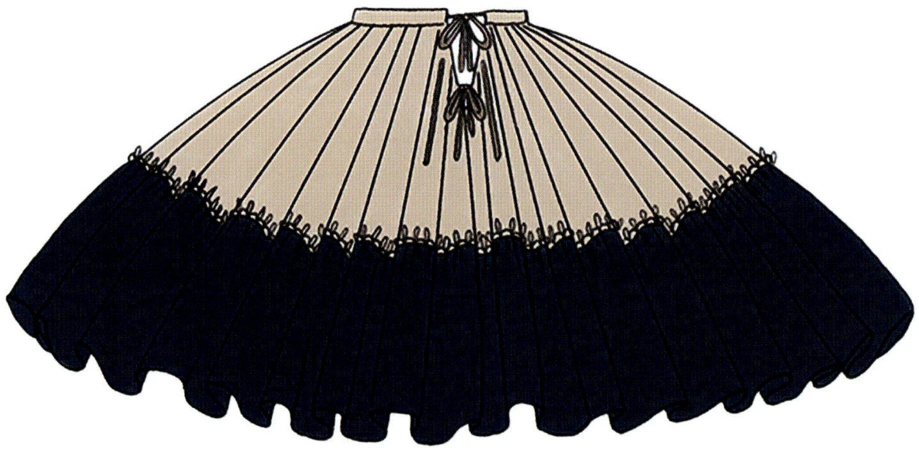

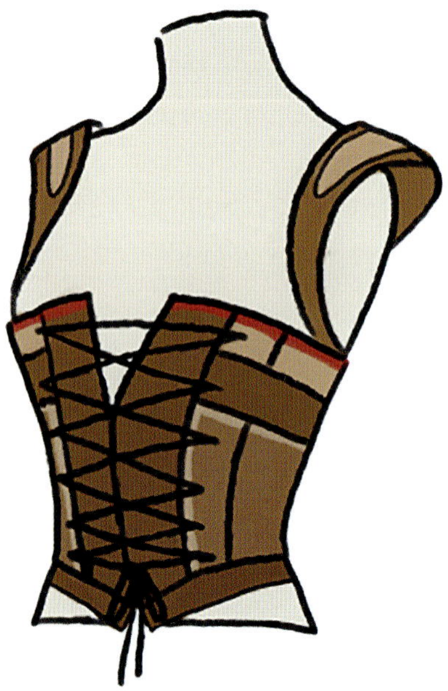

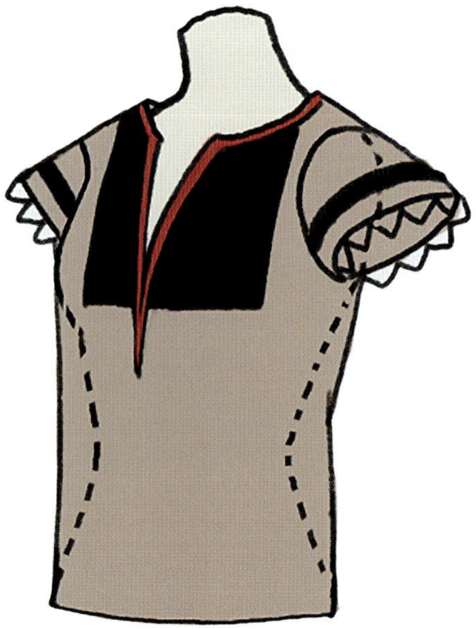

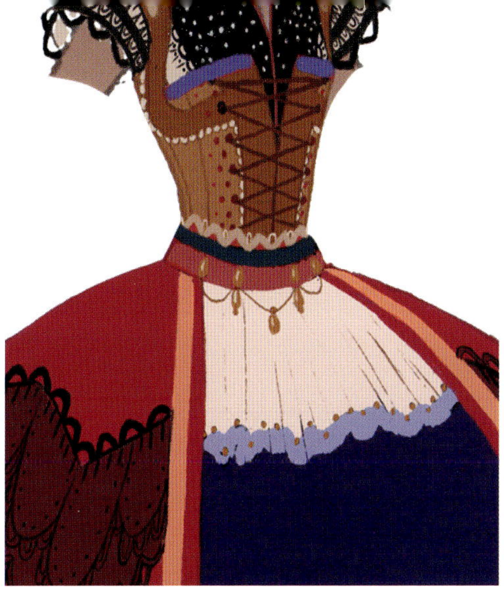

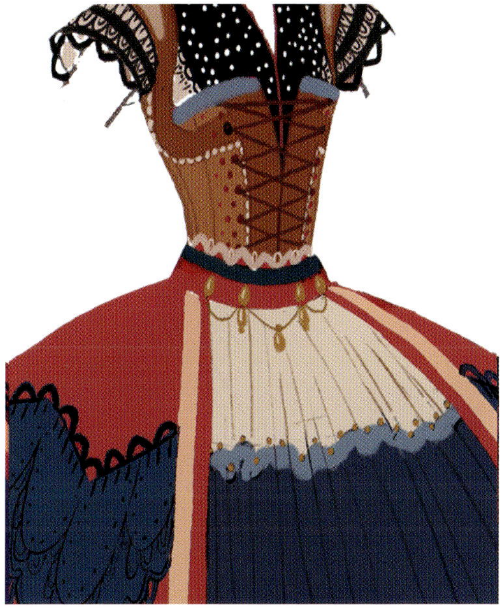

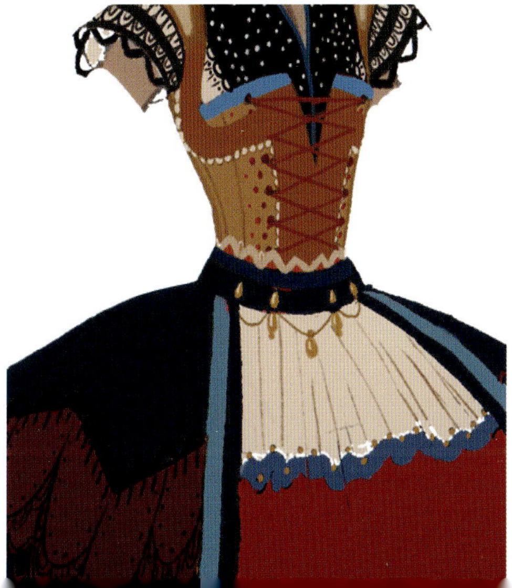

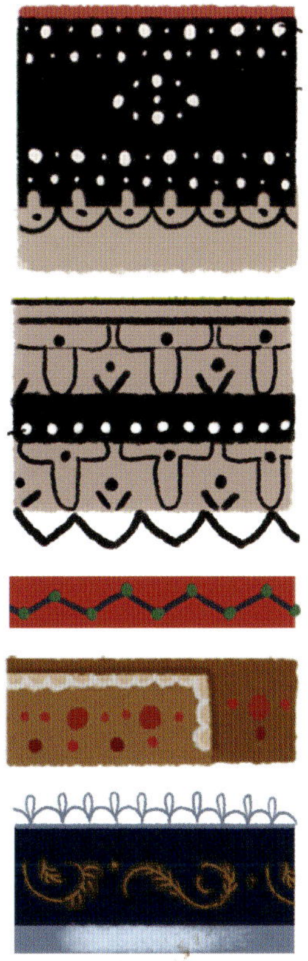

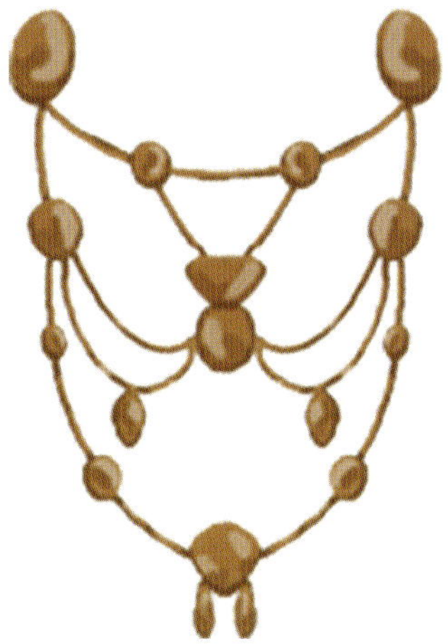

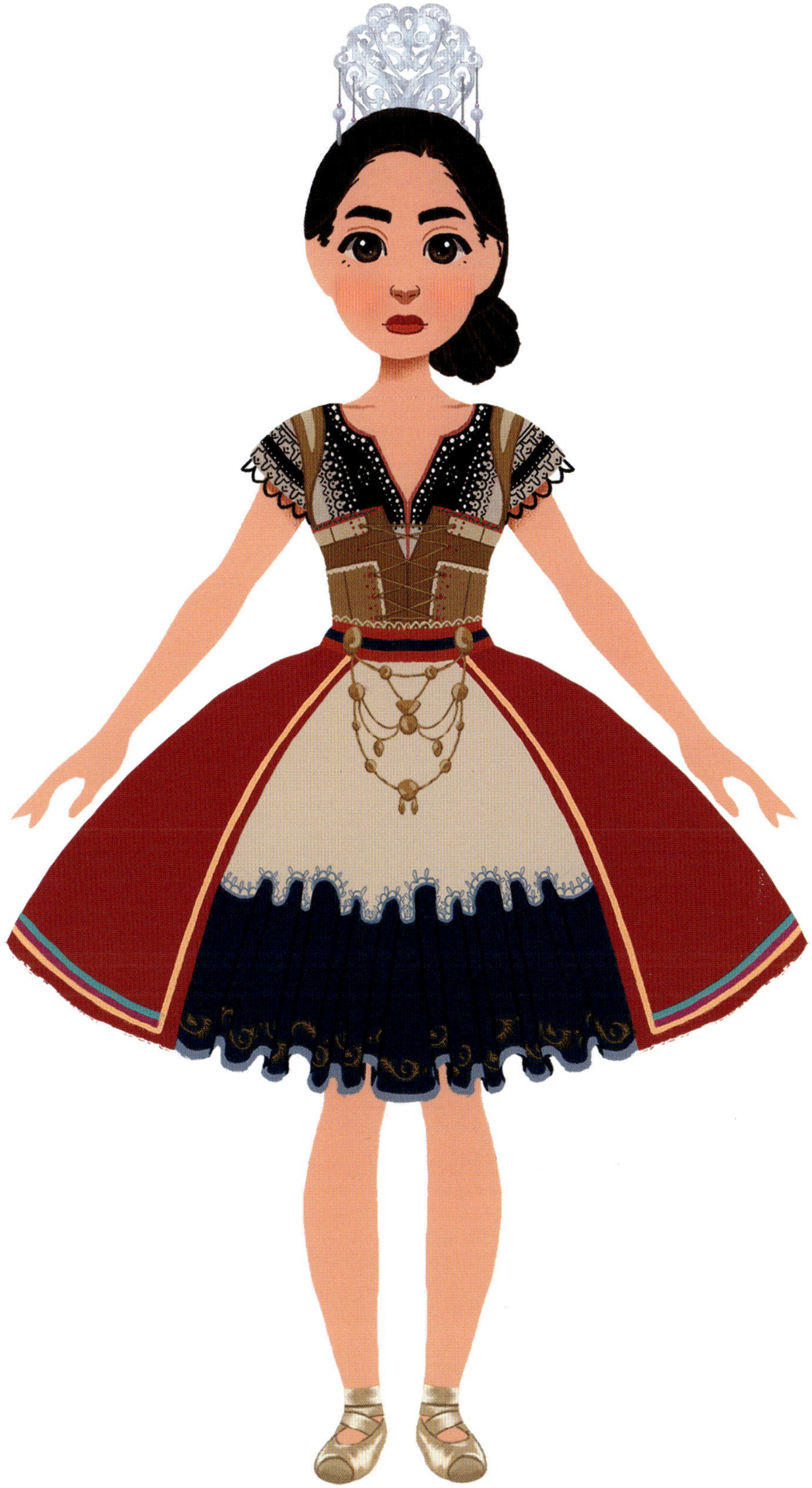

STEP 6: CONCEPT PRESENTATION

During the design process, I also study real ballerinas. This helps me understand the movements and weights of the fabrics and informs me to land on my final concepts and material choices.

As the designs will be finalized by 3D artists, I create concept paintings to communicate the dimension of the shapes and forms of my costumes. I use a simple pose to present the idea and have materials in mind from my research to hand on to a character painter if this direction is approved.

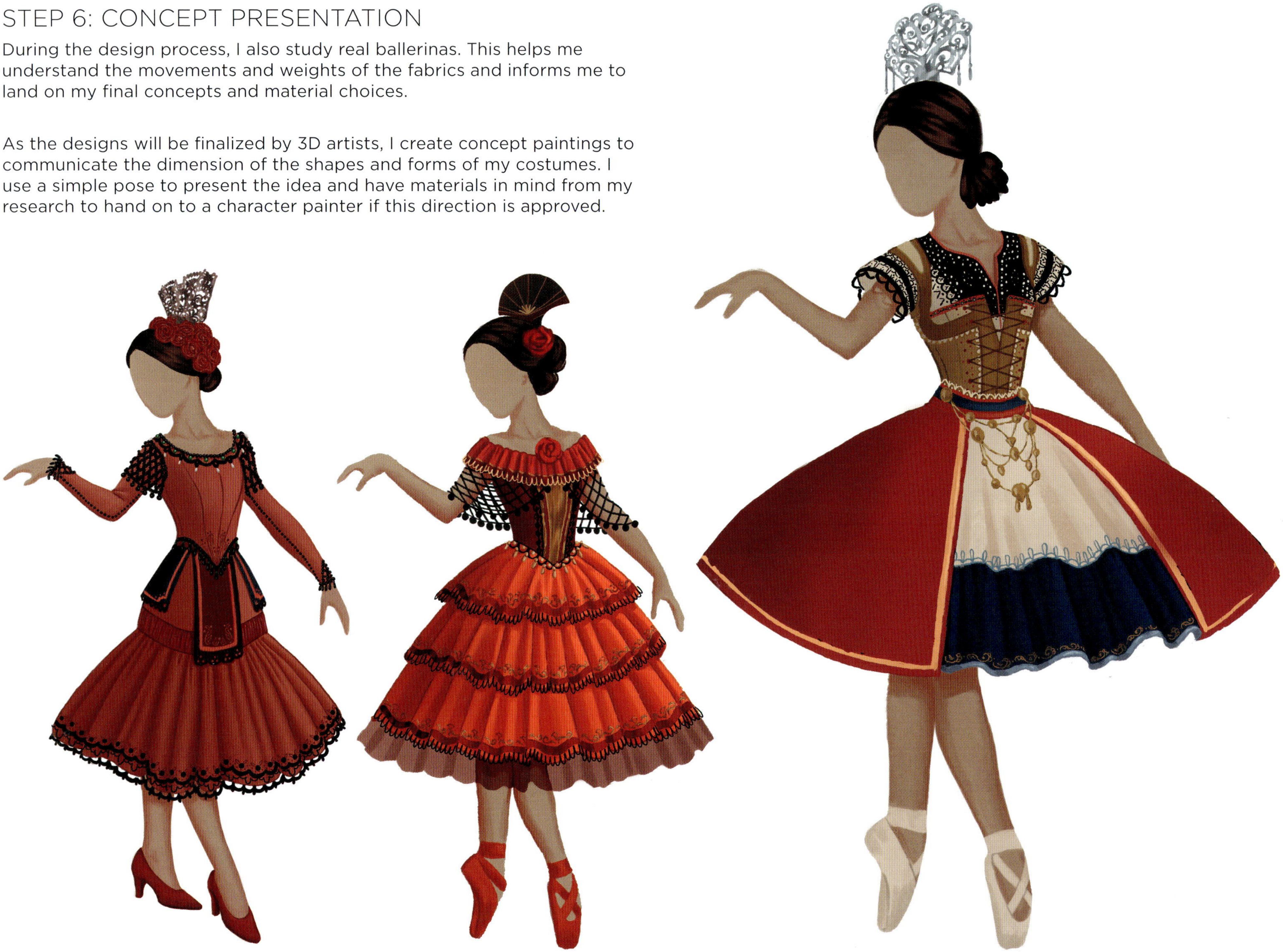

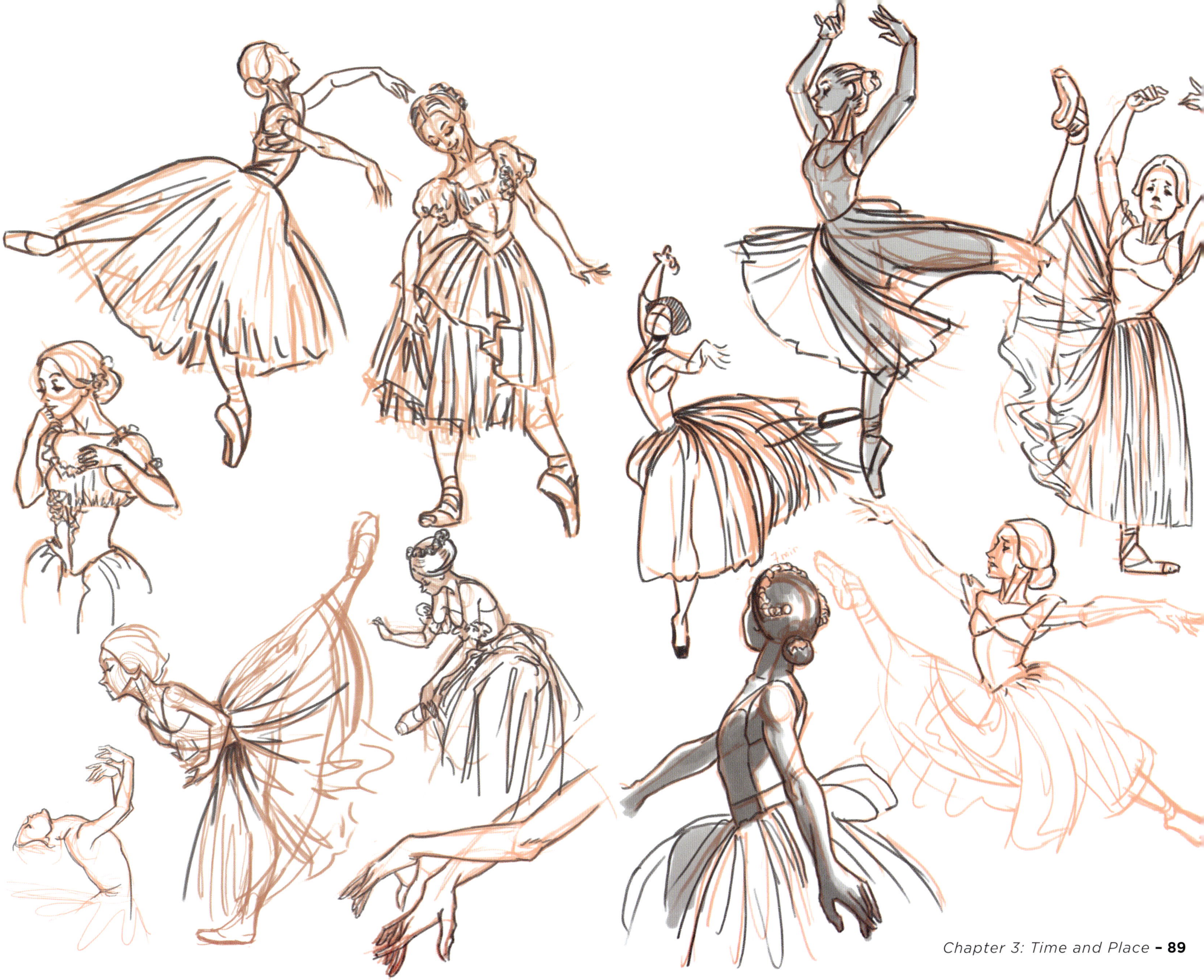

STORY WE WEAR

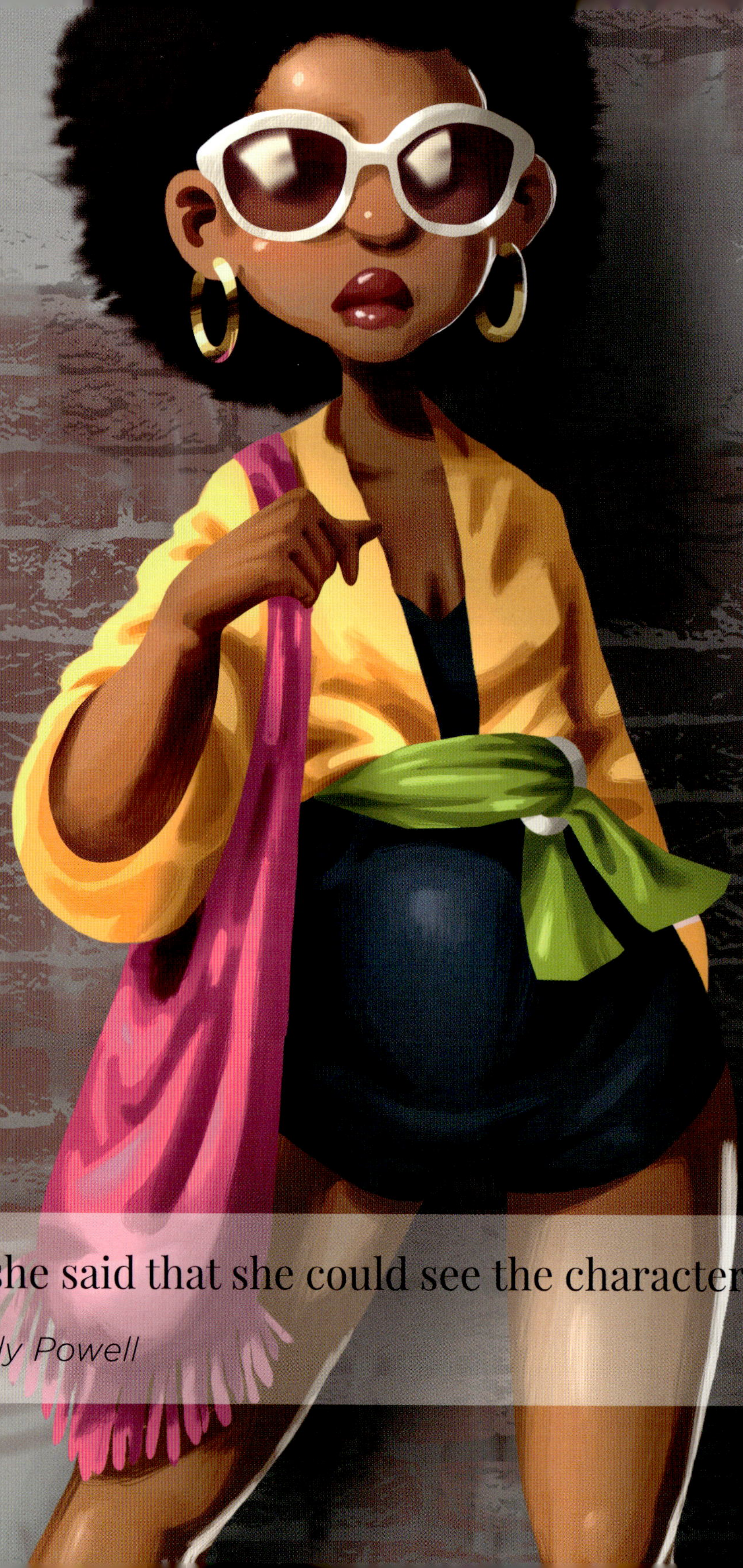

Linework by Blythe Russo, painting by Kevin Scarborough

"The minute she put the costumes on, she said that she could see the character."

—*Sandy Powell*

CHAPTER 4 PERSONALITY

It is human nature to gather information on things and people to understand them, and at times we apply unfair or unflattering labels based on that info. While it's not fair, there's one first impression, and clothing choices factor into it. Would you assume that a character whose clothes are patched and worn is poor instead of adventurous? Or that a character who loves wearing bright patterns is fun and cheerful?

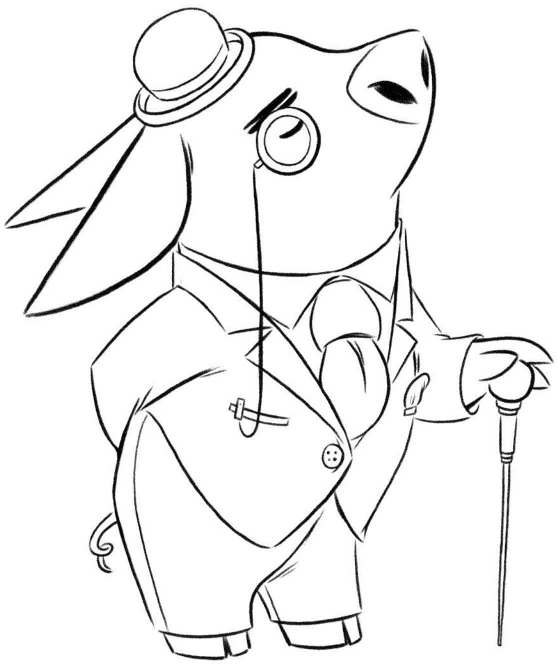

Take this super buttoned-up pig, perfectly put together. Monocle to cane, he is dressed to the nines. Maybe he's stuck up. Maybe he just likes looking good. Maybe this is the uniform he has to wear at the swanky pig hotel where he works.

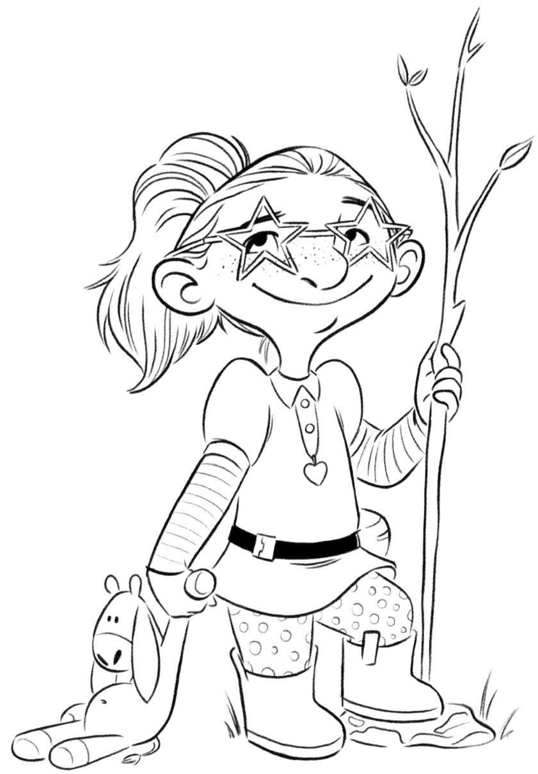

This girl looks incredibly comfortable in this outfit, as if she confidently picked it out herself and is ready for whatever the day brings. Does she play well with other kids? Or is she a lone adventurer who finds comfort in her stuffed animal?

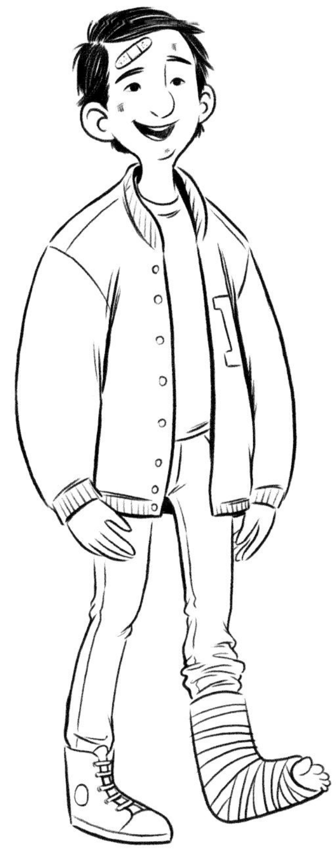

This guy has been through some stuff, but it looks like he's earned that varsity jacket and is happy to be wearing the oversized garment. Or maybe he's putting on a brave face, and he is still feeling the pain from a freshly broken foot. Small details like the jacket patch, Band-Aid, and bruise on his face offer pieces of his story.

What conclusions do you draw about these characters based on their costumes?

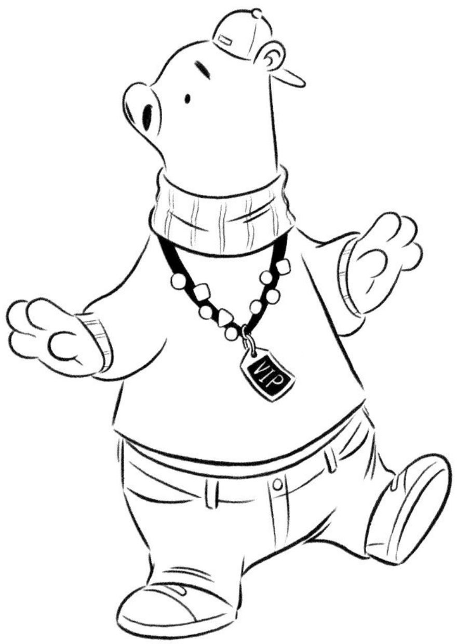

Where do you think this bear is going? Why is he a VIP? What kind of music do you think he listens to?

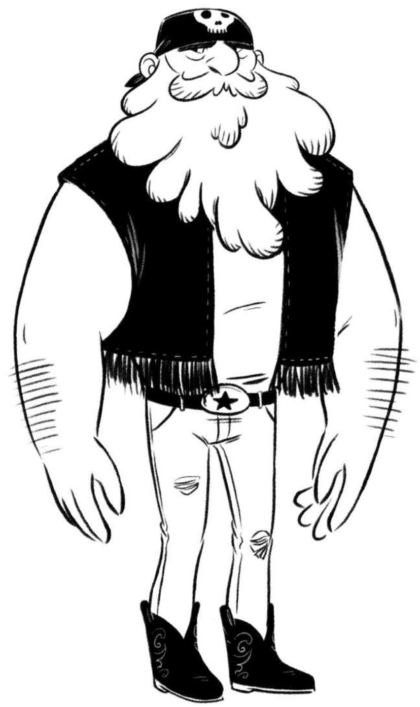

Do you think Mr. Biker Dude is as tough as he looks? Is he even a biker? Or does he just like wearing those kinds of clothes?

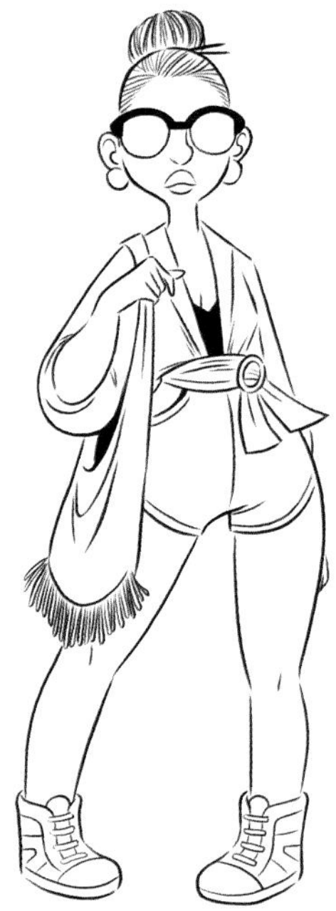

Do you think this woman dresses like this all the time? Do you think she knows about global politics? What do you think she does for a living?

While you were analyzing these character's costumes, did you feel uncomfortable with any immediate assumptions you made about their personalities or what their values are? There are obvious dangers in assuming people are a certain way based on how they're dressed, just as you have to be sensitive about how your costume choices for a character shape the world's perception of them.

In Mark Twain's *The Prince and the Pauper*, a simple switch of outfits results in two boys experiencing vastly different lives. Stereotypes often reinforce negative portrayals of people and can range in their severity. As *Merriam-Webster Learner's Dictionary* puts it, a stereotype is "an often unfair and untrue belief that many people have about all people or things with a particular characteristic." Unfortunately, stereotypes tied to race, sex, class, occupation, and so on can be found everywhere. We all have seen them used in popular culture.

The Use of Stereotypes

It is not just human characters that we've created stereotypes for. There is a long history of anthropomorphizing animals, and in doing so, artists have also applied stereotypes to different species in the animal kingdom: dolphins are friendly, owls are wise, and snakes are evil. Disney's 2016 film *Zootopia* tells the story of the first rabbit cop in the city forging an unlikely partnership with a not-so-law-abiding fox to solve a mystery. The complete plot of the film revolves around the idea of animal stereotypes—and actually flipping them.

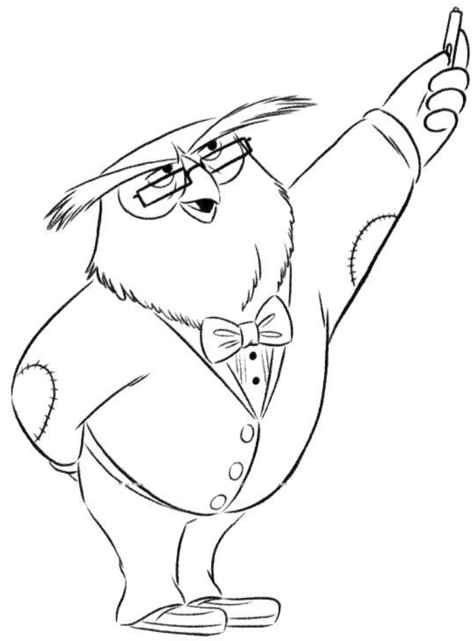

WHY ARE THEY USED?

Creators are often constrained by how much time they have to define a character. With animated features, creators usually have 90 minutes to tell a story, and with picture books, it's 32 pages and around 500 words. With those constraints, pacing becomes even more important. Creators want to spend the majority of their time furthering the story with the main character(s), rather than giving background information on each and every supporting character.

Creators utilize the audience's knowledge of certain stereotypes to limit the need for a character's exposition; they base some characters on stereotypes or archetypes in the hopes the audience automatically understands the general essence of the character at first glance. Ultimately, the first visual impression of that character is all the information the audience needs in order to understand that character and move on with the story.

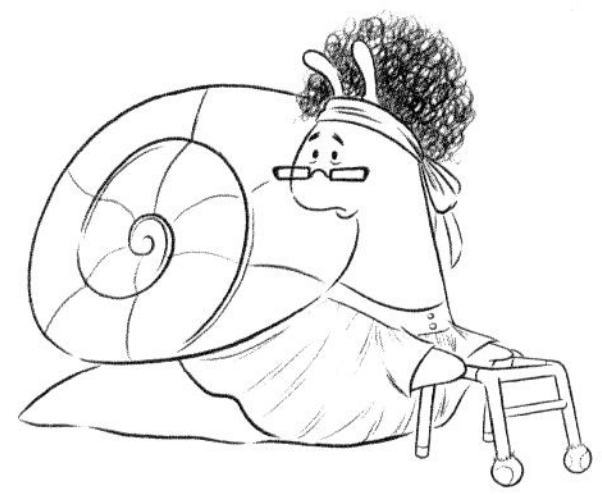

FICTIONAL STEREOTYPES

An archetype is similar to a stereotype but gives you more room to interpret how it's expressed. Oxford Languages defines Archetype in this way:

"(In Jungian psychology) a primitive mental image inherited from the earliest human ancestors, and supposed to be present in the collective unconscious. OR a very typical example of a certain person or thing, or a recurrent symbol or motif in literature, art, or mythology."

As an example, the archetypal attributes of a wizard may include: wisdom, magic, and role as a guiding force. These archetypal ideas transcend cultures and time.

While the stereotypical attributes of a wizard may include: old, male, bearded, solitary, and Caucasian, who wears a robe and pointed hat and carries a magic staff.

Gandalf is a highly recognizable wizard in J. R. R. Tolkien's The Lord of the Rings trilogy. The combination of both stereotypical and archetypal elements simplify his character so we can more easily navigate the vast world that Tolkien created. (See "The Hobbit, A Closer Look" on page 17.)

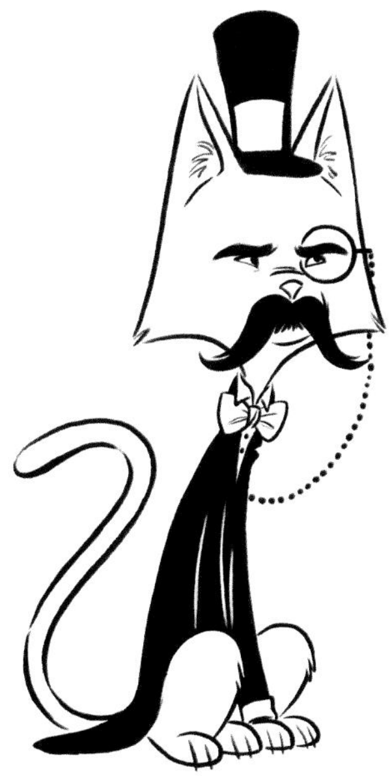

BE AWARE OF THEM AND THEIR POWER

Is it possible to use the quick read of a social stereotype without reinforcing a negative or incorrect story? Some examples of commonly used stereotypes are the ditzy cheerleader, the pristine princess, and the dumb skateboarder. Flat stereotypes like these are extremely overused, and as a result, they don't invite us to learn more about the character. They just aren't interesting to follow because there isn't anything to be surprised by, and we know it. This is the case with the majority of stereotypes used in entertainment. They are not surprising or interesting and do not make for successful characters or stories.

Do you know what is interesting? Conflict. It is the basis of every successful story. You can create conflict within a character by having them go against their own stereotype. A simple way to do this is with the character's clothing choices. Try using your character's costume to reveal the difference between their perceived personality and the reality, whether those assumptions are made by the audience or the character's own world in the story.

What if the cheerleader also moonlighted as a ninja? Even if she was a horrible ninja because she would always forget what she was doing, she would always manage to finish the case. What if the princess loved getting dirty and digging things out of the mud? Princess of the swamplands! What if the skater was a girl? Maybe she's a tomboy, maybe not. Maybe she's into the physics involved in skating. These are just quick examples. Challenge yourself to think up more!

By recognizing the stereotypes and archetypes associated with the character and their narrative, you can decide what elements are true, or false. And since it is easy for us to filter the world through our own perception, when in doubt, learn more about the people you are telling the story about. How do they see themselves and the world?

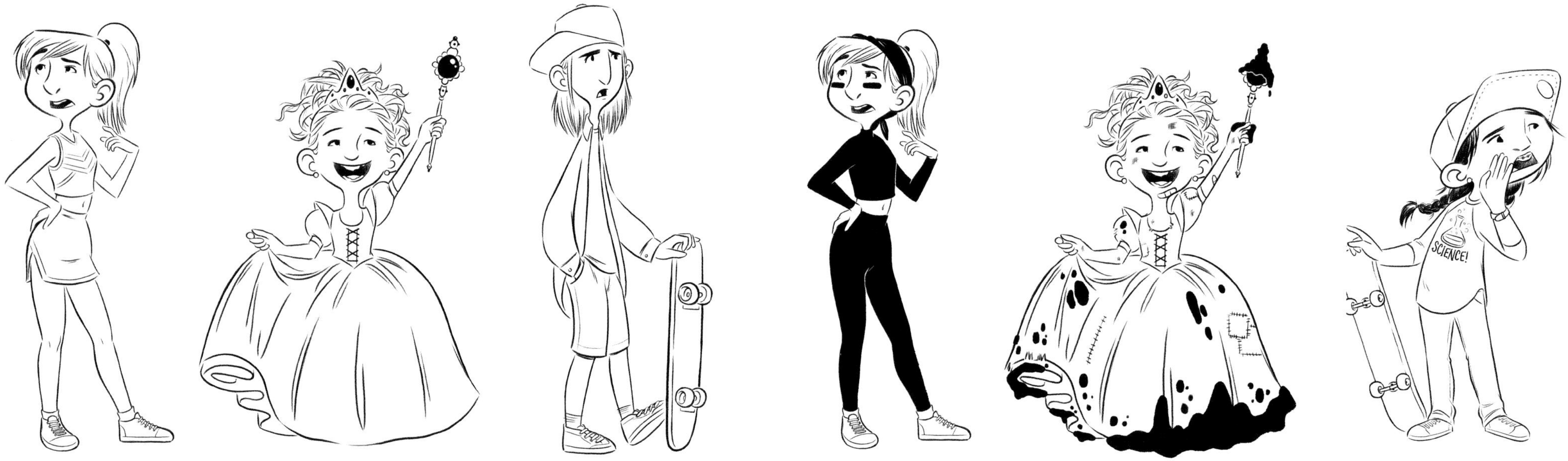

Exercise: Flipping Stereotypes

Create an astronaut, a pirate, and a king based on stereotypes. What gender, race, age, social status, interests, clothing, etc. did you automatically associate with the prompt? Design to the stereotypes that came to your mind first.

Now flip them. Note the things you associated with the stereotype and flip them on their heads by choosing their opposites. You can switch interests, clothing, gender, age, race, social status—push yourself to go beyond your first impressions.

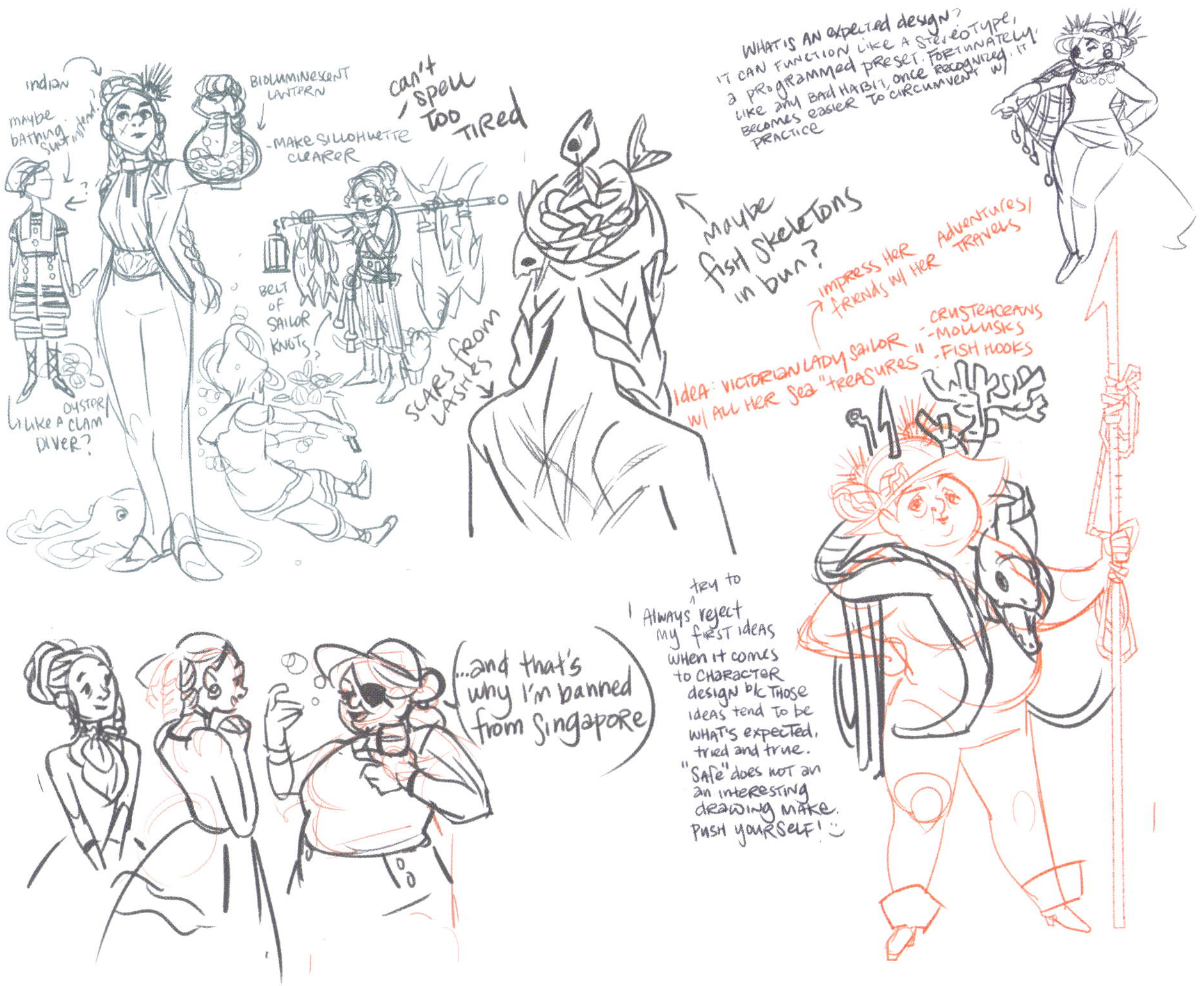

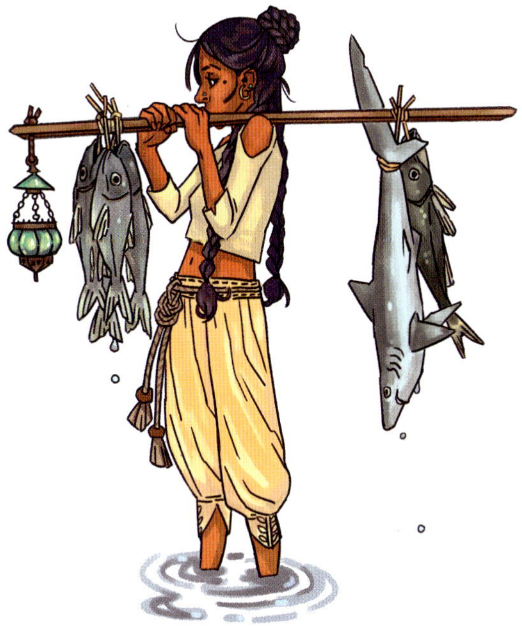

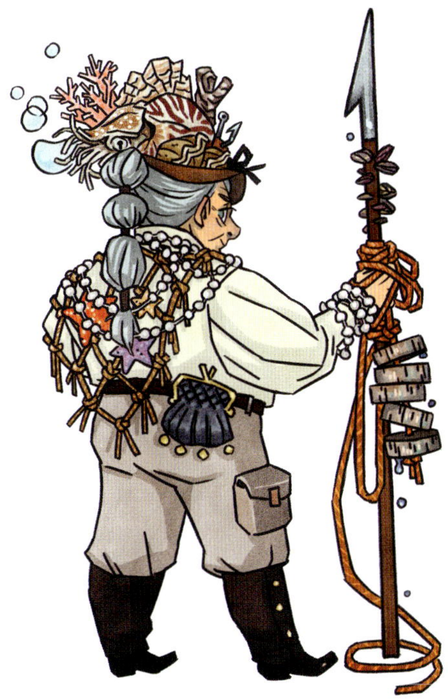

"A Victorian Lady" by comic artist Anissa Espinoza

WHAT'S MY MOTIVATION?

Your character's greatest desire is a direct reaction to their greatest fear (and vice versa).

By knowing the events in the character's past and present that drive their reactions, you can develop compelling visual conflict for any character. However, when you are referencing people from life to design this conflict, you may find that they have a hard time simplifying their stories. It may be too vulnerable to share, or they may feel confused about it themselves. By using simplified psychology tools, we can better notice and create visual shorthand for many of the motivations, traits, and instincts that drive personality and story.

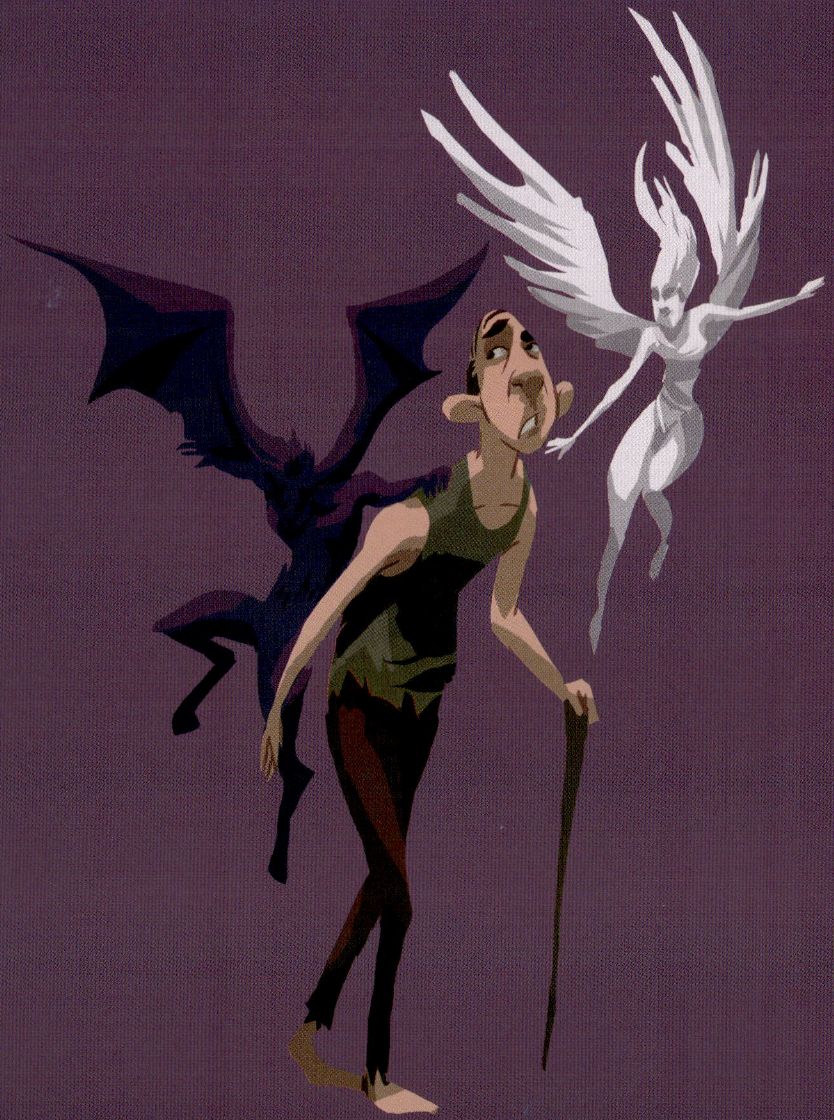

Imagine your character as a child; was there something they just sensed was "true" from the beginning? Part of the fabric of their reality that the character didn't feel they needed to work on to receive? Maybe the character felt the world would support them, that they had worth, that they were loved unconditionally. There was a "virtue" in the world that they resonated deeply with.

But at some point it was lost . . . and a lie was introduced that prevented them from finding it again.

"I am worthless."

"I am unlovable."

"I can't do it alone."

Phrases like these loop in their mind and interfere with the ability to gain their deepest desire. This lie will evolve into your character's "vice".

As they struggle with this internal battle, they build habits and defenses to fight off the lie and force reality back into a lost ideal. When events and scenarios of the plot incite them to run toward or away from certain people, locations, or challenges, each action exposes and clarifies their true motivations to the audience. We learn their greatest need through conflict.

The audience doesn't (usually) hear the internal monologue of the character, but as a costume designer you can hint at that internal battle with visual subtext. You can even create "red herrings": misleading clues that keep the audience on their toes.

The Nine Enneagram Type Descriptions

Enneagram is a personality theory that conveniently sorts motivations like these into three categories: fear, shame, and anger. Within these categories, there are different triggers and nuanced reactions that your character can express. Whether they are a hero or a villain, the following nine core motivations give your characters both virtues and vices that can move them to transform in meaningful ways.

Choose a type for your character or layer multiple types to create a more complex character. There are many great resources out there to help you navigate layering them in interesting and poignant ways. Try the Enneagram Institute or The Narrative Enneagram as a starting point.

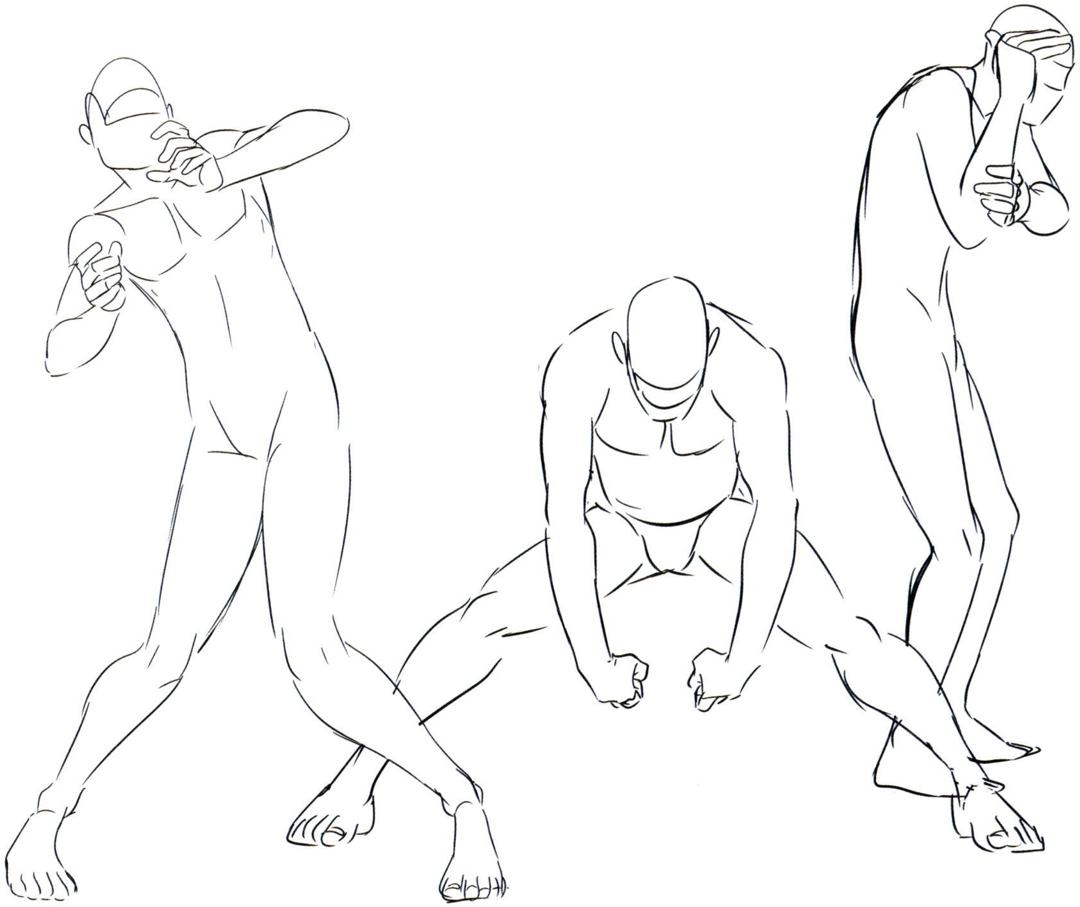

TIP:

Your character can't change their history, but they can rewrite the narrative of what it means to them. They may even rewrite the narrative of a costume element from their past—transforming and polishing fashion styles they've used out of fear, shame, or anger into styles that empower through ownership and victory.

VICE:

GLUTTONY

"I am deprived."

7

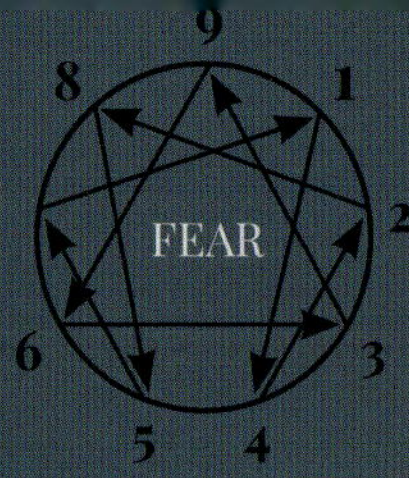

VIRTUE:

SOBRIETY

"I am satisfied."

Indulgent: Lives a larger-than-life lifestyle, often binge shopping for the best, loudest, or zaniest items to show off their wealth. Louis XIV of France was famous for decreeing that only those in his favor could wear red heels. Those who gained the coveted status decorated their shoes with gold and ribbons to show off their status even more.

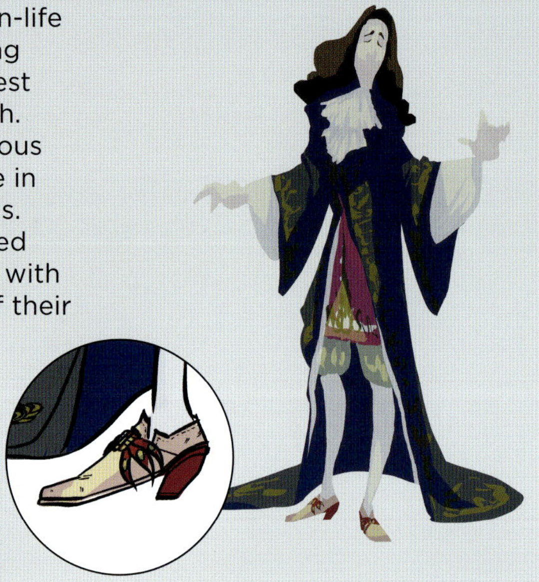

Trendy: Has the "grass is always greener" mentality, changing their wardrobe to follow every trend. When a new pair of sneakers became a status symbol to working class people, this humble shoe soon evolved into a wide variety of styles. These days, many are particularly invested in having the newest high-end, eclectic designs to symbolize conquering a financial limitation.

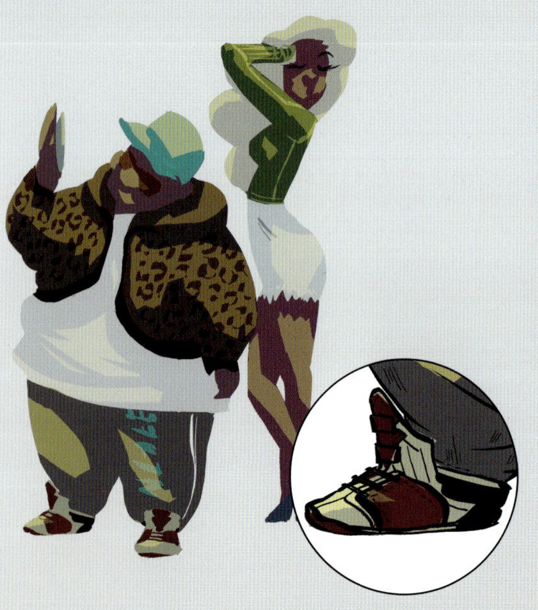

Enthusiastic: Has an exuberant attitude and can transform an eclectic item into a bold statement. Self-described "bionic artist" Viktoria Modesta opts for avant-garde prosthetics in terms of material and design versus a more traditional artificial leg for mobility, challenging preconceived images of what a disabled life (or woman) should look like.

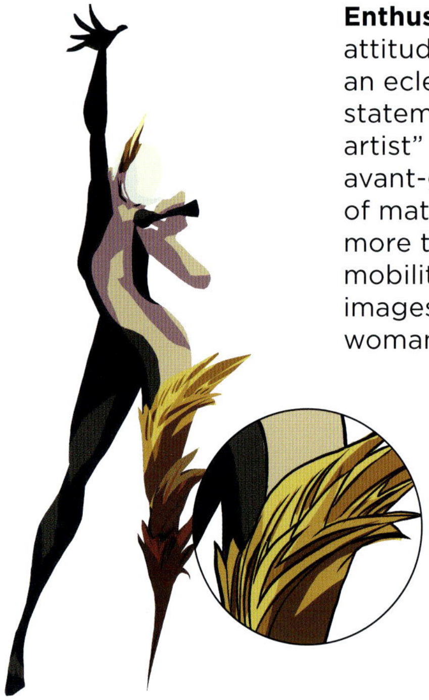

Experiential: Even a go-with-the-flow hippie who appears more minimal on the outside can express their focus on gathering novel experiences with an item bought on their journey to India.

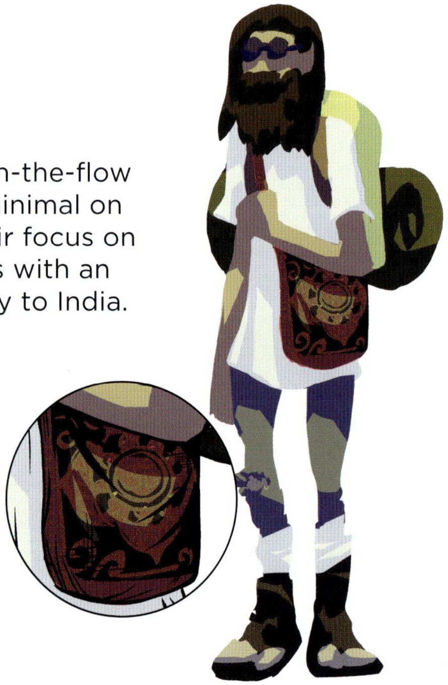

CORE MOTIVATION: SATISFACTION

VICE:

PARANOIA

"I am alone."

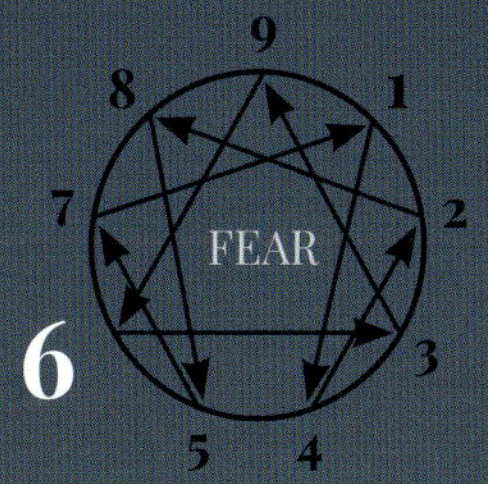

VIRTUE:

LOYALTY

"I am supported."

Conforming: Creates a "perfect" or ideal image to attract and fit into a network of support. Foot binding in China is an example of this. For some 10 centuries, girls would have their feet bound in order to fit them into tiny "lotus shoes" to have what was considered attractive to royalty: small feet.

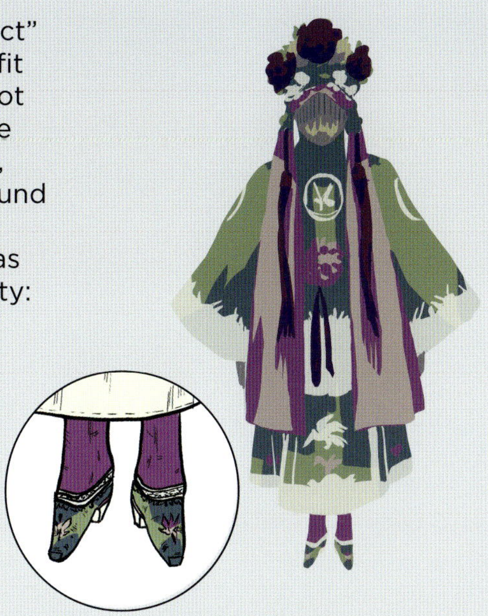

Nonthreatening: Seeks to show others they are not a threat or are in service to them to encourage connection. This mantis spirit wears a sash marked with a contract seal that suggests a commitment and loyalty to a master.

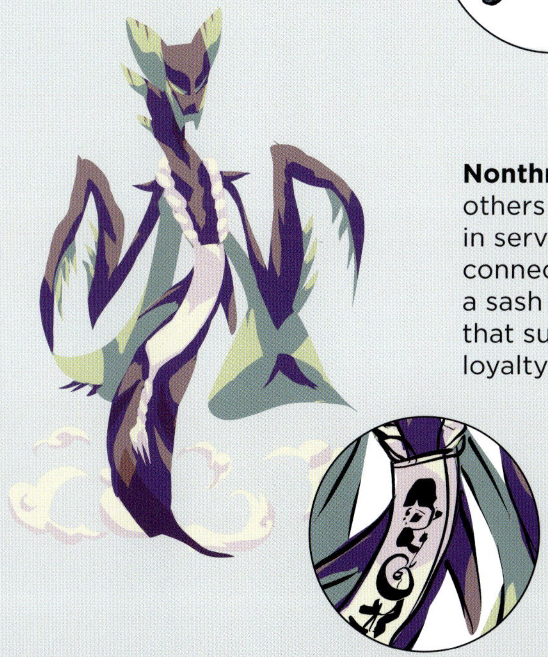

Loyal: Creates a certain order and security to maintain the health of their network. A military uniform not only connects them to a support network, they can also showcase their value to that network, allowing them to become a source of stability.

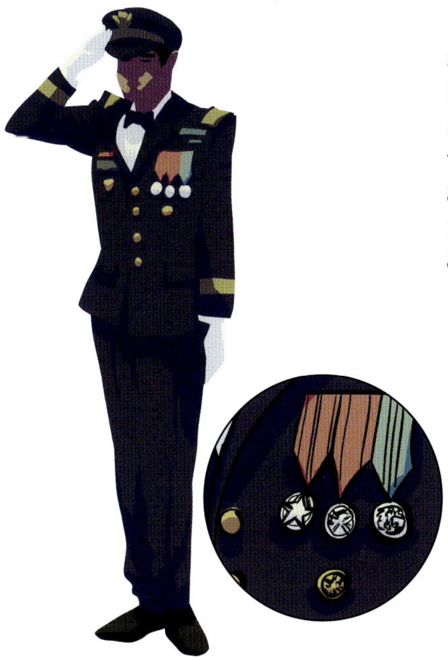

Careful: Working in a competitive office in a male-dominated field, this woman could use a dramatic high heel to give off the message, "I demand to be seen, and I'm up for a challenge," while also emphasizing her femininity to put the competition at ease.

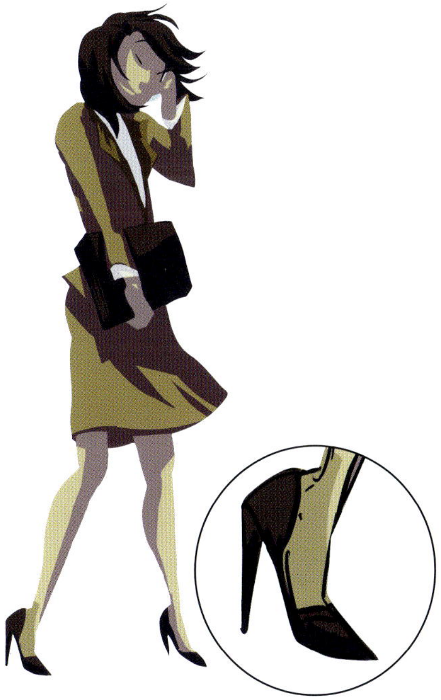

CORE MOTIVATION: SUPPORT

VICE:

GREED

"I am inadequate."

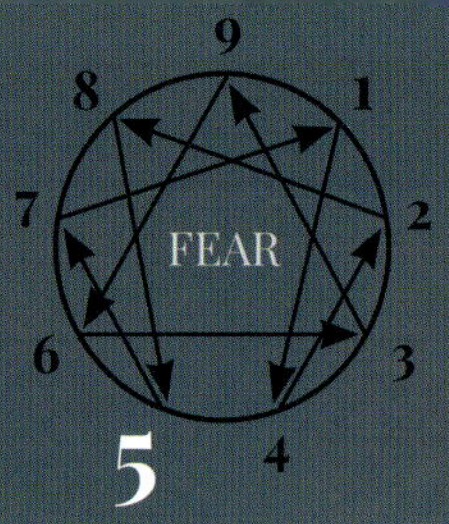

VIRTUE:

TEMPERANCE

"I am enough."

Equipped: Private and obsessive compulsive, they hoard gear and knowledge, curating it into the perfect collection. This treasure hunter wears a dragon cape that alludes to a dragon's inclination to hoard treasure.

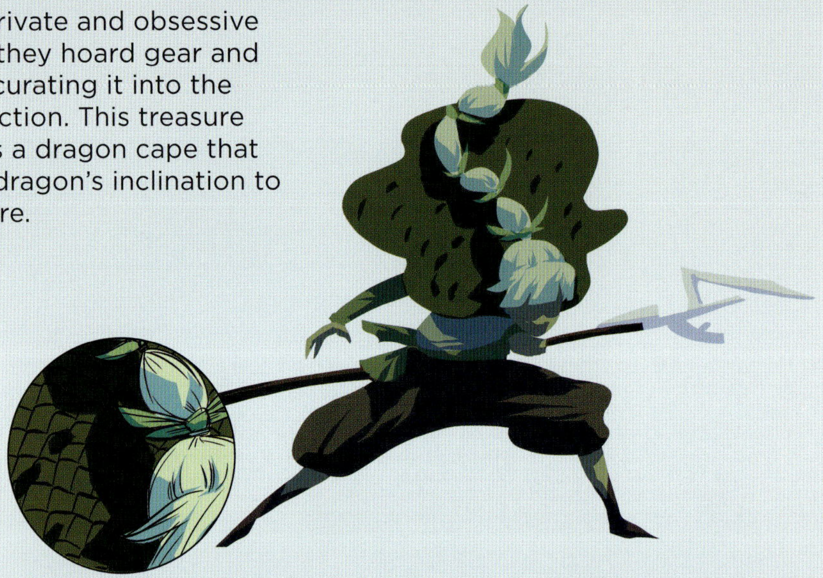

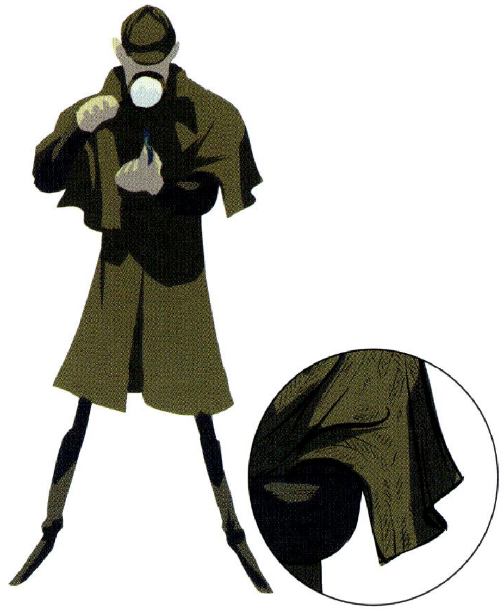

Precise: Spending a lot of money on a few high-quality pieces that they can keep well preserved. Sherlock Holmes's Inverness cape and deerstalker cap became an iconic go-to outfit for the clever detective. Weatherproof and durable, he was ready to face any case.

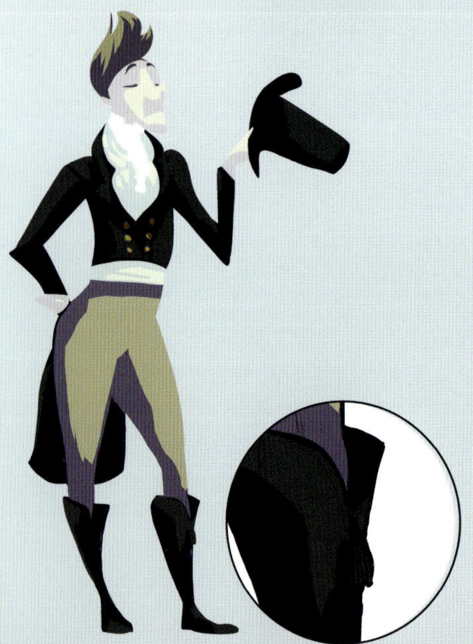

Composed: Not the type to flaunt brand names, they choose appropriate items for each situation that show quality in the details. English dandy Beau Brummell's outfits were famous for being well composed, fashionable, and high quality. He popularized the Hessian boot, which became a necessity for a true gentleman's wardrobe.

Quality-Minded: Appears detached from the world and protects their treasures by hiding the fact that they have anything of value. High-quality choices are apparent, given a closer look. These brogue shoes are a meticulous and expensive choice.

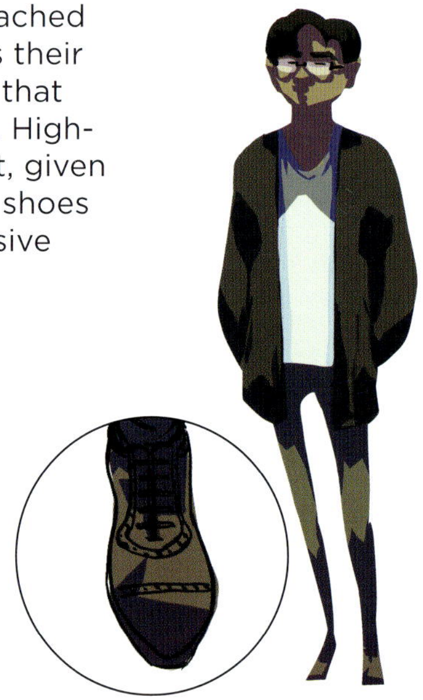

CORE MOTIVATION: CAPABILITY

Exercise: Personality Extremes

Create a set of costumes based on a character's virtue and vice.

- What cultural or societal triggers can you incorporate to give your costume more context?
- What values, objects, or individuals does your character associate with their fears and desires?
- How did you incorporate those into the shape language or details of the design?

FEMININE VIRTUE

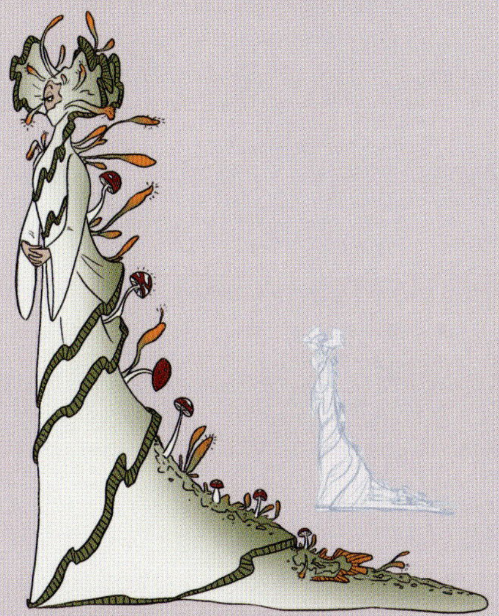

Control • Moderation • Restraint

Cordyceps fungus controls its host but does not destroy it, carefully picking and choosing (moderation, restraint) just enough to keep it alive and to propagate.

Dark, damp environment, lives on dead matter (underworld).

FEMININE VICE

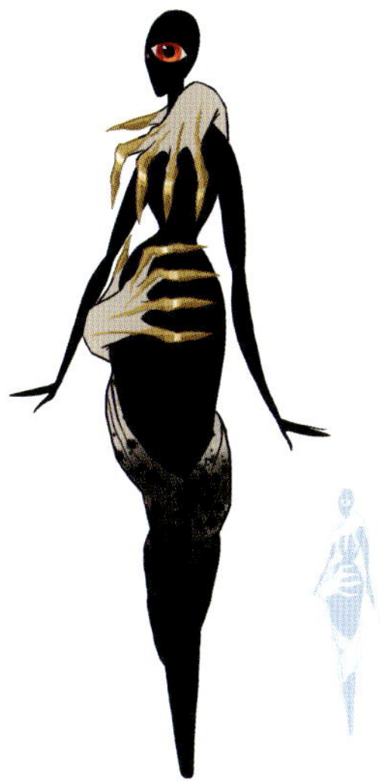

Longing • Excess • Selfishness

Hands dipped in gold to symbolize excess, selfishness.

Inspired by *Birth of Venus* painting.

Eye always watching, longing; greedy type tends to observe more than participate.

MASCULINE VIRTUE

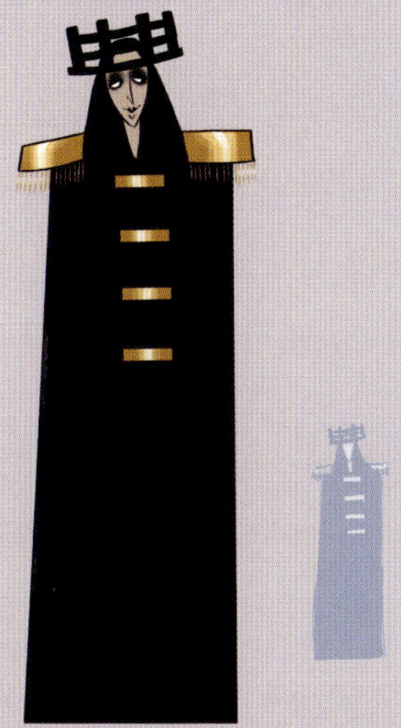

Control • Moderation • Restraint

Pulls from naval uniform and chess pieces for style and silhouette.

Much more minimalist in overall aesthetic (hides fact that they have anything of value).

MASCULINE VICE

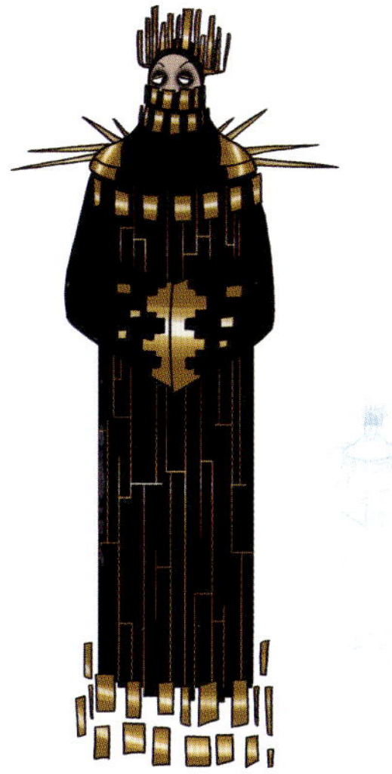

Longing • Excess • Selfishness

More gold to symbolize excess and selfishness. Spiked shoulders create space around her.

Accumulates gold plates around her costume. Well maintained, high quality (precise, everything has its place).

TIP:

Don't be afraid to get conceptual! You can always pull back later and rework your abstract ideas into the details of shape, motif, color, and texture.

VICE:

ENVY

"I am insignificant."

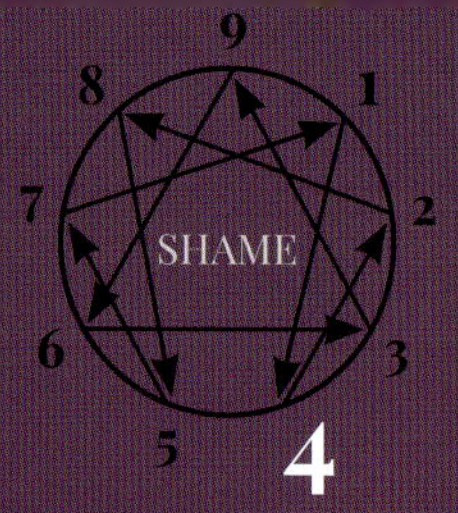

VIRTUE:

EQUANIMITY

"I am special."

Distinct: Uses fashion to make political and personal statements, often pushing others away as a result. "Lolita" fashion returns to the innocence of childhood, a pure look that rejects the sexualization of women. Infant or childish shapes and patterns dominate the look.

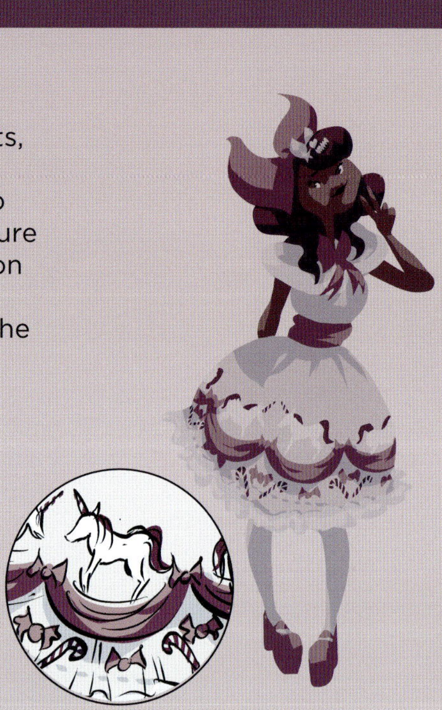

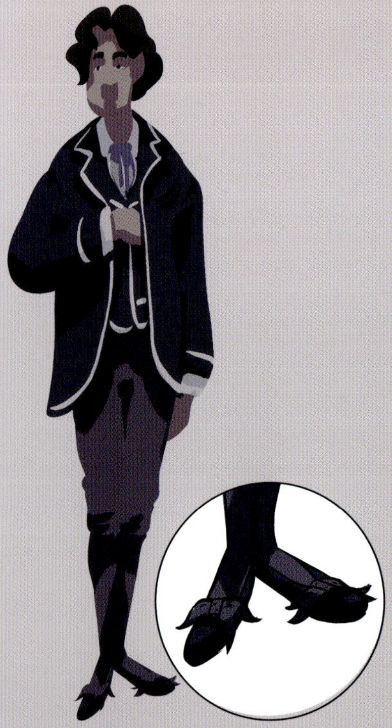

Rebellious: Against the status quo, often wearing clothing that is normal for a different demographic. Oscar Wilde dressed as a child as a symbol of defiance. He wore youthful outfits and house slippers to call back to a time when new ideas, dandies, secularism, and uncommon gender roles were more accepted.

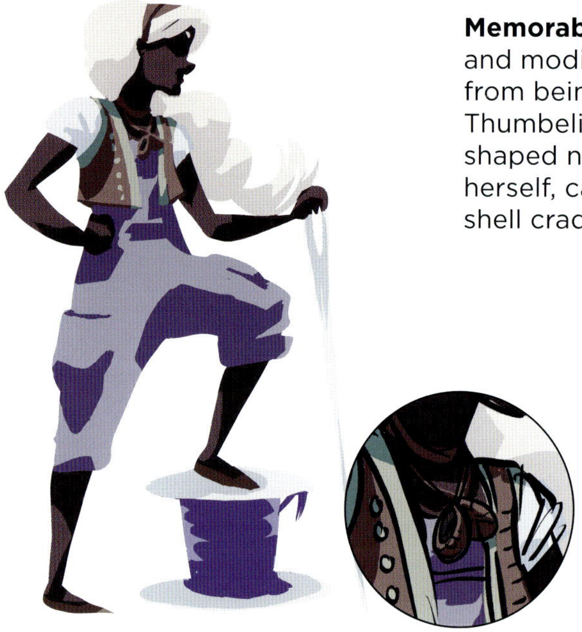

Memorable: Continues to refine and modify their style as a defense from being compared to others. Thumbelina wears a walnut-shaped necklace she fashioned herself, calling back to her walnut shell cradle.

Innovative: Seeks items that help them define themselves to the world. Every item has a rhyme and reason. The Japanese Wamono street fashion style pulls from both East and West, allowing the wearer to create their own unique blend that reflects a new opinion of their tradition and place in a more global context.

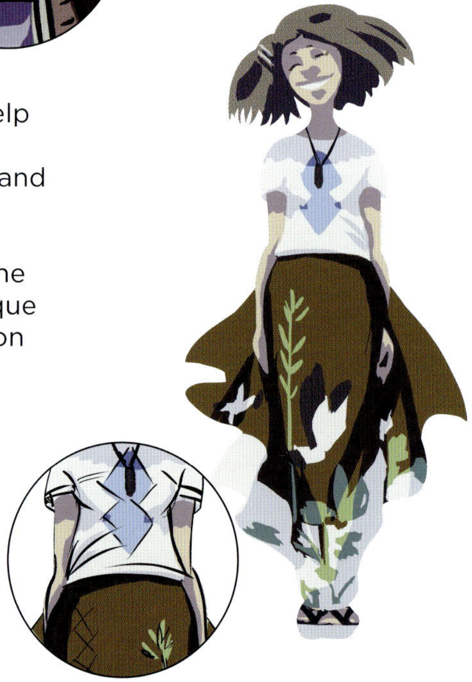

CORE MOTIVATION: SIGNIFICANCE

VICE:
DEECEIT

"I am worthless."

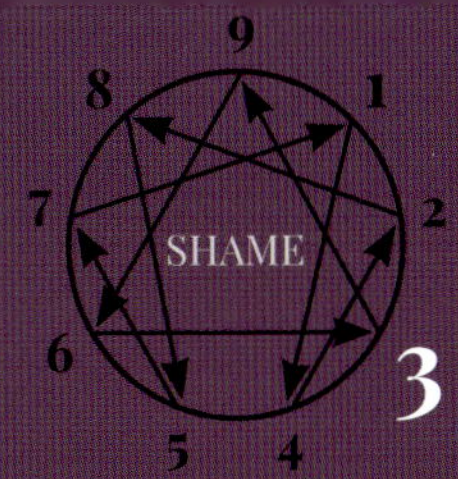

VIRTUE:
AUTHENTICITY

"I am respected/impressive."

Iconic: Vain and drawn to surface beauty, they create and market a version of self that aligns with what society sees as successful. Wearing recognizable classic styles from head to toe, this "Bond Girl"–like character is the perfect accessory for a leading man, from her red dress to her art deco T-strap heels.

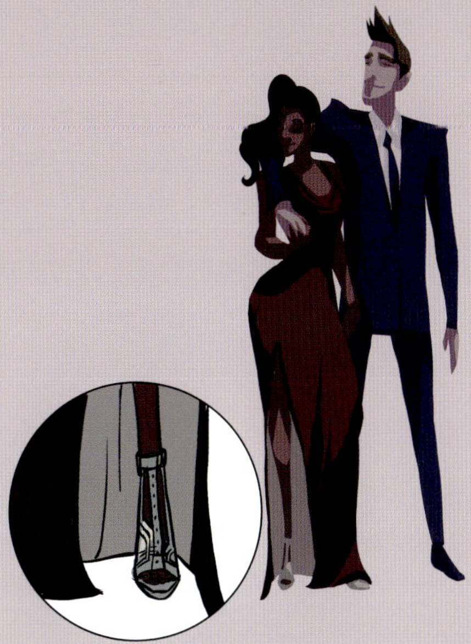

Branded: Works hard to create the best version of their personal image. Greco-Roman ideals also influence this boxer who wants to align with the sportsmanship and mastery associated with gladiators and Olympians.

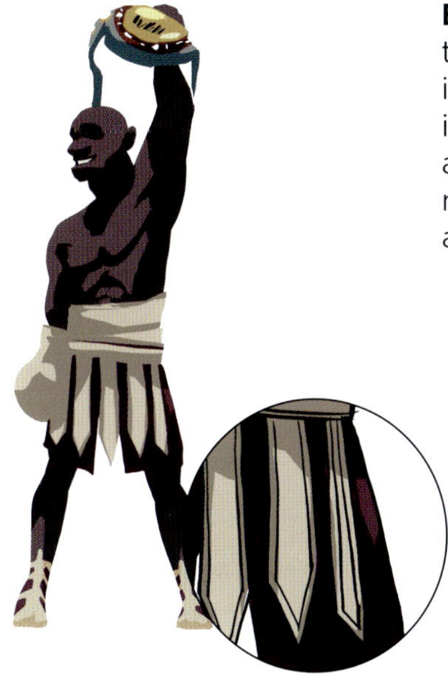

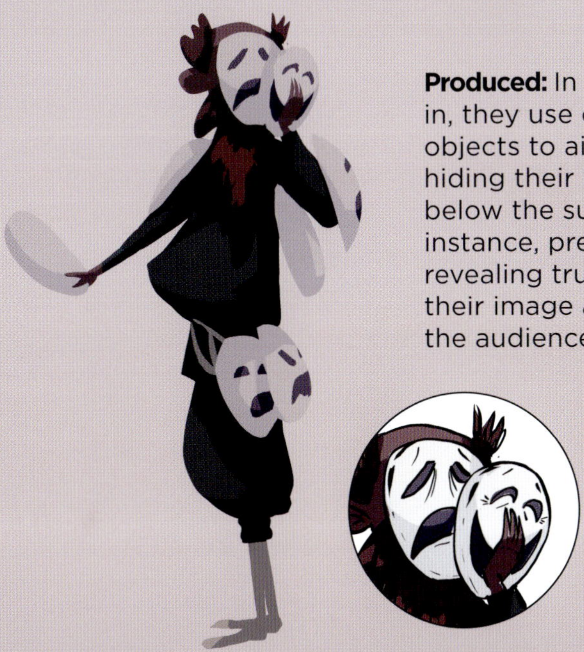

Produced: In any situation they are in, they use clothing, people, and objects to aim for perfection while hiding their imperfect emotions below the surface. A full mask, for instance, prevents this actor from revealing true emotions to control their image and the responses to the audience.

Refined: Relies on the past to identify familiar ideals. They appreciate the impact of iconic, vintage, or retro fashions. French women of the late 18th century, the Merveilleuses, looked for inspiration in the Greco-Roman world and acted out their lives to align with their romantic view of the past. They communicated their ideals quickly with elements like the gladiator sandals.

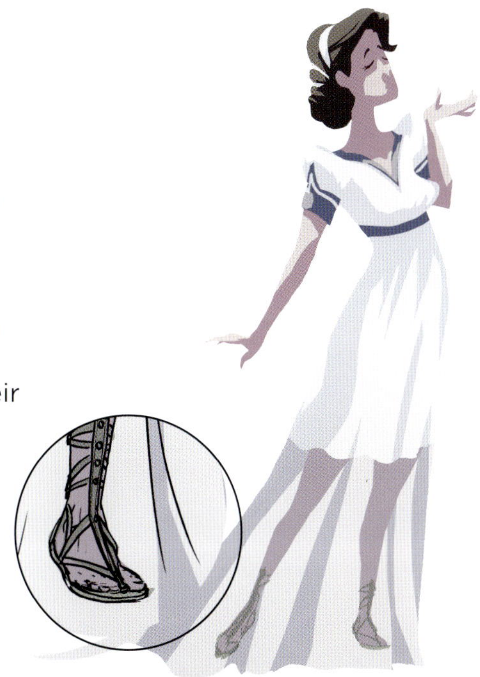

VICE:

PRIDE

"I am unwanted."

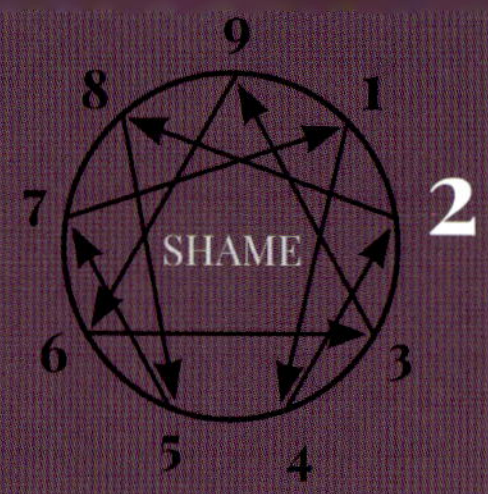

VIRTUE:

HUMILITY

"I am loved."

Practical: Practical clothing items allow them to showcase their focus on providing others with joy. "Loudly" displaying a domestic ideal, this apron shows the character's helpfulness and the frills bring attention to her efforts.

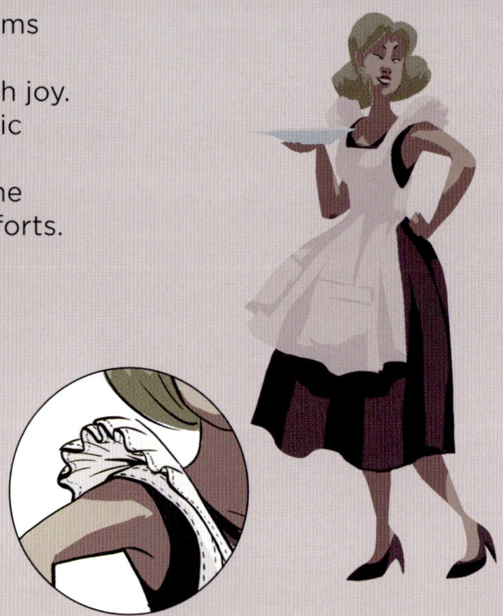

Authoritative: They may look to middle-age or older fashion to assert a persona of gentle authority and nurture trust. For example, part of the uniform for nurses in the military, oxfords have become symbolic of helpful women in the workplace, such as secretaries or librarians.

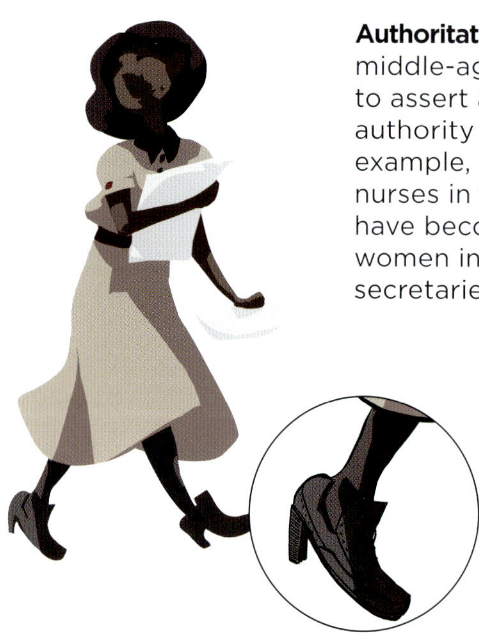

Frugal: Used clothing exhibits their prioritization of others over self. They often wear items until they are worn out. This brownie works hard in hopes of milk or cream from grateful homeowners. He wears an outfit made of discarded teatime items and his shirt is constructed with actual tea leaves that he will wear until they fall apart. You don't want to find out what will happen if you forget to leave out the milk.

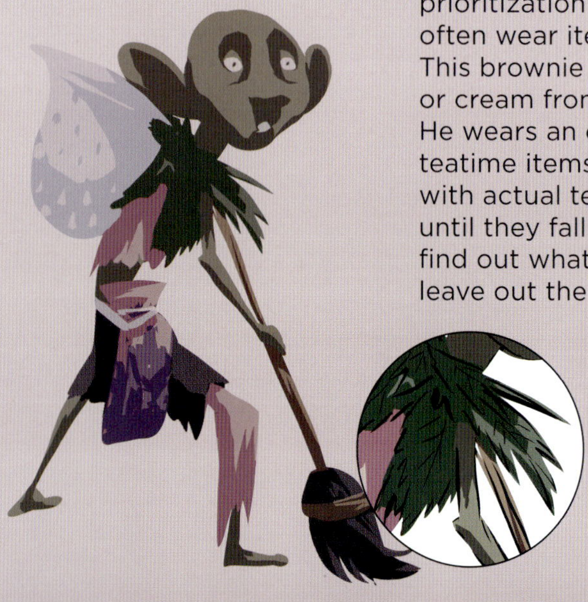

Selfless: They prefer classic, timeless, fashions that are usually available in less expensive but durable materials. A nonslip work shoe popular with nurses, they are worn to help with back and knee pain, allowing them to keep working as long as they can stay awake.

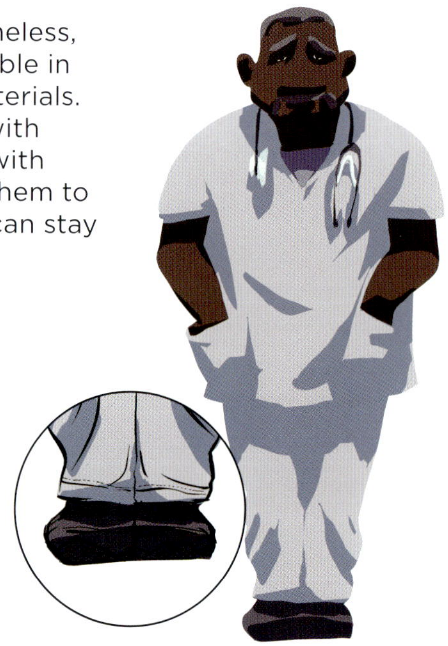

CORE MOTIVATION: BEING LOVED

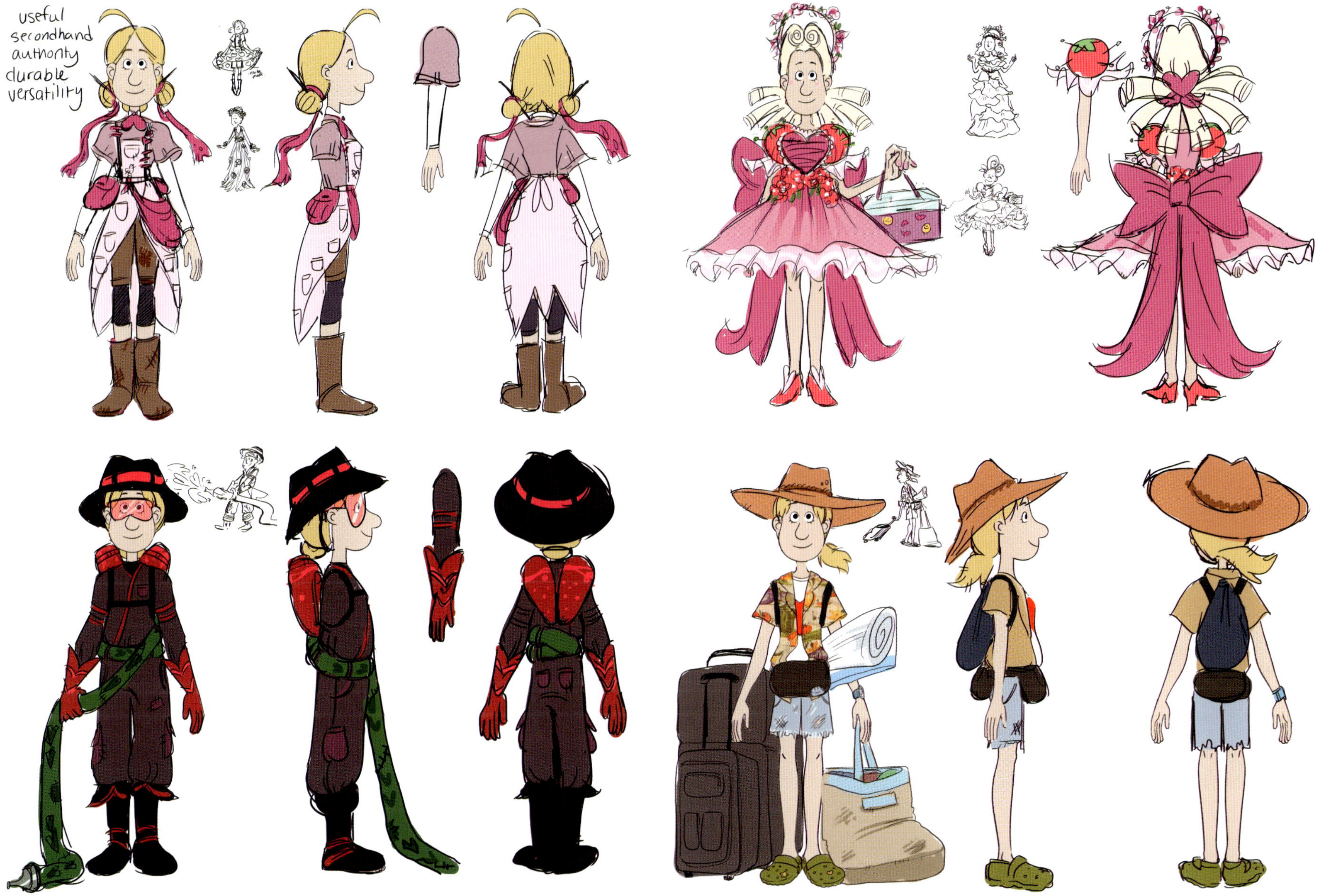

Illustration by Madeline Abatemarco

TIP:

Think of roles they might play in their world, or modernize them to explore more familiar roles and occasions to amplify their attitude. Turn them around to explore side and back elements.

VICE:
FORCE
"I am disempowered."

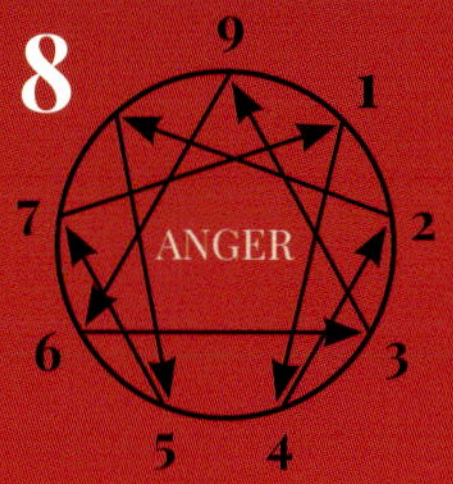

VIRTUE:
INNOCENCE
"I am self-sufficient."

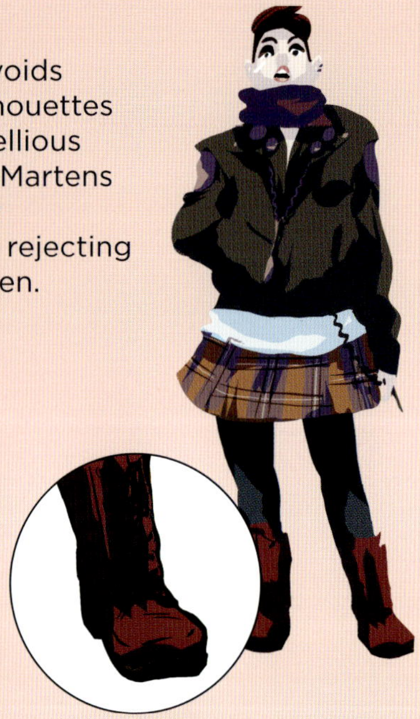

Masculine/Androgynous: Avoids bland attire and chooses silhouettes that make a statement. Rebellious women popularly wore Doc Martens in the 1970s and '80s, loudly announcing their arrival and rejecting the small foot ideal for women.

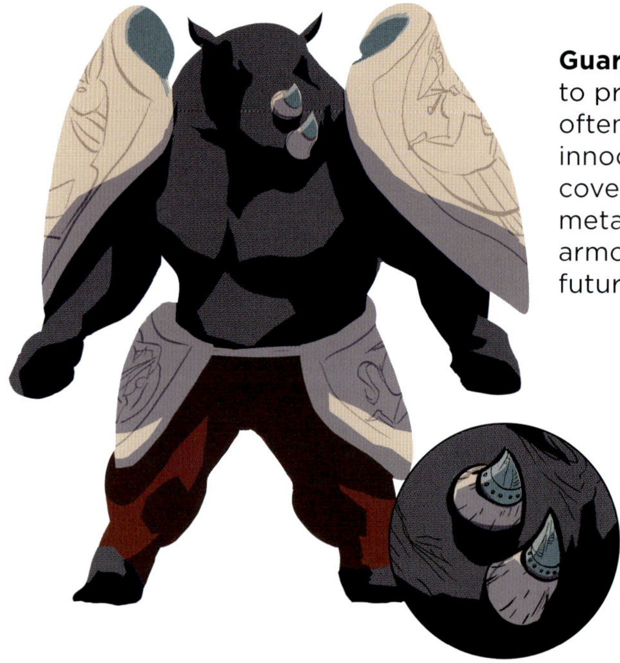

Guarded: Uses their strength to prevent abusive treatment, often defending the weaker and innocent. This "Rhinotaur" has covered his stolen horns with metal replacements, using his new armor to protect the herd from future attacks.

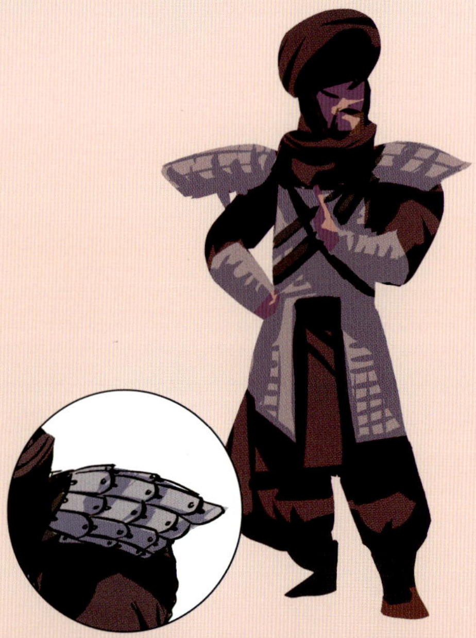

Intimidating: Has a strong presence created by an emotional wall that masks "weak" human shapes. An Arab scimitar warrior protects their body while also creating an intimidating shape on their shoulders.

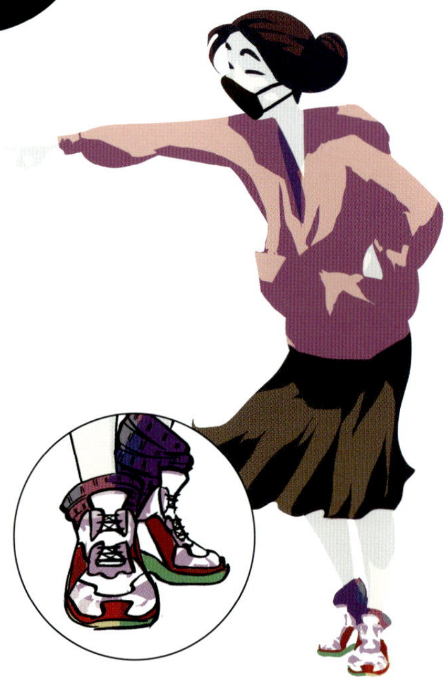

Passionate: Aligns with objective truth, challenging those who distort it. The "ugly-shoe" trend redefines the narrative of beauty and femininity; chunky sneakers are the mascot of this trend.

CORE MOTIVATION: POWER

VICE:

WRATH

"I am corrupt."

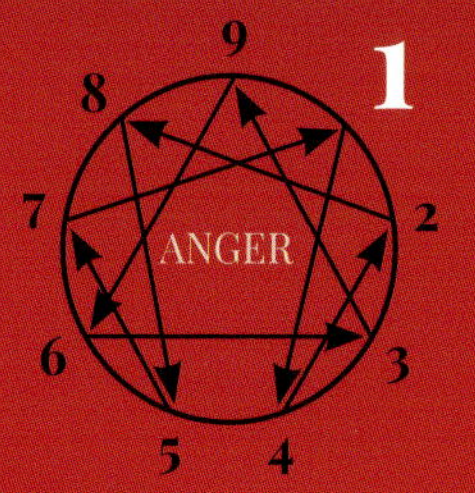

VIRTUE:

SERENITY

"I am good."

Rigid: Seeing the world as strictly good and evil, they seek to align themselves with the side they perceive to be correct, defending it to the death. A symbol of righteous wrath, as mentioned, sabots are famous as the wooden clogs that French workers would throw in the machines that were taking their jobs during the industrial revolution.

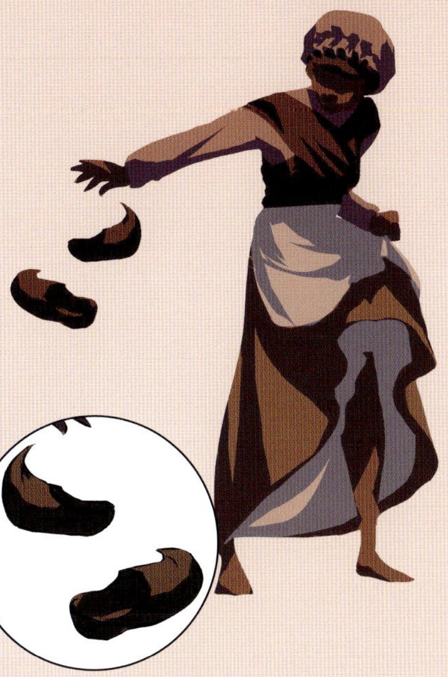

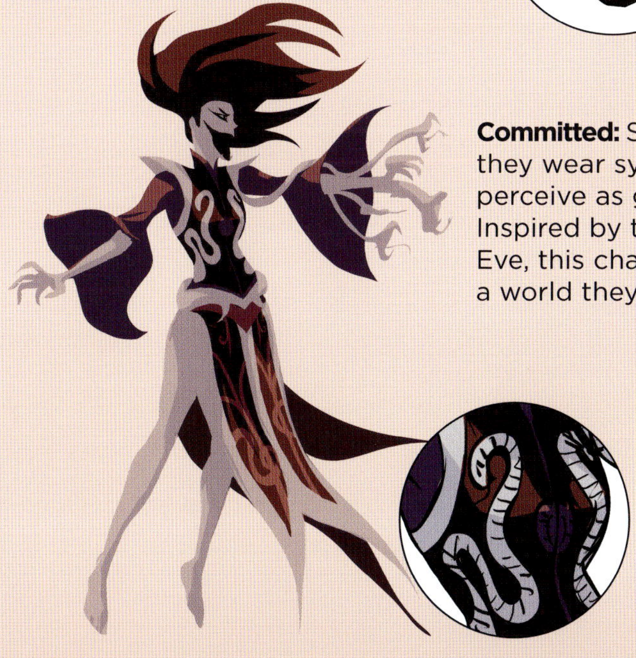

Committed: Showing their choice, they wear symbols of what *they* perceive as goodness and integrity. Inspired by the snake in Adam and Eve, this character seeks to destroy a world they feel betrayed by.

Of the People: Actively chooses items that connect them with disenfranchised groups, such as quality working-class boots. They show that they are still one of the people, uncorrupted by wealth.

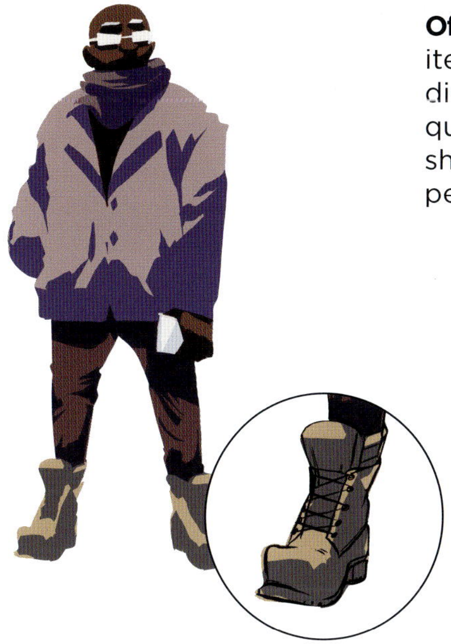

Obedient: Looks for durable, timeless fashion and will prescribe a uniform for themselves that fits their place in society. A knight defending goodness and truth wears a religious cross, showing their alignment with their perceived correctness.

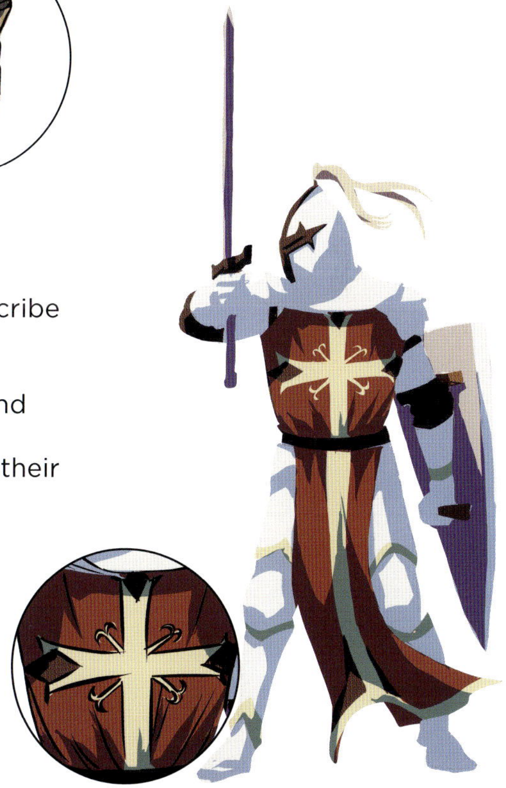

CORE MOTIVATION: INTEGRITY

MASCULINE VICE
I Am Corrupt

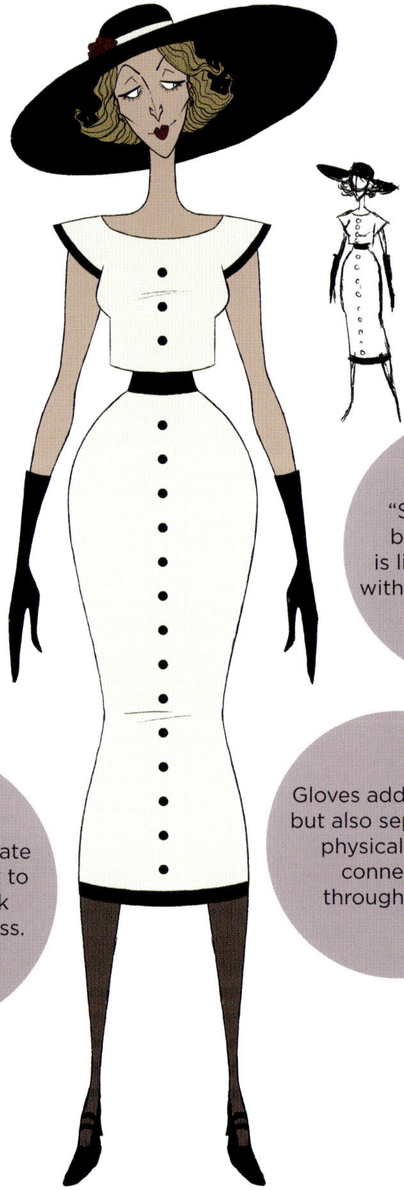

Flowers as symbols often placed somewhere on her person. Believes this represents her goodness.

Dress is more like a power suit than a typical dress. Divides her silhouette.

White is often a color reserved for higher status since it was such a hard material to keep clean, requiring constant washing by housemaids.

Lots of buttons create a fussy sort of look to an otherwise slick and minimalist dress.

"See the world in black and white" is literally portrayed with her color scheme.

Gloves add elegance but also separate her physically from connecting through touch.

MASCULINE VIRTUE
I am Good

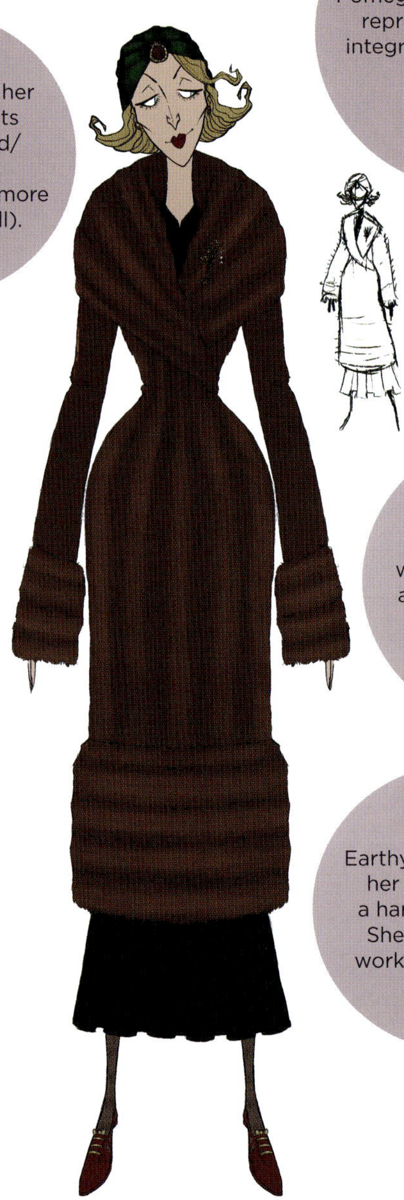

Covers more of her "feminine" traits (hair is covered/ contained and her figure is more covered as well).

Pomegranates as symbols represent loyalty and integrity in her marriage with Hades.

"One of You" Raccoon fur coats were worn to display a certain wealth, but also very common among the youth.

Earthy tones connect her to her role as a harvest goddess. She still does the work she has to do.

TIP:

Explore cultural masculinity and femininity in your costumes, regardless of your character's gender, to push past your first impressions. You may have a tendency towards one or the other in your work so this can be a helpful exercise to expand your visual library.

TAILORED EXAMPLE

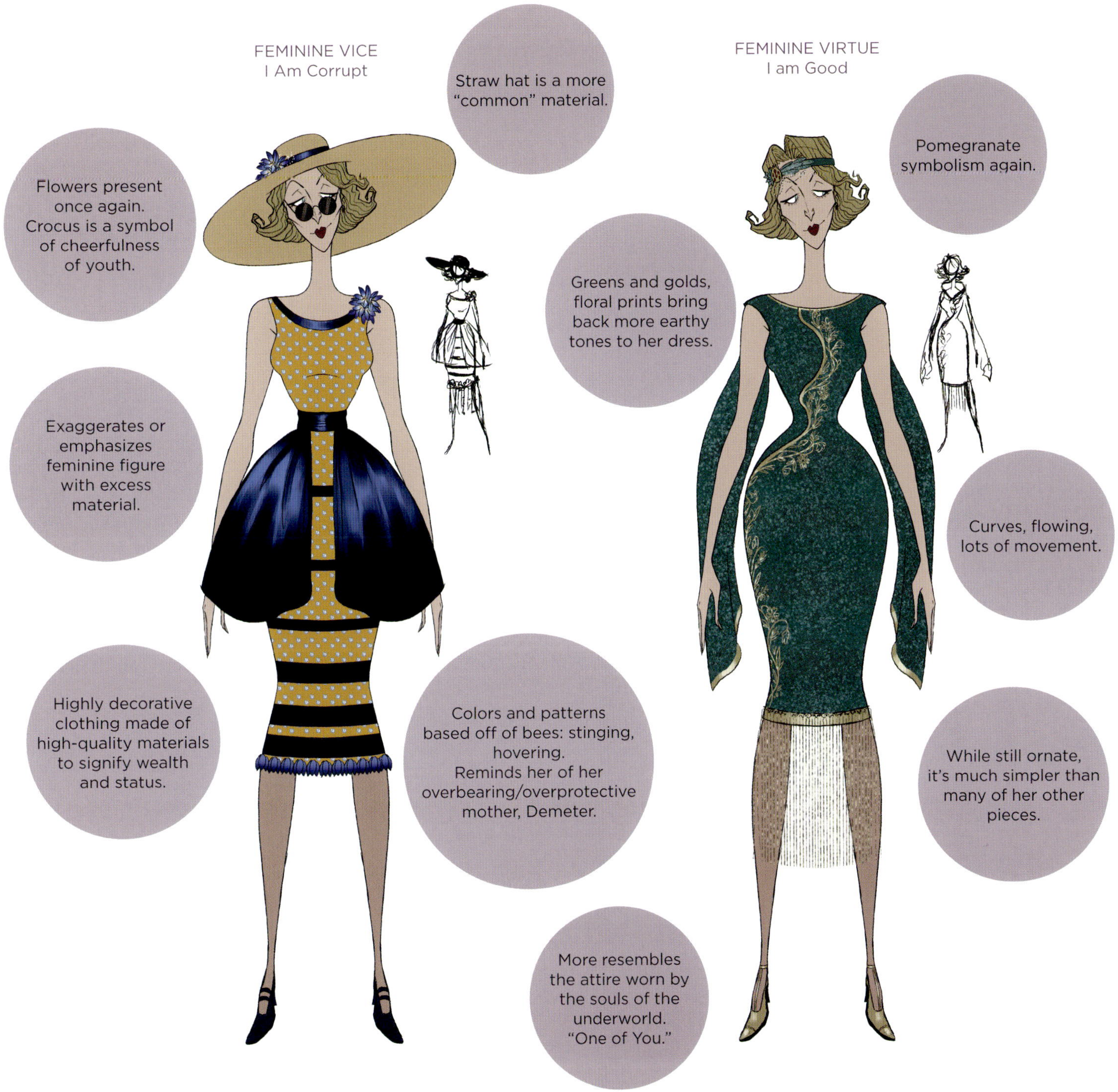

VICE:

SLOTH

"I am lost/fragmented."

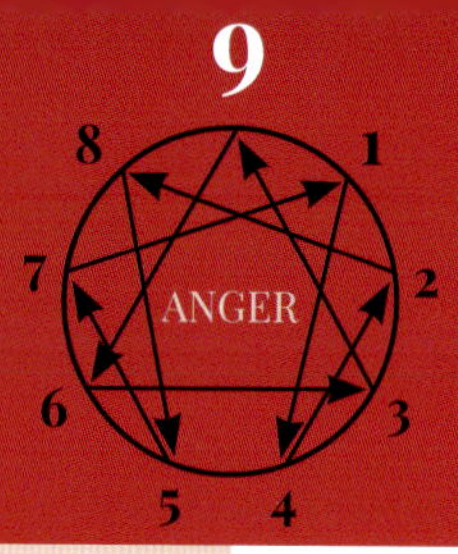

VIRTUE:

ACTION

"I am whole/at peace."

Reserved: Wears layers to mask and minimize their form. They often cover parts of their hands and choose quiet footwear. Built for skateboarding, Vans sneakers have come to represent antisocial youth: a non-choice by those who don't want to, or don't have the opportunity to, engage in society at large.

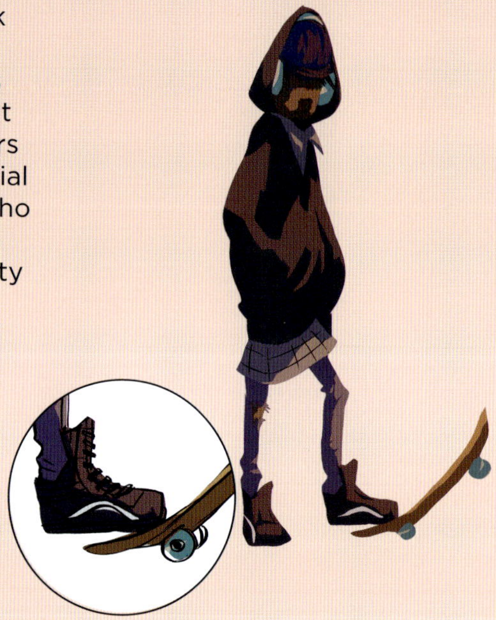

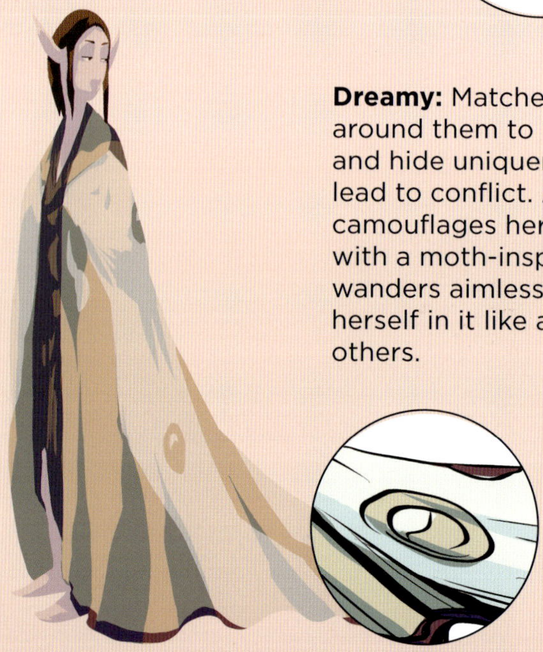

Dreamy: Matches with those around them to "test the waters" and hide uniqueness that may lead to conflict. A dreamy elf camouflages herself in the forest with a moth-inspired cloak. She wanders aimlessly, ready to wrap herself in it like a blanket to avoid others.

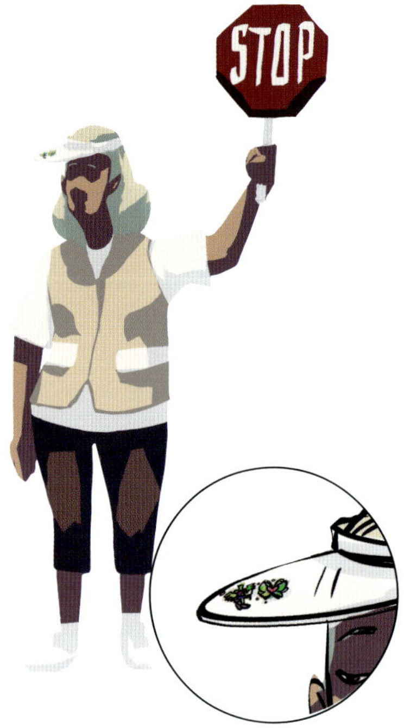

Passive: Complements their quiet wardrobe with a few precious, personally meaningful items. This crossing guard may wear a plain and simple outfit, but the childish stickers on her visor hint that she may care for it more than she gives off.

Harmonious: Seeks harmony and acts as a mediator. Listens to others and puts themselves in others' shoes. This Buddhist monk showcases his viewpoint for others through his outfit of a devout follower, signaling to those around him what his motivations are.

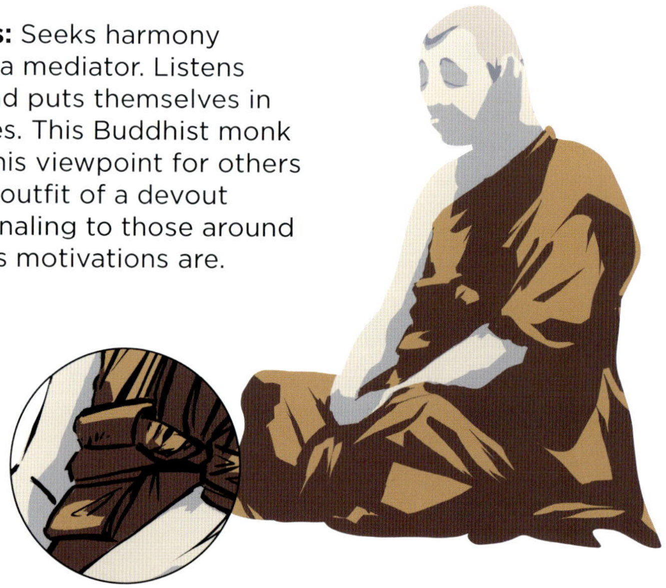

CORE MOTIVATION: WHOLENESS

Problem-Solving Styles

While we are running from our fears or toward our desires, we use our senses, intuition, feelings, and logic to deal with the unfamiliar situations that arise. As you review your character's story, note how they problem solve to move the plot forward. Are they more extraverted in certain situations and introverted in others? Carl Jung developed the cognitive functions as a way to understand this layer of our personality. Also used in the Myers-Briggs Type Indicator, you can learn more on *16 Personalities* or *Geek Psychology's* video series.

SENSES

Your character is thrust into a new environment. Do they . . .

REFLECT

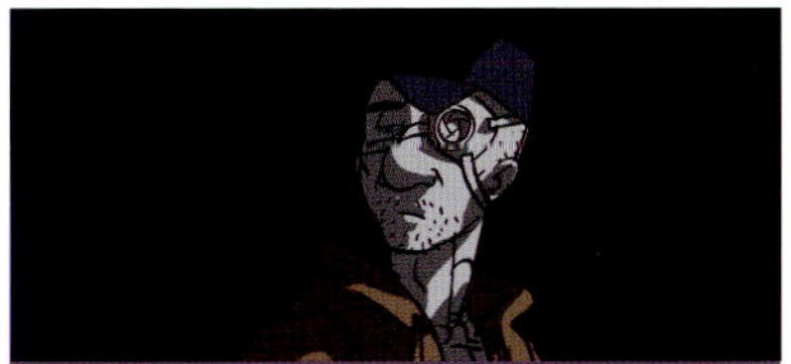

The Guardian

IMMERSE

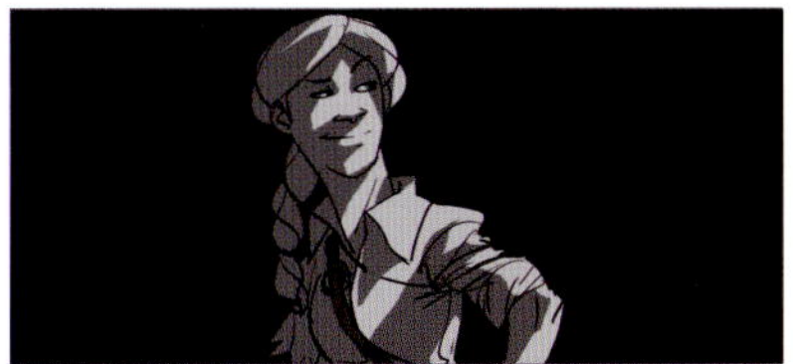

The Adventurer

THINKING

When creating a strategy, do they . . .

ANALYZE

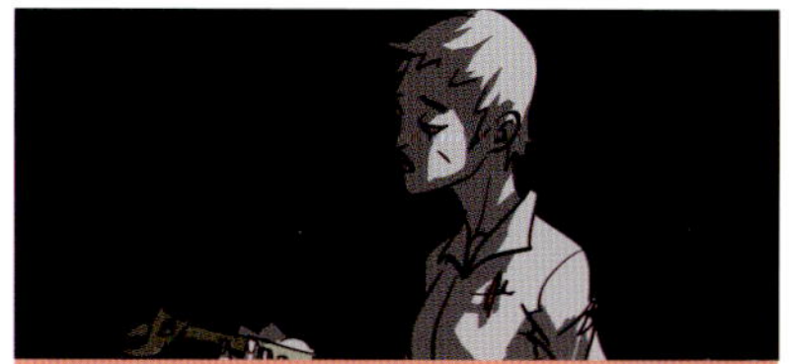

The Technician

LEAD

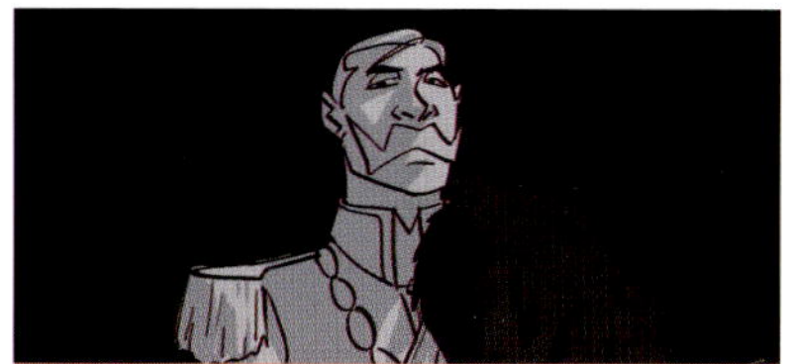

The Commander

INTUITION

Your character has to start a new project. Do they . . .

ENVISION

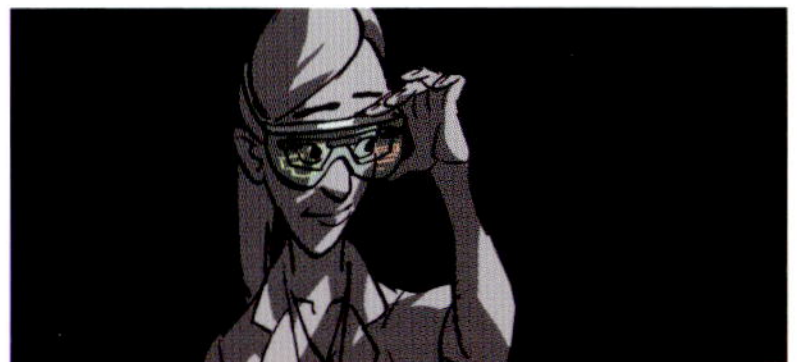

The Visionary

BRAINSTORM

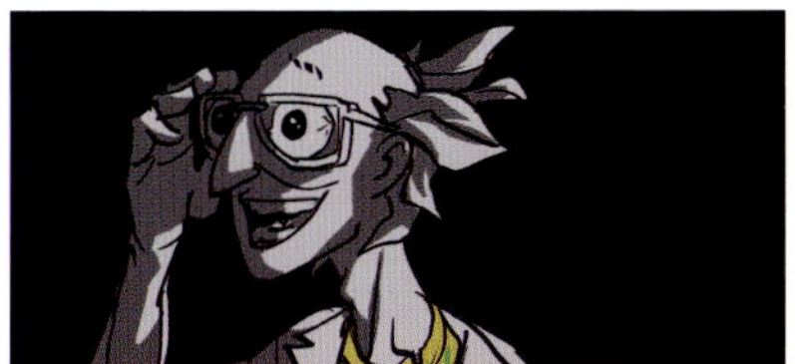

The Innovator

FEELING

When developing a value, do they . . .

SYMPATHIZE

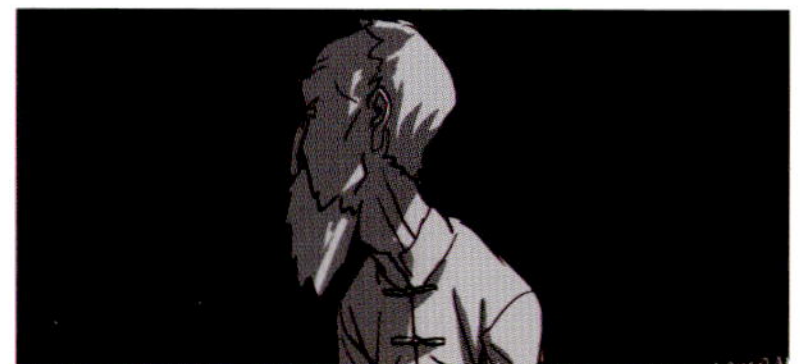

The Appraiser

EMPATHIZE

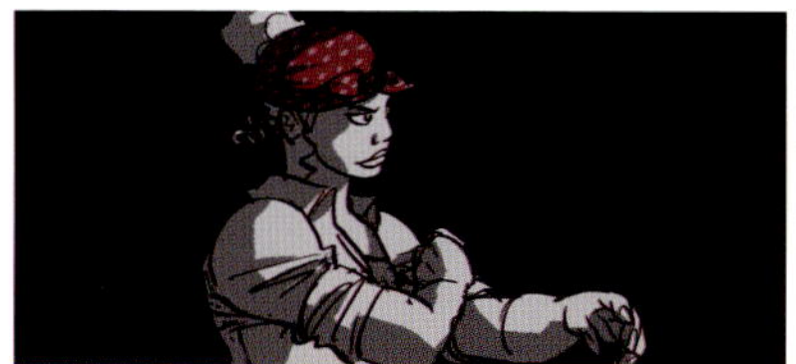

The Ambassador

The Introverts

The Guardian

Batman, Captain America, The Wizard (*The Wizard of Oz*)

The Visionary

Doctor Strange, Sabrina Spellman, Vanessa Ives (*Penny Dreadful*), Miranda Priestly (*The Devil Wears Prada*)

The Technician

Neo (*Matrix*), Wolverine (*X-Men*), Steve Jobs, James Halliday (*Ready Player One*)

The Appraiser

Harry Potter, Scarlet Witch (Marvel *character*), Sugar Plum Fairy (*The Nutcracker and the Four Realms*), Trigun

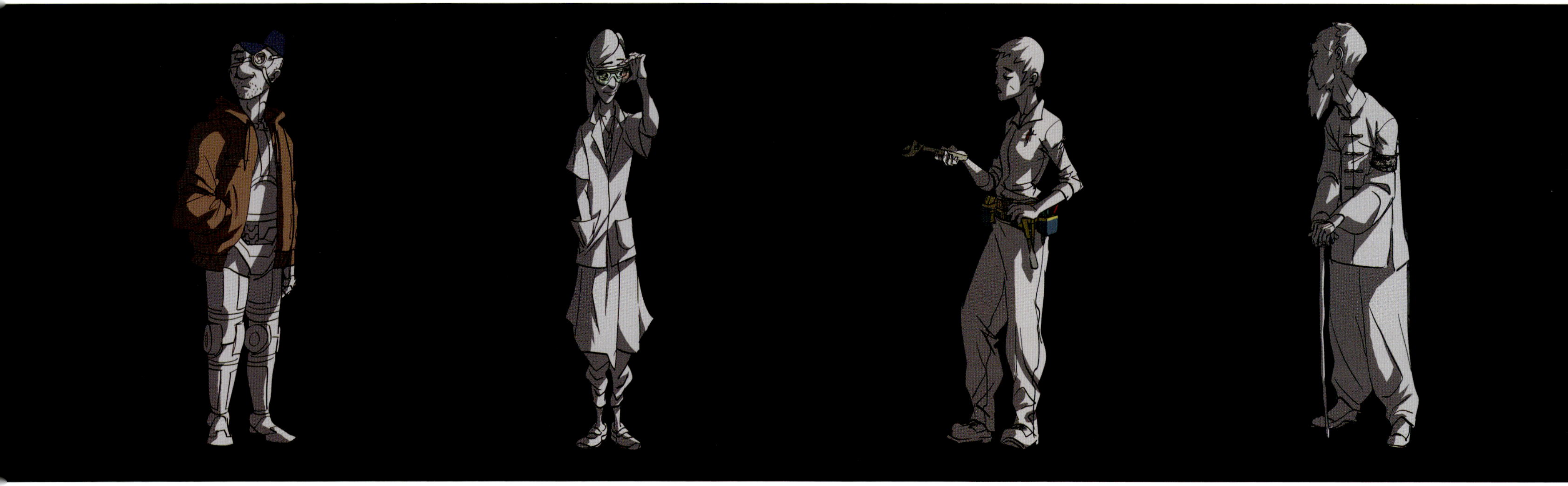

Behavior: Reflects and relies on the experiences of the past to create stability and predictability.

Style: Dresses to match a traditional theme or to express their opinion of the world. Often wears items until they wear out.

Example: A cyborg wears a nostalgic old cap and worn sweater from a long forgotten time in his past.

Behavior: Trusts their flashes of insight that they then envision and develop into detail.

Style: Can anticipate trends and be ahead of others and often have refined fashion with a quiet introspective flavor.

Example: Augmented medical glasses to help a surgeon identify and visualize solutions.

Behavior: Identifies the logical and most accurate action to take through analysis; seeks the perfect/ultimate solution for all their clothing needs and sticks to conclusion.

Style: Clean, minimal, and comfortable; often having multiples of same piece.

Example: A mechanic's tool belt equipped with the exact tools needed for the job.

Behavior: Identifies the emotional reasoning behind decisions, prioritizing the feelings/values of the individual. Treats clothing as reflection of self, so seeks pieces that align with inner self-image; holds onto favorite pieces for a long time.

Style: Fantasy, dreamy, non-conforming, and shifting; tests out different personae.

Example: A mourner "wearing their emotions on their sleeves" with an armband accented with a custom pattern to honor their lost loved one.

The Extraverts

The Adventurer

Maui (*Moana*), Lando (*Star Wars franchise*), Derek Zoolander (*Zoolander*)

The Innovator

Iron Man, Genie (*Aladdin*), Doc Brown (*Back to the Future*), Kaylee (*Firefly*)

The Commander

Furiosa (*Mad Max*), Minerva McGonagall (*Harry Potter*), James Norrington (*Pirates of the Caribbean*)

The Ambassador

Boromir (*The Lord of the Rings* trilogy), Jean Grey (*X-Men*), Elsa (*Frozen*), Sophie (*Howl's Moving Castle*)

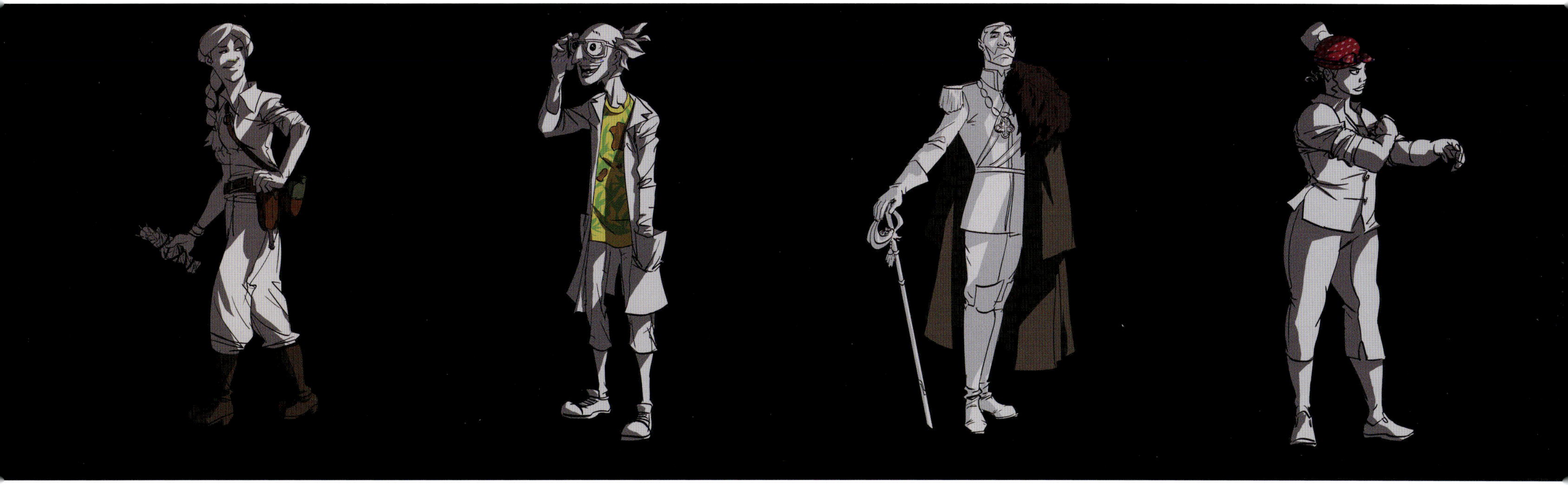

The Adventurer

Behavior: Strives to engage with the activated senses, living in the moment to create a sensory impact on themselves and others.

Style: Current and on-trend fashion; wants to be ready for action and chooses clothing that is equipped for being highly active.

Example: An explorer with active gear made of comfortable and sturdy leather that can withstand their jungle excursions.

The Innovator

Behavior: Sees vast possibilities for how a problem may connect to other ideas, brainstorming new and unexpected options with the current tools.

Style: Explorative and fun, often skimming from many styles, resulting in a quirky mix of pieces.

Example: A mad scientist in a loud shirt from his eclectic collection, covered in stains from his experiments.

The Commander

Behavior: Takes command of a situation by efficiently assessing the survival needs of the group and responding to them; plans, enforces, and follows an organized set of style rules to express dominance.

Style: Practical, suits expectations; chooses pieces that mix easily with everything in its place.

Example: A ruler wearing a fur jacket to show power and dominion. Every element is clean, pressed, and in place.

The Ambassador

Behavior: Leads/advocates for others based on personal assessment of the group's emotional needs, prioritizing the feelings/values of the group.

Style: Welcoming, friendly, and appropriate; dresses to make others feel comfortable around them in order to increase their ability to influence. Expressions of personal style are subtle and serve to help the group identify and remember them.

Example: A volunteer ready to work dons a "We can do it" headscarf to rally team spirit.

EXERCISE: EXPLORING THE FIVE SENSES

As you learn these new tools and types, it can be easy to get stuck in your head. Let's get grounded with our senses for this next exercise.

The "ghosting technique" is a valuable form of artistic meditation that helps you discover real people rather than puzzle-piece archetypes. You can use it for a single character, but it can also be used to explore a community or group through the same process. The steps may appear to be simple, but the process of delving into a character is not always an easy one.

1. **Find a quiet place to think, away from any distractions.**
2. **Bring a piece of paper and a pencil.**
3. **Create a worksheet of the five senses, providing a row for each: sound, touch, taste, smell, and sight.**
4. **Imagine your character navigating the world off-screen.**
5. **Write what the character experiences in each of the five senses.**
6. **Use your worksheet to sketch a series of thumbnail costumes.**

To get the most out of ghosting, here are some tips:

- Avoid stereotypes. If you really explore the character in this way, it will ideally go beyond what is expected.
- Imagine the character in an idle state, doing an everyday task, not actively in a narrative or interacting with anyone else.
- Use your gut to inform yourself about a person, not an archetype. Ghosting employs your artist intuition.
- The more you try this form of exploration, the more you'll be able get into your character with ease. It could take five minutes of silence before you can really let your mind and character wander, or it could take much more the first time.
- You can revisit your character again and again in a specific scenario doing a different task to help you fuel more genuine ideas.
- You can also try this technique with a couple other people, focusing on one character. Have everyone close their eyes in a quiet space and take turns describing what each one senses. This will provide others' perspectives to help you expand your understanding of the character.

Senses	
Sound	
Touch	
Taste	
Smell	
Sight	

Tutorial: Ghosting a Necromancer

I asked Josh Wong, a character artist in Los Angeles, to create two versions of the same character using the following prompt.

PROMPT: A young necromancer apprentice trains hard to become the best her city has ever seen.

Senses	
Sight	High apartments, wire fence, yellow grass
Sound	Bass guitar strumming, heels on pavement, a kiss
Touch	Unkempt, cat fur, rusty metal, a punch
Taste	Flavored lip gloss, fried eggs
Smell	Polluted air, bakery, car exhaust

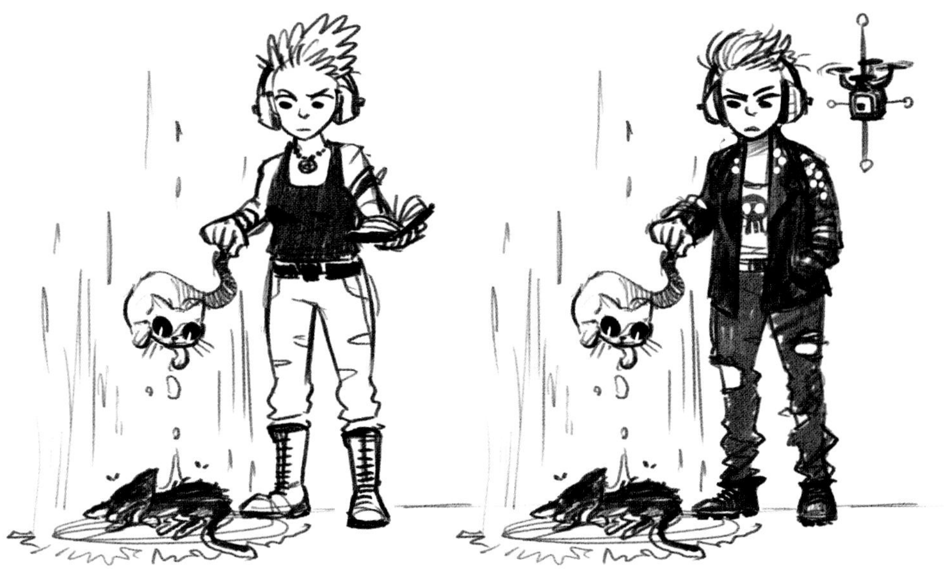

Josh: I think I'm going to change her senses. I don't want a stereotypical punk/goth dark magic girl. Overdone.

Gwyneth: Agreed, but your senses don't have to mean that.

Josh: Maybe she'll be all bubbly and bright colors; it'd be a weird contrast. My senses for her now are kinda gloomy, stereotypical for necromancer. Wouldn't I sense different senses depending on the version? Lower vs. middle class?

Gwyneth: If Ghosting leads you to stereotypes—such as the punky gothy necromancer—then you're doing them wrong. The exercise isn't really about aesthetic so much as character development.

Josh: Yeah. Biases messing with my senses.

Gwyneth: Try again! Don't "choose" to change your senses; let the character speak for herself.

Josh: All I know about her is her environment. Sense from there?

Gwyneth: For example, the best way for me to do this is to imagine them in an idle state, not actively in a narrative. Like an everyday task, not interacting with anyone else.

Josh: Ok.

Gwyneth: Ghosting is what brings your artist intuition back in the game—everything else is analytical pattern recognition. Ghosting allows you to step away from that and use your gut to inform yourself about a *person*, not an archetype. Step away from her environment, and think just about *her*—not her job, not her time period, not her environment.

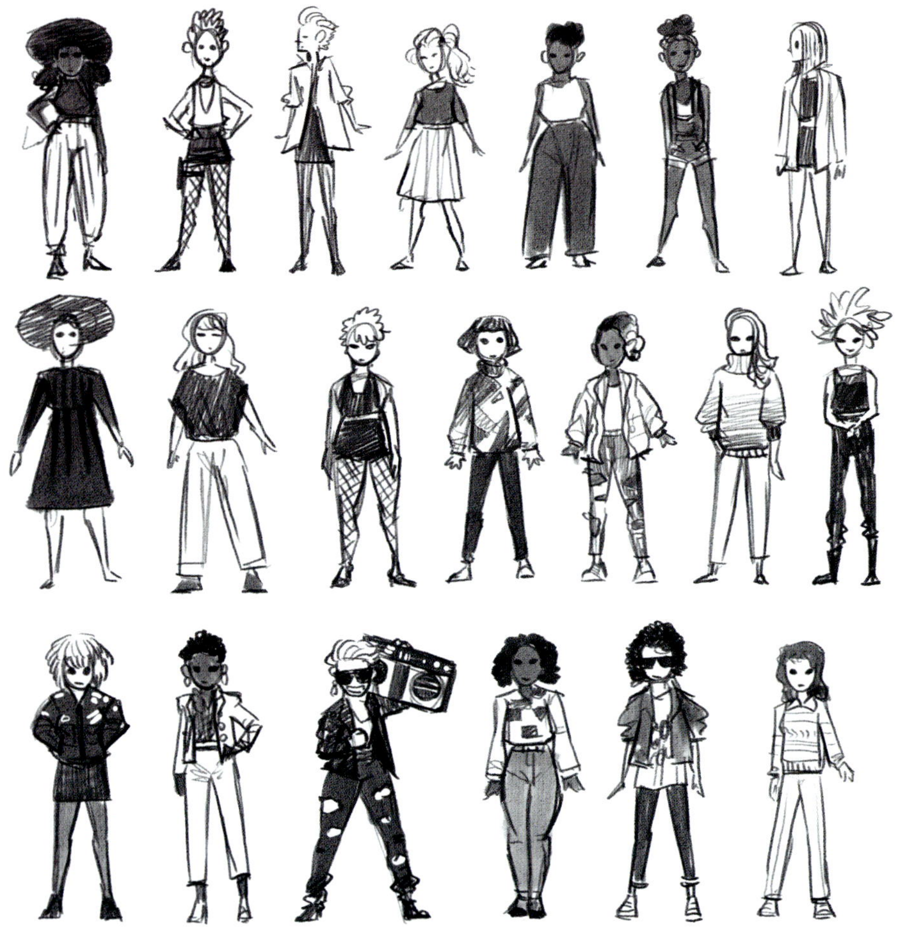

Josh: But she's a blank slate now. I just make up senses that feel right?

Gwyneth: No; she's not blank. She's just a girl, waiting for the bus, or whatever. Try to imagine her before the story has even started. It's more like you're allowing yourself to go a little blank, and letting that person manifest in your head. If she bubbles up in your head doing some task you hadn't expected, then you're probably on the right track. Think of it like artist meditation.

Josh: OK. I'll put on my headphones and ambience.

Gwyneth: I did this exercise for a witch character that lives in a swamp, and she "manifested" filing her nails on the porch. LOL. It was the witch from Hansel and Gretel, so that action is definitely not part of the story, but it's part of the person, and that's equally important.

Josh: Haha cool. Ok. Go blank. Imagine her doing idle things. Don't force the story on her.

Gwyneth: You work well with patterns and analysis as a designer. It's your chance to find the gut instinct part that you already use but just don't know how to control. It's one reason why young artists have good days and bad days without a lot of consistency in the quality of their ideas.

Josh: I see.

Gwyneth: The first dozen times you do this, it'll be much harder and take longer. For me it takes about five minutes of silence to really feel out, and then sometimes I'll return to whatever task I manifested them in and it'll fuel some more genuine ideas later in the process as well.

Josh: Ok.

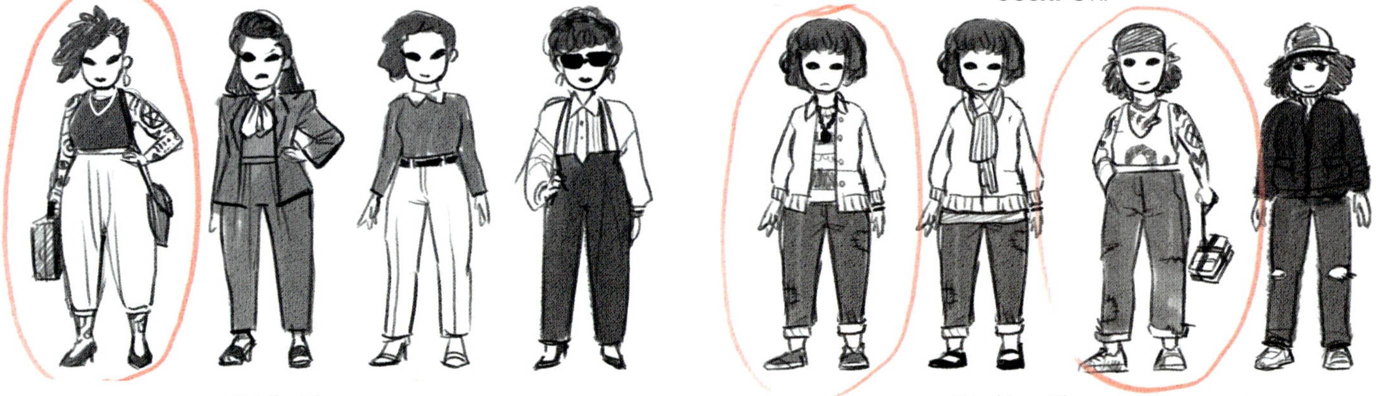

Middle Class

Working Class

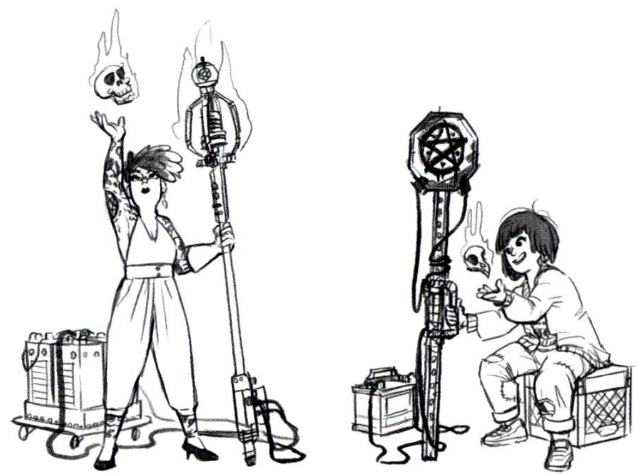

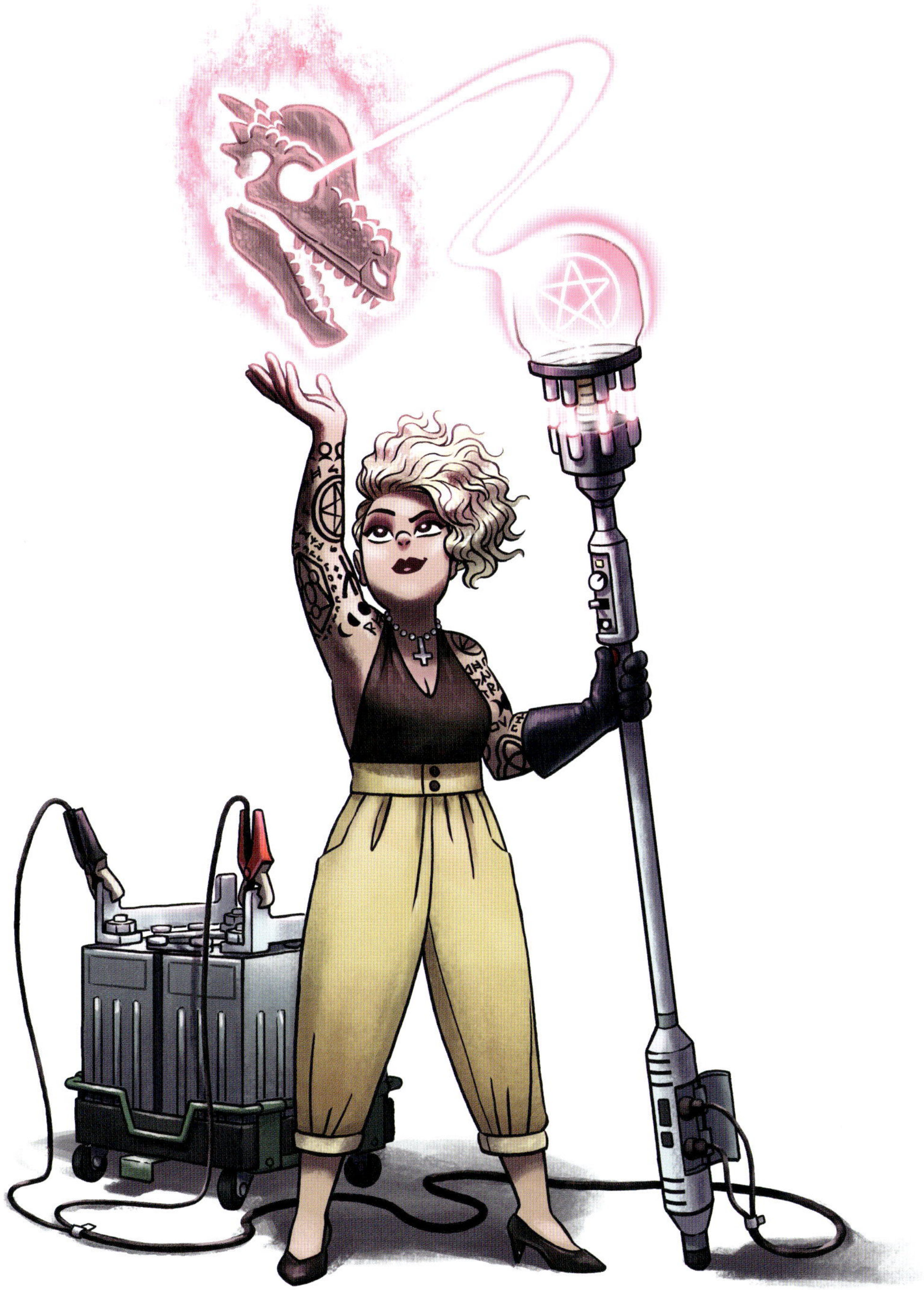

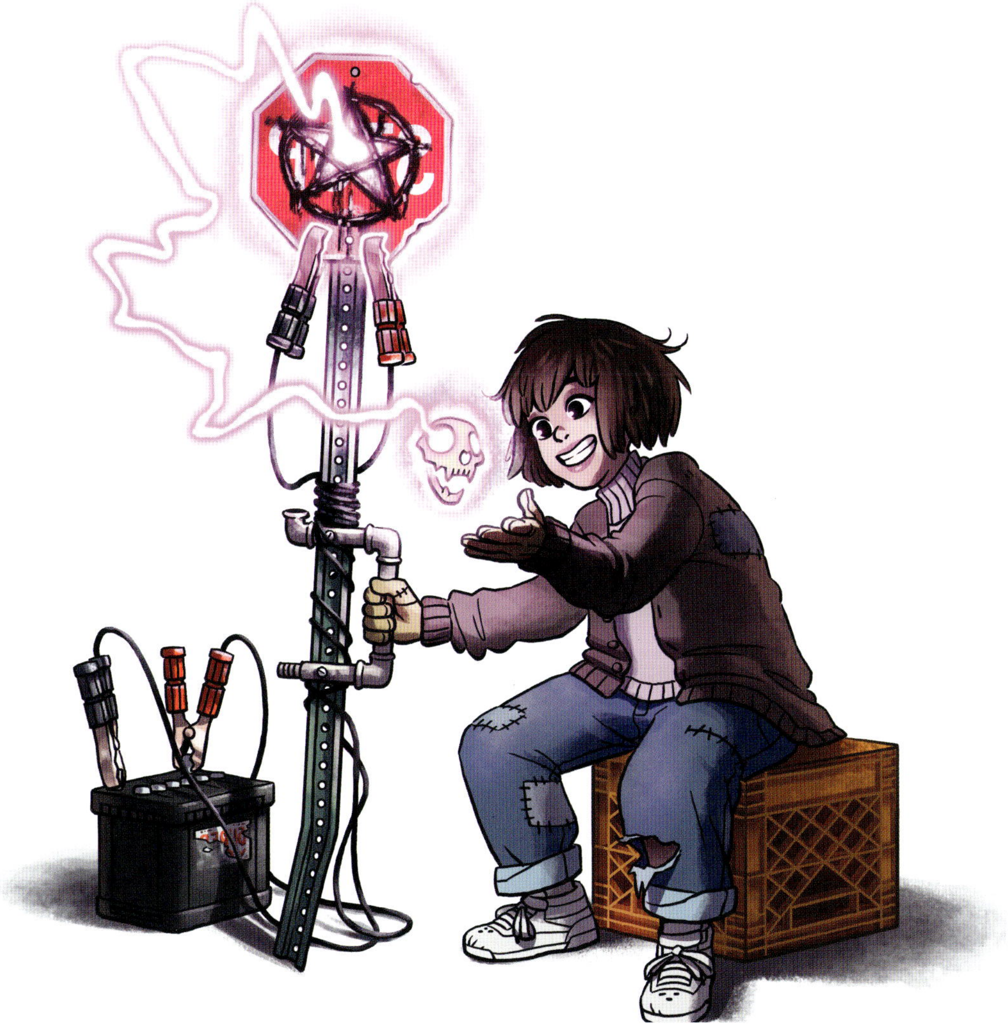

EXERCISE: THE OUTSIDER

Now it's your turn. Try this technique with this prompt: **An aging male cowboy** visiting a new town. Close your eyes and think about the character you're designing. Put yourself in his shoes during the moments the "camera" isn't on him to learn more about his personality. That means not him riding a bronco or in a shootout; instead, he should be still and quiet, just like you are.

Soon after, he'll start to move. He'll do a task you weren't expecting or that you can't quite decipher yet. Now you can start to really sense the person behind the character you want to create a costume for. If you really want to design the first time the audience sees a character, you need to know who the person was before the story began. This exercise is an attempt to see the person without the burden of story. If you approach your design in this way, the character's transformation during their journey will be even more impactful.

Imagine he's about to explore his surroundings. Let your imagination run free rather than chase preconceived ideas. Sound usually comes first. Shuffling, rustling clothes, a sniffle. Be patient for the specific sounds and record them on your paper.

Touch, taste, and smell come next. Interestingly enough, sight should be one of the last things you explore and the most difficult. Sight isn't usually a specific object, but a texture, element, or atmospheric light. If you see that cowboy's horse or spurs, you haven't quite hit the sweet spot. Breathe, clear your mind, and try again.

By the end, you may even be able to feel the character's weight, the creak of his bones, the texture of his skin and hair, how comfortable his shoes are on your own feet. In a way, you become that person's ghost. If this process comes slowly at first, that's alright. Be patient and let it wash over you. It's a more natural experience for those with a performance background. If you have never performed before, you may find it frustrating to start because giving up conscious control is uncomfortable. Many artists feel like they have to push the character into acting. In these cases, practice patience. Once your mind starts to creatively wander (not thinking about grocery lists or doing laundry), you're more likely to be surprised by the character.

Reference your worksheet as you develop some costume designs. Ghosting isn't for everyone, but if it works for you, it will help you develop stronger empathy for your characters, and a more personal connection to their lives and story.

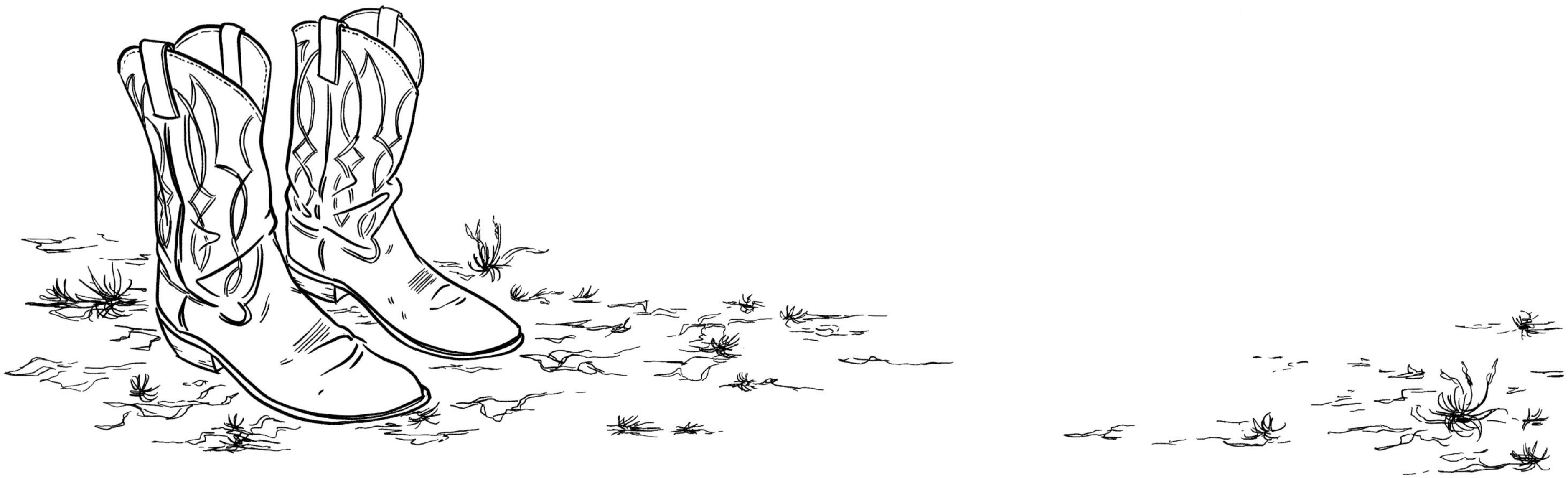

Incorporating Basic Instincts

However civilized your characters are, at their core, they will also feel an internal pull toward an animal instinct to guarantee their survival as they pursue their goals. These instincts may manifest in unique ways: a peacock uses its feathers to attract a mate, a chameleon camouflages itself into its environment, or an ape relies on a group. Think of human behavior that compares to these practices and consider which animal instincts your character will need to rely on more to survive their world and achieve their goal; incorporate them into your design.

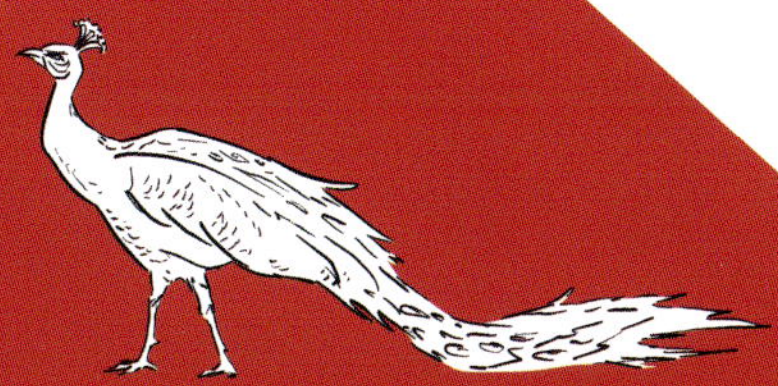

SEXUAL (THE HUNTER)

The sexual instinct compels a person to find and merge with another to create something that will continue their existence, whether it is a child or an idea. Navigating the world with a "you and me vs. the world" mentality, a character driven by this instinct is good at synchronizing with others, supporting, and noticing when someone else is off.

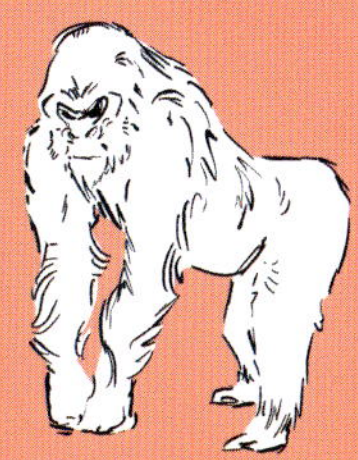

SOCIAL (THE TRIBESPERSON)

The social instinct compels your character to merge with and rely on a group network to access what they need to survive. Concerned with the health and status of her community (tribe), gossip becomes key to knowing what and who is safe, dangerous, desirable, and so on.

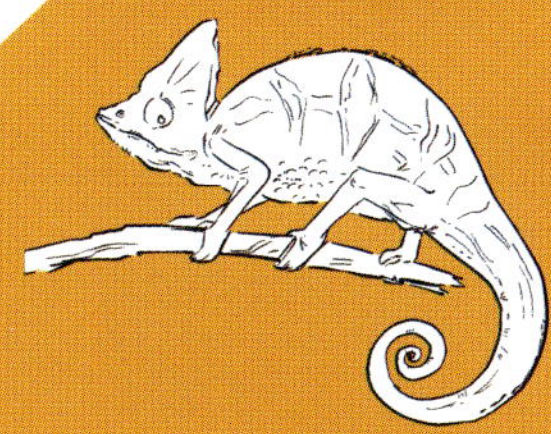

SELF-PRESERVATION (THE SURVIVALIST)

Self-preservation compels your character to rely more on themself, but will join communities to access shelter, food, energy, clothing, money, security, and other resources for basic physical survival. Survivalists monitor their surroundings for potential danger and blend in with their physical environment to feel safe.

Hunters use clothing, like a peacock's feathers, to draw a potential partner to them. They seek chemistry and stimulation so alluring styles or styling is intended to charm those that they are attracted to. **Keywords:** intense, strong eye contact, presence, attractive, stands out, romantic, intimate, impactful, appealing.

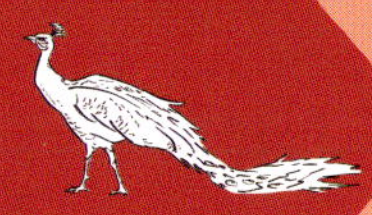

Tribespeople wear clothing that draws the attention and acceptance of their desired network, which means matching with other members of the tribe and following the popular styles. The nature of the chosen tribe will determine the style, so a social instinct can manifest in anything from a business suit or a team jersey to a furry suit. **Keywords:** talkative, watches everyone's moves, knows everyone's name, protects the group, host/hostess.

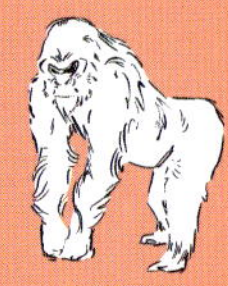

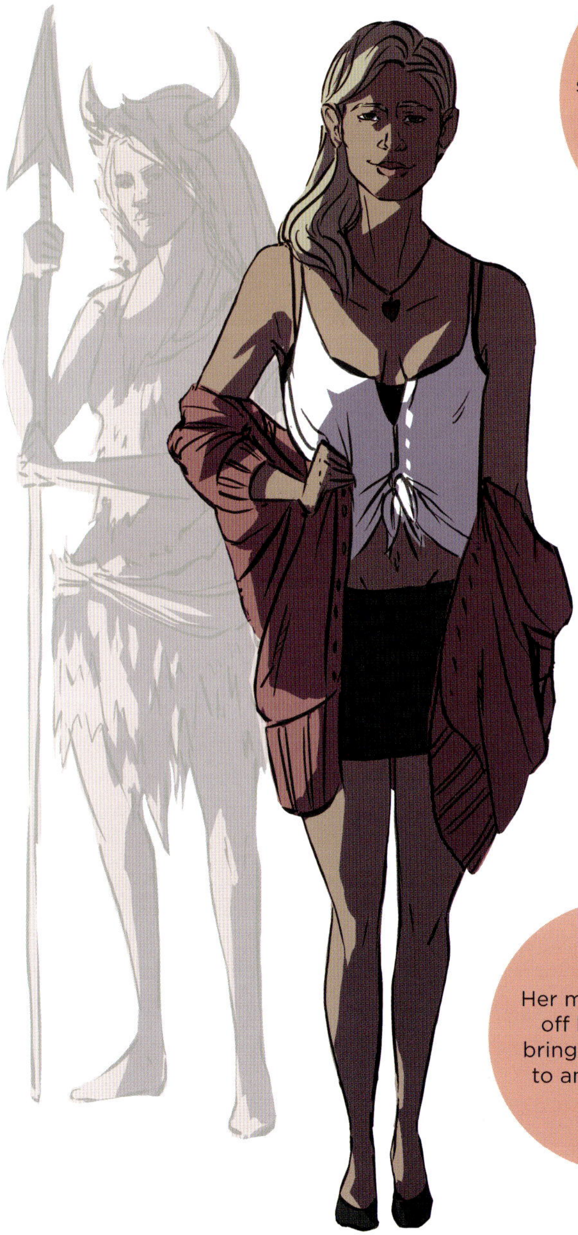

Her hair is pulled to the side, over her shoulder, emphasizing its health and length, and bringing attention to her collarbone.

Her top exposes her bra strap and teases her bra, bringing attention to curves and toned body, with the intention to attract a healthy partner.

The sweater is worn loosely to add movement and to tease a reveal; it is an element that can easily be taken off.

Her miniskirt shows off her legs and brings attention up to an erotic zone.

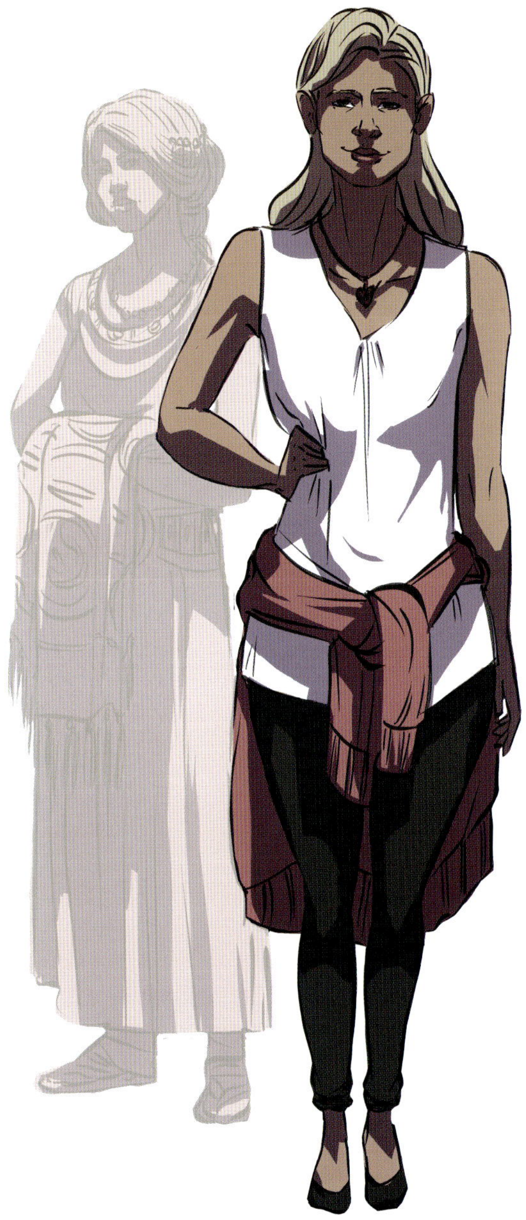

Her hairstyle is relaxed but styled to frame her face and disarm others.

A versatile, white, sleeveless blouse of wrinkle-free polyester blend expresses her minimalistic style while also allowing her to easily layer or accessorize to tailor for multiple social situations: from work to a date to hosting a party at her house.

A pair of black fitted slacks, or yoga pants, gives her the flexibility to modify her look easily.

Survivalists use clothing as a barrier to outside forces and to provide them with a sense of comfort. They can find confidence through covering up more vulnerable areas or dressing to suit the changing needs of their environment. **Keywords:** adaptable, reserved, walled off, practical, careful.

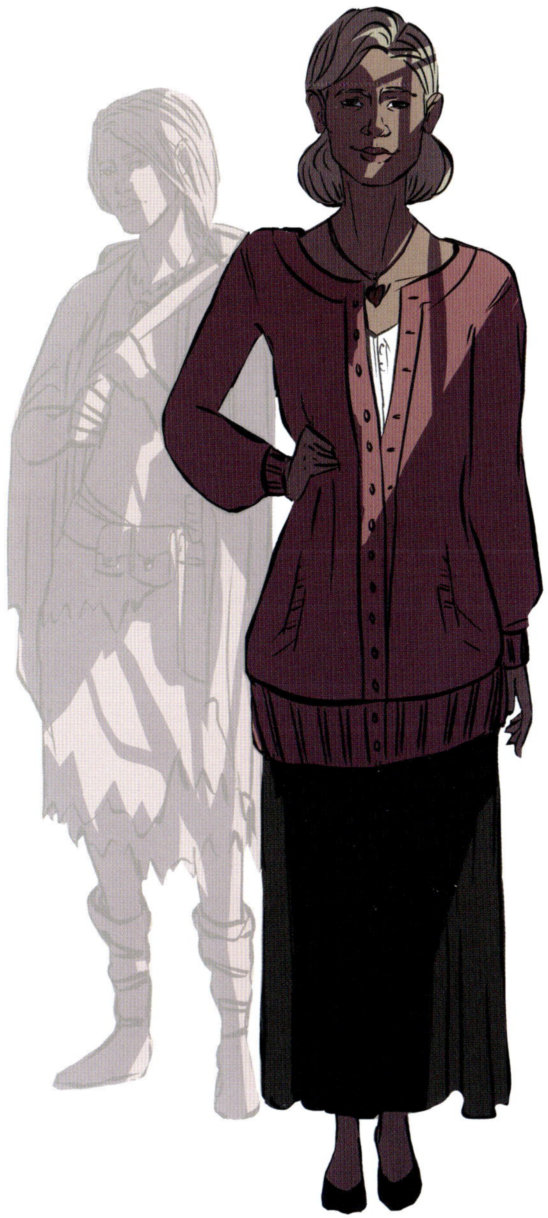

Her hair is pulled back in a safe conservative bun.

All buttoned up, the oversized sweater makes her figure less visible and hides vulnerable areas.

The outfit is layered in comfortable separates that make her feel ready for anything, protected, and sheltered when she is away from home.

Her skirt covers her legs completely and only exposes her ankles. It also emphasizes her traditional femininity to attract a conservative protector.

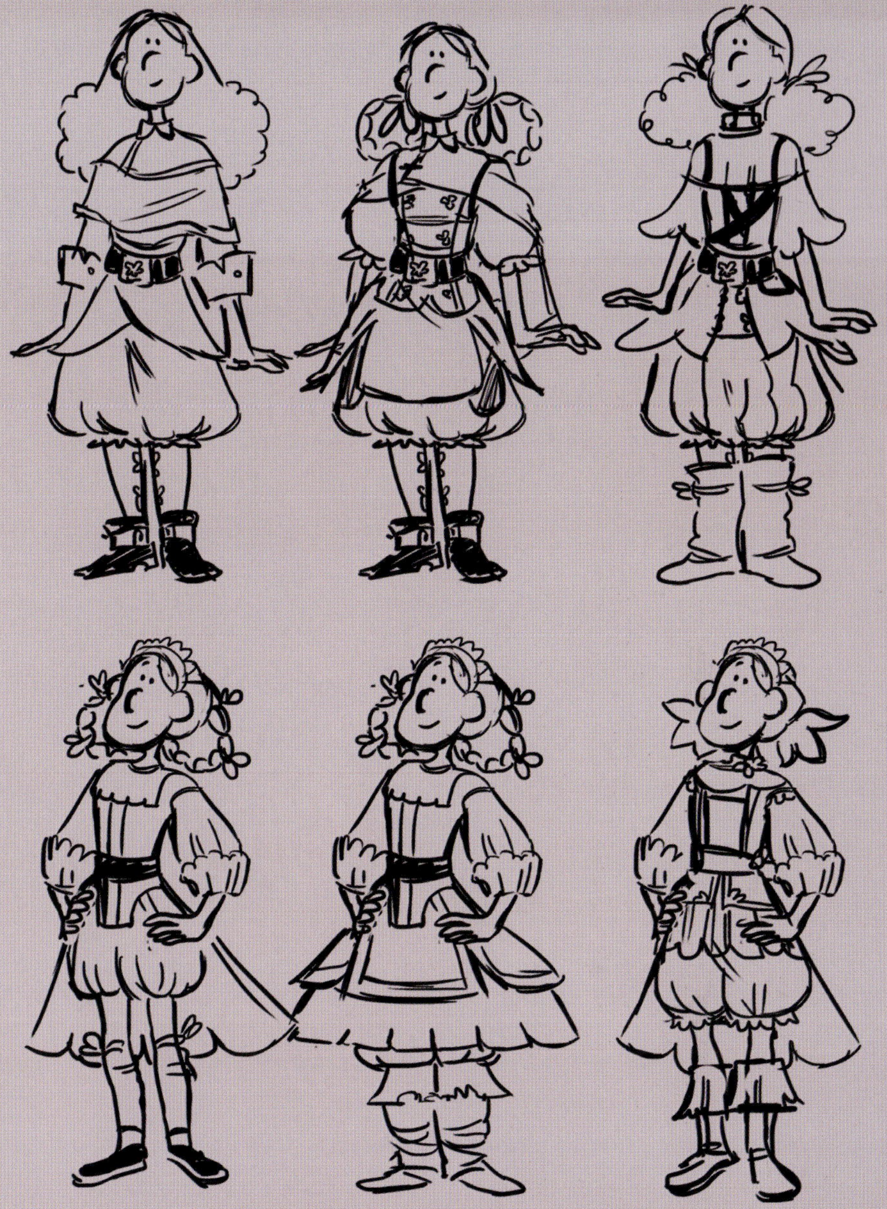

TIP:

You may want or need to caricature one motivation, trait, or instinct for your narrative, but remember, as humans, we use all of these to survive. Adding narratively driven details that allude to more than one will give you more room for subtle visual subtext.

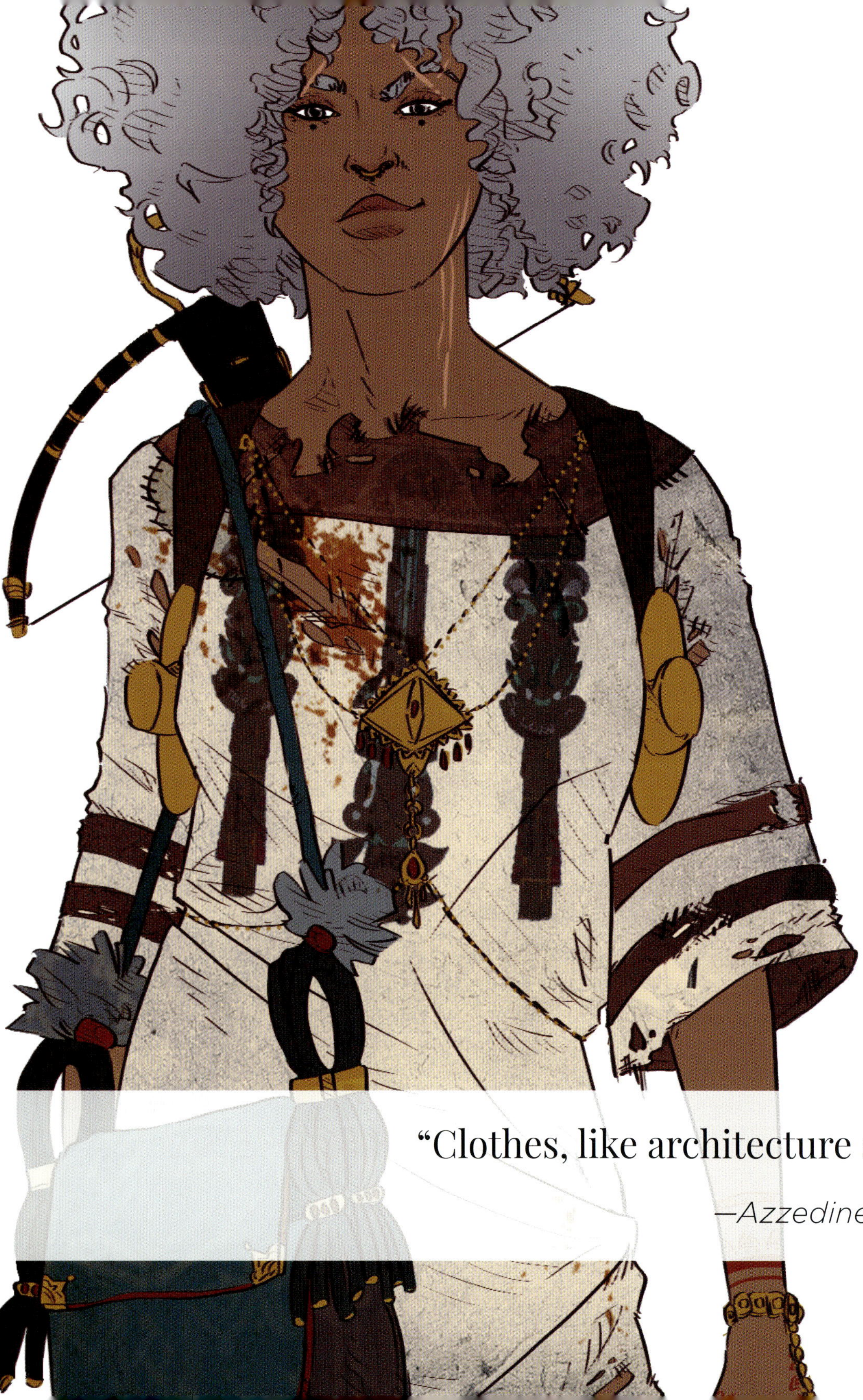

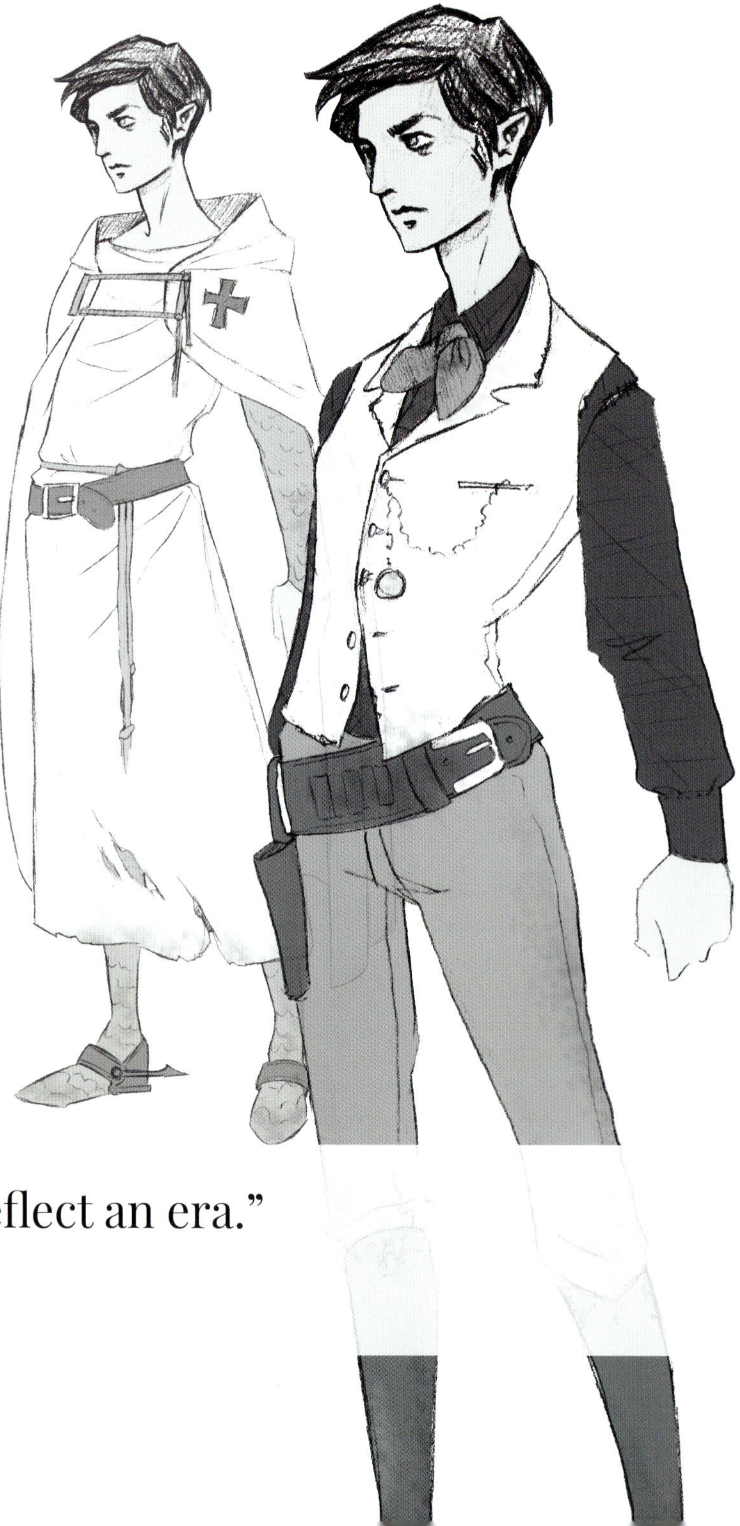

"Clothes, like architecture and art, reflect an era."

—Azzedine Alaïa

CHAPTER 5 PASSAGE OF TIME

Whether a story takes place over the course of an hour, a day, or centuries, a costume can indicate a passage of time. Even if your production doesn't have a budget for multiple costume changes, you can find ways for the costume to change through lighting, color, textural wear and tear, the manipulation of layers, the use of props to change the overall effect, or by changing its relationship to the characters around them in a scene.

In the 2004 animated film *The Incredibles,* Mr. Incredible is an aging superhero and father of three. When he attempts to return to his crime-fighting glory days, he faces an unexpected foe . . . his belt. While his stretchy suit is forgiving of his growing waistline, he battles to close his tightened belt. This not only offers a comedic moment but also reinforces how long he has been out of action.

Here are other examples that reflect specific stretches of time.

MINUTES	**In the 1997 action comedy *Men in Black*, Agent J's suit is covered in amniotic slime when he helps deliver an alien baby.**
HOURS	**An episode of the British sitcom *IT Crowd* (2006-2013) features the character Jen obsessed with wearing a pair of flattering heels, but they only come in a very small size. She hobbles through the day, determined to keep wearing them despite the growing pain.**
DAYS	**In 1993's action film *Jurassic Park,* each character's outfit shows the wear and tear, dirt and grime, of days running for their lives from genetically created dinosaurs.**
YEARS	**The drama series *Downton Abbey* (2010-2015) follows a group of characters' lives and fashion trends between 1912 and 1925.**
CENTURIES	**Stories about vampires (*Being Human* TV series, 2008-2013, and *What We Do in the Shadows* TV series, 2019), time travelers (*Back to the Future* trilogy, 1985-1990 and *Time Machine* by H. G. Wells), or reincarnation, (*Cloud Atlas* by David Mitchell) may span centuries over the course of a production.**

Honoring Period Dress and Norms

We modify the shape of our bodies in different ways to make a statement, and the shape language of every period is embedded with the zeitgeist of the time.

On the left, we see a lady wearing a corset. It brings the breasts up, tightens the thorax and waist, creating the hourglass silhouette of the Victorian period. In 1906, designer Paul Poiret popularized abandoning the corset, resulting in the familiar Edwardian silhouette. Without the corset, the silhouette is less curvy. The breast line is the natural height and the shape of the thorax-waist-hips is not forced or exaggerated like in the Victorian period.

These shape changes not only accommodated the increased mobility needed after the industrial revolution, they also reflected a period of enlightenment that moved society to embrace a more intellectual, youthful, or androgynous figure—replacing the hourglass shape that enhanced the sexual (and therefore fertile) shapes of female, tying them to the home and more conservative philosophies.

An elderly character may prefer the shapes and ideals of the past, a disenfranchised character may be limited to older items from thrift stores, and the nobility may glorify the timeless designs. Trendsetters may even flip the past and present on its head by creating entirely new shapes. Or you may choose to manipulate the body in other ways, not just emphasizing what is the gender ideal, but also minimizing or inverting it—compare a corset that highlights the bust-waist-hips ratio to a binder that flattens everything.

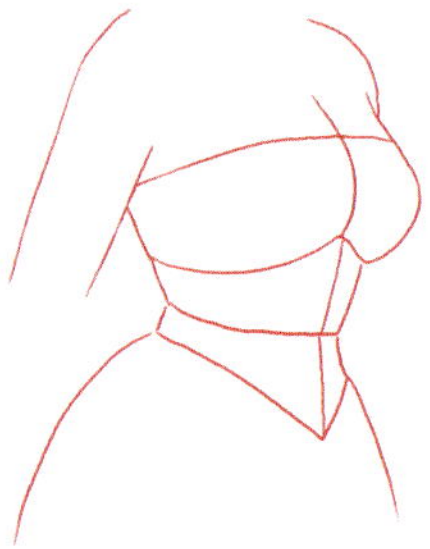

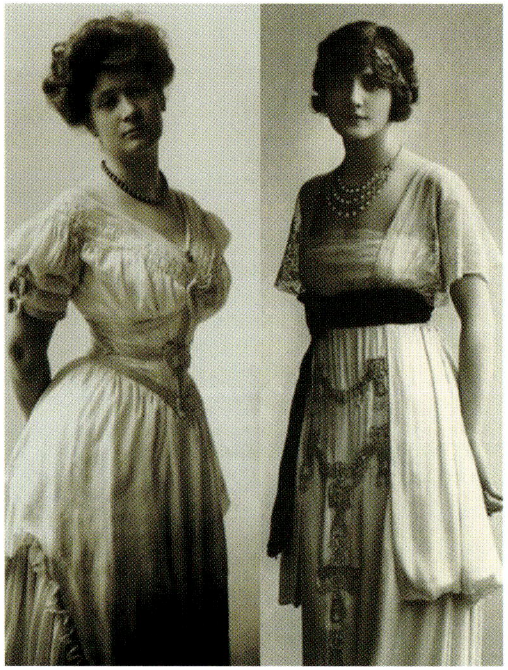

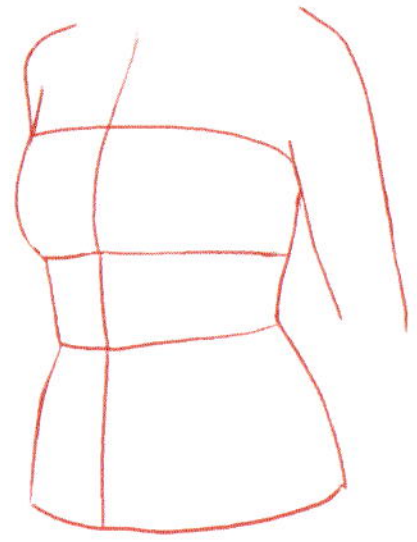

Ima Hogg, photography studio identified as The Elliotts, Austin, TX, 1900

Lily Elsie, photo by Margareta "Rita" Weir Martin

Exercise: Compare and Contrast Fashion Eras

1) Create two costume designs of a character from a familiar fairy tale such as Cinderella. Without referencing any images, set one in 1779 and one in 1799. Now create new versions of these costumes, this time using reference from a reliable museum or book. What is the difference? How does it impact your impression of the character and story? Observe the fit and movement of the costume. Is it consistent with the time period?

2) Compare the popular styles during Queen Victoria's reign (1837–1901) and early 1950s American fashion. Create a fashion board to show the similarities. Did they share silhouettes, a certain hemline, use of material, or specific accessories? Why?

Changing the shapes you use changes the context of the world. And by showing the influence of the past in your world, you create a richer narrative tapestry.

A believable silhouette is created by an internal structure: the framework inside of or underneath a garment that provides the foundational shape. This foundational shape also influences the range of motion that a character has—either to limit or emphasize.

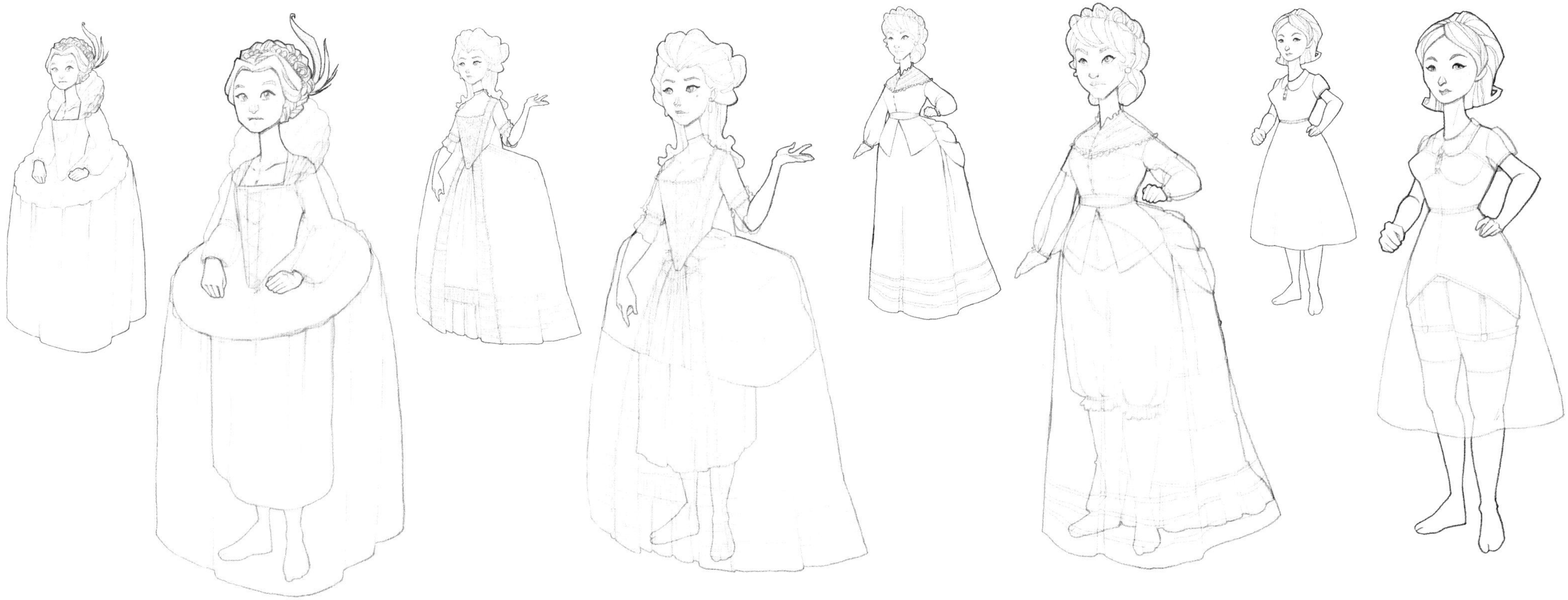

SFX TIP:

Each period has its own list of undergarments necessary to achieve their particular look. Petticoats, stays, hosiery, all apply. Knowing the construction and nature of the under layers will help you know what the character will look like if layers are discarded or damaged. In Disney's *Cinderella*, the dress that her animal friends make for her to attend the ball has a layered skirt. When Cinderella's stepsisters tear the dress apart, the viewer sees one of the under layers exposed.

Exercise: Silhouettes Through the Ages

Design an article of formal clothing for a character living during a certain era, for instance, a Regency dress that was popular from 1795–1820. Research and identify the layers used for your costume by looking at fashion history. Just be careful of referencing more modern underwear and fabrication techniques when you are creating a period piece. They will not give you the same results as bustle cages, panniers, starched petticoats, shoulder supports, chemises, and so forth.

Regency "stays" are there to hold assets up and usually separate them. The cups come up to mid-bust level, and the breasts are contained within the chemise. They look unnatural and high.

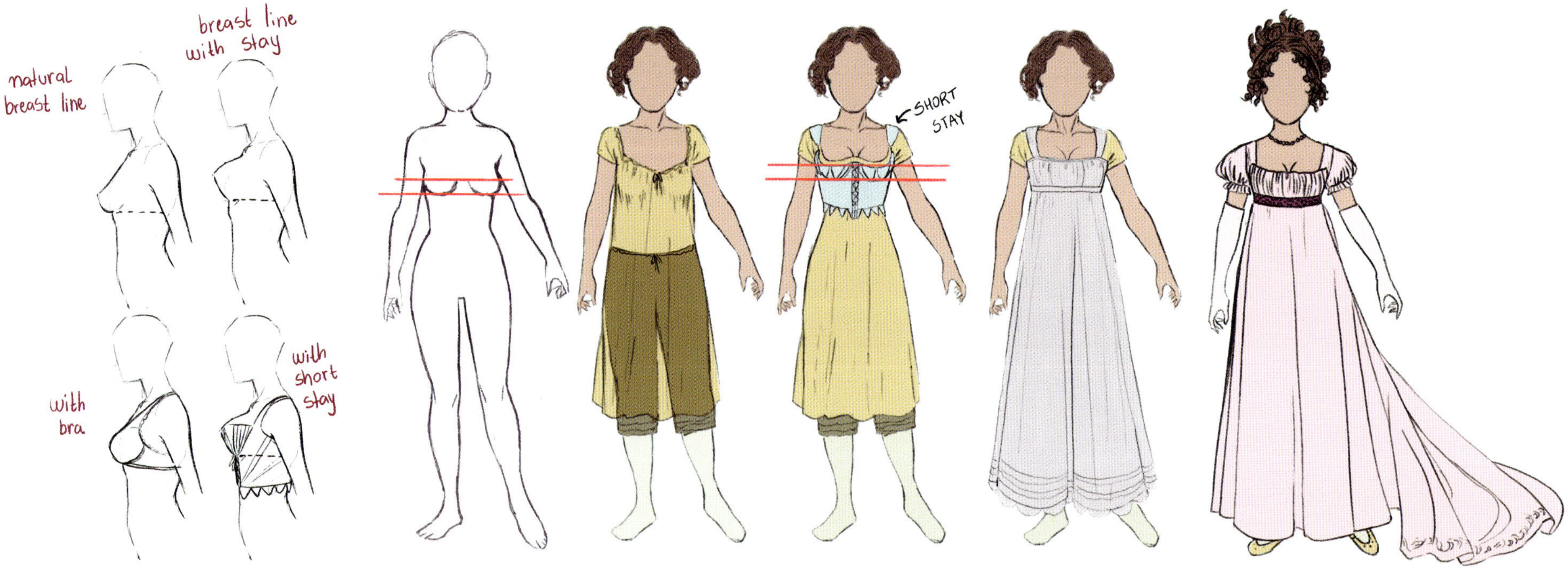

Next, create a sketch breaking down the layers of your chosen piece to better understand how the outer silhouette is affected by the layers below it. Why and how did each shape evolve from the previous one? What historical events and/or people influenced each change in silhouette?

> When you design or animate a costume, understanding and/or designing the internal structure of the costume is just as important as designing the outside.

Finding Relevant Reference

Until the 20th century, the clothing people wore was actually referred to as "costume." Pieces were customized to the client's taste, and the maker was not known as a fashion designer, they were simply a dressmaker. Fashion designers as we know them today have only existed since the makers began what was then considered radical: creating clothing that reflected their own personal vision and perception of the world, and inviting consumers to wear their brand or style.

As designers for narrative, we need to think beyond what a fashion designer does. Our designs are customized to the production and cast, specifically the protagonist. It is not our own perception of the world we are selling, it is the protagonist's, the director's, or even that of a culture. Referencing current fashion trends may make sense for a modern story where we are capturing our protagonist's or society's fixation on certain brand identities for example, but it will fail us if we depend on it too heavily. Even when you look to the past, to costume history, it is necessary to find the broad trends and context of the designs to identify themes.

Copying from a historical painting may give you a sense of the time, but it lacks the narrative meaning. Remember, those designs were created for an individual in history, not custom designed for your character or narrative.

Exercise: Personal Costume Journal

Use your sketchbook or journal to note your observations and impressions of your daily outfits. Observe those around you and imagine the motivations or histories behind the outfits of others. Create a rich reference library of outfit personalities and details to utilize.

You can even reach back into your history, noting any of the memorable outfits of your life. Record how they changed and evolved alongside you, how you felt when you wore them, and note any standout highlights that come out of that. You can write, sketch, dig through old photographs—whatever it takes to get a good landscape of your personal fashion history.

Now draw a linear timeline of your style from childhood to adulthood. For example, you can use your most memorable outfits from five-year increments or choose times in your life where you experienced major changes. As you draw, note the patterns. Did a style or element of clothing repeat more than once or disappear dramatically when your style changed? Why? Gather your insights and sketches to tell a short story about a time of personal transformation through a lineup of outfits.

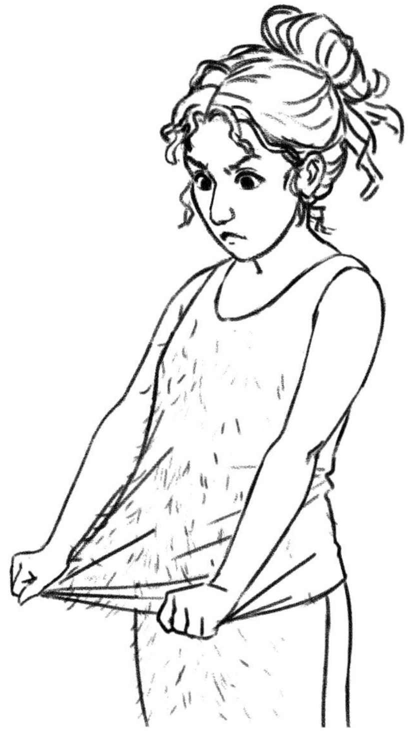

Wear and Tear

Something we commonly see in student portfolios are "shiny characters": designs and renders that are like toys right out of the packaging, brand spankin' new. It's not the worst thing in the world—such assets can be useful for identifying the "default" example or might be needed for marketing purposes (promotional artwork). But how do you combat that kind of blandness in your final design? Consider the character's preference.

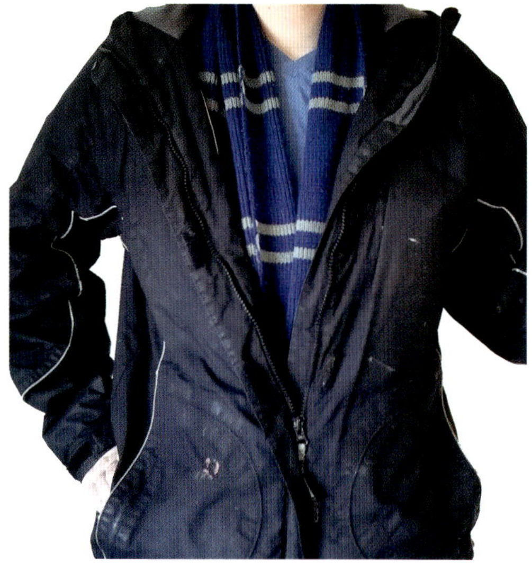

Think about Merida, the main character in Pixar's 2012 animated film *Brave.* There is a distinct difference in how she, the warrior protagonist, wears her everyday green dress and the formal blue gown. There is a comfort level she has established in her favorite frock that visibly changes when forced into the other. Instead of conforming to the occasion and restrictive dress, she rebels by splitting the seams.

Now think about your favorite coat or hoodie. Where did you get it? How long have you had it? Why is it your favorite? Is it too big or too small? Have you noticed the color fading over hundreds of washes? Has the zipper broken from all the times you've tugged it too quickly? Has someone tried to repair it for you? How successful were they? Does it have a meaningful saying or image on it? Are there iron-on patches or clipped-on flashy pins? Does it smell like your gym socks? Do you wrap it around your waist when you realize it's too hot? Would you go out tomorrow and buy a new one? A different one?

Exploring what makes an item unique or meaningful will help pinpoint specific qualities of the garment that make it stand out from one off the rack.

DID YOU KNOW?

A standard pair of jeans will show wear in different locations than a pair of fashion jeans. Fashion jeans with pre-created wear points place them for aesthetics, whereas standard jeans will wear due to natural use. Can you guess which is which? Make sure to reference the relevant wear and tear for your character. A cowboy with fashionable wear points can create an interesting story but will interrupt the immersion if it's unintentional.

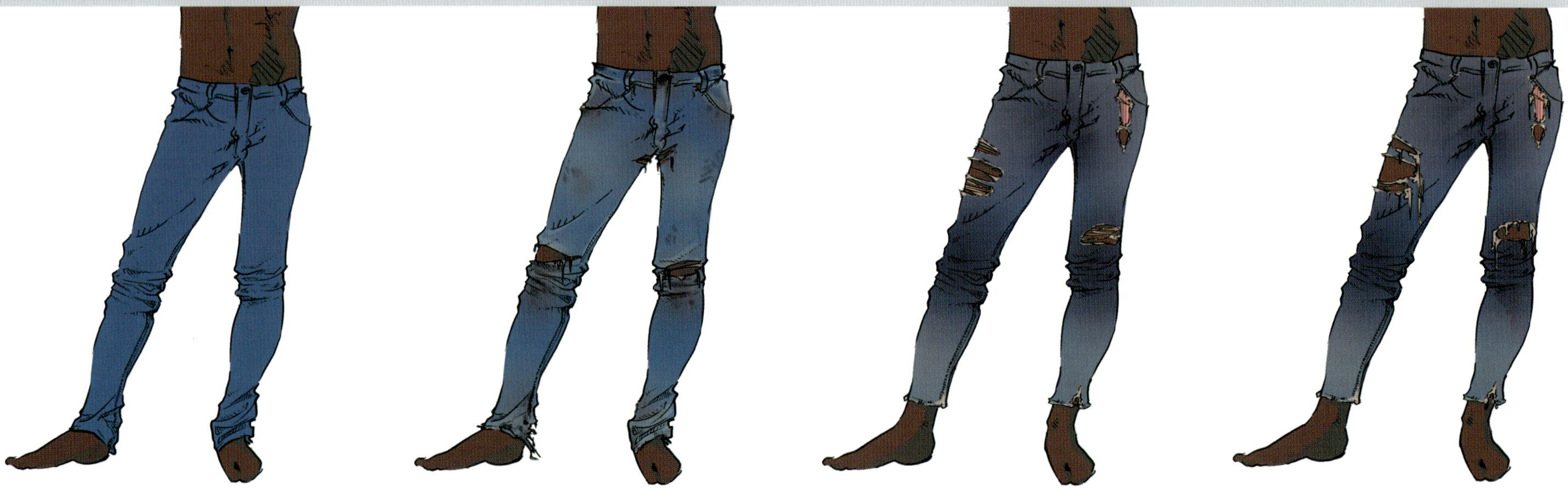

Status Effects (FX) Are Plot Effects

Materials rarely exist in a vacuum and are usually affected by one or multiple status effects during the course of the narrative. A commonly neglected pass, the condition of materials adds a level of immersion into the world and plot that would otherwise halt your audience's suspension of disbelief. Status FX can be permanent, resulting in an evolution of the character, or temporary, fading with time or until washed or repaired/replaced.

When adding detail, it's possible to go overboard. Ask yourself: *Does this help the story, or is it just fluff?*

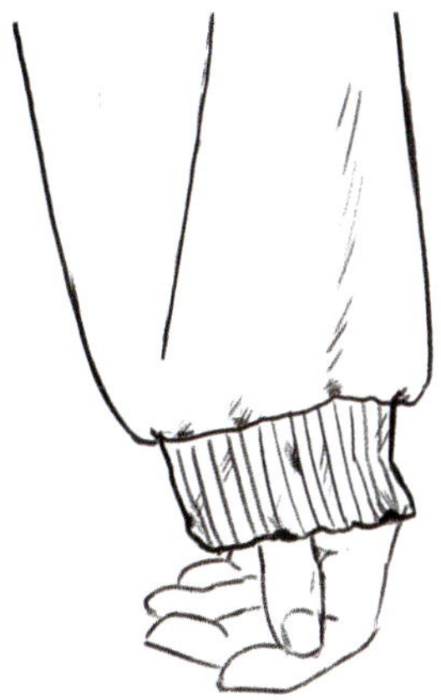

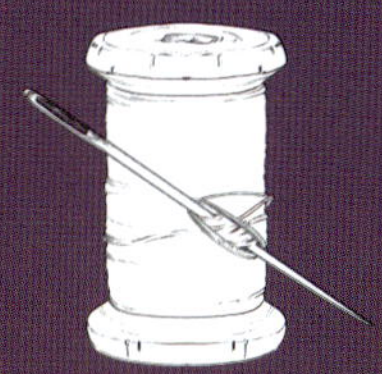

BEHAVIORAL

Wrinkles
Food Stains
Customization
Patches/Repairs

Conflict:
- Tears/Puncturing
- Blood (Old/New)

Common Wear Points (Fraying/Dents):
- Knees
- Heels
- Toes
- Hems
- Elbows

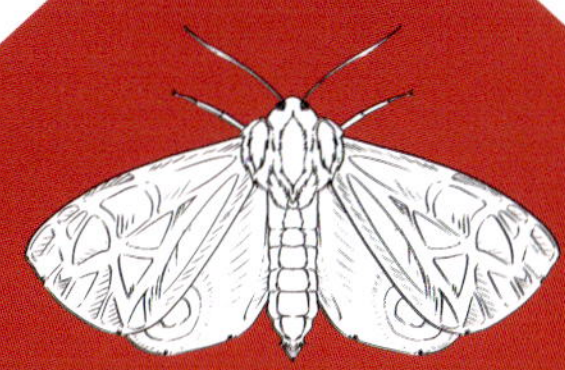

ENVIRONMENTAL

Dirt/Dust
Mud
Rain
Snow
Plant Debris
Insects (Moths)
Charring/Melting

Time:
- Light/Color Fastness
- Rusting
- Fiber Integrity

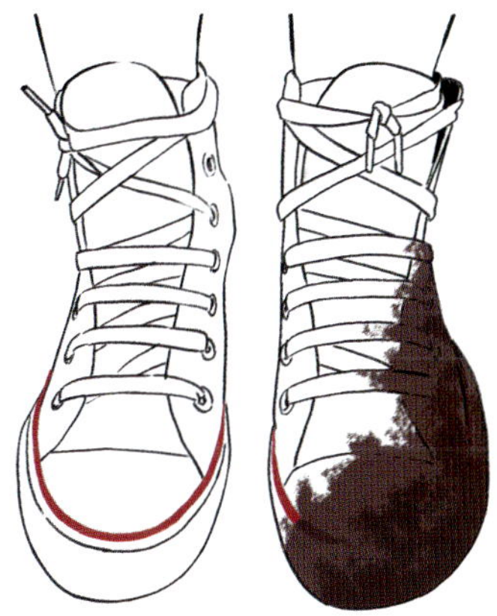

These effects are a direct result of the character's actions or personality, such as Sue's baking adventure on Monday. She wanted to make cookies but found the flour getting away from her and the bowl. Her little apron is wrinkled from where she wiped her hands and a bit stained with the sticky dough.

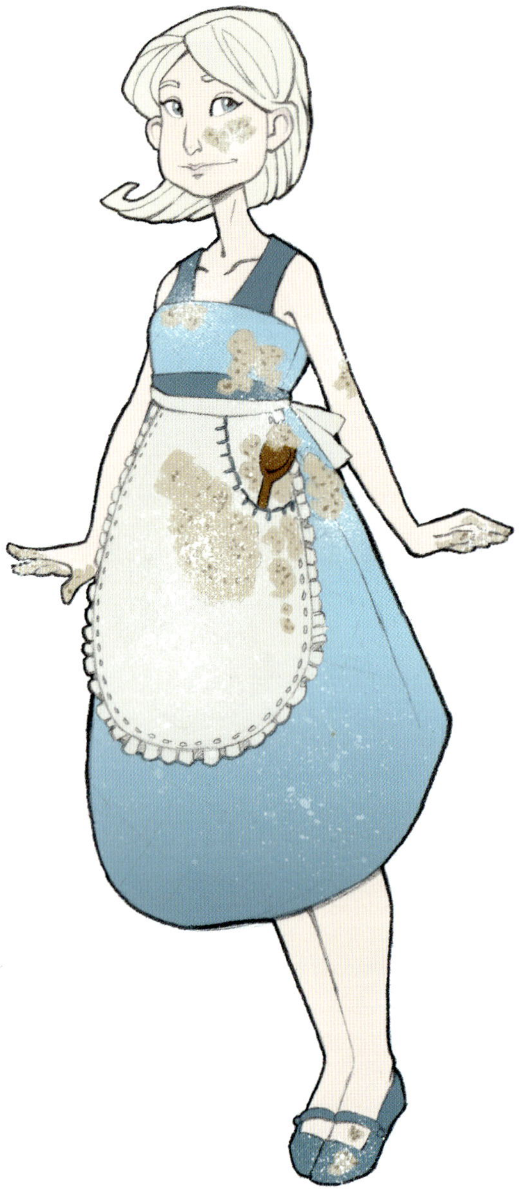

Effects that are caused by others or external forces, such as Sue's unfortunate run-in with zombies, resulting in her zombification.

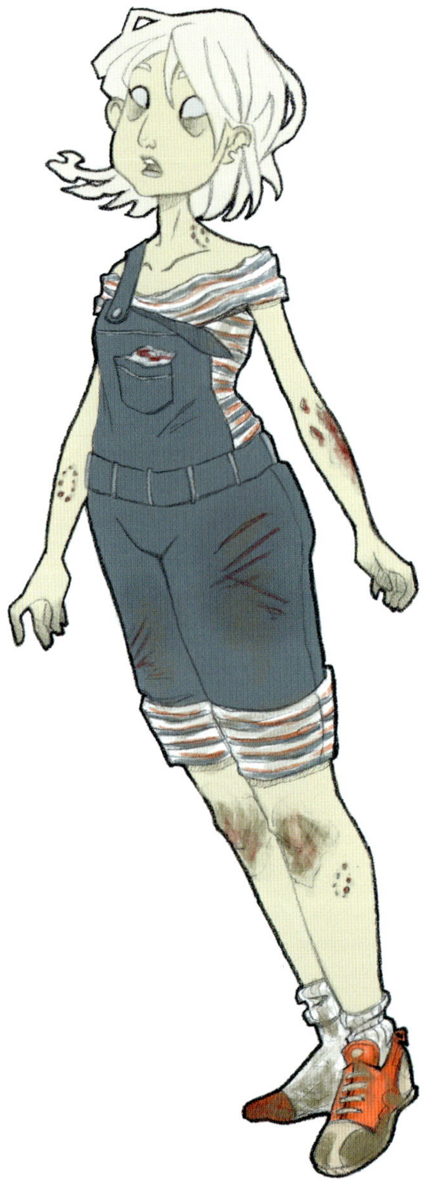

ENVIRONMENTAL

These are caused by external forces of the nature variety, such as Sue's gardening adventure on Wednesday. Her white socks were the first casualty, and then her poor knees, which are starting to wear through. Her gloves are covered with dirt and weed residue, which no doubt will never come out, but at least her carrots are safe.

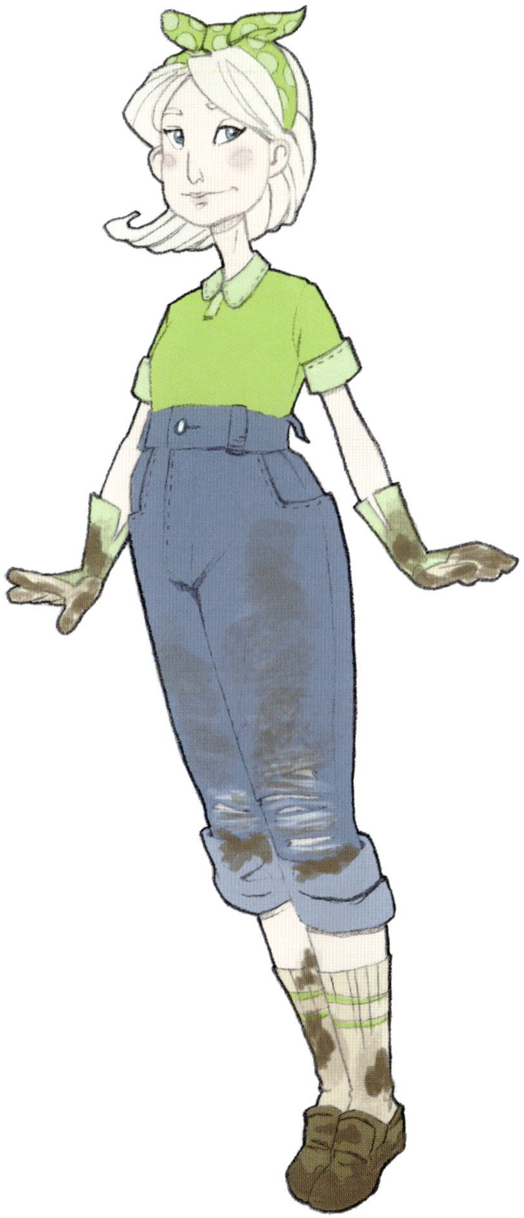

AGING

Effects that are caused from the passage of time and continued use, such as Sue's mending adventure on Thursday. Her black shirt was a hand-me-down from her older sister and has been washed a good number of times. Whites and blacks are notorious for discoloring quickly. The pattern on her hem is starting to pull apart as well. A failing seam has been repaired.

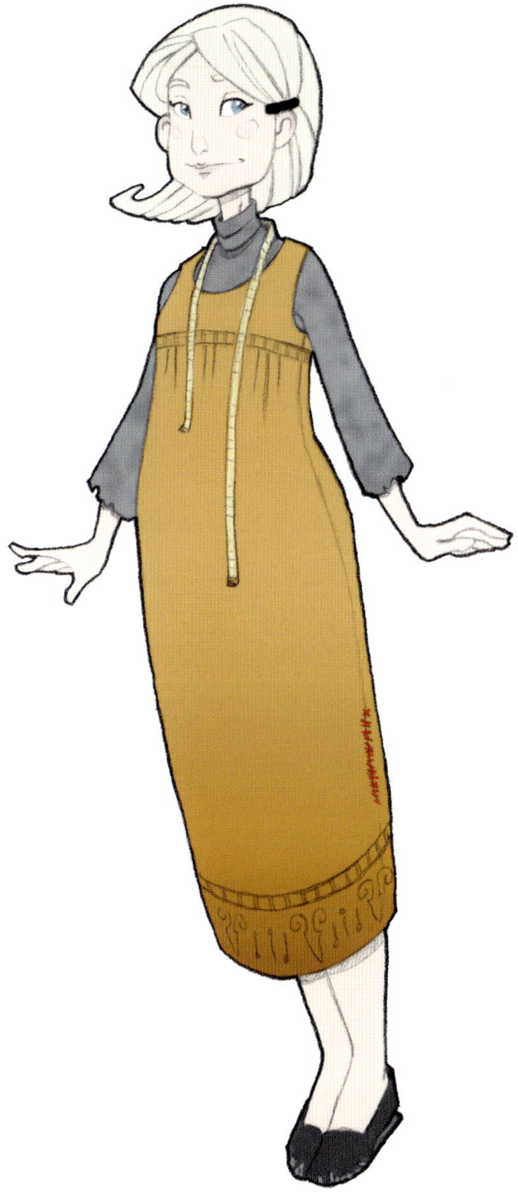

Exercise: Script Breakdown (Visual Development)

When you're handed a script, remember to break it down into scenes and shots. Highlight in various colors if necessary. Then create a spreadsheet to track or map your character's journey and technical needs throughout the production to use as a reference when determining what assets you need to build. This will help you avoid having to go back to the literal drawing board mid-production. Don't be afraid to make several passes through the script to get all the information you need organized.

The spreadsheet can include the following categories:

Scene/shot: Timing of scene
Version: Status FX, the state of the character's clothing
Action: Behavior involved
Notes: Any other special info that would need attention

Let's take a generic Sunbonnet Sue tale "Saturday Visit" with added detail about the state of her clothes.

SCENE / SHOT	VERSION	ACTION	NOTES
1200.0280	Dry	Arrives at friend's house: walks	Excited to see her friend, Sue has a little skip or bounce in her step as she rings the doorbell. The weather is windy, rainy. She may be worried her hat will fly off.
1200.0290	Dry	Teatime: sits	Her friend's table is for dolls, so the chair is undersized. Sue is perhaps a little flustered about how to sit gracefully in her skirt at such a small table.
1200.0300	Wet	Back home: shakes off	Drenched from being caught in the rain on the way home, Sue collapses into a regular-sized armchair. She loved visiting but is relieved to be warm again.

Always ask *why* and *how* your characters are wearing specific clothing. Examining and recording such details will equip you to execute a more successful design.

Exercise: Wear and Tear

In *Rip Van Winkle*, the main character falls into a deep sleep, misses a war entirely, and wakes to find his family and friends 20 years older or killed in the war. Now imagine *Rip Van Winkle* set in the years 2000 and 2020. How would his fashion stand out from others when he wakes up two decades later? What wear and tear would occur during his long sleep?

Create a design that tells us about a character's story and their world through the way the costumes change or deteriorate with time.

1. Start by establishing the components of their costume.

Layer 1: Chemise and Stockings

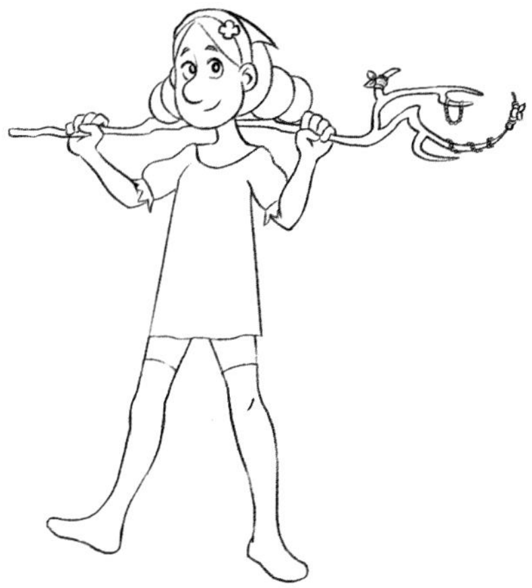

Layer 2: Breeches and Boots

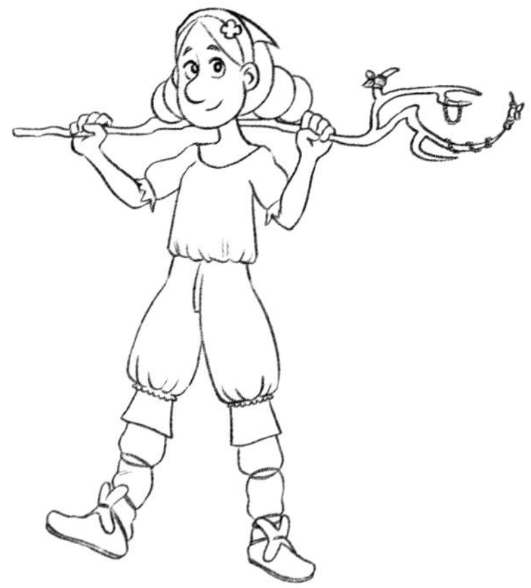

Layer 3: Petticoat

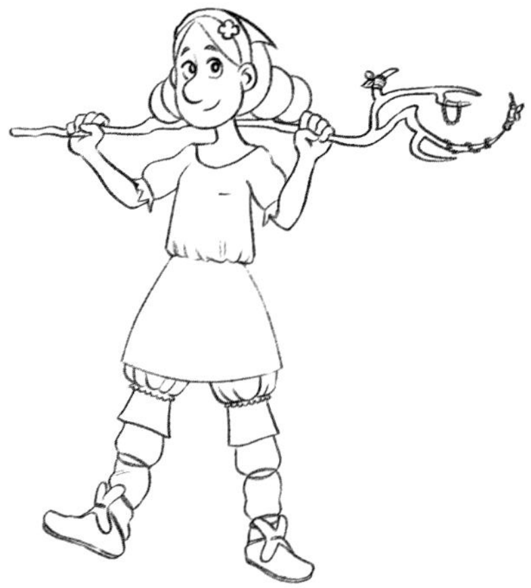

Layer 4: Bodice

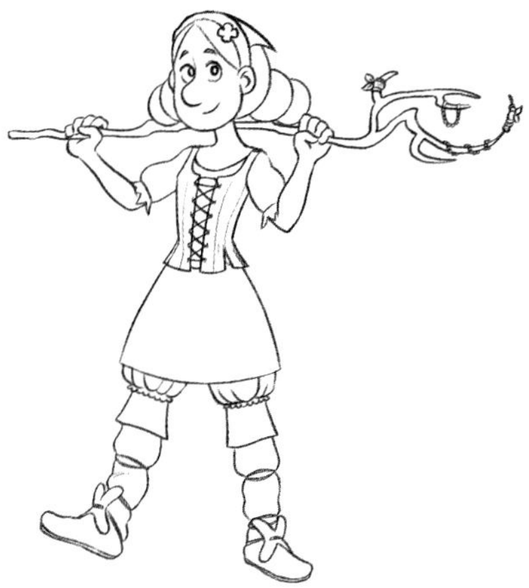

Layer 5: Manteau

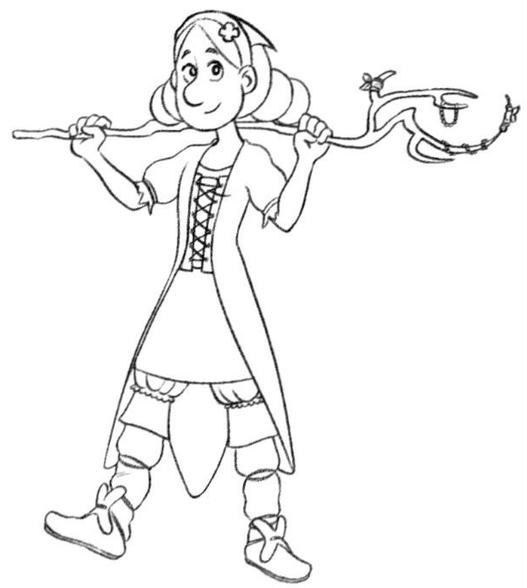

Layer 6: Accessories

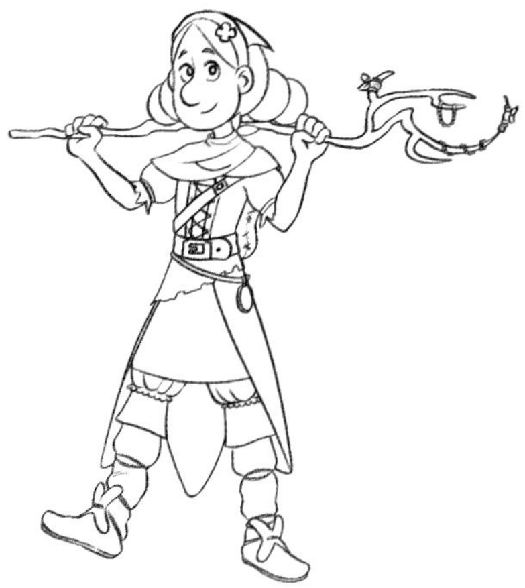

2. Create a lineup of sketches that explore the effects and changes based on environmental and/or behavioral effects. Note significant story structure and social, time, place, or personality considerations that influenced your choices.

YOU	NEED	GO	SEARCH
A character is in a zone of comfort	but they want something;	they enter an unfamiliar situation,	adapt to it,

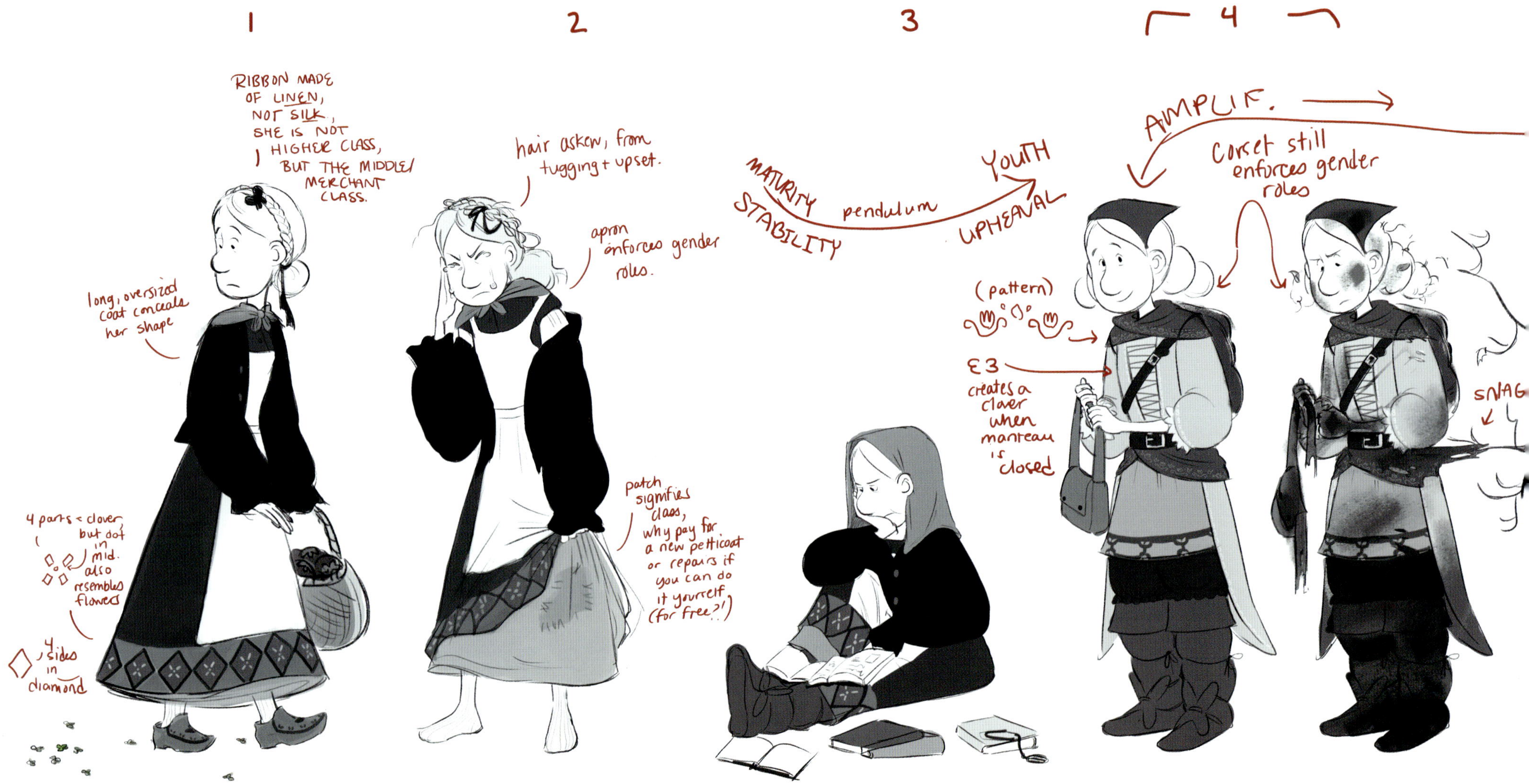

TAILORED EXAMPLE

Madeline Abatemarco uses Dan Harmon's eight-beat story structure to track her character's progression. The eight-beat structure, also referred to as the "Story Circle," is an adaptation of the Hero's Journey. The powerful simplicity of the structure allows us to prioritize what elements to highlight from our complex worlds and emotional motivations without getting too bogged down in details.

FIND
get what they wanted,

TAKE
pay a heavy price for it,

RETURN
and then return to their familiar situation

CHANGE
having changed.

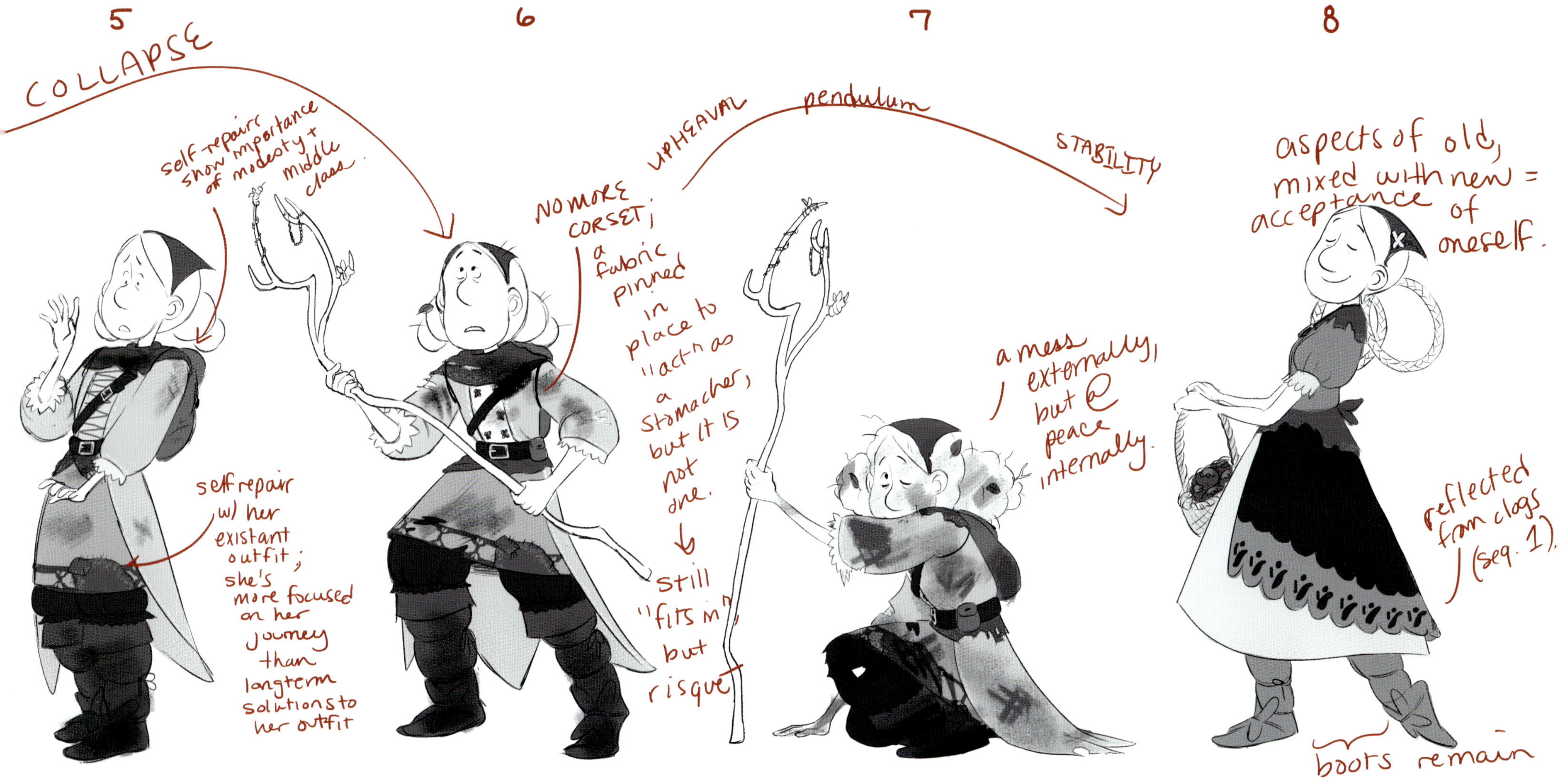

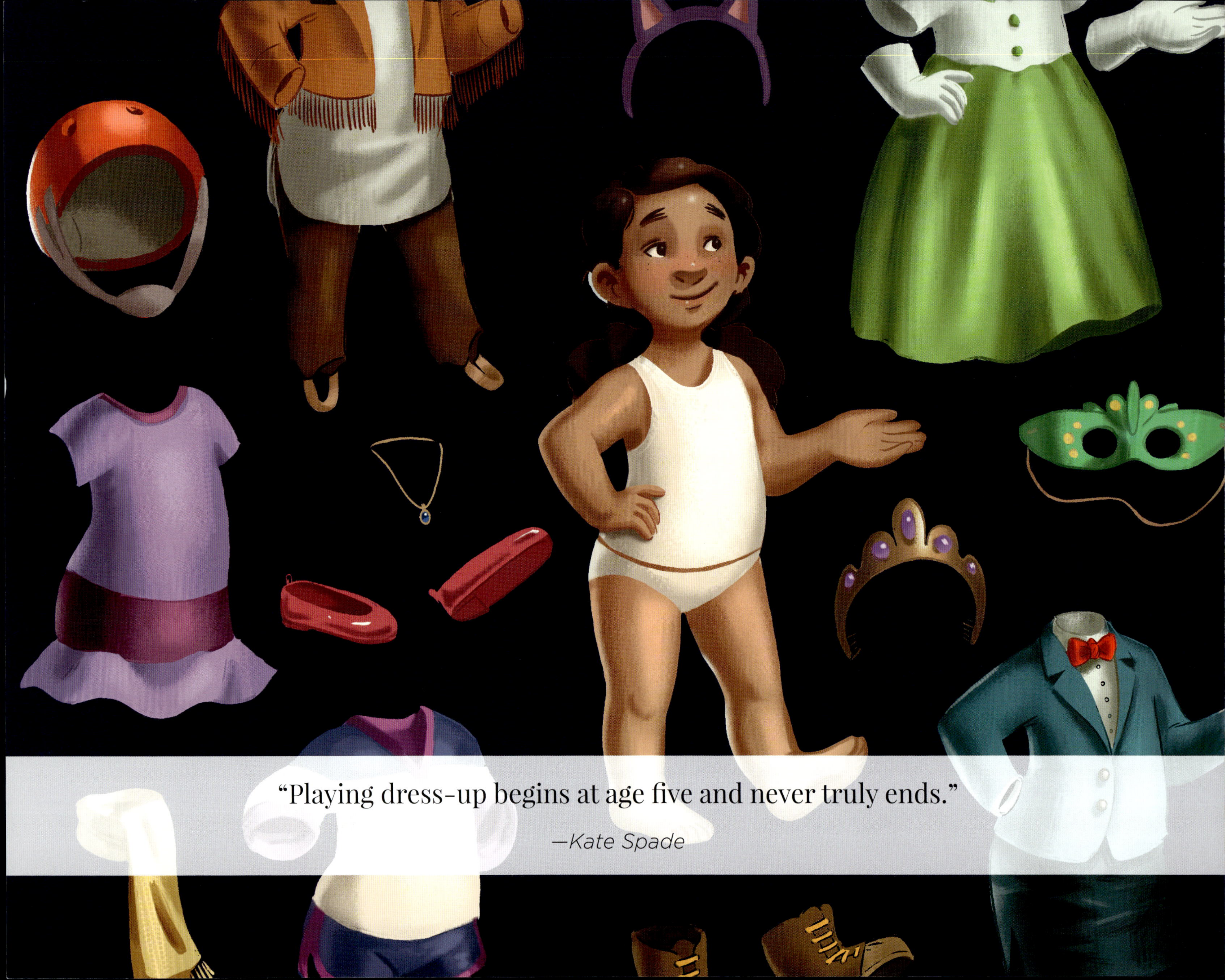

"Playing dress-up begins at age five and never truly ends."

—Kate Spade

CHAPTER 6 STYLING AND SURFACE DESIGN

Costume Design vs. Styling

Not all artists have the luxury of specializing in costume design. Illustrators, for example, often wear multiple hats, acting as writers, character designers, costumers, layout artists, color stylists, and more. Juggling many hats is simply a part of the job description. Unfortunately, this limits the amount of time illustrators have to spend on each part of the process. This means, with costumes, they often use a design shortcut, styling.

DESIGN IS ABOUT GETTING IT RIGHT

Design is a technical and research-based specialism used to tell the story, but with exhaustive detail. Design is highly specific, conveying information about the world in which the characters live, while propelling the story forward. The idea of costume design parallels rightness, whether that is more expressive, historical, or technical.

The research and information needed for good costume design takes notable expertise, money, and time; thus, a longer time frame for more extensive research and a budget for material sourcing are needed. Design may not always be practical—this is dependent on the designer.

STYLING IS KEEPING IT SIMPLE

Styling can be described as a design shortcut. It is the assembly of an outfit instead of the creation of one. When costume styling is chosen over costume design, there is no longer an obligation to create from scratch; existing pieces are used instead of designing and fabricating them. However, this does not mean costume styling doesn't require effort. Research and the acquiring of reference images is integral to both costume design and styling.

Both design and styling are legitimate processes, and you may switch back and forth between them, but understanding which of them you are using at the time will help you understand which questions to ask.

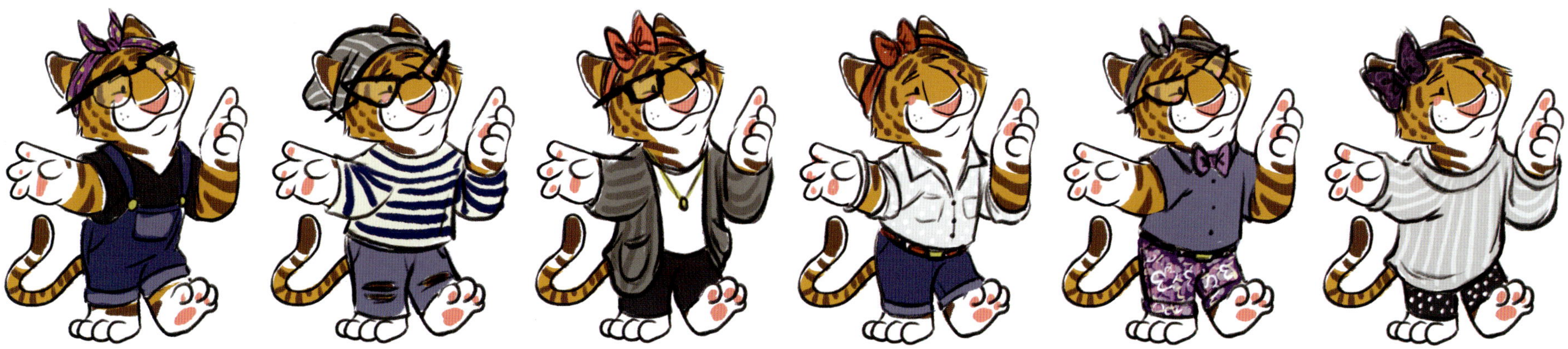

Developing a Character's Style

Think of how you get dressed in the morning. What do you want to wear today? What's already in your closet? What's the weather like outside? Using clothes you already own (the ones typically identifying your personal style), you tell the story of your routine day.

This is the same process in which you style the characters you create. You take existing articles of clothing and put them together to make an outfit your character would wear. Use your story to figure out what's in your character's closet and narrow down your character's clothing choices to help you dress them more quickly and efficiently.

ASK YOURSELF:

- ***How old is your character?*** Whether or not your characters dress themselves is very important. Kids wear different things than adults do, often wilder outfits, but maybe a super eclectic wardrobe fits your character's personality.
- ***Where does your character live?*** If your character lives in downtown Chicago and it's the middle of winter, it's highly unlikely they will be prancing around in shorts and a tank top. What kind of wardrobe does the character have available and what would be placed in storage?
- ***What clothing do you have in common?*** Make a list of things you have in your closet (generally speaking, pants, shirts, dresses, etc.) and highlight the ones your character would also have. Pick a few things off the list you think would fit with the story and start designing a few iterations of each. (If you'd like, you can draw each item of clothing on a Post-it note and mix and match them to see what works best visually). Keep at it until you find the outfit that best fits your character and their story!

Learning how to communicate your personal identity and aesthetic through your own clothing will enhance your ability to give your character an authentic style of their own.

Also:

- What materials are used to make the outfit?
- How does the outfit make the character feel?
- Is the character comfortable in their skin?
- Is this the outfit the character would choose to wear without external prompting?
- Are the clothes comfy and tattered because the character loves to explore?
- Are they made of a stiffer material and highly tailored because the character comes from a high-status family? And how would that shape the character's personality?
- How do the clothes affect the character's posture and movement?

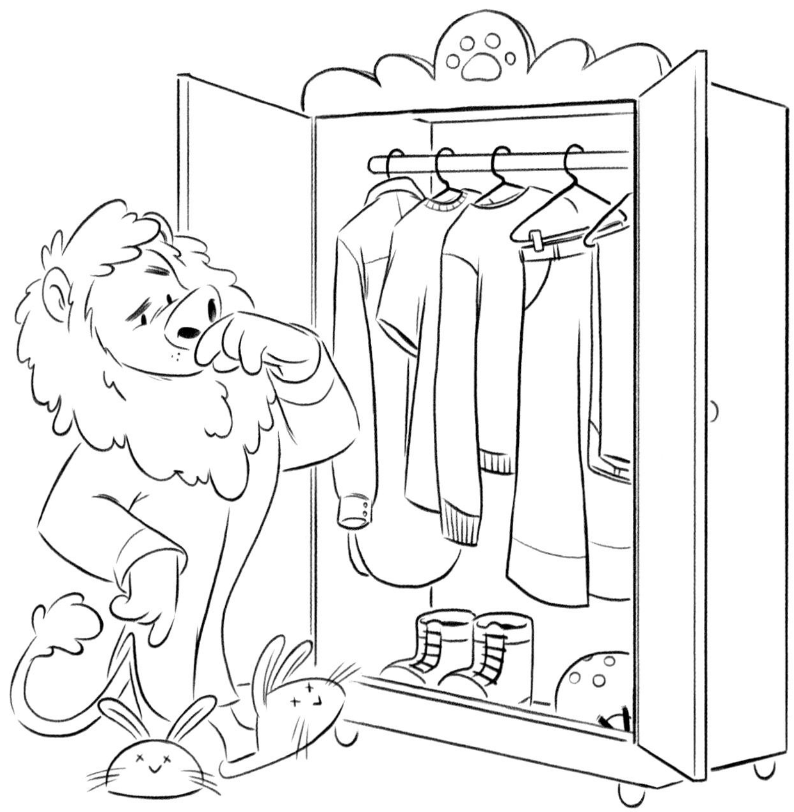

Using Body Language

When choosing items, think about the simple impression they give off. Just as we can show a character rubbing a hand behind their neck to show their resistance to new ideas ("stiffneckedness"), we can translate common body language into costume by bringing attention to areas of the body. Using accessories like enlarged glasses, or rolling up sleeves, can change an existing item from your closet into a costume that expresses the character's attitude and story.

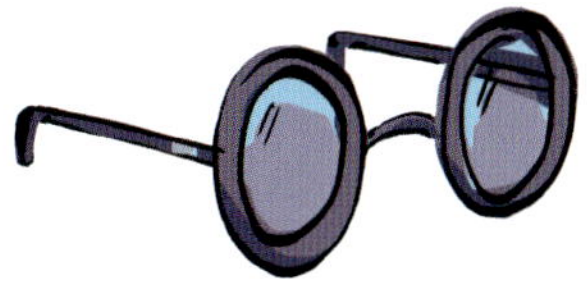

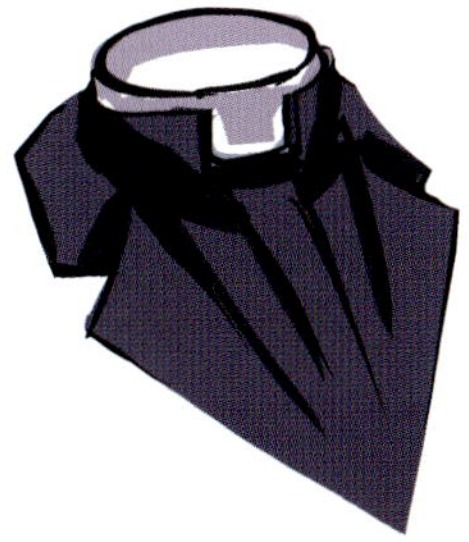

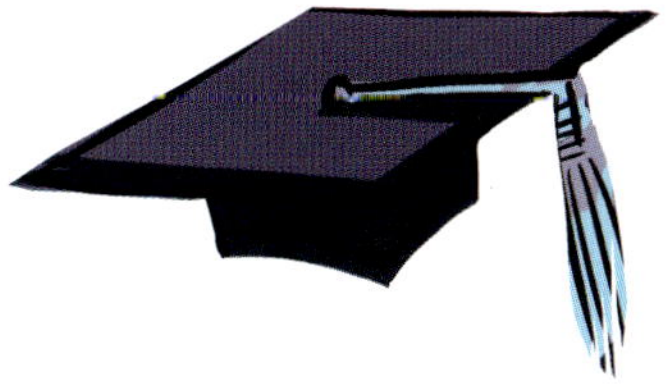

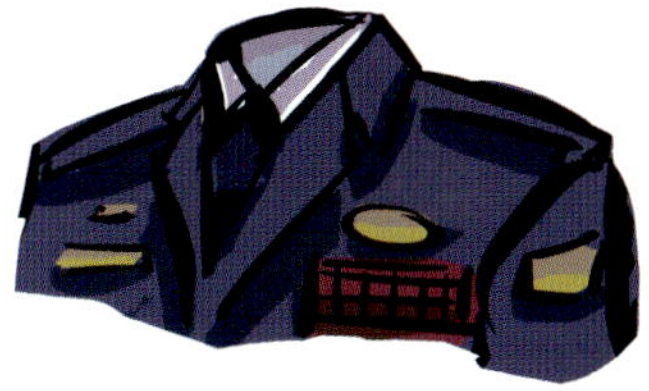

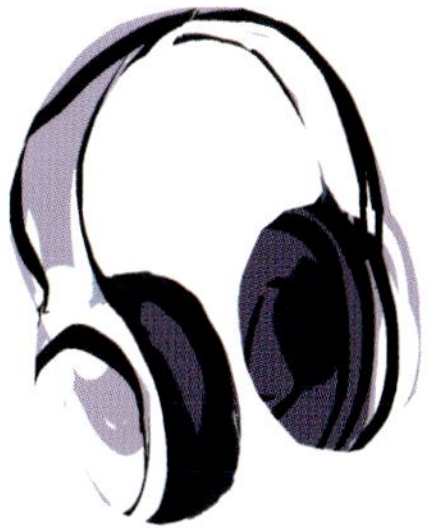

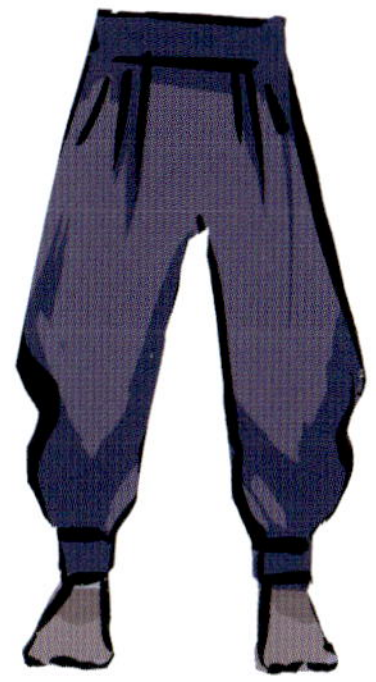

Head	Information
Eyes	Imagination/Curiosity
Neck	Concern/Acceptance of Ideas
Hands	Intent/Protection/Vulnerability/Potential/Action
Ears	Understanding/Learning
Shoulders	Responsibility
Arms	Carrying/Managing Tasks
Legs	Balance/Support/Strength
Feet	Foundation/Intention/Direction

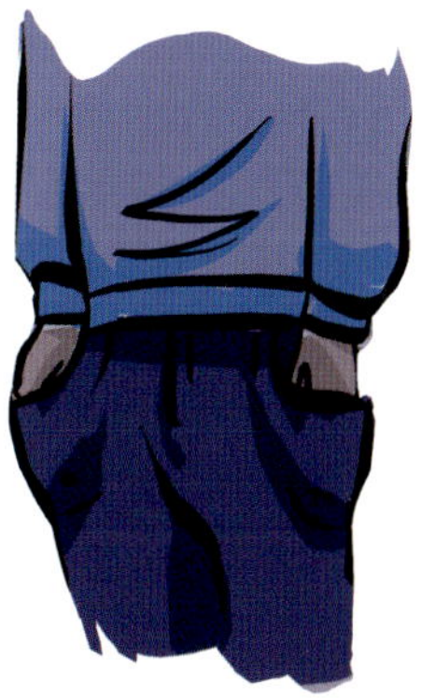

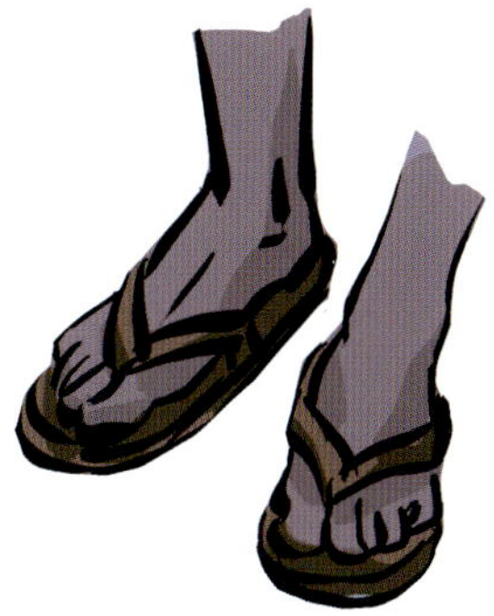

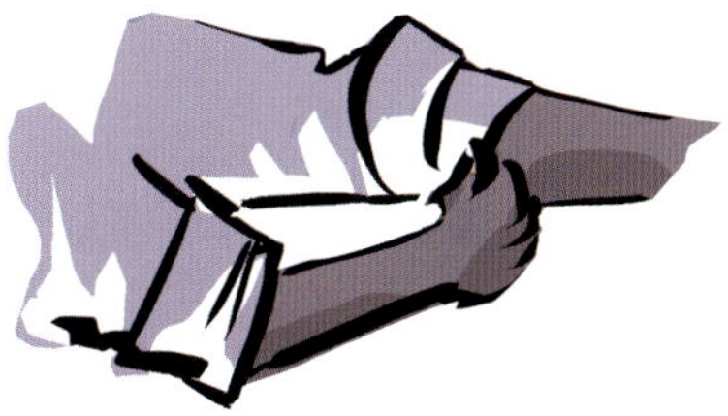

Playing with Proportions and Fit

Proportions refer to how the pieces in an outfit relate to each other as a whole. Is the character wearing a crop top and a long pencil skirt? What about a long T-shirt with knee-high socks? How does the size and shape of each garment look on the character and what happens when you change them?

Fit is exactly how it sounds. How do the character's clothes fit? Is the outfit baggy or too snug? Is it tailored to fit just right? If someone wears clothes that are too tight or too big, what does that say about them?

Study different body types and genders and the way they choose clothing to amplify or minimize certain shapes!

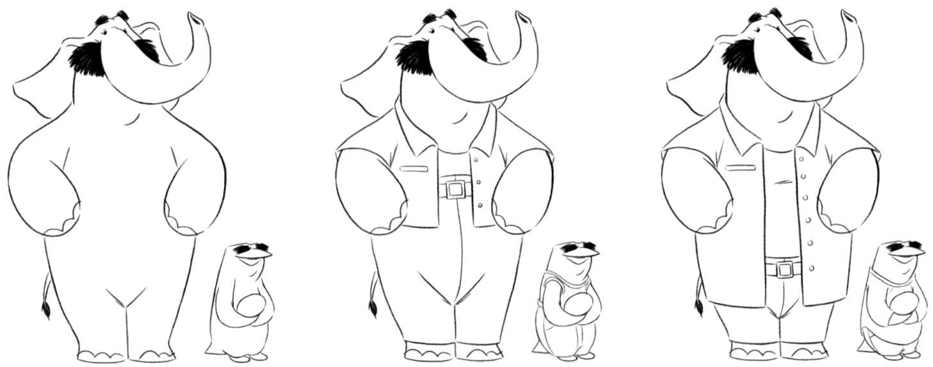

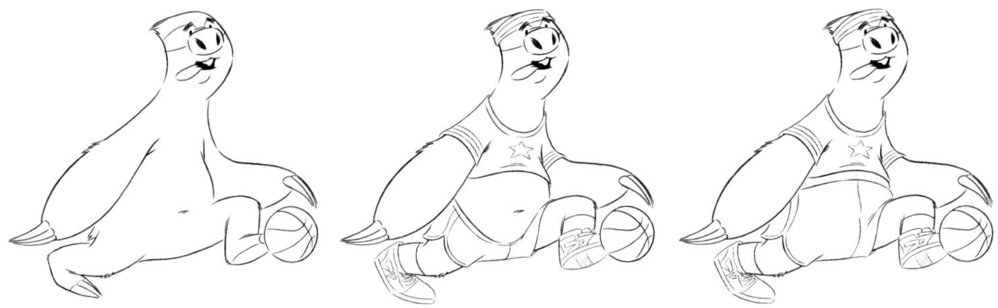

For example, look at the size difference between Elephant and Penguin. If you wanted to accentuate Elephant's larger size, you could play with the proportions of his clothing. For instance, make his pants' waistline higher to elongate his legs or bottom-half, thus making Penguin seem even smaller in scale. You can also make Elephant's torso look longer by placing his waistline where it would naturally sit—near his belly button.

In the second image of Sloth, his basketball uniform is much too small. The proportions of the shirt and the shorts cut Sloth into thirds. When characters wear clothing that's too small, it can showcase a gangly or immature quality, such as an awkward teenage growth spurt. In the third example, the uniform fits better, but the proportions are different. The high waist of the shorts accentuates Sloth's rounded shape and makes him seem more capable.

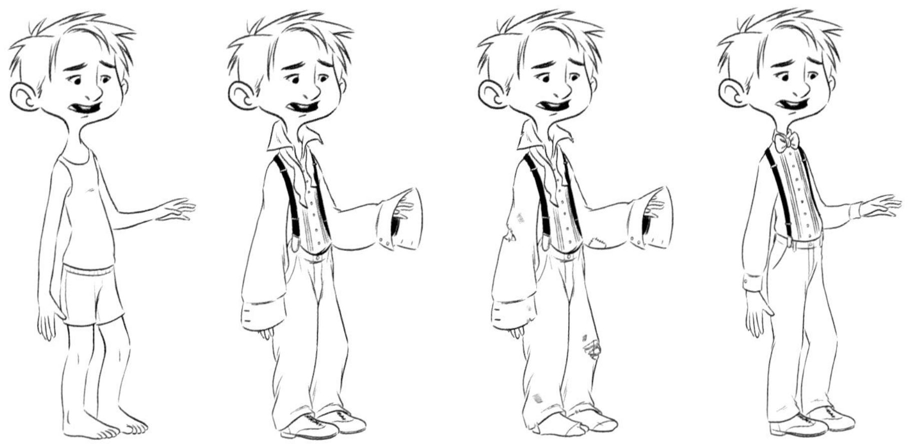

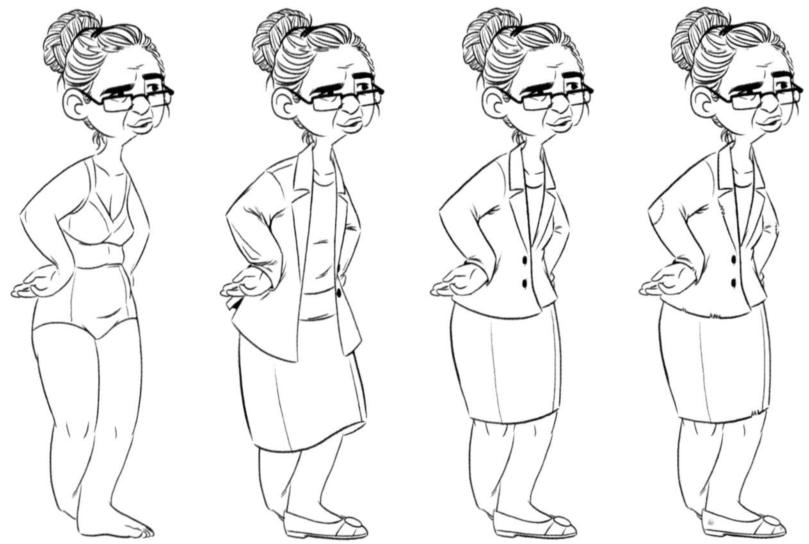

In this example, the boy is wearing dressy attire. In the second image, the clothes are too big. Maybe the outfit is a hand-me-down from an older sibling; maybe his story involves magical realism and he has shrunk. Either way it is ill-fitting and makes the boy look unkempt. In the third image, the unkempt look is intensified by the worn state of the suit. There are patches and holes and frayed edges that could mean that the boy has had quite a day or that the outfit has been worn so often it's in shambles. The fourth image shows the boy in the same items of clothing, but they fit his body to perfection. He looks put together and sophisticated—whether that's the truth is up to the story.

In a similar example, this woman is wearing a business suit. In the second image, the suit fits a little large on her small frame and seems more casual with the suit jacket open. The third image shows an outfit that fits the character's body and proportions very well. The fourth image shows a suit that is tailored to the woman's body, but also one that has been worn a lot. It is frayed and has patches that may reveal the elderly woman's frugality. Or maybe this is her lucky suit?

MAINTAINING SILHOUETTES

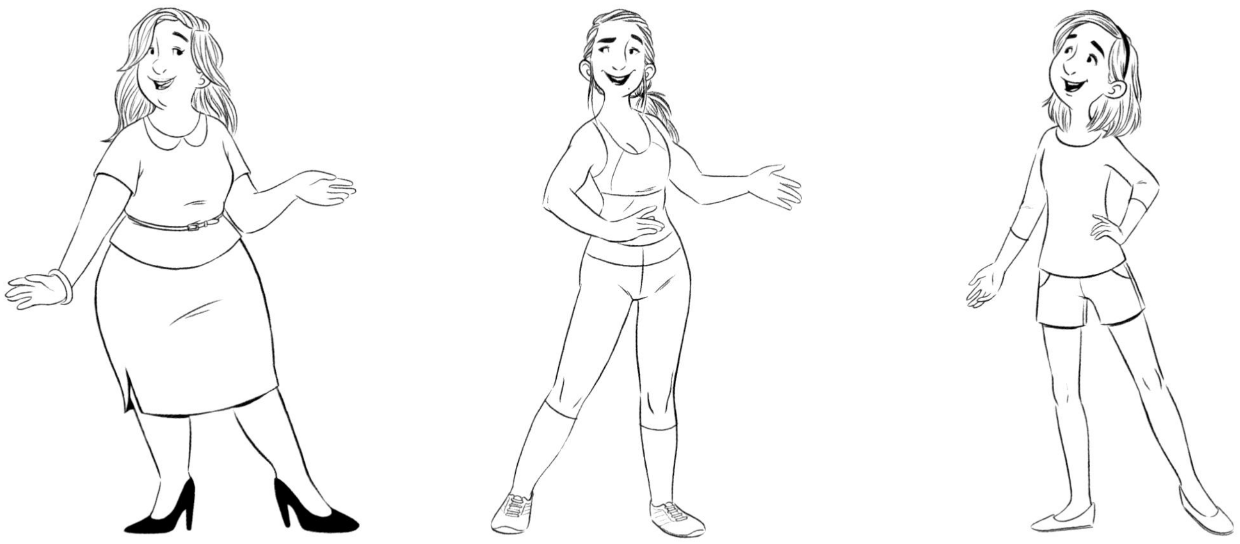

Silhouette not only describes the general shape of a character but also their outfit. Is there a uniquely defined shape? Or is it an unmemorable blob? No matter the media, we want our character's shape language to be readable to the audience. However, the more stylized the media (animation, stop-motion, video games or illustration), the more care we need to take to maintain the overall shapes at a distance, or while in movement.

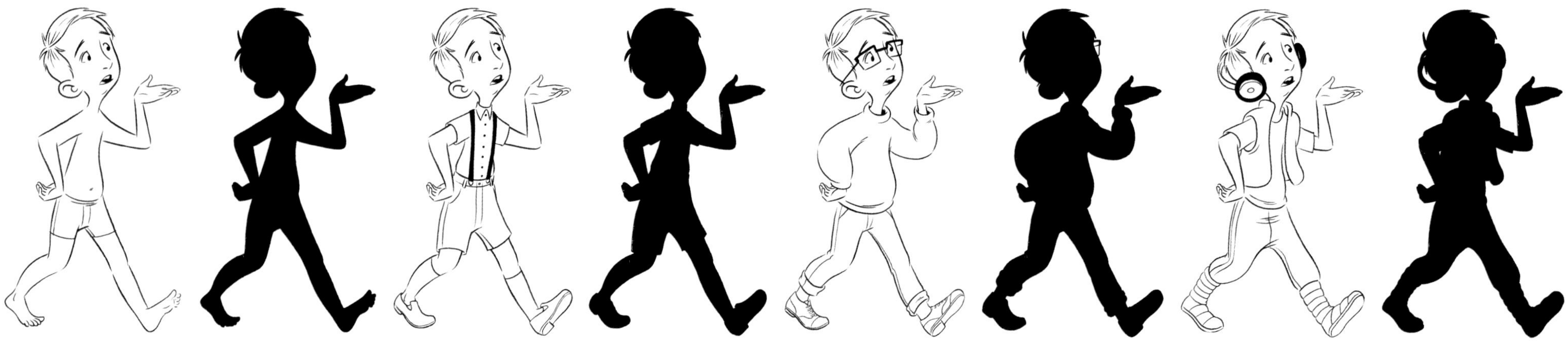

This is the same boy with three different outfits choices, but all three of these silhouettes could be deemed successful because you can determine the pose (and the boy's action) in each one.

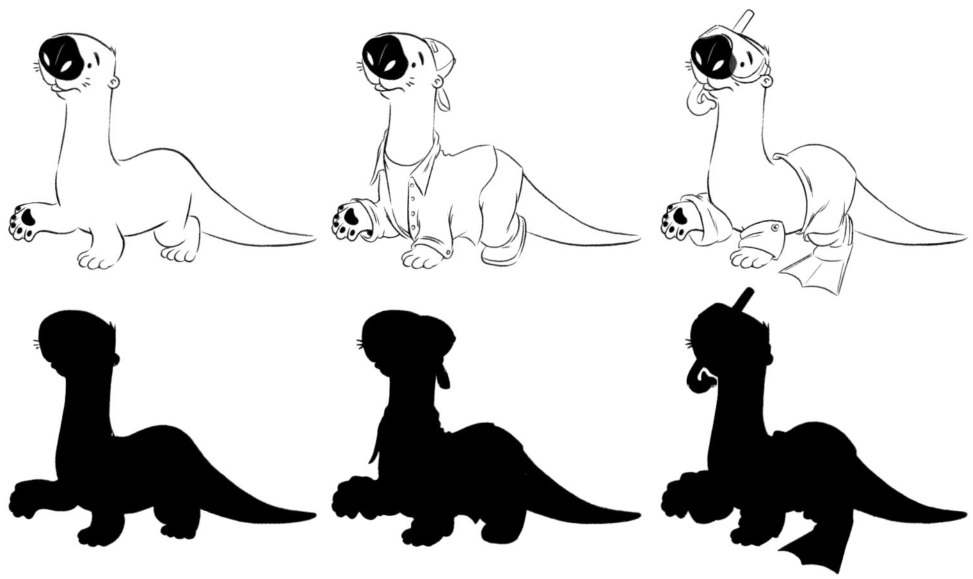

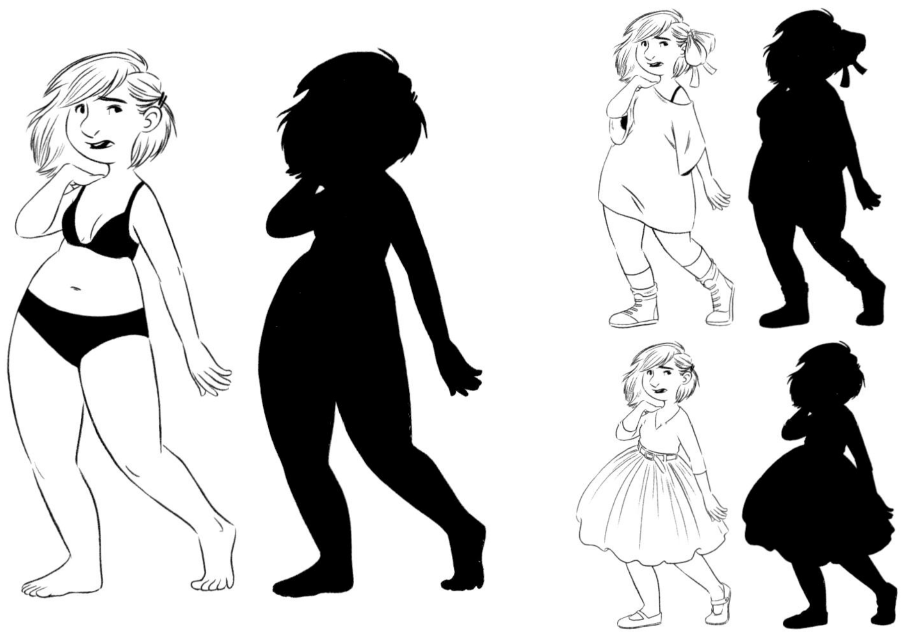

Ask yourself: How does the clothing affect the character's silhouette? Does it muddle the design shape? Does it lessen the impact? Or does the silhouette of the outfit add to the overall shape positively? Otter's basic shape sans clothes is already relatively complex. His legs are short, which is a fun play on anatomical proportions but can cause issues when adding clothing. This is why you see so many costumes conforming to a character's body—to not disrupt the silhouette. In the case of Otter, the first and third silhouettes are the most successful, but the third would probably be better without the floaties on the front legs.

In this example, the baggy '80s outfit of the top-right image distorts the clean silhouette of the character's figure, while the large shape of the skirt in the bottom image adds visual interest. The left and the bottom examples are best because you can, for the most part, decipher exactly what pose she is in/what she is doing. To make the top-right silhouette more successful, one would show the articulation of her hand away from her shoulder.

By exaggerating transitions between body and clothing, it becomes easier to quickly break down the shapes at a glance. This helps us stay "on model" when we need to repeat the same character multiple times from many angles.

Exercise: "Ugly Duckling" Transformation

Books and films are full of ugly-duckling transformations where unfashionable characters have their wardrobes updated to make them more attractive or impressive. For instance, they might go from wearing baggy clothing to tighter garments that emphasize their physiques. This silhouette transformation makes them more identifiable. Even a change from glasses to contacts can modify their overall silhouette. These transformations can also serve to disguise a character if they need to avoid attention or recognition.

Create a narratively driven silhouette transformation. Ask friends or colleagues how they interpret the story to evaluate if your intention is clear.

Exercise: Exaggerate your Silhouette

We can also start from an existing real-world silhouette and push it to add more personality through exaggerating the existing shape language. Identify a garment you want to study and restyle it to fit a personality archetype such as in the Enneagram section. Use your gut impressions of the different types to explore and style new variations. For example, gluttony has lots of decoration, greed is very minimal, etc.

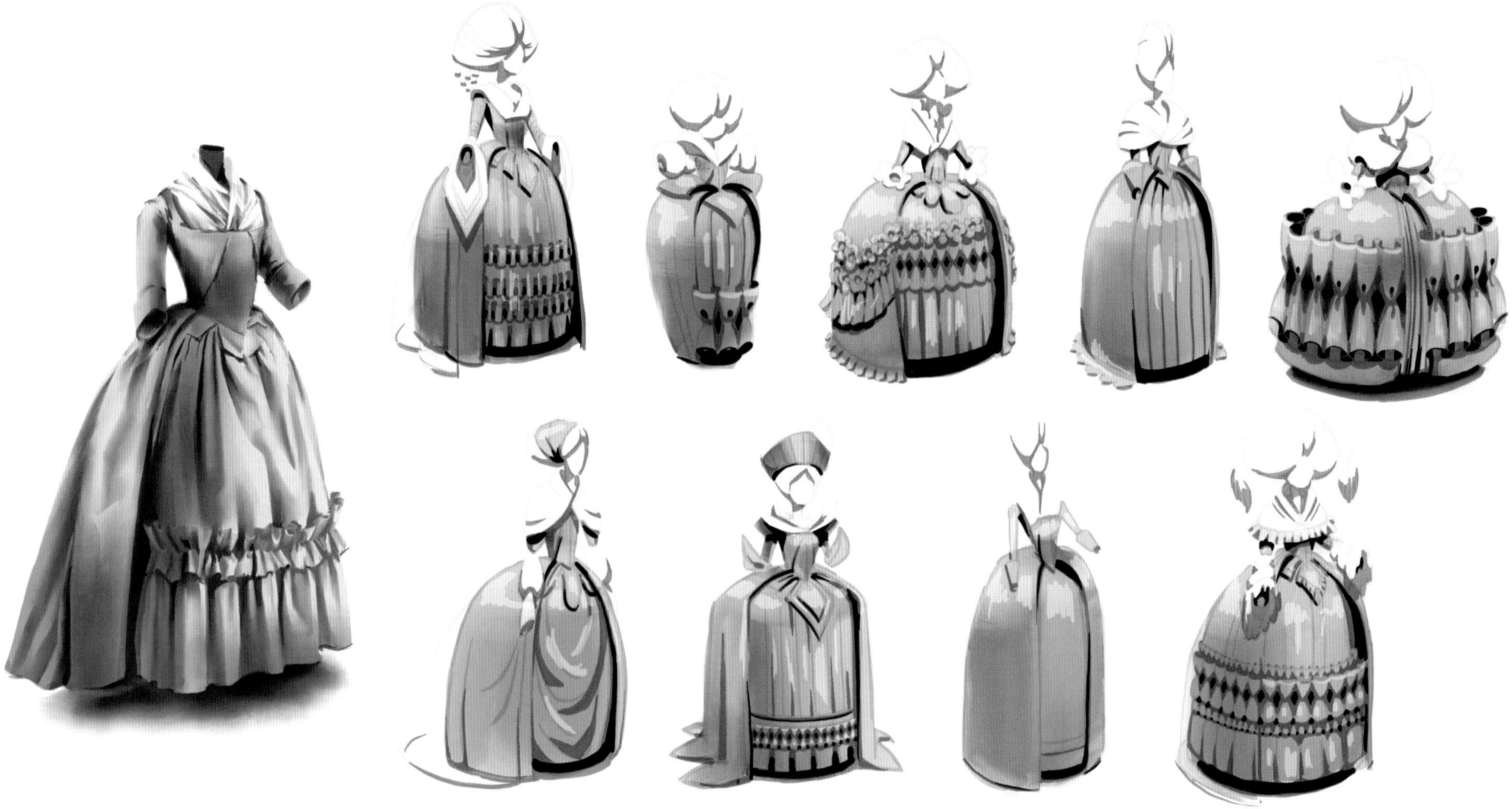

Exercise: Stretch Your Silhouette

FINITE RESOURCES AND TIME

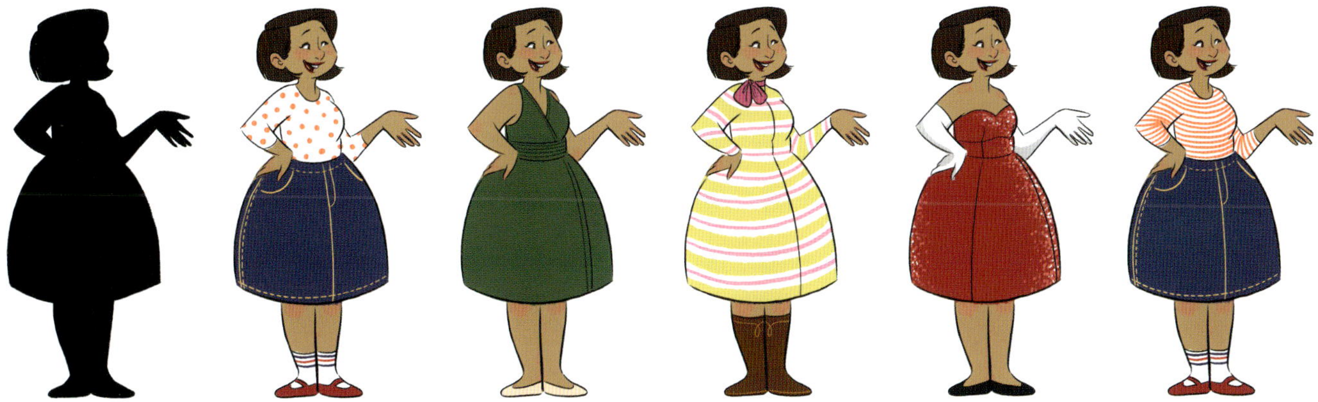

When you break the silhouette of the 3D character, you may be actually requiring a new build of the entire character model. This can chip away at the number of assets a TV show has in its budget, so you need to get creative. Instead of breaking the silhouette for a fun costume that will only be used in one episode, try adding/attaching existing props (such as a bow or flower) to costumes and/or changing the surface texture to break up the interior detail in new ways. You can change the pattern, "apparent" cut, or texture without breaking the silhouette of your character. Running into practical challenges like this can push your creativity and reinforce the value of working from strong silhouette designs in the first place.

A similar principle applies to animated films or games. You might need to mix and match standardized wardrobe pieces to create unique background characters, or create color and texture variations for games with customizable outfits.

1. Take your exaggerated silhouette and without breaking the silhouette create variations that allow your character to fit into different settings in their story.

2. Use common props you might find in your productions assets (jewelry, a backpack) to break the silhouette and add more variety to your options.

3. Create a set of background characters using a limited number of garments you have to mix and match.

4. Modify color and texture of the background characters you developed to create a broader variety of options.

Choosing a Color Palette

Colors are associated with all sorts of symbolism and meaning. Like stereotypes, cultures form common emotional associations with colors. Red can be associated with anger or passion while yellow may allude to happiness or brightness. Choosing colors for a character's outfit depends a lot on the mood of the story. Is the character happy? Or sad? If they're sad, maybe accentuate that fact by having the character dressed in cool blues but surrounded by an environment made up of warm oranges. (Look at color scripts from animated films for great color inspiration.)

You can rely on common color associations or teach the audience to make a new association in your story. Whatever you decide, keeping the costume and motifs simple also helps the character stay recognizable in any setting and allows the audience to quickly comprehend the details as they move through the scenes. In animation and comics, colors have been used masterfully in helping the audience easily identify the villain from the hero, and both groups from secondary characters. In animated productions, colors like purple, turquoise, blue, red, and black are common for villains, and vivid colors often go to heroes.

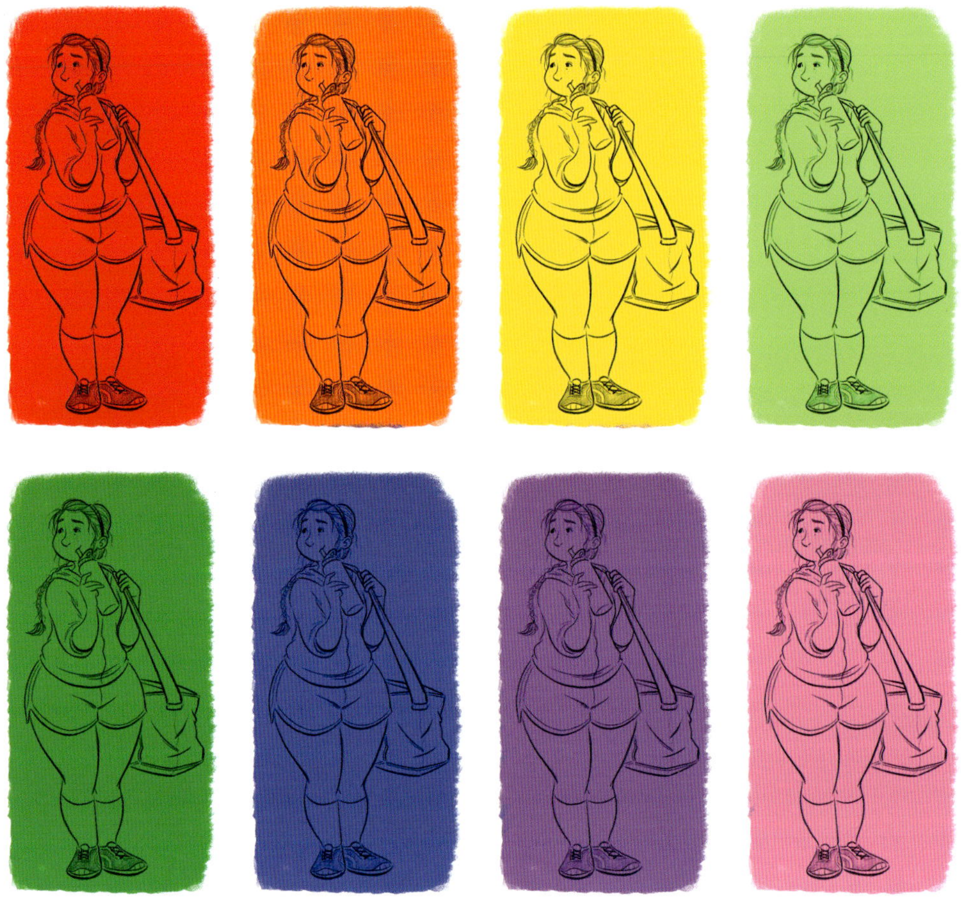

Color Evolution

Once you've established a fundamental palette for your characters, there is another approach you can use to add an additional level of complexity: show the metamorphosis of characters by changing the colors they wear.

In *Black Swan* (2010), the main character Nina (Natalie Portman), a ballerina, opens the film wearing standard uniform shades of pink that capture her innocent and girlish personality. As Nina faces the challenges of becoming a prima ballerina, she evolves into an adult and her palette changes from pink to gray. By the end of the film, her identity has completely transformed from the innocent girl into the seductive, powerful, and confident prima ballerina, leading her to fully embrace a "Black Swan" look.

Character	Film	Year	Character	Film	Year
Peter Pan	*Peter Pan (animated)*	1953	Maleficent	*Sleeping Beauty*	1959
Merida	*Brave*	2012	Jafar	*Aladdin (animated)*	1992
Hiro	*Big Hero 6*	2014	Claude Frollo	*The Hunchback of Notre Dame*	1996
Tulio and Miguel	*The Road to El Dorado*	2000	Ursula	*The Little Mermaid*	1989
Moana	*Moana*	2016	Dr. Facilier	*The Princess and the Frog*	2009
Mulan	*Mulan (animated)*	1998	Yzma	*The Emperor's New Groove*	2000
Nausicaä	*Nausicaä of the Valley of the Wind*	1984	Eris	*Sinbad: Legend of the Seven Seas*	2003
Rapunzel	*Tangled*	2010	Prince Hans	*Frozen*	2013
Chihiro	*Spirited Away*	2001	Mother Gothel	*Tangled*	2010
Toothless	*How To Train Your Dragon*	2010	Lots-o'-Huggin' Bear	*Toy Story 3*	2010
Maria	*The Book of Life*	2014	Scar	*The Lion King*	1994

Color and Lighting

Consider the style of the project, color script, and/or lighting needs to determine how the color might change throughout the narrative or game. This will also help inform material choices as you move forward with your design. Reflectivity may differ, and you might want to adjust the local color choice (local color = actual color in even light) to suit the needs for lighting and environment. This is also an opportunity to check your personal mood board or the team's mood board for colors that are coming through as dominant.

Exercise: Color Shift

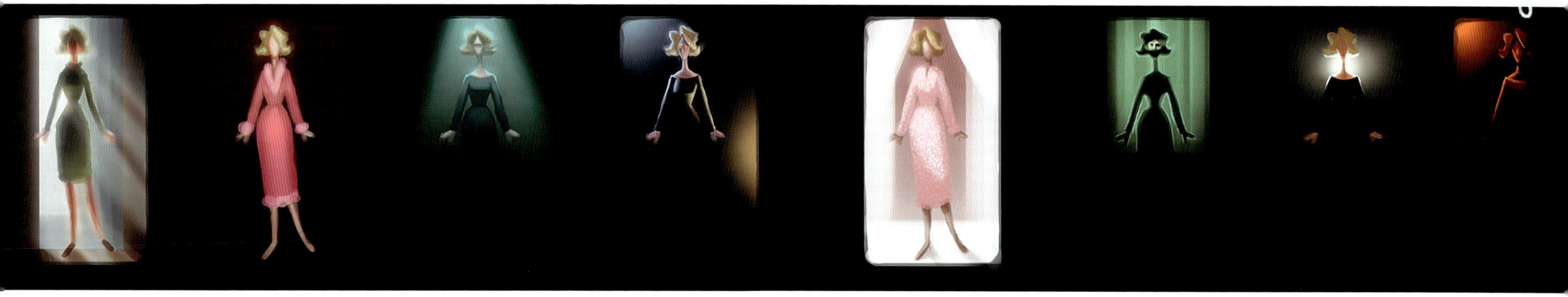

Create a costume or a series of costumes for a character who moves from one extreme emotion to the next, using color to indicate the emotional change. If your character stays in the same costume, study how the fabric would change color as it absorbs or reflects the lighting or contrasts with colors in the environment. For inspiration, watch *A Monster in Paris* (2011). Note how they use the main character's white suit to reflect the colors of the lighting.

Consider the season or locations the costume will be used in. In the examples on this page, Natalia Falciglia used seasonal clothing and dramatic lighting to inform an old Hollywood take on the Greek myth of Orpheus and Eurydice. Here she explores the costume designs of Persephone, a former leading lady.

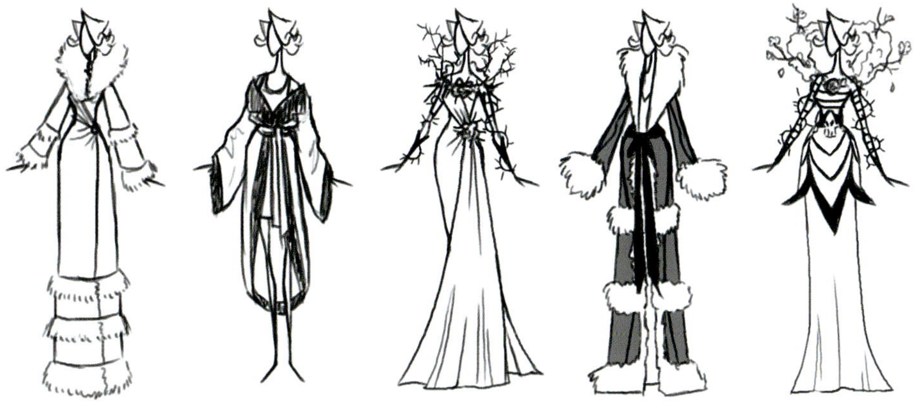

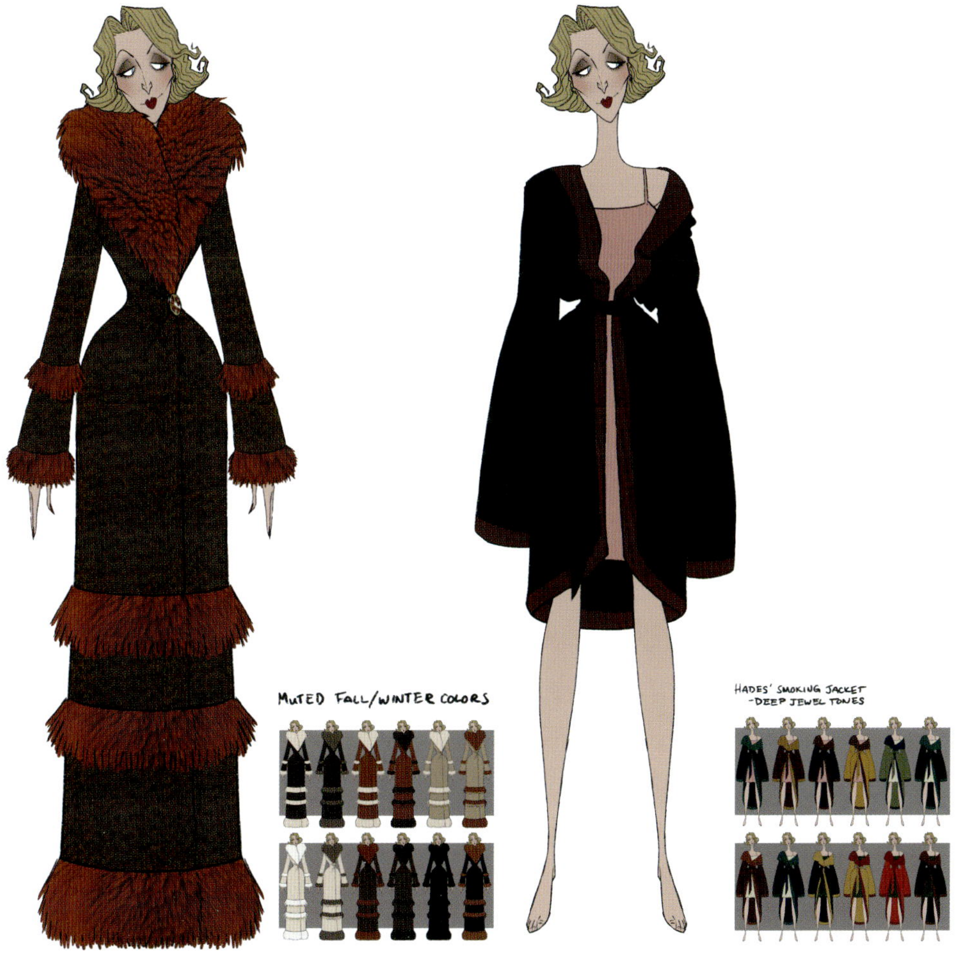
MUTED FALL/WINTER COLORS
HADES' SMOKING JACKET
-DEEP JEWEL TONES

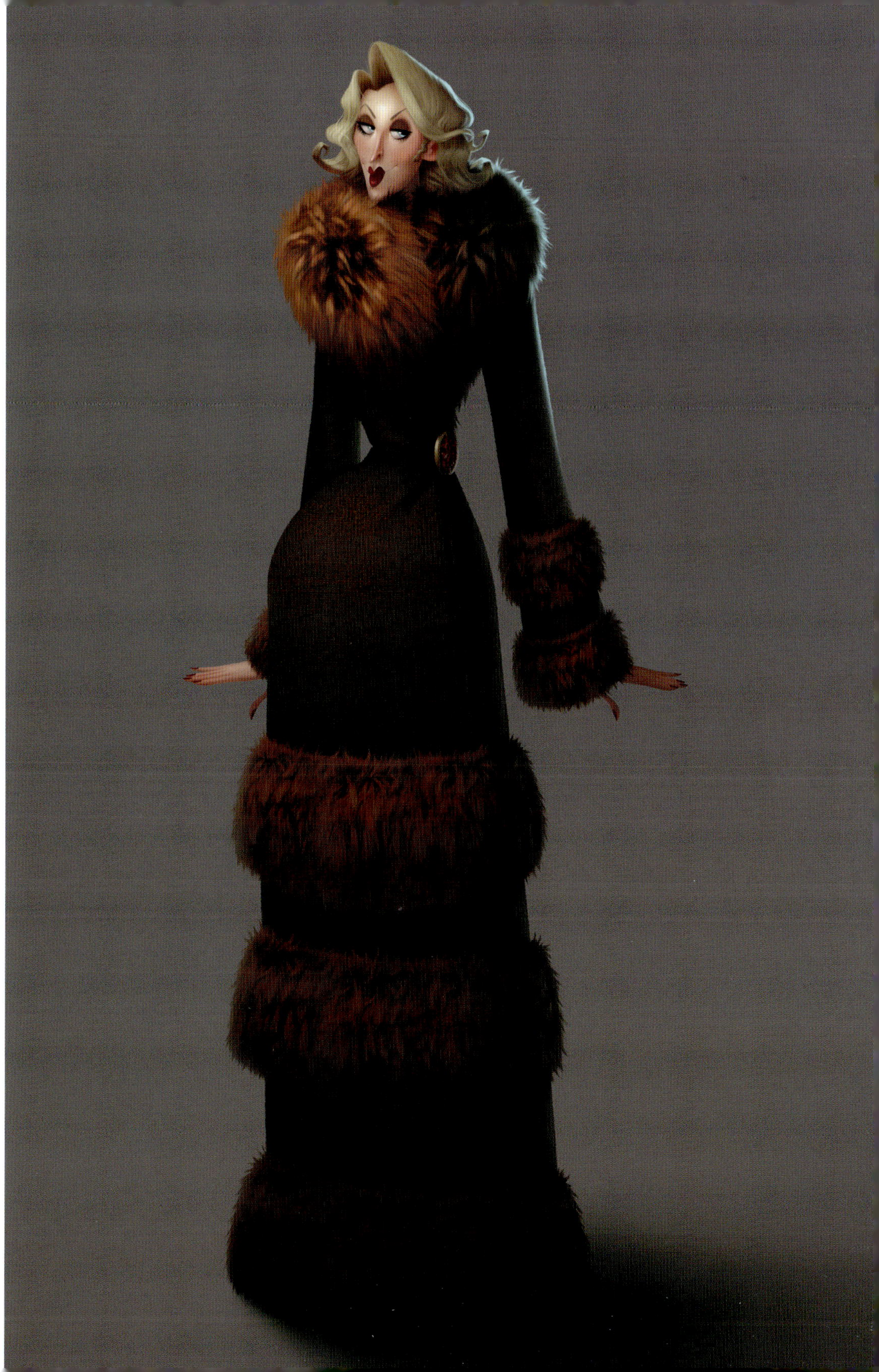

Storytelling Through Surface Design

Embellishments and Status Effects

Surface design (the details) can be utilized to emphasize the character's role in the story. This can be larger design statements, like a loud polka dot, or subtle, such as a contrasting thread.

What qualifies as surface design?

- The use of fabric pigmentation such as dyes, paints, markers, etc.
- Screen printing or fabric printing.
- Laser etching or cutting.
- Controlled distressing.
- Hand embellishments such as lacework, embroidery, etc.
- Fasteners and closures like buckles, buttons, hooks, and zippers.

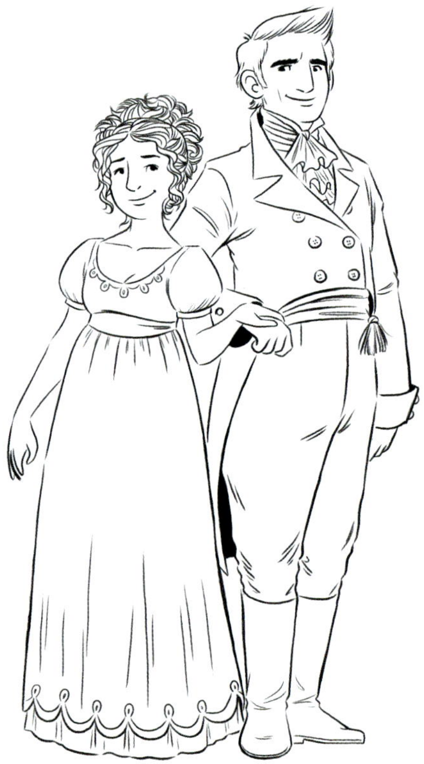

THE POWER OF PATTERNS

Patterns add visual interest and texture to any costume. Whether it's in the subtlety of a weave or obvious in a loud paisley, consider the aesthetic flow of the pattern. To highlight something on a character, using a pattern is a quick way to do so. Notice how the direction of the stripe changes the way the audience notices the action of the child. Experiment to explore the effect on the aesthetic.

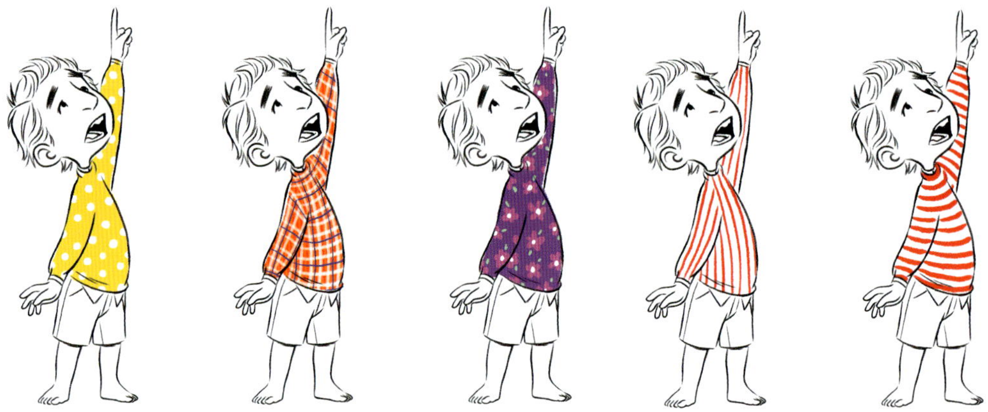

This child picked out his own outfit, not conforming to society's standards for what "matches." Consider a character's preferences. Don't be afraid to mix patterns! Especially if the character is bold or wild. Now, you don't have to use the whole rainbow when mixing patterns; two different patterns with similar color schemes will go together nicely. Likewise, you don't have to go crazy with paisleys or houndstooth—stripes and polka dots are great ways to add texture to an outfit.

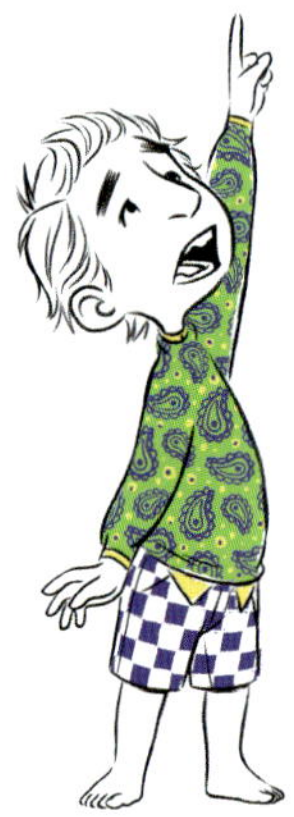

CONSIDER THE SYMBOLISM OF THE PATTERN

Patterns can be used to clarify a character's loyalty, interests, or create red herrings (distractions) as well. As a challenge, create a costume for a con artist who exposes their true nature through a subtle pattern in their clothing. For inspiration, watch *House of Flying Daggers* (2004).

When creating a fictional pattern or symbol, there are some helpful guidelines you can follow.

- The shapes in tribal motifs reflect their physical environment.
- Colors and designs of motifs are often dictated by the available materials in the location.
- Colors were often dictated by the natural vegetation growing in that area.
- Types of patterning (embroidered, woven, or printed) can be exclusive to certain regions. (See Powers Dynamics, page 28, Class Dynamics, page 39, and Trade Dynamics, page 51, for guidance.)

TIPS FOR STYLIZING SYMBOLISM

The connection between the location, culture, and the resulting pattern can capture geography and identity. For example, a village surrounded by mountains could reflect their location by using triangles to represent the mountain range.

But environments consist of more than mountains; additional shapes like clouds can be represented as well. The more elements you add, the more complex the design becomes.

Do you notice how the clouds are represented as angular shapes like the triangles? Each pattern you create will vary according to the material and tool used to create it. When carved on stone, it assumes an angular shape, while it may be more curvilinear or triangular on weaves. Limiting the shapes to suit the tools used to create it and staying true to the simplification of the concept will help your pattern emerge with more integrity.

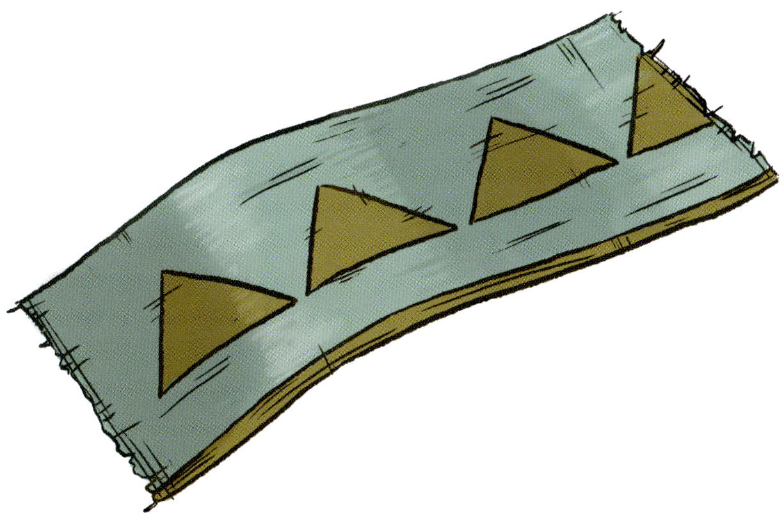

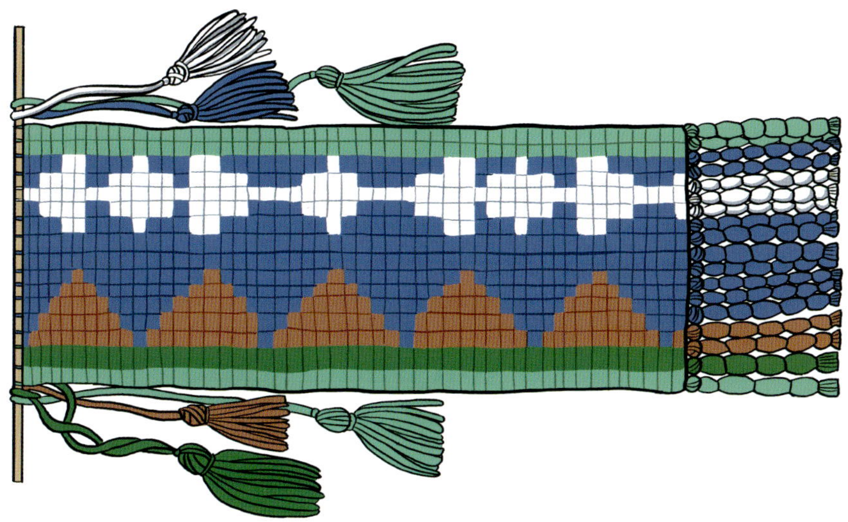

What if your design incorporates motifs that you need to simplify or modify—how can you maintain the essence of the design? Official sports uniforms offer a great example. They change through the decades but manage to keep the essence of the original logo intact; you still recognize the symbol even if it is only partially showing. If you understand the level of familiarity that the audience will have with your motif, you can abstract or edit quite a bit without losing that connection. A more dominant cultural symbol such as a flag will still be easy to recognize at a highly abstracted level. Even if the symbol itself as a shape has to go, you can rely on the colors to act as a symbolic representation.

It's also important to note that if you scale the symbol down too much, it may not be readable at a distance. Additionally, the smaller the garment or prop that you are using it on, the more you may need to increase the size of the motif for the audience to notice it.

Reference the meaning behind existing motifs, like the paisley, to find interesting and charged ways to simplify it, or use them to inspire how you will create or use a new pattern in your design. (Look to the Fear and Fascination/Evolving Symbols, pages 36 and 37 for ideas.) By deconstructing complex motifs into separate elements, you can turn a daunting task into an intriguing puzzle.

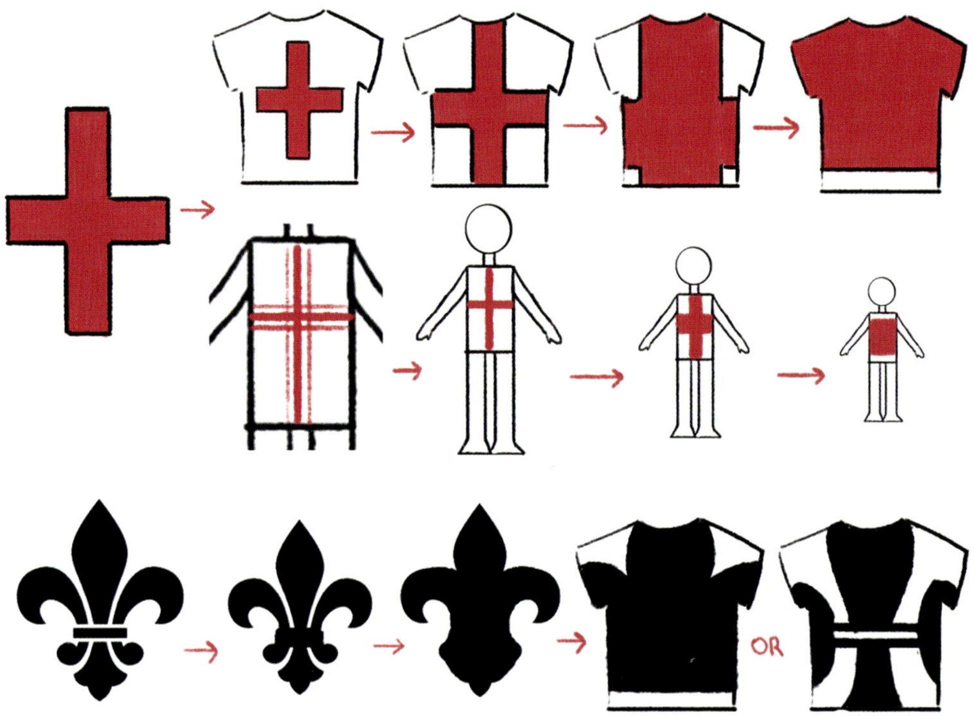

If you understand the level of familiarity that the audience will have with your motif, you can abstract or edit quite a bit without losing that connection.

Using Surface Design to Distinguish Groups

In artist David Lojaya's costume designs for his original story concept, "*King's Tailor*," a take on "*The Emperor's New Clothes,*" he explores the people surrounding his main character: a young, arrogant, and fragile king cursed with a broken, magical, invincible batik cape, using colors and shapes to identify and visually separate the groups.

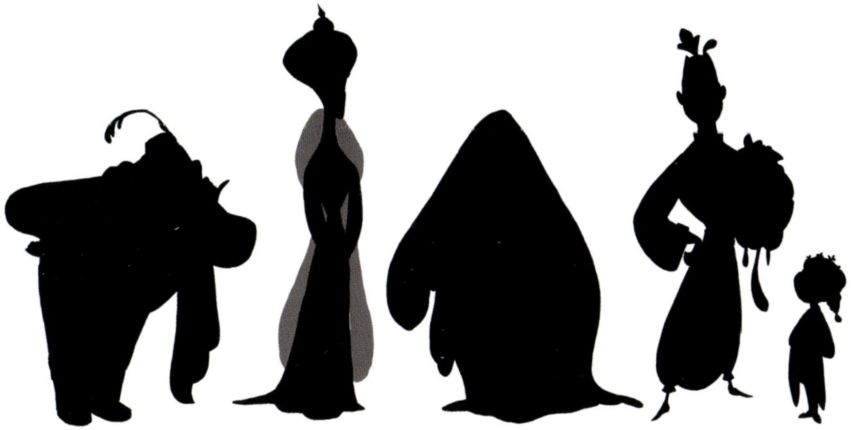

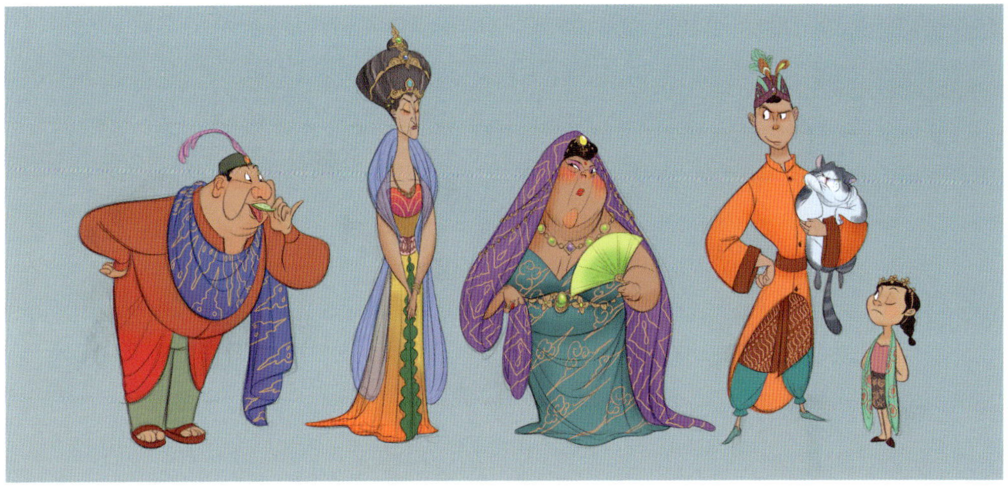

The wealthy wear a variety of vibrant colors and fashion accessories such as scarves and precious jewelry. He's also chosen to distinguish their silhouettes from the sharper-edge designed villagers, by making them rounder. Their batik motifs are more varied as well.

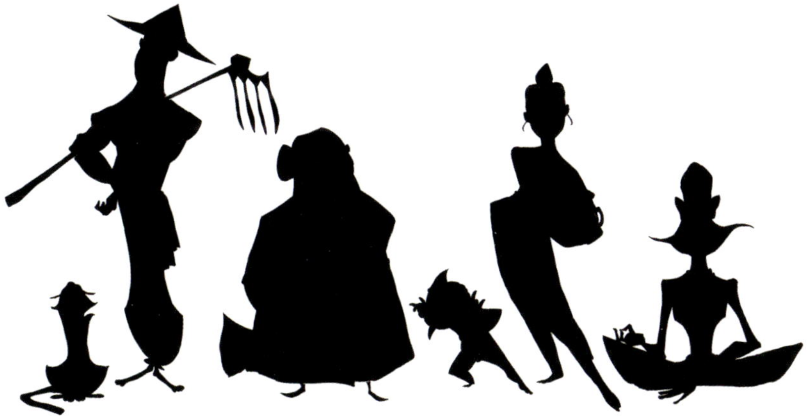

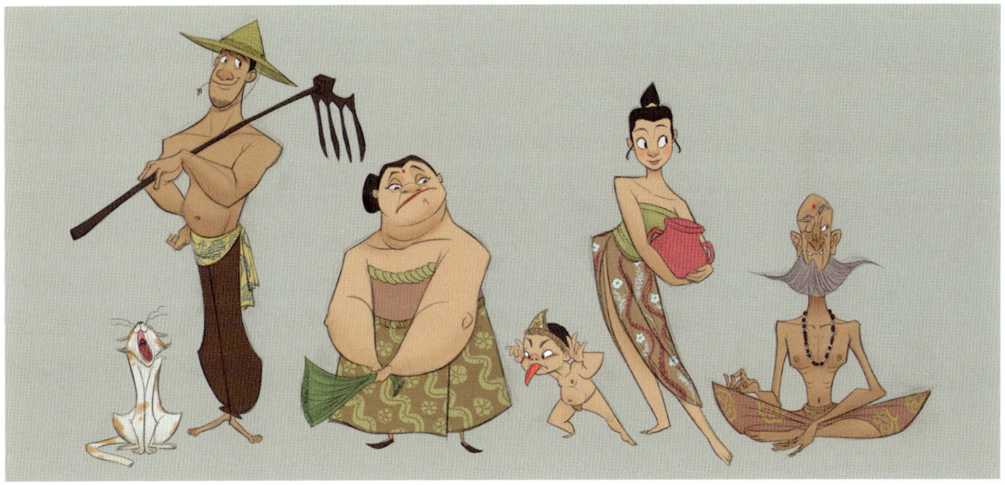

The villagers, on the other hand, wear more traditional clothing in mostly earthly tones like brown, green, and yellow. The batik motifs that they are using are mostly inspired by nature, such as animals and plants.

Transformation Through Motifs

David Ardinaryas Lojaya

Logline (loosely based on *"Emperor's New Clothes"* story)

A young, arrogant, and fragile king cursed with a broken, magical, invincible batik cape, desperately trying to find a batiks tailor to fix the cape and get back to the throne in time.

In my "King's Tailor," the main theme of the story is about a magical "batik," a traditional Indonesian cloth made with a special technique that uses hot wax as the main ingredient. The batik is made into a beautiful long cape for the king to be worn on coronation day. Not only the king, but all the characters, including villagers, are wearing batik, but there are several motif designs that separate them all.

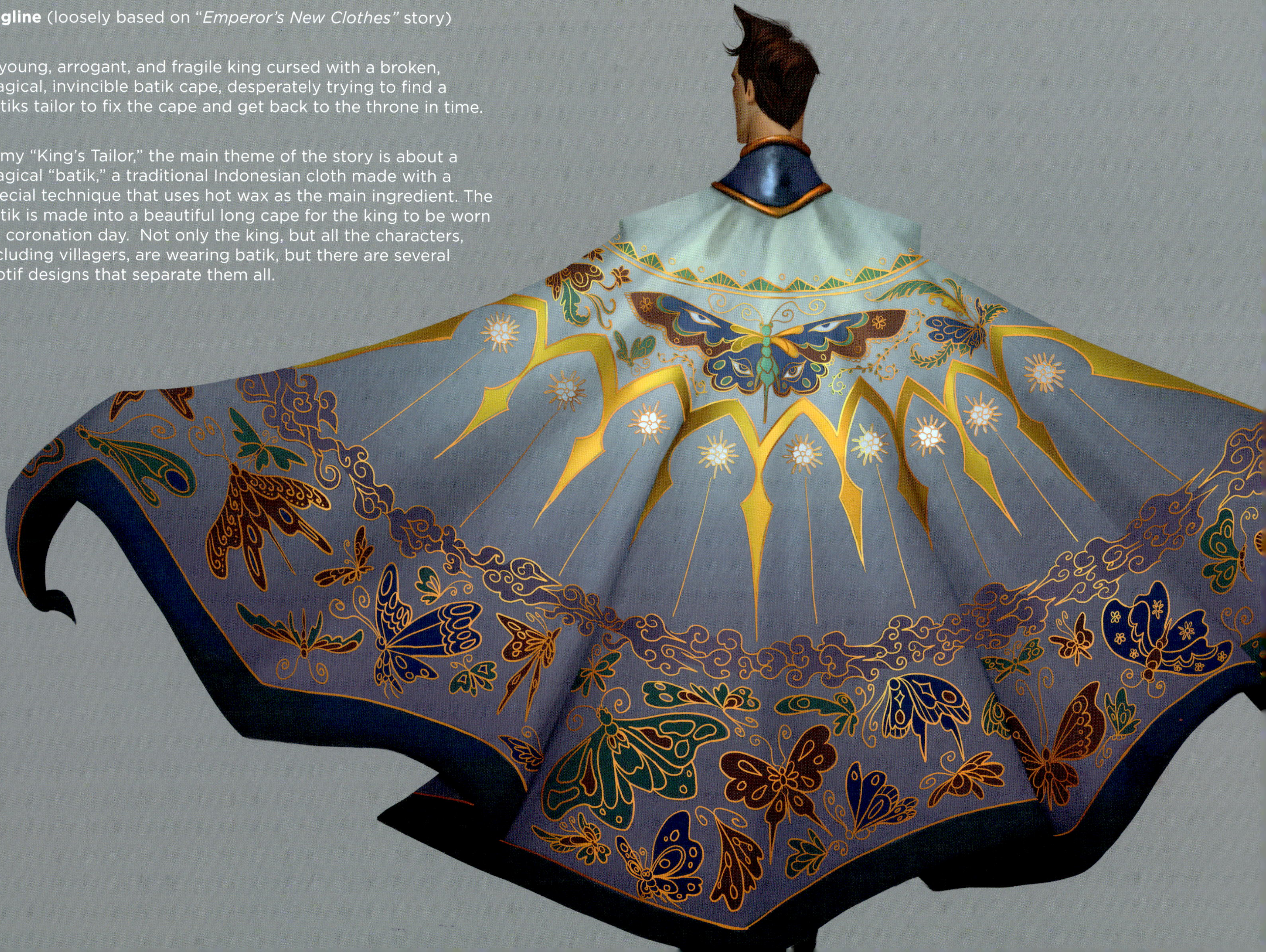

The cape is drawn with a special batik spell consisting of butterflies. It has a unique magic that can make the user appear to be invisible to the naked eye, but can still be seen with a special type of glass. The villain of the story gave the cape to the king to fool him into wearing it. His goal was to kill the king while he was invisible, making it easier to hide the corpse.

The pattern was inspired by the camouflage butterfly and the batik 'Mega Mendung' cloud pattern. The cape has three levels of designs; the first upper part is the head, which consists of the big butterfly and several butterflies that look like a flower. The big butterfly represents the mother of the butterflies on the cape. The second level is the arrow and flower that represent 'giving order.' The third level is the clouds and butterflies, which are the pawns.

The transformation magic starts with the butterflies going from two-dimensional to three-dimensional, slowly leaving the cape a blank canvas. The butterflies coming out are only the golden wax; their color will dissolve slowly along with the king's body. When the user takes off the cape, the butterflies will slowly reappear and "pawn" butterflies will fly into the cape randomly. As a result, the third level always has a different pattern each time it's been used.

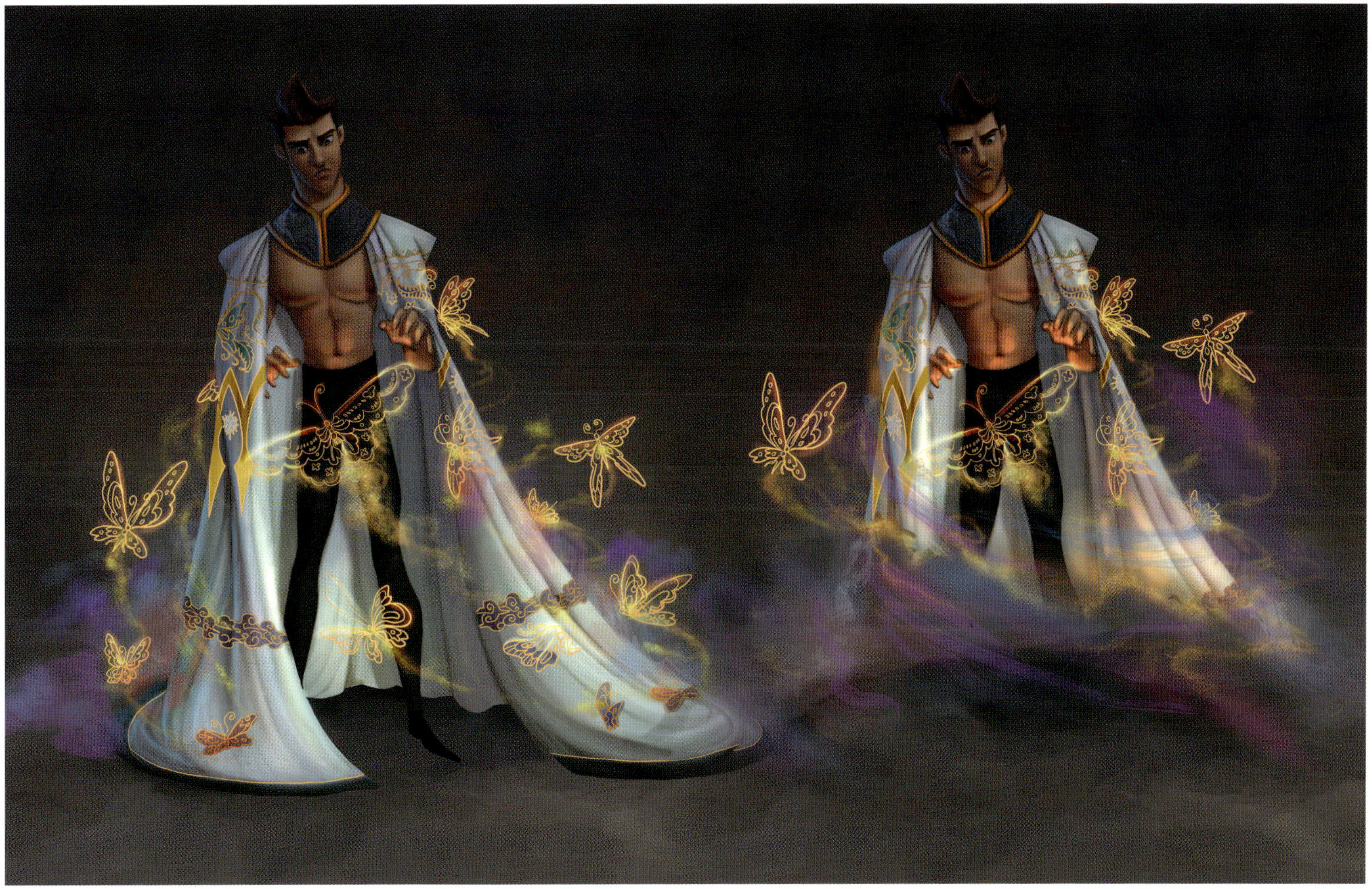

Exercise: Reimagining a Character's Costume

Let's put all the techniques you've learned so far in the book to use on an assignment to stretch your creativity within specific parameters: developing designs for a world that your audience is already familiar with. This comes with challenges and expectations. How can you make your interpretation unique? How can you add an artistic voice to it that makes it stand out from a market flush with visualized versions of that same story?

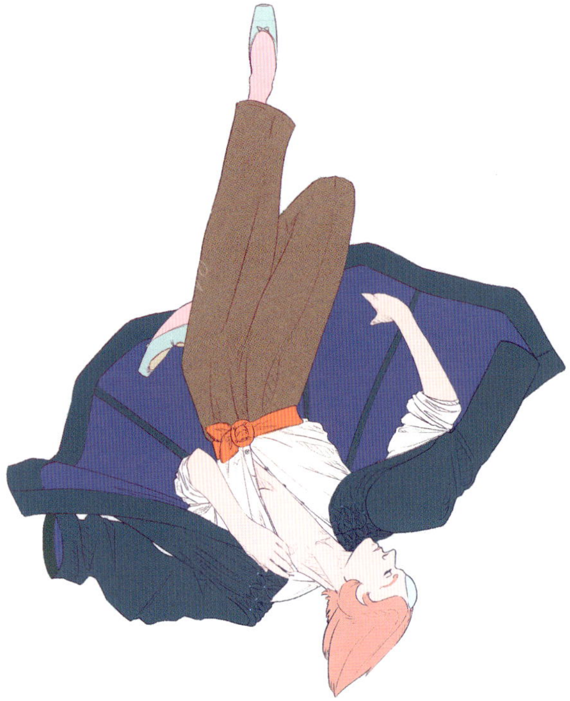

Create a main character costume for an animated remake of a live-action film.

Here is an exploratory checklist to help guide your decisions:

- Conduct adequate research by answering the five functions of costumes presented in this book. (See page 8.)
- Think of ways to bridge the existing designs to your new design.
- Look at what the original/past designer was originally inspired by.
- Incorporate that inspiration into your design.
- Ensure every choice made in your design has a purpose.
- Consider adding your own voice in the nuanced details.

Create a detailed list that justifies specific choices you made.

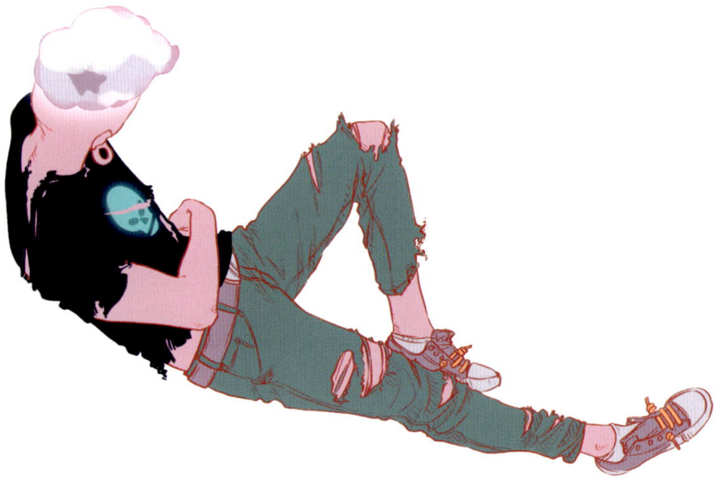

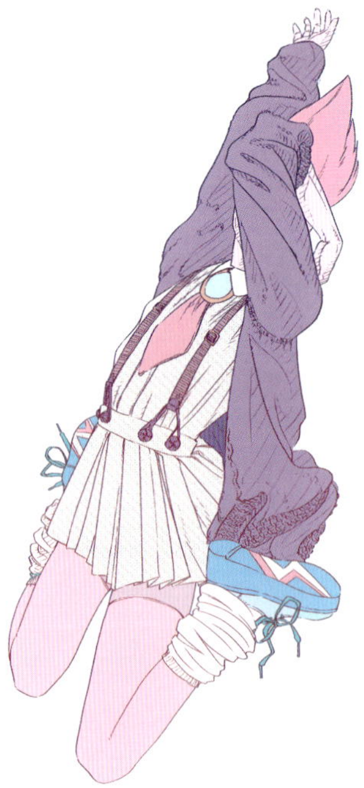

TAILORED EXAMPLE

Cloud Atlas

Josh Wong

These designs are by Josh Wong, inspired by the 2004 sci-fi novel *Cloud Atlas* by David Mitchell. What follows are the stylistic choices he made and why he made them. Your list should be as in-depth as his.

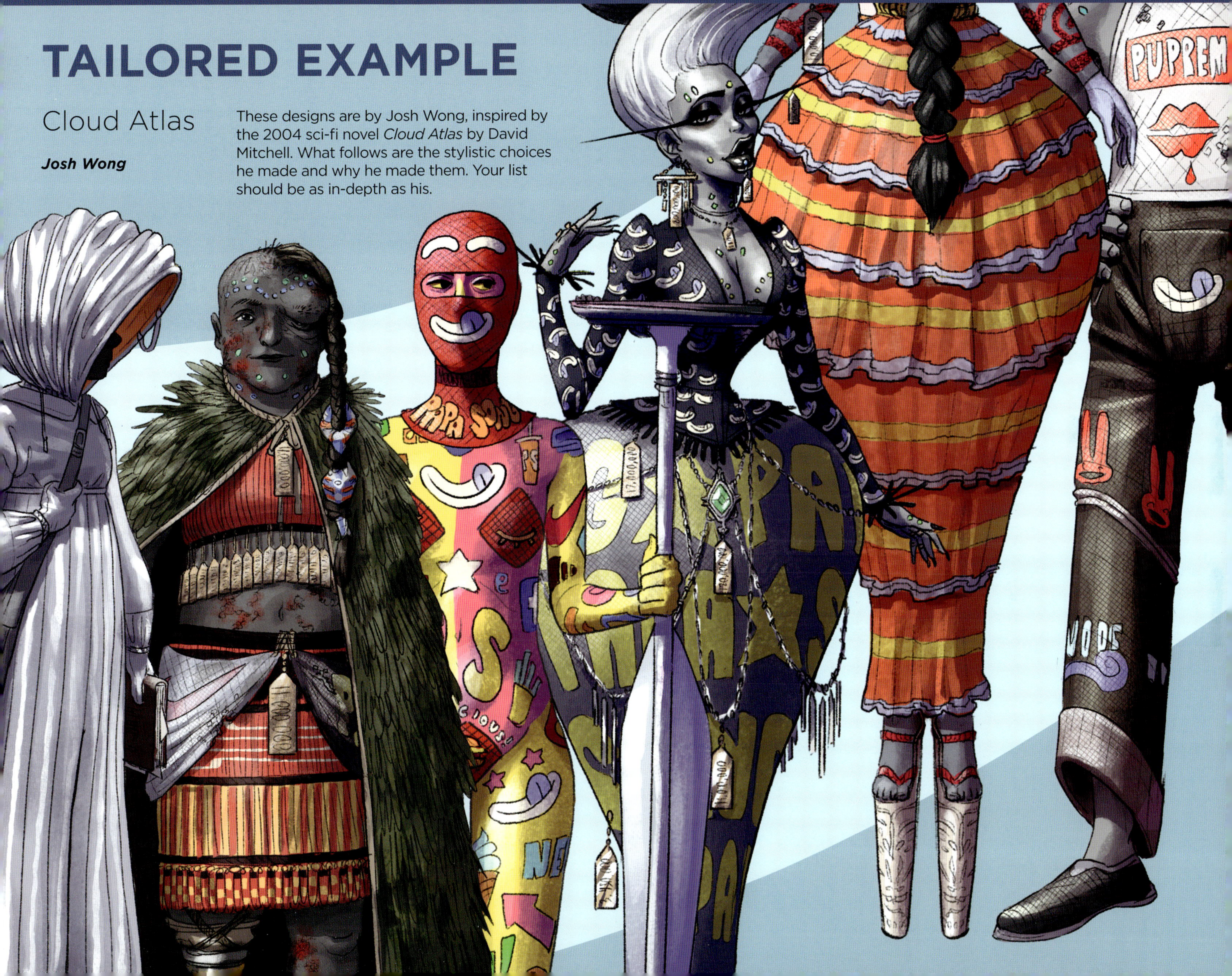

This amount of 3D-printed material would be seen as wasteful being used on a fabricant, but the hood is needed to cover up the fact that Yoona no longer smiles constantly like her coworkers.

Yoona-949's outfit merges overt sexuality with advertising in a way that may seem grotesque or obscene in our world, considering she works at a family restaurant.

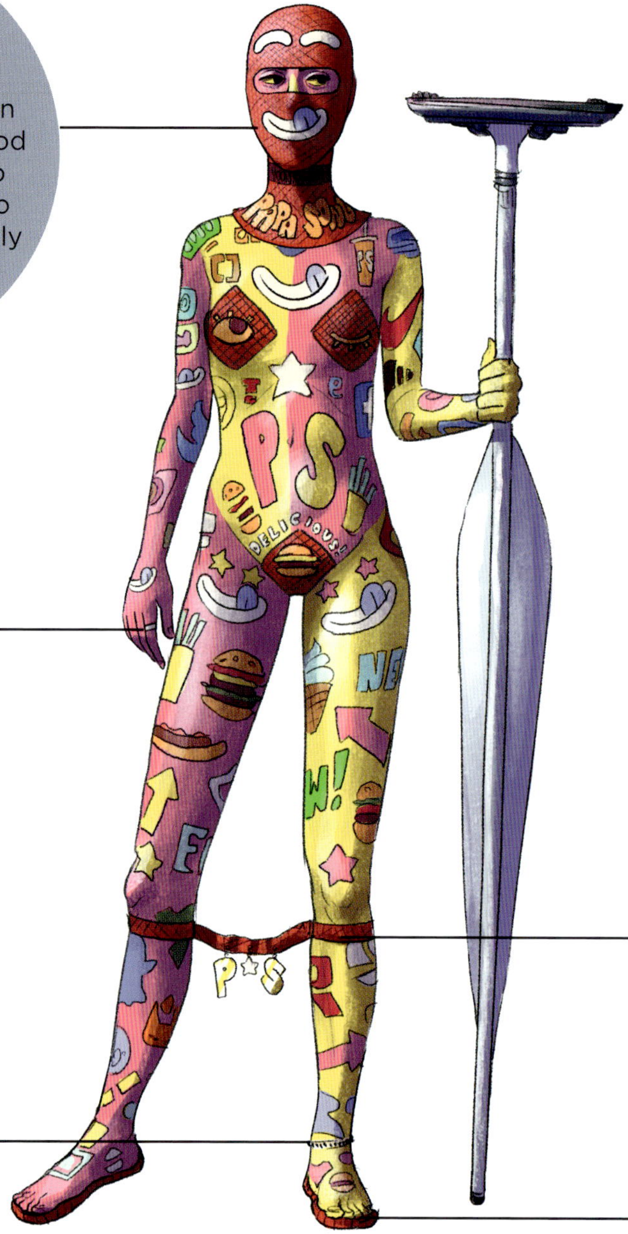

Even with her entire body tattooed in vibrant logos and corporate colors, Yoona-949 displays reminders of her sentience with a ring on her finger and bracelet around her ankle, taken from customers who dropped them.

Leg fetters are mandatory to ensure fabricants walk in tiny steps and do not have the ability to run. Of course, even this garment is also decorated in corporate advertisement.

Due to limited resources in the dying world, fabricants are given the bare minimum of 3D-printed fabric. Shoes are reduced to simple printed soles glued to feet.

YOONA-949 SANITATION FABRICANT - PAPA SONG'S - NEO SEOUL

Rich purebloods have holograms incorporated into their outfits in unique ways. Mrs. Rhee has a hologram of Papa Song dancing in her hair. The logoman being so high symbolizes valuing corporations more than individuals.

Fashion is forced to keep up with the mandatory weekly spending quota. Every week, citizens are required to recycle their 3D-printed clothing and purchase an entirely new wardrobe designed by the fashion corporation. Trends come and go quickly.

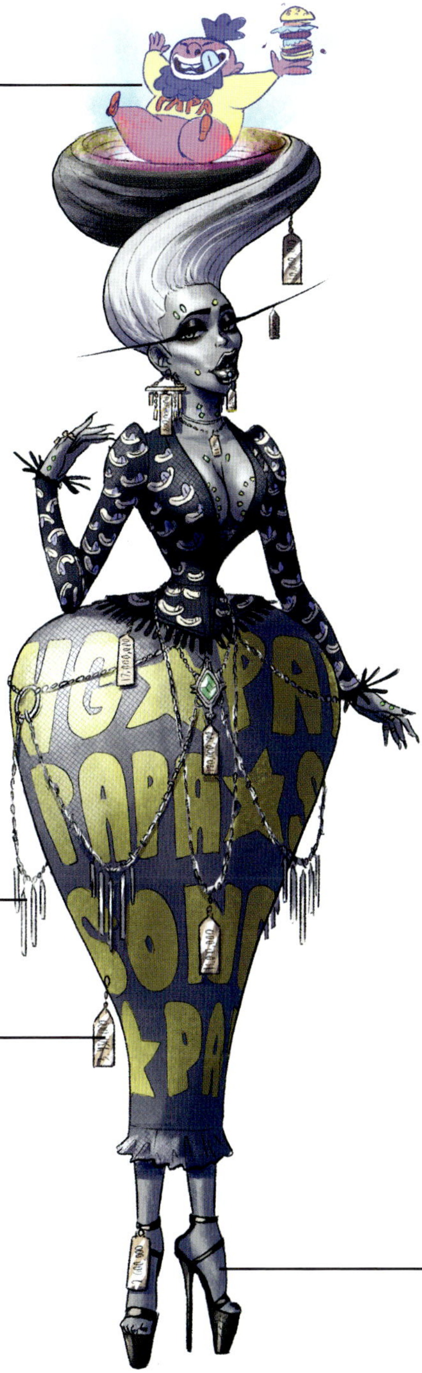

Purebloods wear precious metal price tags on every piece of clothing they purchase. Metal is scarce, so these tags display wealth and social class. They even hang from body modifications, such as Mrs. Rhee's extended lashes and enhanced lips.

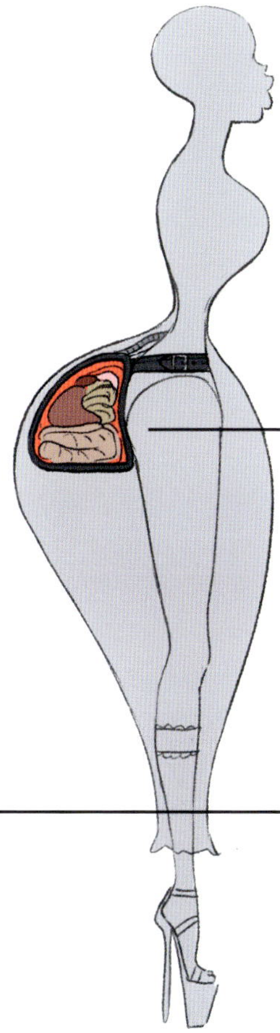

The illusion of a stable society is enforced by returning to traditional gender roles. Women's fertility is highly exaggerated with wide hips and tiny waists. The desirable waist diameter is so incredibly small that abdominal organs must be permanently relocated to a mechanical "false rump" through an expensive procedure.

The amount of metal in a stiletto heel signifies the wearer's wealth due to the material shortage. The higher the heel, the higher your status.

SEER RHEE'S WIFE PAPA SONG'S - NEO SEOUL

Due to the emphasis on traditional gender roles, hypermasculinity is encouraged. Boom-Sook has had many synthol injections in his arms to give the (poor) illusion of muscle mass.

Clothing is only built to last for a single week due to mandatory wardrobe recycling. However, Boom-Sook is lazy and often wears the same wardrobe for weeks on end, which is why the 3D-printed fabric is deteriorating.

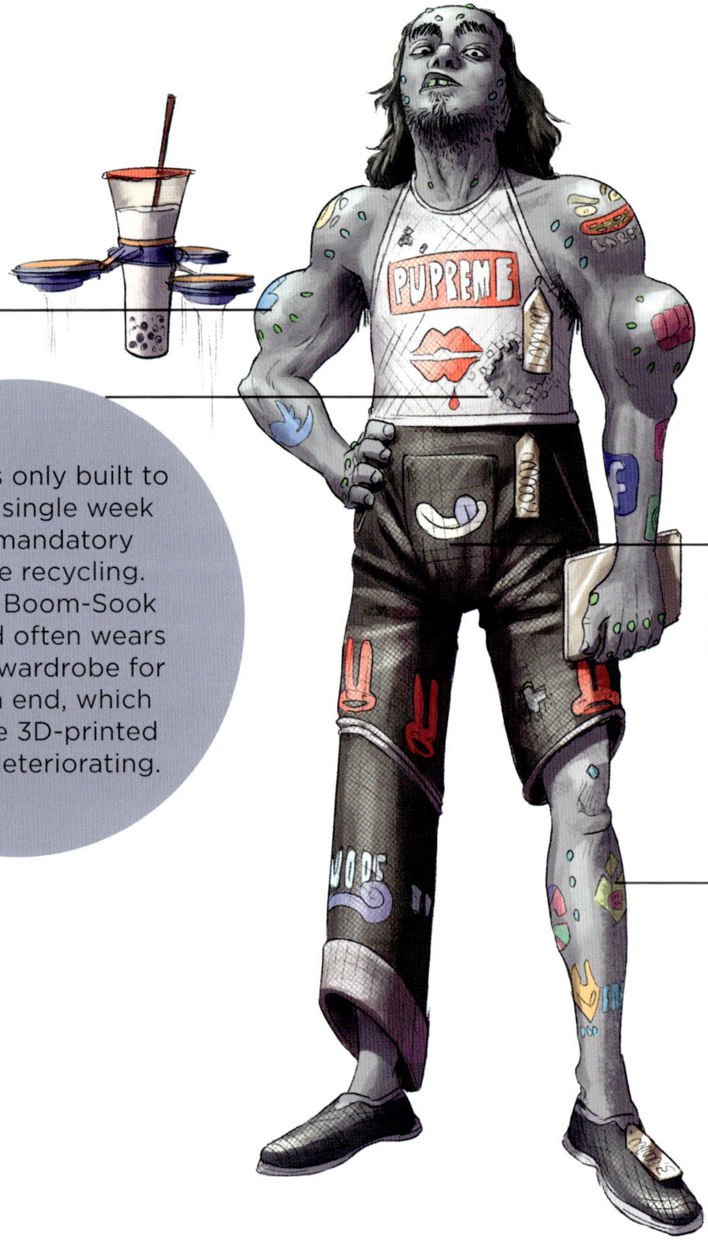

Historically, as society advances, color in clothing becomes more muted. This is taken a step further in corpocratic society, where humans are genetically coded to have greyscale skin, emphasizing the color of the toy-like fabricants and corporate logos instead of individual people.

The fly front is held in place with magnets and can be dropped with ease. Throughout history, men's flies have become increasingly easier to open, causing moral controversy along the way.

Mandatory tattoos and synthetic gemstones cover pureblood citizens' skin, even embedded into tooth and bone. In each gem is a monitoring device that covertly keeps track of citizens' health and adrenaline levels, reporting the data to the government.

BOOM-SOOK KIM STUDENT - TAEMOSAN UNIVERSITY - NEO SEOUL

Meronym's hood, inspired by a calash bonnet, can be pulled down to shield her face from the sun at a moment's notice. Over time, it's become a polite courtesy to keep your hood closed around informal company.

Highly reflective neoprene makes up most of her garments, providing protection from UV rays and other harsh elements.

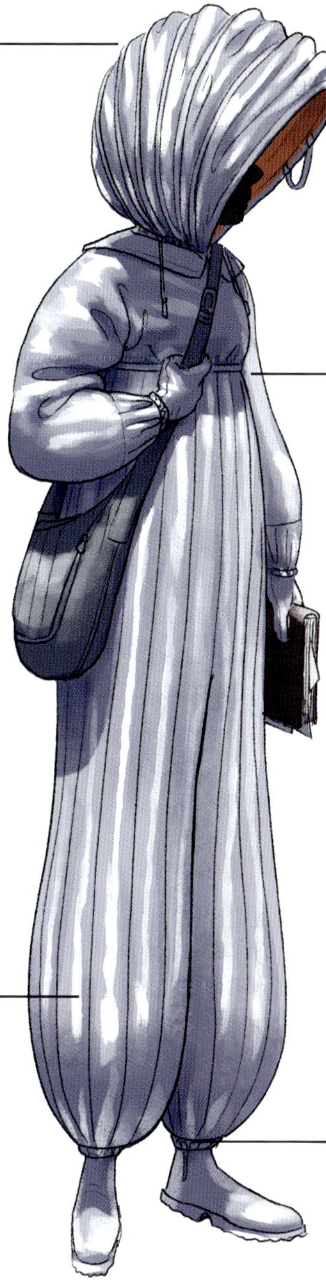

The pants are loose and baggy, allowing for a wide range of movement. Traditional gender roles are not as emphasized in prescient society and the column-shape silhouette reinforces that.

Death by disease is a constant threat in prescient society. Their anxiety is reflected in how high the waistline is on their clothing. This is mirrored in post-revolutionary European clothing having high waistlines.

The hem of the pants and sleeves are drawn tight with elastic, so no foreign contaminants may enter. Having loose sleeves is seen as obscene and shameful.

MERONYM PRESCIENT RESEARCHER - HA WHY

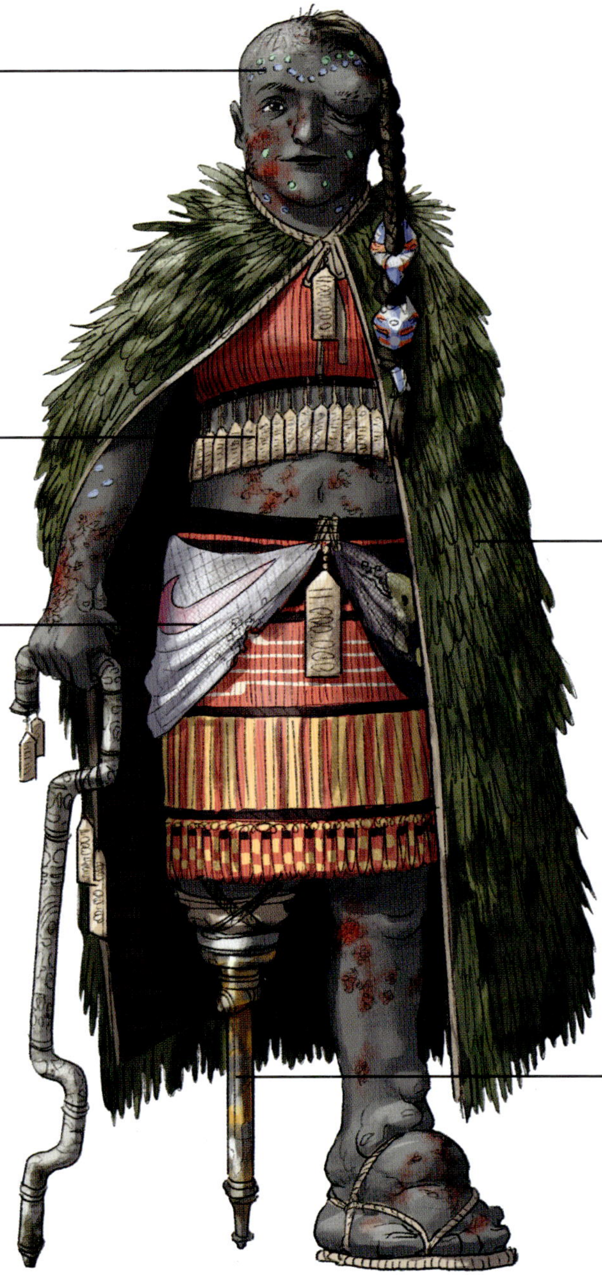

The Valleymen revere the "Old Uns", but the only information about their culture are old rusty advertisements. Things like price tags and gem-embedding are incorporated into Valleymen culture. Important figures such as the Abbess are bestowed with ancient price tags and colorful markings on the skin to resemble gems.

Ancient 3D-printed fabric is a rare artifact that only the Abbess may wear. It's only worn on special occasions, due to the fragility of the material that is crafted to only last a week with normal wear.

With the de-evolution of civilization, vibrant color returns to clothing, a stark contrast to the grey skin of the Valleymen who are descendants of greyscale purebloods.

A peaceful tribe, the Valleymen wear woven-reed cloaks in order to hide themselves among the flora when the Kona people attack.

Due to a heavily damaged ozone layer, Valleymen develop skin cancer at a young age, leading to short lifespans. Extreme bodily mutations have forced the Valleymen to find ways around disability, such as the Abbess's metal leg and uniquely tied sandal.

ABBESS LEADER OF THE VALLEYMEN - HA WHY

The main character, Zachry, envisions Sonmi surrounded by a halo of driftwood, in reverence of nature, and price tags, in reverence of the Old Uns' advanced society.

Sonmi's skin markings resemble skin cancer symptoms of the Valleymen, but are made up of small red flowers. This is a way for Zachry to cope with the red scabs that plague his people.

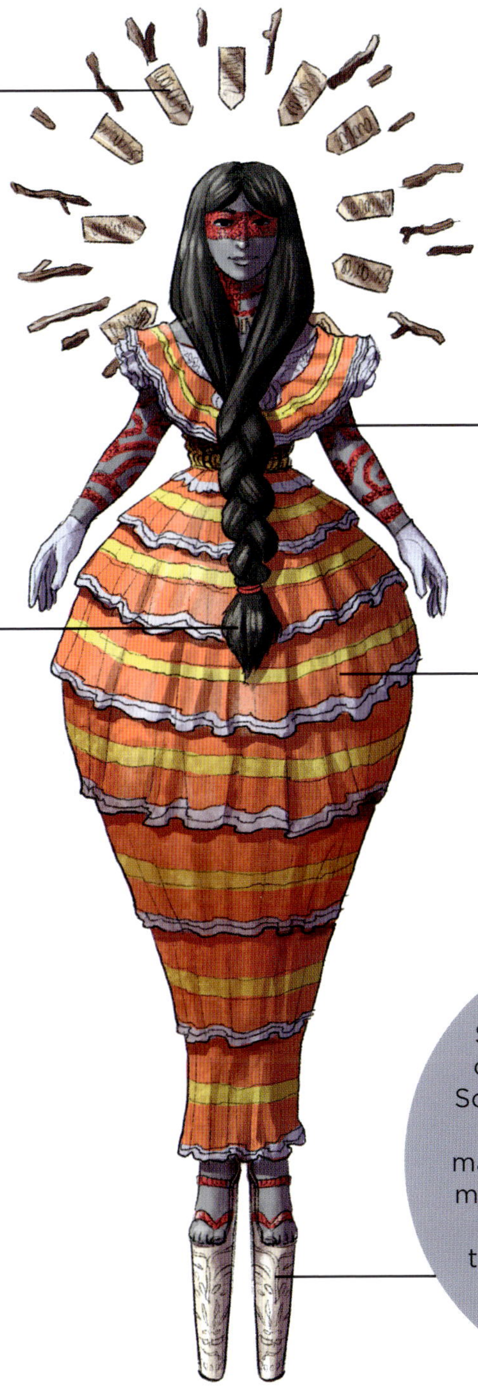

Long hair is a symbol of good health in Valleymen culture, so Zachry imagines Sonmi with a lustrous, healthy braid.

Since Zachry has visions of Old Georgie as a mid-19th-century middle-class man, it makes sense that he would also envision Sonmi's clothing to be inspired from that period. Her late-1850s dress is mixed with the extreme silhouette from corpocracy era fashion.

Since heels were a sign of status in corpocracy, Sonmi's shoes reflect that. Instead of 3D-printed material and metal, they're made of intricately carved bone, reminiscent of the personalized totems Valleymen worship.

SONMI GODDESS OF THE VALLEYMEN (AS ZACHRY ENVISIONS HER) - HA WHY

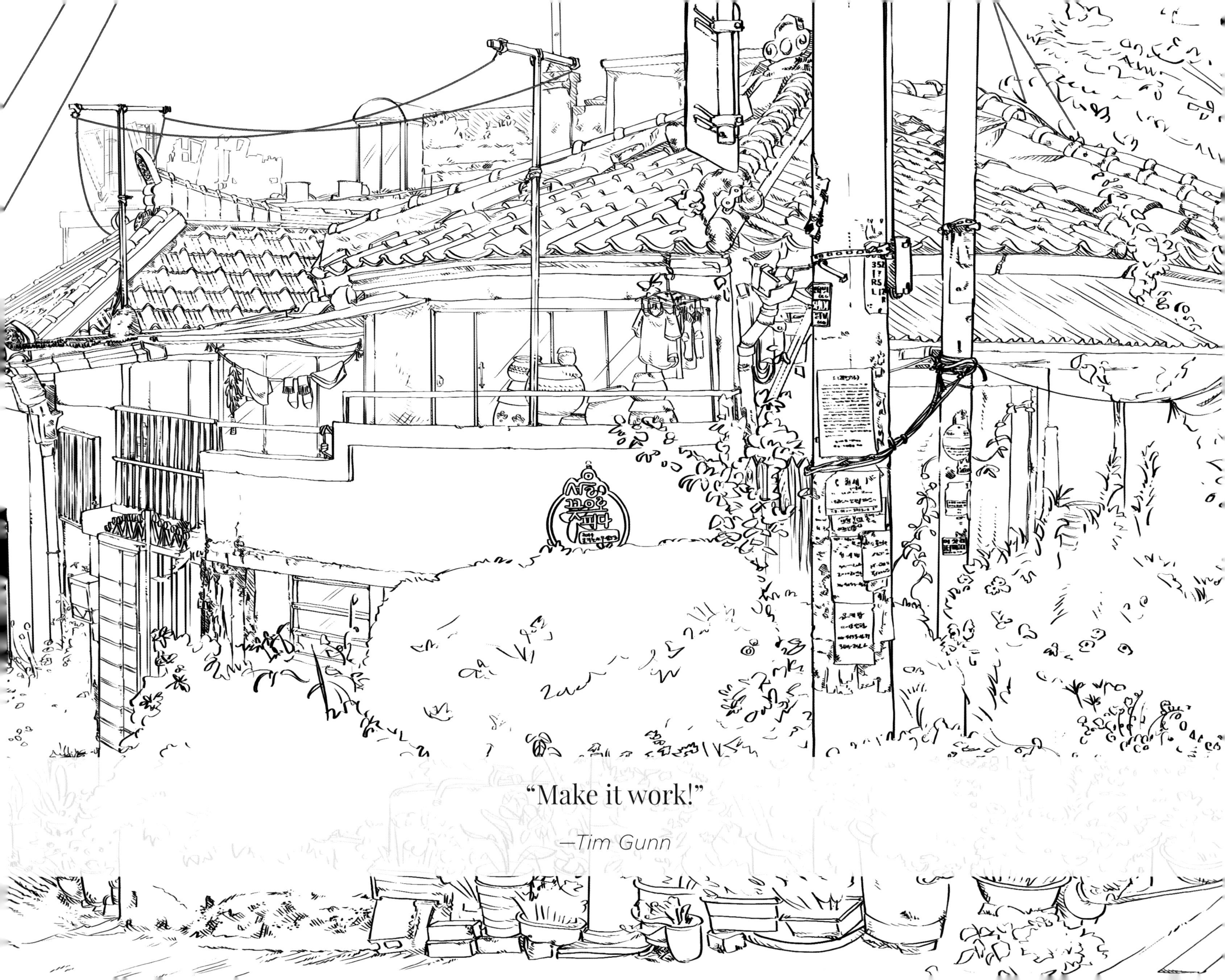

"Make it work!"

—*Tim Gunn*

Pattern Drafting

Understanding how patterns are made is like understanding perspective drawing. Yes, there are painful math numbers, and angles, and lines, and finessing curves, but knowing the fundamentals is important to knowing how to successfully suspend your audience's disbelief and push beyond the ordinary.

It may seem irrelevant but consideration of seam lines and how different decades used seams differently will play a role in helping the audience connect with the time and place you have chosen. Even if they are not trained in patternmaking, the audience will still have an intuitive sense for what looks natural or not. More ancient costumes would have had little to no tailoring, while more modern advances in patternmaking have led to more complex fits and shapes. How advanced your culture is in other aspects of their world, architecture, science, etc. can help you anticipate how advanced their clothing could be.

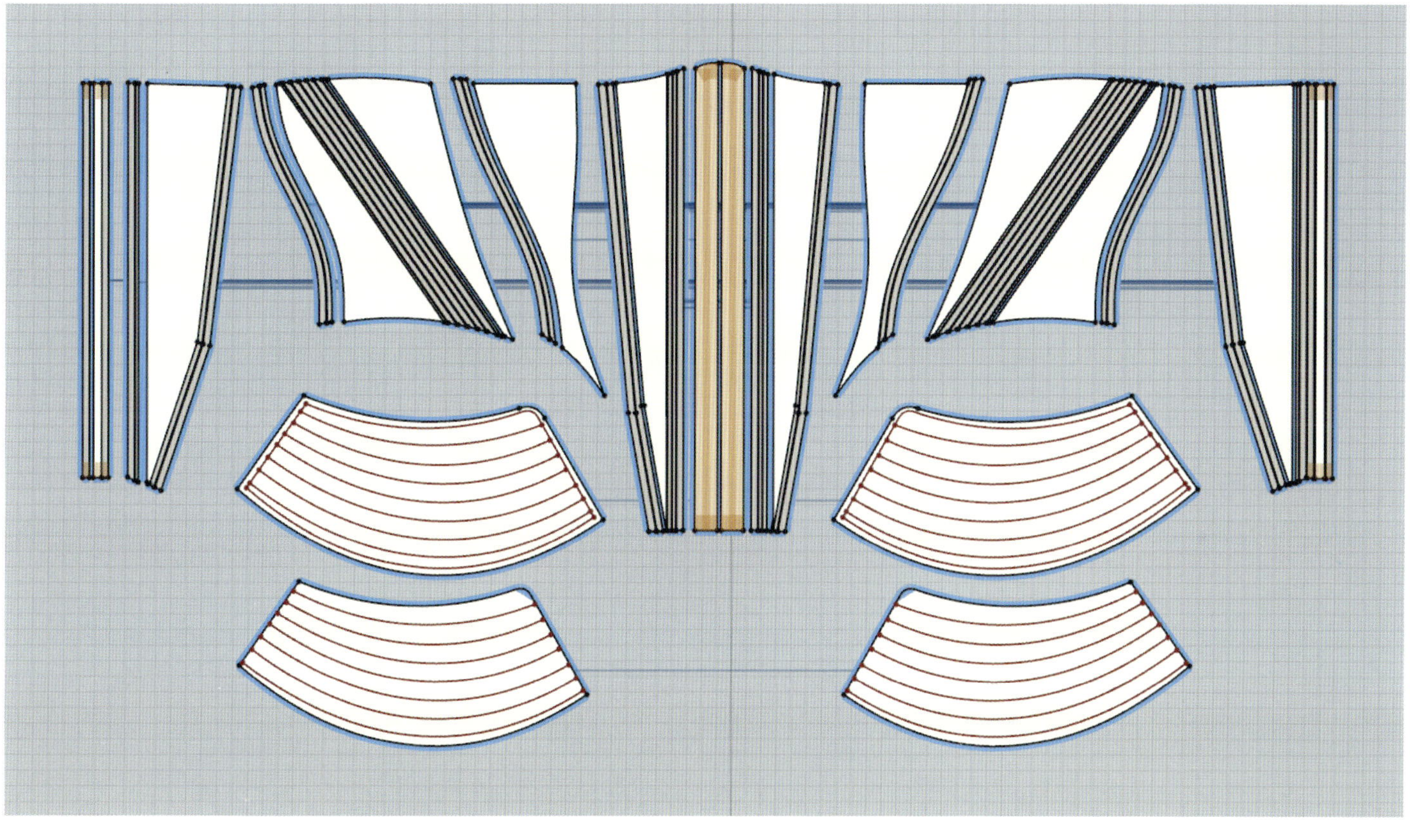

A pattern can make or break a good costume concept.

Whether it's drafting or draping, each fabricator has their own preference for one or the other method of patternmaking. You can use either or both to achieve the best results.

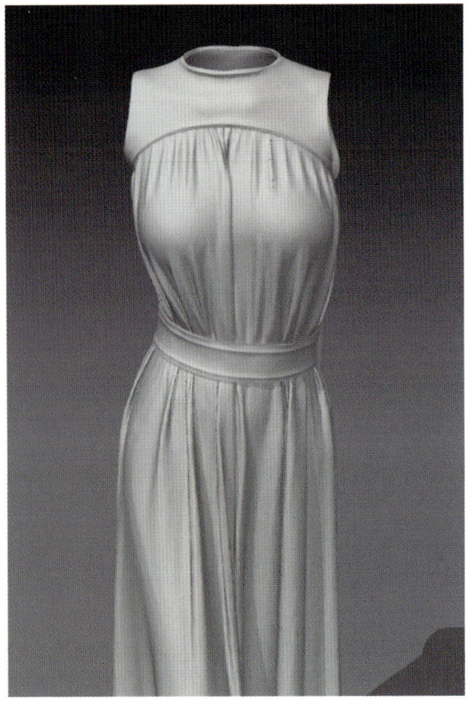

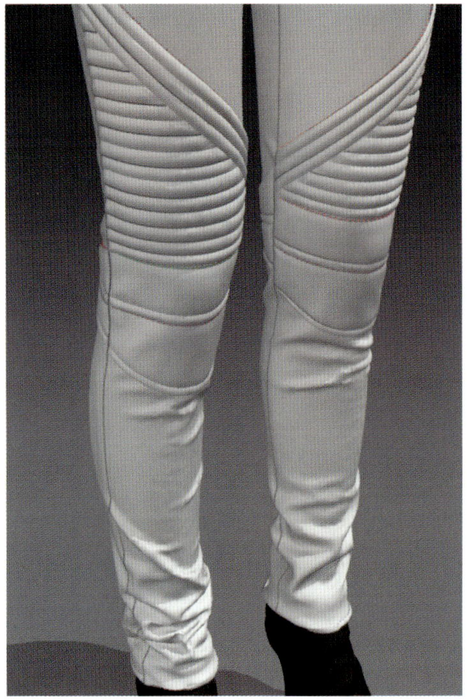

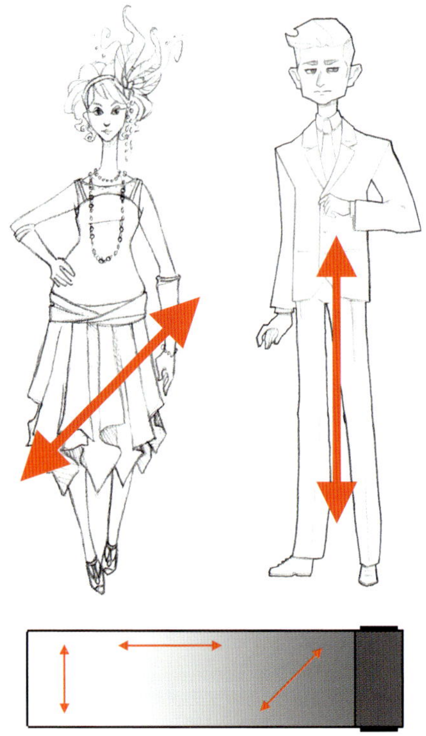

DRAPING

Draping is done by applying fabric directly to the body or form you are costuming, using pins to plot out details. Once roughed out in this way, it is transferred to a paper format. This is usually on a per garment basis and seems to work best for irregular forms—like puppet bodies that don't often adhere to formulas designed for full-sized humans. Most commonly used in womenswear.

DRAFTING

Drafting is done by taking measurements and then applying formulas to those findings to determine how to draw the pattern on paper using the appropriate rulers and curves. Usually one would start this method by creating a sloper (a form-fitting shell—no seam allowances!) that could then be used to make any variation wanted. Knowing how to alter things in this state is helpful if you need to go back to make tweaks to a pattern. Most commonly used in menswear.

GRAIN LINE

The direction of woven threads in fabric creates a grain. The grain line of the fabric and how it is placed in the pattern will determine how well your costume falls on the body. A well-placed grain allows the character to wear the costume naturally as opposed to fighting the grain and creating odd ripples and sagging areas.

Equal to understanding the templates is understanding the material you plan to use. How does the fabric behave? Does it naturally have a lot of body, or does it hang heavy? Will it shimmer uncontrollably on camera with every lighting shift? What kind of stretch does it have? Can you cheat stretch by cutting the pattern out on a diagonal (bias cut)? How will changing the grain line change how the garment hangs, wears, or warps?

Explore how your fabric material behaves and warps over time and study how the pattern aids or decreases the longevity of your constructed piece.

VOCABULARY OF ELEMENTS

Darts: Tucks or folds that are sewn in to create shaping in a garment. They aren't just for women's busts. You wouldn't see darts in early medieval clothing because they didn't have buttons yet. No buttons, no way of getting into and out of fitted clothes; nobody had time for that.

Style Line: Serves to shape the garment to fit the form, like a seam line, but style based. Can be decorative. Absorbs darts.

Cut: Refers to the silhouette. Alternate way to reference the effect of the style lines.

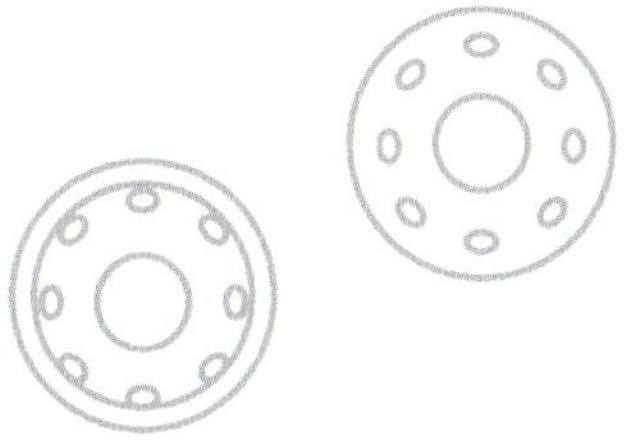

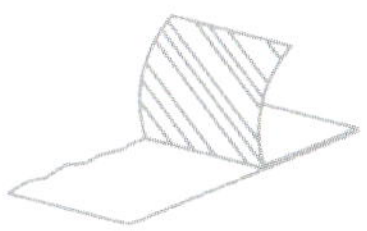

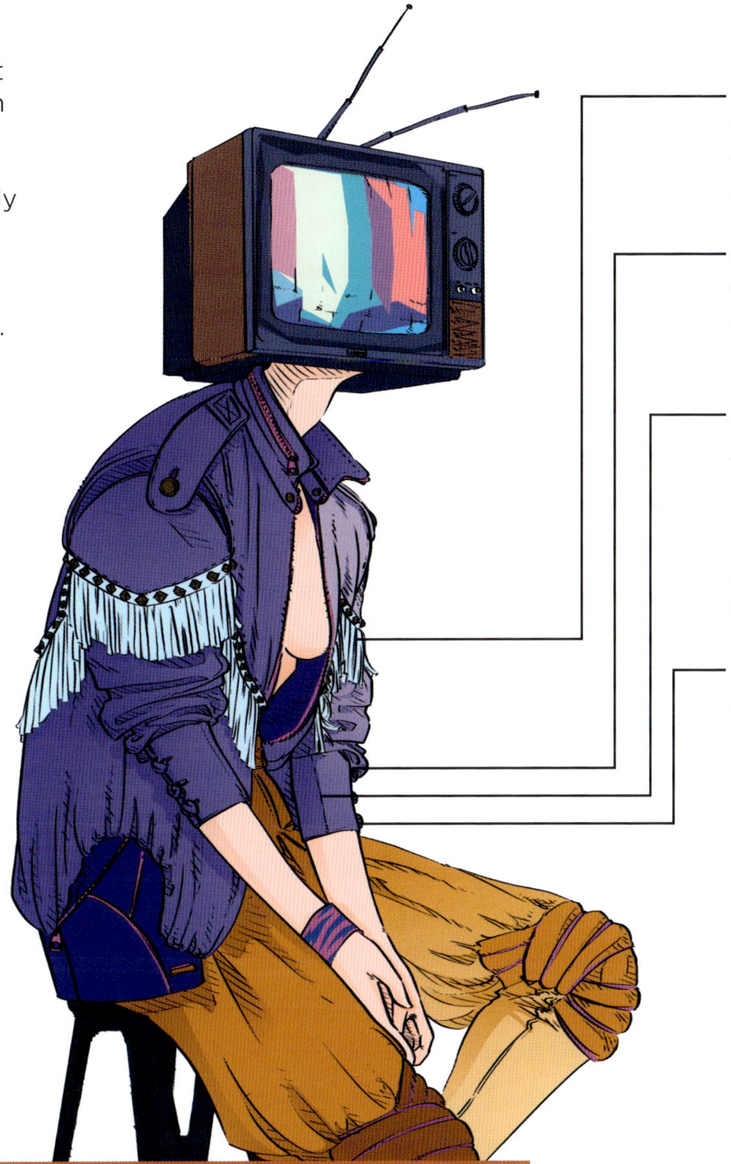

Embellishments: Decorative elements that serve aesthetic rather than function—in this case, fringe, studs, the collar zipper, and the ornamental shoulder details (epaulet).

Closures: Point at which a garment is fastened together, as opposed to a seam where it would be stitched closed. This allows it to open or close, such as zippers, hook and eyes, hook and loops, frogs, buttons, etc.

Seam lines: Where each individual piece of cloth is joined to create a garment. This is generally seen as a line. On a typical T-shirt you would expect to see these lines on the sides from your armpit to the bottom hem, along your various hems, around your arm hole, around your neck if the shirt has a collar, and on the underside of your sleeve.

Hems: A finished edge of a garment, usually folded and stitched in place so it doesn't unravel.

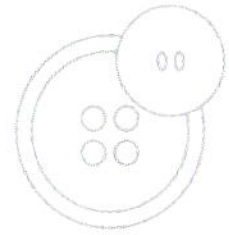

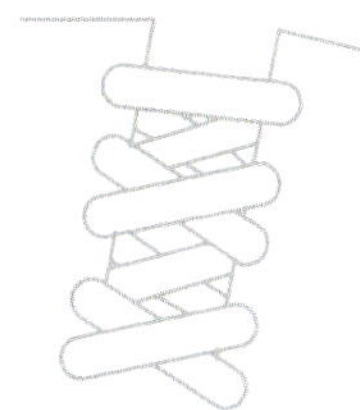

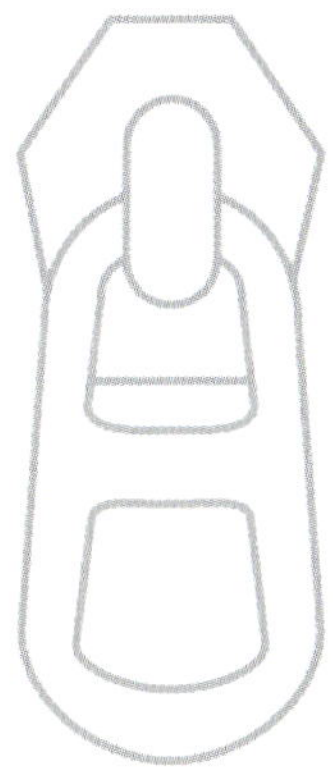

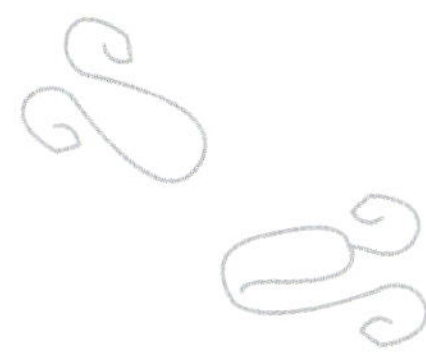

TIP:

Avoid using these closures visibly in a time period before they were invented!

- Buttons—13th century
- Hook and Eyes—14th century
- Snaps—1885
- Zippers—1925
- Hook and Loop (Velcro)—1955

Material Behavior

How you draft, drape, cut, and scale the material will impact our design's movement qualities. Studying different fabrics and fit will help you better understand how the character's movement, posture, and acting may be affected.

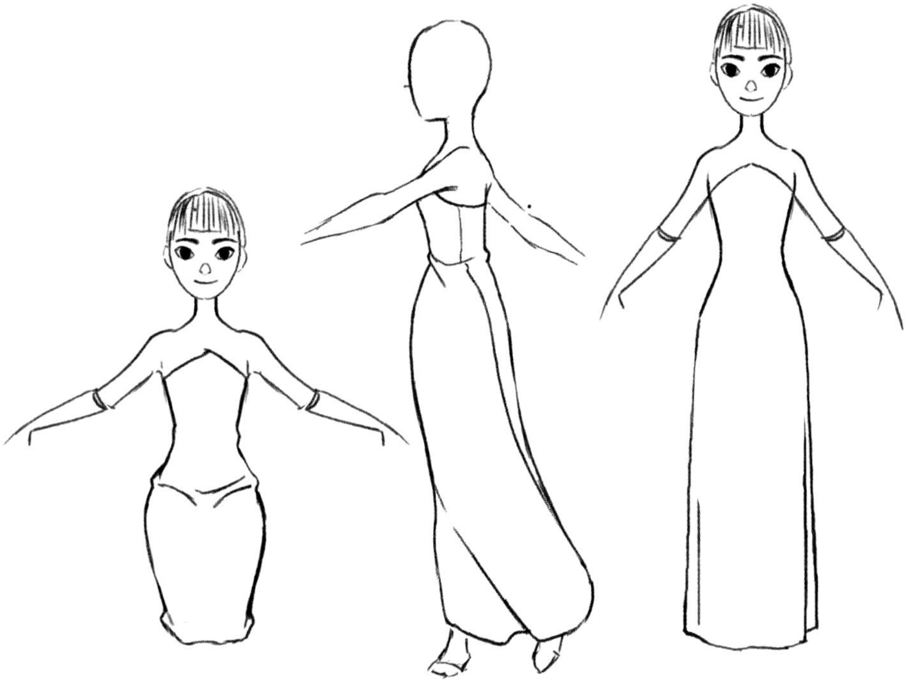

Dress with thick inflexible fabric

Because the textile is inflexible, e.g., cotton, the person wearing a dress of this type would not be able to move as much. Here you see the dress lacks folds and has a smoother look. A common example of this type of dress is a qipao, which has an open skirt so the wearer can move their legs more freely.

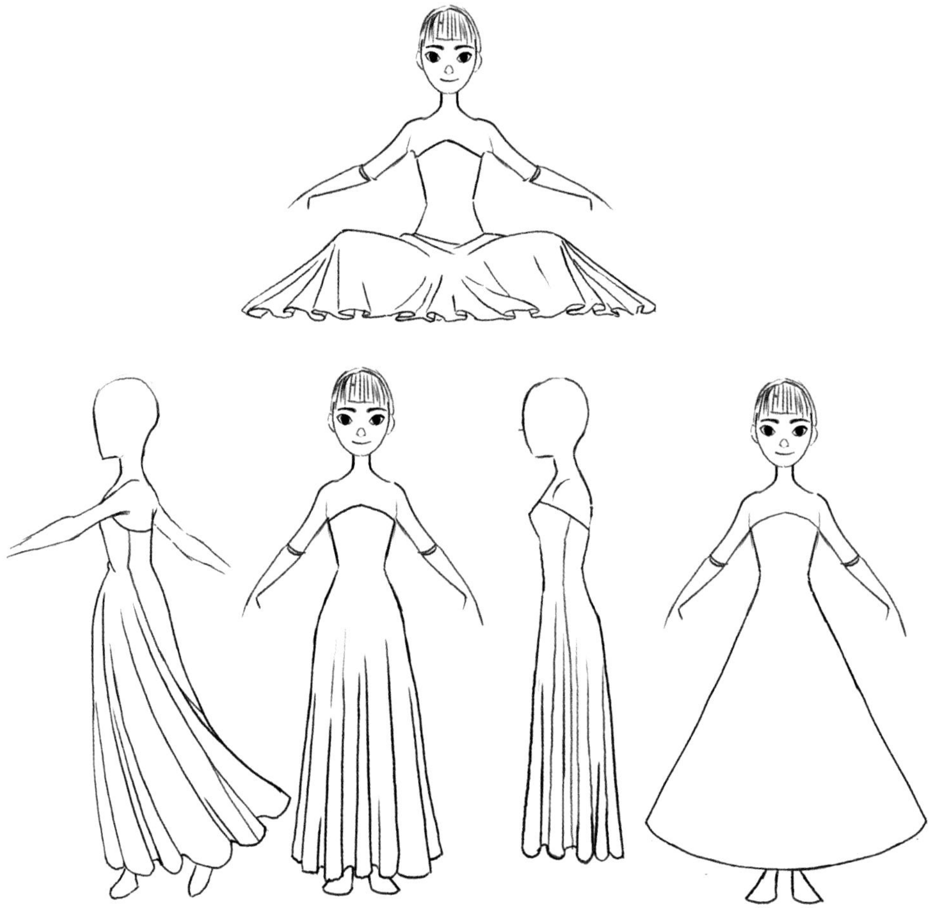

Dress with no volume and thin flowy fabric

Dresses with thin, flowy fabric won't have much volume, but the more fabric you use, the more small folds you will get. You can see this in materials with elastic properties or silks. While standing, it will rest against the body, but when moving or when blown by the wind, the fabric will be able take a larg-er space around the wearer.

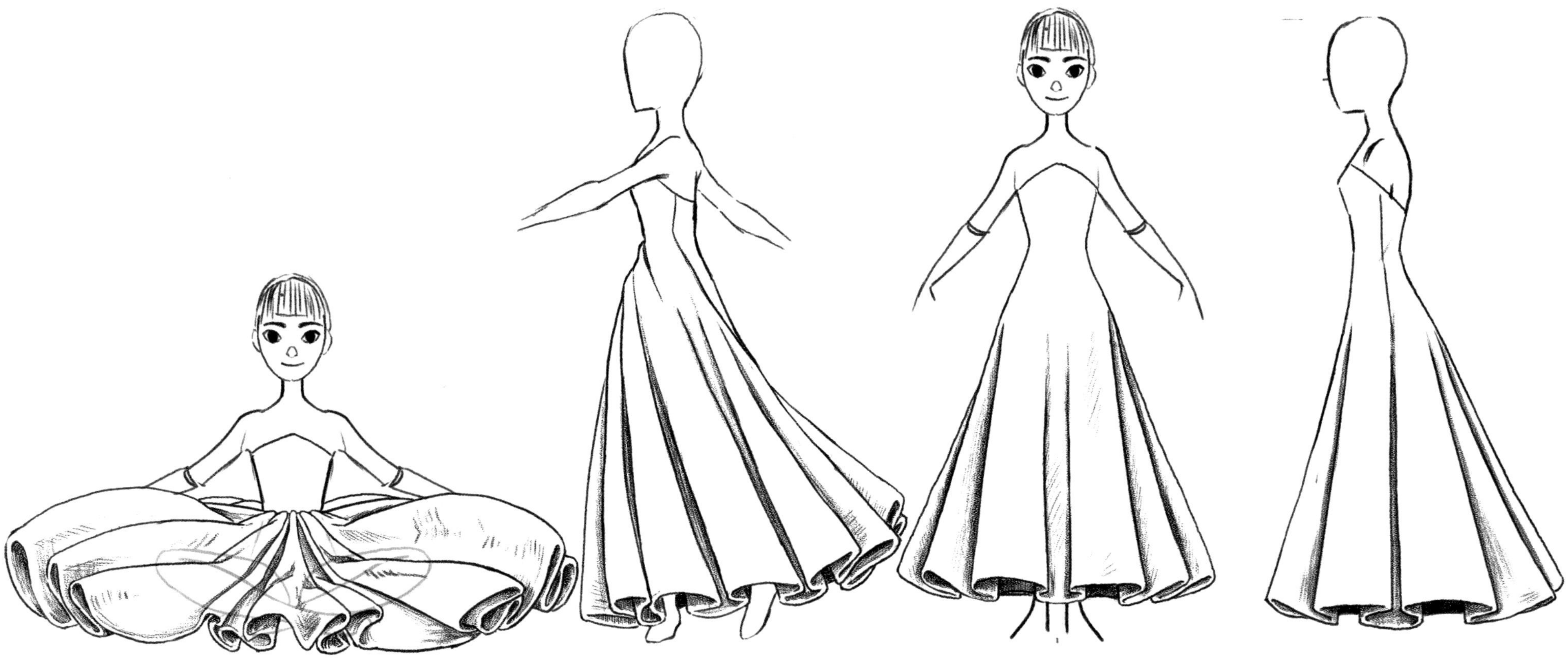

THICKNESS

When the dress to the left is created with a thicker textile, the skirt will create large folds. No underskirt is necessary to achieve the volume. It will have a more triangular shape than circular. Dresses with this type of fabric are more commonly found at formal events and are usually decorated with embroidery, as the fabric can handle a large amount of stitching.

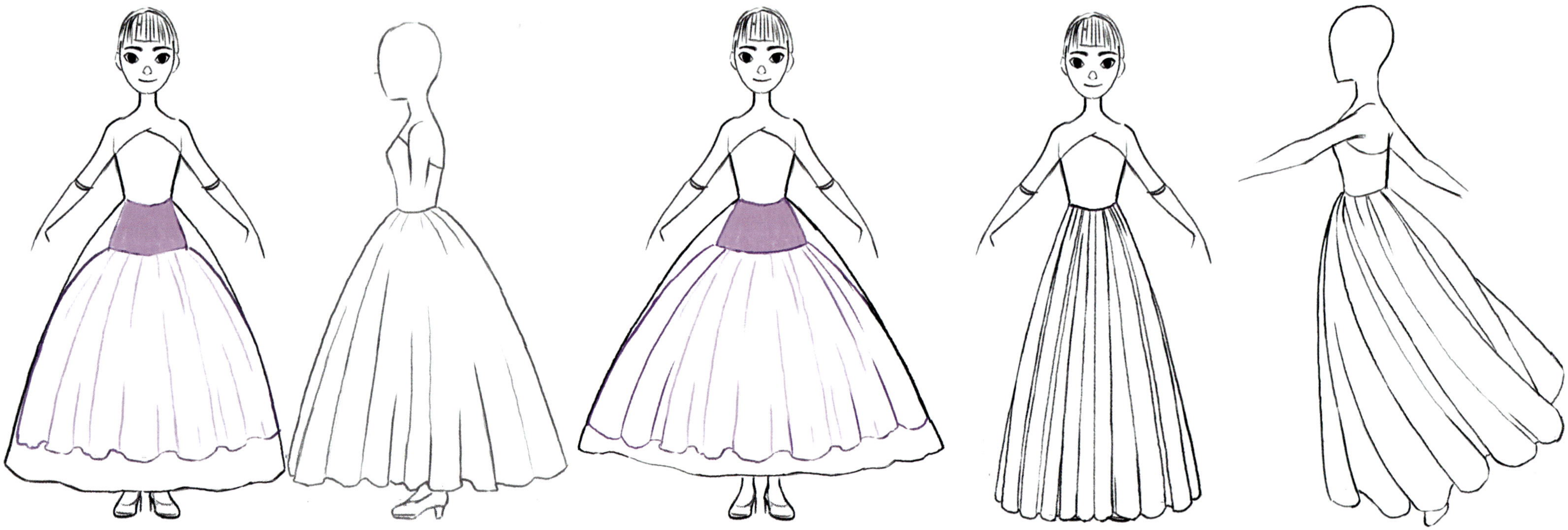

Dress with volume and thin fabric

For the skirt to have volume, a petticoat with layers will give the skirt a rounder appearance. With textiles that are thin, more layers are necessary to achieve volume; for example, the more tulle you add to the underskirt, the bigger the volume becomes. If you remove the petticoat, the skirt will be too long.

When sitting, the underskirt will show.

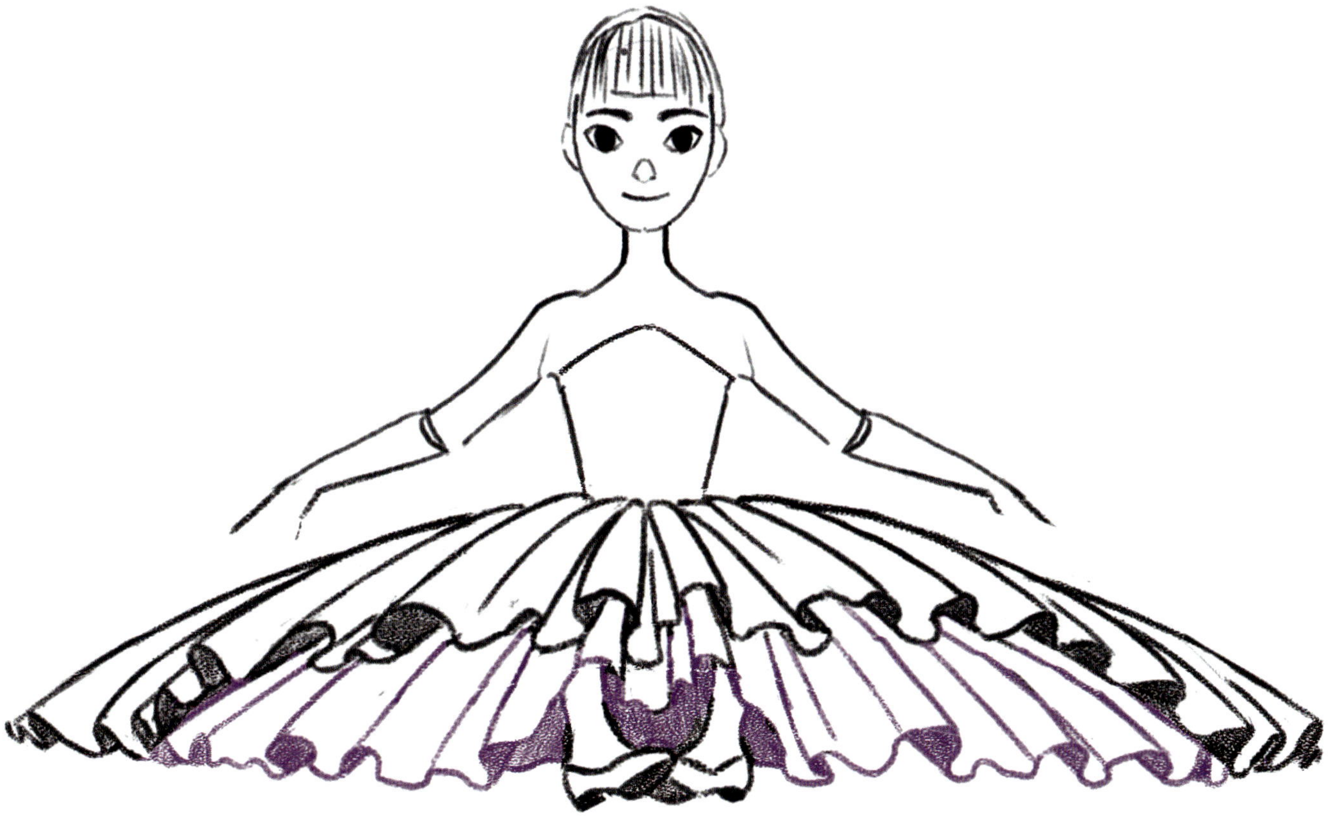

TIP:

With elements like shoulder pauldrons, it can be tempting to create highly decorative pieces, but if your character were to reach up, they could impale themselves. By keeping your character's full range of movement in mind as you design, you'll save the project (and your character) from unnecessary blood, sweat, and tears.

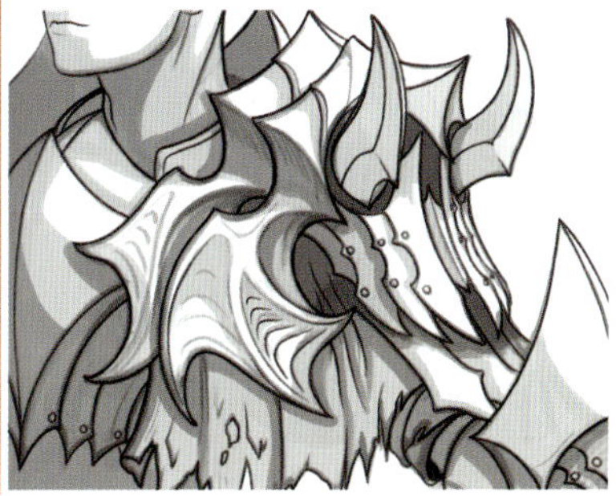

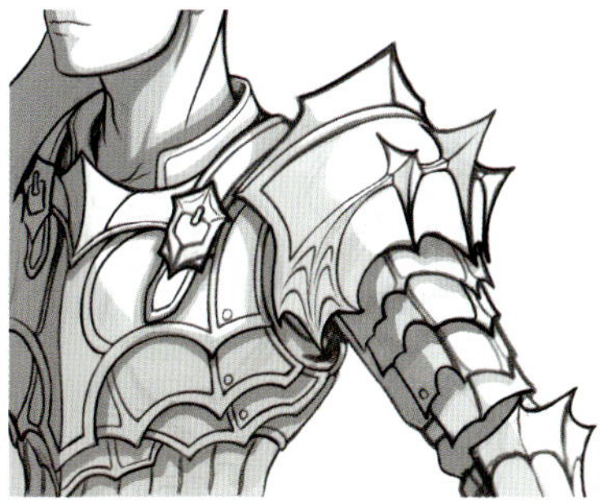

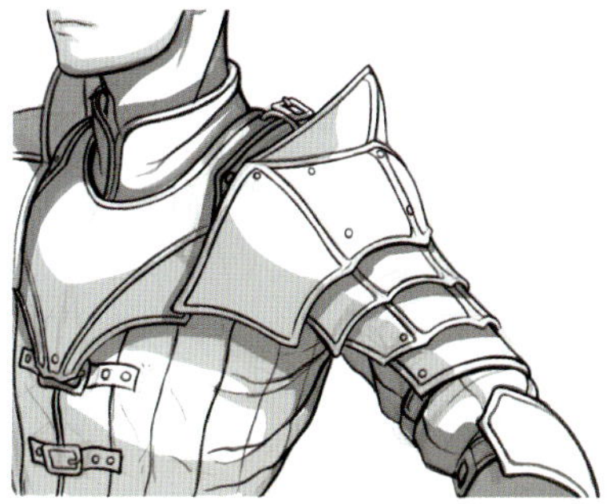

Types of Folds

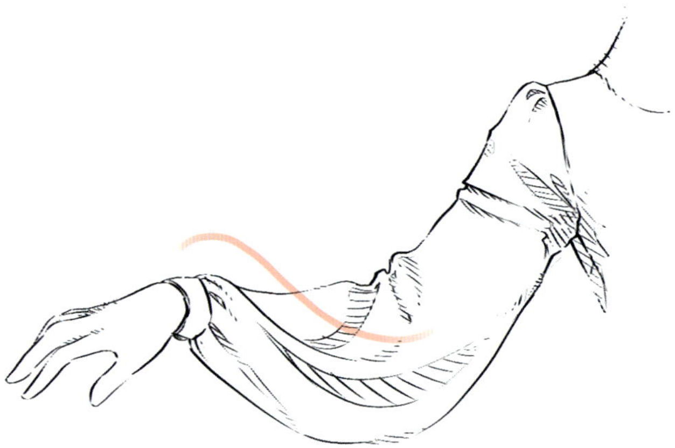

drape fold

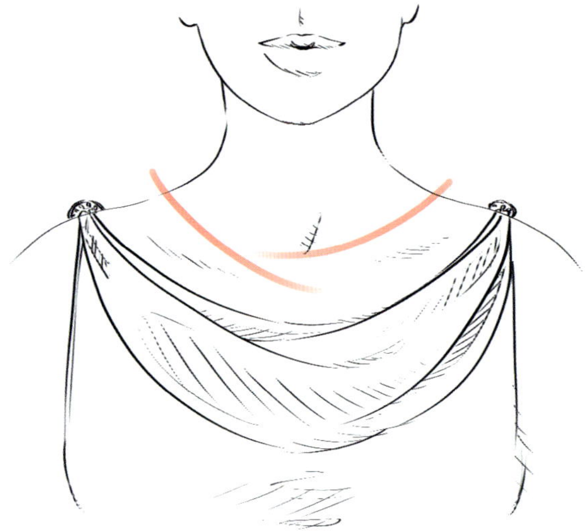

diaper fold

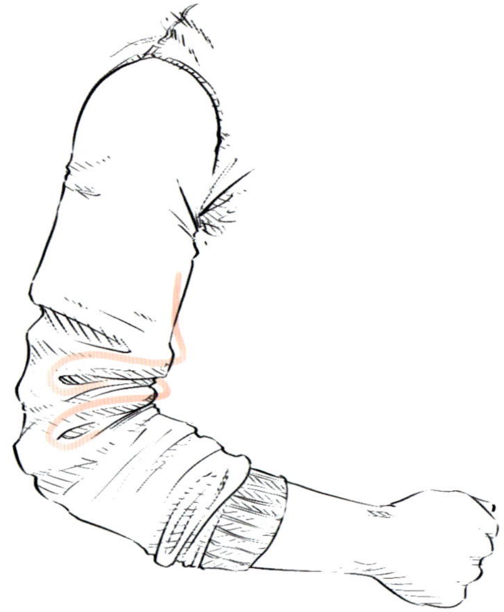

half-lock fold

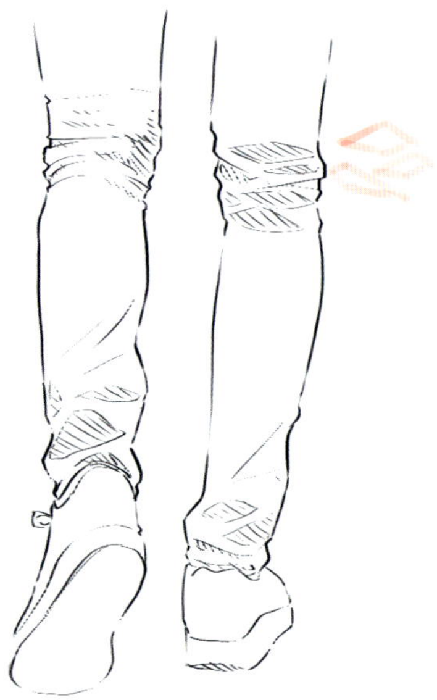

zigzag fold

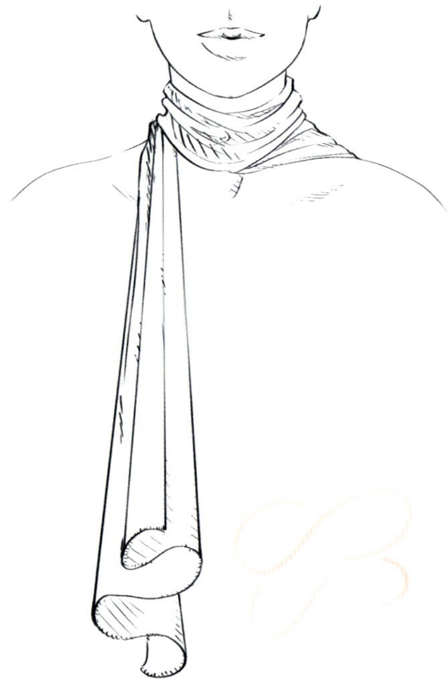

pipe fold

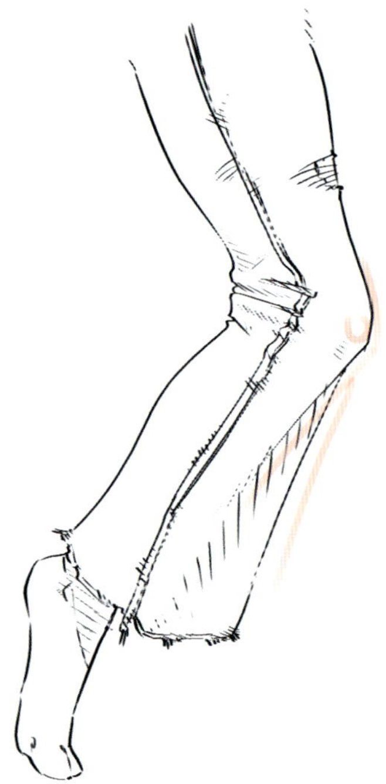

drop fold

EXERCISE: FOLDS IN ACTION

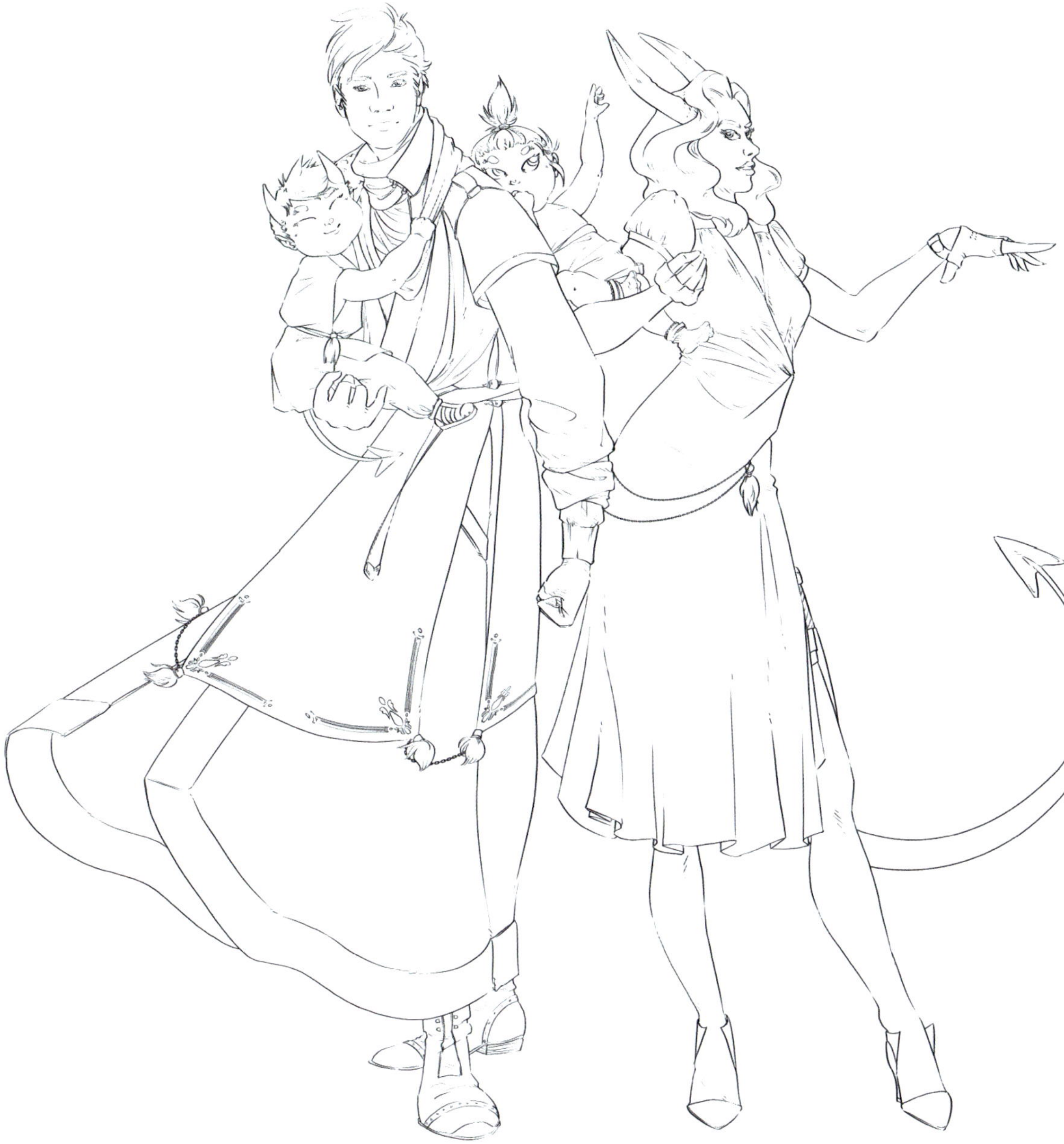

Draw your character(s) in a pose that features one or more types of folds. Gather reference of similar garments in motion to understand the types of folds you will need.

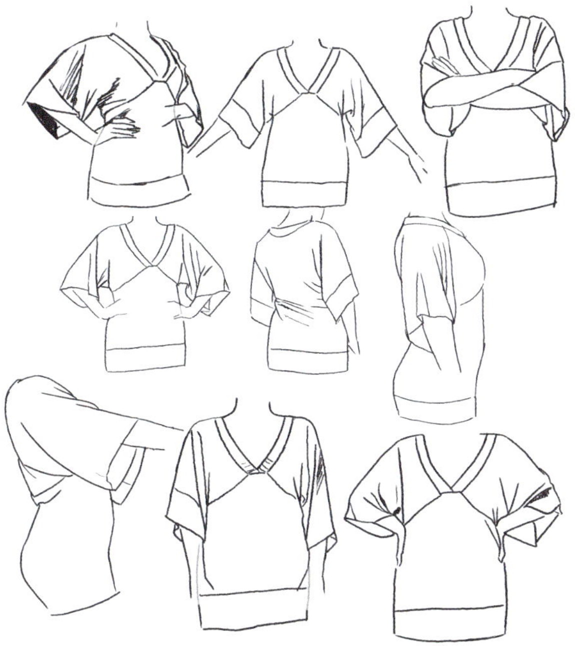

TIP:

Having trouble finding or understanding your reference? Find physical pieces made of similar material to wear as you recreate the poses. Or drape a physical piece of the material to see what would happen to the shapes as the material moves.

EXERCISE: RANGE OF MOTION

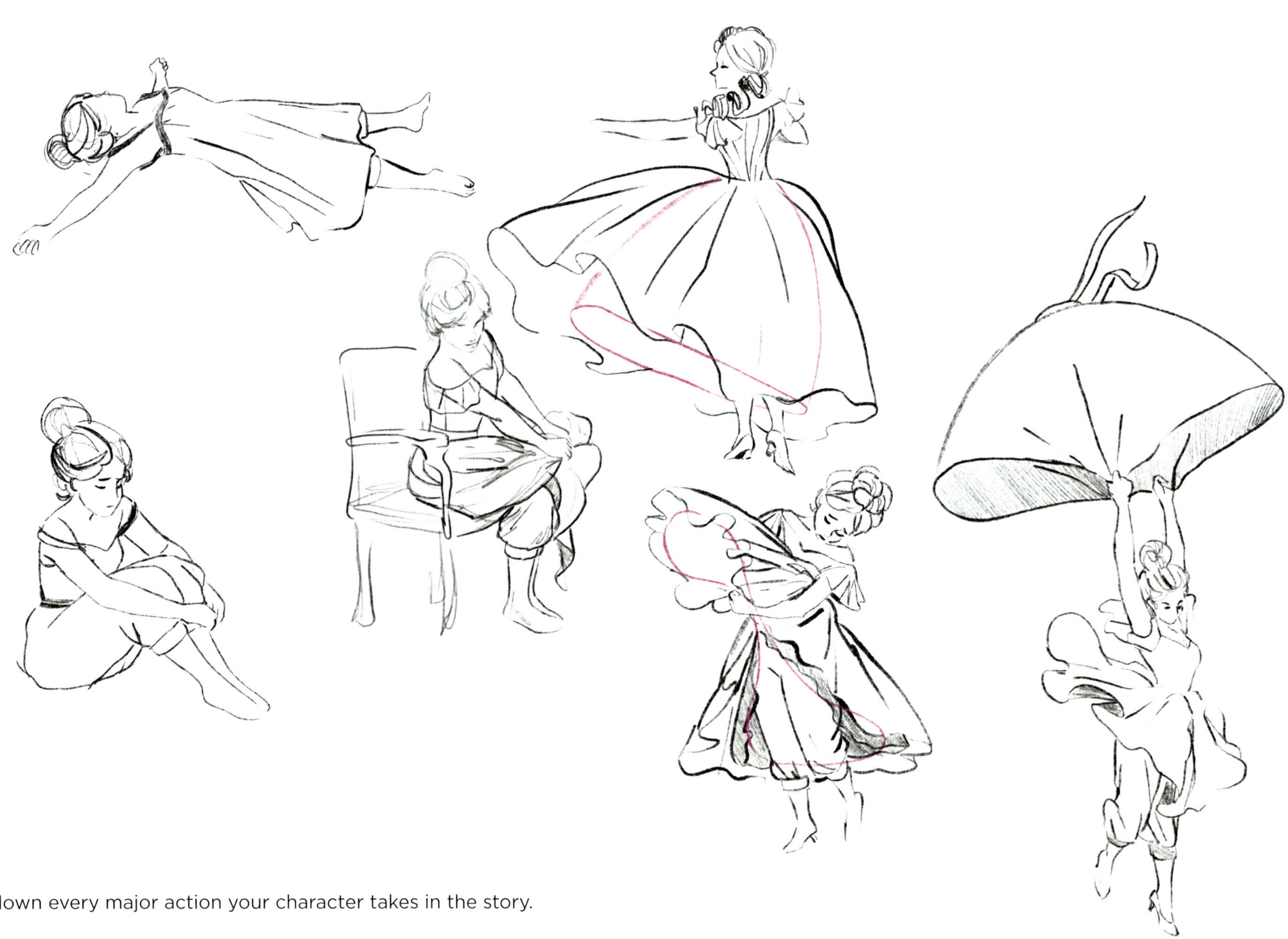

Write down every major action your character takes in the story.

Don't gloss over the details. If the character is sitting, how are they sitting? On the floor? In a chair? On a step? How committed to the sitting action are they? Is the character comfortable? Exhausted? Afraid the chair will break? By breaking down the movements your character will need to make, you'll know exactly what range of motion to build into your costume.

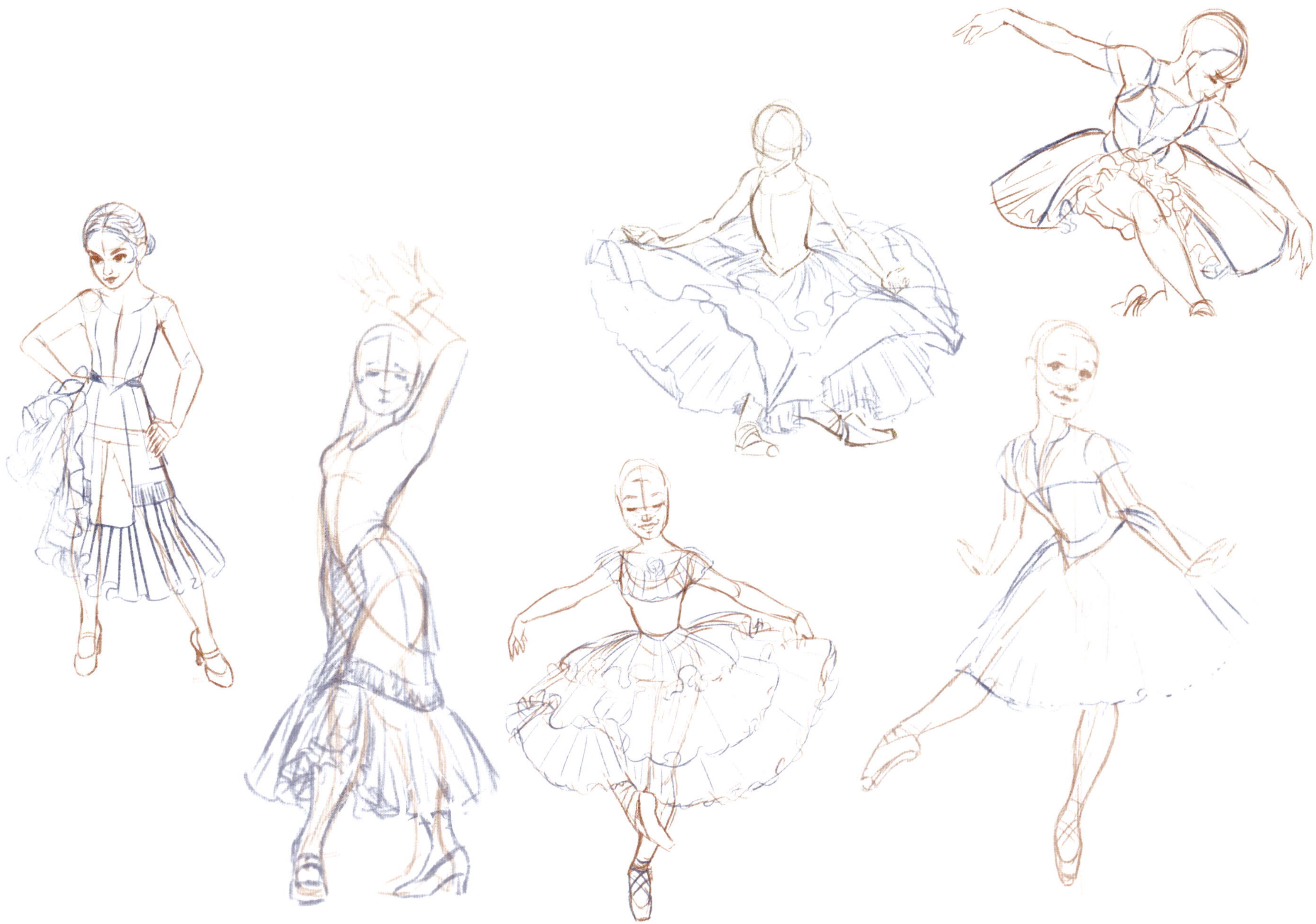

Study your character's range of movement in a set of sketches. For the Dancing Princess on page 80, Maria created these sketches.

As seen on page 89, she also studied real world examples of ballerinas to better understand the material behaviors and find potential poses.

Internal Structure

As shown in passage of time or with the petticoats, fabric lying directly against the character's skin will not always create the desired effect. Some costumes require an internal structure, and understanding its full impact on the movement, along with the traditional fabrication approach, will help you replicate the desired effect more clearly.

Beyond taking formal patternmaking courses, historical pattern books and free online patterns can hold a wealth of insight for your designs. You can also find videos of reproduction fabricators and seamstresses talking through their process to broaden your understanding.

By combining classical training in patternmaking with understanding of 3D/digital garment construction, e.g., Marvelous Designer, Maya, and ZBrush, a costume designer can find tools and tricks that can bridge the gap for mediums like 3D animation.

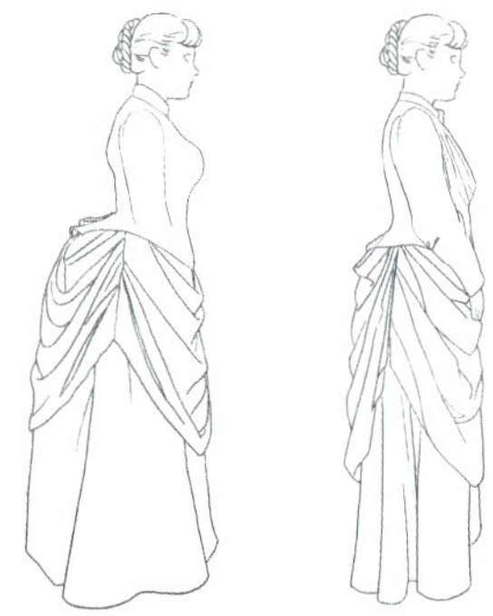

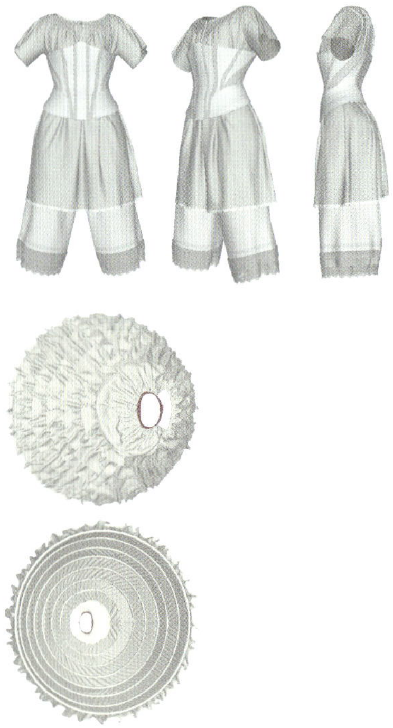

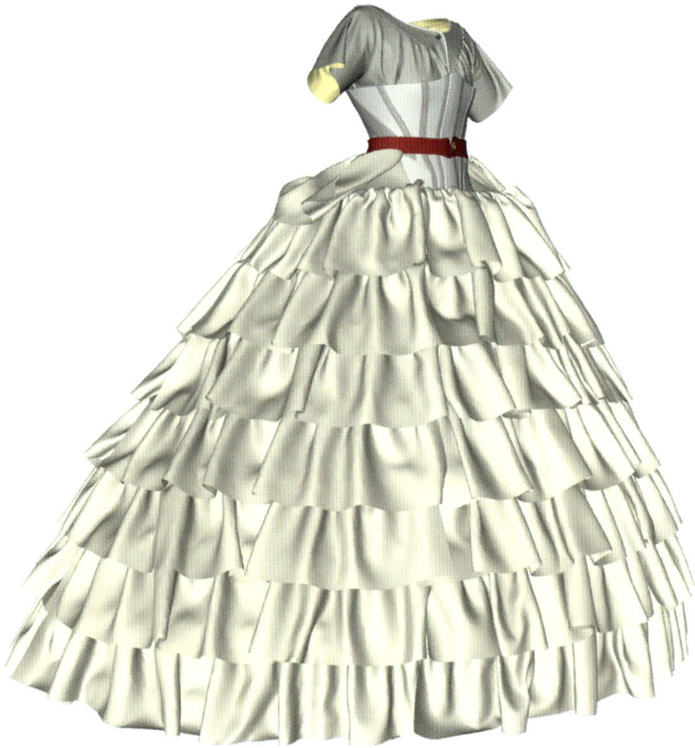

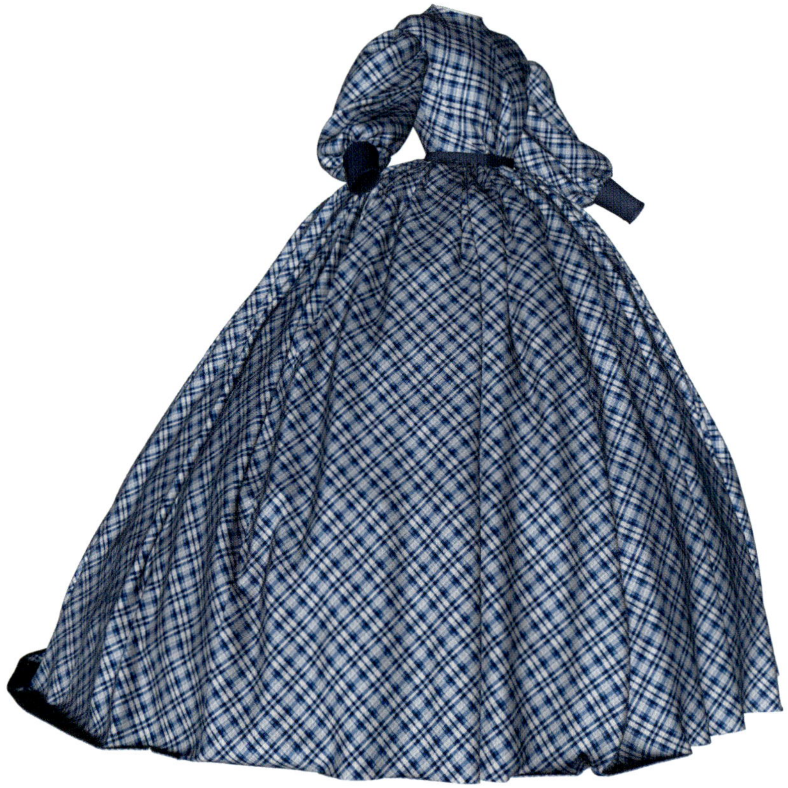

Stylized Bodies

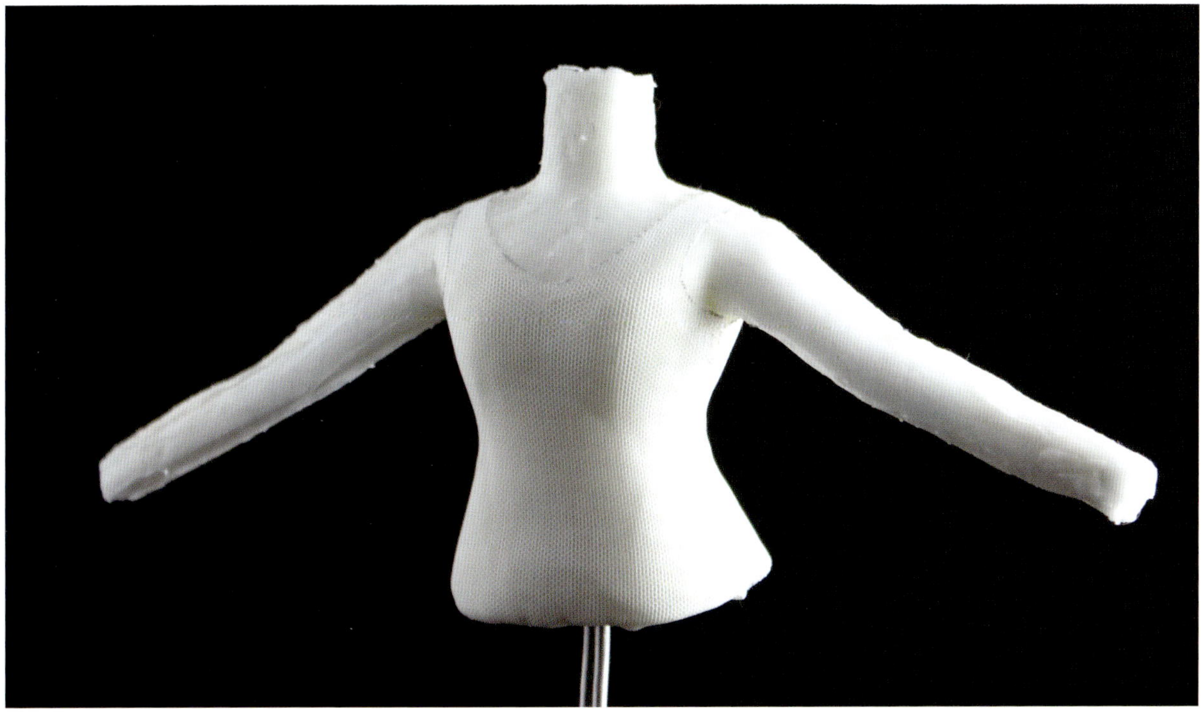

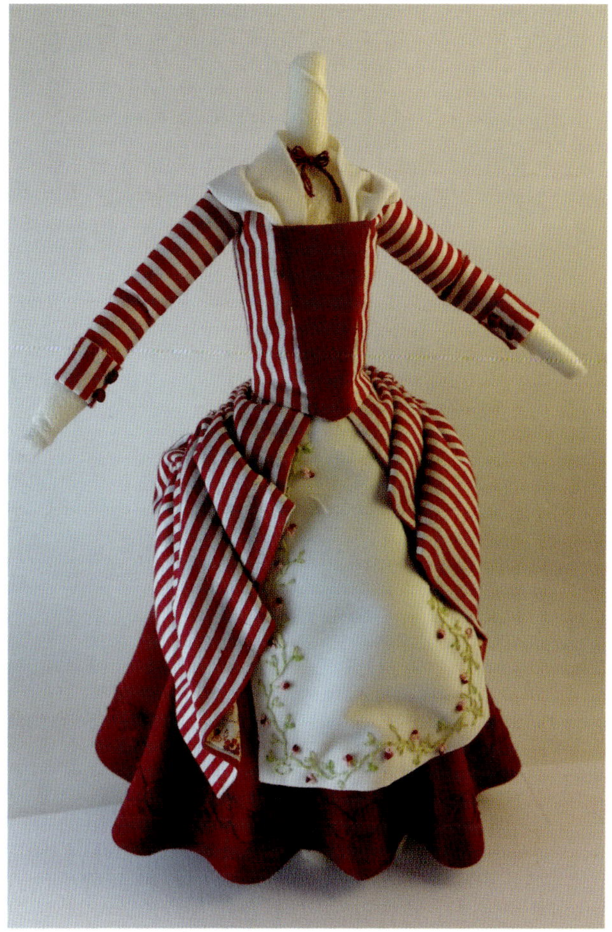

In stylized animation, it's more likely that one will encounter a character body that was already roughly shaped in a particular way (narrow waist or shapely hips). Adding a scaled-down corset on top of an already shaped waist wouldn't serve a purpose. In stop-motion, it would only hinder things and create undesirable shifting, or crawling, as the costume interacted with the corset during animation. It's one thing to sew a pretty dress, another thing entirely to sew one that can move frame by frame with the rest of the puppet or CG model.

For example, how do you secure a garment to a stop-motion puppet if there's no undergarments and you don't want to damage the puppet body itself? A close-fitting mesh bodysuit can provide anchor points and also help replicate gravity at the shoulders. Just make sure you keep your access points clear so you can get back in to increase tension in joints if needed. To preserve the range of movement in a particular high-use area, such as the shoulder, a model would not have pre-shaped shoulders. This is when shoulder pads would be used.

Imagine your design will be stop-motion animated. Based on your range of movement studies, where do you think you would delete or add internal structure vs. building the shape into the character's body?

TIP:

Simply building a pattern that fits the character and/or internal structure in a T pose may be tempting, but the result will lead to odd bunching and strain on the fabric and seams. Create your character in an A pose to improve your pattern.

MOCKING UP A SCALE PATTERN

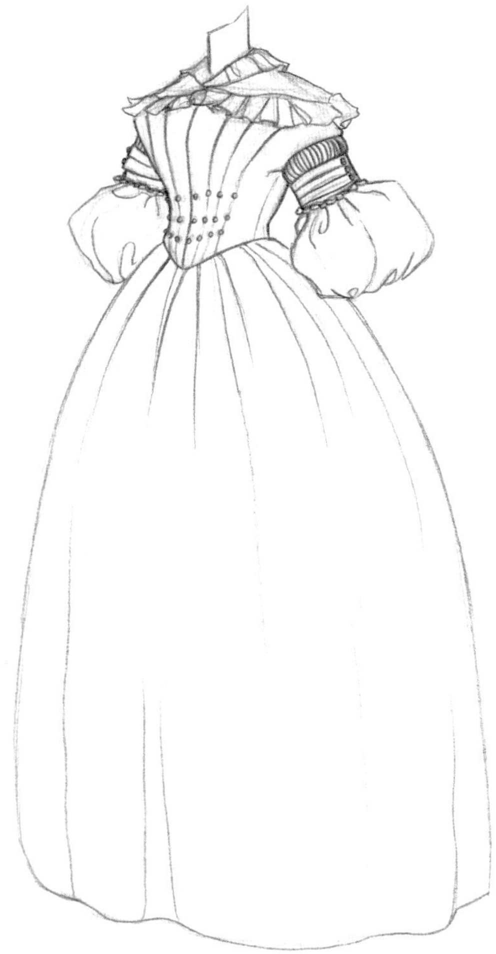

DEVELOP A PLAN OF ACTION.

Say you need to scale down your design for a stop-motion puppet. Just like sketching through an idea to work out the bugs, you can create a small mock-up of your intended design as a test of the materials and techniques.

I chose to interpret a day dress from 1838. It features red silk and wool, and mixed gauze with silk satin piping.

What drew me to this dress was the pleating in the upper sleeves. The main challenge I wanted out of this case study was to see if I could make pleats work on a small scale without becoming so bulky that they restrict movement of the puppet's arms.

START WITH SOLID RESEARCH OF THE TIME PERIOD.

This is where I spend the bulk of my time during the design phase, pouring through books, scouring the Internet, people watching at malls or in parks, anything that applies directly to the brief or sometimes as a tangent to enhance a vague idea. I thumbnail while I research. It's not a separate step for me, which is probably what adds so much additional time to the research step. This will help me understand the elements I will be scaling down so I can retain the most important information as I eliminate and modify details to accommodate the size.

REALLY DELVE INTO THE CHARACTER BY LEARNING AS MUCH AS YOU CAN ABOUT THEM.

Was a character handed to me or am I invited to just go for it? For this example, I initially approached it as mildly tweaking a historical piece outside of the additional restraints that come with designing for a very specific character in a very specific production—which proved impossible as I started sketching. I realized that creating a more realistic versus a more stylized duplication would essentially be establishing a production design. Customizing specific elements took the garment from being a general example to one of personal taste. So I leaned into the time period's ultra-feminine qualities by softening, simplifying, and adding florals, knowing that the tiny lady I was creating this for was some kind of romantic, perhaps with a gardening hobby.

CREATE A BLUEPRINT TO FOLLOW.

The original dress is about ankle length with a voluminous skirt and small waist, which was pretty typical of that time period. The sleeves are pleated near the shoulder with button details and some lace, a poofed (gigot) near the elbow, and the forearms appear to be covered by gloves. There are button details and folds on the front that mimic the shoulder. The collar area is somewhat obscured by an additional covering (fichu).

I added an opaque lower sleeve since I didn't intend to give my dress form hands for gloves and still wanted to cover as much of the form as possible for display. I simplified the collar area. I also removed many of the buttons since pleats were my focus.

I wanted to bring visual interest to the lower skirt, so I repeated the pleating from the upper sleeve along the hemline. I smoothed out the gather around her waist which presented a problem I didn't have time to solve—how would one construct those gathers so they wouldn't alter in between frames and always fall "correctly"?

This blueprint is a rough idea of what I'm going for. I aimed to have all my major forms/layers mapped and breakdowns of possible details, as well as fabric selections. While I do try to be as thorough as possible, I have to keep in mind that this will change as the project progresses. That way I don't end up disappointing myself when things are not exact.

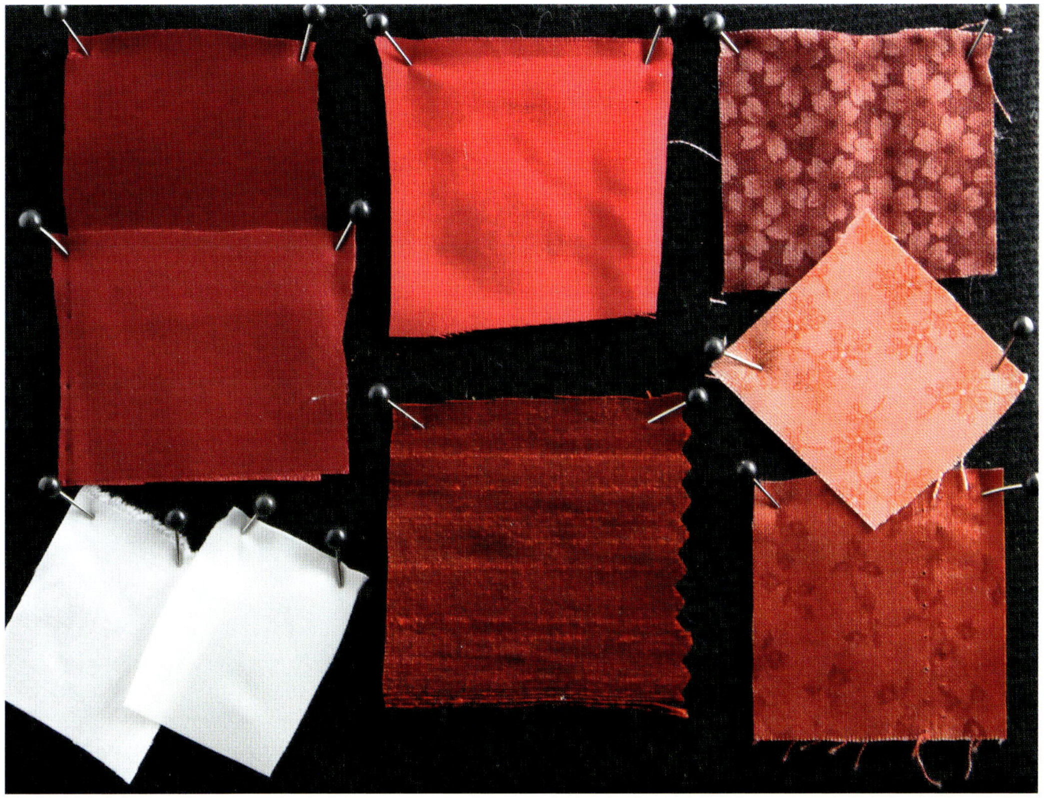

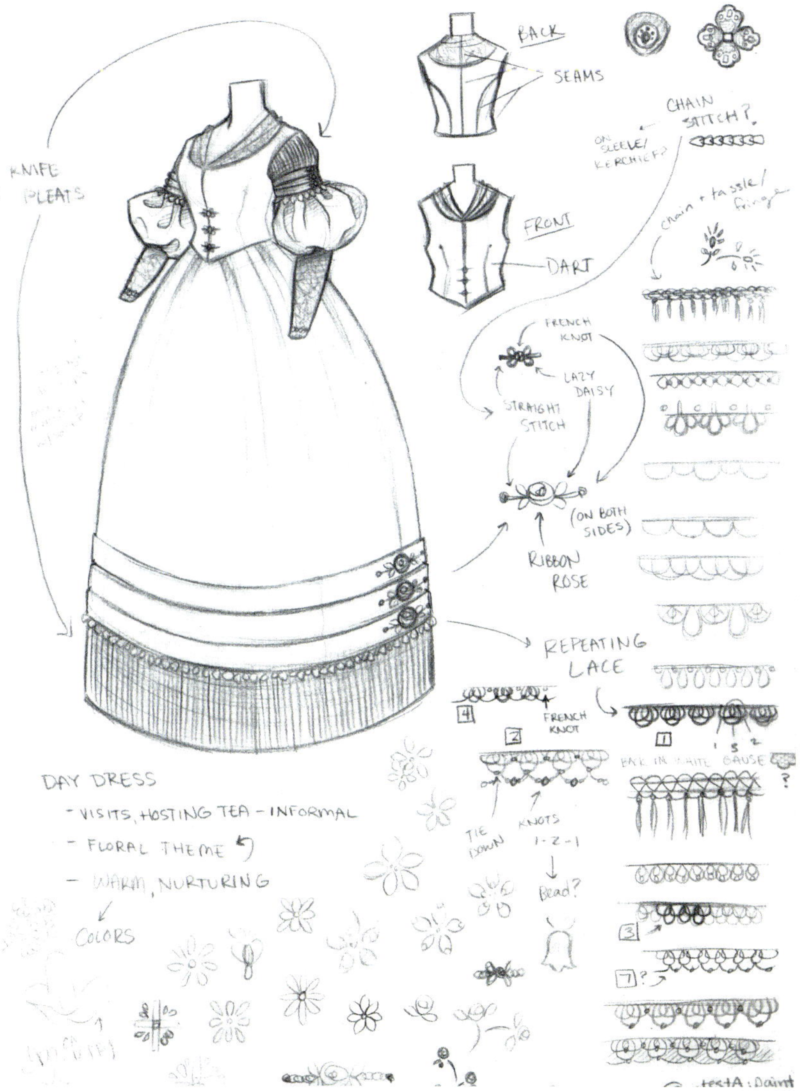

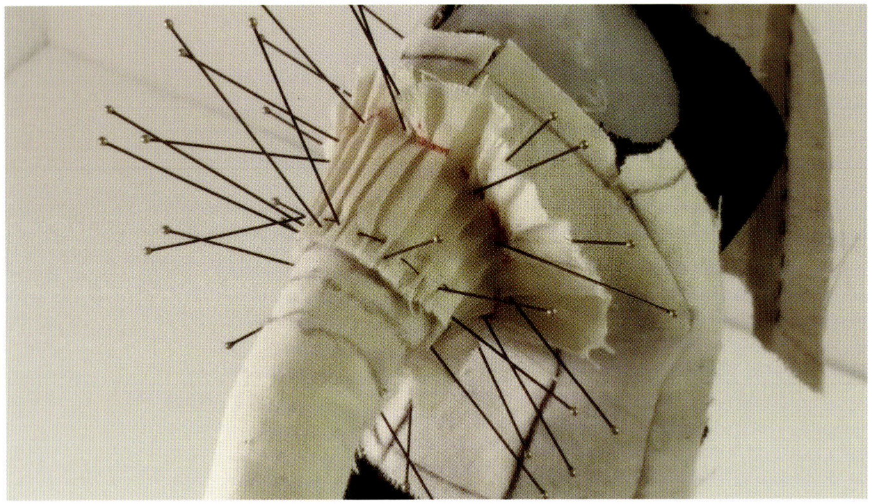

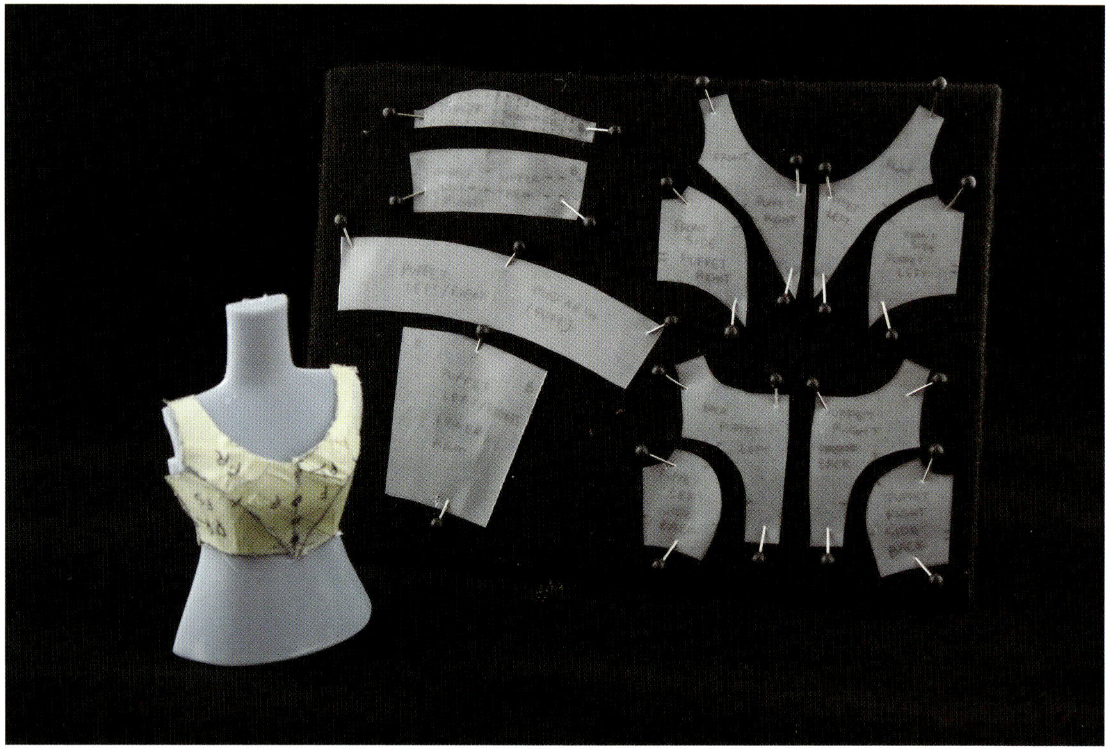

FITTING

In stop-motion, a close fit is important. Mock up on a model as you refine your pattern.

When I finished a section, I sewed together a dummy version to ensure my fit was right. Then, if I needed to make alterations to a seam or length, I could do so easily and save my final fabric.

For this project, I made my mock-ups in muslin, which is inexpensive to come by in large amounts. And I definitely needed quite a bit, as I made several versions, narrowing in on the ideal fit. Something I struggled with in this case study was the need to reduce bulk in the seams—especially in the shoulders and edges. Seams and hems on a regular garment can range in size, but ultimately they lay flat or are stitched down in a way that doesn't become obtrusive. You want as close a fit as possible for stop-motion because a loose (or uncontrolled/unrigged) article will crawl on screen as the animator brushes against it to move a limb or twist a torso.

Mark folds and edges with a pen to serve as guides. While mocking up the sleeves, I pinned everything in place exactly as I wanted it. Then I took a heat erase pen and marked every fold and edge so that when I unpinned it, I still had all the guides in place for the pattern. When the pattern was later assembled, it maintained those original forms that I wanted.

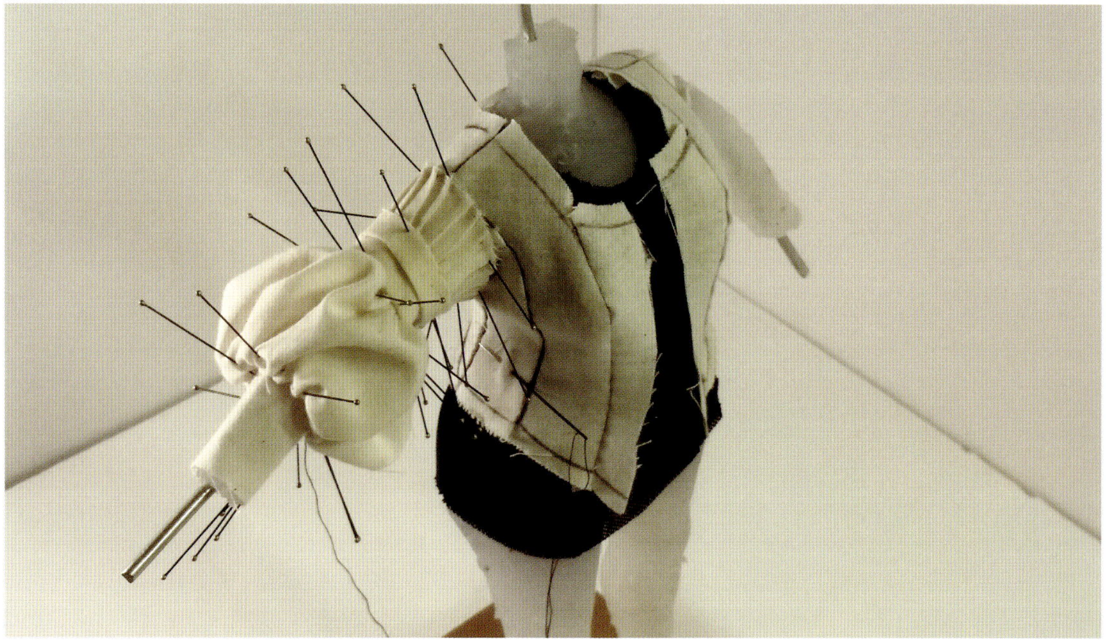

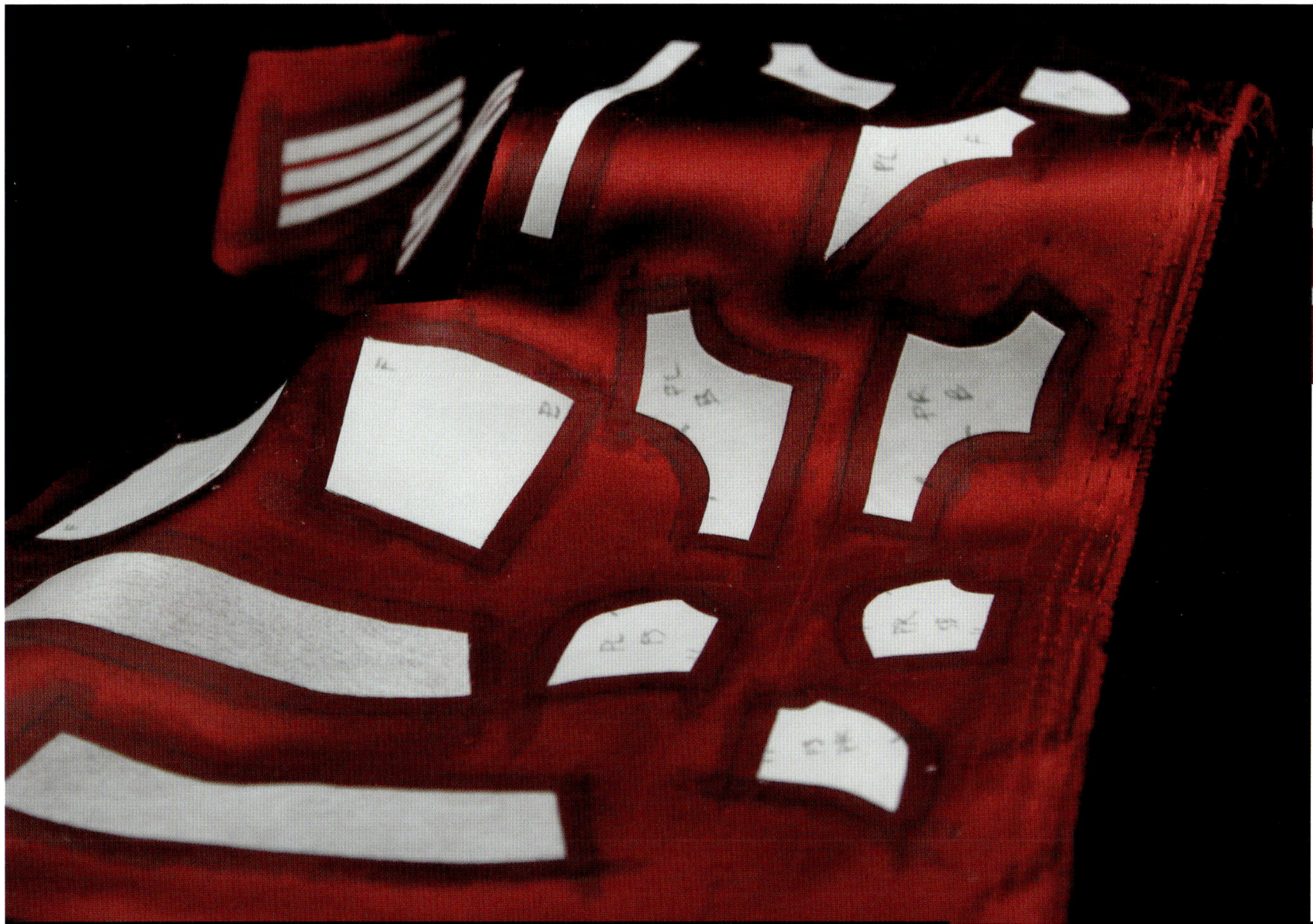

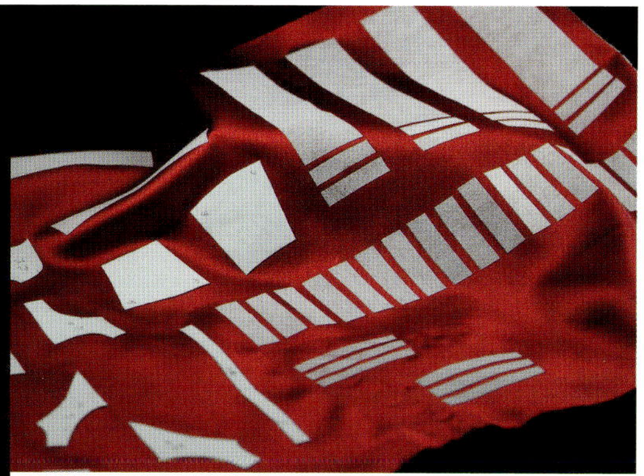

When possible, use the final fabric during the draping/patternmaking state.

I wanted the best fit possible for my form. I combined draping with flat patternmaking to achieve this. It's nice to use the final fabric for draping so you know what kind of finish you'll get, but this can be expensive and frustrating if there isn't some level of visibility when making marks for cuts and darts.

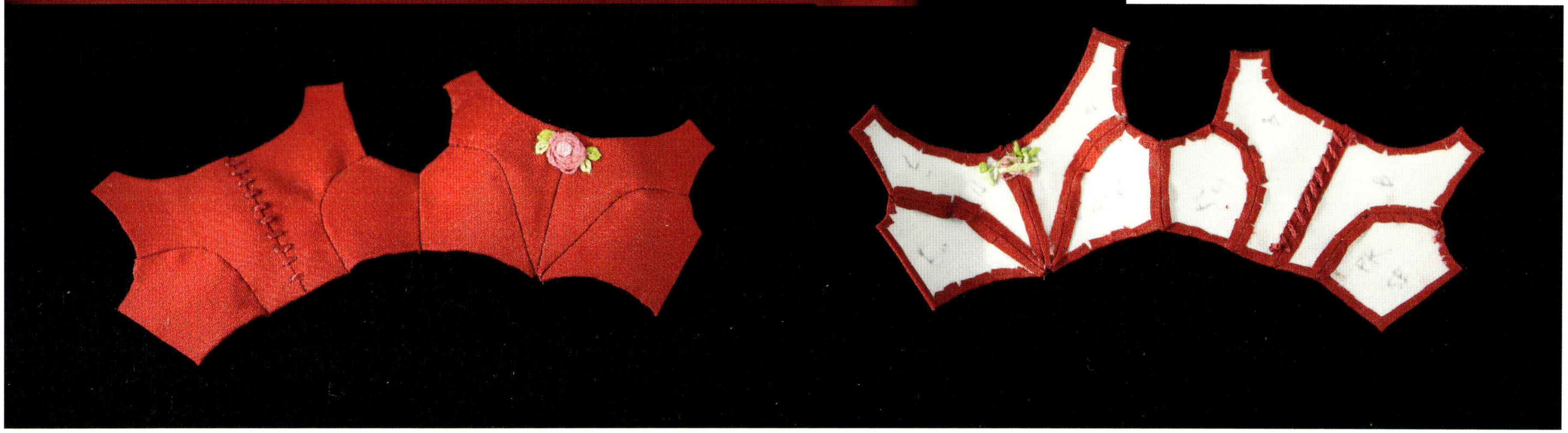

Built for Action

Do you need to replicate gravity at a smaller scale? Is the costume close fitting or loose? Do the desired shapes of the costume match the shapes of the puppet, or will you need padding? How durable does your character need to be? How will you address repairs needed, like replacing hands or tensioning joints underneath the clothes? Do you need to make duplicates of a character? Do individual elements of the costume need their own separate controls? Does the costume need the ability to deform for an action and then return to a neutral shape? Is there a specific movement wanted—like a little bounce in her skirt as she hops up to ring the doorbell? Is there an element that should not move/chatter while other elements around it will be expected to move?

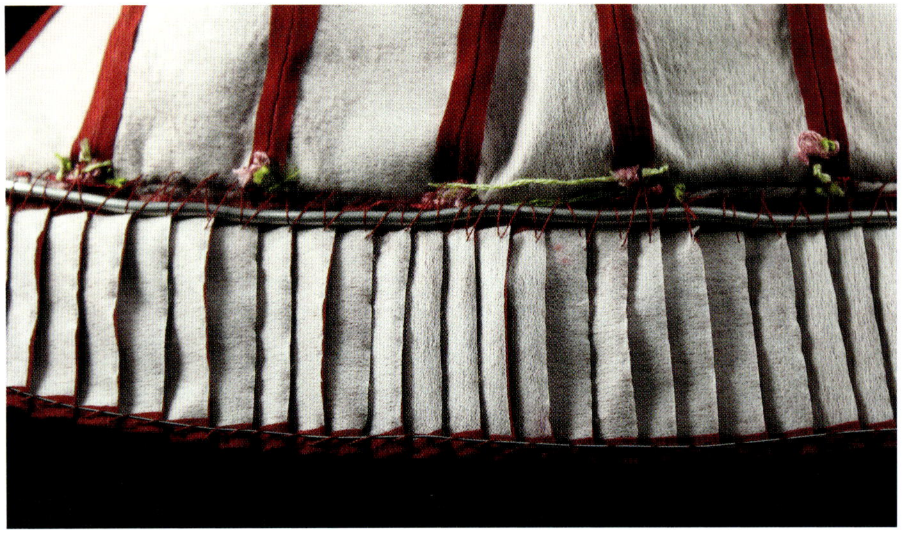

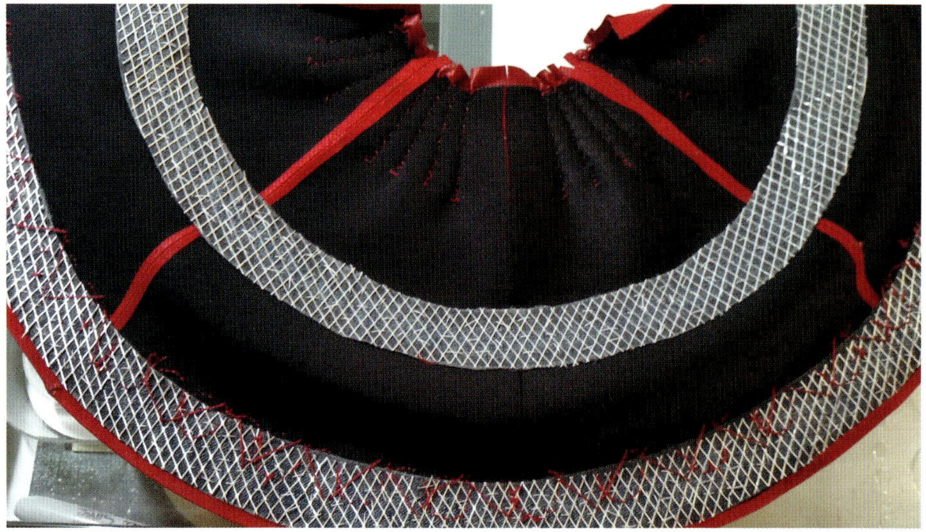

That's the trick of stop-motion—your costume needs to be animated. You have to build in the movement required to tell the story while giving it the stability necessary to keep it from "chattering" every time you brush against it. And with an animator manipulating the limbs and bodies in all manner of poses, the costume also needs to endure a lot of wear and tear.

These things will all affect what kinds of structure types you might want to explore. Each character model is unique like the individual it represents (in the case of puppet duplicates, not every copy will be perfect) and will have its own challenges. What works for one model may not work for another; so much of this is trial and error.

CONSIDER:

The lining material so the stress of motion doesn't eat through your fabric.
How you will emulate gravity on a smaller scale.
How to hold a drape without causing chatter every time an animator touches the puppet to move a hand.
How to ripple or sway with the movement/wind.
How will you access the puppet's joints for tensioning or if you need to replace a hand or foot?

STRUCTURE TYPES	ADVANTAGES	DISADVANTAGES	POSSIBLE MATERIALS
FLEXIBLE	Increased animation mobility; keeps close fitting parts fluid	Thinner fabrics can wear through over extended use; loose fit can give no control over crawl	Silks
STIFF	Decreased crawl; keeps necessary parts rigid	Not always easy to manipulate, especially in close fits	Interfacing, bristol board, wire mesh
WEIGHTS	Emulates gravity	Heavy puppet; more difficult to maneuver	Magnets
WIRES	Increased animation control	Sometimes flimsy, breakable	Floral wire

DETAILS

In stop-motion surface design, the details emphasize story. The unintentionally incorrect scale of details like patterns, buttons, and lace can take a well-constructed garment completely out of context and ruin the effect, so I was careful to get them right.

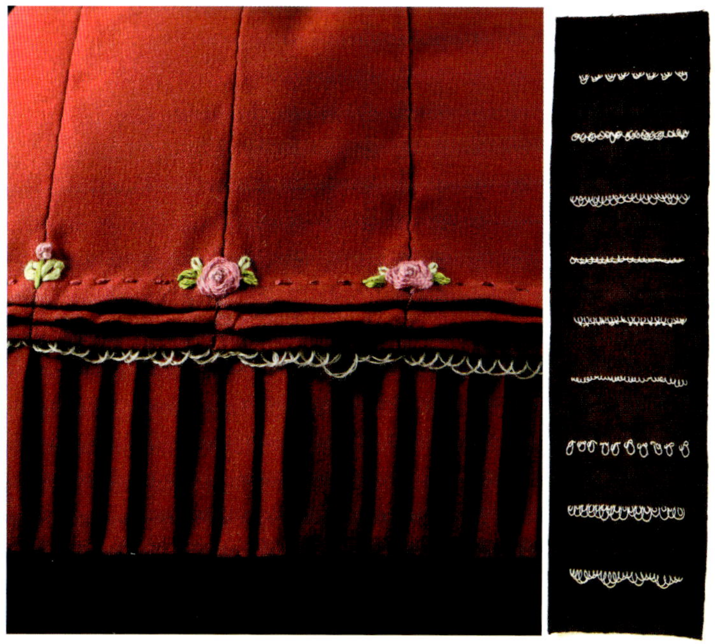

You can't fail if the object of the exercise was just, "Let's see what happens when . . ."

I hand stitched my trim lace here. In the past, I had store-bought laces which could be applied quickly, but they were the wrong scale for the piece and lacked the charm that hand stitching has. I tested various stitches to find one that I thought fit the nature of the dress best—that I knew I could complete as consistently as possible.

I highly recommend doing multiple tests of your intended finishes. Then you can be certain:

- The dyes or paints will be consistent with what you want.
- Intentional frays hold to rigorous movements and handling.
- To maintain the quality of a stitch over a larger area or for multiple copies of a puppet.

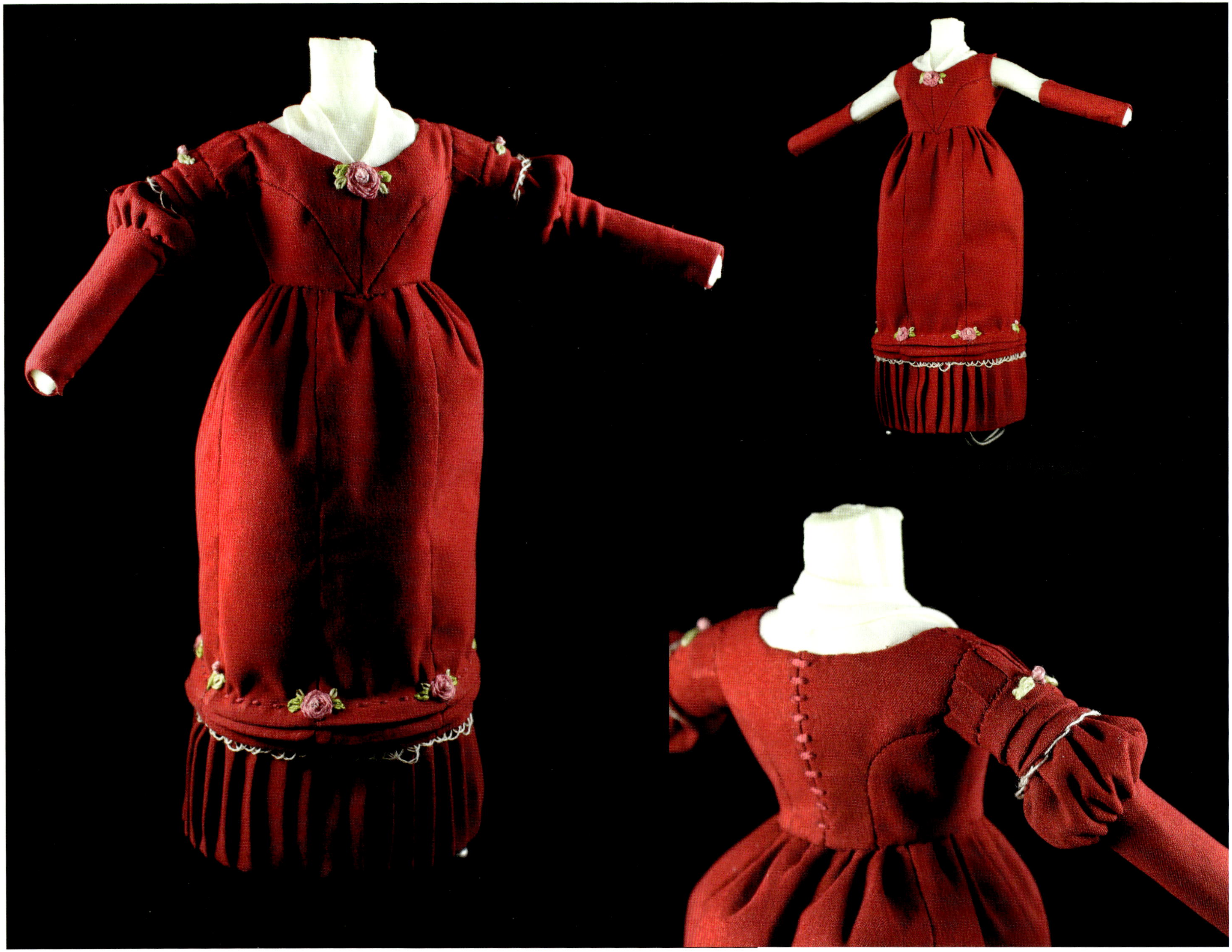

DESIGN TRANSLATION

It's a dark and stormy night, because that's apparently when bad things happen, and your producer walks in and calls for attention. He has decided that instead of a card game based around collecting cute little monsters you are now to make a video game where those monsters are trained to fight to the death. So now what? You've worked so hard on this design, and now, instead of translating it into a 2D space, you have to think in 3D physical terms.

Thunderclap

This would hopefully never happen mid-production, because of budgetary reasons. But how does that change in medium affect your process? What would you need to consider as you accommodate the new format, or any format?

Let's find out! Create three versions of one of your designs. Include relevant pattern detail, surface finishes, and material callouts for each.

Version 1: A slow-paced dramatic feature or game for adults, with lots of details and depth, to give the audience the immersion needed to ground them and allow viewers to relate to the emotions and pain of the characters, e.g., *Detroit: Become Human*.

Version 2: An animated show, picture book, or game targeted at children. Communicate the story more quickly and directly through a simplified design to accommodate their comprehension level and attention span with more exaggerated design and movement, e.g., *Steven Universe*, *Kingdom Hearts*, *Final Fantasy V*. Stuck? Try breaking down the more realistic costume design into fewer strokes. Identify and bring the most important information to the surface, editing out the layers of complexity, e.g., taking a fine-checkered shirt on a more realistically proportioned adult and amplifying the size of the checkers for a 2D animated TV show for children.

Version 3: A stop-motion animation episode or feature, e.g., *Boxtrolls* or *Wallace and Gromit*. Much like in virtual space, the stop-motion costume must be constructed and rigged to move with the animation. Watch your resolution! The application of correctly scaled fiber weaves might not initially seem like an important detail, but consider a normal piece of denim. It looks natural when we wear it, but the minute we stick it on a body that's an eighth of our size, the weave begins to look like finger-thick noodles. Now capture that on film and expand it up to the size of a movie theater screen and those jeans look like they're made from the cable of the Golden Gate Bridge (yikes).

Understanding the unique characteristics and challenges of your role, production style, medium, or format will help you identify what information you can, and should, include in your designs. The following reference guides offer an overview of the basic factors you should consider depending on the format and property.

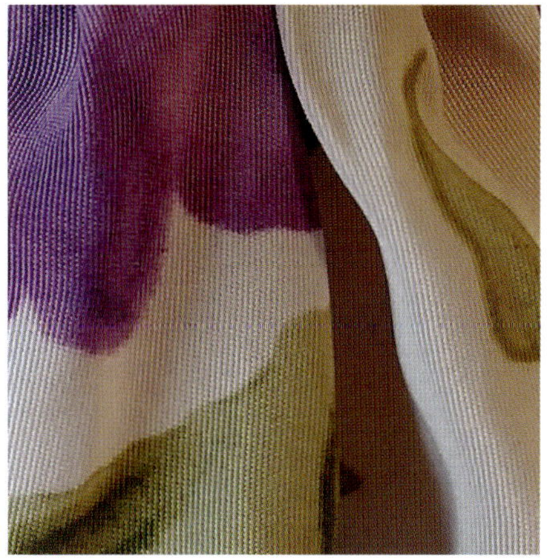

TIP:

Always consider the requirements of the output medium. What looks great on your computer screen may not work for a table banner without the right scaling. This is the original photo taken with a camera phone. When scaled up for a different screen size, the gauzy fabric looks less like silk and more like burlap. Imagine what it would look like on a large movie screen!

Live-Action

WHO DO YOU REPORT TO?

Director

WHO MAKES THE FINAL DECISIONS?

This is tricky! If you're working in commercials, for example, the client may have the final say. If there's a star in the cast, they will have a lot to contribute to final decisions, especially if they're also a producer. Sometimes, if the film is action heavy, a production designer may even be your department head. In any of these scenarios though, the director will always contribute to the final say.

WHO COMES BEFORE AND AFTER YOU IN THE PIPELINE?

Before: screenwriter, director, director of photography; ideally you are brought on at the same time as the production designer, but sometimes they get started before you do.

After: editor, sound designer and foley, color correction.

SOFTWARE THAT'S GOOD TO KNOW:

SyncOnSet, Costume Continuity Pro, Photoshop, Acrobat, Google Drive, Dropbox, Procreate, Excel

WHAT PARTS OF THE PROCESS ARE UNIQUE TO THIS FORMAT?

Actor measurements and mobility, fabric structure and weight, whether or not a fabric will dye/can be cleaned/is durable, availability of local resources, skilled artisans for building the costumes themselves (such as drapers, tailors, stitchers, specialty makers, etc.), driving from location to location in order to do fitting/pick up costume pieces/have maker meetings, and so on. Other questions we have to ask include: Does this costume already exist, or do I need to build it? Is it available to rent, or will I need to piece it together from multiple sources? So on and so forth.

WHAT CHALLENGES DO YOU FACE?

Performer Comfort: We want performers to be comfortable, but in film they may be standing in a cocktail dress and four-inch heels for twelve hours. Finding ways to accommodate their comfort is important to their sanity, but can be challenging when a script calls for them to appear uncomfortable.

Performer Fit and Mobility: Every costume in live-action design is altered to fit the performer as beautifully as possible. Their action may also require more range of motion than the standard period corset or business suit allows for.

Logistics: Perhaps the biggest difference between live-action and more stylized mediums is that we have a lot of physically moving parts in live action. One film may employ people from multiple states to work on the same costume, or perform fittings on opposite ends of the same city. Rentals and purchases may also take you to several rental houses and shopping centers for a single look. This means lots of running around for the designer and their assistants. Hauling costumes, lugging heavy set kits, standing for twelve hours a day . . . it's a very labor-intensive job!

Costume Illustration for Live-Action Film

WHO DO YOU REPORT TO?

Creator (if illustrating for a pitch)

Costume Designer (if illustrating for a production)

WHO MAKES THE FINAL DECISIONS?

Creator or costume designer

WHO COMES BEFORE AND AFTER YOU IN THE PIPELINE?

Before: creator or costume designer

After: costume designer (in the case of working for a creator); costume makers (in the case of working for a costume designer)

SOFTWARE THAT'S GOOD TO KNOW:

Photoshop, Illustrator, ZBrush, Procreate, Blender

WHAT PARTS OF THE PROCESS ARE UNIQUE TO THIS FORMAT?

You are often trying to illustrate not just general concepts but also a specific idea that's in the creator's or designer's head.

If you are acting as illustrator, the details may be dictated to you by the creator or designer. If you are acting as a costume concept artist, you are taking the designer's lead but generating your own design ideas for them to choose from. Keep in mind, the final product for a live-action costume designer isn't the illustration but the performer in a physical costume; your final product illustration is only a tool to communicate and clarify within the process.

WHAT CHALLENGES DO YOU FACE?

Every production is different, and so are the expectations and personalities of the people you work with. While some designers and creators can read drawings very well and "speak your language," others can't at all.

The expectation for a final product can range from stylized to photo-realistic.

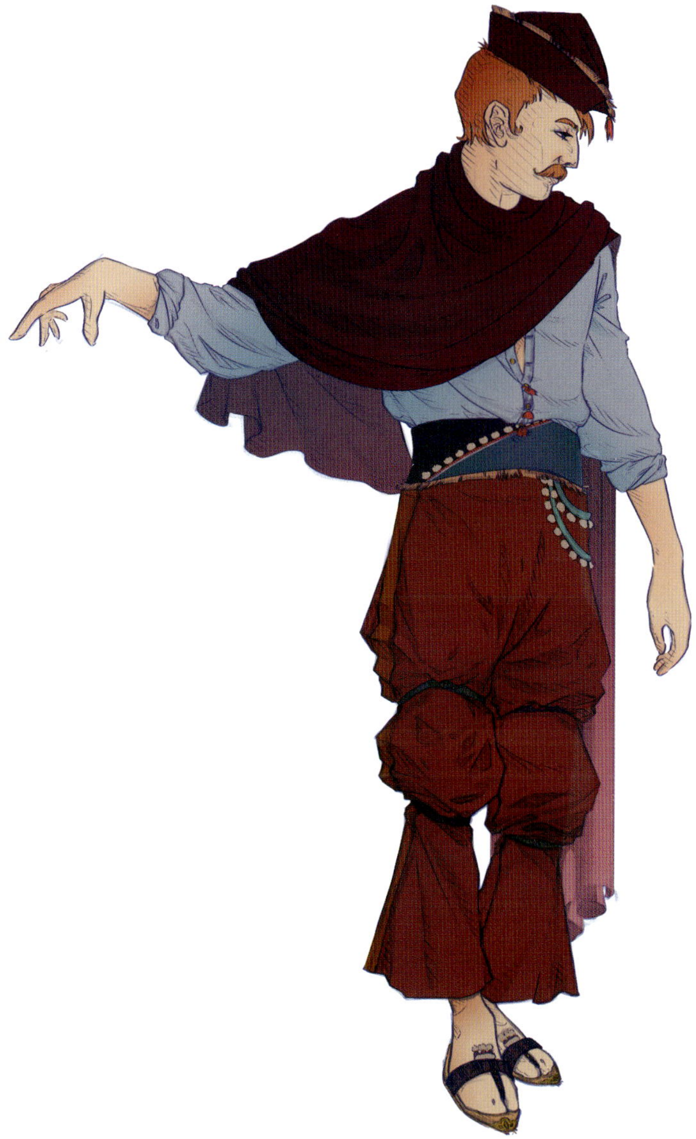

Illustration: Fashion

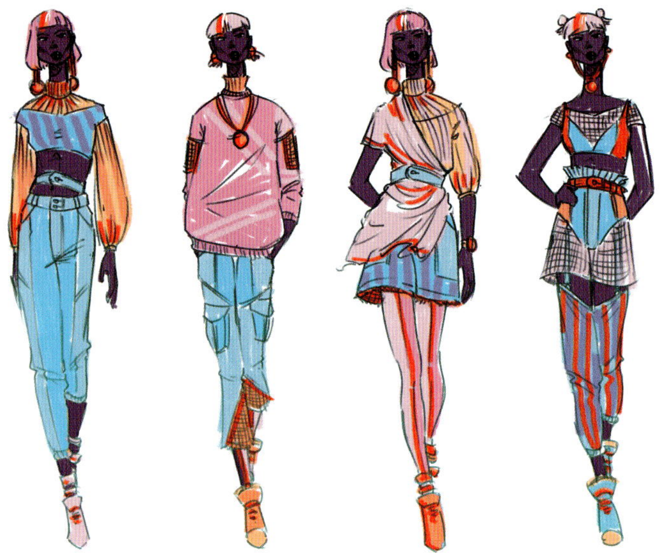

WHO DO YOU REPORT TO?

Fashion designer or label's creative director

WHO MAKES THE FINAL DECISIONS?

Fashion designer or label's creative director

WHO COMES BEFORE AND AFTER YOU IN THE PIPELINE?

Before: fashion designer or label's creative director

After: patternmaker or draper

SOFTWARE THAT'S GOOD TO KNOW:

Photoshop, Illustrator, Procreate

MATERIALS:

watercolor, markers and ink, pencils, pastels, eyeshadow, nail varnish, acrylic, gouache

WHAT PARTS OF THE PROCESS ARE UNIQUE TO THIS FORMAT?

There are three parts to working in fashion illustration. Not all of these skills are required, but they are desirable for any artist a designer might hire:

Fashion Sketches: These are the artistic drawings that a designer uses to sell or communicate the final collection. The style varies drastically depending on who the designer or label is, and who they want to wear their clothing. This requires traditional and digital medium flexibility.

Technical Flats: Once the design has been approved and a patternmaker has created the shape of the garment, most fashion houses will require technical flats created in Illustrator to send to overseas workshops and factories where the bulk of the garments will be made. These are flat line drawings with dimensions, seam lines, and proportions accurate to the final garments. It requires more of an engineer's mind than an artistic hand.

Graphics and Textile Design: Graphics are unique splashes of art that, for example, decorate the front or back of a T-shirt. A fashion illustrator may also be called upon to do textile design, which requires a pattern to repeat at the desired scale, so it can be printed on fabric and cut into a garment.

WHAT CHALLENGES DO YOU FACE?

Fashion figures have to *feel* like the design as well as communicate the actual garments. Glamour figures are often ten to twelve heads high for a more sweeping figure while sportswear might be seven to eight heads high for a more grounded feel. The desired style depends greatly on the type of clothing your designer is creating.

EXERCISE: ON-SCREEN ILLUSTRATIONS

WHO DO YOU REPORT TO? Producer or/and director

WHO MAKES THE FINAL DECISIONS? Producer and director

WHO COMES BEFORE AND AFTER YOU IN THE PIPELINE? Before: director; After: printing team and/or costume designer

SOFTWARE: Photoshop, Procreate

TASK: Create costume illustrations that will be featured in a character's stylized self-portrait illustrations. For example, you can choose a superhero film where the character is designing their outfit (e.g., Spider-Man), or a TV series where a character is a comic book artist (e.g., *Bored to Death*).

NOTES:
The illustrations will be seen on-screen as well as printed for characters to interact with. Work in RGB and deliver the illustration in both RGB and CMYK, so further in the pipeline they can adjust the colors if necessary.

The costumes in the portraits are outfits the character wishes they could wear, so they do not currently exist in the film. You will need to create original designs. However, since the physical costume designs for the character are already established, you will also need to research the costume designer's goals through interviews and behind-the-scenes featurettes.

Note the production design style throughout the movie. Replicate that tone in the outfits used in the illustrations.

Study the character's intentions in the scene your illustration would be featured in, aligning it with the director's vision. Research interviews and featurettes to gain more insight.

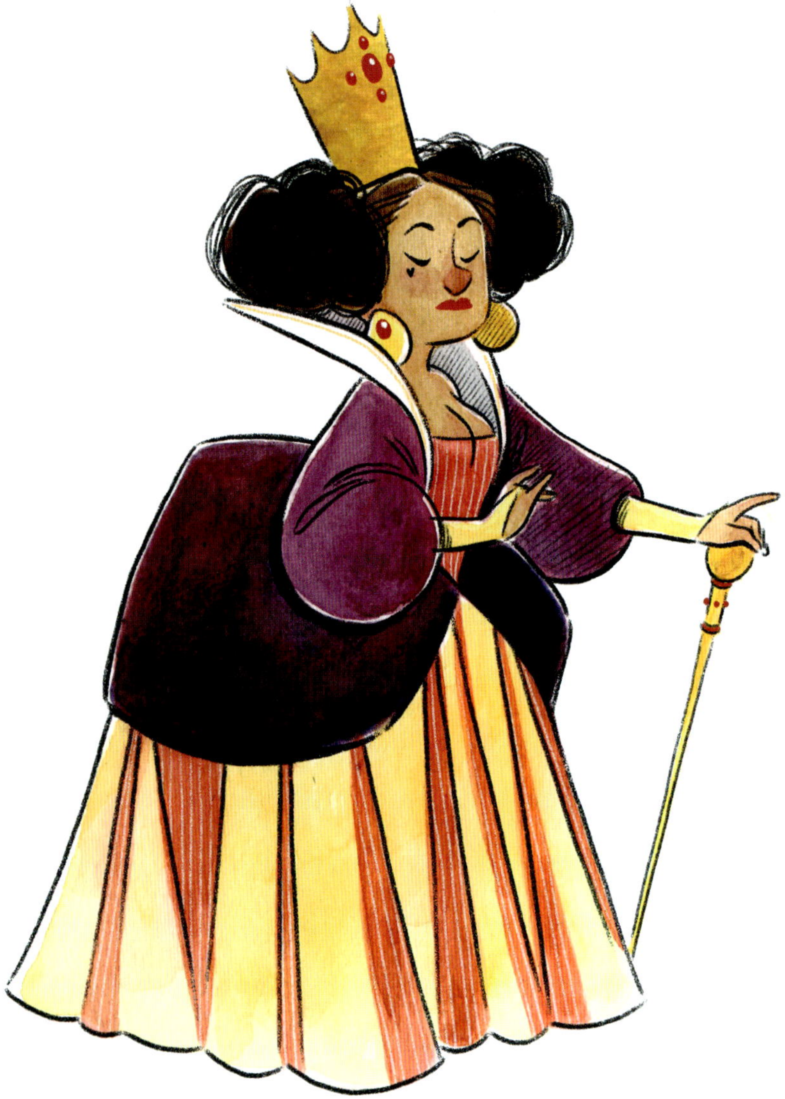

Illustration: Publishing

WHO DO YOU REPORT TO?

Illustrator only: art director

Author/illustrator: editor and art director

WHO MAKES THE FINAL DECISIONS?

Ultimately the publisher has the final say, but there are a lot of people who look at the art before it is approved for layout and sent off to print.

WHO COMES BEFORE AND AFTER YOU IN THE PIPELINE?

The editor acquires an author's manuscript and then works with the art director to hire an illustrator. The art director and illustrator start planning the art, which includes costume along with every other visual aspect. Once the final art is submitted and approved by the editor and art director, the book is usually sent to the designer for layout.

SOFTWARE THAT'S GOOD TO KNOW:

The sky's the limit. Books have been illustrated using both digital (Photoshop, Illustrator) and traditional media (watercolor, acrylic, pencil, collage, etc.), and 3D illustration (Maya, ZBrush) is also becoming more common. Traditional 3D illustration is also on the rise, including illustrating with cake! Photoshop and InDesign are also great programs to know for editing and layout purposes.

WHAT PARTS OF THE PROCESS ARE UNIQUE TO THIS FORMAT?

Print is the one format in which the color you envision your work to be in can be matched in the final product. Essentially your (color) vision can be implemented and seen by the viewer, unlike a TV, phone, or movie screen that can have varying settings.

WHAT CHALLENGES DO YOU FACE?

Color Matching: If you are working digitally, you will definitely face color calibration problems. What you see on your screen won't necessarily match what you print. This will be resolved by hard-copy color proofs you can review before the art is sent to print, but it can cause some additional back and forth between you and your art director.

Making Art Evergreen: Producing books can take a long time. You can be working on one book from months to years, and then the printing process will generally take a minimum of three months. So don't illustrate based on what's currently trendy because it's already old. And there will always be a popular art style that is taking over bookshelves and magazines.

Sequential Comics: Keep the details simple and the silhouette clear. Like 2D animation, the amount of times you need to redraw the character requires the design to be highly repeatable and recognizable. Also, as your reader flows through the frames and pages, you don't want an overly complex costume to interrupt that rhythm.

Cover Illustration: Style needs to fit the tone of the text to set the correct expectations. Because it is a static illustration, though, the reader will look at the single image longer and you have more opportunity to create rich detail and depth in the design (appropriate to the tone of the story).

Illustration, Paper Doll (Publishing or Apps): Keep an eye on that silhouette! Be mindful of overlapping elements to make sure the costume can stack well. Photoshop layers are your friend, so label wisely and test thoroughly.

When a project is small, there are often no art directors to translate the desires of the director/app developer for you. You can find yourself working directly with the project director or even in committee meetings when the developer or funders are more involved. You'll not only need to interpret the project needs yourself, e.g., how many outfits to create and what style, but you'll often need to create your own design prompts as well.

Because you are likely working more directly with a non-artist, you'll need to know how to clarify the expectations for the amount of pieces they can fit in their budget, timeline expectations, and practical limitations of the costume range (pieces need to hide behind the silhouette of other pieces); and you'll need to interpret the language a non-artist director uses to describe their vision. There is a lot of back and forth in these scenarios, and pricing effectively can be a challenge. Make sure to include revisions in your budget and limit the number of revisions. With multiple costumes needed for paper dolls, the earlier you define and lock the style down the better. Troubleshoot the tech with a test costume set as well if it's an app in order to avoid excessive revisions.

Live Puppet Theatre: Hand Puppets

WHO DO YOU REPORT TO?

(Art) director

WHO MAKES THE FINAL DECISIONS?

Director

WHO COMES BEFORE AND AFTER YOU IN THE PIPELINE?

Before: whoever is in charge of writing the script.

After: director and the puppeteers.

TECHNIQUES THAT ARE GOOD TO KNOW:

Sewing, flat patterning, and construction

WHAT PARTS OF THE PROCESS ARE UNIQUE TO THIS FORMAT?

You aren't ever really finished with the puppets until the show's run is over. Puppeteers can be really rough with the puppets (especially if on a traveling show), and so the puppets will need constant repair/cleaning.

WHAT CHALLENGES DO YOU FACE?

As in most productions, there are always changes happening. Changes in the script can lead to changes in a puppet's use, which can lead to a change in design.

CHANGES IN USE/NEEDS:

Sometimes you can't tell if something works or not until you are pretty far into the process. This doesn't happen too often and it doesn't always mean a total redo, but it does occur. You just have to be flexible. You may even need to create duplicates or variations of a puppet (with or without legs) for specific scenes.

WEIGHT/HANDLING:

Always remember to make puppets as light and durable as possible to start out, because elements and reinforcements are added and puppets can easily get too big and/or too heavy. Puppeteers need to be able to perform with the puppets, so it can be a challenge to make them usable but also visually appealing.

Other puppets used in live-animation formats: animatronics, rod puppets, and marionettes.

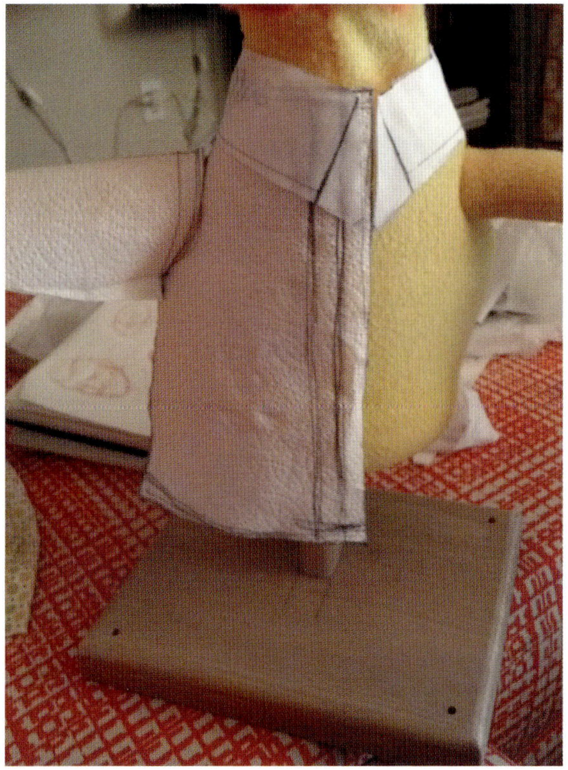

Draping can be difficult, and it takes some practice. Use scrap fabric or inexpensive fabric like muslin to experiment. If you don't have muslin, try draping using duct tape or paper towels. Make it work.

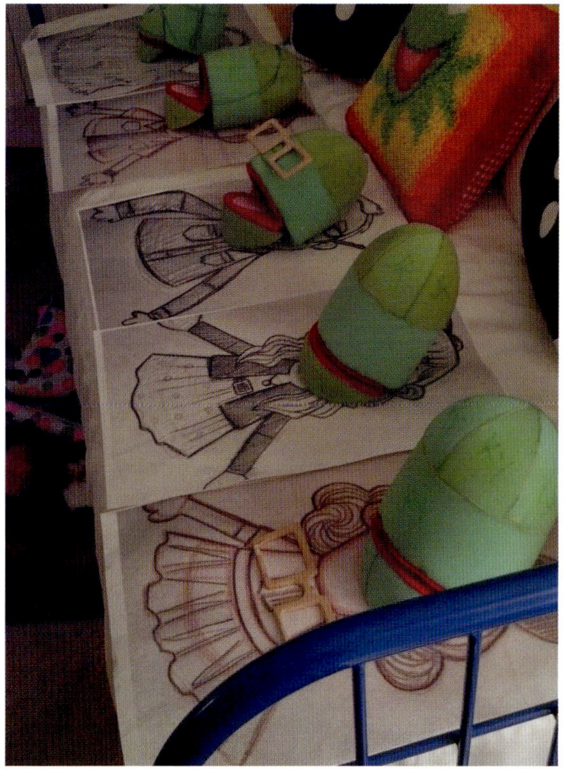

Creating large-sized prints of your design can help you stay organized and to scale.

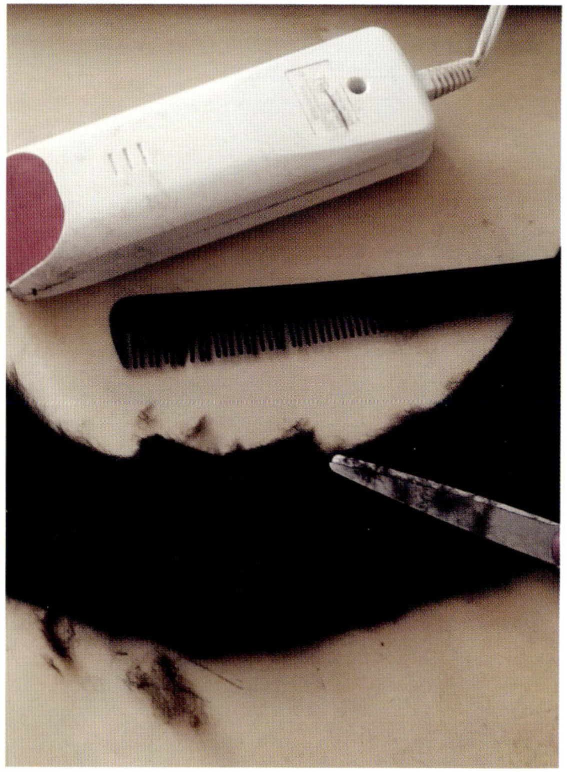

Modify materials to suit your project. When modified, this faux fur can be used to create a beard.

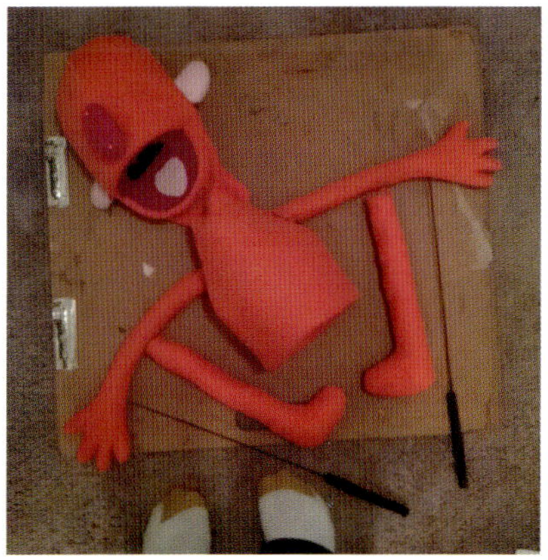

Figure out how you want your puppet to move.

What does this puppet need to do?
How will it perform?

Using applications like Photoshop to visualize your design can help you troubleshoot function, design, and fabric choice without wasting material later on.

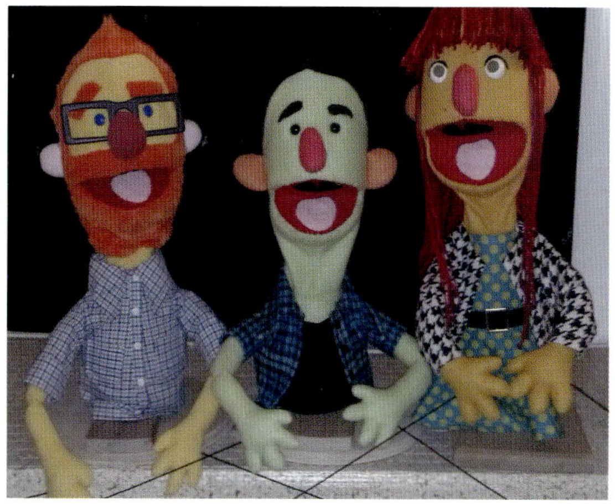

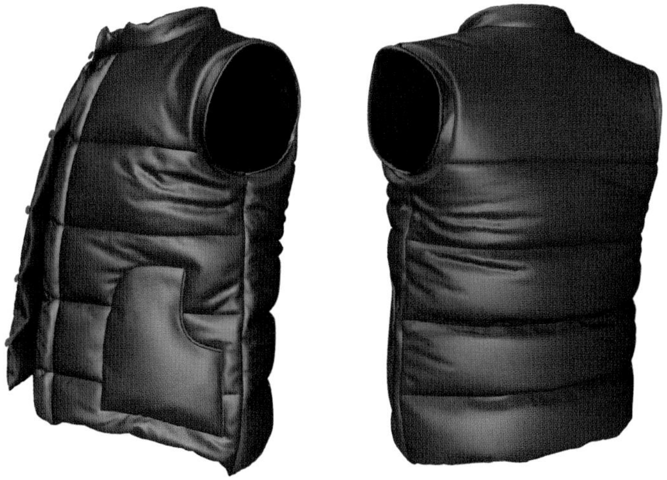

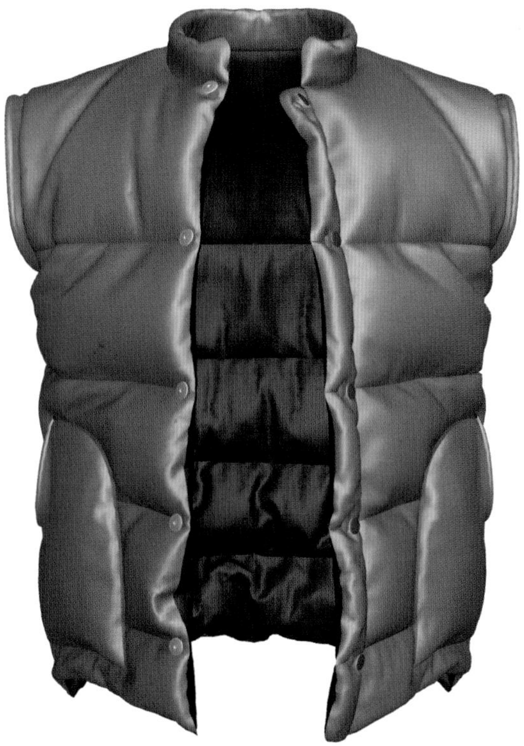

Feature and TV Animation

2D/CG Comparison

WHO DO YOU REPORT TO?

Department lead or supervisor

WHO MAKES THE FINAL DECISIONS?

Art director

WHO COMES BEFORE AND AFTER YOU IN THE PIPELINE?

2D/3D Design
Before: writer or storyboarder

After: storyboarder or animator

3D Simulation
Before: modeling, to create the character anatomy and basic walk cycle.

After: modeling, to fine tune the sculpt with costume, fur, and hair accounted for.

SOFTWARE THAT'S GOOD TO KNOW:

Maya, Qualoth, Marvelous Designer, Toon Boom, 3ds Max

WHAT PARTS OF THE PROCESS ARE UNIQUE TO THIS FORMAT?

2D: The costume has to be easily replicated for inbetweening the key frames—nothing too varied in terms of physics. The costume also needs to be scalable for easy recognition at far distances and close up. Think of social media emojis and icons—no matter the size, they're still readable without detail.

3D Simulation: Costumes can either be constructed like an actual garment, meaning patterned flat on a CAD screen and then stitched together, or directly sculpted in a program like Maya or 3ds Max.

WHAT CHALLENGES DO YOU FACE?

TV: These include limited time to develop characters in the shorter form narrative, budget limits due to a longer run of episodes requiring designs to be simpler/reusable, and designs needing to be created on the fly when a script or storyboard requires a new asset. Costumes may need to be repurposed for budget and time, so new textures, patterns, or colors are used on old costume silhouettes to change the appearance of the piece.

Feature: When working early in the process of development, you have more time to develop concepts; but more frequent script changes will require a completely new direction, and many concepts are discarded. Staying motivated, flexible, and efficient is key. Longer time on screen and in the same linear narrative means more SFX will impact the same costume (i.e., deterioration of a costume).

2D: Simplification of details requires better understanding of which elements from your costume research should be retained to maintain the appropriate context. You need to command the meaning embedded in the details rather than rely on the inclusion of all of the details.

Complete control of the costume can free up the stylistic and transformative possibilities but also requires you to stretch your conceptualization abilities. The lack of limitation is a challenge in and of itself. When you want to maintain believability, understanding basic pattern construction, FX, and even physics will help increase the efficiency of your exploration as you manipulate the shapes or form of the costume.

3D: Character shapes vary greatly in 3D animation. Although sewing patterns for real people are helpful in starting your cloth simulation, they won't answer every question for you. It's best to take a sewing class or two so that you can understand how patterns and fit work together. Don't rely only on your 3D experience.

Once you understand patterns, using programs like Marvelous Designer will let you get a more natural drape with fabrics, because the tactile characteristics are directly incorporated into the simulation. Programs also help with a more natural fit on character models and a more flexible workflow—for example, you can zip and unzip a hoodie in the program, so you don't need to create new simulations. Programs allow you to see the simulation as you work, whereas, when you sculpt, it requires you to move between different spheres of the program. Going straight into a program like Marvelous Designer lets you simultaneously simulate and alter your work.

More technically, it allows you to choose between quads or triangle meshes, or move in between them without having to do it manually; and you can import animation cycles to simulate.

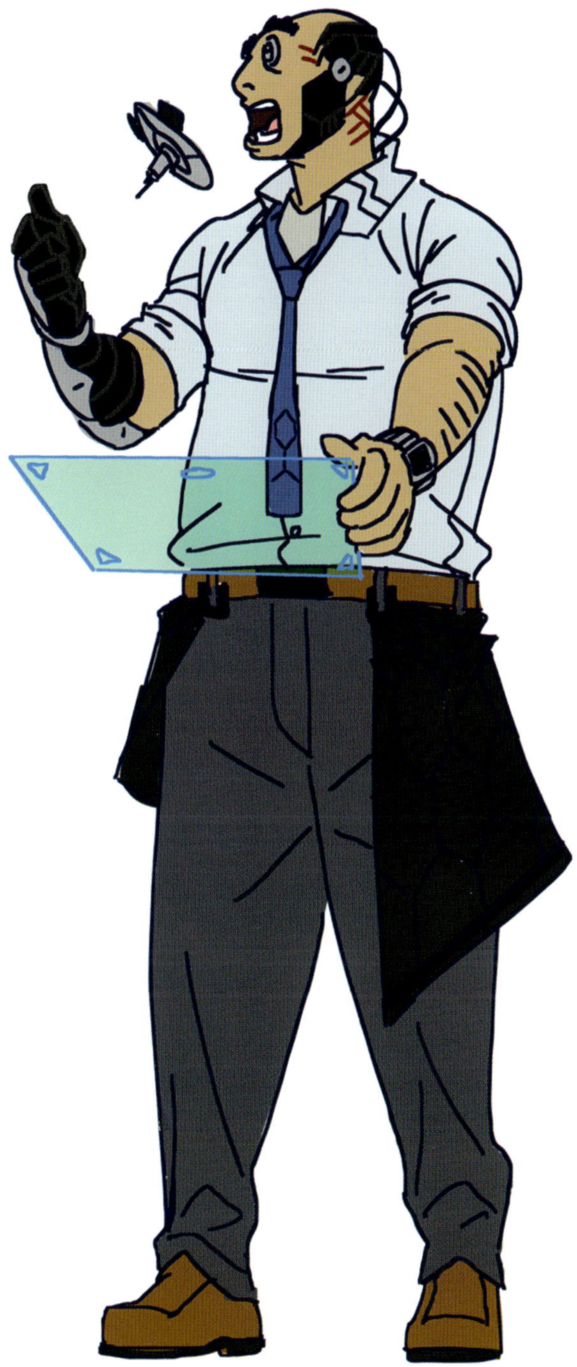

Stop-Motion Feature Animation

WHO DO YOU REPORT TO?

Hierarchy: costume lead > head of costume > costume designer > production designer > director

As the costume designer for a stop-motion production, you would report directly to the director/producers. You would work with other design staff, such as the production designer, character designer, and look dev team to create the designs which would be passed to the costume fabricators for prototyping and further construction. Some designs will need revisions in construction based on needs from the animation department—these challenges are often solved by the fabricators.

As a regular costume fabricator, you would report directly to the lead or head of the costume department and the larger puppet fabrication department's production manager. Coordinators and assistants facilitate communication and deliveries between departments. Wranglers will check in when there are immediate needs such as repair/maintenance work or marketing. You would also work directly with the costume designer, production designer, animation department (and occasionally others), and director/producers when it comes to launching and getting stage approvals. As a costume design assistant or costume look dev artist, you would report directly to the costume designer.

WHO MAKES THE FINAL DECISIONS?

Some very small decisions might be left up to the individual artist (designer or fabricator), but most approvals travel up the chain to the head of department (HOD). Directors/producers have final say depending on who is available.

SOFTWARE THAT'S GOOD TO KNOW:

Adobe Illustrator, Photoshop, and Embrilliance (a machine embroidery program that has a similar feel to Illustrator and can import Illustrator files), but new technologies are being implemented all the time, so it's good to expand/be curious about new opportunities.

WHO COMES BEFORE AND AFTER YOU IN THE PIPELINE?

Before: scriptwriter

After: look dev/fabricators

A designer is brought in early, once there is a script, working in tandem with other development roles to create assets for the fabricators to work with in prototyping.

Before a costume can be prototyped by a fabricator/look dev artist, the puppet body must pass through the earlier fabrications stages of armatures and then silicone casting/cleanup. Hands and feet usually come along separately. Heads do not pass through costumes unless they require a hat—which is coordinated with relevant departments (e.g., hair and rapid prototyping fabrication).

Once a prototyped costume is approved, a polished final version will be made to photograph for reference when making duplicates. A smart fabricator will have copious notes that are easy to follow so duplicating is streamlined. After a costume is approved to move forward, it will pass to paint for final touches/treatments and then on to stages for animation.

WHAT PARTS OF THE PROCESS ARE UNIQUE TO THIS FORMAT?

Physical Construction at Smaller Scale: Nothing is free; even gravity must be "invented."

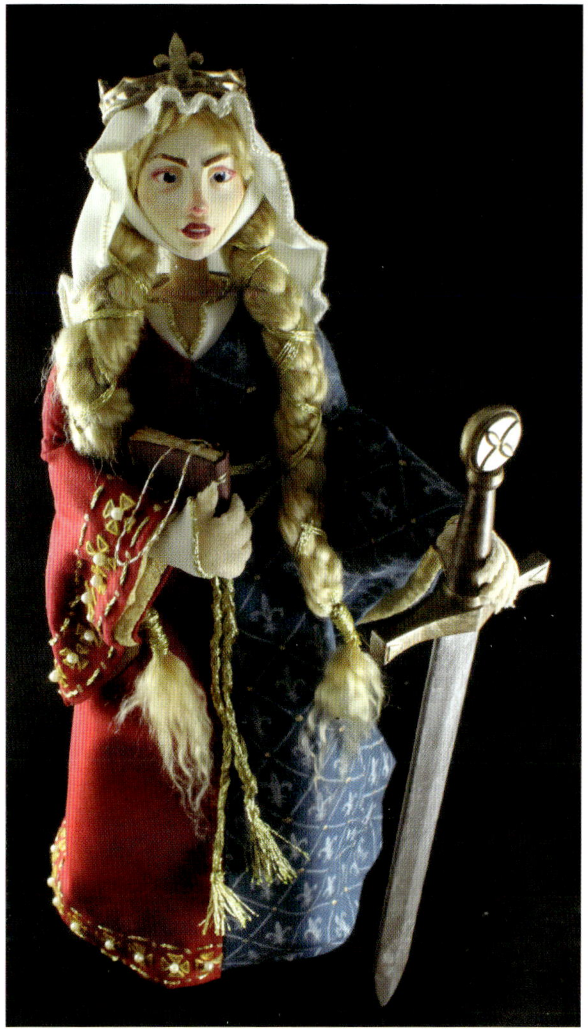

Internal Structures: Similar to digital formats, stop-motion costumes must be rigged to control all possible movement. But the similarities end there; the amount of wiring, lining, and rigging is far more intensive and must be hidden creatively—no bulky seams or adhesive residue.

Collaboration: Similar to other mediums, multiple animators may work on the same character. So duplicate puppets/puppet components are made—sometimes 30 of one character—to stay on schedule. However, puppets are not assigned to specific animators, so if one animator prefers to have increased tension in an elbow or requests an additional rig to be added, that change comes back to the fabricators in the costume department between shots. Once the scene is shot and the puppet moves on, it usually comes back to the fabricators to have the additional rig removed for the next animator, etc.

WHAT CHALLENGES DO YOU FACE?

Real-World/Small-World Physics: Imitating believable gravity is always a problem, as are finding fabrics with a usable weave scale and amount of stretch—both of which will influence performance.

Adhesives: They have to be invisible, flexible, durable, and preferably nontoxic.

Color Matching: Interpreting the concept/character art and replicating that accurately on camera in stage lighting can be challenging. Do they really mean the color in the highlight/shade? Is the printout from the art department color correct? How many kinds of lighting are there?

Maintenance: Physical things break down with use, and some animators wear down equipment more/faster than others.

Marketing: Hopefully you made multiple neckties for a character because marketing just came in and took the one you were going to put on the stage puppet for a press display.

Flattering Fit That Functions: Puppet bodies are not human bodies. A solid understanding of pattern drafting and draping will get you only so far.

Stylization: How sharp are the edges and corners? How deep are the creases and folds? How do you control those things?

Video Game

WHO DO YOU REPORT TO?

Art director

WHO MAKES THE FINAL DECISIONS?

Art director, chief creative officer, CEO

WHO COMES BEFORE AND AFTER YOU IN THE PIPELINE?

Before: art director

After: 3D art team

SOFTWARE THAT'S GOOD TO KNOW:

Photoshop, any number of 3D programs

WHAT PARTS OF THE PROCESS ARE UNIQUE TO THIS FORMAT?

The level of interactivity that the consumer has. The amount of time invested in video games often spans into the tens and hundreds of hours and can span long, vast storylines, or can be a short, brief but powerful experience depending on the type of game.

Needing to design costume changes or costume options on some games, e.g., *Horizon Zero Dawn* or MMORPGs.

WHAT CHALLENGES DO YOU FACE?

Never quite knowing how players are going to interact with your designs. Beyond cinematics, you cannot control how someone is going to play your game; you can only give them as many visual cues as possible so the experience is enjoyable.

Cinematics aside, everything you design can be viewed up close and 360 degrees around. Often with player characters, you only really see the backs of the character for most of the game, and you must take into account things like the camera angle (multiplayer online battle arenas, for example, are mostly top down cameras, so designing good silhouettes from that angle is key).

There are many disciplines involved in game design; narrative, gameplay, combat, tech art, concept, 3D art. This can often end up in a lot of design by committee and having to compromise the pure artistic design of something to help make some of those departments happy.

Games often have technical limitations, and good concept artists will work with those creatively.

Beyond Costume: Thoughtful Design is Universal!

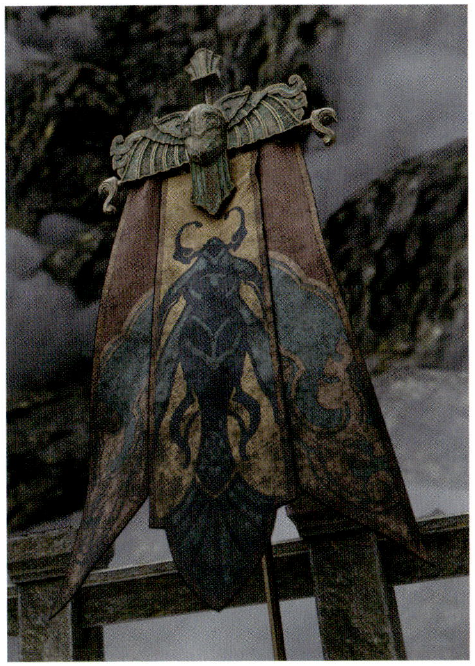

Not every studio or project will have room for a dedicated or full-time costume designer, but the principles in this book can be applied to all types and stages of world-building design. You can use the character costume skills more directly in illustration, visual development, character design, or concept art. Or you can translate the same principles to look dev, prop design, environment design, and texture art.

Raul Ramos demonstrates how he can incorporate narrative values, motifs, and surface effects to a banner asset.

"I wanted to create a banner that looked like it could have been made by a culture that had a strong association with water or a water deity. I imagined that this culture would incorporate water motifs and/or representations of their water goddess on the items they created, including this banner.

I pull from my surroundings when texturing a model. Living in the Pacific Northwest, it's easy to see the effect that a lot of moisture has on various surfaces. Imagining how this prop would age in this type of environment led to a unique look that I might not have chosen otherwise."

Raul Ramos currently works in the video games industry. He has spent several years creating illustrations for online trading-card games such as *The Elder Scrolls: Legends TCG* and *Eternal* card game. His work can be found at raulramosart.com.

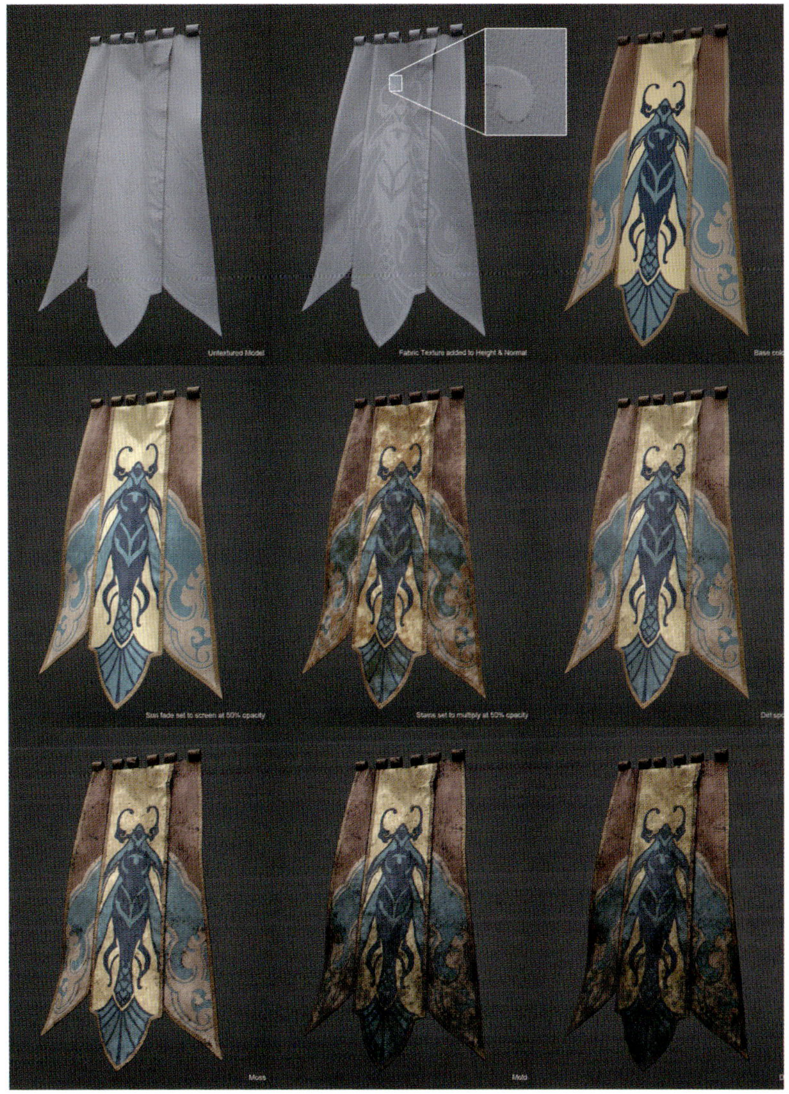

Raul Ramos

TIP:

Apply some of the concepts from your costume into a prop or environment design to deepen your understanding of the design principles, build your versatility, or improve your collaboration skills.

WHEN DOES THE COSTUME SPECIALIST COME IN?

Whether the production requires a year of development, a fast, three-month research to design approach, or a simple one-day consultation, there are many stages of production and/or needs where a costume specialist can offer their unique tool set.

VISUAL DEVELOPMENT

Research
Costume Concepts
Costume Props
Culture Building
Design Stylization
Surface Design
Status Effect Design
Material Callouts
Texture Packs
Turnarounds

CINEMATIC EFFECTS AND MODELING

Garment Fit and Analysis
Technical Flat Patterns
UV Maps
Cloth Behavior
Continued Research
Design Analysis
Thinking in the Round
Resource Acquisition
Under Structures
Model Styling

FABRICATION

Look Dev
Garment Patterning
Garment Construction
Garment Fit
Animatable Structures
Access and Maintenance
Material and Detail Scaling
Surface Finishes
Material Manipulation
Advanced Technologies
Aging and Dyeing
Handwork
Cobbling
Millinery
Other Specialty Skills

ANIMATION

Motion Studies
Material Behavior
Performance

CONCEPTUAL SKILLS

VISUAL LANGUAGE BUILDERS:
2D to 3D Spatial Thinkers
Unique Approach to Material, Texture, and Structure

WORKING KNOWLEDGE:
Highly-Skilled Researchers
Add Historical and Social Context
Extreme Aesthetic Versatility

NARRATIVE:
Psychology of Costume
Performer Collaboration

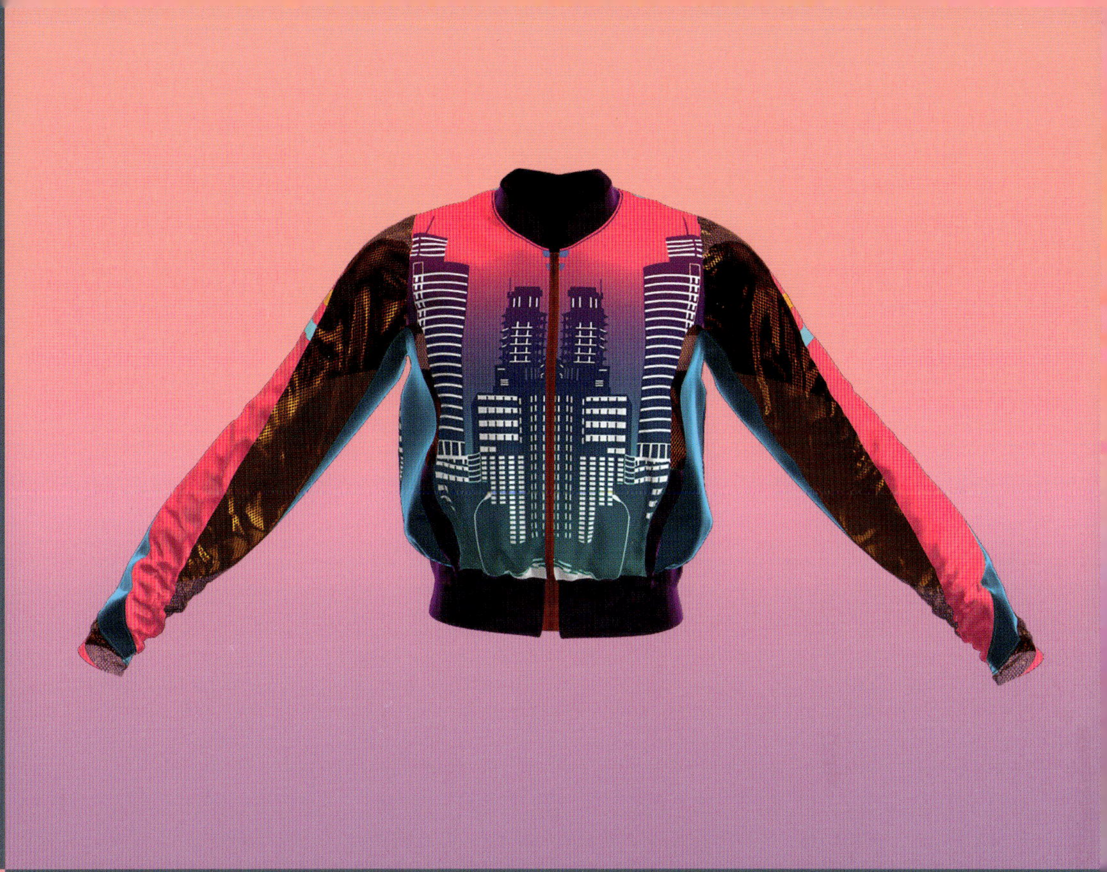

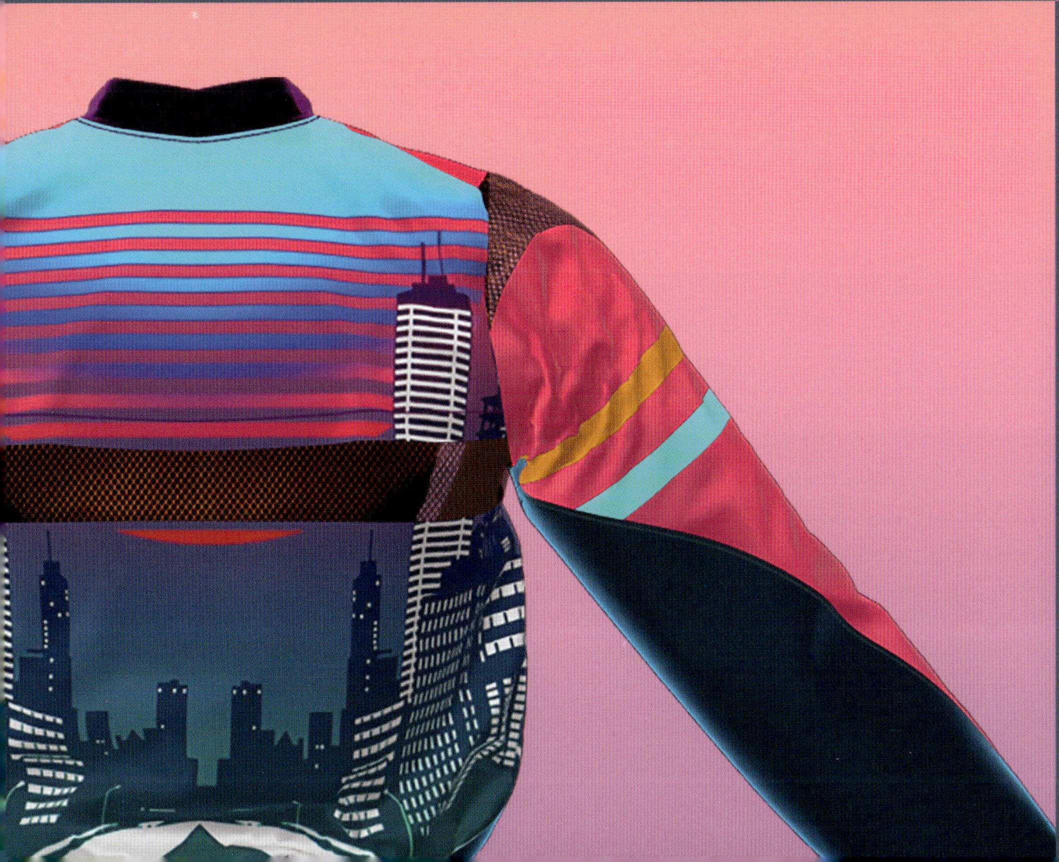

TECHNICAL SKILLS

ANALYSIS:
Contextualizing Story
Introducing Strong Research Methodology
Garment Fit

DRAFTSMANSHIP:
Generating Patterns
Fabrication
Master Techniques

TRANSLATION:
Adapting to Multiple Mediums
Maintaining Design Integrity
Interpreting Historical/Cultural Reference as Story

Tackling a Video Game Character Concept Brief

Sam Hogg is a veteran concept artist working in the video game industry. She has worked on *Forza Horizon, Injustice: Gods Among Us,* and *RuneScape,* as well as *James Bond, Star Wars,* and *Transformers* video games. www.artofsamhogg.com

PHANTOM: A VIDEO GAME CHARACTER CONCEPT

Briefs can range from short sentences or bullet points to longer narratives that multiple people have a say in. For key characters, the process can be long and iterative and involve a lot of feedback. Oftentimes you may be working with ideas that aren't fully formed, so it's important to be able to find little stories in the designs as you work that may help ignite discussion or spawn entirely new ideas.

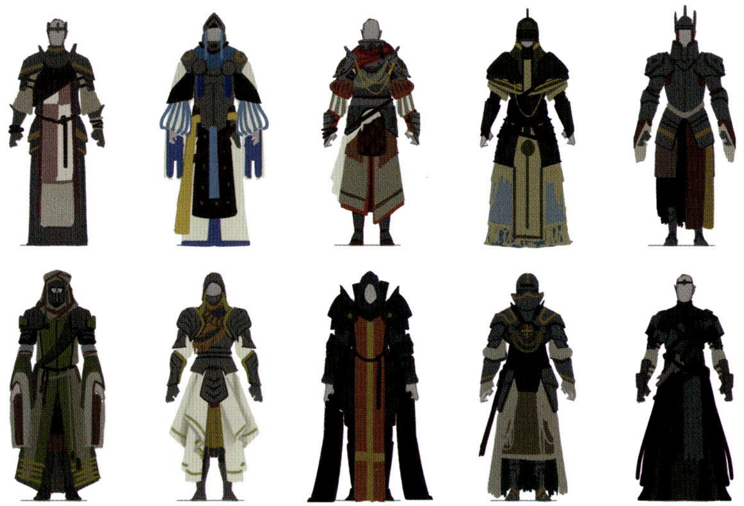

THE BRIEF

Game: realistic, Western fantasy RPG

Character: Phantom

A ghostly Caucasian male knight. He is an actual human, not otherworldly, but has lived longer than most humans do. He wears armor inspired by Western 15th- and 16th-century designs, with elements of Moorish patterning or clothing.

Known Backstory: A knight who has served many rulers and survived countless battles over an unnaturally long time, Phantom is now an elusive, isolated figure who protects the town his long-dead family lived in. He occasionally helps those he deems worthy. Phantom is to be a major questline character who helps the player advance the story. He is perceived as neither good nor evil.

The Importance of Visual Cues

Games often rely on visual cues to show the player how to advance, e.g., using light sources, colored surfaces, or specific enemy silhouettes. Bad visual design can lead to players feeling confused or frustrated when visual patterns are set and not followed. Starting from a place of simple blocks of color and value will help you avoid getting too caught up in the bells and whistles like texture and lighting. Symmetry is a great way to get these designs down quickly, but don't forget to add some asymmetry if you are looking for more real-life, believable costumes. People rarely wear things symmetrically.

In Phantom's case, I've focused on a muted palette inspired by Moorish mosaic and wall patterns that help sell the ghostly and "past-his-prime" aspects of the brief. My designs concentrate on detail and bulk around his head, shoulders, and chest, suggesting a physically powerful character. The complexity of layers shown suggest that he isn't just an infantry soldier or mercenary; the embellished tabards suggest he once served a particular monarch or duke.

The Man Behind the Armor

Sketching poses helps me find the right gesture for the character. Extreme action wouldn't have fit the brief as well as these introspective poses. Use these rendered poses as a base to expand on your designs and help speed up your workflow. (You won't have to repaint the body every single time you flesh out one of the thumbnails.)

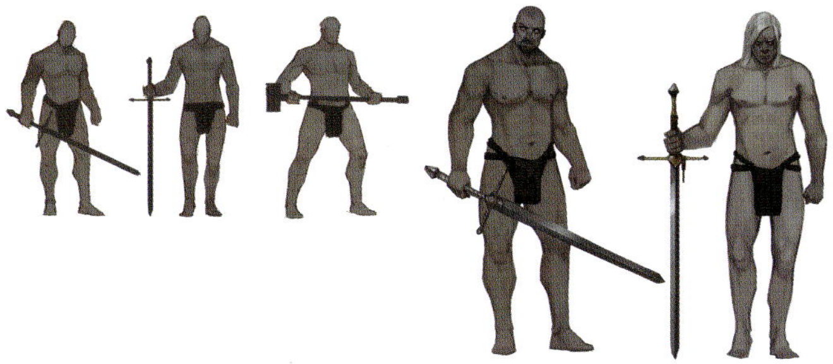

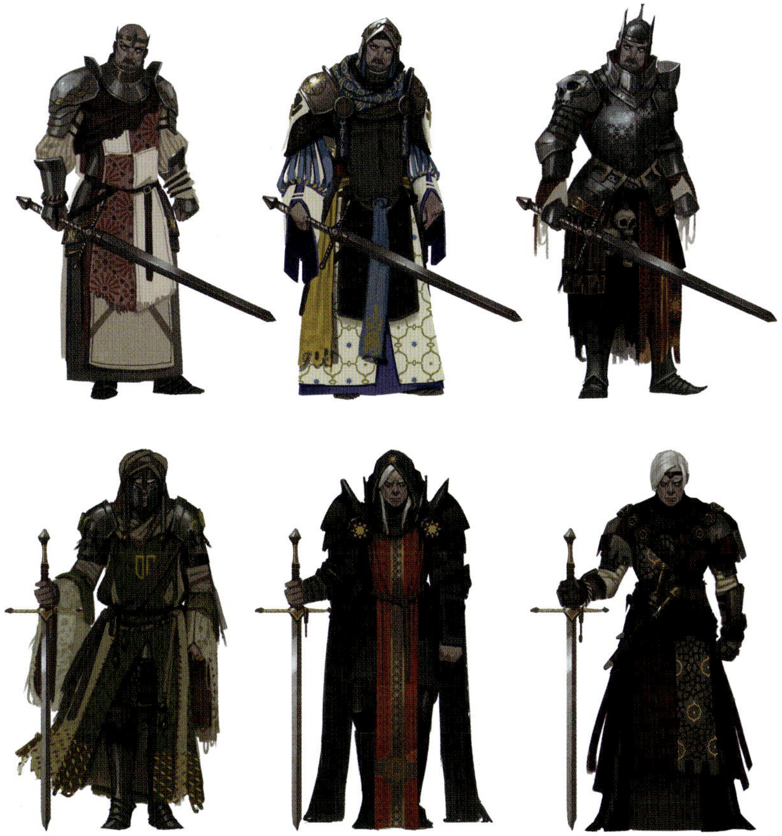

The heavily armored look strengthens the fact he is now an isolated figure: the armor is one more barrier to the outside world yet also suggests he still has a fondness for whatever capacity he previously served in as a knight. It might be that he was a standard bearer, a king's guard, leader of the king's guard, or a knight who fought for a smaller landowner/lord. This societal standing might influence the kinds of clothing/materials he had available to him.

These are all signs that might be subconsciously picked up by the player before they've even had chance to interact with him. Is he dangerous or just world weary? Does he care what the outside world thinks of him or not? Each one of these designs is a variation on the core concept.

Without a brief that describes exactly what kind of person he is, it's important to give a number of choices to pick from to the client, the art director, or other developers. The best thing is when your designs spark excitement and conversation in your coworkers, and players really connect with them because of the thought that you invested in the characters—from their costumes to their psyche.

Detailing the Design

This is where you get to the details that really sell the story of the character. As I redraw the designs, I start considering many things:

what it feels like to wear armor like this;
where it gets damaged;
how many weapons he carries;
what sorts of trinkets he might have collected in his many battles;
and whether he really cares for fancy fabrics or not.

DID YOU KNOW?

A major questline character is an important character, with whom the player may spend a lot of time interacting, so he should visually stand apart from other non-player characters (NPCs) who just populate the world as visual background noise.

Working with a Specialist: A Case Study of Costume Collaboration in Animation

LACUNA by Moonraker Studios

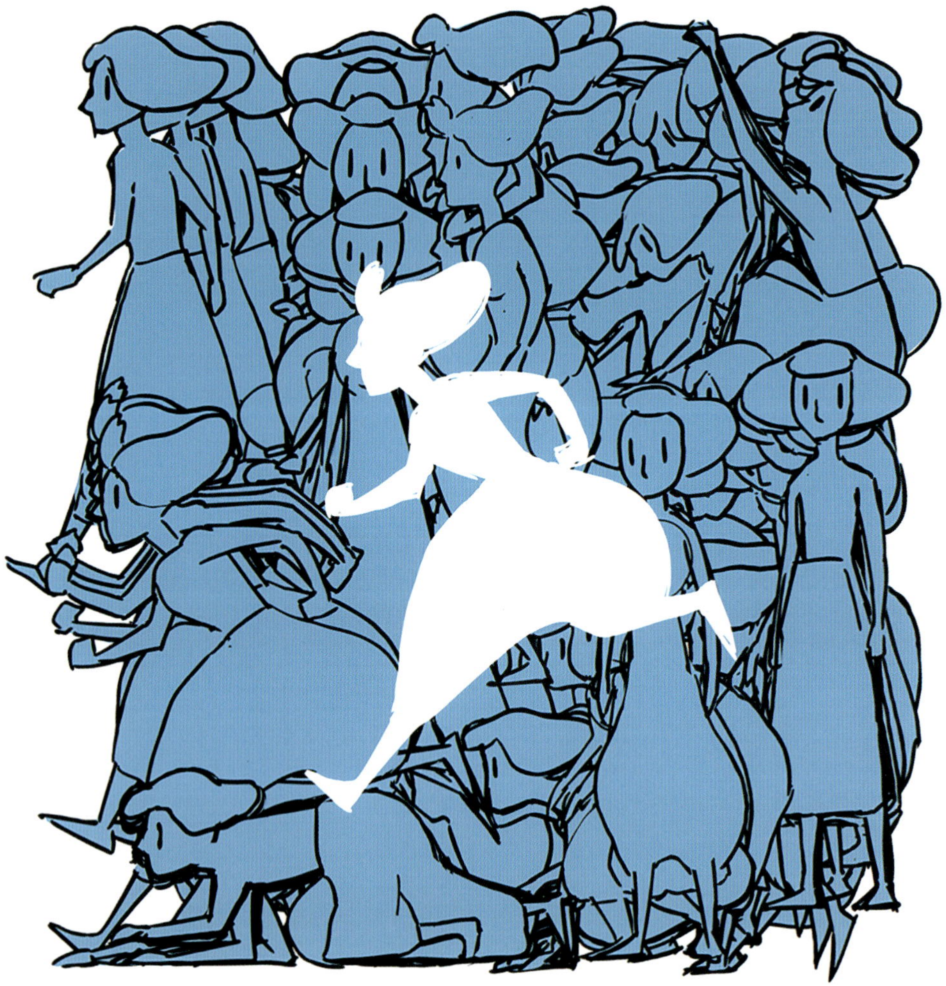

By Gwyn Conaway

Lacuna, created by Akili Pomian, is the story of Haro, a girl whose world is broken apart by a comet that collides with the earth. “The Fall,” as she calls it, was actually the destruction of the gate between the spirit world and her own.

While her parents snoozed on an early train back to the city, Haro was wide awake, eager to see the massive, ancient stone giants that were carved into the desert cliffs. After sneaking into a private observation deck, she looked up in terror. A blinding white light streaked toward her city from a dark, perilous sky. In the aftermath of the catastrophic shock waves, Haro awoke to find herself the sole survivor of the derailed train. Following the train tracks toward home, she soon realized that the world was no longer as it had been. Dangerous, broken spirits roamed the deserts, the ruins, the abandoned towns. Pockets of time floated about the landscape, revealing not the desert she knew but a vast Mediterranean sea. With the help of a mysteriously sentient broken spirit, she embarks on a journey to save her parents and heal her world.

We were inspired by a range of people, from Turkish and North African to Peruvian and Mongolian. High elevation, Mediterranean climates, vast grasslands, dry orchards, and dilapidated harbors were key environments for us to consider. We wanted to draw from cultures with a long history that faced harsh living conditions with vibrant color palettes, woven textiles (rather than leather or felt), and diverse ornamentation.

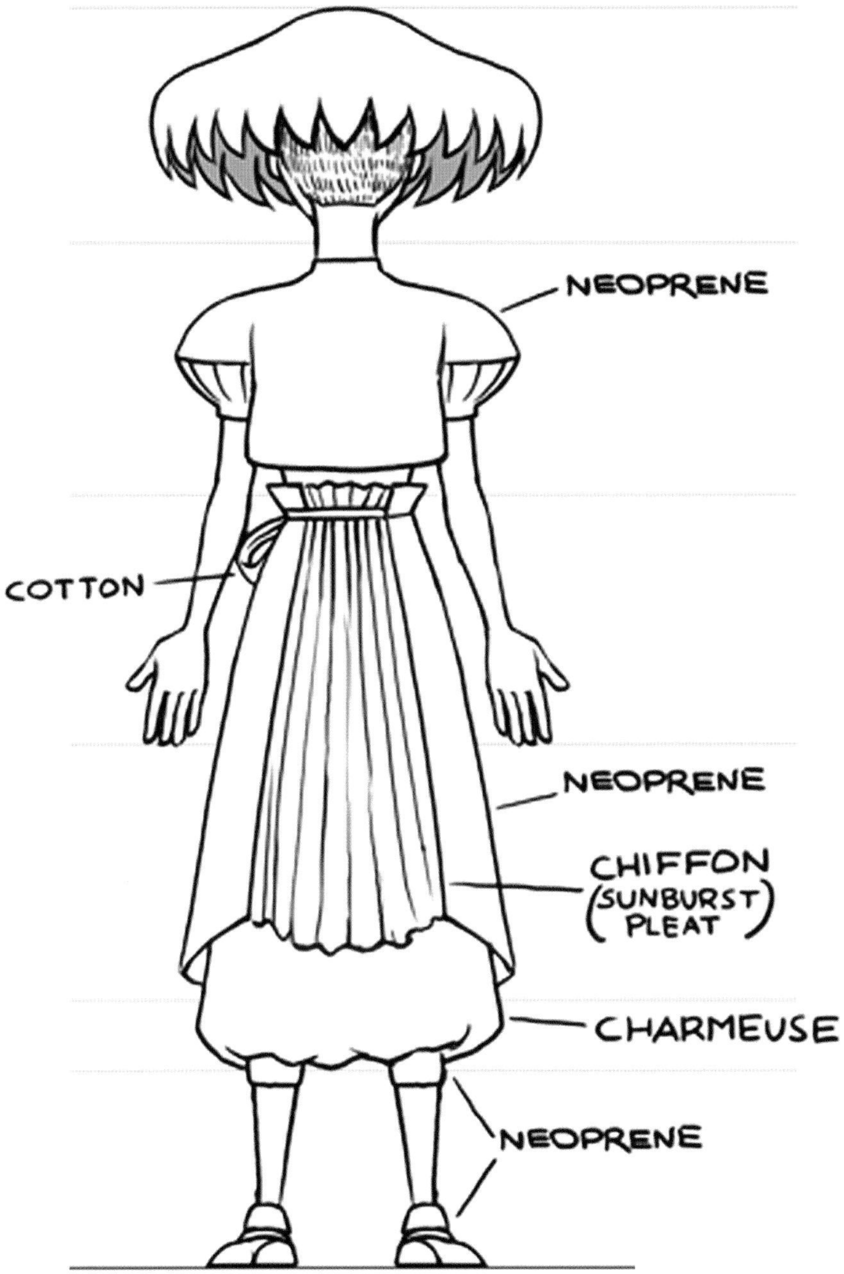

Lacuna was originally a blue sky project for a 2D scroller game a group of my friends came up with during an online chat. We organized into Moonraker Studios, but rather than finishing the project, we dedicated ourselves to an addictively supportive critique circle that lasted nearly four years. We focused on personal growth and enthusiasm for each other's success. It was an incredible way to share our personal works, continue group projects, and grow as artists.

When I was elected the art director at Moonraker, I knew that defining the world through costume was something we would pursue. The resulting collaboration with our character designer and lead animator, Josh Wong, and character artist and animator, Maria Kercher, was a true testament to the potential of costume specialists in the entertainment industries.

FABRIC CHOICES

My initial Haro designs were used to inspire Josh's final design. The fabrics I'd chosen remained intact:

Neoprene (used for wet suits; supports large smooth shapes and movements): relates to themes of water, which were important to the creator, Akili Pomian. The pockets of time Haro had to navigate took her back to a world in which her desert nation was actually a verdant coastline.

Chiffon (light, airy fabric with some structured body): creates dynamic movement when paired with the more bell-like movements of the neoprene; sunburst pleats create an angular visual that contrasts the large neoprene shapes of the skirt and top.

Four-ply moiré charmeuse: The charmeuse is thick and buttery with mercurial movement; the moiré pattern creates organic pattern interest in contrast to the linear and geometric details throughout the rest of the costume. This also relates back to water, as moiré is also referred to as "watered silk" for the water stains found in wood.

LACUNA
by Moonraker Studios

HARO

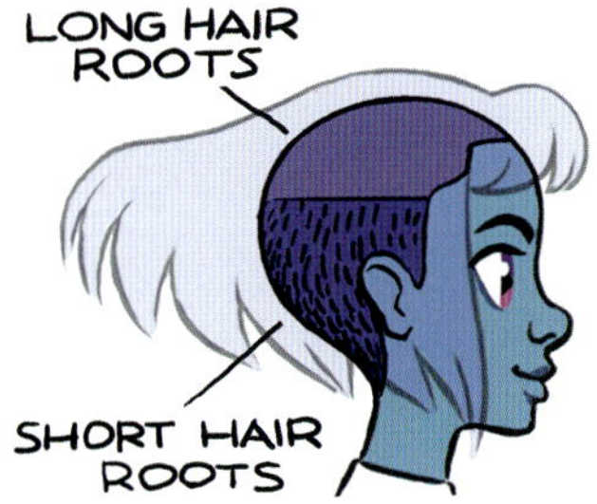

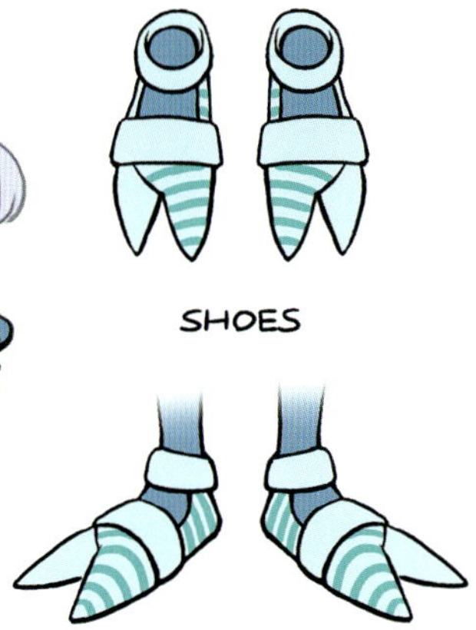

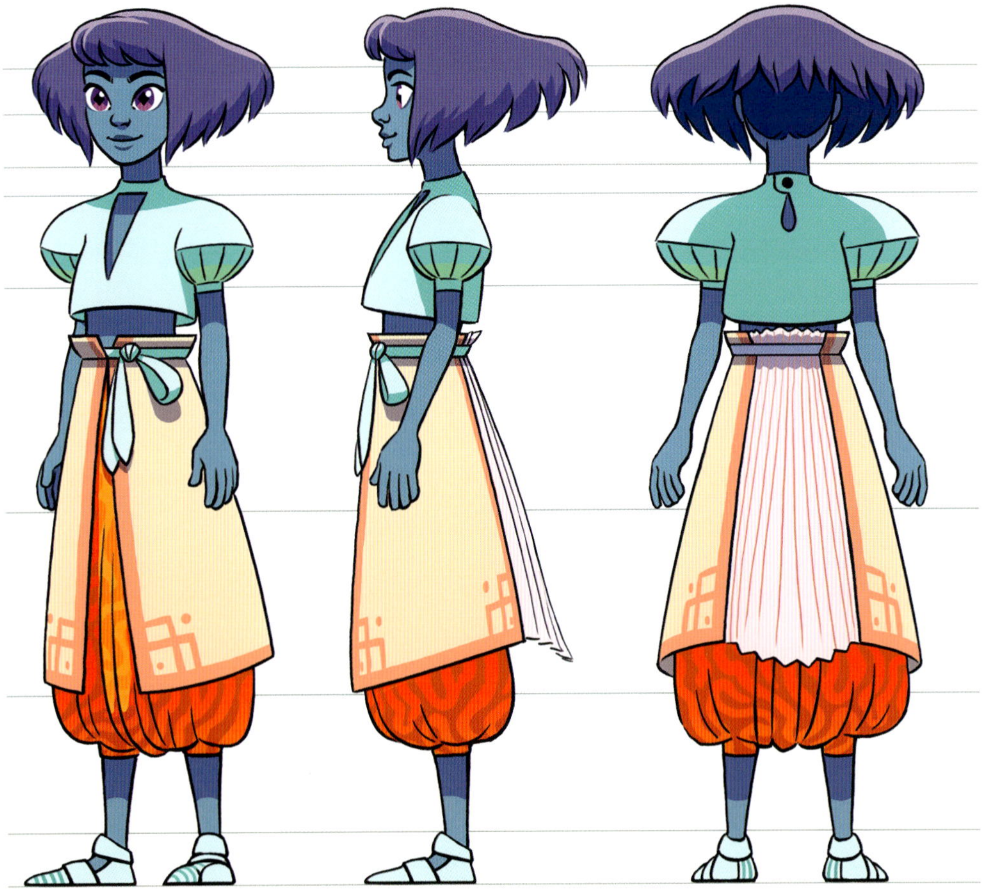

UNDER STRUCTURES AND THE EFFECT ON ANIMATION

When Josh first drew Haro with her arm extended, we had a discussion about its shape. This is a common consideration for live-action designers, but in 2D animation, real-world limitations don't apply, so he had drawn it simply falling below her bicep. I suggested that the sleeve actually be supported by a sleeve crinoline. These were worn during the Crinoline period (1850–1865 or so) to support the giant sleeve shapes.

This ended up affecting the look of Haro's animation cycles significantly, as the sleeve behaved with more weight and structure rather than "floating" without definition.

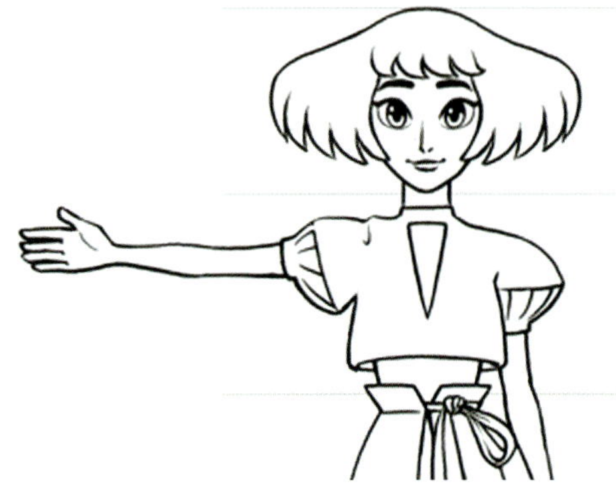

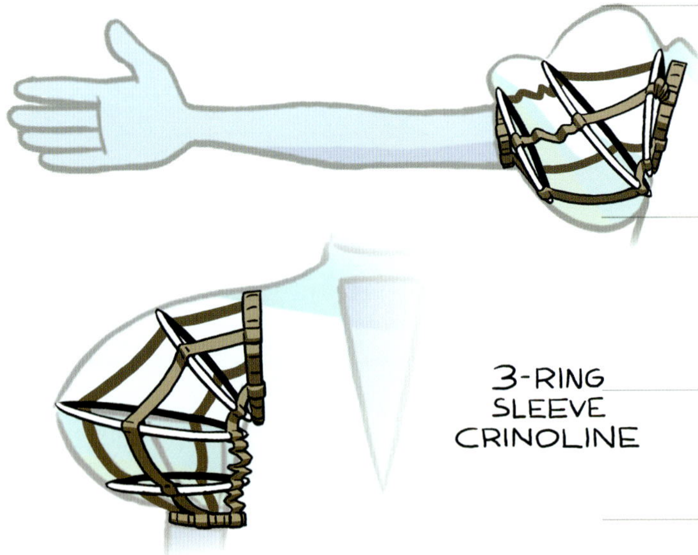

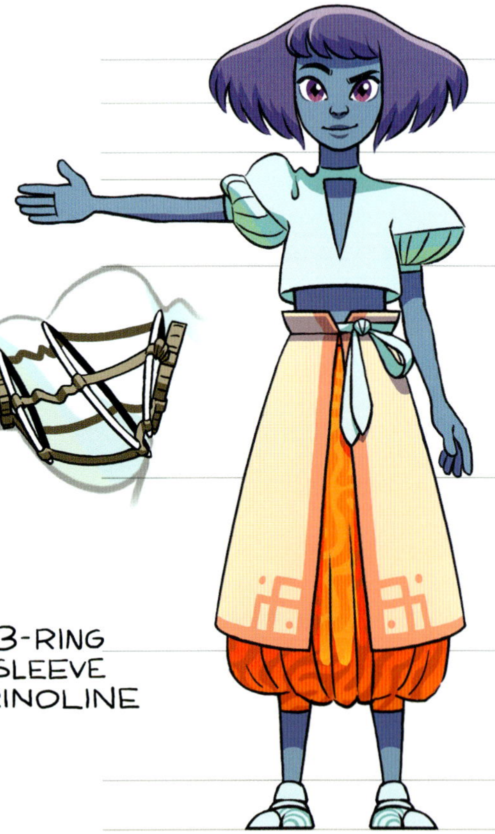

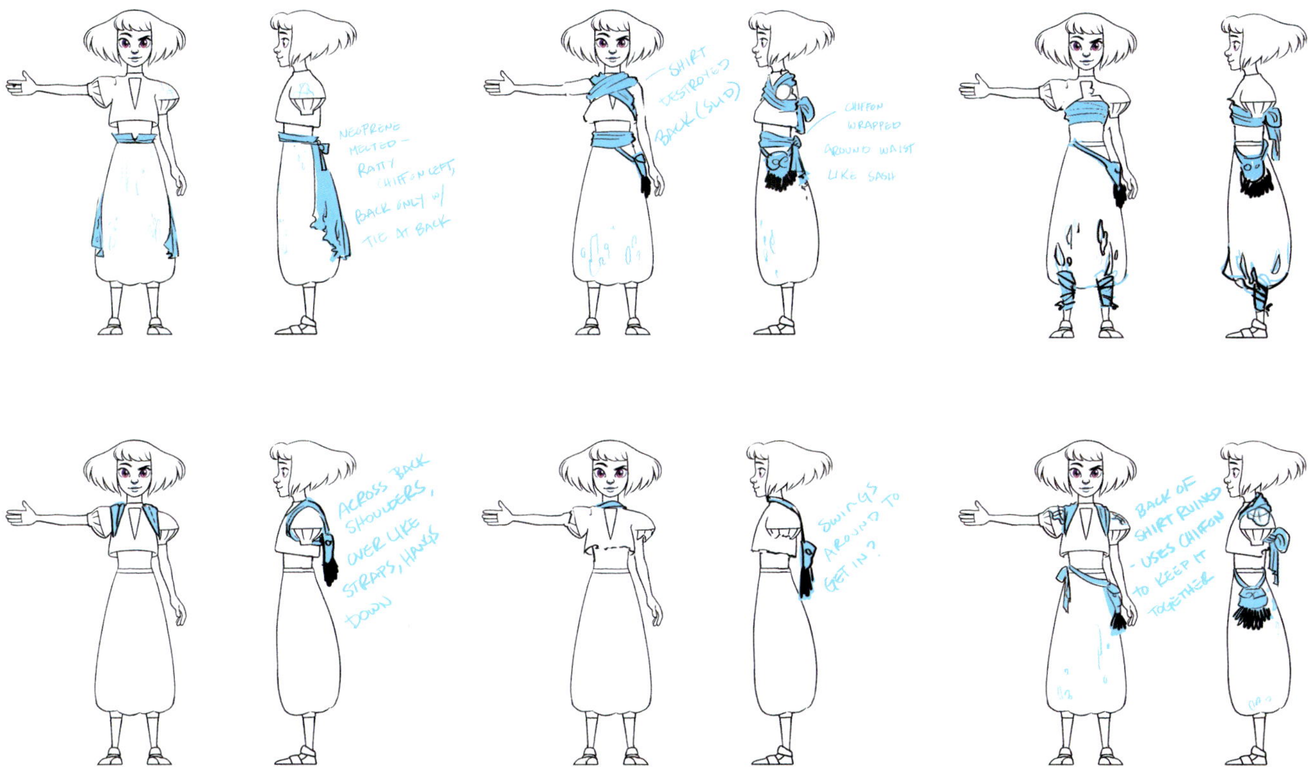

REAL WORLD AIDS

HARO'S HAREM PANTS

In addition to designing, Josh was also tasked with Haro's animation cycles. To help him with movement, I built a pair of Haro's pants for him to wear. Although the animation fabric in my mind is a four-ply moiré charmeuse, this fabric does not exist in real life. As a result, we built the pants from a moiré polyester for the correct reflectivity and pattern. I also sent him home with a bolt of chiffon to acquaint himself with the weight of her skirt's movement.

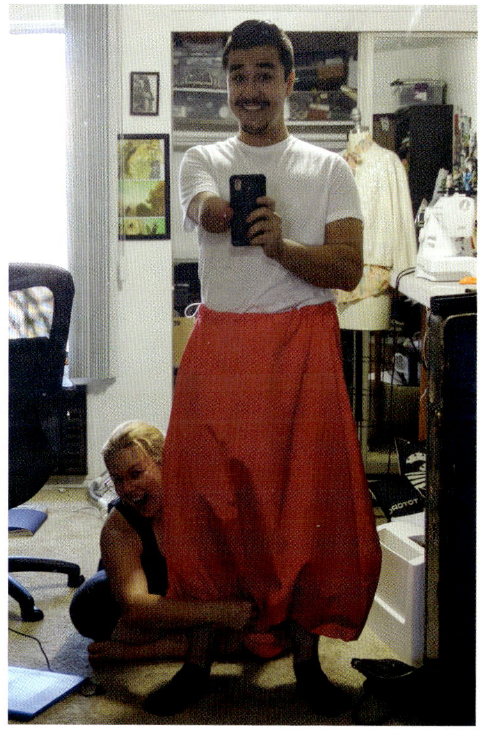

DISTRESS AND ITERATIONS

We decided that Haro's costume needed to evolve after The Fall. The environment would have electrical fires, rugged terrain, and sprays of water. Josh's initial instinct was to poke some holes in the skirt and pants, but each sketch was compositionally flawed from one side or another. Since he was experiencing artist's block, he asked me to sketch some iterations to help train his eye.

Rather than poking holes in her clothing, I tried to think instead of what happened. She was thrown about, skidded across dirt and rocks, and was pelted with potted ferns, snack carts, and luggage. Her soft overskirt wouldn't have survived, and she'd probably have damage on her knees and burn marks. Her top is made of neoprene and would potentially melt. The triangular keyhole might get snagged and tear too.

I decided she'd use the remains of her skirt functionally: protection from flying sparks, wrapping her loose top more tightly, and strapping on important items so she could climb.

COMMUNICATING CULTURE

The very beginning of the game was our only chance to introduce Haro's culture. The sleepy train was filled with carefully calculated characters to introduce some basic elements of modern-day Lacuna. Inclusion was important to us as a group, as well, so our train represented a wide variety of people in her world. This was a challenge, as every character was also asleep. This meant our characters had to speak through their luggage and clothing.

One particular group we discussed in depth was business people. The train was full of commuters returning to the city on a red-eye express from one end of the desert to the other. In a sense, this train represented our own modern day. Every sleeper wore casual lounge clothes with diverse haircuts, color palettes, and luggage. Everyone, that is, except for the business people. They were crammed together on a single bench, hugging their briefcases, wearing matching haircuts.

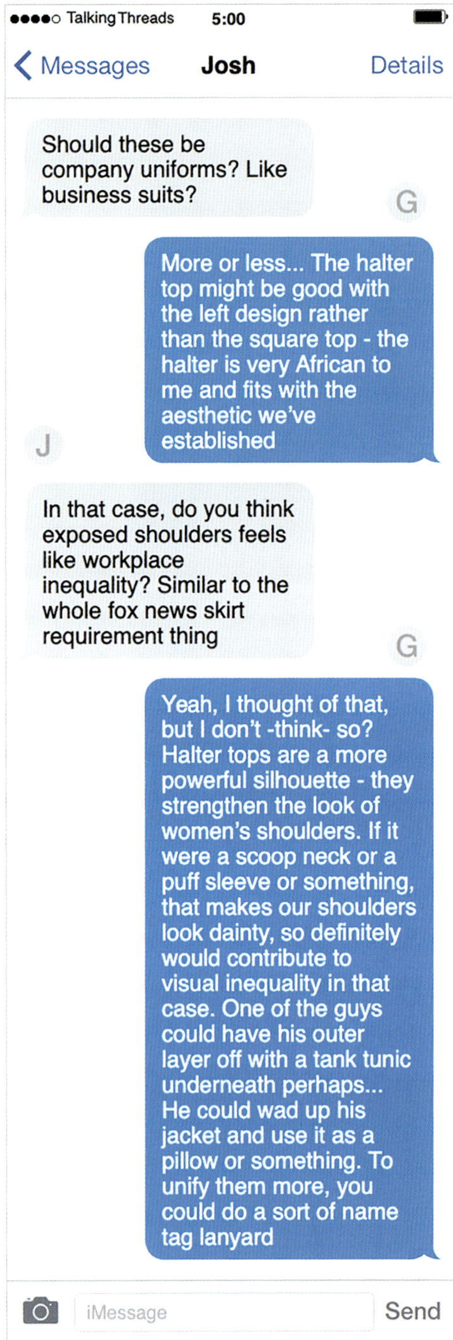

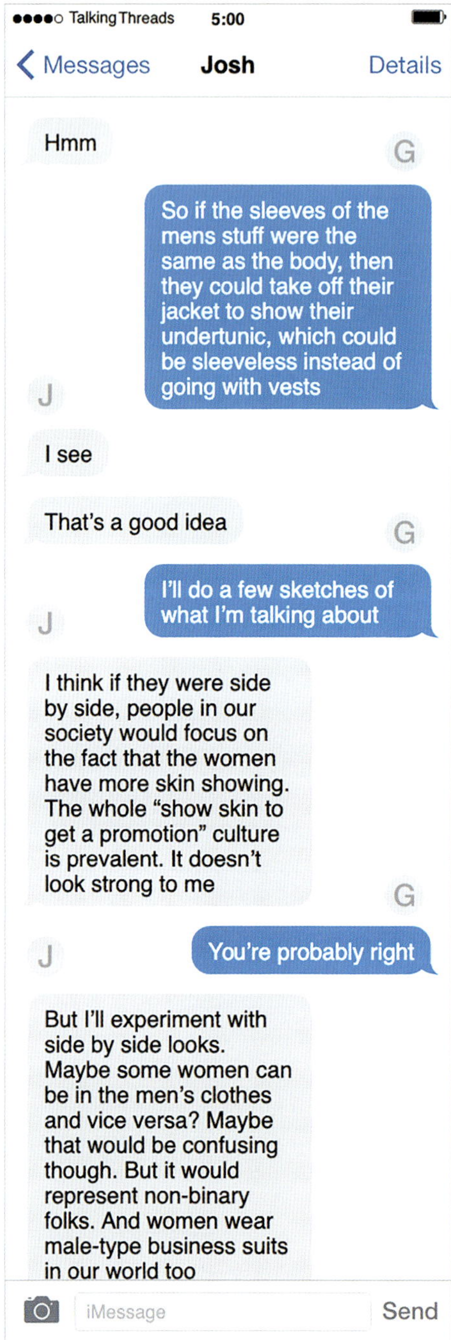

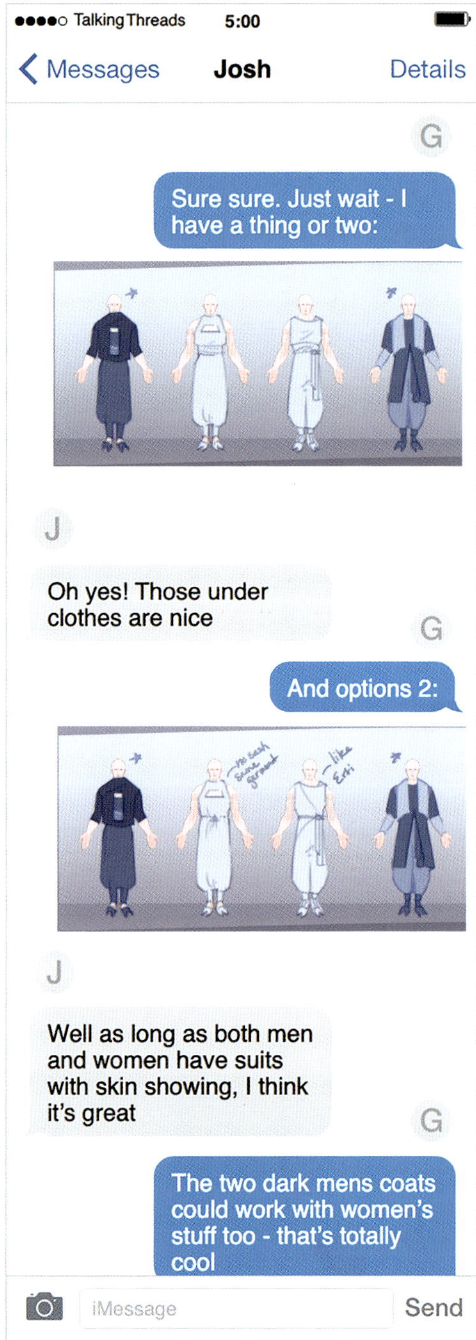

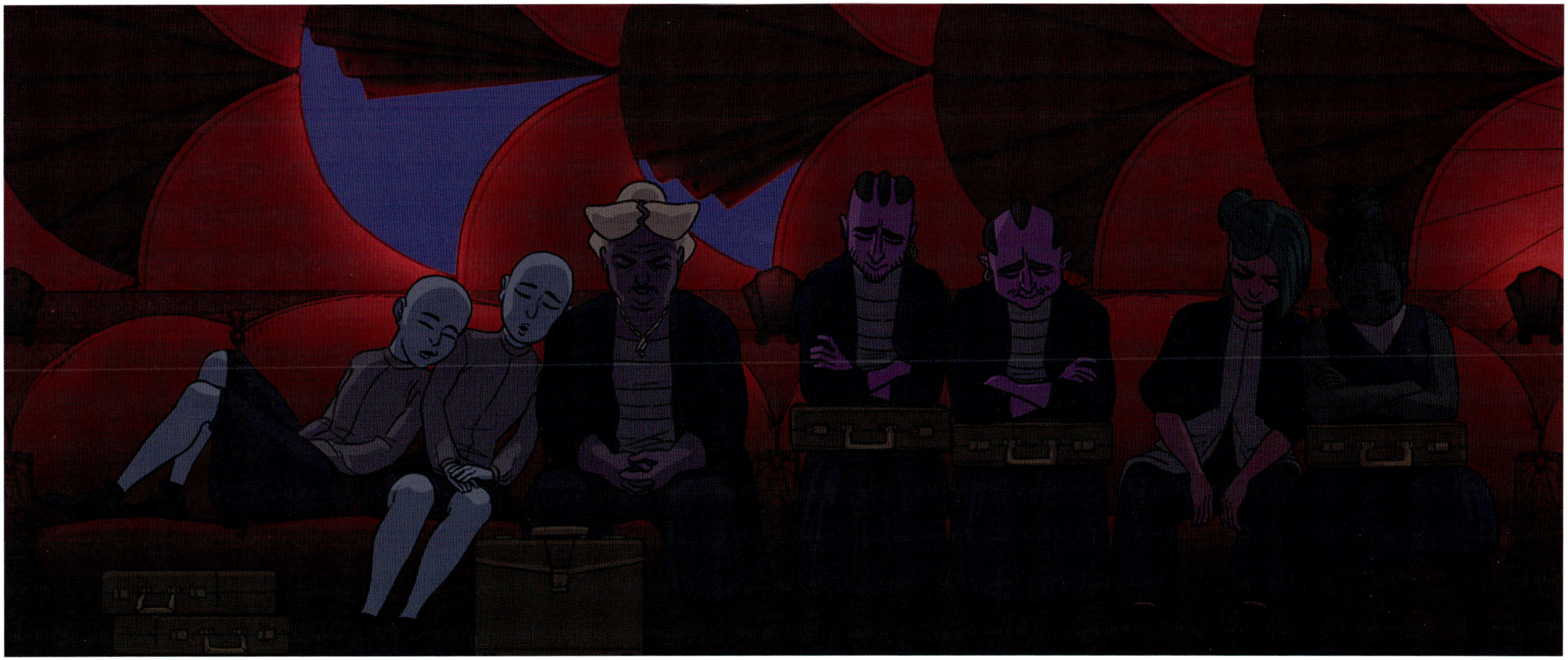

It was a challenge, to say the least. Some things we learned or considered along the way:

Having artist's block is normal, even in a professional environment. When you have artist's block, reach out to a colleague that understands the unique obstacles you're facing. Josh and I worked very closely to create the costume language, and complemented each other's skills as a team.

Ten to fifteen minutes: This is how much play time we expected to have to introduce all of our sleeping passengers and define Haro's culture before The Fall. This gave us a little cushion to really define each sleeper. In fact, to make it fun for ourselves, many of the sleepers are modeled after the team! Finding places to lay Easter eggs that don't deter from the story can keep your team (and audience) engaged.

Diversity: This was very important to our group. We wanted to represent a wide variety of people, orientations, relationships, and so on. We talked at length about representation, finally deciding to use cool skin tones rather than fleshy colors, so that any young girl could see themselves as Haro.

Equality: Josh and I had an ongoing discussion about the business people especially. It's common to design a world with more gender separation in entertainment because it creates visual contrast that's pleasing to look at—a pair of pants standing next to a skirt, for example. We didn't want to fall into this pithole for Lacuna, though, especially since Akili modeled Haro's culture as a matriarchy. Simple decisions had to be closely considered.

What does a scoop neckline vs. a halter neckline say? While scoop necklines are curvy and feminine, a halter neckline makes women's shoulders look strong. A scoop neckline with a cap sleeve feels modern and athletic, while a scoop neckline with puff sleeves feels childish. Each costume element had a lot to contribute to how we view our characters.

CONTRASTING TIME AND CULTURE

I wanted there to be a strong difference between the metropolis Haro grew up in and the ancient pockets of reality she stumbles into.

Like the business people sleeping on the train, modern people camouflage themselves into the tones and textures of their cities, just like we talked about in societal terrain. In contrast, I pushed Josh and our other character artist, Maria Kercher, to create a vibrant and exciting world for Haro to explore after the train accident. It was important to the group that her journey be both challenging and full of wonder.

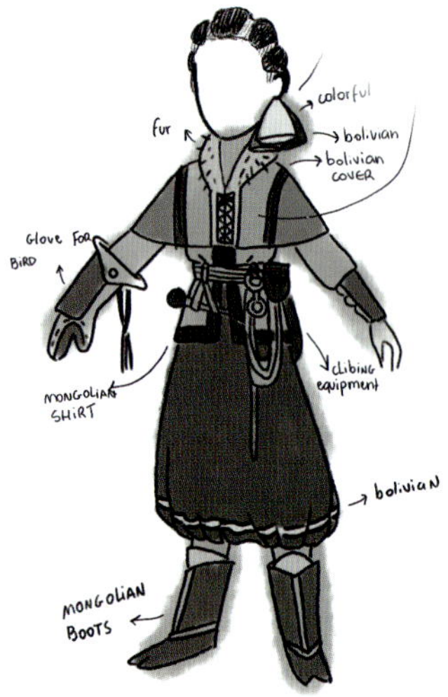

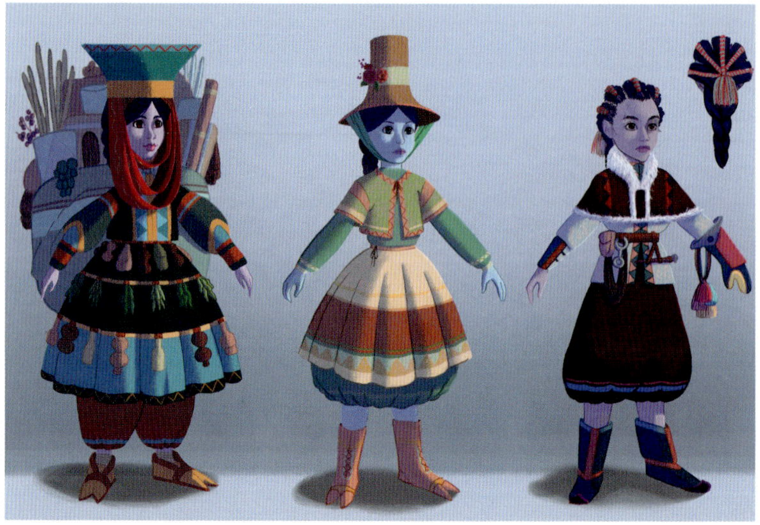

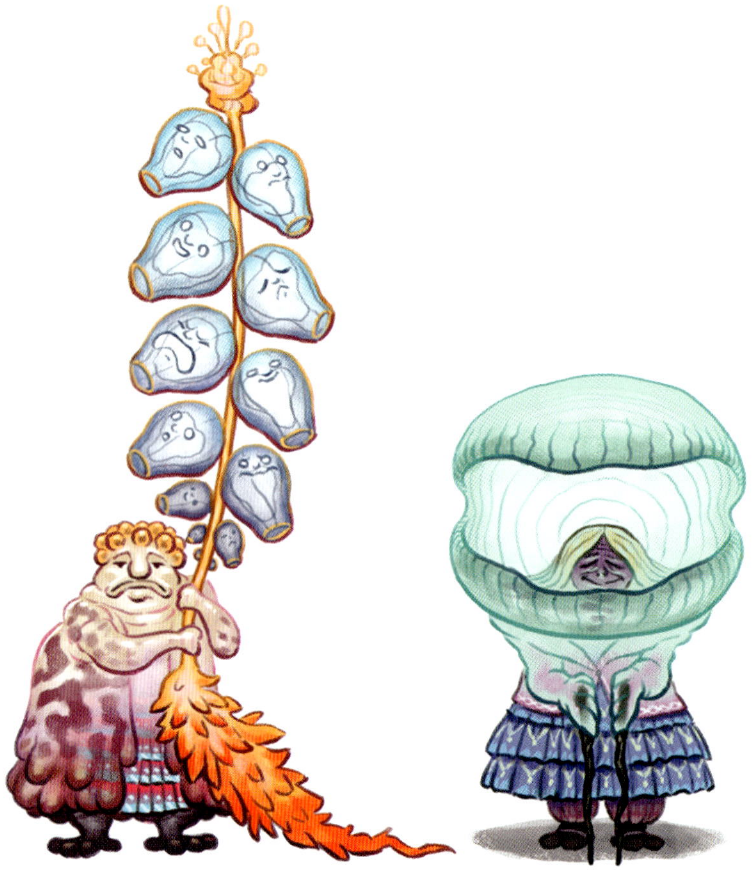

Our real ancient civilizations used bold patterns, shapes, and palettes to signify their village, ruling lords, deities, and other important information in a way modern people don't anymore. I wanted to see this infused into the world of Lacuna in the same way the spirits and ancient denizens have also melted together. Here you can see some ancient villagers that resided in Lacuna before The Fall and some broken spirits Haro discovers after.

Tasked with designing the ancient humans, Maria turned to our overall production inspirations of Turkish, Peruvian, Mongolian, and North African aesthetics. Our goal was to create a unique and unified culture rather than a civilization that felt collaged or pulled from many sources. With this goal in mind, we looked for cultures that had political and cultural similarities and stuck to our guns.

In indie or personal projects, artists often default to referencing other intellectual properties as a shorthand for creating exciting content, but in Lacuna we worked hard to make sure every choice supported the world in a genuine way. Rather than referencing to other entertainment, we drew our inspiration from the places and people that supported our story. As a result, our blue sky project had a unique flare with strong foundations that allowed us to explore a wide variety of possibilities without feeling like our visual language was spread too thin.

Letter from a Character Artist

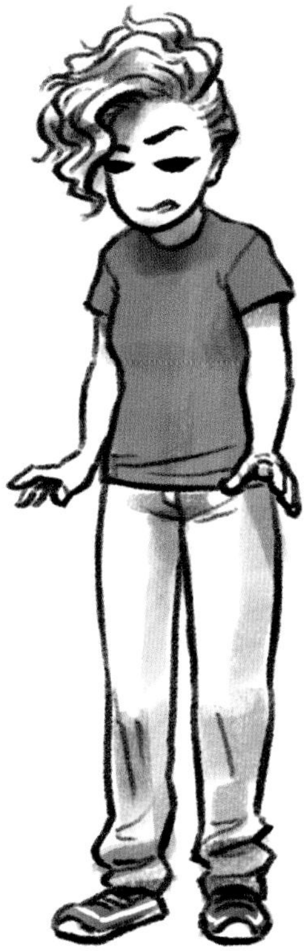

Josh Wong, head animator for Lacuna, the 2D scroller game currently in production at Moonraker Studios, discusses costume design from the perspective of a character artist.

My character designs have improved tremendously. The biggest factor in this? Working alongside an experienced costume designer, Gwyn Conaway.

Before I signed on to Lacuna, I had absolutely no concept of costume design. My human characters were well drawn, but for reasons unknown to me at the time, they didn't feel authentic. It was as if they were specifically designed to fill a plot point or character archetype, instead of being living, breathing people.

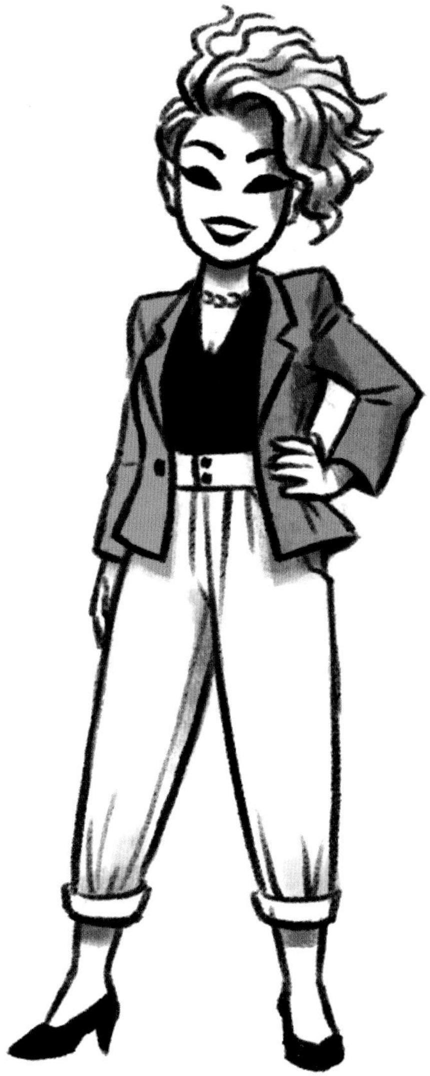

I've always loved drawing heads and faces, but when it came to drawing clothes, I always locked up. I drew a simple T-shirt or flannel, or maybe something from a TV show I had watched. The world of fashion was an unknown to me. (My own wardrobe consists of T-shirts and basketball shorts.) I didn't know I should be thinking about costume design at all.

When I started working with Gwyn, my third designer eye opened. Aesthetically, I started learning about things such as the inseam, shoulder seam, and back yoke—little details that make clothing look more realistic in a design. On a deeper level, Gwyn taught me about the history of certain garments, and what factors influenced their popularity. This was very useful for creating fantastical characters and their other-worldly garments. All design draws from real life, after all.

Bouncing designs off of Gwyn for her expert advice lifted all the stress of designing a character's clothing off my shoulders. I learned things I wouldn't have thought to research before, such as an intricate sleeve crinoline, the beautiful moiré pattern rolled onto some polyesters and silks, or the way chiffon sunburst pleats sway in a gentle breeze. I literally discover something new every time we collaborate.

Now, my character designs are stronger than ever, and the clothing they wear reveals an inner depth to their personality. Working alongside a costume designer has opened a door for me, leading me out of a cramped closet full of stereotypical designs into a world rich with history, culture, and endless possibilities.

The Stories We Tell

On average, 75 percent of a character canvas is clothing. As a costume designer, you have the unique opportunity to work on the most personal piece of design that the characters interact with. The challenge is at the same time exciting, fascinating, and intimidating. But the challenge is worth the payoff—because when you can use your costume knowledge with command and confidence, you elevate and strengthen the impact of the narrative.

Story changes the world. We rely on it to help us cope with our fears, see hope in overcoming trials, and learn how to relate to others with vastly different experiences or points of view. It opens us up to new connections and remedies the lies we tell ourselves. The stylized narratives and formats allow us to take it a step further, immersing audiences in a touch of fiction that opens us up to the analogies or allegories that will help us find new meaning in life. Every type of story has its purpose, but we open up to the fantasy, the alien, and the stylized mediums in ways that we just don't in more realistic visual stories.

As knowledge and tools become more and more available to indie creators or freelancers, we have even more opportunity to push the boundaries of what we've done in the past. We can create stylized stories with powerful costume designs that will not only entertain and enrich children but will also raise the bar (and increase the interest) in stylized stories created for adults as well. The more costume expertise we bring to the mediums, the more power we give a broader variety of stories to impact the world in new ways.

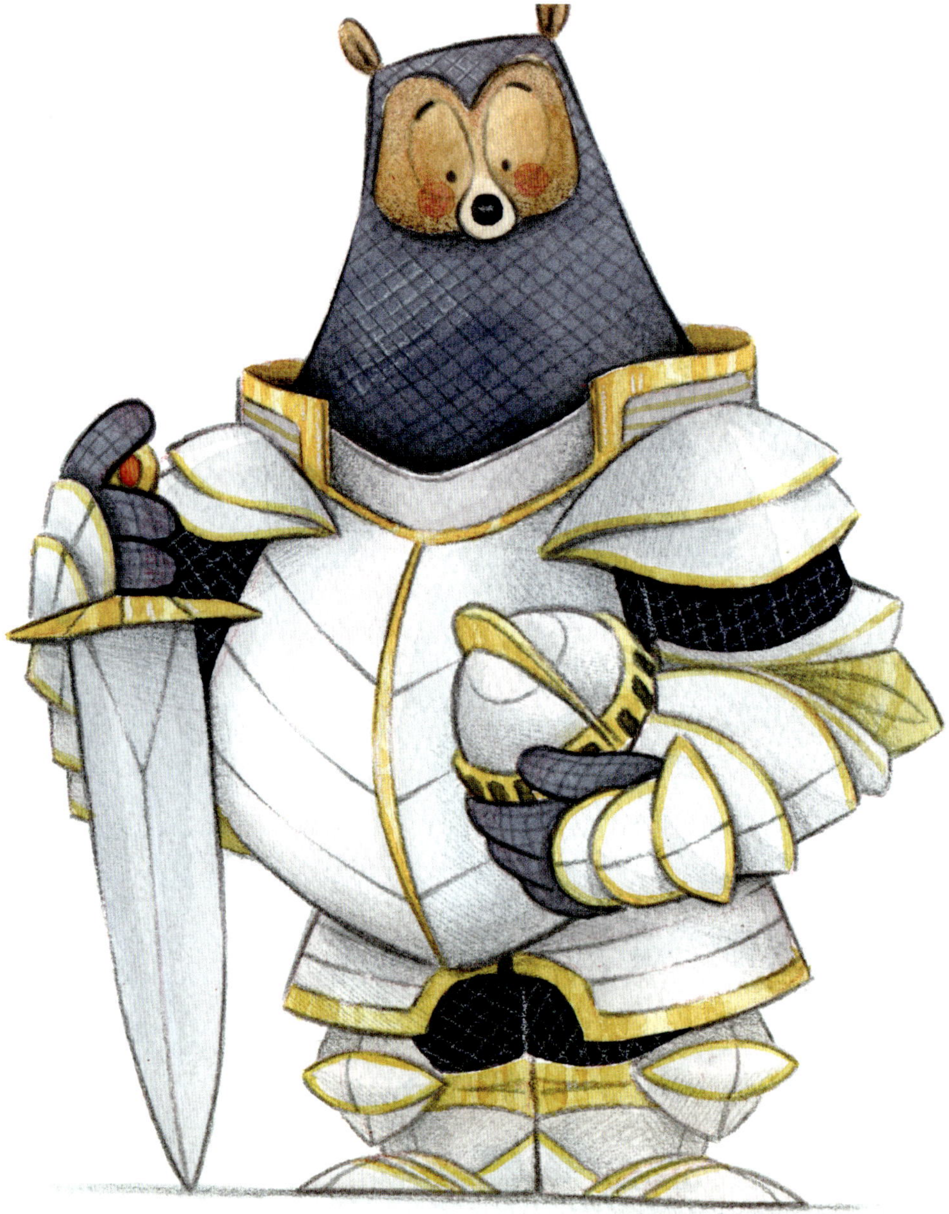

TAKEAWAYS

BIOGRAPHIES

Look in the mirror. Think about what clothing means to you and how you use it. We all communicate through our clothing; understanding the messages you are sending out into the world through your personal design choices will aid your ability to see clothing as a language.

Observe the world around you. Understand how shapes and designs in fashion reflect the fears and fascinations of a society or culture (or your own fixations). Study the context behind what's popular or what was popular in the past, and you will become stronger at using clothing to build context for your world.

Notice change. Notice where you wear through your clothing and why. What causes us to change our clothing choices during a week? What triggers a change in a trend? Fashion is never static, and the more you observe those changes, the better you can incorporate them into a story about change.

Know your format and medium needs. Understand how your design needs to be modified to fit the limitations of a project. Be considerate of your collaborators, respect the script and prompt, and acknowledge the capability they have of translating your design into the next stage. Learn their unique lingo and gain a basic understanding of their roles to find new ways to design and save them time.

Find your own niche. Build out from there. Once you understand how to approach things from your strengths, you can use the principles to learn other aspects of design. This book covers a variety of design approaches and questions. We each started somewhere. Translate the principles, and you can just as much ask them to refine your unique costume niche or improve your character, environments, or prop design strength.

"There's no such thing as a stupid question."
Jessie Kate Bui

"Equip yourself."
Gwyn Conaway

"Give yourself permission."
Maria Ferreira Kercher

"Wing it!"
Blythe Russo

"You're more legit than you think."
Rebecca Black-Gliko

Jessie Kate Bui

http://jessiekate.com

Jessie Kate is a design and story mentor. Her past experience has been in freelance design, educational program design, production coordination for TV animation, creative direction for startups, and indie project development. Working with her father, a master craftsman and furniture designer, gave her experience with complex creative problem-solving at an early age, and her mother's love of creating moods through design and music in her environments nurtured a love of immersive entertainment. When she brought her curiosity and analytical approach to the animation industry and found a gap in the costume design education, she decided to fill the void by gathering a team of specialists to create this book. Driven by stories that fight stigma and support personal transformation, Bui specializes in using personality psychology to develop authentic character arcs and immersive costume designs. Bui co-instructed History of Fashion at ArtCenter College of Design with Gwyn Conaway before creating her own online course, guiding her mentees through narrative analysis, practical research methodology, and concept development. She continues to create and share new exercises, challenges, and downloadable templates for designers and writers through her website.

Tools: Sakura Pigma Micron .25mm pen, cardstock, index cards, and Macbook Pro laptop so I can research, write, and edit on the go. Photoshop, SketchBook Pro, Grayscale Copic Markers, Intuos Pro Paper, Cintiq. Charcoal, oil paints, pastels, and Sculpey to tap back into the senses and bring in more organic chaos when the digital perfectionism hits too hard.

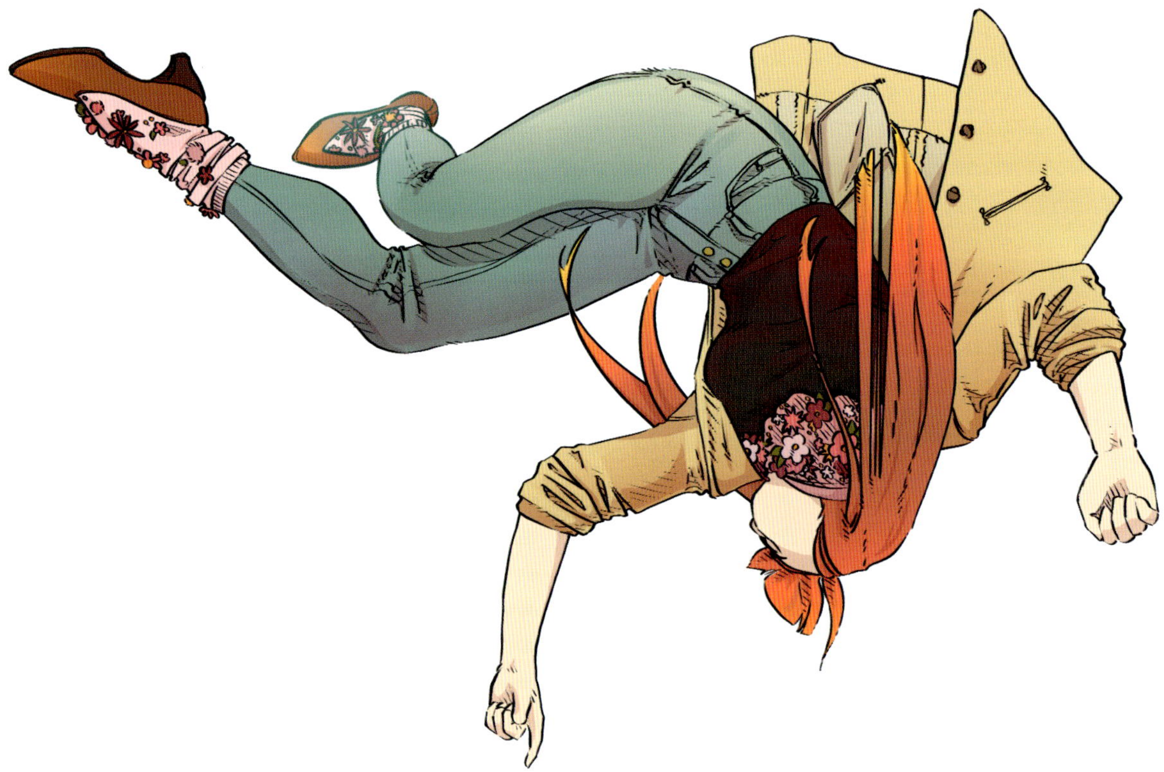

Gwyn Conaway

http://gwynconawayart.com

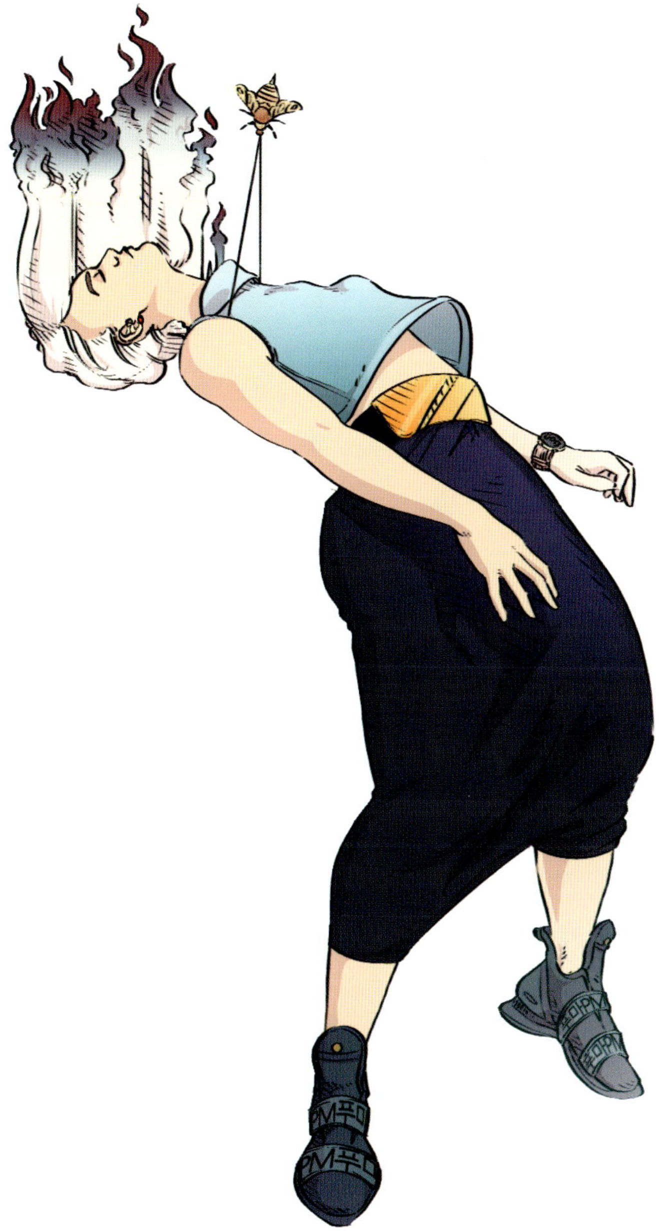

Gwyn is a member of the Costume Designers Guild Local 892. She's a costume designer, fashion historian, and culture specialist living in Southern California. Although she works primarily in historical and dramatic film, she also consults on costume simulation for major animation and gaming studios. She specializes in Marvelous Designer and garment model fit. Considered an authority on the intersection between clothing and social psychology, Conaway is on the cutting edge of how the entertainment industry thinks about costume and culture as a visual language. She is often called upon to design and consult for conceptual projects in post-apocalyptic and fantasy settings. Conaway is faculty at ArtCenter College of Design in Pasadena, CA. Her course, History of Fashion, is the first of its kind. Geared directly towards entertainment design students, the class explores Conaway's burgeoning expertise: building cultures for film, television, and gaming from the ground up.

Tools: Marvelous Designer, Photoshop, ZBrush, Maya, Bic pens, M. Graham Watercolor, Korean calligraphy brushes, Sakura gel pens, Pentel Fude brush pens, Copic markers, nail varnish, Intuos Pro, SyncOnSet (or another continuity program), truckloads of jasmine green tea.

Maria Ferreira Kercher

http://mariakercher.com

Maria is a visual development artist specializing in material behavior and cultural stylization for animation. She has also worked in design for indie games and illustration for live-action film. Born and raised in Brazil, Maria visited the opera and ballet frequently and participated in dance and figure skating competitions that nurtured a fascination with how costumes are used to enhance performance. Through figure skating, she gained an interest in how countries or people can be represented through simplified shapes, colors, movement, and music. Learning to sew from her mother, she began exploring her fascination through fashion. When her father introduced her to animation in the U.S., she fell in love with the idea of breathing life into a fictional world and came to the U.S. to study animation. Now based in Seattle, WA, Maria is focused on expanding her knowledge of materials and world cultures to better connect audiences to each other.

Tools: Photoshop, Procreate, Cintiq 13, Pentel brush pen, Copic markers, Copic pens, pencils.

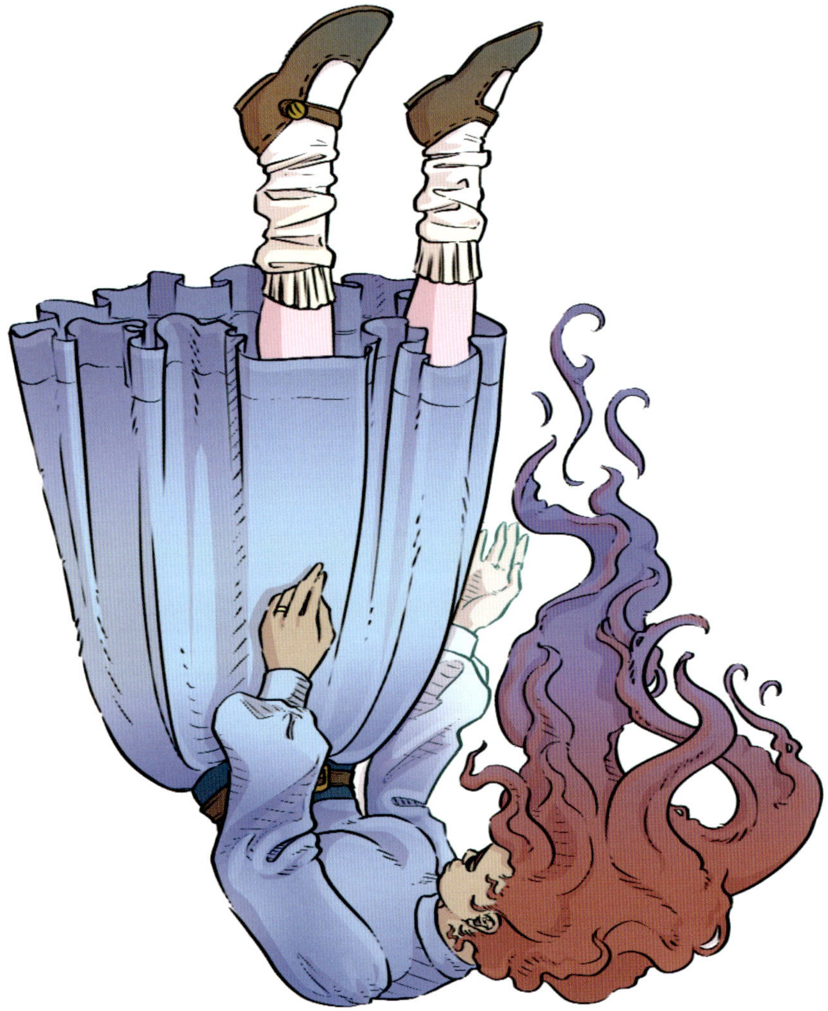

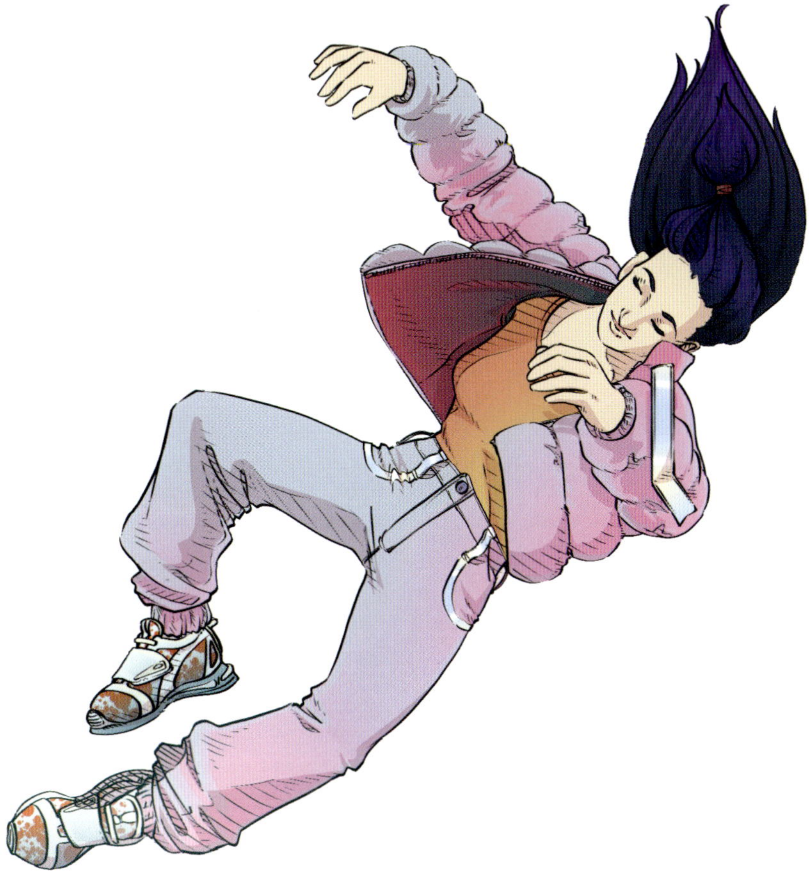

Blythe Russo

http://blytherussoillustration.com

Blythe is an illustrator and puppet builder living in Ohio. She holds a masters in illustration from the Savannah College of Art and Design and is an active member and supporter of the kidlit community. She made her debut as a children's book illustrator with the counting book *One More Wheel!* (Macmillan/August 2019). Blythe's favorite stories to tell are ones of friendship that give the reader both the giggles and the warm fuzzies. Blythe is also a self-taught puppet builder who has worked as the lead puppet builder for Madcap Puppets. She has designed/fabricated pieces for a variety of their shows, including *The Case of the Kidnapped Backpack*, *The Wonderful Wizard of Oz*, and *Pinocchio*. She's also been known to teach a puppet-building class every so often.

Tools: pencil, paper, Photoshop.

The most basic tools are needed for ideating/designing; how a person executes the designs/ideas is extremely dependent on taste/comfort level.

Rebecca "Beki" Black-Gliko

http://cosmicjingleart.com

Beki descends from a long line of quilters and thus has been sewing in some form or another from a very young age. Her devotion to learning led to a degree in illustration as well as studying abroad in Japan and New Zealand. Beki has worked for Laika on *Kubo and the Two Strings* and *Missing Link* in both the rapid prototype and costume departments. She currently lives in Oregon with her husband Raul Ramos and continues to work on projects that explore and combine a variety of mediums. She is currently working on a stop-motion educational book, *Building Character,* as well as a stop-motion graphic novel, *Oni-san,* that combines her love of animation, illustration, and stop-motion. Beki enjoys the challenge of translating a design on paper into a functional final product, whether the end result is digital or physical, and choosing the format that best translates the intentions of the narrative.

Tools: Photoshop, Illustrator, Intuos4/Cintiq, machine specifics like Embrilliance for embroidery machines.

Disclaimer: these tools are accumulated over a long period of time. Work to your budget and find clever new ways to use what you have: various fabrics, parchment paper, wax paper, Pros-Aide, Hi Tack, Clover Mini iron, regular iron, hair dryer, wax carver with adjustable heat and various tips, scissors, beading needles, respirator and filters, noise-canceling headphones, yoga block, nitrile gloves, silicone sheet, various wires, bug pins, ruler, tweezers, various brushes, rubbing alcohol, sewing machine, thread magic, heat erase pen, chalk pen, fray check, fabric stiffener, Kahl hat stiffener, various dyes, various markers, Invisafil, embroidery floss . . . pretty much anything handy. Each project is different so . . . the list could be quite long.

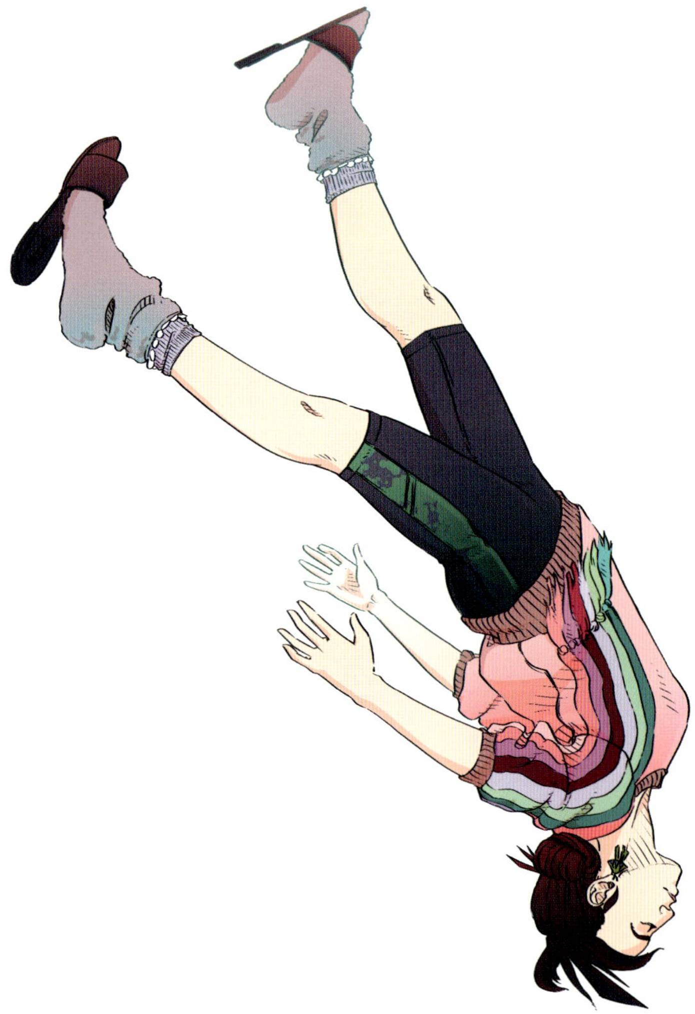

INDEX

OUR RESEARCH LIBRARY

Adorned in Dreams: Fashion in Modernity, Elizabeth Wilson, 2013

The Art of Frozen, Charles Solomon, Disney, 2013

The Art of Tangled, Jeff Kurtti, Disney, 2010

August Sander: Seeing, Observing and Thinking, Agnes Sire, Gabriele Conrath-Scholl, and Thomas Schatz-Nett, 2009

"Cinderella," Brothers Grimm, 1812

"Costume Design as an Essential Part of the Narrative," Araujo da Costa

"Costumes and Cinema: A Didactic Experience in the Academic Education of Fashion Designers," contribution by Marcel Martin

The Dan Harmon Story Circle

The Enneagram: A Christian Perspective, Richard Rohr and Andreas Ebert, 2001

Fashioning Fashion: European Dress in Detail, 1700–1915, Sharon Sadako Takeda, LACMA

Fear and Fashion in the Cold War, Jane Pavitt, 2008

Forgotten London: A Picture of Life in the 1920s, Philippa Lewis and Elizabeth Drury, 2011

Geek Psychology, MBTI and Enneagram Consultant

The Golden Thread: How Fabric Changed History, Kassia St. Clair, 2019

The Hero's Journey: Joseph Campbell on His Life and Work, Joseph Campbell, 2014

Illustrations of Norman Rockwell

Individuality in Clothing Selection and Personal Appearance, Mary Kefgen and Phyllis Touchie-Specht, 1986

Interviews with Oscar Ichazo, Oscar Ichazo, 1982

Invisible Ink: A Practical Guide to Building Stories that Resonate, Brian McDonald, 2017

Joanna Johnston, Back to the Future III Costume Designer

katherinefauvre.com, Enneagram Consultant

Looking at Textiles: A Guide to Technical Terms, Elena Phipps, 2012

Master your Influence: Body Language, 3keyelements.com

Merriam-Webster's Learner's Dictionary

A Midsummer Night's Dream, William Shakespeare, 1600

narrativeenneagram.org

personalityhacker.com

Prior Attire, www.priorattire.co.uk

Reigning Men: Fashion in Menswear, 1715–2015, Sharon Sadako Takeda, Kaye Durland Spilker, and Clarissa M. Esguerra, LACMA

16personalities.com

Taxing Visions: Financial Episodes in Late Nineteenth-Century American Art, Leo G. Mazow and Kevin M. Murphy, 2010

Understanding the Enneagram: The Practical Guide to Personality Types (revised edition), Don Richard Riso and Russ Hudson, 2000

The West: An Illustrated History, Geoffrey C. Ward, 2003

Back to the Future III Costume Designs (used as reference, pg 61), Joanna Johnston, Costume Designer

CC41 Utility Label, c. 1944

Cinderella and the Fairy Godmother, William Henry Margetson (1861–1940), c. 1904–1910

Day Dress, c. 1838, photo by Taishi Hirokawa, The Kyoto Costume Institute

With and Without Bustle (used as reference, pg 176), Izabela Pitcher, Prior Attire, www.priorattire.co.uk

Sans Culotte, Louis-Léopold Boilly (1761–1845), c. 1792

Sugarcane, Eva Elijas

The Wicked Witch Melts, William Wallace Denslow, 1900

THANK YOU

Deborah Landis
Anissa Espinosa • @redribbonrobot
David Ardinaryas Lojaya • @ardinaryas
Keith Zoo • keithzoo.com
Kevin Scarborough • kevinscarborough.com
Kristen Morefield, LMFT
Madeline Abatemarco • madelineabatemarco.com
Matt Sherman • geekpsychology.com
Natalia Falciglia • nataliafalciglia.com
Raul Ramos • raulramosart.com
Samantha Hogg • artofsamhogg.com
Shaun Bryant • art-bomb.com
Tegan Clancy • teganclancy.com
Tom Parrish • www.tomparrish.co.uk
Tong Bui • tongbui.com

The Design Studio Press team

Lacuna Artistic Team

Akili Pomian
Alex Hadfield
Diogo Cambrian
Amilton Macedo
Josh Wong
Anastasia Castle
Maria Ferreira Kercher
Tiago Carneiro

And our awesome ArtCenter and Costume Mentorship students who've already put the principles from the book into action!

THE TALKING THREADS

For resource recommendations and videos, check out thetalkingthreads.com.

OTHER TITLES BY DESIGN STUDIO PRESS

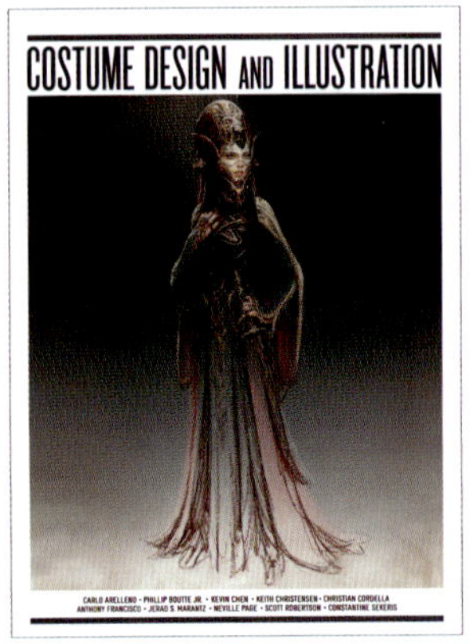

isbn 978-1933492-58-2

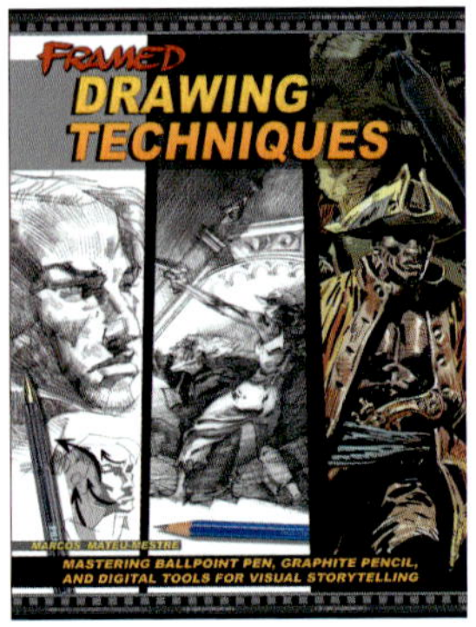

isbn 978-1624650-40-6

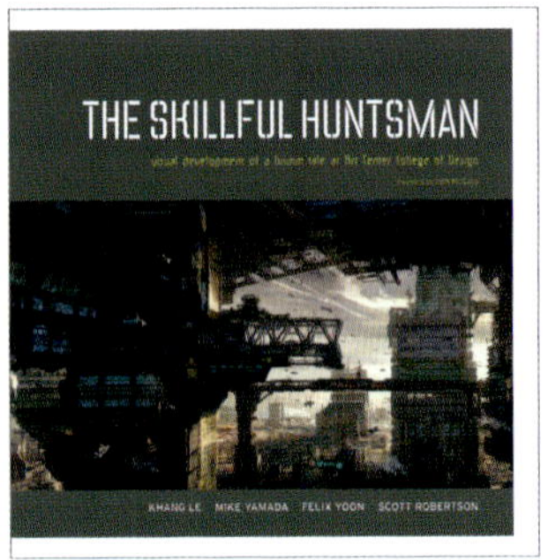

isbn 978-0972667-64-7

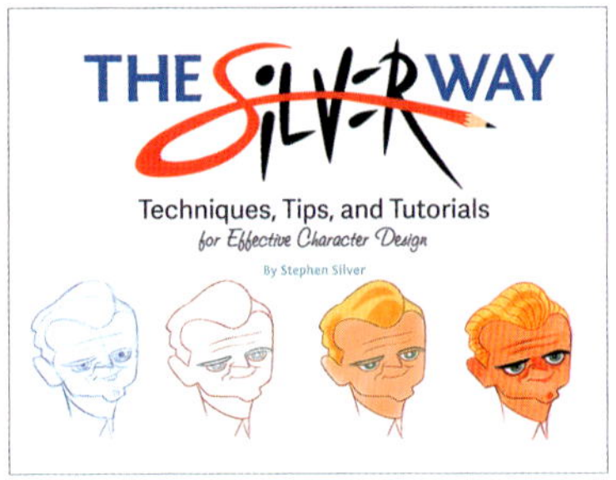

isbn 978-1624650-34-5

To order additional copies of this book and to view other books we offer, please visit: www.designstudiopress.com

For volume purchases and resale inquiries, please email: info@designstudiopress.com

Telephone: 310.836.3116

facebook.com/designstudiopress

@designstudiopress

@DStudioPress

designstudio PRESS